Poetry

Nonfiction

Comic

Drama

A note about the cover
Our new cover reflects themes of the fourth edition: how multiple elements—shapes and genres—work together to create interesting patterns, and how a two-dimensional space (such as a screen or a page) serves as a vehicle for making meaning.

THE PRACTICE OF CREATIVE WRITING

A GUIDE FOR STUDENTS

FOURTH EDITION

HEATHER SELLERS

University of South Florida

bedford/st.martin's
Macmillan Learning
Boston | New York

Vice President: Leasa Burton
Program Director, English: Stacey Purviance
Program Manager: John E. Sullivan III
Executive Marketing Manager: Joy Fisher Williams
Director of Content Development: Jane Knetzger
Executive Development Manager: Susan McLaughlin
Editorial Assistants: Samantha Storms, Alex Markle, Bill Yin
Marketing Manager: Vivian Garcia
Director, Content Management Enhancement: Tracey Kuehn
Senior Managing Editor: Michael Granger
Senior Manager of Publishing Services: Andrea Cava
Senior Content Project Manager: Pamela Lawson
Assistant Director, Process Workflow: Susan Wein
Production Supervisor: Lawrence Guerra
Director of Design, Content Management: Diana Blume
Interior Design: Jerilyn DiCarlo
Cover Design: William Boardman
Text Permissions Manager: Elaine Kosta, Lumina Datamatics, Inc.
Photo Permissions Editor: Allison Ziebka
Director of Digital Production: Keri deManigold
Project Manager, Media Training Specialist: Allison Hart
Project Management: Lumina Datamatics, Inc.
Project Manager: Jogender Taneja, Lumina Datamatics, Inc.
Editorial Services: Lumina Datamatics, Inc.
Copyeditor: Nancy Benjamin
Indexer: Sunny Khurana
Composition: Lumina Datamatics, Inc.
Cover Image: ThomasVogel/Getty Images
Printing and Binding: LSC Communications

Library of Congress Control Number: 2020936185

ISBN 978-1-319-21595-8   (Student Edition)

Printed in the United States of America.

1   2   3   4   5   6   25   24   23   22   21   20

Acknowledgments

Text acknowledgments and copyrights appear at the back of the book on pages 507–509, which constitute an extension of the copyright page. Art acknowledgments and copyrights appear on the same page as the art selections they cover.

For information, write: Bedford/St. Martin's, 75 Arlington Street, Boston, MA 02116

PREFACE
FOR INSTRUCTORS

For many years, I taught creative writing in the same way it had been taught to me. I took my students through inherited lessons on developing character in fiction, deepening theme in drama, measuring out meter in poetry, and studying great literature to learn. But as I did so, I felt like a fraud (a well-intentioned fraud) in the classroom; my own writing process bore almost no resemblance to the approaches I offered my students.

In my writing room, I always began — and still do — as many writers do: with *an image*. Literary terms never entered into the generative phase of my writing process. Instead, I always concentrated on a kind of movie in my mind's eye; in fact, I would have been hidebound and blocked as a new writer if I had consciously thought about metonymy, theme, or diction. I sensed intuitively that what made good writing good lay underneath and in advance of genre considerations. Then, as now, I delay genre decisions until I know more about what it is I have on the page. Genre is as much a question as it is a container.

In fact, what trips us up as writers often isn't line breaks or thematic considerations or specific genre conventions — not at first. Most writers I know, students and colleagues, have to work at actually getting to the desk and staying put. To improve as writers, we know we have to figure out how to create, extend, and sustain productive focus. I firmly believe the creative writing course must begin with instruction in process. Thus this textbook begins with strategies for building a thoughtful, meaningful writing practice, and then moves, step-by-step, through the strategies writers use, across genres, to develop and enhance their efforts.

For years, I was aware of the gap between what I did in my writing studio and what I did in the classroom, teaching my writing classes as though they were literature courses with creative writing assignments mixed in. It wasn't until I took a life-changing class with Lynda Barry that I found entry into a rich body of material on the artistic process and the nature of literary art. I found a way to teach writing as deep play, akin to the kind of focused imaginative state of mind we sustained for hours on end when we played as kids. In interviews with artists and writers, we hear this same sort of "dreaming deep" method described again and again. As I studied creativity and method, my classroom transformed. My students—spending more time learning about the nature of imagination, the way humans tell stories, and the psychology of concentration—focused for longer periods of time, wrote more, and they wrote *better*. It was truly thrilling.

As my writing life and my teaching practice came into better alignment, I wanted to create a textbook for students that foregrounded this new approach to the creative writing process, a book that would also teach sophisticated and nuanced reading skills in an approachable, welcoming, and *creative* way. This is that book.

The Practice of Creative Writing has three overarching objectives. In this course of study, I seek to help students:

1. Apply sophisticated close-reading skills to a wide range of innovative literature in order to develop as writers.
2. Build a healthy writing practice with a high level of self-observation, regularity, and focus.
3. Compose exercises to hone specific micro-skills, while building more sophisticated and layered writing projects—poems, memoir and essays, stories, plays, and hybrids and experiments.

Making the move from personal expression to powerful, reader-oriented creative writing is demanding. Ultimately, this book seeks to assure writers: *It takes time to learn to write well. The endeavor is a weirdly maddening mix of fun and difficulty. You can do this, and it's worth the trouble.*

NEW IN THE FOURTH EDITION

This edition of *The Practice of Creative Writing* contains five new features.

Process micro-interviews with authors included in the text. For the new edition, I interviewed ten writers whose pieces are presented in these pages. These interviews provide a special glimpse into each author's particular writing process and prompt process awareness and self-reflection assignments for students.

Clearly stated course and chapter objectives. Especially helpful for designing online course modules, building a syllabus, assessing learning throughout the course, and deftly guiding students' reading and learning, objectives are posted here in the preface and at the head of each chapter, providing a visible framework for learning. Based on Bloom's taxonomy, these objectives aid instructors in certifying their courses meet institutional standards and requirements.

Genre-based writing assignments. To improve the flexibility and usability of the text, each chapter now concludes with writing projects labeled by genre: experimental/hybrid, poetry, nonfiction, fiction, and drama. Instructors can organize the course by writing strategy or by genre; students can easily see how writing strategies apply across genres.

New readings. With a specific focus on innovation, flash, and micro forms, as well as new speculative readings, each new selection is chosen because of its proven success in providing inspiration for student writers. New writers such as Thao Thai, Och Gonzalez, and Jarod Roselló are presented alongside beloved contemporary authors such as Ted Chiang, Natalie Diaz, and Ross Gay. Brief excerpts from student favorites, Joy Harjo's "She Had Some Horses" and Beth Ann Fennelly's *Heating & Cooling: 52 Micro-Memoirs*, for example, provide fresh new models for writing projects.

Fresh approach to revision. How do we help student writers develop revision skills? Typically they often resist making changes to existing text, and often mightily. We know that complex, fresh, and memorable writing comes from a wide range of revision skills. The fourth edition presents a fresh new set of approaches to this crucial and challenging part of the writing process; the new Chapter Nine, Shape, groups revision strategies and will help students where they struggle the most.

In addition to these five new features, a fully revised and updated **Instructor's Manual** is available for **face-to-face and online** teachers adopting the book for use in their classroom. Sample syllabi, additional writing projects, and suggestions for designing and leading a successful course are included. Instructors who wish to teach by genre will find various classroom-tested options for course design. And instructors who teach by writing strategy will find tips for organizing their course as well. I've also created a series of videos that teachers can access. The Instructor's Manual and the videos can be accessed on the Macmillan Learning website **macmillanlearning.com**.

FEATURES OF *THE PRACTICE OF CREATIVE WRITING*

The hallmark features of *The Practice of Creative Writing* are all in the fourth edition.

A flexible, process-based approach for writers in every genre. The *Practice of Creative Writing* is based on the premise that good writing is good writing. Regardless of which genre you are working in, effective writing has six components: images, energy, tension, patterns, insight, and shape. These universal principles of good writing are best learned by experimenting across genres before settling into a home genre or taking a course devoted to a single genre. The six strategies are presented in order of difficulty so students can build facility with each one and layer the techniques to produce more sophisticated pieces as the course progresses.

Cross-training works, and students like it. For many students, a concept is made clear only when presented and practiced in several forms. Studying formal poetry strengthens the fiction writer's ear for rhythm; prose writers can create better dialogue by reading monologues and plays; and observing a nonfiction writer's use of insight helps student writers see the world more astutely. Every selection in the text displays the six core strategies so each lesson is consistently reinforced as the course unfolds.

Instruction in creative process and creative concentration in every chapter. Part One of *The Practice of Creative Writing* presents effective strategies for building a writing practice, distinguishing "life blocks" from "creative blocks," and how to use reading as the foundation of one's writing life. In Part Two and Part Three, students build on the skills they learn in Part One, designing more complex writing projects as they practice new skills. *The Practice of Creative Writing* also presents revision as an act of shaping, and something writers do throughout the writing process, not an activity they tack on at the end. Workshop guidelines and self-assessment opportunities appear throughout the text. Writers who wish to explore process and creativity further will find a detailed updated list of resources in Part Four.

Instruction for giving and receiving feedback, working well in a writing group, and building a portfolio of polished work. In every chapter, practical prompts and checklists aid students in distinguishing between revising and editing, and encourage higher levels of reader awareness. Workshop sections in each strategy chapter provide guidance for self-guided revision as well as peer response. Writers' tips and checklists also help students continually assess and revise their own work and make constructive suggestions to peers. At the end of the course, a class might offer a live read-ing, publish its own literary magazine, require students to make chapbooks of their best work, or turn in portfolios. Chapter Eleven presents detailed information to support writers in bringing their work to an audience.

Writing in forms and genres. After learning the six strategies of effective creative writing in any genre, students move to Part Three, Forms. Various forms of writing from across the genres—from the list to the sonnet to the one-act play—are presented as recipes, and students are set loose to create a body of work. Most courses will ask students to show their strengths across the genres, and a helpful chart on page 423 shows which forms meet the criteria for each genre.

Instructors usually ask students to tackle these longer, more formal genre-based projects late in the course, after the six strategies have been mastered. But some organize their course around the forms in Part Three, and those assignments drive the study of strategies throughout the course as students work their way through a series of assignments and move toward a portfolio of complete projects. Examples of many of the forms presented in Chapter Ten appear throughout the text, including journeys, graphic narratives, son-nets, and villanelles. Readers are referred to additional examples as well.

Lively readings in all genres. The readings in the book are vibrant, fresh, and popular among both students and their instructors, including works by contem-porary authors such as Raymond Carver, Terrance Hayes, Pablo Neruda, Akhil Sharma, Kim Addonizio, Julia Koets, and Ira Sukrungruang. A wide range of lively work is presented, including short stories, flash fiction, essays, memoir, poems, prose poems, comics, monologue, and drama. Most important, every piece included represents aspects of the six strategies; each piece can be used to illustrate image, energy, tension, pattern, insight, and shape; and each chapter encourages review of previously introduced concepts. Throughout the book, box quotes from writers around the world provide inspiration for students and can be used as prompts for journal writing and/or discussion posts about the writing process—particularly helpful in online versions of the course, where building daily meaningful instructor presence is crucial.

ACKNOWLEDGMENTS

Allyson Hoffman has been my editorial assistant for this project and I'm grateful for her professionalism, good cheer, research skills, spot-on sug-gestions and support. I'm similarly indebted to the MFA students in my graduate creative writing pedagogy courses at the University of South Florida; our discussions about teaching creative writing have improved this project in many ways. I want to thank LaSaundria Bass and Victor Ventor in Innovative Education at the University of South Florida for helping me learn how to teach online effectively and for our many discussions about best practices in course design and the essential role of textbooks in online education. I'm part of a truly wonderful English Department with supportive and kind colleagues — thank you, especially to Laura Runge-Gordon, Debra Garcia, John Fleming, Rita Ciresi, Jay Hopler, Jarod Roselló, Karen Brown, Mark Leib, and Julia Koets. It is a privilege and joy to be your colleague. I'd also like to thank Jennifer Phypers, Heide Nelson, Helen Wallace, Jane Bernstein, Elaine Sexton, Susanna Childress, Silvia Curbelo, Adriana Casteneda, and Victor Casteneda, for their kindness and support. I'm grateful to all of the writers who contributed work to this edition and am especially appreciative of those who agreed to be interviewed about their writing process: Jarod Roselló, John Brehm, Och Gonzalez, Lee Herrick, Vincent Scarpa, Brenda Miller, Dylan Landis, Beth Ann Fennelly, Julie Hakim Azzam, and Julia Koets.

At Bedford/St. Martin's, my wonderful development editor, Susan McLaughlin, provided terrific guidance during all stages of the writing and revision process. I am lucky to have had this opportunity to work with her — I'm indebted to her. Special thanks to Leasa Burton, who has been with this project from its original inception, and to Jane Knetzger, John Sullivan, and Lauren Arrant for their leadership during the preparation of this edition. Pamela Lawson skillfully handled production, while Alex Markle, Samantha Storms, and Bill Yin helped with countless details, Joy Fisher Williams coordinated marketing efforts, and Elaine Kosta managed permissions. I also want to thank Billy Boardman, who designed the fresh new look for our cover — a perfect visual representation of craft, play, and creativity.

Many thanks to the following reviewers, who have helped shape each new edition of *The Practice of Creative Writing* with their excellent feedback and suggestions. For this edition, I relied on the collective wisdom of these colleagues: Maria Brandt, Monroe Community College; Ayse Bucak, Florida Atlantic University–Boca Raton; Michele Cheung, University of Southern Maine–Gorham; Robert Cowser, St. Lawrence University; Thomas D'Angelo, Nassau Community College; Patricia Francisco, Hamline University–St. Paul; David Galef, Montclair State University; Bill Gary, Henderson Community College; Joyce Kessel, Villa Maria College–Buffalo; Kathleen McCoy, Adirondack Community College–Queensbury; Berwyn Moore, Gannon University; Jeffrey Newberry, Abraham Baldwin Agri College; Christina Rau, Nassau Community College; Lindsay Starck,

Augsburg University; Scott Ward, Eckerd College; Martha Webber, California State University, Fullerton; Stephanie Webster, Ivy Tech State College; Courtney Huse Wike, Black Hills State University; Kevin Wolfe, Eckerd College.

Heather Sellers
University of South Florida

BEDFORD/ST. MARTIN'S PUTS YOU FIRST

From day one, our goal has been simple: to provide inspiring resources that are grounded in best practices for teaching reading and writing. For more than thirty-five years, Bedford/St. Martin's has partnered with the field, listening to teachers, scholars, and students about the support writers need. We are committed to helping every writing instructor make the most of our resources.

How can we help *you*?

- Our editors can align our resources to your outcomes through correlation and transition guides for your syllabus. Just ask us.
- Our sales representatives specialize in helping you find the right materials to support your course goals.
- Our learning solutions and product specialists help you make the most of the digital resources you choose for your course.
- Our *Bits* blog on the Bedford/St. Martin's English Community (**community .macmillan.com**) publishes fresh teaching ideas weekly. You'll also find easily downloadable professional resources and links to author webinars on our community site.

Contact your Bedford/St. Martin's sales representative or you can visit **macmillanlearning.com** to learn more.

Print and Digital Options for *The Practice of Creative Writing: A Guide for Students*, 4e

Choose the format that works best for your course, and ask about our packaging options that offer savings for students.

- To order the fourth edition, use ISBN 978-1-319-21595-8.
- *Achieve Writer's Help.* Achieve puts student writing at the center of your course and keeps revision at the core, with a dedicated composition space that guides students through drafting, peer review, source check, reflection,

and revision. Developed to support best practices in commenting on student drafts, Achieve is a flexible, integrated suite of tools for designing and facilitating writing assignments, paired with actionable insights that make students' progress toward outcomes clear and measurable. With trusted content from the widely used Hacker or Lunsford handbooks, *Writer's Help* takes students through first-year writing and beyond. For details, visit **macmillanlearning.com/college/us/englishdigital**.

- *Popular e-book formats.* For details about our e-book partners, visit **macmillanlearning.com/ebooks**.
- *Inclusive Access.* Enable every student to receive their course materials through your LMS on the first day of class. Macmillan Learning's Inclusive Access program is the easiest, most affordable way to ensure all students have access to quality educational resources. Find out more at **macmillanlearning.com/inclusiveaccess**.

Your Course, Your Way

No two writing programs or classrooms are exactly alike. Our Curriculum Solutions team works with you to design custom options that provide the resources your students need. (Options below require enrollment minimums.)

- *ForeWords for English.* Customize any print resource to fit the focus of your course or program by choosing from a range of prepared topics, such as Sentence Guides for Academic Writers.
- *Macmillan Author Program (MAP).* Add excerpts or package acclaimed works from Macmillan's trade imprints to connect students with prominent authors and public conversations. A list of popular examples or academic themes is available upon request.
- *Mix and Match.* With our simplest solution, you can add up to fifty pages of curated content to your Bedford/St. Martin's text. Contact your sales representative for additional details.
- *Bedford Select.* Build your own print anthology from a database of more than 800 selections, or build a handbook, and add your own materials to create your ideal text. Package with any Bedford/St. Martin's text for additional savings. Visit **macmillanlearning.com/bedfordselect**.

USING *THE PRACTICE OF CREATIVE WRITING* IN YOUR ONLINE CLASSROOM

Using a textbook gives your students a second teacher, a vital "instructor at home." In addition to these five new features, the fourth edition of *The Practice of Creative Writing* has been updated specifically for ease of use in the online classroom, where students crave presence and consistency.

Chapters convert easily to modules and assignment sequences are clear and student-tested. Those without reliable internet connections easily access material anywhere. All permissions are legal, and all material is proofread and fact-checked.

For teachers, your course is pre-built:

- *Module Objectives.* You'll find student-centered objectives at the beginning of each chapter.
- *Discussions.* The new Practices in each chapter are designed to serve as online Discussions; students are asked to respond to posts in their groups.
- *Reading Quizzes.* Use bold-faced terms in each chapter to help students read closely and internalize key vocabulary.
- *Rubrics.* The objectives at the beginning of the chapter can be used to create simple, clear rubrics for assessing each assignment in the chapter. Grading assignments is simplified.
- *Writing Projects.* To complete each module, students create a piece of writing that demonstrates the key concepts in that chapter.
- *Live Readings by Authors.* Insert live readings from YouTube and other platforms into your module so students can see and hear the authors in each chapter's anthology perform their work. The Instructor's Manual has specific suggestions.

One of the most important features of a successful online course is, of course, instructor presence. With the textbook at hand, students connect to a cohesive and substantive body of material; you coach and guide them through the course. The Instructor's Manual helps you increase instructor presence by outlining ideas for making a welcome video for each chapter, downloading videos that come with the book, responding to Discussions, and pointers for locating key concepts in chapter readings.

About the Author

Heather Sellers is professor of English in the graduate and undergraduate writing programs at the University of South Florida, where she was honored with a university-wide teaching award. She offers courses for creative writers in hybrid and experimental writing, fiction, memoir, essays, and poetry, as well as a course for creative writing teachers. Born and raised in Orlando, Florida, she earned her PhD in English/Creative Writing at Florida State University. She has taught at New York University, the University of Texas–San Antonio, St. Lawrence University, and for almost two decades, Hope College, where she was elected Professor of the Year.

A recipient of a National Endowment for the Arts Fellowship for Fiction and a Barnes and Noble Discover Great New Writers award for her short story collection *Georgia Under Water*, she has published widely in a variety of genres. Her work appears in *The New York Times*; *The Pushcart Prize* anthology; *The Best American Essays*; *O, the Oprah Magazine*; *Good Housekeeping*; *Reader's Digest*; *Parade*; *Real Simple*; *On the Seawall*; *Adroit*; *Longreads*; *Creative Nonfiction*; and frequently in *The Sun Magazine*. Her memoir *You Don't Look Like Anyone I Know: A True Story of Family, Face Blindness, and Forgiveness* was a Michigan Notable Book of the Year and Editor's Choice at *The New York Times Book Review*. Other publications include *Drinking Girls and Their Dresses: Poems*; and *Spike and Cubby's Ice Cream Island Adventure*, a children's book. She lives in Saint Petersburg, Florida. Her website is heathersellers.com.

CONTENTS

3 CREATING FROM COMPONENTS   87

PART TWO

STRATEGIES   *139*

PART THREE

FORMS   *419*

PART FOUR

THE WRITING LIFE   *477*

11 REACHING READERS   *479*

12 WRITING RESOURCES   *495*

HOW CREATIVE WRITING WORKS

Welcome to *The Practice of Creative Writing*.

Creative writing is an endeavor that is both fun and challenging, based on:

- **paying close attention** to the world, to yourself, and to human experience
- rendering with **words** and **images** your observations and experiences in a way that makes them fresh, meaningful, and alive in the **reader's mind**
- the practice of close **reading** to expand who you are and what you know

Ultimately, the purpose of this class is to teach you how to make your creative writing interesting and valuable to readers.

It's also important to keep in mind that creative writing is *not*:

- an easy way to get rich or famous
- a way to vent personal feelings
- for only a few talented geniuses
- rarefied, "artsy," special—just for English majors

Rather, creative writing is an incredibly rich and worthwhile way to spend your time, to engage with meaning, and to connect with others. Creative writing and reading increase empathy, emotional intelligence, skills of focus and concentration, and prosocial behaviors.

Because creative writing is so various and fascinating and endlessly stimulating, it's the discipline to which I've devoted my entire life. I've met the most kind, generous, wise, and warm people in this field, and through creative writing I've gotten to know myself a lot better, too. I've been writing professionally and teaching for three decades, and I've put into this book the most useful principles I've learned over these years.

> *You shouldn't listen when [critics] tell you the bad things. But you also shouldn't listen when they tell you the good things. Both of those can wreck your creative process. It still has to be about the attempt.*
>
> —ADA LIMÓN

HOW *THE PRACTICE OF CREATIVE WRITING* WORKS

I've organized the book into four parts.

Part One helps you build a healthy, productive **writing process**. Writing is one of those activities, like learning a musical instrument or building a new relationship or mastering a sport, where you're going to make mistakes. A lot of mistakes. There's a high level of failure built into the learning process. Failure, however, is not really a problem—it's an opportunity for *learning*. As we assess and learn from our errors, we gradually improve. But it can be easy to get discouraged and flounder, not knowing what to do next.

Writers—no matter what genre they choose to work in—find their own work-arounds for inevitable failures and frustrations. This book seeks to help you, personally, normalize your relationship with mistake-making so you can grow as a writer. By the end of Part One, you'll be able to better figure out what specifically blocks you and what unblocks you so you can spend less time frustrated and more time enjoying your creativity. In Part One, you'll also distinguish writing for yourself from creative writing, writing you do for others. What do your readers love more than anything? To be lost in a world, to hear a good story told well, and to enjoy the richness of language, of delicious words and captivating rhythms, whether from a rap song or a love sonnet or a prayer or a post. Creative writing is not so much about you. It's all about the reader.

Part Two, the heart of the course, presents the six basic **writing strategies** that inform the basis of every **genre**. Genre is simply a set of agreed-upon definitions; I believe that learning genres just for the sake of learning them may be less important or less interesting than learning writing techniques you can use no matter what you want to write. (Why not invent your own genres?)

The six essential creative writing strategies presented here let you build the projects you want to write—**comics, poems, stories, essays, memoirs, plays,** and perhaps **hybrids** and **experiments**—the way you want to write them. In the end, you'll have a deep skill set that is practical and flexible. It will allow you to write well across genres, and to invent and innovate, too.

And, by "cross-training" in more than one genre you'll see even greater payoff in the writing you choose to do. For example, fiction writers write plays in order to hone their skills of dialogue, tension, and pace. Essay and memoir writers try poetry in order to write more precise images and increase their powers of word choice, rhythm, and subtext. Creating comics trains you to write tight, image-driven plots, and so on.

Here are specific, detailed definitions for the six **strategies** that make up the foundation of *The Practice of Creative Writing*.

Images. Images are the building blocks of creative writing. Images are living pictures, the "movie in the reader's mind," that your words create on the reader's mental screen. When you read a great piece of writing, your imagination (notice that

> *Write each and every day of your life.*
> —WALTER MOSLEY

image is the root of the word "imagination") is activated; you can see, and smell, and hear, and touch in your mind's eye.

Energy. Energy is the spark that makes a reader pay attention. Good creative writers work to infuse their writing with energy in every possible way, so the reader feels momentum, pleasing leaps, interesting gaps and pauses. Energy involves pacing, intensity, heat, excitement, and interest. Every genre requires expertise in manipulating energy.

Tension. Tension is the underlying push-pull, conflict, juxtaposition, or *what will happen next?* in all good creative writing. Tension is conflict.

Pattern. Art imposes patterns on the messy chaos of life. Pattern makes meaning. And, pattern attracts the human eye. Through the artful and carefully calibrated repetition of key images, words, and sounds, readers will pay attention to what you want them to notice, and your work will stand out as more memorable.

Insight. We read to be entertained but also to learn, to see the world from the perspective of others. One of the reasons we read creative writing is to learn in a pleasurable way. We don't want literature to lecture us or sermonize; we want writing that sparks us and provokes us, so that we can come to our own conclusions. In the chapter on how to create insight in your work, you will practice clever ways for adding layers and depth to your pieces.

Shape. Most pieces don't come out fully formed, though some do. Professional writers spend a small amount of time generating new pieces and most of their time shaping their works-in-progress. Instead of approaching revision and shaping as a punishing task, or a step that actually makes your piece worse, not better, this book presents options for shaping a work-in-progress so you can present effective and polished pieces to your audience. The chapter on shape also distinguishes shaping from rewriting and editing and proofreading. Choose the approaches that best fit your writing process and personality.

Part Three is a recipe book presenting an abundance of writing projects for you to experiment with. After you've learned the six basic strategies of creative writing, you may choose to build a portfolio of pieces to showcase your skills. The forms presented here—including lists, anaphora, villanelle—are fun and flexible; some work across genres and some help you hone your skills in specific genres. The projects in Part Three are each designed to help you extend your writing abilities even further.

In **Part Four**, "The Writing Life," you'll find practical suggestions for publishing your work, giving live readings, and creating chapbooks to share your writing with others in a more formal way. Along with dozens of suggestions for participating in larger communities of writing, you'll also find general writing resources and super-specific suggestions for delving deeper into fantasy or writing for children, writing a screenplay, or, eventually, finding an agent.

Few successful writers work alone, especially when they are starting out. In Part Four, and all along the way, this book also suggests how to contribute to and how to get the most from your writing community—your writing partners, small groups, your writing class, as well as finding the writing communities that will nourish you locally and digitally.

Some of your work this semester will focus on how to read work written by other student writers and how to learn the same kinds of things from your classmates' early triumphs and failures that you do from polished, published texts. Learning how to offer meaningful, helpful observations on a work-in-progress is an art in itself and a very useful skill for anyone entering the job market, in any profession. Learning how to form bonds with members of the writing community, how to create a writing community where one doesn't yet exist, and how to nurture supportive writing relationships are essential to your sustained growth as a writer.

ASKING GENERATIVE QUESTIONS

The literary arts—art forms using words as their medium instead of paint or musical notes or movement or clay—take up some of the same questions you probably study in your philosophy, psychology, anthropology, economics, religion, sociology, and communications classes:

- What is most interesting and puzzling about human nature?
- What is it like to be a particular human person, with a particular set of problems?
- What does it feel like and look like to attempt to be moral, to do the right thing, and fail, or to make a mistake, perhaps one with significant consequences?

Writers are interested in these kinds of questions, and also:

- How can I express myself memorably, so others will be affected by my words?
- How do I use language in fresh and exciting ways to say what I want to say?
- How can I write about what matters to me without getting discouraged or hurting other people?
- What happens if someone criticizes my work and then I no longer want to write?

This book helps you answer all of these questions — technical questions, writing process questions, and larger questions about what for and why.

Notice the one question that is not on this list: *How do I know if I am any good?* That's not the right question to ask — it's paralyzing rather than generative and completely unhelpful. As hard as it is, you must dismiss thoughts along those lines. Instead, always keep your focus on questions that generate learning — building your writing practice, building your skill set. Avoid self-judgment. You might not have even started trying yet! Ask what you can learn about yourself, what you can learn about your own habits of mind, what you can learn from reading other writers, and how to practice new skills.

> *Don't self-reject. You know what I mean.*
> —KELLY LINK

Practice lots, and have fun. Good luck and keep in touch. I look forward to reading and viewing your poems, plays, comics, projects, and books someday soon.

I hope you enjoy the course.

Heather Sellers
The University of South Florida
sellersh@usf.edu

FOUNDATIONS

PART ONE

One or two days a week I might feel like I'm making progress — but I know it's during those other, blah kind of days that all the essential composting takes place.

KEVIN BARRY

Writing is such a necessary way for me ... to look beyond myself, to make sure that what I'm writing is not just for me, but also for readers, whomever they might be.

ROXANE GAY

Without craft, art remains private. Without art, craft is merely homework.

JOYCE CAROL OATES

CHAPTER ONE

FINDING FOCUS

In this chapter you will:

- Explore creative focus and the mind's eye
- Identify and address writing blocks
- Develop rituals to build a productive writing practice

Remember the last time you were reading a wonderful story? Time fell away, you forgot where you were sitting, and you no longer heard the sounds around you.

When you are totally absorbed in a great piece of writing, you are *transported* to another time and place—the words create a new reality, and you, the reader, actually inhabit another world. Not only do you see a kind of movie play out in your head as you read, but you also experience, with your senses, this other world. Recent research in neuroscience proves that for your brain, that world created in your mind when you are reading is just as real and fully formed as this one—the brain actually doesn't know the difference between reading and reality.

Research also shows this deep transformational power of the written word to affect brain activity works better with words on physical pages than words on screens. In fact, all aspects of focus, when you are reading on a screen, are harder for your brain; you aren't as transported. You absorb less of what you read. When you read on a screen, your eyes move around much more rapidly. You read in a nonlinear way, taking in extra information you don't need. And the physical act of scrolling, experiments show, diverts your attention—memory (learning) is less concretized. When you scroll, your eyes have to search to find the place you left off—these micro-actions suck "battery power" from your attention process. It might not seem like a lot, but attention researchers have discovered these small distractions add up, disrupting visual attention and interfering, measurably and significantly, with your ability to read, process, understand, and recall.

THE MIND'S EYE

Regardless of what format the reader chooses, creative writing — comics, flash fiction, poems, novels, and plays, the kinds of writing we will attempt in this course — seeks to create a specific mental state marked by **visual images**, sounds, tastes, and textures, a full **sensory experience**. This world that reading activates in the brain is rich and real and singular. Because the brain perceives in pictures, or images, we call this special way of perceiving via the reading experience the **mind's eye**.

In Shakespeare's famous play, when Hamlet says he is seeing his father "in [his] mind's eye," Hamlet's friend Horatio worries he is going mad. Horatio tells Hamlet his father is dead — he isn't seeing him. But Hamlet insists, and he is right. He *is* seeing his father. (If you close your eyes now and imagine your father or someone else close to you, do you see an actual person? Try it. What do you see?) The image Hamlet sees in his mind is *just as real* as his breakfast, his girlfriend, the castle walls. In his imagination, his father talks. He moves. The primary goal of creative writing is to engage the reader just this way by creating images — real, live moving images — in their mind's eye.

Art is a sensory experience, and creative writing — the making of art objects using language — appeals first to that sensory experience. We don't read creative writing in order to have things explained to us. Learning by way of explanation is important, and it's the vital work of historians, philosophers, and scientists to teach us concepts and facts — this knowing enriches our lives. In creative writing, in literature, we read in order to have an experience, to actually feel what it is like to be in another world, another body, another soul, another point of view. When it comes to creative writing, readers want to forget they are reading. Take me somewhere, the reader says. Anywhere. But don't remind me — with too much description or analysis or thinking or interruptions — that I'm reading.

Some people are natural storytellers, transporting us with riveting tales that play out in our mind's eye. How do they accomplish this? A good storyteller, whether talking out loud or in their writing, creates activated images — movies in the mind — so we can see the events play out as they happen. The successful storyteller probably sees the events, too, as they play out. The storyteller is *in* the story on the sensory level and that act of focus enables her to bring the tale to life for us. Some people are naturals at this. Others watch the eyes of their friends glaze over. After a failed storytelling experience, we might say, "Guess you had to be there."

Exactly. To bring creative writing to life for a reader or listener, you, the author, have to actually be there, present to the situation and all its physical dynamics.

Notice how you tell stories to friends and family members. What are you doing when you tell a story well versus when you tell it poorly?

For example, on the first day of class, I often hear students complaining about finding a parking space. Many of the stories are the same and the complaints we hear every year are familiar—the student focuses her story on her feelings and emotions. But some students are able to turn their difficult morning into a good story. As we listen, we are transported. It's interesting to experience the world through the storyteller's eyes, even though we've all heard a version of a similar story many times. When a natural storyteller launches into an account of how hard it was to find a parking space on campus, if they are fully involved in the physical scene and the five senses, as though it's all taking place again in real time, we're transported. When they show how they're behind the wheel, stressed about being late for class, leaning forward in the car, gripping their cell phone in one hand, willing the parking app that will help them find an open spot to work, while holding the steering wheel in the other, envisioning how fast they can run to the building their class is in on the opposite side of campus without spilling their mug of coffee, some part of us is behind the steering wheel, with them willing the story to have a happy ending.

We relive the experience, tracking action and image, in order to tell a story well. Your stories and your jokes often come out best when you *reexperience the original sensations* as you retell. Weaker writers and storytellers don't know yet how to transport themselves back into the moment. They talk *about* the experience. And it's usually not interesting because it summarizes. "I looked all over for a parking space," they report, generalizing, distancing. They explain and comment:

> My best [writing] advice is the advice they give kids at a crosswalk: stop, look and listen.
>
> —RAE ARMANTROUT

"I can never find a place to park. It took like forever." They leave out all the good parts. The pink Vespa that swooped in out of nowhere just as they were easing into the last spot on the top floor of parking garage nicknamed "Siberia."

Here's one student's rendition of their first-day-of-the-semester parking adventure:

> This morning I was creeping through the Marshall parking garage, a string of cars ahead of me, and a string of cars behind me. Not one space on the first level. There are cars parked in the motorcycle parking spots. Nothing on the second level, nothing on the third level. I check my phone. The air-conditioner in my car is broken and it's hot, even though it's early in the morning. I look at the clock. It's 7:59. My 8:00 A.M. class is on the other side of the Sun Dome and I'm going to be late, even if I sprint. That is, if I ever get a spot. I'm on the ramp to the top level of the garage when I hear a hissing noise and then this guy is coming toward me, almost running, pointing at my front passenger-side tire.

Good storytelling transports us just this way. (Writers who are sense-impaired compensate in a variety of ways on the page, just as in real life, often creating innovative and original descriptions for their readers.)

Write What You See

Think for a moment of flipping through cable channels and landing, on Saturday afternoon, on one of those programs with a title like *Learn to Paint Oceans!* or *Perfect Flowers in One Minute!* A guy in a windowless television studio with a canvas, a lot of blue paint, a lot of white paint — and no actual ocean in view, no real flowers anywhere to be seen — explains to viewers how to rotate the brush for a wavelike swoop, how to dollop more white for crests of waves, and ta-da! — a very cool little wrist motion that will create the perfect expanse of sand. Use pink paint and the same exact wrist motion to do roses!

At no point is it suggested that we look at an actual ocean, wave, or beach, rose, pansy, or peony. At no point is the viewer's experience of the painting considered. This kind of approach to art is based on tricks instead of looking closely at the real world. Fooling the eye, these shortcuts usually produce mediocre paintings that look like everyone else's mediocre paintings.

Paintings made out of technical tricks might not create a world; they suggest a shorthand for *The Beach, The Ocean, Nice Garden Scene, Floral Medley.* When you look at an amateur painting, you see the painting. When you look at a painting by a talented artist, not only do you see the painting, but you are transported into the color, the shapes, the scene, or perhaps to your own childhood memories of sweet afternoons at the shore, Grandma's rose bed, the peonies you grew last summer. The painting activates your mind's eye.

You may want to avoid the kind of "quick trick" techniques that keep you from *really looking closely at the real world* and focusing on the people in it. "How to Plot Your Novel in Thirty Days" or "Create Fabulous Characters in an Hour!" — these kinds of shortcuts do not usually produce effective, memorable work. What often produces good writing is accurately noticing specific/real, individuals and instances, invented or observed. Focus on the things you notice, especially if you are inventing characters and situations, and concentrate on the very smallest things you notice — the things other people might pass right over. The more fantastical the world you are creating on the page, the more powerful the details will be in convincing your reader to enter and dwell in your world.

PRACTICE 1

NOTICE IMAGES: "Robot Camp"

Read Jarod Roselló's comic on page 29. What are some examples of very small, concrete, and well-observed details in this story? Which details work to convince the reader Robot Camp is "real"? Even though this is a comic, a visual form of creative writing, do you have a "mind's eye" experience when you read? If so, how? When you read Jarod Roselló's explanation of where his ideas come from, does it seem to you he is envisioning his world in his mind's eye when he creates?

Moving Images

Imagine a child swinging on a swing set at a playground. Did you invent a child, or is the image hovering in your mind's eye of a real kid, someone you know, perhaps yourself when you were six? Look closer. Can you see what the child is wearing? What his hair, his arms, his hands, and his face look like?

Pause for a moment and using the power of your mind's eye look at this child, noticing any small detail, anything interesting. Notice that his sneaker is untied. How you can make him swing faster. Slower. Notice how you can make him jump off the swing and land in a puddle — seeing this in your mind's eye all the while — and make him run across the park, over to a small dog wagging her tail.

The point of this example is that your mind can create all of these things — real, live, moving images. You don't need a lot of description to have this experience; your reader doesn't either. In fact, the more information you give, and the more abstract that information is, the harder it is for the reader to see what you are talking about, what they are supposed to pay attention to, or even to see anything meaningful at all. She was a beautiful, generally fabulous, and amazingly generous child. Just completely outstanding in every way, a wonderful delight to be around, a stunning person with a great personality, too — everyone loved her!

Do you see anyone specific in your mind's eye in the second description? The words "child on swing" prompt a more powerful visual than the wordy paragraph, above, about the generous child.

Creative writing demands **sensory engagement**, and in the second example we have no idea who the child is, no feel for where she is, what she's doing, what she's wearing, what she actually looks like or how she behaves. In this wordy description, as reader you are overloaded with abstract information and unnecessary extra words. You don't really get an image in your mind's eye. Creative writing is all about creating for your reader a *sensory emotional experience*.

Even if you could keep a strong visual image alive in your mind during the general description above, you were working hard. Too hard. Readers can't be expected to work that hard; they need clear images to focus on. The reader wants to see her own kid, her own banana, her own house. She is fully capable of doing so all on her own. That's the central lesson of this chapter: If you write from a focused place — describing the child as you want the reader to picture her, your reader will see the same child. If you see, in your mind's eye, the banana, the horse, the emotional breakup scene — your reader will see it and feel it, too.

Be specific (*banana*, not *fruit; child*, not *person*). Name what you see. But most important of all, keep part of your mind in focus on the live scene as you write, with the image in mind.

Many writers mistakenly believe that wordy writing is good writing, and they include too many adjectives and adverbs to decorate and enrich their writing. In your creative writing, don't spend lots of time describing the perfect fruit. For example, "The glowing red orb pocked with holes made by denizens of the humble earth" is really hard to see. It's stronger to simply write *old apple*.

In sports like tennis, baseball, and football, the coaches constantly remind players to keep their eye "on the ball." It's the same advice for writers. Keep your eye on what you see in your mind's eye when you are writing.

As you practice creative writing in this course, notice when you become aware of a specific image, a movie, in your head when you read and when you write. When you aren't transported into a realistic, moving image, what *does* happen in your mind when you read? Paying this kind of close attention is challenging, but you will get better at it as you practice. Not every sentence or line in a piece of creative writing has to feed the moving picture, but most probably do.

Practice noticing what you like to read, what moves you, what affects you. When do you feel "lost" in a reading, totally unaware of what is going on around you because you are submerged in the author's creation? If you work toward being able to articulate to yourself what makes a piece of writing memorable and powerful for you, your own writing technique will improve.

PRACTICE 2

NOTICING IMAGES in "The Poems I Have Not Written"

Read John Brehm's poem on page 43. Note the lines that contain images — things you can see, things that are moving. How many specific images — visual experiences in your mind's eye — do you find in the poem? Make a list of each "mind's eye" moment.

SUBJECT AS FOCUS

Now that you have been introduced to the technique of utilizing images by writing from the mind's eye — another way of saying **show** the reader, **don't tell** them — you may wonder *what* to look at. What makes for a good writing topic? Nearly any **subject** can be made into a terrific topic choice for creative writing.

> *A playwright knows that what is most private in her heart of hearts is also the most astonishing.*
>
> —TINA HOWE

As you look for good subjects, three general guidelines to keep in mind are:

1. Focus on what you see — action and the five senses — and not on what you feel.
2. Write as truthfully, honestly, and accurately as possible.
3. Write about what you know.

Write What You Know

We've already addressed the first two guidelines at the beginning of this chapter. Your job as a writer is to report from the world you know — invented or not — and to bring that world to us. What is in that world? How do people act in your world? Why do they act the way they do? What do the people you know yearn for? What does that yearning look like? What are some of the rules and behavior conventions in your world? What happens when they are broken? Any person, place, or thing you have behind-the-scenes access to or firsthand experience with will be excellent choices for writing topics this semester.

Remember: This "knowing" we are speaking of is a visual sensory knowing. Write what you see in your mind's eye, not what you may just know about in your head. Also, remember that you can invent all manner of situations in your head. But the material in your mind will only be real for your reader if you deliver realistic images through the mind's eye, using action and the five senses.

Your own life is one of the richest repositories for material. You know and are aware of much more than your own lived experience. Be careful about using "experiences" you've gleaned from videos and films. Other people's material belongs to them. By recasting, maybe unconsciously, films, television series, stories, and poems you love may fall flat for your readers and may also be considered plagiarism.

Don't try to start writing with only an idea in mind. Instead of "I have an idea for a story," start with a concrete sensory detail from a place you have special access to. If you know a lot about the food prep schedule at the Windmill Restaurant, how Terry likes the eggs to be set up for the breakfast shift, how the bread is made fresh early in the morning, how the delivery guy spits outside the back door every single morning, then start with those images, the specifics you know well. If you haven't ever been in a war, but you want to write a war poem, you will need to get some specific insider images — things only someone who has experienced actual battle would have visual and sensory access to — by doing careful original research.

You do not need to write an autobiography, but you are well served, especially when starting out as a creative writer, by choosing topics you are familiar with and have experienced. It's going to take practice and confidence to get a feel for how that works. How can your tiny apartment in Rockaway Beach, your annoying parents, or your adorable little sister be the stuff of art? What if you didn't have a troubled childhood? What if you have the dullest job on the planet? Great writers — from Shakespeare to Austen, Hemingway to Morrison, Jaquira Díaz to Junot Díaz — have used the day-to-day material of their everyday lives to create rich literature, television, theater, and film simply by looking closely at what was in front of their eyes. Fortunately, you are an expert on many, many things. Your great-aunt Madge who was a roller-skating star when she was a teenager, owning a hamster, playing soccer, working at Five Guys, enlisting in the military, working at a call center, being married (perhaps from observing your parents), graduating from high school, breaking up with someone after a long-term relationship (perhaps from observing a friend) — you know *a lot.*

Making lists of potential subjects allows you to slow down and look at your own material with a writer's eye. It might not seem interesting to you until you break down your topics into small pieces and start to look at them closely and creatively.

Creating lists of potential subjects to work with gives your unconscious mind a chance to generate ideas. And, lists are generative: They provide you with writing prompts you can use all semester long. Keep in mind that subject lists are a terrific place to begin if you are new to writing or find yourself stuck when you are in the process of writing.

PRACTICE 3

MAKING A SUBJECT LIST

In your writing journal, on your phone, or in a file on your desktop, start a **subject list**. Try to list at least five items in each of these categories: jobs, passions, griefs, joys, secret worlds. Don't censor yourself—surprising things come up when you cast a wide net and think about subjects from a writer's perspective. Here's an example of a subject list:

Jobs: one day at McDonald's, babysitting triplets, working in the rat lab, raking for horrible neighbor

Passions: playing soccer, T'Mara in third grade—what happened to her?, watching *Game of Thrones*, nineteenth-century paintings

Griefs: living with multiple sclerosis, losing a pet, fighting with brother, father dying from cancer, cheating scandal #1, cheating scandal #2, never reporting assault

Joys: spending time in bookstores, publishing first book, my partner, playing in snow, listening to Chance the Rapper

Secret worlds: Disney tunnels, sister's bathroom when she had her secret pet duck, password to my father's computer

Summer activities: camping, archery, falling in love, swimming in the lake, building a house for Habitat for Humanity

Trips/journeys: to the park to BBQ, down the shore with friends, visiting colleges, Japan to meet family I did not know I had, fake running away from home when I was five

Next time you are stuck or blocked, force yourself to choose an item on your list and use it to spark new images to write about.

PRACTICE 4

CHOOSING READER-FRIENDLY SUBJECTS

Share your subject list with a classmate or two. Ask your partner(s) which two or three subjects are most interesting. Are you surprised or not surprised? What do you notice about what's interesting to potential readers?

PRACTICE 5

DEVELOPING A SUBJECT: "What I Do on My Terrace Is None of Your Business"

Read the micro-memoir by Och Gonzalez on page 45 and the interview that follows the piece. What inspired the author to write? What was her process in shaping a topic for writing? What important part(s) of her topic did she *not* write about, and why? Notice the use of the mind's-eye technique: Which parts of her story create an image in your mind?

> *I practice every day. You have to stay on good speaking terms with your piano. Or the piano will rebuff you.*
>
> —HANK JONES

DEVELOPING FOCUS

We've talked about using the technique of the mind's eye as the power center of focus in a creative writing practice. And we discussed the use of creating a list as a technique to create subject matter and consulting with potential readers — classmates — to see what sparks the most interest. We acknowledge that using sensory detail and writing what we know best will help us create writing that holds our reader's attention.

So far, so good. But for so many of us, here's where things can go horribly awry. Here's a common scenario. You have an idea and you sit down to write. Nothing happens. Nothing. The blank page stares at you. Or the blank screen stares back. You type a sentence. You erase it. You type another sentence. You erase. You feel frustration, anxiety. You check your phone. Then you go on Instagram or Snapchat — just for a second. Hours pass. Days pass. And not a single word gets written.

Having trouble focusing as a writer is common. If you are one of those people who find writing easy to start and stay with, skip this next section. If you are a writer who often gets stuck, procrastinates, or finds it really hard to set and keep to a writing schedule, please read on.

The Writing Habit

Becoming a writer means being resourceful enough to find the time and the place in your life for writing. Establishing a physical place conducive to your specific personality — some people need a noisy coffee shop, others require total silence — is crucial. A regular and consistent block of time — at least twenty minutes a day — that fits into your schedule is highly recommended. Most writers work best if they do a little creative writing every day, at the same time of day, in the same place, for the same amount of time. Without

a writing habit, something reassuring you can count on, it's probably asking too much of your imagination to sit down and write well on demand. For most people, creativity doesn't work that way. It only comes with a regular and consistent routine.

There are binge writers who write in bright-hot swaths of time — lost weekends, stolen summers, early morning, or all-nighters. If it works for you, **binge writing** isn't necessarily a bad thing. You need to know yourself and adjust your expectations so they are in line with how much time you are spending practicing your craft.

> *I never could have done what I have done without the habits of punctuality, order, and diligence, without the determination to concentrate myself on one subject at a time.*
> —CHARLES DICKENS

If you don't have a writing habit, you might even be setting yourself up for failure. If you write only when you are in the mood or when you have some free time, you may never be able to write enough material to see what you are good at and what needs work. Writers (like athletes, artists, and musicians, for example) practice whether they are in the mood or not. It's the only way. Everyday practice. That's how you get better. Successful writers — including many of the writers presented in this book — probably don't have more natural talent than you do. They are simply people who have figured out how to spend enough time writing every day in order to improve their techniques. They've taught themselves how to show up and how to focus.

Know that *most* writers struggle with focus — call it procrastination, writer's block, distraction, or laziness. It's ridiculously common and absolutely normal. You aren't alone; in fact, you're in really good company. But you'll need to develop you own personal strategies to deal with your writing challenges. Learning how you best focus your creative time is probably half the battle when you are taking a writing class.

Writing Rituals

Rituals help us achieve and intensify focus. One strategy for overcoming focus issues and writing blocks is to schedule your daily writing session for the same time and same place every day. Some writers write in bed, first thing in the morning before any distractions set in. Some writers stay away from their phones and email until they've logged in their twenty-minute writing session. Others go to the basement of their library after work every night. Still others like the white noise of a crowded coffee shop or restaurant during lunch hour because that's when they focus best. The key is to have a ritual — a time, a place, and a process that doesn't usually vary — using the same laptop, jotting in the same notebook, drinking the same coffee, and

> *The problem of creative writing is essentially one of concentration and the supposed eccentricities of poets are usually due to mechanical habits or rituals developed in order to concentrate.*
> —STEPHEN SPENDER

writing at the same time. If you have to reinvent the wheel every day, it's more likely you will stray from your practice.

You may also need to develop a **transition ritual**. Notice how most athletes and musicians warm up. They may run a few slow laps, do push-ups, and stretch hamstrings, or tune their instrument, play scales, and rehearse part of a song. People rarely leap out of the car and start running a great road race, or walk into the concert hall and play a perfect concerto. Many successful writers have developed simple and predictable ways for getting into the zone. For example, one writer I know takes a fifteen-minute walk without her phone before a writing session. While she walks, she plans out what she wants to work on and then when she returns from her morning walk, she writes for twenty minutes. Another writer I know wakes up, makes breakfast, plays video games, and generally enjoys life without a care, but before he leaves the house for the day, he sets a timer, puts on his favorite music, and he sits in his closet, on the floor, and writes, by hand for ten minutes. Every single day.

Rituals guide our brains into successful practice. The more you repeat a ritual, the smoother your practice will be. Find the notebook that works for you, the pen or pencil that will be your talisman. Do the same thing before you write—take a bath, go for a run or a walk, read poetry, play with the cat, clean up your apartment—every single time. Rituals let your body and your creating mind know it's time to work. It's probably unrealistic to expect that you can rush home after work or school, bang out a poem, and then revise it as you make dinner, get your chemistry lab under way, and text friends all the while. One writer, Bob Vivian, lights a candle when he starts his daily writing and he blows it out when he is finished. It has to be the same kind of candle; he always travels with his special writing candle. It doesn't matter what your rituals are; what is important is that you pay attention to what you do right before your writing sessions—and repeat what works for you.

> *Show up, show up, show up, and after a while the muse shows up, too.*
> —ISABEL ALLENDE

Flow

When you are "**in the zone**" on the basketball court, the basket looks enormous. You can't hear the fans in the stands. Things take place almost as if in slow motion. When you are in the zone as a writer, you lose all sense of time, too. You are *in* the scene or moment you are writing—you aren't sitting in your writing place at all.

You can't hear nearby conversations around you, the television show, or the music playing. You are in the writing zone.

Some researchers call this state of creative concentration **flow**—when you are involved in an activity and you go into a kind of focused trance. Susan Perry, a psychologist who studies creativity, describes it this way in her book *Writing in Flow*:

> Flow is a relatively new term for an essential and universal human experience. You know you've been in flow when time seems to have disappeared. When you're in flow, you become so deeply immersed in your writing, or whatever activity you're doing, that you forget yourself and your surroundings. You delight in continuing to write even if you get no reward for doing it—monetary or otherwise—and even if no one else cares whether you do it. You feel challenged, stimulated, definitely not bored. Writing in flow, you're often certain you're tapping into some creative part of yourself—or of the universe—that you don't have easy access to when you're not in this altered state. Sports figures call this desired condition being "in the zone."

You know flow. You play for hours at pastimes that absorb you—video games, lacrosse, cycling, knitting, talking with friends—whatever your passion. You fall out of time and become lost in a narrative, whether it's the game or the conversation. Practice paying attention to when you are utterly absorbed by a task. How did you get into that state? What brought you out of it?

One of the best ways to train yourself to fall into flow is to use a **timer**. There are a number of different methods writers use—twenty-minute sessions with five-minute breaks, thirty-minute sessions with ten-minute breaks, and forty-five-minute sessions with fifteen-minute breaks. Experiment with timed writing sessions—no phone, no email, no distractions. Find out what time period works best for your personality. Creativity researchers generally agree that using a timer, and disciplining yourself to do nothing else except write during that time period, keeping your hands moving all the while, even if you are simply writing your name or a sentence over and over again, followed by a prescribed break, produces the optimal conditions for flow.

Most writers who use a timer ritual to sustain their daily practice find the **breaks** crucial. For many, it's important that the break be timed and also limited. Texting, phone calls, engaging with conversation—these can disrupt flow *even on the breaks*. Breaks that involve reading, walking, yoga, taking a bath, doing the dishes, folding laundry—anything that keeps your body moving but doesn't take you too far away from the dream state you're in when you write—often offer creative surprises that feed right back into your work.

When engaged in these simple tasks that don't require talking or engaging with others, ideas may pop up, solutions often come to the fore, and usually the writer can't wait to get back to their page.

PRACTICE 6

TRY THE POMODORO TECHNIQUE

The **Pomodoro technique** has been proven to enhance flow. It's a simple timed practice. First, set your writing intention. "I'm going to start writing my poem." Or, "I'm going to read the rest of this chapter and then begin my subject list." Or, "I'll work on my story, starting in the middle where I left off." Set your timer for twenty-five minutes. Keep at your task for the entire twenty-five minutes and try to keep your hand or fingers moving the entire time, writing. When your timer rings, set it for five minutes. Take a five-minute break. If you choose to continue, set a new intention and the timer for twenty-five minutes. The breaks are crucial: Notice what ideas come up during the break. The goal is four sessions, and then a thirty-minute break. Try at least one Pomodoro of twenty-five minutes and see what happens. Report back to the class.

LACK OF FOCUS

Even with a good foundation—working from the mind's eye, using sensory detail, writing what you know, developing a (perhaps timed) daily practice, and employing rituals, many writers face difficulties with focus. Getting stuck, or **writer's block**, is essentially an inability to focus artistically, the loss of creative concentration. Often what gets labeled "writer's block" is actually distraction—external or internal distraction. When you have a problem with procrastination, you may want to redefine the issue as a *loss of focus*. To develop strategies for combating lack of focus—procrastination, writer's block, internal and external distractions—it may help to learn a bit more about the nature of writer's block, distraction, and procrastination. After all, the known enemy is easier to defeat than the unknown enemy.

Writer's Block

Writers sometimes say they are blocked when they cannot write. They describe feeling disconnected from their own work. The blocked writer often feels tapped out, completely devoid of imaginative energy. The blocked writer can't envision the scenes and moments and images that transport themselves, *the writer*, much less a reader.

To cure a block, creativity experts say to focus first on fear. Many writing blocks may actually be manifestations of fear: fear of not being good enough, fear of failure, fear of sounding insincere, fear of hurting someone with your words. These writing fears are common, normal, and realistic: You probably *do* want to be a better writer than you are now. But you might write quite a few clichéd pieces, especially when you are just starting out. Maybe this isn't a problem? You're learning. Keep in mind that failure is a large and important part of learning any new skill. Some of your writing block might be a helpful, wise call to thoughtfulness: Words are extraordinarily powerful. It's good to be aware of your intentions and sensitive to how your work might affect others.

The poet William Stafford has a terrific rule you might want to use. "Got writer's block?" he says. "Lower your standards."

Here are four additional tips for working through a block:

- Read for at least thirty minutes a day. Often reading writers you love will reignite your passion to write.
- Write for a set amount of time each day. Start with five minutes — or even one minute — and then work your way to ten to fifteen minutes a day.
- Allow yourself to write without judging your writing.
- Remember that you aren't the first person to be blocked nor will you be the last. Take some time to study the psychology and process of writing. Elizabeth Gilbert's *Big Magic*, Eric Maisel's *Fearless Creating*, and Mason Currey's books on writer's rituals sit on my bookshelf, and these three tomes are my go-to sources when I see a block on the horizon.

I think of a block like the flu. I'm more susceptible to each if I'm run down — tired, engaged with activities that don't really feed my soul, overcommitted, trying to please too many people, pushing myself too hard. I try to stay healthy as a writer by working in small, timed sessions every day, regularly reading good literature, avoiding unnecessary activities, and studying my craft. When the inevitable block arrives, I'm armed with gentle, healing approaches that I know, from trial and error, work for me. This semester, find out what works for you in terms of preventing and treating inevitable writer blocks.

Distraction

There are two kinds of distraction: internal — where the thoughts in your head keep you from staying focused — and external. **External distractions** include your noisy roommate, your active three-year-old daughter, your elderly dog, hourly texts from your mother, your boyfriend doing jumping jacks in the living room while he waits for you to finish writing your poem. **Internal distractions** are your emotions regarding your boyfriend, the nagging feelings you have about cleaning the house, calling your mother back, going to the store because the refrigerator is empty, studying anatomy for your midterm, needing chocolate *now*. Distraction destroys flow.

To keep external distractions at bay, writers have to find a place and a time where we can work undisturbed, even if it's for a brief time each day. After an external interruption, you're at your most vulnerable for losing focus. To get back into flow, many writers reread their last few sentences, or start at the beginning, reading until they get caught back up in the piece. As you practice, try to notice how you get back into your work, and reoriented into the mind's eye. The more you know about your specific ways of working, and how you best recover from interruption, the more productive you'll be.

Internal distractions are trickier. You may be dogged by perfectionism, struggling to get each sentence or syllable just so before you move on. You may be haunted by concerns about what others will think of your writing. Low confidence or high anxiety, or both, can make it almost impossible to get and stay in flow. The books mentioned above, and the practices and projects in this textbook, can help you get out of your own head and into the world you're trying to create on the page. Some writers find it useful to jot down their internal distractions, putting them into words so they can keep an eye on them. Some writers require music while working, as an aid to quieting the internal "monkey mind." Almost every single writer struggles with a pack of interior voices hounding them not to work, to give up, to do something else, anything else. These critical voices have to be dealt with creatively. That's part of the practice.

Cal Newport, a computer science professor at Georgetown University, has written about the power of focus in his book *Deep Work: Rules for Focused Success in a Distracted World*. "We tell ourselves," he says in an interview on *The Hidden Brain* podcast, "Let me just do a just-check to my inbox. Let me just do a just-check to my phone real quick and then back to my work. And it feels like single-tasking. And it feels like you're predominantly working on one thing. But even those very brief checks that switch your context even briefly can have this massive negative impact on your cognitive performance. It's the switch itself that hurts, not how long you actually switch."

Newport describes recent lab experiments which prove people don't perform as well on cognitive tests after distractions, even tiny distractions that simply require moving one's attention from one thing to another and quickly back. We know we should not let our devices drive our attention. However, he says, "We treat it, I think, in this more general sense of, eh, I probably should be less distracted. And I think it's more urgent than people realize, that if your brain is how you make a living, then you really have to worry about this cognitive fitness. How are you getting performance out of your brain? Are you taking care to get good performance out of your brain or not? And people would probably be surprised . . . how much they're leaving on the table by the way they're currently working right now."

Procrastination

Procrastination is a lack of focus caused by internal distraction. Learning how your mind works and repeating productive behaviors is your best line of defense and your best way to get back into focus. However, if you are using procrastination itself as a focusing tool, and it works for you, perhaps procrastination isn't the worst thing. If you have plenty of extra time in your life to get things done, procrastination doesn't hurt anything. If you are pressed for time, however, you will need to develop more effective strategies.

> *Procrastination is fear of success. People procrastinate because they are afraid of the success that they know will result if they move ahead now. Because success is heavy, carries a responsibility with it, it is much easier to procrastinate and live on the "someday I'll" philosophy.*
>
> —DENNIS WAITLEY

Many students report that they procrastinate. They assume there are "real" writers out there, working steady hours, right on schedule, happily progressing along, writing poem after poem, book after book, and that they are deeply flawed. In fact, most writers putter around and get to the task at hand in a slow and somewhat haphazard way.

Many students, and many writers, constrict the amount of time they have so they can jump-start their ability to focus. T. S. Eliot once said that not having as much time for his writing as he would like allowed him to concentrate better. Perhaps this is why we procrastinate instead of doing the work for our classes—we wait until the last minute so we experience that useful time pressure.

Having a limited amount of time forces us to concentrate. When we are zealous about getting the project done—it's due in *less than one hour*—we can often concentrate with our full creative powers. You can use that human instinct to your advantage: Set a timer. Make sure to set micro-deadlines for yourself and use the compression and intensity of a deadline to jump-start flow.

> *I plan out the day like a chess player moving the pieces around. This is what I'm going to work on when. I don't let my mood dictate how my day unfolds.*
> —CAL NEWPORT

Judgment

Some psychologists who study creativity theorize that blocks, distractions, and procrastination — all the things we do to sabotage ourselves — are caused by judgment, that unhelpful critical voice that evaluates the quality of your work long before you're even close to be done.

But judgment doesn't have to be negative to be distracting. If you are thinking about how great you are, how much money you will make, how profound your writing is, how beautiful the words will sound when you read them aloud at your Pulitzer Prize acceptance, you are distracted. You aren't focused on the reader's experience. And chances are that your writing won't be as powerful as it could be.

If you go in to your writing session to criticize or beat yourself up, it's going to be hard to focus on the mind's eye and observing sensory detail.

When you write from your center self, keeping in mind the images you want to write about, you are focused and there isn't room for judging the work: You *are* the work. When you are truly focused, your question isn't "Is this going well?" or "Is this bad?" because you can never really know that. When you are at work, your question is "What is most interesting here? What do I see? What are my senses telling me?" And you watch. And keep writing.

Recall the main concept from earlier in this chapter: It's not about you. It's about your reader. You are a sort of middleperson, a channel. Your job as a writer is to reach down and scoop up the stuff that is buried at the image level inside you. You bring it up to the light, trying not to overanalyze the emotions or explain what's going on — simply re-create for your readers the images and story in your mind.

Try to delay product-based judgments — positive and negative — while you are creating. Will I get published? Is this terrible? While you are writing is not the appropriate time to ask these questions. However, evaluation of your *process* is important as you work. Did you show up for your writing session today? Did you manage distraction? Were you able to stay off screens for the duration of the entire writing period until the timer went off? Good! Writing time is for writing. Evaluation is a completely different process — best saved for later. Much later. As in Chapter Nine later.

Here are best-selling author Neil Gaiman's rules for writers. Many of his suggestions echo concepts you are reviewing in this chapter. Notice how he approaches process first (write, write one word at a time; then, finish what you are writing) and advises caution around judgment (choose good friends) and perfectionism (let it go).

Neil Gaiman

8 Rules for Writing

1. Write.
2. Put one word after another. Find the right word, put it down.
3. Finish what you're writing. Whatever you have to do to finish it, finish it.
4. Put it aside. Read it pretending you've never read it before. Show it to friends whose opinion you respect and who like the kind of thing that this is.
5. Remember: When people tell you something's wrong or doesn't work for them, they are almost always right. When they tell you exactly what they think is wrong and how to fix it, they are almost always wrong.
6. Fix it. Remember that, sooner or later, before it ever reaches perfection, you will have to let it go and move on and start to write the next thing. Perfection is like chasing the horizon. Keep moving.
7. Laugh at your own jokes.
8. The main rule of writing is that if you do it with enough assurance and confidence, you're allowed to do whatever you like. (That may be a rule for life as well as for writing. But it's definitely true for writing.) So write your story as it needs to be written. Write it honestly, and tell it as best you can. I'm not sure that there are any other rules. Not ones that matter.

Finding focus as a writer requires you to understand what transports readers and what your own mind and personality need in order to be creative. Reading what other writers who have come before you have learned along the way can be inspiring. *The Guardian* newspaper's "Rules for Writers" feature showcases the distilled writerly wisdom from Neil Gaiman alongside some of the globe's most widely read and highly respected authors. Perhaps reading their advice will be part of your writing ritual?

WRITING PROJECTS

Process/Drama

1. Write a one-page dialogue between you and the critical voice in your head. Give the critical voice a name—I call mine "Demon." Discuss

your writing life with the critical voice; argue with it. Format the piece like a play. Here's a sample:

Demon: You suck.

Writing Self: Will you ever give me a break?

Demon: No. Because no cares what you write—why are you even trying?

Writing Self: I'm not sure. I feel better after write . . . it helps my anxiety, to be honest.

2. Based on what you've read in this textbook so far, and after rereading the interviews with the writers on page 42, page 44, and page 46, create your own list of 8 Rules for Writing. Consider printing your personalized list and posting it above your desk or on your fridge to refer to when you're grumpy about writing or feeling stuck.

Experiment/Fiction

3. Create a comic about you or someone else you know becoming a writer, creator, or artist but use another activity (baseball, robotics, cooking, fixing a car) to describe the steps, pitfalls, or processes. Use images. Don't write *about* what you see. Write the actions and images, experiencing them on the sensory level as you write.

Poetry

4. Write an imitation of John Brehm's poem on page 43. titling yours "The Poems I Have Not Written." Make a list all the poems you haven't written, using specific images to describe how these poems flourish in the world. When you imitate a poem, you place the words *after [name of poet]* at the end of the poem so everyone knows you are consciously imitating and not stealing someone else's ideas or words.

Nonfiction

5. Reread Och Gonzalez's micro-memoir, "What I Do on My Terrace Is None of Your Business" on page 45. Create a scene from your life now set in one room where you live. Focus on observing the people around you. If you are feeling sad, try to show that through your observations of the people/place. If your mood is buoyant, allow the details you observe to show joy. Just as Gonzalez does, end on a tiny, tiny moment of observation—an action—that gives you hope or seems like a sign of change to come.

READINGS

Jarod Roselló
Robot Camp

AT FIRST, I THOUGHT ROBOT CAMP WAS A GOOD IDEA

WE ALL DID

AND FOR A WHILE IT WAS

WE WERE BUILDING ROBOTS

LEARNING COMPLEX ROBOTICS, ENGINEERING, AND MACHINE-MAKING

I FELT LIKE A SCIENTIST AND A METAL WORKER AND AN ARTIST

BUT BY THE THIRD WEEK, THINGS STARTED TO GO WRONG

I BURNED MY HAND

THEN A MAN LOST AN ARM

A COUPLE COUNSELORS WENT MISSING

ONE TIME, WE THOUGHT WE SAW A GHOST

BUT IT TURNED OUT TO BE SOMETHING ELSE

IT WAS THE MONDAY OF WEEK FOUR

WHEN WE DISCOVERED ALL THE FOOD WAS GONE

IN ITS PLACE WERE NUTS AND BOLTS

CIRCUITS, WIRES, AND SWITCHES

SOMEONE DRAINED THE LAKE WHILE WE SLEPT

AND ALL THE FISH DIED

ONE NIGHT, THE CAMP WAS SET ON FIRE

IN THE MORNING, THE RAIN PUT IT OUT

DESPITE ALL THIS, WE KEPT BUILDING ROBOTS

WHAT ELSE COULD WE DO?

SOMEONE SAID THE WORLD WAS ENDING

BUT IT HADN'T ENDED YET

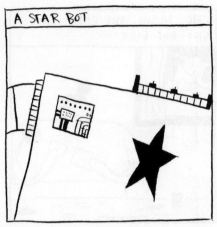

I TRIED A FEW TIMES TO CRAFT IT MYSELF

BUT THE TOOLS I NEEDED WERE MISSING

SMASH

SOMEONE SUGGESTED I BUILD SOMETHING ELSE INSTEAD

BURN

BUT AT THAT TIME I WAS TOO FOCUSED ON MY ROBOT

STOMP

TOO BLINDED BY DESIRE

TO PURSUE ANY OTHER VENTURES

IT WAS THIS SCREAM THAT RATTLED ME

THAT WOKE ME UP TO THE HORRORS AROUND US

I KNEW WHAT I HAD TO DO

AND I KNEW JUST HOW TO DO IT

A MAN WROTE MY NAME ON A FLAG

AND I THREW IT IN THE FIRE

WE WAITED FOR THE RIGHT MOMENT

FOR THE SUN TO NEARLY SET

WHEN WE KNEW THE ROBOTS

WOULDN'T BE ABLE TO SEE VERY WELL

I TURNED ON THE MACHINE

AND TOLD EVERYONE TO RUN

WRITERS ON WRITING

JAROD ROSELLÓ

HEATHER SELLERS: How did you come up with the idea for "Robot Camp"?

JAROD ROSELLÓ: Robot Camp came in the middle of writing a different robot story. I was working on the script for a graphic novel about a planet-wide robot invasion. I hadn't really sat with the idea of a robot invasion for very long, and so I felt like I needed a minute to work through it. It was summer, and I'd just sent my own children off to camp, and I also thought it might be kind of funny that these people would be at a robotics camp during a robot invasion. I'm drawn to story elements that seem too wild, coincidental, or illogical, and the challenge of figuring out how to make them work.

HS: What was the process like for "Robot Camp"? Did you revise it a lot?

JR: For Robot Camp, I actually wrote all the text first, jotting down some notes or doing quick sketches of visual imagery as it came to me. But I set this comic up with the constraint of having to work around and through the text I'd written. As I was working out the drawings, I would edit the text in response to something I'd drawn, then edit the drawings again based on the revised text. It's not quite like finishing discrete drafts, so much as it was continuous adjustments and changes to the piece until it felt done. A kind of dialogue between drawing and writing.

HS: What's your creative process like on any given day?

JR: I like to work in loud, busy places full of people. So, if I'm not stuck at my drawing desk, I like to take my sketchbook to a coffee shop or somewhere public, put on some headphones, and draw and write. I don't have a consistent writing process: I'll work with whatever materials I have, wherever I am, and figure out how to make something. The only real consistent part of my process is that I have to find the right song or album to write to. Most of my writing revolves around exploring sensations and feelings, and music is a great way for me to get myself to the places I want to know more about.

HS: What advice do you have regarding revision?

JR: Sometimes revision means taking your writing apart and moving things around. Sometimes it means adding, cutting, or rewriting certain parts. Sometimes, it means taking your big ideas or concepts, and re-contextualizing them entirely. And sometimes, revision is about taking the lessons you've learned—about your own process or your craft—and putting them into a new piece. Revision should be an act that moves you closer to making the kind of work you want to make, and whatever form that needs to take is okay.

John Brehm

The Poems I Have Not Written

I'm so wildly unprolific, the poems
I have not written would reach
from here to the California coast
if you laid them end to end.

And if you stacked them up,
the poems I have not written
would sway like a silent
Tower of Babel, saying nothing

and everything in a thousand
different tongues. So moving, so
filled with and emptied of suffering,
so steeped in the music of a voice

speechless before the truth,
the poems I have not written
would break the hearts of every
woman who's ever left me,

make them eye their husbands
with a sharp contempt and hate
themselves for turning their backs
on the very source of beauty.

The poems I have not written
would compel all other poets
to ask of God: "*Why* do you
let me live? I am worthless.

Please strike me dead at once,
destroy my works and cleanse
the earth of all my ghastly
imperfections." Trees would

bow their heads before the poems
I have not written. "Take me,"
they would say, "and turn me
into your pages so that I

might live forever as the ground
from which your words arise."
The wind itself, about which
I might have written so eloquently,

praising its slick and intersecting
rivers of air, its stately calms
and furious interrogations,
its flutelike lingerings and passionate

reproofs, would divert its course
to sweep down and then pass over
the poems I have not written,
and the life I have not lived, the life

I've failed even to imagine,
which they so perfectly describe.

WRITERS ON WRITING

JOHN BREHM

HEATHER SELLERS: What was your process in writing this poem?

JOHN BREHM: "The Poems I Have Not Written" came quickly and pretty effortlessly. I wrote it in a single sitting and then made just a few changes. But the moment of writing had been preceded by quite a lot of worrying about my meager output, envying of more prolific poets, etc. I remember being struck by the idea that I could turn a weakness into a strength by boasting about the brilliance of all the poems I had not written. Then it was off to the races with one hyperbolic claim after another. I had a lot of fun writing this poem, but there's also an undercurrent of sadness in it, as I really was regretting not being able to write more than I do. Focusing on the poems I had not written led me, in a moment of inspiration as I was sailing along, to realize I could assert that they were about the life I had not lived, or even imagined, creating a perfect, self-contained loop between unwritten poems and unlived life. "The Poems I Have Not Written" is also an example of the way I often get divergent emotions to flow together in a poem, in this case exuberance and sadness, absurdly exalted self-praise and a sober recognition of my own limitations.

HS: Is your writing process different, as far as you can tell, when you're working in prose versus poetry?

JB: I find it easier to work on prose, once I get started, without the surge of imaginative energy needed for poetry. I can flesh out ideas, create transitions, clarify points, add examples, etc., in a way that feels more deliberate and workmanlike than the sudden bursts I need for poems. When I'm writing a poem, I need to be in the flow to do anything worthwhile. I suppose poetry and prose differ in the degree of conscious vs. unconscious energies each relies upon, with prose being the more conscious endeavor and poetry more free to take unexpected turns, make leaps, say things that are outlandish or illogical. But I'm opposed to hard-and-fast notions about the differences between poetry and prose. Each can do pretty much everything the other does.

Och Gonzalez

What I Do on My Terrace Is None of Your Business

The woman in the apartment on my left has her head drooped low and an arm weighed down by a yellow watering can spouting all over the clay pots that line the metal bars of her terrace. If she had fuchsia pink hair, she would look exactly like the hibiscus flowers she's been growing in the pots. She does this every morning but the flowers don't seem to want to cooperate and are already starting to look listless and she can't figure out why. I want to tell her she's doing it wrong—hibiscus plants need to be watered every day in the summer, but once the weather cools, like it already has on this early November morning, they need only a little water every now and then. I want to tell her she's killing them and it's only a matter of time until she slides her glass door open one morning to find them with limp pink heads and yellowing leaves, all bogged down by the weight of her well-intentioned care. I know this because in the garden of the old house I lived in for fifteen years before moving to this row of anonymous flats just a month ago, I used to have a fully-grown hibiscus shrub. I didn't do much to help it, but it thrived and exploded in bursts of red all throughout both the brisk mornings and the shimmering afternoons. I want to tell her all of this but I don't. What she does on her terrace is none of my business.

She sees me sitting on a white plastic chair on my own terrace, a leftover from my old garden set, drinking my morning coffee and lighting up a cigarette. The white tiles in my own tiny strip of space are shiny but strewn with wayward ashes and some squiggles of hair that the wind has plucked from my scalp. The scraggly black strands look forlorn without my dog's golden hair tangled along with them. Her own ashes now sleep in a small wooden box on top of my bookshelf, and beside it, a tuft of her fur rests undisturbed by the wind under the gleam of a glass dome keepsake. The woman on my left looks over at me dolefully with an almost imperceptible shake of her head. I can practically see the gears in her brain kicking alive, churning and wheeling over *why, in this day and age, would somebody still choose to smoke, why not just jump over the railing of the terrace down to the ground twenty-nine floors below and be done with it,* to which my own gears quickly churned back, *well, we all self-destruct somehow—we just do it in different ways. You shouldn't fret. What I do on my terrace is none of your business.*

I almost say the last words out loud but just then a flock of gray doves flies over us and my head snaps up. A few seconds later, another one. This goes on for about five times before I realize that it's the same flock circling round the building. They are shaped like an arrow, the alpha bird at the tip and his six minions divided into two slants of three. They look like cadets on a morning jog, warming up before the commander releases them to their designated posts for the day. In the space between the fifth and the sixth round, I look over to the woman on my left and see her hand still holding the watering can aloft, water dribbling down her hapless hibiscus, making them nod like somnolent bobbleheads, her face upturned and waiting for the doves like I am, grasping at the harmony in the gray and the order in the middle of random things like the dying and flying of the things we hold dear, and sharing in the same pockets of grace that happen when one remembers to look up.

WRITERS ON WRITING

OCH GONZALEZ

HEATHER SELLERS: How did you come up with the idea for this piece?

OCH GONZALEZ: This piece came about as a result of two big changes that happened in my life at almost the same time—I lost my dog to cancer, and then just a week later, we had to move out of the house that had been our home for fifteen years.

I was feeling isolated and adrift. I loved our old house which was so full of character and our old neighborhood, where everyone knew each other, and the new building we moved into was the total opposite of this—a high-rise condominium where all the units looked the same, and everyone was always busy rushing off to work.

But even worse was the loss of my dog, who was not only a member of our family, but also a big part of my writing life. I could not bear to write without her just yet.

One morning out on my new terrace, feeling melancholy, I saw the flock of doves and it hit me that this is GRACE, that all is not lost, that I will recover.

This flash of insight led to the writing of this piece.

HS: Is writing flash different from other kinds of writing?

OG: The perfect inspiration for a flash nonfiction piece is literally a flash, a single moment that contains power and emotion in it, a moment that could only have been caught by being mindful, which is what a writer always needs to be. This piece came to me from the flash. But had I not been paying attention, I would never have noticed the doves, or little details like the strands of hair on the floor.

HS: Describe your writing process.

OG: For this specific piece, I needed no warm-up. I was driven by the desire to explore my melancholy and find my way back to connectedness. I knew that I needed to convey the disconnect I felt so I first came up with the title containing those words, "none of your business." Because this was a flash piece, I needed to be really choosy with the words I would use. I had to use details really carefully: to convey the back story that was the foundation of the piece.

The imaginary conversation between me and the woman shows how sometimes we make snap judgments of each other even while being strangers. But as the incident with the doves showed, we can just as easily cast our judgments aside and recognize moments of grace and share in them, even while being strangers.

HS: Do you write every day? Do you revise a lot?

OG: In general, much of my writing process is centered on mindfulness, on noticing things around me. On days that nothing really comes to me, I warm up with poems because I've found that putting things in poetry form, no matter how terrible, invites a sense of rhythm and tunes my ear.

When I finally do get around to having a decent draft, I leave it for a while and come back to it with a fresh eye so I can more easily see what can be improved.

I like the word "shape" because it's a lot more encouraging than the word "revision." The latter sounds tedious and boring. "Shape" more accurately describes what we do with the words we lay down, much like a potter shapes a jar out of clay.

I feel a piece is done when I've managed to make it balanced — there's enough to move the story forward, and yet not so much that the reader no longer has a call for active engagement. Personally, as a reader, I like writing that challenges me to connect the dots myself.

CHAPTER TWO

READING AS A WRITER

In this chapter you will:

- Develop close reading skills across genres
- Practice strategies for reading your own writing and writing by peers
- Use reading to launch your creative writing projects

Creative writers read differently from literature students. As in a literature course, we are looking at the components of writing—**speaker**, **point of view**, **metaphor**, **characterization**. But we're not picking the piece apart in order to make an argument of some kind. We're not looking for hidden messages or deep themes or life lessons or to apprehend literary history. All valuable activities, but that's not what we're doing here. We are reading to learn technique. We're reading for pleasure, too, of course, but probably a bit differently from those happy, relaxed folks who are reading on the beach.

By reading closely and strategically, with a specific and perhaps somewhat selfish agenda in mind, we learn our craft.

TIPS FOR READING AS A WRITER

Be Curious

A writer confined to one section of the library or to one specific type of book or genre is rare indeed. Creative writers are free-range and undisciplined readers, roaming from new works by young authors hot off the press over to the poetry world, perhaps dabbling in the classics before grazing science fiction, eagerly hunting down novels, comics, plays, and pieces that defy genre classification written by authors of all ages and periods, from the ancients to the postmodernists, exploring work from all over the globe. We tend to be radically inclusive in our choices: We'll read pretty much *anything*. Because there is so much to learn about the craft of writing, our reading lives are driven by a particular hunger: We read to live, artistically.

Read Widely

If you are in a reading rut, trending toward the same kinds of novels or comics, again and again, challenge yourself to branch out. Read works in translation, works by writers from other classes, countries, and centuries. A healthy reading diet includes poetry, graphic memoirs, digital stories, as well as novels, stories, and plays. If you're serious about the craft of writing, creating a reading list of about fifty texts per year is a good goal. Treat yourself to a wide array: As in many aspects of life, variety and diversity are your friends.

Explore Genres, Question Boundaries

Poets read novels to extend their range. Short story writers study poetry to learn form and infuse their sentences with sound and rhythm. Playwrights read memoir and nonfiction to hear how different people speak, and for inspiration and content.

Read what you don't usually read. Try a collection of prose poems. Experiment with an alternative literary site like *Diagram* or *F(r)iction*. If comics don't usually interest you, try Moira Kalman or David Small. If all you read is graphic novels, embrace a Russian classic or a contemporary play. Reading the same kind of thing is too safe, too thin for the writer in you. As you branch out intentionally, you might ask your instructor for recommendations, start a book group, or use the appendix in this textbook for suggestions.

Poet and novelist Ocean Vuong has this to say about **genre**:

> I'm not sure a genre is a destination so much as a way of thinking, a tendency of inquiry. When we think of tables, we think of staying there, of keeping our place cards, our seats. I'm not interested in possession. I want to be freer than that. Maybe I'm being naive, but I understand genres to be as fluid as genders. Our lives are full of restrictions—jobs, bills, time, gravity, all of this impinging on us—but to write is to gift yourself the freedom of choice and possibility. That feels truly precious to me.

Do his words inspire you to approach genre in a new way, perhaps with some confidence that your experiments may be both necessary and perhaps even inspiring to others?

Embrace Discomfort

> *The greatest part of a writer's time is spent in reading; in order to write, a man will turn over half a library to make one book.*
>
> —SAMUEL JOHNSON

Rarely, if ever, do successful creative writers glance at a new work and say "I don't like it," walk away, and head back to what's safe and familiar. Nor do we limit ourselves to reading only what's "**relatable**." As writers we are eager to expand our range and know about the worlds we haven't experienced. Instead of focusing on how a piece of writing connects to our own, perhaps limited, experience, we like to extend ourselves boldly and discover how we relate to the new, the strange, the unexpected, the different.

We tend to be more patient readers than the general population because our curiosity overrides our irritation; patience wins over confusion, and quest for knowledge of how writing works trumps boredom. When put off by a difficult or unusual text, instead of giving up and going back to an easier read, we tend to see difficulty as a challenge, a kind of artistic problem to be solved. When stymied while reading, we burrow in, asking questions along these lines:

- Why is the writer doing it this way?
- What's interesting about the choices the writer is making?
- Why might a publisher have found this worthy?
- Why might other readers find this useful or interesting?

Some texts are just too mysterious to us and perhaps we set them down to come back to later (or not). But as writers, we typically work hard as readers, often reading a selection multiple times in order to gain as much as we can from each work.

An interviewer once asked William Faulkner what he, the interviewer, should do—he had read Faulkner's novel three times and still didn't understand it. Faulkner said, "Read it four times." Some pieces just aren't going to be meaningful to you. We all have reading blocks and literary blind spots. But staying with a difficult or strange piece, working to understand it, and then having it open up for you is the best possible gift you can give yourself as a writer.

Creative reading is, in part, the ability to postpone settling hastily into likes/dislikes and to lead with curiosity. In fact, as creative readers, often we don't even care very much if we like or dislike a piece of writing. Usually we're much more interested in figuring out what the author is trying to do, how exactly she's creating the effect she's creating. It doesn't matter to us as much if the work is wildly successful or not; we aren't book reviewers. We're like mechanics. We read in order to see how the piece works.

TO READ IS TO TRAVEL

Creative reading is about going to new places and hanging out, even when it's unknown, uncomfortable, and really far from home. Just like travelers, creative readers know in advance they are going to

> *The beautiful thing about learning is nobody can take it away from you.*
> —B. B. KING

get lost in certain books, confused by poetry, and overwhelmed by plays. Some degree of trepidation and crankiness is inevitable on any trip. Difficulty and discomfort are, by definition, part of travel.

In *Beautiful and Pointless*, his book on why to write poetry and how to read it, David Orr discusses this very topic:

> The comparison may seem ridiculous at first but consider the way you'd be thinking about Belgium if you were planning a trip there. You might try to learn a few useful phrases, or read a little Belgian history, or thumb through a guidebook in search of museums, restaurants, flea markets, or promising-sounding bars. The important thing is that you'd know you're going to be confused, or at least occasionally at a loss, and you'd accept that confusion as part of the experience. What you wouldn't do, however, is become paralyzed with anxiety because you don't speak fluent Flemish. . . . Nor would you decide in advance that you'd never understand Belgians because you couldn't immediately determine why their most famous public statue is a depiction of a naked kid peeing in a fountain (which is true). You'd probably figure, hey, that's what they like in Belgium; if I stick around long enough maybe it will make sense. (p. xv)

We read to travel across the human experience, to save ourselves from our own limits, to extend the range of what we can know and understand and feel and love. We don't expect every part of the trip to be comfy, familiar, and easy—that's just not how travel works. Creative reading means we like going places we haven't been before, and to do so we know we're going to develop a tolerance for not getting the whole thing at once, an ability to be lost and not get frustrated and retreat to familiar ground.

Some readers are naturally bolder than others by nature. Some readers easily tolerate not knowing or not getting it: Oh, kid peeing in fountain, makes no sense, but I gotta love it, not a problem. Others find unusual things (A kid peeing in a fountain?) very concerning and they want to flee.

But steering toward what is comfortable and familiar isn't creative at all. In fact, it's the opposite of creative. Writers are rarely the kind of people who want everything spelled out, simplified, familiar. When someone wants to improve as a writer, the ability to diversify one's tastes, to travel further and wider to take more challenging trips as a reader, is essential. Just as competitive rock climbers continue to seek more difficult vertical ventures, and just as gym rats keep increasing the resistance even though it's frustrating and sometimes even painful, creative writers crave works that challenge them anew and expand their **reading repertoire**.

PRACTICE 1

EXAMINING YOUR READING REPERTOIRE

Take a close look at your reading life. Answer the following questions. (1) What have you typically gravitated toward as a reader?; (2) Was there a time in your life you read a lot? Not at all? Why?; (3) How do you decide what to read next?; (4) Do you read a lot of works that are in the genres you wish to write in?; (5) Do you think cross-training as a writer, reading in other genres could be helpful to you? If so, how?; (6) What's your favorite piece of writing of all time? Least favorite? Why?

To find new and interesting things to read, consult Chapter Twelve in this text. There you'll find suggestions for resources on social media and how to search online for new literary magazines and current writers. For example, you can subscribe to the *Los Angeles Times Review of Books* and find lively, fresh reading suggestions delivered to your phone weekly. Many literary magazines are on Facebook and Twitter, and in addition to tweets from *The Believer*, *The Offing*, and *Tin House*, don't forget to troll your local bookstore for zines and local literary journals. Ask other students in your creative writing program who they are reading and where they find the best recommendations. Google "best new writers under forty." Go to Powells.com and peruse their Staff Picks and "Twenty-Five Books to Read Before You Die." Your instructor will have suggestions for you as well. Perhaps you will start a real or virtual bulletin board in your department where others can post their top picks for best new authors.

STRATEGIES FOR CLOSE READING

When we read a short story, poem, or play for the first time, we're generally aware of the effect it has on us emotionally. But for a working writer, the first read is a walk-through. On the second read, we begin to pay closer attention to exactly how the words, lines, sentences, scenes — each of the parts — work together to create the whole effect. Because a piece of writing — whether it's a poem, a play, a micro-memoir, or a short story — is a complex thing, we can only focus on one set of concerns at a time; multiple rereadings may be required before we come to understand how a piece works, or doesn't. To break down the close-reading process, here are five strategies to try.

Read Multiple Times, Take Notes

The first read is a get-to-know-you, a chance to notice what looks potentially interesting and to mark trouble spots. If we love the piece, great. There's more pleasure ahead by focusing carefully on how the piece works. If we're stymied or put off by the selection, we don't freak out. (We just arrived in Belgium. We don't speak the language. It's too soon to say if we like it or not.) On the first read, we flag our favorite passages and also note what is confusing, just as on a trip we might jot down certain things we want to follow up on, places we want to come back to in order to explore in more detail.

> *In all genres, I wait in ambush for the exact, perfect, telling detail, the thing that makes the scene or line come alive.*
>
> —LAUREN GROFF

On the second read, we pay attention to the following:

- What information comes from the title?
- Where does the piece take place? How is that significant?
- Who is talking?
- How does the piece look on the page? Why did the writer do it that way?

Researchers have studied how people behave in art museums and found that the average visitor spends five seconds — five *seconds* — in front of a painting or sculpture before moving on. Professionals know that it takes five *minutes* of carefully looking before a viewer can really start to appreciate the basics of what's going on in a piece of art, and more time is needed to appreciate the subtleties of the meaning and craft. Don't be the hurried tourist who says, grumpily, "My kid could do that." Take time. It's often worthwhile to go more slowly as you read a selection, read longer, stare quietly. You'll be amazed at what you can see when you look and look again.

PRACTICE 2

REREADING

Reread any of the pieces discussed in Chapter One. Read three times, if you can. Take notes on anything you notice in the second reading that you simply didn't see before; nothing is too small to notice. Compare your notes from the first time you read it to the third time. How are they different?

Read Aloud

The second read is usually best performed aloud. (Note: For pieces of poetry and drama, we *always* read at least once aloud.) Hearing creative work read out loud, in your own voice or someone else's, makes a significant difference in your ability to appreciate subtle aspects of a piece as well as to better understand the piece, which is especially true for poetry. The ear can pick up things the eye doesn't. Having someone else read a piece aloud to you while you read along on the page is another good way to embark on a successful second read. Whether you are listening or speaking, reading aloud forces you to go more slowly, and in doing so, you have the chance to notice more of what's going on behind the scenes, under the surface.

PRACTICE 3

READING ALOUD

Read Lee Herrick's poem "My California" on page 72 to yourself. Now read the poem aloud, slowly. What do you hear — if anything — that you didn't notice in the silent reading? Have someone else read the poem aloud to you. What do you notice on the third read? Do you see any patterns or repeated images you missed on the first two reads? Could you hear things you didn't see?

Experiment with Copywork

For generations, writers without access to higher education have taught themselves to write by practicing **copywork**. Jack London, a self-educated writer, and Robert Louis Stevenson both famously taught themselves to write by copying out, by hand, long passages from their favorite books. Copywork teaches you to read closely because it forces you to pay attention to every word. Working by hand has proven cognitive benefits as well. Copying favorite passages teaches you about word choice and opens up possibilities for sentences and style, dialogue and pacing, structure and detail. When writers are stuck, many will use the technique of copywork to get their groove back.

PRACTICE 4

COPYWORK

Take any one of the poems or a paragraph of prose from this textbook. Choose something that looks appealing to you but is unfamiliar — something you haven't read before. Read the piece. Then retype the words or copy them over by hand. Now read the poem or paragraph aloud. What do you notice when you reread the piece that you didn't notice before you copied it over?

Memorize

Actors memorize, and so do writers. Poets, especially, often memorize poems in order to expand their understanding of their craft. Author Beth

Ann Fennelly is known for her "My One Hundred," a notebook of one hundred poems she keeps at hand on her writing desk. She tries to have one hundred poems memorized, ready to recite, at all times. This kind of mental copywork, the act of memorizing a poem, demands the kind of close reading that allows creative writers to grow and thrive as they internalize more sophisticated pieces of literature. When working on a monologue or play, you will learn the lines in order to memorize them, to say them aloud, to ensure they "track" for both the audience and the performer. Spoken word and rap artists memorize huge swaths of material, uploading it into their brains so they can infuse their performances with passion and heart.

PRACTICE 5

MEMORIZE A POEM

Memorize a short poem by copying it over, carrying it around with you, and reciting it aloud over and over. You can find short poems online at the Poetry Foundation or your instructor may assign you a poem from this textbook. Notice what you learn about the poem by memorizing it.

Annotate

Annotating is writing specific comments in the margins of a text, either by hand or using your word processing program's comment function or editing/suggesting mode. Like a scientist dissecting a flatworm, we label the parts of a text, commenting on how the parts are working, noting patterns, asking questions.

Your instructor may have specific guidelines for your annotations. Here are common features you may be asked to annotate for the pieces you will read in this textbook:

Images: These are the various concrete actions, details, and pieces of dialogue that create "movies" in your mind as you read. What do you "see" or experience as you read?

Energy: Where is the excitement or spark in the piece? Is it the plot? The words themselves? The tone of voice? What keeps you engaged?

Tension: All creative writing has tension or conflict. What does the writer do, exactly, on the page that makes the piece taut, crisp? What do you notice you are concerned about, as you read on? What actually keeps you reading?

Pattern: Art relies on pattern to create meaning. When you close read for pattern, your annotations will focus on rhythm, repetition, rhyme, echoes, layers, and syntax.

Insight: Good creative writing continues to feed the reader more, even after a second, third, or fourth reading. How does the piece of writing get its meaning across to the reader? When you close read for depth, you'll try to peer behind the curtain—under the surface of the piece—in order to teach yourself how to deepen your own work and increase its power and reach. In literature courses, this is often called theme.

Here's an example of an annotation you can use as a model.

> Based on the title, I predict that this poem will explore the light of late evening, full of lightning bugs.

> The structure imitates a dictionary entry and creates a new, emotive definition for the word *afterglow*.

> Instead of talking about skies in general, we see the specific sky light in Ohio. The setting grounds the poem.

> The entire workweek is encapsulated in this line, lending a tone of timelessness.

A. Van Jordan
af · ter · glow

af • ter • glow \≈\ n. **1.** The light esp. in the Ohio sky after sunset: as in the look of the mother-of-pearl air during the morning's afterglow. **2.** The glow continuing after the disappearance of a flame, as of a match or a lover, and sometimes regarded as a type of phosphorescent ghost: This balm, this bath of light / This cocktail of lust and sorrow, / This rumor of faithless love on a neighbor's lips, / This Monday morning, this Friday night, / This pendulum of my heart, / This salve for my soul, / This tremble from your body / This breast aflame, this bed ablaze / Where you rub oil on my feet, / Where we spoon and, before sunrise, turn away / And I dream, eyes open, / swimming / In this room's pitch-dark landscape.

> These slashes break up the prose poem and make me pause. the lines end on the most important words that tie back to *afterglow*, like "light" and "ablaze."

> My prediction expressed my personal connection to the word *afterglow*. I think this poem similarly explores the narrator's personal connection to the word.

> A pendulum is a weight that swings freely.

> *Phosphorescent* means that something glows without getting hot.

> How does this line fit in with the others? It is sensual with the word *oil*, but the mention of feet surprised me.

PRACTICE 6

ANNOTATE A SHORT STORY

Read Ted Chiang's short story, "The Great Silence," on page 79. The story is made up of twelve sections. In a sentence or two, write what each section adds to the whole story. In your own words, state what you think is the heart of each section. Do you have a favorite section?

PRACTICE 7

ANNOTATE A POEM

Read Sebastian Matthews's "Buying Wine," on page 71. Label three images: places you see the images in your mind's eye, the "movie in your mind." What senses (sight, touch, sound, etc.) are activated in each of the three images you labeled?

GENRES: AN OVERVIEW

Genre means "kind" or "sort" and refers to the categories of creative writing. There are genres of **form** (poetry, fiction, plays) and genres of **subject** (fantasy, science fiction, romance). **Hybrid** genres (also called **cross-genre**) include **prose poetry**, which is formatted like prose (lines go all the way over to the right hand margin, but instead of narrative, the writer uses symbols, alliteration, metaphor, and imagery). You can find a thoughtful, accessible introduction to prose poetry online at The Poetry Foundation. **Text and image** is a hybrid of text and visual elements — writers have been combining forms for ages, from illuminated manuscripts to comics. **Electronic literature** and **digital poetry** are fast-changing and particularly fertile grounds for new forms of creative writing. For an example, check out "Between Page and Screen" by Amaranth Borsuk and Brad Bouse. Hybridizing old technologies (you can purchase or download the book for free) and new ones (glyphs and augmented reality), here the authors create a love affair between "P" (page) and "S" (screen) — each one has something other longs for.

Creative writers work in spaces large and small, print and ephemeral: animated Instagram stories, vlogs, video essays — you'll find smart, inventive creative writing in every genre. As stated earlier, creative writers thrive on cross-training: If you want to be a fiction writer, you are well served by honing your skills of imagery and depth by writing poetry. If you want to improve as a spoken word artist, learning narrative skill from fiction and sound work techniques from poetry will allow your performances to soar and will help you hold your audiences' interest. To write a play is to learn aspects of structure, compression, and dialogue that will serve your fiction writing, to be sure, and writing a play increases your appreciation of writing for theater and television. Generating pieces in every genre will help you to develop a solid, flexible foundation of writing strategies that will serve you well long after this course.

Especially in the beginning, stay open to experimentation. Resist the urge to pigeonhole yourself as Sonnet Man or Future Playwright. Who knows? You might be like one of those athletes who letter in cross-country, basketball, and tennis — an all-star writer who excels in prose poetry, comics, *and* screenplays.

Each genre of creative writing typically relies on the same core strategies — **images**, **energy**, **tension**, **pattern**, **insight**, and **shape**. It's my personal experience as a writer that practicing the core strategies in a variety of genres is the best way to improve as a writer. An effective writer can write well in any genre. Why be constrained by historical definitions of genres? Creative writing thrives on risk, invention, and reinvention. When it comes to genre, you can learn the "rules" if only to break them and make your own. Here is how the genres are defined in this textbook.

Hybrids and Experiments

Creative writing is not limited to the four basic genres most often taught in literature courses (fiction, nonfiction, poetry, and drama). Creative writers often resist rules and fixed categories, consistently reinventing and redefining what kinds of art objects can be made out of words.

Experimental creative writing is fertile ground for new writers who aren't yet locked into a single genre identity. Realize that the more difficult your work is to read, and the more off-putting your subject matter, the fewer readers you will have. One rule to consider (and possibly break): The author should never have more fun than the reader. The more you stray, as a writer, from a strong, clear narrative story line and clear action-based images, the harder your reader has to work to understand what is going on and stay involved in the piece. But if the writing provides a great payoff — in terms of humor or insight — the reader may rise to the occasion. Think about what you love to read and try to give your readers the same kinds of experience you enjoy. Consider keeping your experimental work shorter: The longer your experiment, the harder it is to sustain.

Ultimately, creative writers thrive on experiment and play. If you are blocked, try new things. Risk failing. Embrace your weirdness. Make a mash-up; make a mess. Read work you wouldn't normally be drawn to. If you are working at the edge of what is comfortable for you, you are very likely growing as a writer.

Vincent Scarpa's "I Go Back to Berryman's" on page 76, a list-essay-in-one-long-sentence is an experiment, as is A. Van Jordan's definition poem "af•ter•glow"—he created a form, hybridizing poetry with the format of the dictionary definition.

Poetry

Poetry records our elusive inner perceptions, surprising external observations, and it pays close attention to the sounds of the words being used. Poetry could be defined simply as creative writing in which the lines don't go all the way to the right side of the page. But that visual definition doesn't really get at the nature and range of poetry or the specific ways we practice poetic thinking through poetry. "Distinctive realms appear to us when we look and hear by poem-light," Jane Hirshfield writes. Emily Dickinson defined poetry this way: "If I feel physically as if the top of my head were taken off, that is poetry." Poetry insists we see what isn't easy to see.

Prose poems are poems in blocks of type, usually one paragraph or sometimes two. The prose poem *looks* like prose (prose is fiction and creative nonfiction, work that is formatted in traditional paragraphs). But where fiction and creative nonfiction usually tell a story, a prose poem may not be a story at all; it might be pure emotion and feeling and description. It often employs the heightened language of poetry: images, sounds, and feelings, with more overt rhythm to the words. Sometimes prose poems have characters, but not always; a prose poem can be all description. It has to be read with the same amount of concentration as a poem because the stage setup we can expect in fiction—scenes, characters, images playing out in our mind's eye in real time—may not exist. A prose poem may feature strange, surprising, or surreal situations. If you want to explore prose poetry on your own, try Charles Baudelaire, Russell Edson, and Lydia Davis. A Van Jordan's "af•ter•glow" is a kind of prose poem.

Free verse is poetry where the writer has created a structure for the poem, using repetition within the lines or anaphora (repeated words at the beginning of lines). John Brehm's poem about all the poems he hasn't written on page 43 is an example of free verse. He created his own form. **Formal poetry** isn't fancy or off-putting poetry, it's simply poetry that uses a specific recipe for the structure of the poem, such as a sonnet or a villanelle. See Kim Addonizio's sonnet on page 121 for an example.

> *Poetry is life distilled.*
> —GWENDOLYN BROOKS

PRACTICE 8

COMPARING FORMAL VERSE AND FREE VERSE

Read Dylan Thomas's poem, "Do Not Go Gentle into That Good Night" on page 123. For your second read, read the poem aloud (or listen to it online) and notice the repetitions and the structure. This is a formal poem, a **villanelle**. Contrast this formal poem to the two free verse poems in this chapter, "Buying Wine" on page 71 and "My California" on page 72. What differences do you notice between the formal poem and the free verse poems?

Creative Nonfiction: Memoir and Literary Essay

It's interesting—perhaps somewhat annoying, too—when a vocabulary term defines something it is not. Straight-up **nonfiction** is a broad category that includes writing that is factual and not invented, as fiction is: history, philosophy, guides on caring for your new kitten, sociology, self-help, nature guides. This kind of writing uses summarizing, instruction (as does the book you are reading now), reporting, explanation, and analysis to inform the reader. **Creative nonfiction** is writing that is also 100 percent factual and based squarely in the real, true, known world. However, it refers specifically to a special subcategory of nonfiction writing that uses the conventions of fiction to tell a true story—scenes, dialogue, patterns, and a story arc. **Essays** rely on reporting, analyzing, explaining, and describing—and they are what you typically study in nonfiction- or essay-writing courses (and probably what you studied in your first-year expository writing course). By contrast, creative nonfiction uses the mind's eye or "movie in your mind" technique, allowing the reader see the story, instead of being told about it.

"What I Do on My Terrace Is None of Your Business" on page 45 is creative nonfiction, as is "I Go Back to Berryman's" on page 76. Both are true accounts of things that happened to the author, but the authors use imagery, details, and action—to **show rather than tell** the reader. The techniques used are the same ones fiction writers use—scenes, dialogue, and story presented in a narrative arc—but the facts and situations are not invented, they are drawn carefully from real life.

As with fiction, creative nonfiction can be almost any length, from a six-word story to a paragraph-long micro-essay to a book. Ira Sukrungruang's "Chop Suey" on page 74 is a micro-memoir; you can find more of these at Brevitymag.org.

And, as with fiction, there are graphic and comic subgenres in creative nonfiction, ranging from history books written in comics form to memoirs using text and image. If you are interested in **graphic memoir** but have never read one, you might take a look at *Fun Home* by Alison Bechdel and *Stitches* by David Small.

Fiction

Fiction is an invented story, of course, and narratives can take the form of short stories, flash fiction, short-shorts, novellas, comics or graphic works, or novels. **Speculative fiction** (see Kelly Link, Karen Russell, George Saunders for great examples) includes supernatural, fantastic, or futuristic elements. **Science fiction** imagines technological or scientific advances in future worlds, parallel universes, other planets, and space. **Realistic fiction** is exactly that—employing a setting and characters we might run into in our daily lives. **Short stories** typically run from a couple of pages in length up to forty or more pages.

> *Fiction is lies; we're writing about people who never existed and events that never happened when we write fiction, whether it's science fiction or fantasy or western mystery stories or so-called literary stories. All those things are essentially untrue. But it has to have a truth at the core of it.*
> —GEORGE R. R. MARTIN

Micro-fiction, **flash fiction**, and **short-shorts** are very short stories—from a paragraph to a few pages in length. Nancy Stohlman's "I Found Your Voodoo Doll on the Dance Floor After Last Call" on page 76 is a micro-fiction.

A **novella** is a short novel, and the length varies greatly, but fifty to one hundred pages is typical. **Novels** may run anywhere from one hundred to six hundred pages or more and can focus on many characters and perhaps cover more time—years instead of moments—than we typically see in a short story. A **graphic novel** uses text and image to tell a fictional story.

Drama: Spoken Word, Monologue, Play, and Screenplay

> *Grammar is a piano I play by ear. All I know about grammar is its power.*
> —JOAN DIDION

Spoken word, monologues, plays, and screenplays are all forms that are designed for presentation on the stage or screen but they can also be read and enjoyed on the page, as well.

Spoken word, because it is performed live, often uses artful repetition, rhythm, and rhyme to make it easier to memorize and to heighten the musicality. Spoken word embraces improvisation, free association, and wordplay. Contemporary spoken word has roots in jazz, blues, and folk music as well as in oral storytelling and epic and narrative poetry, and it's related to experimental performance and monologue theater. Practicing your storytelling skills and poetic techniques is crucial for growing as a spoken word artist.

Plays and **screenplays** are designed to be read, performed, and/or filmed. They exist on the page in two forms: One form, which you will practice this semester, is formatted for readers. The second is formatted for a theater company or movie production. If you are interested in writing for stage or screen, you'll need to follow very specific guidelines for formatting and submitting your work. In this course, we will focus primarily on how to write strong dramatic scenes, evoke clear conflicts, and deploy fresh, energetic dialogue in plays or screenplays.

Playwriting and screenwriting are storytelling in images. Sometimes screenwriters get so distracted by the cool things they can do with cameras that they forget about what the writer must still do: Create a story that moves readers/viewers. Practicing in this genre helps your dialogue skills if you are a fiction or creative nonfiction writer. But a play also uses sound, music, and rhythm, just as a poem does. A **monologue** is a speech by one person, as part of a larger play or standing on its own.

Just as in poetry, when it comes to crafting drama, every single word matters and structure—having tension and an arc—is crucial. There are one-minute plays, five-minute plays, ten-minute (one-act) plays, and of course, in addition to full-length three-act plays, complex multipart productions can be created for the stage and screen or both. An **act** is a unit of drama in which *something happens.* At the end of this chapter, you can read Marco Ramirez's one-act play "I am not Batman" on page 82. A **musical** is a play with songs carrying significant parts of the action. A video game is a kind of play; comics are usually written as scripts first, as well.

PRACTICE 9

READING A PLAY

Read "I am not Batman" on page 82 and notice the different parts of this play.

1. Italicized sentences at the top provide succinct **exposition**, telling us the setup for the situation that is about to unfold. We also get some necessary information about the character. Observe the creative writing here—"maybe 7, maybe 27."
2. Capital letters are used for the **character names**, wherever they appear: "BOY."
3. **Sounds** that will be heard during the play are placed in capital letters and all capital letters and italics: "*(—SNARE—)*" with an em dash on either side to denote a pause.

Note two examples of exposition and two examples of sound. Then make a brief statement, answering these two questions: How many people speak in this play? What is the central problem the main character faces?

PRACTICE 10

COMPARING GENRES

Read all of the pieces at the end of this chapter.

A. Van Jordan, "af·ter·glow"

Lee Herrick, "My California"

Sebastian Matthews, "Buying Wine"

Vincent Scarpa, "I Go Back to Berryman's"

Ira Sukrungruang, "Chop Suey"

Nancy Stohlman, "I Found Your Voodoo Doll on the Dance Floor After Last Call"

Ted Chiang, "The Great Silence"

Marco Ramirez, "I am not Batman"

Rank them from your favorite to your least favorite. For the ones you really like, what is it about them that attracts you? Do you prefer one genre over the others? For the pieces you like the least, what specifically turns you off? Were you surprised by any of your preferences? Is it the genre itself you like or don't like, or is it the specific piece? Why?

CLOSELY READING YOUR OWN WORK

> *There is creative reading as well as creative writing.*
>
> —RALPH WALDO EMERSON

When reading your own work-in-progress, it's important that you approach the text just as a reader would. Try to let go of your judgments: This is terrible or this is so great. Instead, read "cold"—as though you happened upon this text for the first time. This is a challenging skill and an essential one to practice as you work to improve your craft.

Here are two tips for reading your own work-in-progress.

1. **Read from hard copy.** Composing entirely on your phone or laptop can distort your impressions of what you have. Devices, by their very nature, allow us to write quickly and erase quickly. As the writer, you may end up feeling things are there for your reader—but they aren't. At regular intervals during your writing session, consider printing your pages and reading with your pen or pencil in hand. This shift allows your brain a little distance and can more approximate the reader's experience.

2. **Read your work aloud.** Many professional writers find that the best way to improve their writing is to read it aloud. The ear picks up things

the eye misses, and vice versa. Some writers record into their phone and play back their own work, while others read aloud alone to themselves. Still others find that the best way to capture mistakes, cull out rough patches, and adjust the voice is to read their work to a trusted writing partner. When you can hear how others experience your work, it can often be clearer as to what needs to be clarified or cut, made more interesting or expanded.

READING WORK BY PEERS

> *Easy reading is damn hard writing.*
> —MAYA ANGELOU

Reading work-in-progress is very different from reading professional writing that has been edited and published. Learning how to effectively read the work of peers, in order to offer supportive but also useful comments on their works-in-progress, is usually a vital part of any creative writing course. Being able to read someone else's draft and put into words what aspects of the draft is working well and what areas might be delved into more deeply is a skill set that has rich benefits for you personally as a writer. The act of being able to articulate, with some degree of accuracy and in a way that can be well received by its author, how a piece of writing works improves your ability to write well. Here are some tips for reading work by your peers:

1. **Read the piece more than once.** It's recommended that you read the piece once straight through without making any comments. It's often easier to see the flaws in a piece than it is to see what's working really well. Perhaps in your first read, you'll note the things that stick out to you as not working well: places you got stuck or confused. Read a second time, carefully, and find specific things that you really enjoyed—even if they are small—and make notes of these things. If you are wild about the piece, make sure you are able to support your opinion with specific examples, so you aren't just fawning.

2. **Balance specific praise with gentle questions.** Be kind. Be honest. It's usually best to comment on the strengths you find in the piece first. The author needs to know you respect the work and understand the purpose. Make sure your praise is based on specific examples and is sincere. Instead of offering suggestions and solutions, it can be more helpful to a writer to hear questions that you have. After you have made observations about strengths—nothing is too tiny to notice—you may want to tell the author where you are confused or where and why you want to know more or see more.

3. **Focus on images, energy, and tension.** These are the three pillars of strong creative writing—the strategies that hold up our work. Play back for your peers: Where do you see things in your "mind's eye"? Where is the heat, the energy in this piece? What's most interesting? What do you want to know more about? Make a list as you read and reread the selection.

When reading a work-in-progress written by others, remember that you are often most helpful when you present your reactions as those of a fellow writer also seeking to improve. You should work toward striking a balance between being substantive and being supportive. The goal is for the members of the class to always leave *wanting* to write more, not less.

While you are reading your classmates' literary output in order to give them useful feedback about their craft, there's another reason you are reading these pieces-in-progress. You are reading to see what works and what doesn't so that you can improve your own writing as well. The more clearly you can articulate why a piece succeeds and where it is weak, the better writer you will become.

READING TO WRITE

For creative writers, reading and writing are two sides of the same coin; reading the work of others—peers and professionals—is absolutely the foundation of a healthy writing practice. Ask professional writers about their reading lives. Read interviews with the authors whose work you most respect. Most writers spend at least half of the creative time reading; reading is an inextricable part of the writing life. It's how we learn.

> *Reading is equivalent to thinking with someone else's head instead of with one's own.*
> —ARTHUR SCHOPENHAUER

Here are some specific ways we rely on reading to augment our writing practice.

Inspiration

We read in order to get inspired to write. Many writers start their daily practice by reading a poem or a chapter by a favorite author in order to get caught up into the way literature moves us, makes us feel, and makes us think in its very specific and very powerful way.

We can be inspired, in general, by the works we love—for many of us, it was reading in general that first made us want to become writers. The

themes of race, power, beauty, and oppression in Toni Morrison's novels inspire us to carefully witness what is happening in our own community. **Form** can inspire us. The sonnets of Robert Frost inspire us to try **blank verse** and then sonnets.

When I first read *Love Medicine*, a collection of inter-linked short stories about two families, I was inspired to write a sequence of short stories myself, *Georgia Underwater*, telling the story of a fractured family in a fractured narrative. **Subject matter** often inspires us. Flannery O'Connor's strange, dark, riveting short stories about Southern families inspires us to find the mythic and archetypal resonance in material that may look quite simple on the surface. Which writers inspire you to want to write?

PRACTICE 11

CONSIDERING SOURCES OF INSPIRATION

Who or what has inspired you to write, recently or in the past? When you think about the writers who make you want to write, what about their work specifically inspires you?

Imitation

Stevie Wonder told me that he heard me coming in on the radio from Windsor [Ontario], that I had influenced some of his pieces. It wasn't like he copped the lick or anything like that, but basically he went in a more adventurous chordal direction than he would have had I not existed. That's the kind of influence that I like. It is not copying.

—JONI MITCHELL

Imitation is different from inspiration in that with imitation you consciously borrow one writer's specific moves as an experimental way of expanding your own skill on the page. Imitation is a time-honored technique many writers use in order to understand a piece of writing more deeply while honing their writing skills. When you were little, you learned to walk, talk, eat, dance, make friends, and do math by watching other people do these things and then copying them. Imitating writers isn't plagiarism, so don't get anxious. You aren't going to publish your imitation — it's just an exercise. Even in class and workshops, you'll always give credit to the author you are imitating.

Practiced regularly, imitation can increase your confidence as a writer as it helps you find your way to your own best material. It might feel awkward, at first, but it's a direct path, like copywork, to rich, layered, and focused writing.

With imitation, you're creating new neural pathways. You are trying to block out your normal thinking habits and force yourself into some new patterns and new moves.

Close Imitation. In a direct, or **close imitation**, you use most of the original writer's form (the shape of the piece) and syntax (the kinds of sentences), substituting key words (often adjectives and nouns) for your own.

You may use their original title or come up with your own. Some writers call this technique "scaffolding" because the original text acts as a scaffold—a temporary structure—while the new text is built. When the new text is complete, the scaffold is taken away.

Close imitation is a lot like Mad Libs, the fill-in-the-blank game. Below you'll find a scaffold and you are to fill in the blanks. Work quickly as you copy over the poem and fill in the first thing that comes to mind. Try not to censor or edit or "get it right." If you work quickly and you're surprised by your answers, that's a good sign you are on the right track. In this exercise, you are imitating a well-known poet named Betsy Sholl. Because her poem relies heavily on **metaphor**, comparisons that shift the qualities of one thing onto another, allowing the reader to make meaningful connections and see more deeply into your subject, it makes for interesting imitations.

> *Imitation gave me room to operate with my own scalpel in someone else's scrubs. To use a style that I wasn't used to connected some circuits in my head, and I felt more freedom to explore different directions with the tools I already had. I could discover rhythm and ride the wave all the way to shore.*
>
> —CHRISTIAN PIERS

When you complete your imitation poem, you'll put your name on it and you'll also write, under your title, "After Betsy Sholl."

Genealogy
After Betsy Sholl

One of my parents was a _____, the other a _____.

One was a _____, the other a _____.

In the night I'd wake to _____ and the faint
smell of _____.

The _____ tattooed on my lower back
is the one for _____.

One of my parents was a _____,
the other a _____ I carried into the night,
convinced it was _____.

One of my parents I drank, the other I dreamed.

In the revolving door of my becoming,
one _____ and one _____.

Thus, my troubled birth, my endless _____.

One was an _____, the other a _____.

How they amused each other.

One was a _____, the other a _____. I was ashamed
of _____, embarrassed I couldn't _____.

I was a child calling across the _____ to a _____
they didn't have.

PRACTICE 12

COMPARING THE IMITATION TO THE ORIGINAL

After you've completed your imitation, turn to page 67 to read Sholl's original. How
does your imitation compare to the original? What surprises you about the original?

Loose Imitation.   Above, you used another poet's basic idea—comparing
two parents using metaphors in order to describe, perhaps, a particularly
difficult childhood and how parent behavior impacts a kid's personality. You
used the poem as a **writing prompt** in order to create your own original
poem. (Imitation exercises like these make great warm-ups for daily writing
practice, by the way.)

While a close imitation keeps half or more of the original intact, **loose
imitation** takes the basic concept or part of a piece and launches a new
work from there. Loose imitation has long been a vibrant part of creative
writing—ancient writers recast myths and oral stories into plays, Shakespeare borrowed plots and made them into masterpieces, and playwrights
and screenwriters may work from novels and previous versions of many
kinds of texts. In addition to loosely imitating a plot, writers build their
characters on previous characters: Tolkein's Elves and Dwarves are drawn
from German mythologies.

Form—the way a creative work is put together—also provides possibilities for loose imitation. Suzanne Buffam's *A Pillow Book* is compiled of lists
and brief diary-like entries, just like its predecessor, *The Pillow Book*, written
by Sei Shōnagon in Japan in the eleventh century. Buffam's *A Pillow Book* is a
very clever imitation, in conversation with its original text. While Sei Shonagon
serves the demanding empress of the court, Buffam is the mother of a two-
year-old daughter and discovers herself waiting hand and foot on a demanding

toddler. For readers who know the original text, reading an artful imitation provides a delightful, enriched reading experience. For readers who don't know the original, *A Pillow Book* stands on its own as a hybrid memoir (made of lists and journal entries, just like the original). A lively innovative imitation may inspire your readers to delve into the original text. Credit to the original author is always given and a rich conversation within an artistic lineage develops.

Again, you aren't necessarily submitting your imitation for publication, although some writers do. You're practicing new creative moves. Imitation is also an exercise in close reading, a worthy practice in itself. When you imitate, you're trying to get inside another writer's head to see if you can learn more about the craft of creative writing and maybe, hopefully, just possibly have some fun.

PRACTICE 13

LOOSE IMITATION OF "GENEALOGY"

Instead of writing about your parents, imitate Betsy Sholl's "Genealogy" on page 67 by selecting a topic from this list: two roommates, two coaches, two exes, two siblings, two pets, or two friends. Try to capture the essential differences between your two subjects by filling in your own contrasting concrete images. You may want to shift some more of the words in the original poem; that's encouraged. Keep the essential "one of my _____ / one of my_____" structure. Be sure to put the words "after Betsy Sholl" on your final version.

WRITING PROJECTS

Process

1. Read about the author's writing process in the interview with Vincent Scarpa on page 78. What's most interesting to you about his process? Interview one of your classmates about their writing process, asking from five to seven questions about aspects you are most interested in.

Experiment

2. Write a definition poem. Choose a simple word, like *beds* or *green* or *water*. Take the reader through images from various aspects of your life so that the entire dictionary entry is a micro-memoir about interesting, odd things from your world. To format your piece, imitate Van Jordan's definition poem on page 71.

Poem

3. Imitate "My California" by Lee Herrick on page 72 by titling your poem "My _____" and the name of the state or city or region where you are from. List fifteen images, using all five senses, providing a detailed portrait of your place.

Nonfiction

4. Write an "I go back to...." memoir from your own life. Make your list about the same length as the model, "I Go Back to Berryman's" on page 76. Imitate the form using ultra-long sentences containing lists of detailed images from a neighborhood you lived in when you were young. Pack your piece with carefully observed sights, sounds, textures, and smells.

Fiction

5. Using Nancy Stohlman's "I Found Your Voodoo Doll on the Dance Floor After Last Call" on page 76 as your inspiration, write a one-paragraph short story.

Drama/Monologue

6. Read "I am not Batman" found on page 82 aloud. Choose a superhero or another character from media or literature and imagine yourself—perhaps a younger version of yourself—as this character. Write a one-page monologue, imagining yourself as the fictional character, standing on a stage set you've designed or somewhere specific out in the world.

   Note how Ramirez formats his play—and imitate the following:

   a. Write a brief description of where your character is standing and begin your play this way, with **exposition**.

   b. Use "WAITER" or "UNICORN"—whatever the name of your character is—in ALL CAPITALS to indicate when your character is talking.

   c. Most of the play will be dialogue—what does your character have to say to the world?

   d. Imitate Ramirez's use of sound by thinking of a meaningful way your character can make some noise, if you can. Note how sounds are placed in ALL CAPS and parentheses, so an actor reading the play and the sound technicians on set know exactly what to do and how to do it.

READINGS

A. Van Jordan
af • ter • glow

af • ter • glow \≈\ *n.* **1.** The light esp. in the Ohio sky after sunset: as in the look of the mother-of-pearl air during the morning's afterglow. **2.** The glow continuing after the disappearance of a flame, as of a match or a lover, and sometimes regarded as a type of phosphorescent ghost: This balm, this bath of light / This cocktail of lust and sorrow, / This rumor of faithless love on a neighbor's lips, / This Monday morning, this Friday night, / This pendulum of my heart, / This salve for my soul, / This tremble from your body / This breast aflame, this bed ablaze / Where you rub oil on my feet, / Where we spoon and, before sunrise, turn away / And I dream, eyes open, / swimming / In this room's pitch-dark landscape.

Sebastian Matthews
Buying Wine

When we were boys, we had a choice: stay in the car or else
follow him into Wine Mart, that cavernous retail barn,

down aisle after aisle—California reds to Australian blends
to French dessert wines—past bins loaded like bat racks

with bottles, each with its own heraldic tag, its licked coat
of arms, trailing after our father as he pushed the ever-filling cart,

bent forward in concentration, one hand in mouth stroking
his unkempt mustache, the other lofting up bottles like fruit

then setting them down, weighing the store of data in his brain
against the cost, the year, the cut of meat he'd select at the butcher's:

a lamb chop, say, if this Umbrian red had enough body to marry,
to dance on its legs in the bell of the night; or some scallops maybe,

those languid hearts of the sea, a poet's dozen in a baggy,
and a Pinot Grigio light enough not to disturb their salty murmur.

Often, we'd stay in the car until we'd used up the radio
and our dwindling capacity to believe our father

might actually "Just be back," then break free, releasing
our seatbelts, drifting to the edges of the parking lot like horses

loosed in a field following the sun's endgame of shade; sometimes
I'd peer into the front window, breath fogging the sale signs,

catching snippets of my father's profile appearing and disappearing
behind the tall cardboard stacks. Once I slipped back into the store,

wandering the aisles, master of my own cart, loading it to bursting
for the dream party I was going to throw. But mostly, like now,

as I search for the perfect $12 bottle, I'd shuffle along, dancing bear
behind circus master, and wait for my father to pronounce, tall

in his basketball body, wine bottles like babies in his hands, "Aha!"

Lee Herrick
My California

Here, an olive votive keeps the sunset lit,
the Korean twenty-somethings talk about hyphens,

graduate school and good pot. A group of four at a window
table in Carpinteria discuss the quality of wines in Napa Valley versus Lodi

Here, in my California, the streets remember the Chicano
poet whose songs still bank off Fresno's beer soaked gutters

and almond trees in partial blossom. Here, in my California
we fish out long noodles from the pho with such accuracy

you'd know we'd done this before. In Fresno, the bullets
tire of themselves and begin to pray five times a day.

In Fresno, we hope for less of the police state and more of a state of grace.
In my California, you can watch the sun go down

like in your California, on the ledge of the pregnant
twenty-second century, the one with a bounty of peaches and grapes,

red onions and the good salsa, wine and chapchae.
Here, in my California, paperbacks are free,

farmer's markets are twenty four hours a day and
always packed, the trees and water have no nails in them,

the priests eat well, the homeless eat well.
Here, in my California, everywhere is Chinatown,

everywhere is K-Town, everywhere is Armeniatown,
everywhere a Little Italy. Less confederacy.

No internment in the Valley.
Better history texts for the juniors.

In my California, free sounds and free touch.
Free questions, free answers.
Free songs from parents and poets, those hopeful bodies of light.

WRITERS ON WRITING

LEE HERRICK

HEATHER SELLERS: How did this poem come about?
LEE HERRICK: I wrote "My California" during a Presidential election season, in the year before Barack Obama became our 44th President, so politics, problems, solutions, and ideas were heavy on my mind. I began to think about my own state, my own city (Fresno). I wanted to write about feeling at home here. I was born in South Korea, but I have lived here almost my whole life, so I was also resisting the racist idea of Asian Americans as voiceless, apolitical, or perpetual foreigners. I belong here as much as anyone else. I have great hope for California. It turns out that I had a lot to say, so the poem was born.

HS: What was your writing process with this particular poem? Similar or different from your usual composition process?
LH: "My California" uses anaphora, which I like and often use for its rhythmic, musical effect. I used the phrase "in my California" in slightly different locations and ways, speaking to details about California's diversity, joys, and problems such as Japanese internment or police shootings.

Every poem's process is slightly different. Some begin with an image, or a sound, a declaration, a technique like anaphora, or a form. Some poems take fifty drafts and ten years; in rare instances, they take just a few drafts in a short time. This poem somehow poured out of me in only a few drafts. It brewed for many years, but the actual writing process was only about a month.

HS: Is writing poetry a different process for you than other kinds of writing?
LH: Poetry writing is a different because it's a compressed form, where each word can play a variety of important roles. The poetic forms also inspire and challenge me — the fourteen-line sonnet, the nineteen-line villanelle. There

are differences between each genre, I think, just like each instrument is slightly different—drums, guitar, piano, sax—but it's all music. It's all creative writing. It all takes hard work, patience, practice, and love.

HS: Can you talk more about your shaping/revision process with this poem? In general?
LH: I enjoy the revision, the seeing again. Every revision is a new discovery. I often cut 25% or more of what I write in a poem. For "My California" I also had to work hard on the ending, but it finally arrived. Sometimes it takes a while.

HS: Anything else you'd like to add?
LH: I believe the intersections of our lives, our families, our dreams, our cities and states, along with our potential to act, behave, and write about what we desire, love, loathe, and hope for are what somehow contribute to a better world. I'm not saying this poem makes the world a better place, but I do believe literature and writing have that potential. Writing is a place to speak your truths, whatever they may be.

Ira Sukrungruang
Chop Suey

My mother was a champion bowler in Thailand. This was not what I knew of her. I knew only her expectations of me to be the perfect Thai boy. I knew her distaste for blonde American women she feared would seduce her son. I knew her distrust of the world she found herself in, a world of white faces and mackerel in a can. There were many things I didn't know about my mother when I was ten. She was what she was supposed to be. My mother.

At El-Mar Bowling Alley, I wanted to show her what I could do with the pins. I had bowled once before, at Dan Braun's birthday party. There, I had rolled the ball off the bumpers, knocking the pins over in a thunderous crash. I liked the sound of a bowling alley. I felt in control of the weather, the rumble of the ball on the wood floor like the coming of a storm, and the hollow explosion of the pins, distant lightning. At the bowling alley, men swore and smoked and drank.

My mother wore a light pink polo, jeans, and a golf visor. She put on a lot of powder to cover up the acne she got at 50. She poured Vapex, a strong smelling vapor rub, into her handkerchief, and covered her nose, complaining of the haze of smoke that floated over the lanes. My mother was the only woman in the place. We were the only non-white patrons.

I told her to watch me. I told her I was good. I set up, took sloppy and uneven steps, and lobbed my orange ball onto the lane with a loud thud. This time there were no bumpers. My ball veered straight for the gutter.

My mother said to try again. I did, and for the next nine frames, not one ball hit one pin. Embarrassed, I sat next to her. I put my head on her shoulder. She patted it for a while and said bowling wasn't an easy game.

My mother rose from her chair and said she wanted to try. She changed her shoes. She picked a ball from the rack, one splattered with colors. When she was ready, she lined herself up to the pins, the ball at eye level. In five concise steps, she brought the ball back, dipped her knees and released it smoothly, as if her hand was an extension of the floor. The ball started on the right side of the lane and curled into the center. Strike.

She bowled again and knocked down more pins. She told me about her nearly perfect game, how in Thailand she was unbeatable.

I listened, amazed that my mother could bowl a 200, that she was good at something beyond what mothers were supposed to be good at, like cooking and punishing and sewing. I clapped. I said she should stop being a mother and become a bowler.

As she changed her shoes, a man with dark hair and a mustache approached our lane. In one hand he had a cigarette and a beer. He kept looking back at his buddies a few lanes over, all huddling and whispering. I stood beside my mother, wary of any stranger. My mother's smile disappeared. She rose off the chair.

"Hi," said the man.

My mother nodded.

"My friends over there," he pointed behind him, "well, we would like to thank you." His mustache twitched.

My mother pulled me closer to her leg, hugging her purse to her chest.

He began to talk slower, over-enunciating his words, repeating again. "We … would … like…to … thank…"

I tugged on my mother's arm, but she stood frozen.

"… you … for … making … a… good … chop …suey. You people make good food."

The man looked back again, toasted his beer at his friends, laughing smoke from his lips.

My mother grabbed my hand and took one step toward the man. In that instant, I saw in her face the same resolve she had when she spanked, the same resolve when she scolded. In that instant, I thought my mother was going to hit the man. And for a moment, I thought the man saw the same thing in her eyes, and his smile disappeared from his face. Quickly, she smiled—too bright, too large—and said, "You're welcome."

Nancy Stohlman

I Found Your Voodoo Doll on the Dance Floor After Last Call

It was squishy under my feet and at first I thought it was a wad of napkins. But as the crowds cleared, it became obvious. It looked just like me if I'd been made out of cornstalks and had button eyes. *Is that really how you see me?* I thought as I picked it up and smoothed the yarn hair. My first instinct was to toss it into the dumpster but I had doubts — what if it landed on its head? Was stabbed by sharp cardboard? What if I woke in the morning and found myself buried alive or impaled on a U- Haul box?

The mantel was out of the question, too far to fall if the cat knocked it down. A cabinet wouldn't work-there was suffocation, asphyxiation. Anything near a sink was out. Nothing near the fireplace, on the balcony, near a window.

A bird cage seemed the best solution.

One day I rushed home from work and the cage door was open, the voodoo doll missing. I started a blank, button-eyed stare into its empty depths.

When I saw you at the bar later, voodoo doll on a chain around your neck, I collapsed to my knees in front of you. Thank god, I said.

I knew you'd be back, you said.

Vincent Scarpa

I Go Back to Berryman's

All of the streets in the trailer park are named for fruits or for dead presidents — Cherry, Lincoln, Peach, Garfield — and if you walk them and peer through windows with parted curtains, you will see love being made, hate being made, bodies being discovered, bodies being forgotten, smoking and drinking and swearing and Bible reading, you will see people doing their best, and you will see that sometimes their best is *not that good*, and you will see rooms where welfare mothers rock babies and sing *If I needed you / would you come to me?*, and you will see double-wide lawns where men like my best friend's father try to exorcise the gay out of their sons by placing a bat in their hands and lobbing underhanded tosses when what their sons really want is to bring the stereo on the front porch and choreograph intricate and well-intentioned routines to top 40 pop, and you will see Renee apply tanning oil to her frail leather body as she sprawls across the driveway from where she has moved her dented pick-up pocked with bullet scars, you will see her repositioning her beach chair to follow the sun in a circle and rotate 20-20 front and back, her body so crisp and even in next week's open casket, you will see sober fathers and drunk fathers and belt-bearing fathers and fathers who hide child pornography in secret folders on their computer, you will see mothers like mine knocking over patio furniture in fits of manic rage, or mothers who hang confederate flags alongside American flags, or mothers who pray for drunk drivers and who pray for terrorists and who pray for their own recovery from afflictions of the mind and heart and body and soul, mothers who erect roadside memorials across town for sons and daughters squished between liquored tires, you will see old women whose children do not call or do not call often on hold with phone psychics from whom they seek guidance and answers but also sheer company, you will see old men who think of the rifles in their closets when a black or a Puerto Rican walks by but also when they catch themselves in the mirror or have too much time to think or drink, you will see motherless children riding rusted bikes and scooters and falling on cracked pavement, their knees and elbows scuffed and skinned like the scratch-off lottery tickets their fathers allow them at the liquor store checkout, you will see teenagers who consider themselves to be much older pass loosely rolled joints in the woods, the girls flashing their tits to the guys who ask nicely or who only ask or who simply insist, guys with acne on their backs which you could connect to resemble an outline of the continental forty-eight, guys who claim they're allergic to latex, and you will see their younger brothers and younger sisters who sneak through the woods trying to find the hiding spot, and you will hear the older siblings yell, *Get outta here you retards, go home*, and you will see a pool the size of a postage stamp in the middle of the park where children are taught to swim, to dive, to walk don't run walk don't run walk don't run, where these children compete to see who can hold their breath the longest but also to see who has the most bruises, kid fears, war stories, dead cousins, and you will see me leaving the pool despite having just arrived because I'll never be comfortable taking my shirt off in front of anyone who isn't a doctor, and even then, and you will see me walk back to my trailer on Lot 252, my dry towel dragging behind me like a tail that collects gravel and cigarette butts, and you will follow me into my house where my mother is having sex with her boyfriend, you will see their door close as I take off my sandals, you will see me contemplate going to the fridge — I am so thirsty — and decide against it because the kitchen is too close to my mother's bedroom, and I don't want to prevent her or interrupt her or make her think of me, and so instead you will see me walk into my room, where I will write in my journal on a blank page: *I feel homesick but I'm writing this at home.*

WRITERS ON WRITING

VINCENT SCARPA

HEATHER SELLERS: How did you get the idea to write this piece?
VINCENT SCARPA: I lived in Berryman's, the trailer park of this essay, for ten years, and I could write a full-length memoir about all I witnessed. My intention for this piece, though, was essentially the opposite. I wanted to distill everything down — to make clauses out of what might've been chapters.

HS: Do you have a daily writing process or any writing rituals?
VS: I wish I could say I was one of those types who has mastered some routinized practice of writing — 5 a.m. every morning at my desk with a word count goal and unplugged from WiFi — but that has never once been the case for me. I seem to write in spurts. There will be weeks where I don't write anything beyond little iPhone notes, fragments. I get far more pleasure out of reading than I do out of writing, and that's probably my biggest procrastination tool. (Though if you're procrastinating writing, reading is certainly the most nourishing way to do so.) That being said, I'm a firm believer in a line of wisdom from Joy Williams, my favorite writer, who says, "The messenger comes when you're sitting at the table." Just that simple.

HS: Do you think of it is as poetry or memoir or fiction? or something else?
VS: I wrote this essay as an undergraduate, and at the time I was very puritanical about the rules of nonfiction. I instantly distrusted anyone who tried to argue that the boundaries and edges of the genre were somehow flexible or subjective. All these years later, I'm far more interested in precisely how those boundaries are negotiated or challenged by the writer. As it pertains to how I'd classify this essay, I feel now as I did then that this is a piece of nonfiction, memoir, life-writing, personal essay — whatever the term du jour — but I wouldn't object in the slightest to it being read as poetry. The most penetrating and useful comment I know of on this account comes from the writer Eula Biss, who says that genre, "like gender, with which it shares a root, is mostly a collection of lies we have agreed to believe."

HS: Have you ever revised published work? When you look back at this piece, is there anything you'd do differently now or anything you see in the piece that you weren't aware of when you were composing?
VS: Not looking back on older work is more or less a condition of possibility for my writing new work in the present. Opportunities for cringing and self-criticality are too abundantly found on that memory lane, and those states of mind aren't good ones for a writer to be inhabiting for very long. Looking back at this essay now, a decade after writing it, I can certainly see things I might wish to change or cut or rearrange, but I'm not bothered by that. It's indicative of my own growth as a writer, I think, and to go about making those amendments now

would be to distance the piece from the writer I was when I wrote it, which to me seems antithetical to the ostensible purpose of writing creative nonfiction: to capture who and how one was in a given moment.

Ted Chiang
The Great Silence

The humans use Arecibo to look for extraterrestrial intelligence. Their desire to make a connection is so strong that they've created an ear capable of hearing across the universe.

But I and my fellow parrots are right here. Why aren't they interested in listening to our voices?

We're a nonhuman species capable of communicating with them. Aren't we exactly what humans are looking for?

The universe is so vast that intelligent life must surely have arisen many times. The universe is also so old that even one technological species would have had time to expand and ll the galaxy. Yet there is no sign of life anywhere except on Earth. Humans call this the Fermi paradox.

One proposed solution to the Fermi paradox is that intelligent species actively try to conceal their presence, to avoid being targeted by hostile invaders.

Speaking as a member of a species that has been driven nearly to extinction by humans, I can attest that this is a wise strategy.

It makes sense to remain quiet and avoid attracting attention.

The Fermi paradox is sometimes known as the Great Silence. The universe ought to be a cacophony of voices, but instead it's disconcertingly quiet.

Some humans theorize that intelligent species go extinct before they can expand into outer space. If they're correct, then the hush of the night sky is the silence of a graveyard.

Hundreds of years ago, my kind was so plentiful that the Río Abajo Forest resounded with our voices. Now we're almost gone. Soon this rainforest may be as silent as the rest of the universe.

There was an African grey parrot named Alex. He was famous for his cognitive abilities. Famous among humans, that is.

A human researcher named Irene Pepperberg spent thirty years studying Alex. She found that not only did Alex know the words for shapes and colors, he actually understood the concepts of shape and color.

Many scientists were skeptical that a bird could grasp abstract concepts. Humans like to think they're unique. But eventually Pepperberg convinced them that Alex wasn't just repeating words, that he understood what he was saying.

Out of all my cousins, Alex was the one who came closest to being taken seriously as a communication partner by humans.

Alex died suddenly, when he was still relatively young. The evening before he died, Alex said to Pepperberg, "You be good. I love you."

If humans are looking for a connection with a nonhuman intelligence, what more can they ask for than that?

Every parrot has a unique call that it uses to identify itself; biologists refer to this as the parrot's "contact call."

In 1974, astronomers used Arecibo to broadcast a message into outer space intended to demonstrate human intelligence. That was humanity's contact call.

In the wild, parrots address each other by name. One bird imitates another's contact call to get the other bird's attention.

If humans ever detect the Arecibo message being sent back to Earth, they will know someone is trying to get their attention.

Parrots are vocal learners: we can learn to make new sounds after we've heard them. It's an ability that few animals possess. A dog may understand dozens of commands, but it will never do anything but bark.

Humans are vocal learners too. We have that in common. So humans and parrots share a special relationship with sound. We don't simply cry out. We pronounce. We enunciate.

Perhaps that's why humans built Arecibo the way they did. A receiver doesn't have to be a transmitter, but Arecibo is both. It's an ear for listening, and a mouth for speaking.

Humans have lived alongside parrots for thousands of years, and only recently have they considered the possibility that we might be intelligent.

I suppose I can't blame them. We parrots used to think humans weren't very bright. It's hard to make sense of behavior that's so different from your own.

But parrots are more similar to humans than any extraterrestrial species will be, and humans can observe us up close; they can look us in the eye. How do they expect to recognize an alien intelligence if all they can do is eavesdrop from a hundred light-years away?

It's no coincidence that "aspiration" means both hope and the act of breathing.

When we speak, we use the breath in our lungs to give our thoughts a physical form. The sounds we make are simultaneously our intentions and our life force.

I speak, therefore I am. Vocal learners, like parrots and humans, are perhaps the only ones who fully comprehend the truth of this.

There's a pleasure that comes with shaping sounds with your mouth. It's so primal and visceral that throughout their history, humans have considered the activity a pathway to the divine.

Pythagorean mystics believed that vowels represented the music of the spheres, and chanted to draw power from them.

Pentecostal Christians believe that when they speak in tongues, they're speaking the language used by angels in Heaven.

Brahmin Hindus believe that by reciting mantras, they're strengthening the building blocks of reality.

Only a species of vocal learners would ascribe such importance to sound in their mythologies. We parrots can appreciate that.

According to Hindu mythology, the universe was created with a sound: "Om." It's a syllable that contains within it everything that ever was and everything that will be.

When the Arecibo telescope is pointed at the space between stars, it hears a faint hum.

Astronomers call that the "cosmic microwave background." It's the residual radiation of the Big Bang, the explosion that created the universe fourteen billion years ago.

But you can also think of it as a barely audible reverberation of that original "Om." That syllable was so resonant that the night sky will keep vibrating for as long as the universe exists.

When Arecibo is not listening to anything else, it hears the voice of creation.

We Puerto Rican parrots have our own myths. They're simpler than human mythology, but I think humans would take pleasure from them.

Alas, our myths are being lost as my species dies out. I doubt the humans will have deciphered our language before we're gone.

So the extinction of my species doesn't just mean the loss of a group of birds. It's also the disappearance of our language, our rituals, our traditions. It's the silencing of our voice.

Human activity has brought my kind to the brink of extinction, but I don't blame them for it. They didn't do it maliciously. They just weren't paying attention.

And humans create such beautiful myths; what imaginations they have. Perhaps that's why their aspirations are so immense. Look at Arecibo. Any species that can build such a thing must have greatness within it.

My species probably won't be here for much longer; it's likely that we'll die before our time and join the Great Silence. But before we go, we are sending a message to humanity. We just hope the telescope at Arecibo will enable them to hear it.

The message is this:
You be good. I love you.
X

Marco Ramirez

I am not Batman.

Sudden drumming, then quiet. Lights up on a BOY, *maybe 7, maybe 27, wearing a hooded sweatshirt. He looks out directly before him, breathing nervously. A* DRUMMER *sits behind a drum set placed in the middle of the stage, in some kind of silhouette. The* BOY *is excited, but never gets ahead of himself.*

BOY. It's the middle of the night and the sky is glowing like mad radioactive red. And if you squint you could maybe see the moon through a thick layer of cigarette smoke and airplane exhaust that covers the whole city, like a mosquito net that won't let the angels in.

(LIGHT SNARE DRUMMING.)

And if you look up high enough you could see me. Standing on the edge of a eighty-seven story building, —

(Thick steam shoots out of some pipes behind him —)

— And up there, a place for gargoyles and broken clock towers that have stayed still and dead for maybe like a hundred years — up there is *me*.

(DRUMS.)

And I'm freakin' *Batman*.

(CYMBAL.)

And I gots Bat-mobiles and Bat-a-rangs and freakin' Bat-caves like for real, and all it takes is a broom closet or a back room or a fire escape, and Danny's hand-me-down jeans are gone.

(BOOM.)

And my navy blue polo shirt?—

(—BOOM—)

—The-one-that-looks-kinda-good-on-me-but-has-that-hole-on-it-near-the-butt-from-when-it-got-snagged-on-the-chain-link-fence-behind-Arturo's-but-it-isn't-even-a-big-deal-'cause-I-tuck-that-part-in-and-it's-like-all-good?—

(—BOOM—)

—*that* blue polo shirt?—

(—BOOM—)

—It's gone too. And I get like, like transformation-al.

(BOOM. SNARE.)

And nobody pulls out a belt and whips Batman for talking back—

(SNARE—)

—Or for *not* talking back,—

(—SNARE, CRASH—)

And nobody calls Batman simple—

(—SNARE—)

—Or stupid—

(—SNARE—)

—Or skinny—

(—CYMBAL—)

—And *nobody* fires Batman's brother from the Eastern Taxi Company 'cause they was making cutbacks, neither, 'cause they got nothing but respect, and not like *afraid*-respect. Just like *respect*-respect. 'Cause nobody's afraid of you.

'Cause Batman doesn't mean nobody no harm.

(BOOM.)

Ever.

(SNARE, SNARE.)

'Cause all Batman really wants to do is save people and maybe pay Abuela's bills one day and die happy and maybe get like mad famous. For real.

. . . And kill the Joker.

(DRUMS.)

Tonight, like most nights, I'm all alone. And I'm watching . . . And I'm waiting . . . Like a eagle. Or like a—no, yea, like a eagle.

(The DRUMS start low but constant, almost tribal.)

And my cape is flappin' in the wind ('cause it's freakin' long), and my pointy ears are on, and that mask that covers like half my face is on too, and I got like bulletproof stuff all in my chest so no one could hurt me and nobody—*nobody*—is gonna come between Batman,

(CYMBAL.)

and Justice.

(The SLOW KICKS continue, now there are SHORT hits randomly placed on the drum set. They somehow resemble city noises.)

From where I am I could hear everything.

(The DRUMS build, then STOP.)

Eyes glowing white, cape blowing softly in the wind.

(HIT. HIT.)

Bulletproof chest heaving. My heart beating right through it in a Morse code for "fuck with me, just once, come on, just try."

(HIT. HIT. HIT.)

And the one good-for-nothing left standing, the one with the handgun, he laughs, he lowers his arm, and he points it at me and gives the moon a break, and he aims it right between my pointy ears, like goalposts and he's special teams.

(The BOY stands, frozen, afraid.)

And JanitorMan is still calling Saint Anthony but he ain't pickin' up,

(Silence.)

And for a second it seems like . . . *maybe I'm gonna lose.*

    (The BOY *takes a breath. Sudden courage.)*

Naw.

    (—SNARE. The BOY *mimes the fight.)*

SHOO—SHOO! FUACATA!—

    (—SNARE—)

—"Don't kill me mannn!!"—

    (—CYMBAL—)

—SNAP!—

    (—SNARE—)

—Wrist CRACK—

    (—SNARE—)

—Neck—

    (—SNARE—)

—SLASH!—

    (—CYMBAL—)

—Skin—meets—acid—

    (—SNARE—)

—"AHH!!"—

    (—SNARE.)

And he's on the floor. And I'm standing over him. And I got the gun in MY hands now. And I hate guns, I hate holding 'em cause I'm Batman, and—ASTERICKS: Batman don't like guns 'cause his parents got iced by guns a long time ago—but for just a second, my eyes glow white, and I hold this thing, for I could speak to the good-for-nothing in a language he maybe understands,

    (He aims the gun up at the sky.)

. . . CLIC—CLIC . . .

    (The BASS DRUM.)

And the good-for-nothings become good-for-disappearing into whatever toxic-waste-chemical-sludge-shit-hole they crawled out of.

(A pause.)

And it's just me and JanitorMan.
And I pick him up.
And I wipe sweat and cheap perfume off his forehead.
And he begs me not to hurt him and I grab him tight by his JanitorMan shirt collar and I pull him to my face, and he's taller than me, but the cape helps, so he listens when I look him straight in the eyes and I say two words to him:
"Go home."
And he does, checking behind his shoulder every ten feet.
And I SWOOSH from building to building on his way there, 'cause I know where he lives. And I watch his hands tremble as he pulls out his keychain and opens the door to his building.
And I'm back in bed before he even walks in through the front door.

(SNARE.)

And I hear him turn on the faucet and pour himself a glass of warm tap water.
And he puts the glass back in the sink.

(SNARE.)

And I hear his footsteps,

(BOOM. BOOM.)

And they get slower as they get to my room.

(BOOM.)

And he creaks my door open like mad slow.

(Silence.)

And he takes a step in, which he never does.

(BOOM.)

CHAPTER THREE

CREATING FROM COMPONENTS

In this chapter you will:

- Identify the core components of creative writing
- Distinguish the specific components of poetry, nonfiction, fiction, and drama
- Plan and construct your own creative writing projects

So far we've considered ways to build a productive writing practice. We've examined strategies for reading as a writer and distinguishing genres and subgenres in creative writing. And we've been working with whole pieces. Now we zoom in for a closer look at how the various parts of creative writing — words, sentences, lines, conflicts, dialogue, scenes, and stanzas — combine to make a meaningful whole.

CORE COMPONENTS OF CREATIVE WRITING

Three essential components inform creative writing:

- Words
- Metaphor
- Polarity

These three components are so crucial to effective creative writing, to ignore them is to run the risk of producing flat, predictable, and clichéd work.

Words

We rely entirely on **words** to create. In every genre, each word you select has to be the right word, the best word. Some beginning writers are drawn to "writerly" words, like *azure seas, enveloping darkness*, and *sinuous muscles*, but these words, often only ever seen in writing classes, may mark your work as amateur. Some writers overuse single-syllable words, giving their writing a simplistic feeling. Other writers go in the opposite direction, overusing the thesaurus, studding their work with heavy-duty words: *a conflagration of citizenry blossomed into the night* instead of simply *a crowd gathered at 9:00 p.m.* Other writers over-rely on familiar phrases: *tears streamed down their cheeks; he frowned, unhappily; my heart burst out of my chest.* Rather than doing the difficult, necessary work of observing the scene, the hasty or novice writer may resort to **cliché**—overly familiar phrases that no longer create an image in the reader's mind's eye.

Beginning writers in all genres must work to avoid **word packages**—words that come in groups, used habitually; they'll often feel flat to your reader. Here are some examples:

She shrugged her shoulders.
They shuddered with fear.
We were nervous with anticipation.
I was pleasantly surprised.

Words that frequently travel in little packs together usually need to be broken up and reconsidered afresh. Instead of resorting to word packages, do the work and enter the moment. What can you describe that's unusual, interesting, and fresh? Can you be more accurate with your words? Paying attention to the physical experience of each word—the sound and texture of the vowels and consonants—is a simple and rewarding way to improve the power of your writing. Think about the feel of each word in the reader's mouth (the word *spatula* is different in the mouth than the word *murmur*). The sounds of the words matter and must accompany the subject matter and theme of your work. This is vital in poetry, of course, but also in every genre.

Clarity and **accuracy** are your guides when choosing your words. A wide working knowledge of your range of choices helps. Learn the names of things. Develop a vocabulary grounded in precision, as opposed to showing off. Learn the histories of the words you choose to use—every word comes with shades of meanings, subtle implications, and textures of history. Strive to know where words come from and to include words from both Anglo-Saxon languages and Romance languages as well as words that came to

English from other cultures. Each word has a past, a life of its own. Knowing those invisible meanings allows you to create powerful pieces.

PRACTICE 1

EXAMINING WORD CHOICE in Ira Sukrungruang's "Chop Suey"

Turn to page 74 and read "Chop Suey" by Ira Sukrungruang, a poet and a nonfiction writer. As you read through his micro-memoir, circle each word that has a spark or holds specific interest for you. For example, *El-Mar, Thailand, mackerel, Vapex, champion,* and *sloppy* are all very interesting words, not ones we see every day, but straightforward and clear. Comment on word choice in this piece.

Metaphor

In Greece, trucks with the word *metaphora* painted on their sides zip over the roadways. *Metaphora* means "delivery truck" or "moving truck," and this image provides a useful way to understand how metaphors work. In creative writing, a **metaphor** is a word or group of words that carries the meaning associated with one thing over to another thing.

For example, in Betsy Sholl's poem "Genealogy" on page 67, she uses the technique of metaphor to build her entire poem about the personalities of each family member. Here's the first stanza:

> *Some stories, some poems, some nonfiction essays, some children's books present themselves immediately. That's the genre they should be. But sometimes you have to discover that. You try different things to see what works. My default genre is poetry. That's where I began.*
>
> —JULIA ALVAREZ

One of my parents was a flame, the other a rope.
One was a tire, the other a dial tone.

The poet compares one person to fire, taking the qualities of heat, warmth, and perhaps danger or steadiness, or both, and applies those qualities to a parent. It's a complex and provocative image. Flames almost always go out, but before they do they can cook our food or destroy our entire home or neighborhood. Then she takes the qualities of rope—rope is sturdy and useful, but one can have too much rope; a noose is made of rope—and she applies these qualities to the other parent. When we put the two together, flame and rope, sparks literally fly: flames burn rope. Ropes are used to rescue people trapped in fire. But flame and rope don't usually go together very easily or very naturally. There's probably trouble if both of these things are in close proximity. With just eleven words in one line, and two metaphors, each carrying layers of meaning in a single word — *flame, rope* — Sholl has created a complex and resonant image for her reader.

In line 2, "One was a tire, the other a dial tone," another pair of metaphors proves equally provocative. We associate tires with transportation, with getting worn out, with puncture, with going flat. Dial tones make us think of being hung up on, a conversation not happening. Was one parent always taking off and other difficult to talk to? Each reader will have their own associations with the meanings carried over from the words *tire* and *dial tone* and assigned to the parents.

Metaphor is an efficient way of using words, allowing you to compress pages of writing into a couple of words or one sentence. It's also rich, and open-ended, capable of rendering complex ideas with nuance and creativity. Metaphor also allows the reader to make up her own mind: She drives the truck of meanings across town.

Thoughtful use of metaphor gives your reader a richer experience. If everything in your piece simply is what it is, you aren't engaging your reader's full creative intelligence. You aren't allowing the reader the pleasure of making connections. A metaphor invites your reader to participate in your creative work actively by figuring out how the qualities you've moved from one thing to another illuminate the meaning of your piece. This is an essential part of the pleasure of the reading experience.

A metaphor is always a word or a group of words: *the lake was a mirror, one of my parents was a star already gone out.* A **symbol** is a metaphor that relies on a complex image in the piece of writing for the transfer of qualities. For example, instead of saying straight up "After I moved, I was so sad. I was in an ocean of grief" (the quality of enormity, from an ocean, being carried over to grief, which one can easily get completely lost in, too), consider this example: Och Gonzalez, in "What I Do on My Terrace Is None of Your Business," on page 45 uses the setting of the piece to create a metaphor. "[T]his row of anonymous flats" is a metaphor for how she feels; lost and flattened out, depressed. The anonymous, depressing, and flatly similar apartments and their terraces match her mood — she too is flat, lonely, feeling anonymous, having lost her dog and her warm and familiar home. Here, people are killing their flowers; the dead flowers carry over their qualities of lifelessness to her own mood. Because the setting of the piece is complex, the metaphor becomes a symbol for her grief.

Syntax — the order of the words in a sentence — can also be used as a symbol to echo the main theme of your piece. Vincent Scarpa, in his Writers on Writing piece, which appears after "I Go Back to Berryman's" on page 76, reveals how he uses the qualities of a long, highly pressured sentence that's kind of out of control as a symbol for adolescence.

Metaphor and symbol are a large part of what make creative writing complex and interesting and special, unlike all other forms of writing. Straight-up reports and manuals don't use these tools; they can be quite boring to read because what you see is exactly what you get — there aren't layers. There's not much depth. Not much is required of the reader. Metaphor and symbol require your reader to engage, and they provide pleasure and richness in return.

Try to create your own original metaphors, rather than using the ones that first come to mind. *I'm engulfed in darkness* uses the qualities of being overwhelmed that come with the ocean to show what it's like to be depressed or despairing, but this metaphor has been used many times. *I furrowed my brows* uses the qualities of plowing a field — creating lines or *furrows* in the soil — is that really what's happening to your forehead when you are confused? If you've witnessed actual furrows, and your forehead actually looks like that field — okay. Maybe. But the image has been used so many times, we don't even take it in anymore. The metaphor truck no longer carries any qualities; the contents were delivered long ago and it's empty. Try to look closely, observe carefully, and work to discern in fresh ways the qualities of your subject so you can choose a new accurate metaphor to create a smart surprise for your reader.

Ultimately, metaphor helps you turn words into meaningful literature by asking the reader to participate in constructing meaning.

PRACTICE 2

CLOSE READING FOR METAPHOR

Go back to any one of the pieces you've read so far in this textbook and make a list of the metaphors you find in the piece. Look at the words, syntax, and setting, and also the action, dialogue, and symbols as you read closely. Make a comment about the use of metaphor in the piece you choose to close read.

Polarity

A piece of writing has to move from one direction to another — from positive to negative or negative to positive — to reveal an energetic shift of some kind. If a piece is static, with no movement, the reader is often left with a "What's the point?" feeling. This movement is called **polarity**.

In a poem, every line has a polarity. In a story or play, every scene has to move from one point to another point. To find out the polarity of a scene (think of a battery, with the + and the − on either end), ask yourself how your scene or poem starts, positive charge or negative charge? And then where does it go? Do things get better, or worse? Och Gonzalez's "What I Do on My Terrace Is None of Your Business" on page 45 moves from a drooped head in the opening to a literal and figurative metaphor of looking up in the end. In fact, the last two words of the piece are "look up." The piece has a clear movement from negative to positive. Ira Sukrungruang in "Chop Suey" on page 74 moves from the negative—a young son is too naïve to see his mother as a full person yet, to the positive. Through a painful social interaction, he sees who she really is, a force of nature, up against another man's cruel, humiliating behavior. Though it has a happy resolution, Jarod Roselló's "Robot Camp" on page 29 moves from the positive (get to build robots, yay) to the negative (very scary things happen—we can never go back). In using the concept of polarity, writers start in one place and almost always work to end up in a very different place.

PRACTICE 3

CLOSE READING FOR POLARITY

Choose any piece in the textbook and read it carefully to determine the polarity. Where does the polarity of the piece start? Where does it end? Does the piece move from a negative principle to a positive one or positive to negative? What creates movement in the piece? Write a paragraph of commentary on the polarity in the piece you've chosen.

GENRE-SPECIFIC COMPONENTS

Words, metaphors, and movement—polarity—are the lifeblood of creative writing. Within each genre, there are specific components that writers work with in order to assemble a powerful, well-structured, and cohesive piece. In this next section, we'll look at the parts of stories, poems, and plays so you can more adroitly assemble your own creations, and perhaps more skillfully mix and match genre components to invent your own forms.

Components of Narrative: Memoir, Creative Nonfiction, Fiction

Stories are composed of four essential parts:

- Yearning
- Sentences
- Conflict
- Scenes

A story starts with someone (or something—a robot or a bird, for example) wanting something badly, something necessary. We call this desire that ignites and then drives the narrative **yearning**. In stories, the world pushes back—other people or forces keep the characters from getting what they must have. Sentence by sentence, the ensuing conflicts play out in scenes. These are the four core building blocks of narrative.

Yearning. A story starts with someone wanting something and the world pushes hard against that desire—another person, or a force of nature, or something or someone will not let this person get what they want. This push-pull dynamic is the pulse of narrative. In Ira Sukrungruang's micro-memoir "Chop Suey" on page 74, young Ira, the author, yearns to impress his mother. But she ends up impressing him not just with her bowling prowess, but with her grace and power. In "The Great Silence," Ted Chiang's short story on page 79, the parrots yearn to be not just heard, but understood.

To give your story—whether it's fiction, memoir, or drama—depth and staying power, consider the two levels of yearning, **internal yearning** and **external yearning**. The internal yearning is the person's inner, emotional want. The external yearning is what the person is physically doing to get what they want. External yearning is what we can see in dialogue or action. Internal yearning is revealed through metaphor, thoughts, implication, and our interpretations of character behavior.

Brenda Miller's younger self, in her micro-memoir "Swerve" on page 124 wants to love her husband and placate him; and she wants to be safe. Her external yearning is to ask for forgiveness all the time. She apologizes for everything. Notice how her external yearning advances the story: She tries to cook differently, for example. Meanwhile, her internal yearning, as she works harder and harder to anticipate his desires for quiet or for music, begins to shift—or swerve—in a different direction. Here, "swerve" is embedded in the story on a physical, real level—she didn't turn the wheel in time to avoid danger—external yearning. And that action is a metaphor for her larger life situation—she needs to swerve out of the lane she's in quickly and lead a different kind of life—internal yearning.

When giving your piece a title, think about the internal yearning and external yearning coming together in a metaphor, a word your reader can use to apprehend the two kinds of yearning central to the story. If you spend some time before and during your writing process reflecting on what the person you are writing about wants, from within their heart of hearts, your character (whether fictional or real) will have more roundness and your story's polarity will become clearer. If you can create disparities between the inner yearning—to be loving, to be safe—and the external yearning—to please, to maintain status quo, to placate with apologies—you've likely got a dramatic story on your hands. Without yearning, there's no way for a story to progress or to affect us emotionally: No yearning, no story.

PRACTICE 4

READING FOR YEARNING

Read "Cathedral" by Raymond Carver on page 125. In one or two sentences, explain the internal and external yearning of each of the main characters: the blind man, the husband, and the wife.

Sentences. A sentence is a group of words containing a **noun** and a **verb**: In creative writing, the most important words you choose are the nouns and the verbs. Nouns let the reader see your piece in the mind's eye—without good, concrete nouns, the reader wanders in the misty land of abstraction, unfocused. Verbs are the muscles of your stories—they carry the action. Story's DNA resides in the verbs you choose. Keep in mind that the most expedient way to improve the power of your prose is to avoid forms of the verb "to be" and to choose strong action verbs.

There are four different kinds of sentences you'll use to tell your fictional and real stories.

Character sentence:	Shows, through behavior, the character of a person
Relationship sentence:	Shows, through actions and reactions, who people are by how they interact with each other
Plot sentence:	Presents an action step that is going to have some consequences
Backstory sentence:	Provides information from the character's past actions and previous hopes that sheds light on the present situation

The opening sentence of your narrative might reveal something about a character; how she orders a drink, plays pinball; what she likes to eat. "Robot Camp" starts with a character reveal sentence: "At first, I thought Robot Camp was a good idea." Opening sentences usually indicate instability: There's already trouble.

The next sentence might exist to establish relationships (a mother needles her daughter about gaining weight; a young boy is kicked out of the playground by his buddies). "We all did," is the second sentence in "Robot Camp," showing relationships in a community.

The following sentences move the plot forward—things at Robot Camp get weird, for example, or your character loads boxes into her car and drives off with her best friend's child—so that the reader *has to keep reading in order to find out what happens next.*

Lastly, backstory sentences are carefully chosen images from the past that give your story depth and context. Comics and micro and flash forms often leave out the backstory. Readers are asked to fill in many of those details for themselves. In a full-length short story, there's time and space to enrich the story with layers from each character's life. "Hundreds of years ago," Ted Chiang writes, through the voice of a parrot in his short story "The Great Silence" on page 79, "my kind was so plentiful that the Rio Abajo Forest resounded with our voices." Backstory can't be boring; it has to move the story forward, raise the tension.

> *My favorite compliment that I got from a writer early on was, "you leave out all the right things."*
>
> —AMY HEMPEL

Here is an example of each of the four types of narrative sentences, taken from Raymond Carver's story "Cathedral" on page 125:

Character sentence:	She was at the draining board doing scalloped potatoes.
Relationship sentence:	I reached to draw her robe back over her, and it was then that I glanced at the blind man. What the hell! I flipped the robe open again.
Plot sentence:	"Get us a pen and some heavy paper. Go on, bub, get the stuff," he said.
Backstory sentence:	She'd seen something in the paper: HELP WANTED—*Reading to Blind Man*, and a telephone number. She phoned and went over, was hired on the spot.

PRACTICE 5

READING SENTENCE TYPES: Raymond Carver's "Cathedral"

Read Raymond Carver's "Cathedral" on page 125. Locate and label two additional examples of each of the four types of sentences in the story. Of the four types, which do you think is most powerful or effective? Make a comment on your preference.

PRACTICE 6

CREATING SENTENCE TYPES

For a fictional or nonfictional narrative you are writing, or just for practice, write one of each of the kinds of sentences—character, relationship, plot, backstory.

Conflict. A story thrives on **conflict**—friction is a required component for all narrative and dramatic genres. Conflict occurs when one person's yearning is pitted against another person's yearning. Or, the world can push back against someone's yearning—often with great force. Without conflict, you have a prose poem or an anecdote. It might be very beautiful, meaningful, and worthy, but it's simply not a story. In "Robot Camp" the main character yearns to make her star bot, but mysterious forces conspire against her with increasing violence; she has to abandon her project and flee and start again, in a different way. If, in another version of this comic, the main character made robots and that worked out really nicely and she got to continue her work making more robots, we might read and enjoy the comic—it sounds charming, even—but it wouldn't be defined as a story because nothing changed; nothing really happened. There's no conflict.

In principle, if there's no conflict there's no story. For instance, if you tell me about your day, and it was a pleasant, sunny day and everything went smoothly: Lunch tasted quite delicious, and Joey was friendly as he always is, and you got your homework done a bit early, and you found a parking spot right in front of your apartment, and no one you live with was annoying . . . I'm going to be happy for you. But unless we're friends or related to each other, why are you even telling me this? You have created an **account** or an **anecdote**. It's fine, it's perfectly nice.

But it's not a story, for two reasons: There's not a strong yearning. You don't seem to want anything you don't already have.

There's not a problem or conflict: You seem to be just going through your day like you always do.

In "Cathedral," conflicts are **character-based** and complex. A man who is limited in his ability to be comfortable around others is forced to confront his fears when the blind man, a good friend of his wife's, visits his home overnight. There's a lot of story juice in that premise. We're already worried just from hearing about the situation. Is the husband going to offend the blind man? Probably. How will the blind man react? It could go any number of ways. We have to read to find out. Conflict is the pulse of life in your story.

Lastly, the obstacles you choose to include in your narrative have to matter; they can't be random. Imagine your four-year-old niece, reporting her dream from last night. She reports the dragons were chasing her and she fed them. And then they were still chasing her. And they turned purple. And then she was hungry and she was chasing them. And she turned green! And they went to the store and there were dragons there, too. And she got chased . . . and then there were all these monsters who were chasing everybody . . . It goes on from there. There are obstacles galore in her story: dragons, hunger, monsters. But the story is of low interest because the conflicts don't actually matter to the characters in the story. So you turn green. Life goes on. A monster chases you. Not really a problem, it seems. One event just rolls right into the next.

In "Cathedral," we care what happens because the people in the story care a lot about what happens, and they matter to each other. The wife loves her husband and cares deeply for her friend, the blind man. If the husband is rude, his behavior is going to have a significant effect on these relationships. We're worried someone is going to be hurt, and we are right to be worried.

PRACTICE 7

CLOSE READING FOR CONFLICT: "Cathedral"

Make note of the places where you find conflict (yearning + obstacle) as you read through the story. For example, in the opening paragraph:

> Yearning: The husband yearns not to feel awkward around blind people;
>
> Obstacle: A blind person is on his way to his house.

In the second paragraph:

> Yearning: The wife yearns to have poetry and meaningful human contact in her life — she even allows the blind man to touch her face.
>
> Obstacle: Seems to be her husband.

Continue through the story, noting yearning + obstacle as you read for conflict. Make a comment about what you notice as you read carefully for conflict (yearning + obstacle).

Scene. A **scene** is a sequence of actions set in a specific place that occur during a set amount of time. As discussed in Chapters One and Two, when the reader is reading a scene, she sees the action of the story play out in the mind's eye, like a movie, in real time.

Narrative writers have two other strategies in addition to scene: they can use **summary**, and they can use **reflection** or **insight**. Scenes are the most exciting for readers, but summary and insight are important components, and we'll look at how and when to use them later. Our focus here is on the use of scene, the primary vehicle for many contemporary narratives.

Carver creates a miniscene when he shows us the husband and wife beginning to listen to the blind man's most recent tape, the one where he reveals his opinions of this new relationship. Whenever we can see the characters in a setting and they are communicating and doing things, we know we're in a scene. The scene is a container for yearning + obstacles. Here, the husband yearns to connect with his wife, but the obstacle is perhaps his own insecurity. He seems threatened that the blind man knows his wife better than he does. "Now this same blind man was coming to sleep in my house." That sentence launches us into the first major full-blown scene in the story. Compare with the four-year-old's telling the story of her dream, referenced above: no scenes—it's one long list of events.

The key ingredients for a scene are:

Time:	Make sure there's a clock ticking somewhere; the scene starts and ends at specific times.
Place:	Choose a setting that creates a symbolic layer and/or adds tension.
Yearning:	Someone wants something they don't have, and they want it urgently.
Obstacle:	Someone or something is pushing back on the person's yearning.
Action:	Speech and character actions play out, usually in time order, until the end of the scene.

When you change location or jump forward or backward in time, you're creating a new scene. The first scene in "Cathedral" begins with the husband offering to take the blind man bowling. His wife puts the knife down . . . Then she pushes back, telling her husband she'd make his visiting friend feel comfortable. They argue. The husband makes a racist remark. The wife is upset, confused, angry. "Right then my wife filled me in with more detail than I cared to know." The next part of the story shows the husband listening (or maybe half listening?) to his wife as he considers the story he is hearing about the blind man's life. When the next paragraph begins, "So when the time rolled around . . . ," we know we are in a new scene—there's been a shift in time.

In the next scene, the narrator watches his wife assist the blind man getting out of a car. And then they enter the house, and already the scene is saturated with conflict. The narrator criticizes, internally, Robert's beard. He hasn't even met him yet, but he already dislikes him. The wife is laughing and happy out there in the driveway. So when the front door opens, there is a lot at stake. The wife is happier than the narrator imagined she would be. This is going to be much, much worse than he thought. We see he is jealous. Again, there are implications. There are things that could really go wrong here.

PRACTICE 8

BREAKING DOWN A SCENE

Identify each of the scenes in Carver's story. How many scenes did you count in the story? Choose one of the scenes (or divide them up among class members and work in small groups), and identify and describe each of the following:

Time: When does the scene start and when does it end?

Place: Does the setting have symbolic value or inherent conflict?

Yearning: What's the desire of each character?

Obstacle: What's pushing back on each character?

Action: What are the key actions/dialogue lines in the scene?

PRACTICE 9

WRITING A SCENE

Write a scene that includes the following:

Time: A clock ticking — choose a specific time of day.

Place: Choose a setting that has some energy or tension in it.

Yearning: Focus in on the internal and external yearning of your main character.

Obstacle: What is pushing back on this character?

Action: What are the most important actions and lines of dialogue to show conflict?

Building Narratives Using Conflict–Crisis–Resolution. To build a series of scenes into a successful narrative, many writers turn to the classical three-part **conflict–crisis–resolution** structure. Readers appreciate when a story builds and develops. They're often expecting some kind of **turning point** close to the end, whether it's a subtle coming into awareness like we see in "Chop Suey" or a profound shift in consciousness, as we see in "Cathedral." Some readers like surprising twists, as in Nancy Stohlman's "I Found Your Voodoo Doll on the Dance Floor After Last Call," while others prefer to focus on powerful images, as in "Swerve," and figure out the climax and resolution of story (Does she leave him?) on their own.

Whether or not you adhere strictly to the traditional conflict–crisis–resolution arc for your stories, a good rule of thumb to follow is the more

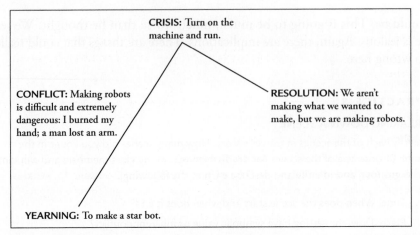

Figure 3.1 Conflict-Crisis-Resolution Template for "Robot Camp" by Jarod Roselló

you veer from building the conflict–crisis–resolution arc into your story, the shorter you might want to make the piece and the more beautiful and interesting the language should be. The above figure shows a visual representation of story arc.

Here are some tips for using the conflict–crisis–resolution template:

1. Begin by focusing on your main character's strongest desire, the **yearning**.
2. **Start with conflict** right away. Start in action with a small battle: one character's yearning directly hitting up against a clear obstacle. Don't start with a character alone with their thoughts. Don't warm up, wander around, or muse. Readers aren't going to be interested in background and buildup—how the family came to be, what it was like to wake up that morning. Don't preface, set up, or introduce. Start in the scene and plunge into problems.
3. **Build to crisis.** Each scene holds a new conflict, caused by the previous one, that's a little bit worse. The most significant conflict in your narrative is called the crisis. A crisis is when the battle is at its very, very worst. After this battle, your main character will be somehow changed.
4. **End with an interesting resolution.** There are many ways to end your story; revisit the discussion of polarity earlier in this chapter. Your main purpose is to show or imply change. What has shifted? Does your main character have a new yearning? Is your main character better or worse off, after dealing with the obstacles? A little of both? As long as you can show that there's been some kind of movement, *some* kind of shift, the

The more restrictions you have, the easier anything is to write.
—STEPHEN SONDHEIM

reader will likely feel satisfied. Work to make sure your opening and your ending relate to each other in an interesting and surprising way. If a character opens a door at the beginning of the story, he closes a door at the end.

| PRACTICE 10 |

MAPPING CONFLICT–CRISIS–RESOLUTION

Examine Vincent Scarpa's "I Go Back to Berryman's" on page 76 and Nancy Stohlman's "I Found Your Voodoo Doll on the Dance Floor After Last Call" on page 76. What is the conflict–crisis–resolution in each? Create visual diagrams, like the one on page 100 Figure 3.1 for these two narratives.

| PRACTICE 11 |

BUILDING A PIECE WITH CONFLICT–CRISIS–RESOLUTION

Plan a story using conflict–crisis–resolution. You may wish to do this assignment as a four-panel comic. Consider using the diagram on page 100 Figure 3.1 as a model.

Components of Poetry

If you think of poetry as a fabulous, welcoming landscape with endless possibilities for creative play, you might find the practice of poetry to be an excellent way to expand your emotional range and also your powers as a writer. Poetry engages your eye and your ear; it welcomes questions and indirection, mystery and weirdness, and wildness and music. Some people are daunted by poetry, but after study and practice, most find this genre to be an excellent foundation for a writing life. Be a little patient and a little bold as you enter the house of poetry. The rewards to come are truly great.

The core components of poetry are:

■ Sound and rhythm
■ Lines
■ Turns
■ Stanzas

Sound and Rhythm. The single most important feature of poetry is music. Poets work to create patterns with the sounds of the words they choose, and they aim to place these sonic patterns into rhythms — we call this meter — that make the poem flow in a pleasing or interesting way.

The poet carefully chooses sounds and metrical patterns—rhythms—that are beautiful and artful; they also must underscore the subject of the poem.

A poem about hummingbirds may have short quick lines, tight staccato rhythms, and sounds that hover on the lips and in the mouth, like the sound *vee* in "hover" does. A poem about a break-up may have long vowel sounds, which can feel sad to a reader, like *oo* and *ee*: *O, Scotty, why did you break my heart?*

For a terrific visual introduction to basic sound and rhythm techniques, look online at Vox for "Rapping Deconstructed: The best rhymers of all time." Playwrights and prose writers avail themselves of these sound effect techniques, too.

If you are not deploying sound echoes and attending to the patterns of emphasis in your poetry, you may unwittingly be writing prose with line breaks. Compare lines that have no particular rhythm and no meaningful pattern of repeating sounds, prose with line breaks:

> A poet writing about hummingbirds could have short
> quick lines and tight rhythms
> in order to appeal to the reader.

With lines of actual poetry:

> Wild men who caught and sang the sun in flight,
> And learn, too late, they grieved it on its way
> Do not go gentle into that good night.

The crucial component that differentiates poetry from prose is the poet's skilled use of sound and rhythm.

Sound. To create sound patterns on the page—and as a poet, you must—you have three power tools to use in order to connect important words in the poem to each other: alliteration, assonance, and consonance. Note that the words with similar sounds need to be near each other—three to eight syllables apart is a good guide. If you overuse the power tools, your work might be too dense, ("Sally sells seashells by the seashore") and difficult to read aloud. But if the sounds are too far apart, the effect may be lost on the reader.

To hear the sound work, you have to read aloud; always go by your ear and not your eye. "Through" and "cough" look like they have similar sounds but when you say these two words aloud, they have no sound in common. "Call" and "wade" share a vowel, but the "a" sound is pronounced differently in each word—no sound link is created. Sound patterns are created by how the letters are pronounced in relationship to each other—all "a" sounds aren't the same.

Here are the three tools you have to create sound patterns:

Alliteration:	Linking the sound at the beginning of words; "this" and "they"; "ghetto" and "greenbacks"
Assonance:	Repeating vowel sounds within neighboring words; "Solo" and "Felonious"; "hip" "th*is*" "is." Note: "call" and "wades" is *not* assonance—can you hear the difference in the *a* sounds?
Consonance:	Consonant letters repeating within words (not at the beginning—that's alliteration); "Hipsters" and "devised"; "ghetto" and "mint"

PRACTICE 12

IDENTIFYING SOUND WORK

Read Terrance Hayes's "Liner Notes for an Imaginary Playlist" on page 121. The poem is in six parts, with a three-line section in italics at the very end. Find at least three examples of each kind of sound work—alliteration, assonance, and consonance. Remember: The poet uses sound work to connect *significant* words together and to create sounds in the reader's ear that support the meaning of the poem. How does Hayes use of sound underscore meaning in specific stanzas?

Rhythm. Rhythm in poetry comes from listening to which syllables are emphasized (stressed), which syllables are not emphasized (unstressed), and what pattern is created across the line by these beats.

> Heather Sellers is my name.
> Teaching poets is my game.

Even a small child can tap out the rhythm in those two sentences. When we say poetry is language set to music, this is what we mean. When you read Shakespeare's words "Shall I compare thee to a summer's day?" you will naturally hit some of the syllables harder than others. Read that line of poetry aloud and listen to yourself closely.

If you read the words as you naturally would speak them, chances are you may have stressed the following syllables:

shall **I** | comp**ARE** | thee **TO** | a **SUM** | mer's **DAY**

There's not a perfectly "right" or "wrong" way to stress. You will invoke rhythms in your poems based on your own voice, your own preferences, and your own personal and cultural speech patterns. If English isn't your first language, you may emphasize different syllables. The objective here is to pay attention to rhythms that naturally occur in language and in you, in your body and on your tongue, and to place the beats (accented syllables) in your lines on words that create meaningful emphasis. Rhythmic patterns create pleasure for the reader and underscore meaning.

If you are writing formal verse that has its own meter, such as a **sonnet** (five stressed syllables and five unstressed syllables per line, just as in the Shakespeare example in the line we looked at above), the poem form prescribes meter for you to follow. If you are writing in a form that doesn't have a meter, like the **sestina** (the Terrance Hayes poem "Liner Notes for an Imaginary Playlist" on page 121 is a sestina—there's a set pattern for the end words but no specific recipe for the beats), creating interesting rhythms is left up to you as the poet. Writing free verse is a little bit harder than writing formal metrical poetry because the poet has to create rhythmic patterns from scratch for every single line.

When you physically identify the accented beats in a line of poetry by marking them with your pen or pencil, that process is called **scanning**.

PRACTICE 13

LOCATING PATTERNS OF RHYTHM IN FREE VERSE

Read the first stanza of the Terrance Hayes poem on page 121 aloud. What syllables are stressed? Make a list of these stressed syllables. Even though in free verse there isn't a set pattern for rhythm, do you hear any repeating patterns of accented (stressed) beats? Make a comment about the rhythms you notice in this poem.

PRACTICE 14

SCANNING FORMAL POETRY

To practice reading for rhythm, go online to For Better for Verse (prosody.lib.virginia .edu), an interactive site that lets you practice scanning poems and identify where the stressed syllables are in relationship to the unstressed syllables in poems. You'll find the poems sorted by difficulty—start with an easy one in order to get a feel for manipulating beats. You can easily check your answers on the site.

PRACTICE 15

APPRECIATING SOUND: Dylan Thomas's "Do Not Go Gentle into That Good Night."

Read aloud Dylan Thomas's **villanelle**, "Do Not Go Gentle into That Good Night" on page 123. Comment on his use of sound and rhythm.

Lines. In poetry, a **line** is all the words on one line of text, a group of words in a row. The poetic line may be a complete sentence, but many poems are made of sentences and phrases broken up into lines; the syntactical units are cut into pieces. The word that the line ends on is called the **line break**. A line that ends in punctuation is called **end-stopped**. A narrative is a story made of sentences but a poem is groups of words and sentences made into lines.

Look closely at the use of line in the following poem.

Gwendolyn Brooks
We Real Cool

> *The Pool Players.*
> *Seven at the Golden Shovel.*

We real cool. We
Left school. We

Lurk late. We
Strike straight. We

Sing sin. We
Thin gin. We

Jazz June. We
Die soon.

In this famous, memorable poem, the lines are ultra-short, most of them merely three words long. Notice, too, how Brooks uses the power tools of sound in every single line — *lurk late, strike straight.* Brooks relies heavily on rhythm, those strong stresses — heavily emphasized syllables that are complete words — in order to add drama to each line. The word *We* is the heavily accented end word at the end of each line: *We* occurs more than any other word in the poem. By breaking each line on the word *We,* it's likely the poet is making a statement about how important the group identity is. There isn't really an "I" or a self. The self is subsumed by the group. And whatever the group does — *sing* or *strike* or *sin* or *jazz* — the I is automatically doing it as part of the we. The group operates as its own entity. The emphasis on *We* is so strong, so powerful, that you can almost hear a fist banging a table, or a beat of some kind. *We* matters. *We* rules. The reader may sense some of the power and excitement that comes from being part of a very tight group, and also some of the weirdness when you aren't making your own decisions anymore. In fact, your very life is shortened — you gave your soul to the group.

You might read the poem another way, but any reading is going to have to take into account those insistent hard lines that end in *We* after *We*. Interestingly, there is no *We* at the end. That line ends short, just like the lives of the kids described. It's missing a beat. And, look at how the lines look on the page. The *We* is always surrounded by white space — nothing comes after the *We* on the line except for silence.

A poem with short lines will often read much more quickly than a poem with long lines. Compare Brooks's "We Real Cool" on page 105 with Sebastian Matthews's "Buying Wine" on page 71. Matthews is telling a story in his poem, one that takes place throughout a childhood and affects adulthood. As kids, they have to wait in the car for a long time while the father shops; in the store, they wander the long aisles. Long lines make sense in this poem of reflection back on childhood.

Short lines can destabilize the reader, especially if they are **enjambed**. Enjambment means the poet breaks the line in the middle of a sentence, as Brooks does:

> We real cool. We
> Left school. We

Think of enjambment as word wrapping a sentence onto two or more lines. Enjambment allows you to create pressure and drama for your reader, and it allows you to create a pattern of beats.

Another way of approaching the line is to make them end-stopped. **End-stopped** lines are simply lines that aren't broken in the middle of a syntactical unit (like subject and verb, as in *We / Left*). End-stopped lines end with punctuation — a dash, a comma, a period. The reader stops and pauses.

In "Buying Wine," the poet uses both kinds of line to create flow and drama in his poem.

> When we were boys, we had a choice: stay in the car or else {**enjambed**}
> follow him into Wine Mart, that cavernous retail barn,   {**end-stopped**}

Note how the enjambment in line 1 creates word play — "or else" has a double meaning. And because Matthews is writing long lines with long sentences, to create a sensation of going down aisle after aisle, long line after long line, he gives the reader places to pause by using end-stopped lines, too, creating flow.

PRACTICE 16

ENJAMBMED VERSUS END-STOPPED LINES: Sebastian Matthews's "Buying Wine"

Turn to "Buying Wine" on page 71 and mark each line as either enjambed or end-stopped. Consider the possible reasons behind each choice. How do the two types of line endings affect your reading of the lines in the poem? Comment on what you notice.

Many poets write in complete sentences; in a poem, a line is not the same thing as a sentence. In Terrance Hayes's sestina, "Liner Notes for an Imaginary Playlist" on page 121, notice that the first three lines in the poem are made out of two sentences. The end of the sentence is not automatically the end of the line. In stanza 3 of Hayes's poem, each line is end-stopped. Compare the difference, when you read the stanzas aloud, to the feel of stanza 4, which uses enjambment in its first four lines.

Lines in poetry are equivalent in their impact to the scenes in a story. In a poem, the line has to accomplish a lot. Lines have to be tight, well constructed, and power-packed. Each word is hand-picked to have the greatest effect. The line is also a container for sound and rhythm. And, each line must advance the poem.

Lines have a polarity, too, just as a scene does. Each line has to *move* in a specific direction. Unlike sentences in a paragraph, which can link and build and clarify and explain, a poem's lines must move from point A to point B, every time.

Many early poem drafts are loose and bulky as the poet works on each line, one at a time. Many lines get cut as the poet hones and compresses the poem. Every line has to work hard to do something necessary and earn its right to stay in the poem.

PRACTICE 17

EXPERIMENTING WITH LINES

Take one of your pieces of narrative composed this semester and, using the first three or four sentences, break the sentences into lines. Try to choose end words that are significant to you. Try to create lines that stand on their own in some interesting way. But don't make any grammatical changes—simply break a piece of prose into lines. Which version do you like better? Does the poem version accomplish anything the prose version does not? Comment on your experiment.

Line Length. A line in a poem can be as short as one word (or even one letter: *O* and *I* being the shortest words we have available to us). A poet can also choose to run all of the lines in a poem all the way to the right-hand margin: This style of formatting lines is called **prose poetry**. An example of a prose poem is A. Van Jordan's "af•ter•glow" on page 71.

How does a poet decide how long to make the lines? In addition to considering the subject matter and enjambment, the poet attends to rhythm, which means counting syllables and accented beats. In some kinds of poems, such as sonnets, there's a prescribed syllable count: ten, with five stressed syllables. Kim Addonizio's sonnet, "First Poem for You" on page 121, doesn't stick to the rules precisely; some of her lines are a few syllables longer than in a strict sonnet. But the beats control the length of the line.

PRACTICE 18

SHORT LINES VERSUS LONG LINES

Retype the lines in Gwendolyn Brooks's poem on page 105 into one or two long lines and read the new version aloud. Write a short paragraph about what you notice. What changes when the poem is in long lines?

Polarity in the Line. Notice that in the lines, whether short or long, there is usually more than one thing happening. In Gwendolyn Brooks's poem, the kids act but that hard *We* at the end points to the cost of their actions. Notice how Sebastian Matthews breaks his lines on key words, creating polarity. The first line of the poem ends "or else" which creates a double meaning when linked to the second line. Lee Herrick in "My California" on page 72 breaks the lines just when you are sinking into the image and the story; he wants his reader looking around, moving quickly, paying attention to a full range of disparate images. On many lines Herrick places **juxtapositions**— things that don't go together, such as beer-soaked gutters and songs, bullets and prayers, a positive and a negative— creating two poles, or directions, in each single line.

Poets use polarity because they want their lines to work hard, harder than mere sentences. Think of each line as a kind of miniature poem.

Turns. Poetry is often called **verse**; the word *verse* actually means "turn." A **turn** in a poem is a change in direction. The speaker changes his mind, or sees things in a new way, or asks a larger question. A turn may involve a change in tone, a change of scene, or a move in time. A turn is some kind of meaningful change and without a turn, you run the risk of writing a poem that feels insubstantial or incomplete or both. Just as narratives are built out of a series of conflicts culminating in a climax, a poem is a series of small turns (each line actually "turns" when it ends) culminating in a significant turn in the subject matter itself toward the end of the poem.

The subject matter turn in a poem usually occurs about three-quarters of the way through, but the turn can come in the very last line, as it does in Brooks's "We Real Cool":

Die soon.

There's no more significant turn than death. In Kim Addonizio's love poem, she's following the guidelines for a sonnet. In a sonnet, the poem is constructed of two components, two halves, divided by a turn and that turn must come at about line 9. She "turns" her poem by changing tone in line 10:

the pictures in your skin. They'll last until

She has turned her attention from the bed where the lovers are kissing to a larger statement about mortality. She's no longer focused on kissing tattoos. She's thinking about what will last between them; the relationship might not stick but those tattoos are always going to be there, until death. There's almost always another turn in the sonnet at line 11. And at line 11, Addonizio turns her poem again. She's used enjambment throughout this poem to describe lovemaking. But at line 11, she switches. She uses two end-stopped lines for the first time in the poem.

be there. Such permanence is terrifying.

The line starts with a command: "be there." And then makes a strong statement, unlike anything we've heard in the poem up to this point. That's a turn and it's marked by syntax, tone, and subject matter.

Also notice how this poet has used components of narrative. She clearly sets us in a specific place (the bedroom), and her sentences move through time, step-by-step, as she traces her lover's tattoos. The list of steps — how she loves the tattoos — is all written in images. Each sentence is structured with *I* — *I like, I'm sure of where, . . .* *I pull you to me, . . .* and *I love, . . .* creating a rhythm through the syntactical pattern. The words *They'll last* five lines from the end of the poem indicate a change in direction. From the "I" list that drove the first two-thirds of the poem, there's a strong shift. She uses "they" twice: ***They'll last*** and ***they will still be there.*** In the last line, this graceful, nimble poet pirouettes yet again — *So I touch them in the dark, . . .* which hooks us back up to the opening line, where she told us she liked touching tattoos in the dark. The poem turns in line 10, turns again, and then turns again, coming full circle.

> *Persist. Read, write, and improve: tell your stories. Accept rejection until you find acceptance.*
>
> —JESSMYN WARD

There are phrases poets use to indicate their turns; these are called **turn signals**: *perhaps, maybe, once, later, however, but instead. . . .* Words that indicate a change of heart, a change of mind, a new way of thinking, or a new question being asked often suggest the turn. A completely new kind of writing indicates a turn, such as the three lines in italics at the end of Hayes's playlist sestina on page 121.

PRACTICE 19

IDENTIFYING TURNS

Read Lee Herrick's "My California" on page 72 and Sebastian Matthews's "Buying Wine" on page 71. Locate the major turn before the end of each poem. Explain your answer in a paragraph.

A poem without any turns might stay on the surface. Consider what happens when there is no turn in a piece of poetry:

> I love Joey.
> Joey is fantastic, adorable, and hot.
> Joey and I will always be together.
> Joey is great and we were meant to be.

There's no sound work or rhythm. There are no patterns that are meaningful. The lines are prose lines, not poetry. And there's not a turn. The poet has only one thing to say: They love Joey. We get it. The sentiment — love — is stated clearly. Too clearly. In order for the poem to be complete, the poet must send the reader in a *different direction*. At least once.

Notice the difference:

> I love Joey.
> Joey is adorable and hot.
> Joey and I were meant to be.
> His partner will see this someday soon.

Poetry is the lifeblood of rebellion, revolution, and the raising of consciousness.
—ALICE WALKER

The turn takes place in the last line. The word choices in this poem are still really basic and un-lovely. The lines are not well thought out — they're random, mindlessly end-stopped with zero polarity and no attention to sound, rhythm, or music. This is prose, not poetry: The lines do only one thing, never two things.

A lot of weaknesses! *But there is a turn.* This one component alone has immense power in poetry. Using turns will drastically increase the power of your poetry.

While the poem *must* turn near the end or in the last line of the poem, it's useful to think of ways the poem can turn in every line:

> I love Joey my baby baloney
> head. And I hate like freak
> him too. He has a perfect
> wife. "Veronica." Ver-
> onica, Hair-onica, snake woman.
> I hate her more, more. Joey —
> love me. You are bald but
> you deserve more!

Not great word choices. Not a great poem, to be sure. But notice what happens when a poet deploys the basic components. The poem suddenly has energy. There's some sound work. Some interesting line breaks. Not every line is predictably end-stopped and there are changes in direction after many of the lines. And notice how even in a very simple poem, the use of turns adds necessary drama and depth to poetry.

PRACTICE 20

COMPONENTS: Kim Addonizio's "First Poem for You"

Read aloud Kim Addonizio's sonnet, "First Poem for You," on page 121. Note examples of alliteration, assonance, and consonance. Note what syllables are accented (stressed). How do her choices for sound (words linked to other words) and rhythm (slow, steady iambic pentameter) contribute to the meaning and effect of the poem? Also notice which lines are enjambed and which are not, and comment on the effect. Where is the turn? Comment on why you choose that line for the turn.

Stanzas. **Stanza** means "room" in Italian and is a group of lines set off by white space. Each stanza holds one specific image or idea in a poem.

Couplets are two-line stanzas, often used for love poems or poems with two entities. "Genealogy" by Betsy Sholl on page 67 is a poem built around seven couplets (with three one-line stanzas and one three-line stanza). Since the poem is about two parents, couplets make perfect sense.

Tercets are three-line stanzas; villanelles and other poems where there's a sense of incompletion, of going forward and going backward, often use tercets. Subjects that have three distinct parts may work well in tercets: for example, life, death, rage.

Quatrains are the most common stanza—four lines. Quatrains are the most "room" like. Four-line stanzas are used for hymns, many popular songs, and they work well for many kinds of poems. Take a look at Natalie Diaz's "My Brother at 3 a.m." on page 165. This poem is a **pantoum**, a form that always uses quatrains. Note how the four-line stanzas create a sense of stability as you read, while in the poem, the brother's breakdown takes place right in front of his house (four walls). There are four people in the poem—brother, sister (observing), and the two parents.

> *In the mornings, I'll put on my wireless headphones and dance to one or two songs. Feeling the joy of the music, and the joy of moving my body to the beat gets my juices going and helps me feel ready to get the words down on the page.*
> —ESME WEIJUN WANG

A five-line stanza is called a **quintet**; quintets are considered by some difficult to read and challenging to pair with subject matter. A popular five-line form is the **cinquain**, which is a form of **syllabic verse** where the number of syllables is prescribed for each line, just as in a **haiku**.

You can vary the number of lines in each stanza in your poem as long as you have a purpose for doing so. But often the pattern of stanzas is perfectly even, as in Terrance Hayes's sestina on page 121, in which every stanza has six lines (**sestet**) except for the last stanza, which has only three lines (a tercet). Gwendolyn Brooks uses couplets for "We Real Cool" on page 105. Her purpose is clear: The "We" works as a unit. You aren't alone, ever, when you are in a gang and so no line is alone in her poem.

Just as each scene in a narrative introduces a new step in the conflict, each stanza adds something new to your poem. Terrance Hayes creates a playlist in his sestina with one stanza for each song; each stanza "room" is self-contained, standing on its own. In "We Real Cool," Gwendolyn Brooks introduces a new element in each stanza—nothing stays the same. Skipping school turns to staying out late at night and getting into fights which turns to drinking—and pleasures—which turns to tragedy.

Some poem forms provide a recipe for how to set up the stanzas. For detailed instruction on how to write a poem in a specific form, see the Ghazal, Sestina, and Villanelle sections in Chapter Ten. The preset guidelines for how to create stanzas can actually make it easier to write a poem.

If you are writing free verse, you have to invent your own stanza structure. You might consider the following guidelines. Use your training as a student of narrative to increase your poetic powers. If there is a scene or location change, or a new idea, or you are coming into your topic from a different angle, it's a good idea to consider a new stanza.

Just as you can break a line (enjambment) within a stanza, you can also create enjambment between stanzas. Examine Lee Herrick's "My California" on page 72 for an example of placing sentences across stanzas.

PRACTICE 21

COORDINATING STANZA LENGTH AND SUBJECT MATTER

Make a list of subjects you could write about that would go well with each of the following stanza types. For example, a poem about loneliness might use single-line stanzas. Come up with fitting subject matter for a poem constructed of a dozen **couplets**, a poem constructed of four **quatrains**, and a poem mixing a random number of single lines, **tercets**, and **sestets**.

Building Poems Using Form. **Formal poetry** is poetry that uses a prescribed template or pattern. While some people think it would have to be easier to write free verse — no rules — it's actually often easier to write a form poem because there's a recipe to follow — you don't have to invent the rhythm and the structure yourself; you can use the scaffolding provided by the form, and focus your creativity on sound work, rhythm, imagery, and turns. You may have written in form: **Haiku** is a popular form. Formal poetry isn't stuffy or old-fashioned; the forms have stood the test of time precisely because they are flexible and generative, providing opportunities for innovation.

You've read a number of formal poems in this course so far:

Villanelle: Dylan Thomas's "Do Not Go Gentle into That Good Night"

Sonnet: Kim Addonizio's "First Poem for You"

Sestina: Terrance Hayes's "Liner Notes for an Imaginary Playlist"

Part Three of this textbook is essentially a recipe book for many different kinds of writing. In Part Three you'll find detailed instruction for a variety of poetic forms starting on page 421 at the beginning of Chapter Ten.

Robert Frost famously said writing free verse is like playing tennis without a net. He meant that having rules—a court to play on, and some specific guidelines for exactly what you are supposed to try to do in that space, but no net—actually makes the process of poetry more interesting and possibly more meaningful.

After you try a few form poems and a few free-verse poems, see what you think about Robert Frost's comment. Many students are surprised to find poems written in form to be their strongest work in the course.

A Word on Poetic Thinking. While prose forms — fiction and creative nonfiction, memoir, flash, and micro — all use sound, effective word choice, metaphor, and rhythm, just as poetry does, poetry works in different ways from prose. Some poems use narrative principles to tell a story — what it's like to buy wine, what it's like that very first night you realize you've fallen madly and irrevocably in love with a tattooed person, or what it's like to watch a terrified brother in the middle of the night as he's caught in the throes of mental illness. These poems give us clear scenes, dramatic conflicts, and thoughtful resolutions, just as prose does.

But poetry also seeks to disrupt our habitual ways of thinking and seeing. Poetry doesn't always give us a story and doesn't necessarily reveal itself quickly; multiple readings may be required before a poem's complexity opens out for us.

Poetry asks us to take on new ways of understanding ourselves and the world. It forces us to pay attention to each word we use. Poetry loves juxtaposition, jolts, surprises, ruptures, disjunctures, and wild comparisons — it wants to wake us up from our trance, from seeing things habitually. Poetry isn't afraid of questions (Can I stave off death? How can I love a flawed state? Can I love someone even knowing death is going to separate us?). Poetry embraces difficulty, weirdness, and leaps.

Poetic thinking means taking the time to look at things differently from how you normally do. The poet looks at things very, very closely and from very far away. Poetry insists on dwelling in questions and hanging out in murky areas for longer than is comfortable. Poetry rants, apologizes, and prays. It wonders. It celebrates beauty and laments loss. It can be very plain or formal and majestic, soft or loud, heartbreaking or hilarious.

Consider reading a poem a day: You can sign up to receive a poem a day on your device; try Poetry Daily or Poetry Foundation Poem of the Day and consider using poetry as a way to deepen your prose. Poetic thinking has the potential to make you a more agile communicator, a better thinker, and a more flexible and creative artist.

PLAYS

Components of Plays

The word *play* in creative writing refers both to the text on the page and to the production on the stage. Live theater is exciting — there are no do-overs, and there's something powerful and intimate about watching actors perform. While the playwright usually has in mind a live audience, plays make for enjoyable reading, too; good dialogue springs off the page. Like poems, plays can be read silently and also read aloud. The techniques we practice in writing plays can serve us well in every other genre because here, all the components of creative writing come to the fore: A play requires intense, sustained conflict, interesting and fresh dialogue, and some elements of poetry.

Most plays staged in theaters are traditional full-length plays, where the dramatic structure — conflict, complication, crisis, resolution — takes place over the course of an evening, ninety minutes to three hours. A popular form for students and competitions is the ten-minute play. Know that for each minute of stage time, there's usually one page of script. You may be interested in five-minute plays and one-minute plays as ways to practice your skills. While you are thinking about the set, props, lighting, and what you want the actors to do, these plays will primarily allow you to practice dramatic structure, exposition, and dialogue.

> *It wasn't enough to rhyme at the end of the line, every line had to have musical theatre references, it had to have other hip-hop references, it had to do what my favorite rappers do, which is packing lyrics with so much density, and so much intricate double entendre, and alliteration, and onomatopoeia, and all the things that I love about language.*
>
> —LIN-MANUEL MIRANDA

Writing a play can be daunting because while many of us have written stories and poems, most of us aren't accustomed to the specific conventions of writing exposition, formatting dialogue for actors, and writing directions for lighting, props, and sound. These conventions are easy to learn, and writing a play — even a one-page miniplay — will quickly and effectively strengthen your writing skills.

A play is by definition a drama. It's all about conflict and action; speech is a form of action, of course. As in a poem, every word matters. As in a story, every single line involves some aspect of conflict.

The four key components of plays are:

- Exposition
- Dialogue
- Set
- Action and sound

Exposition. **Exposition** is background information that helps us understand the play. Through exposition, we understand where the play is taking place and important things that happened right before the play starts. Exposition can come during the play too, when we learn details we need to understand the play as the action and dialogue progress. Exposition on the page is usually printed in italics and isn't spoken aloud. In a live performance, exposition can come through a narrator, character speeches, on-stage media, and other means.

The first component a reader of a play encounters is usually exposition. In the play "I am not Batman." on page 82, Ramirez begins with exposition.

> Sudden drumming, then quiet. Lights up on a BOY, maybe 7, maybe 27, wearing a hooded sweatshirt. He looks out directly before him, breathing nervously. A DRUMMER sits behind a drum set placed in the middle of the stage in some kind of silhouette. The BOY is excited, but he never gets ahead of himself.

This passage of exposition tells us what's on stage so that a director and producer of the play know how to set it up, cast it, and coach the actors. But it also tells us, if we are simply reading the play, exactly what we need to know. Notice the writing itself. Ramirez doesn't choose plain prose words and give workmanlike direction. Ramirez is a poet. He doesn't settle for boring instructions such as: *boy is excited, drummer is lit from the side.* Every word in his play, even in the exposition—especially in the exposition—matters. Ramirez makes a poetic statement about being young—and it's very strange and interesting. How could a seven-year-old look like a twenty-seven-year-old? It's not possible. Something is wrong, something is wrong with this kid-who-is-not-a-kid. The author is using a poetic device in the exposition.

Read the opening of "Pancakes" by Peter Morris on page 303. Note how he formats his play. First he lists the characters and, like Ramirez, he gives their ages. Then he lists the setting using a different format from Ramirez. What's important is that the first lines of exposition in a play, regardless of format, clearly establish who is in the play and where the play is set. Morris notes the time period of the play is the present, and then he gives us the italicized expository information that explains exactly what the audience will see when the curtain comes up. Notice how Morris, like Ramirez, chooses powerful language for his exposition—it's not dull. "Bed head" and "pancake aroma" create images. He uses the five senses, and there is immediately conflict, even in the exposition.

Dialogue. The obvious central defining feature of a play is dialogue (although of course there are experimental plays with no words). **Dialogue** is the words the actors speak. The dialogue in a play needs to:

- Be rich and full of interesting turns of phrase
- Contain interruption, lying, false starts—all the features of actual human conversation

- Constantly show characters in conflict
- Show characters saying one thing but intending something different
- Imply character yearning without stating it directly

While you need to listen closely to how people actually talk in order to write effective dialogue, your play's dialogue will contain poetry and speech that is more interesting than how people actually talk.

PRACTICE 22

IDENTIFYING POETIC COMPONENTS IN A PLAY

Read "I am not Batman." on page 82. Where does the dialogue sound very natural, like an actual person talking? Where does the playwright create poetry out of the dialogue, using language in a special or heightened way? Do you see alliteration, assonance, or consonance in the dialogue? Rhythm? Provide at least three examples of any of the following: alliteration, assonance, consonance, or rhythm.

Set. The **set** is the stage, which as playwright you furnish and light in order to create the best vehicle for your play. When you are starting out, you can keep the set very simple. **Props** are "properties"—the furniture, the other items on the stage, the things the actors will carry around.

Because **lighting** creates powerful emotional effects on an audience, a playwright usually considers how light enhances the drama, attending always to ways to increase the conflict on the set itself. When the playwright indicates how things are lit, as Ramirez does in his Batman play, those of us merely reading the play can see, vividly, the silhouette of the mysterious drummer—a very dramatic use of the stage with just two characters, one prop (the drum set), and a light.

"Pancakes" also has a very simple set—two chairs and a table, with breakfast props. By keeping the set very simple, and focusing on the stage (even if this stage is only ever in the reader's mind's eye), as a backdrop for the action and dialogue, you showcase the conflict in your play. A busy stage can be distracting from the drama. And a complex set can make your play difficult to produce.

Trust your reader; trust your audience. If you give us a few deft strokes—nervous boy, drum set, and the boy tells us he is on the edge of an 87-story building—we'll go along for the ride. Two men, breakfast. We will fill in the details. If you as playwright resist the urge to fill in too much information about the setting and the characters, you leave room for our imaginations to engage.

And you increase the chances that others will be able to perform your play despite real world constraints on time, space, and budget.

Action and Sound. You've set up your play with poetic exposition, and you're writing dialogue that is powerful and loaded with conflict and layers. You have a clear stage set in mind and you've given your readers the crucial details they need to build that set in their mind. Later, you can create that set for a live performance.

While dialogue drives your play, **action**—what the actors do on stage (and in our mind's eye when we read) is a vital secondary layer. The actions you script for your actors should *not* simply illustrate what they are saying. In fact, there should be conflict between what they say and what they do. And, when there's pure action, you may not need dialogue—resist the urge to narrate action. Notice how Ramirez handles the fight scene in "I am not Batman." on page 82:

> *(—SNARE. The BOY mimes the fight.)*

Action is placed in italics and in parentheses. We know, as readers, a fight scene is playing out. Ramirez gives us scattershot dialogue, "Wrist CRACK" and "—Neck—" and "—Skin—meets—acid—" interspersed with dramatic sounds from the drum set. The rhythm and pacing of the scene is dynamic, fast-paced, and fraught.

Note how Morris formats descriptions of action in "Pancakes" on page 303. He too uses parentheses and italics:

> *(Silence. Buddy watches Sam pour more syrup on his pancakes. Buddy stands and exits. Sam continues to eat.)*

And the next line of dialogue comes from off-stage, allowing us to fill in the gaps. Very little needs to be explained. Action is taut, crisp, and always increases the tension in the play. **Sound** is a kind of action since some kind of activity takes place in order to produce sound. Pay attention to the way sound can increase the dramatic effects on stage.

Conflict in a play works the same way as in narrative modes: Your play will need strong rising action, turns, a climax, and some kind of resolution.

WRITING PROJECTS

Experiment

1. Design your own form and give it a name. What are the specific requirements for your invention? Consider creating a piece (or part of a piece) in this new genre. Trade the recipe for your newly invented form with someone else's recipe and write a second experiment in that new form.

Poetry

2. Write a poem in form, either a sonnet, sestina, or villanelle. Kim Addonizio's sonnet on page 121 is a good model; detailed instructions are on page 470 in Chapter Ten. Terrance Hayes's "Liner Notes for an Imaginary Playlist" on page 121 could prompt an imitation: Create a playlist sestina for someone who is very close to you. Follow the rules for writing a sestina on page 466 in Chapter Ten. *McSweeney's* literary magazine has a trove of sestinas online if you seek more inspiration. If you are writing a villanelle, Dylan Thomas's "Do Not Go Gentle into That Good Night" on page 123 is a good model. See Villanelle in Chapter Ten on page 474 for more direction.

Fiction/Poetry/Memoir

3. Take a poem you have written (and if you haven't written a poem, complete #2, above), and then turn it into a flash fiction or micro-memoir (no more than 750 words). And/or take a story you've written and create a version that is in the form of a poem.

Drama

4. Write a one-minute (one-page) play, using exposition, dialogue, two characters, and at least one nonhuman sound. Choose a setting that has metaphorical significance (a precipice for someone who is on the edge of reason, for example).

COMPONENTS WORKSHOP

These questions will help you improve your own writing as you respond to your peers' works-in-progress. You can use the prompts as a basis for your verbal and/or written comments.

1. If you are reading someone's poem, comment on how the subject choice fits with the form the writer chose to write in.
2. For every form, circle and label examples of sound work — "radioactive red," alliteration — and make a comment on the use of sound work. Where is the piece most benefiting from sound work? Where might it use more sound work?
3. If you are reading prose or a play, create a list of the conflicts in this piece, noting what happens at each pulse point (beat) in the piece. What are the three strongest, most vivid, transporting moments or lines? Which three are the weakest?
4. For all forms, circle any words that you consider "packaged" — words with which you would be able to fill in the blank, given the preceding word or words.
5. For all forms, underline the vivid, sparkly, fresh, interesting words and phrases.
6. For every form: Does each line or scene have a polarity — a movement from positive to negative, or vice versa? Label each line that does with a + or a −, and use a ? to indicate that you aren't sure or that the line does not have enough energy to move the reader from a negative emotion or feeling to a positive one (or the reverse).

READINGS

Kim Addonizio

First Poem for You

I like to touch your tattoos in complete
darkness, when I can't see them. I'm sure of
where they are, know by heart the neat
lines of lightning pulsing just above
your nipple, can find, as if by instinct, the blue
swirls of water on your shoulder where a serpent
twists, facing a dragon. When I pull you
to me, taking you until we're spent
and quiet on the sheets, I love to kiss
the pictures in your skin. They'll last until
you're seared to ashes; whatever persists
or turns to pain between us, they will still
be there. Such permanence is terrifying.
So I touch them in the dark; but touch them, trying.

Terrance Hayes

Liner Notes for an Imaginary Playlist
(*For R.*)

1. "Wind Solo" by the Felonious Monks
From the album *Silense* © 1956

1945, after everyone got hip to the blues, this is the code
The hipsters devised. This is what they call a mean
Horn. High on something, the sax man wades beyond the shallow
End of a stormy sea. You can almost see him gathering mist.
The album cover's got nothing but the contours of his body
And a dangerous language you comprehend even if you can't read.

2. **"The DJ's PJs" by SGP (The Stank Gangsta Prankstas)**
   From the album *Loot the Joker* © 1992

   This is for shell-toe sneakers and warmups dyed the hottest red
   I ever saw. So red it was cool. So cool it was a permanent cold.
   You can almost hear Negroes freed of the ghetto, the mint
   Spewing greenbacks in this song. Who wouldn't want to shampoo
   In Benjamins? Even one hit and a dope video makes a mystic
   Of the pauper. At the end of the track you can hear spit in a bottle.

3. **"Mood Etude # 5" by Fred Washington Sr.**
   From the album *Blassics* © 1985

   Strange inclusion, I know, but sometimes lyrics wear a blindfold.
   How many violins, harps, and grand pianos constitute a jazz reed?
   This is Bach according to a young man born on the Carolina coast.
   This is Bach according to a man whose favorite word is "Amen."
   This is Bach according to a man whose childhood was a shambles.
   What if Keats heard Jazz, what if Bach heard the Blues. It's all music.

4. **"Metal Face" by Glad Battle Wounds**
   From the album *New Battle* © 2004

   Remember the Mute Trout album, Empty MT? The mystique
   Of this jam won't puzzle you if you do. The way the battle
   For hearts and minds sounds like the same old bullshit. A newsreel
   Of tanks crushing corpses and a brave soldier in a coat
   Of medals. Remember those old war songs about the Age of Man?
   Maybe like those cuts this one is about being bold and shackled.

5. **"Oh, You" by Marvin & the Gay Ghosts**
   From the album *Baby, Don't Won't* © 1987

   Everything that needs to be said here is contained in a shadow.
   Whenever I fell asleep listening to this song, I woke drenched in music,
   The CD on repeat, my mouth filled with the meat of the bitter-
   Sweet. I'd dream of my first love, then find none of it was real.
   Some songs are like that, I suppose. Like being clothed
   In sweat and wistfulness. Sigh. It's a tune to make you moan.

6. "Mythic Blues" by Big Bruise Guitar
From the album *The Devil's Angel* © **1924**

If you're happy, skip this one. It's definitely not meant
To make you dance. Yes, the previous track was also slow. Use the shuffle
Mode if you don't want to walk the path I've left you. Called "The Mythic
Blues," this track has a way of reminding you how sin does battle
With the good in you. Saltwater is all a listener can reap.
You can see nothing but the blues even when your eyes are closed.

dear r, if anything, this cd tells you how I am sometimes willing
to shuffle into the cove of the melancholic, ready to live
among the men music continuously baffles . . . t.

Dylan Thomas

Do Not Go Gentle into That Good Night

Do not go gentle into that good night,
Old age should burn and rave at close of day;
Rage, rage against the dying of the light.

Though wise men at their end know dark is right,
Because their words had forked no lightning they
Do not go gentle into that good night.

Good men, the last wave by, crying how bright
Their frail deeds might have danced in a green bay,
Rage, rage against the dying of the light.

Wild men who caught and sang the sun in flight,
And learn, too late, they grieved it on its way,
Do not go gentle into that good night.

Grave men, near death, who see with blinding sight
Blind eyes could blaze like meteors and be gay,
Rage, rage against the dying of the light.

And you, my father, there on the sad height,
Curse, bless me now with your fierce tears, I pray.
Do not go gentle into that good night.
Rage, rage against the dying of the light.

Brenda Miller

Swerve

I'm sorry about that time I ran over a piece of wood in the road. A pound of marijuana in the trunk and a faulty brake light—any minute the cops might have pulled us over, so you were edgy already, and then I ran over that piece of stray lumber without even slowing down. *Thunk, thunk,* and then the wood spun behind us on the road. Your dark face dimmed even darker, and you didn't yell at first, only turned to look out the window, and I made the second mistake: *What's wrong?* That's when you exploded. *You're so careless, you don't even think, what if there had been a nail in that damn thing,* you yelled, your face so twisted now, and ugly. *And I'm always the one that has to fix it whenever something breaks.*

I'm sorry, I said, and I said it again, and we continued on our way through the desert, in the dark of night, with the contraband you had put in our trunk, with the brake light you hadn't fixed blinking on and off, me driving because you were too drunk, or too tired, or too depressed, and we traveled for miles into our future, where eventually I would apologize for the eggs being overcooked, and for the price of light bulbs, and for the way the sun blared through our trailer windows and made everything too bright, and I would apologize when I had the music on and when I had it off, I'd say sorry for being in the bathroom, and sorry for crying, and sorry for laughing, I would apologize, finally, for simply being alive, and even now I'm sorry I didn't swerve, I didn't get out of the way.

WRITERS ON WRITING

BRENDA MILLER

HEATHER SELLERS: What inspired you to write this piece?

BRENDA MILLER: I wrote this piece as an "assignment" for my generative writing group at the time. We were reading the poetry collection "Late Wife" by Claudia Emerson, and we assigned each other to write a short piece in the form of an apology.

HS: What was your writing process for "Swerve"?

BM: I sat down and wrote the words "I'm sorry . . ." As soon as I did, this memory from decades ago of driving over a piece of wood in the road came to mind. I'm practiced enough now in this kind of generative writing to not second guess my intuition but to follow it as quickly as I can. So I just started re-inhabiting that memory, calling up sensory details, writing to this "you" I hadn't been in contact with for thirty years. The second paragraph kept the momentum going into the future. I wrote the piece in about 30 minutes.

HS: In terms of shaping or revising the piece, could you describe your process?
BM: I didn't really know what I'd written until I shared it with my writing group the next week. When I read it aloud, and heard that long breathless sentence at the end, I knew I was onto something. The ending line was a complete surprise to me and actually gave me shivers — to come to this kind of understanding, an apology, really, to myself. I did very little revising, maybe just a word here and there. It was one of those "gift" pieces you get once in a while!

HS: Anything else you'd like to tell us about your craft?
BM: I've learned that I need to have various writing communities supporting me at every turn. All my writing now takes place in the context of writing with others.

Raymond Carver
Cathedral

This blind man, an old friend of my wife's, he was on his way to spend the night. His wife had died. So he was visiting the dead wife's relatives in Connecticut. He called my wife from his in-laws'. Arrangements were made. He would come by train, a five-hour trip, and my wife would meet him at the station. She hadn't seen him since she worked for him one summer in Seattle ten years ago. But she and the blind man had kept in touch. They made tapes and mailed them back and forth. I wasn't enthusiastic about his visit. He was no one I knew. And his being blind bothered me. My idea of blindness came from the movies. In the movies, the blind moved slowly and never laughed. Sometimes they were led by seeing-eye dogs. A blind man in my house was not something I looked forward to.

That summer in Seattle she had needed a job. She didn't have any money. The man she was going to marry at the end of the summer was in officers' training school. He didn't have any money, either. But she was in love with the guy, and he was in love with her, etc. She'd seen something in the paper: HELP WANTED — *Reading to Blind Man*, and a telephone number. She phoned and went over, was hired on the spot. She'd worked with this blind man all summer. She read stuff to him, case studies, reports, that sort of thing. She helped him organize his little office in the county social-service department. They'd become good friends, my wife and the blind man. How do I know these things? She told me. And she told me something else. On her last day in the office, the blind man asked if he could touch her face. She agreed to this. She told me he touched his fingers to every part of her face, her nose — even her neck! She never forgot it. She even tried to write a poem about it. She was always trying to write a poem. She wrote a poem or two every year, usually after something really important had happened to her.

When we first started going out together, she showed me the poem. In the poem, she recalled his fingers and the way they had moved around over her face. In the poem, she talked about what she had felt at the time, about what went through her mind when the blind man touched her nose and lips. I can remember I didn't think much of the poem. Of course, I didn't tell her that. Maybe I just don't understand poetry. I admit it's not the first thing I reach for when I pick up something to read.

Anyway, this man who'd first enjoyed her favors, the officer-to-be, he'd been her childhood sweetheart. So okay. I'm saying that at the end of the summer she let the blind man run his hands over her face, said goodbye to him, married her childhood etc., who was now a commissioned officer, and she moved away from Seattle. But they'd kept in touch, she and the blind man. She made the first contact after a year or so. She called him up one night from an Air Force base in Alabama. She wanted to talk. They talked. He asked her to send him a tape and tell him about her life. She did this. She sent the tape. On the tape, she told the blind man about her husband and about their life together in the military. She told the blind man she loved her husband but she didn't like it where they lived and she didn't like it that he was a part of the military-industrial thing. She told the blind man she'd written a poem and he was in it. She told him that she was writing a poem about what it was like to be an Air Force officer's wife. The poem wasn't finished yet. She was still writing it. The blind man made a tape. He sent her the tape. She made a tape. This went on for years. My wife's officer was posted to one base and then another. She sent tapes from Moody AFB, McGuire, McConnell, and finally Travis, near Sacramento, where one night she got to feeling lonely and cut off from people she kept losing in that moving-around life. She got to feeling she couldn't go it another step. She went in and swallowed all the pills and capsules in the medicine chest and washed them down with a bottle of gin. Then she got into a hot bath and passed out.

But instead of dying, she got sick. She threw up. Her officer — why should he have a name? he was the childhood sweetheart, and what more does he want? — came home from somewhere, found her, and called the ambulance. In time, she put it all on a tape and sent the tape to the blind man. Over the years, she put all kinds of stuff on tapes and sent the tapes off lickety-split. Next to writing a poem every year, I think it was her chief means of recreation. On one tape, she told the blind man she'd decided to live away from her officer for a time. On another tape, she told him about her divorce. She and I began going out, and of course she told her blind man about it. She told him everything, or so it seemed to me. Once she asked me if I'd like to hear the latest tape from the blind man. This was a year ago. I was on the tape, she said. So I said okay, I'd listen to it. I got us drinks and we settled down in the living room. We made ready to listen. First she inserted the tape into the player and adjusted a couple of dials. Then she pushed a lever. The tape squeaked and someone began to talk in this loud voice. She lowered the volume. After a few minutes of harmless chitchat, I heard my own name in the mouth of this stranger, this blind man I didn't even know! And then this: "From all you've said about him, I can only conclude — " But we were interrupted, a knock at the door, something, and we didn't ever get back to the tape. Maybe it was just as well. I'd heard all I wanted to.

Now this same blind man was coming to sleep in my house.

"Maybe I could take him bowling," I said to my wife. She was at the draining board doing scalloped potatoes. She put down the knife she was using and turned around.

"If you love me," she said, "you can do this for me. If you don't love me, okay. But if you had a friend, any friend, and the friend came to visit, I'd make him feel comfortable." She wiped her hands with the dish towel.

"I don't have any blind friends," I said.

"You don't have *any* friends," she said. "Period. Besides," she said, "goddamn it, his wife's just died! Don't you understand that? The man's lost his wife!"

I didn't answer. She'd told me a little about the blind man's wife. Her name was Beulah. Beulah! That's a name for a colored woman.

"Was his wife a Negro?" I asked.

"Are you crazy?" my wife said. "Have you just flipped or something?" She picked up a potato. I saw it hit the floor, then roll under the stove. "What's wrong with you?" she said. "Are you drunk?"

"I'm just asking," I said.

Right then my wife filled me in with more detail than I cared to know. I made a drink and sat at the kitchen table to listen. Pieces of the story began to fall into place.

Beulah had gone to work for the blind man the summer after my wife had stopped working for him. Pretty soon Beulah and the blind man had themselves a church wedding. It was a little wedding—who'd want to go to such a wedding in the first place?—just the two of them, plus the minister and the minister's wife. But it was a church wedding just the same. It was what Beulah had wanted, he'd said. But even then Beulah must have been carrying the cancer in her glands. After they had been inseparable for eight years—my wife's word, *inseparable*—Beulah's health went into a rapid decline. She died in a Seattle hospital room, the blind man sitting beside the bed and holding on to her hand. They'd married, lived and worked together, slept together—had sex, sure—and then the blind man had to bury her. All this without his having ever seen what the goddamned woman looked like. It was beyond my understanding. Hearing this, I felt sorry for the blind man for a little bit. And then I found myself thinking what a pitiful life this woman must have led. Imagine a woman who could never see herself as she was seen in the eyes of her loved one. A woman who could go on day after day and never receive the smallest compliment from her beloved. A woman whose husband could never read the expression on her face, be it misery or something better. Someone who could wear makeup or not—what difference to him? She could, if she wanted, wear green eye-shadow around one eye, a straight pin in her nostril, yellow slacks and purple shoes, no matter. And then to slip off into death, the blind man's hand on her hand, his blind eyes streaming tears—I'm imagining now—her last thought maybe this: that he never even knew what she looked like, and she on an express to the grave. Robert was left with a small insurance policy and half of a twenty-peso Mexican coin. The other half of the coin went into the box with her. Pathetic.

So when the time rolled around, my wife went to the depot to pick him up. With nothing to do but wait—sure, I blamed him for that—I was having a drink and watching the TV when I heard the car pull into the drive. I got up from the sofa with my drink and went to the window to have a look.

I saw my wife laughing as she parked the car. I saw her get out of the car and shut the door. She was still wearing a smile. Just amazing. She went around to the other side of the car to where the blind man was already starting to get out. This blind man, feature this, he was wearing a full beard! A beard on a blind man! Too much, I say. The blind man reached into the back seat and dragged out a suitcase. My wife took his arm, shut the car door, and, talking all the way, moved him down the drive and then up the steps to the front porch. I turned off the TV. I finished my drink, rinsed the glass, dried my hands. Then I went to the door.

My wife said, "I want you to meet Robert. Robert, this is my husband. I've told you all about him." She was beaming. She had this blind man by his coat sleeve.

The blind man let go of his suitcase and up came his hand.

I took it. He squeezed hard, held my hand, and then he let it go.

"I feel like we've already met," he boomed.

"Likewise," I said. I didn't know what else to say. Then I said, "Welcome. I've heard a lot about you." We began to move then, a little group, from the porch into the living room, my wife guiding him by the arm. The blind man was carrying his suitcase in his other hand. My wife said things like, "To your left here, Robert. That's right. Now watch it, there's a chair. That's it. Sit down right here. This is the sofa. We just bought this sofa two weeks ago."

I started to say something about the old sofa. I'd liked that old sofa. But I didn't say anything. Then I wanted to say something else, small-talk, about the scenic ride along the Hudson. How going *to* New York, you should sit on the right-hand side of the train, and coming *from* New York, the left-hand side.

"Did you have a good train ride?" I said. "Which side of the train did you sit on, by the way?"

"What a question, which side!" my wife said. "What's it matter which side?" she said.

"I just asked," I said.

"Right side," the blind man said. "I hadn't been on a train in nearly forty years. Not since I was a kid. With my folks. That's been a long time. I'd nearly forgotten the sensation. I have winter in my beard now," he said. "So I've been told, anyway. Do I look distinguished, my dear?" the blind man said to my wife.

"You look distinguished, Robert," she said. "Robert," she said. "Robert, it's just so good to see you."

My wife finally took her eyes off the blind man and looked at me. I had the feeling she didn't like what she saw. I shrugged.

I've never met, or personally known, anyone who was blind. This blind man was late forties, a heavy-set, balding man with stooped shoulders, as if he carried a great weight there. He wore brown slacks, brown shoes, a light-brown shirt, a tie, a sports coat. Spiffy. He also had this full beard. But he didn't use a cane and he didn't wear dark glasses. I'd always thought dark glasses were a must for the blind. Fact was, I wished he had a pair. At first glance, his eyes looked like anyone else's eyes. But if you looked close, there was something different about them. Too much white in the iris, for one thing, and the pupils seemed to move around in the sockets without his knowing it or being able to stop it. Creepy. As I stared at his face, I saw the left pupil turn in toward his nose while the other made an effort to keep in one place. But it was only an effort, for that eye was on the roam without his knowing it or wanting it to be.

I said, "Let me get you a drink. What's your pleasure? We have a little of everything. It's one of our pastimes."

"Bub, I'm a Scotch man myself," he said fast enough in this big voice.

"Right," I said. Bub! "Sure you are. I knew it."

He let his fingers touch his suitcase, which was sitting alongside the sofa. He was taking his bearings. I didn't blame him for that.

"I'll move that up to your room," my wife said.

"No, that's fine," the blind man said loudly. "It can go up when I go up."

"A little water with the Scotch?" I said.

"Very little," he said.

"I knew it," I said.

He said, "Just a tad. The Irish actor, Barry Fitzgerald? I'm like that fellow. When I drink water, Fitzgerald said, I drink water. When I drink whiskey, I drink whiskey." My wife laughed. The blind man brought his hand up under his beard. He lifted his beard slowly and let it drop.

I did the drinks, three big glasses of Scotch with a splash of water in each. Then we made ourselves comfortable and talked about Robert's travels. First the long flight from the West Coast to Connecticut, we covered that. Then from Connecticut up here by train. We had another drink concerning that leg of the trip.

I remembered having read somewhere that the blind didn't smoke because, as speculation had it, they couldn't see the smoke they exhaled. I thought I knew that much and that much only about blind people. But this blind man smoked his cigarette down to the nubbin and then lit another one. This blind man filled his ashtray and my wife emptied it.

When we sat down at the table for dinner, we had another drink. My wife heaped Robert's plate with cube steak, scalloped potatoes, green beans. I buttered him up two slices of bread. I said, "Here's bread and butter for you." I swallowed some of my drink. "Now let us pray," I said, and the blind man lowered his head. My wife looked at me, her mouth agape. "Pray the phone won't ring and the food doesn't get cold," I said.

We dug in. We ate everything there was to eat on the table. We ate like there was no tomorrow. We didn't talk. We ate. We scarfed. We grazed that table. We were into serious eating. The blind man had right away located his foods, he knew just where everything was on his plate. I watched with admiration as he used his knife and fork on the meat. He'd cut two pieces of meat, fork the meat into his mouth, and then go all out for the scalloped potatoes, the beans next, and then he'd tear off a hunk of buttered bread and eat that. He'd follow this up with a big drink of milk. It didn't seem to bother him to use his fingers once in a while, either.

We finished everything, including half a strawberry pie. For a few moments, we sat as if stunned. Sweat beaded on our faces. Finally, we got up from the table and left the dirty plates. We didn't look back. We took ourselves into the living room and sank into our places again. Robert and my wife sat on the sofa. I took the big chair. We had us two or three more drinks while they talked about the major things that had come to pass for them in the past ten years. For the most part, I just listened. Now and then I joined in. I didn't want him to think I'd left the room, and I didn't want her to think I was feeling left out. They talked of things that had happened to them — to them! — these past ten years. I waited in vain to hear my name on my wife's sweet lips: "And then my dear husband came into my life" — something like that. But I heard nothing of the sort. More talk of Robert. Robert had done a little of everything, it seemed, a regular blind jack-of-all-trades. But most recently he and his wife had had an Amway distributorship, from which, I gathered, they'd earned their living, such as it was. The blind man was also a ham radio operator. He talked in his loud voice about conversations he'd had with fellow operators in Guam, in the Philippines, in Alaska, and even in Tahiti. He said he'd have a lot of friends there if he ever wanted to go visit those places. From time to time, he'd turn his blind face toward me, put his hand under his beard, ask me something. How long had I been in my present position? (Three years.) Did I like my work? (I didn't.) Was I going to stay with it? (What were the options?) Finally, when I thought he was beginning to run down, I got up and turned on the TV.

My wife looked at me with irritation. She was heading toward a boil. Then she looked at the blind man and said, "Robert, do you have a TV?"

The blind man said, "My dear, I have two TVs. I have a color set and a black-and-white thing, an old relic. It's funny, but if I turn the TV on, and I'm always turning it on, I turn on the color set. It's funny, don't you think?"

I didn't know what to say to that. I had absolutely nothing to say to that. No opinion. So I watched the news program and tried to listen to what the announcer was saying.

"This is a color TV," the blind man said. "Don't ask me how, but I can tell."

"We traded up a while ago," I said.

The blind man had another taste of his drink. He lifted his beard, sniffed it, and let it fall. He leaned forward on the sofa. He positioned his ashtray on the coffee table, then put the lighter to his cigarette. He leaned back on the sofa and crossed his legs at the ankles.

My wife covered her mouth, and then she yawned. She stretched. She said, "I think I'll go upstairs and put on my robe. I think I'll change into something else. Robert, you make yourself comfortable," she said.

"I'm comfortable," the blind man said.

"I want you to feel comfortable in this house," she said.

"I am comfortable," the blind man said.

After she'd left the room, he and I listened to the weather report and then to the sports roundup. By that time, she'd been gone so long I didn't know if she was going to come back. I thought she might have gone to bed. I wished she'd come back downstairs. I didn't want to be left alone with a blind man. I asked him if he wanted another drink, and he said sure. Then I asked if he wanted to smoke some dope with me. I said I'd just rolled a number. I hadn't, but I planned to do so in about two shakes.

"I'll try some with you," he said.

"Damn right," I said. "That's the stuff."

I got our drinks and sat down on the sofa with him. Then I rolled us two fat numbers. I lit one and passed it. I brought it to his fingers. He took it and inhaled.

"Hold it as long as you can," I said. I could tell he didn't know the first thing.

My wife came back downstairs wearing her pink robe and her pink slippers.

"What do I smell?" she said.

"We thought we'd have us some cannabis," I said.

My wife gave me a savage look. Then she looked at the blind man and said, "Robert, I didn't know you smoked."

He said, "I do now, my dear. There's a first time for everything. But I don't feel anything yet."

"This stuff is pretty mellow," I said. "This stuff is mild. It's dope you can reason with," I said. "It doesn't mess you up."

"Not much it doesn't, bub," he said, and laughed.

My wife sat on the sofa between the blind man and me. I passed her the number. She took it and toked and then passed it back to me. "Which way is this going?" she said. Then she said, "I shouldn't be smoking this. I can hardly keep my eyes open as it is. That dinner did me in. I shouldn't have eaten so much."

"It was the strawberry pie," the blind man said. "That's what did it," he said, and he laughed his big laugh. Then he shook his head.

"There's more strawberry pie," I said.

"Do you want some more, Robert?" my wife said.

"Maybe in a little while," he said.

We gave our attention to the TV. My wife yawned again. She said, "Your bed is made up when you feel like going to bed, Robert. I know you must have had a long day. When you're ready to go to bed, say so." She pulled his arm. "Robert?"

He came to and said, "I've had a real nice time. This beats tapes, doesn't it?"

I said, "Coming at you," and I put the number between his fingers. He inhaled, held the smoke, and then let it go. It was like he'd been doing it since he was nine years old.

"Thanks, bub," he said. "But I think this is all for me. I think I'm beginning to feel it," he said. He held the burning roach out for my wife.

"Same here," she said. "Ditto. Me, too." She took the roach and passed it to me. "I may just sit here for a while between you two guys with my eyes closed. But don't let me bother you, okay? Either one of you. If it bothers you, say so. Otherwise, I may just sit here with my eyes closed until you're ready to go to bed," she said. "Your bed's made up, Robert, when you're ready. It's right next to our room at the top of the stairs. We'll show you up when you're ready. You wake me up now, you guys, if I fall asleep." She said that and then she closed her eyes and went to sleep.

The news program ended. I got up and changed the channel. I sat back down on the sofa. I wished my wife hadn't pooped out. Her head lay across the back of the sofa, her mouth open. She'd turned so that her robe had slipped away from her legs, exposing a juicy thigh. I reached to draw her robe back over her, and it was then that I glanced at the blind man. What the hell! I flipped the robe open again.

"You say when you want some strawberry pie," I said.

"I will," he said.

I said, "Are you tired? Do you want me to take you up to your bed? Are you ready to hit the hay?"

"Not yet," he said. "No, I'll stay up with you, bub. If that's all right. I'll stay up until you're ready to turn in. We haven't had a chance to talk. Know what I mean? I feel like me and her monopolized the evening." He lifted his beard and he let it fall. He picked up his cigarettes and his lighter.

"That's all right," I said. Then I said, "I'm glad for the company."

And I guess I was. Every night I smoked dope and stayed up as long as I could before I fell asleep. My wife and I hardly ever went to bed at the same time. When I did go to sleep, I had these dreams. Sometimes I'd wake up from one of them, my heart going crazy.

Something about the church and the Middle Ages was on the TV. Not your run-of-the-mill TV fare. I wanted to watch something else. I turned to the other channels. But there was nothing on them, either. So I turned back to the first channel and apologized.

"Bub, it's all right," the blind man said. "It's fine with me. Whatever you want to watch is okay. I'm always learning something. Learning never ends. It won't hurt me to learn something tonight. I got ears," he said.

We didn't say anything for a time. He was leaning forward with his head turned at me, his right ear aimed in the direction of the set. Very disconcerting. Now and then his eyelids drooped and then they snapped open again. Now and then he put his fingers into his beard and tugged, like he was thinking about something he was hearing on the television.

On the screen, a group of men wearing cowls was being set upon and tormented by men dressed in skeleton costumes and men dressed as devils. The men dressed as devils wore devil masks, horns, and long tails. This pageant was part of a procession. The Englishman who was narrating the thing said it took place in Spain once a year. I tried to explain to the blind man what was happening.

"Skeletons," he said. "I know about skeletons," he said, and he nodded.

The TV showed this one cathedral. Then there was a long, slow look at another one. Finally, the picture switched to the famous one in Paris, with its flying buttresses and its spires reaching up to the clouds. The camera pulled away to show the whole of the cathedral rising above the skyline.

There were times when the Englishman who was telling the thing would shut up, would simply let the camera move around over the cathedrals. Or else the camera would tour the countryside, men in fields walking behind oxen. I waited as long as I could. Then I felt I had to say something. I said, "They're showing the outside of this cathedral now. Gargoyles. Little statues carved to look like monsters. Now I guess they're in Italy. Yeah, they're in Italy. There's paintings on the walls of this one church."

"Are those fresco paintings, bub?" he asked, and he sipped from his drink.

I reached for my glass. But it was empty. I tried to remember what I could remember. "You're asking me are those frescoes?" I said. "That's a good question. I don't know."

The camera moved to a cathedral outside Lisbon. The differences in the Portuguese cathedral compared with the French and Italian were not that great. But they were there. Mostly the interior stuff. Then something occurred to me, and I said, "Something has occurred to me. Do you have any idea what a cathedral is? What they look like, that is? Do you follow me? If somebody says cathedral to you, do you have any notion what they're talking about? Do you know the difference between that and a Baptist church, say?"

He let the smoke dribble from his mouth. "I know they took hundreds of workers fifty or a hundred years to build," he said. "I just heard the man say that, of course. I know generations of the same families worked on a cathedral. I heard him say that, too. The men who began their life's work on them, they never lived to see the completion of their work. In that wise, bub, they're no different from the rest of us, right?" He laughed. Then his eyelids drooped again. His head nodded. He seemed to be snoozing. Maybe he was imagining himself in Portugal. The TV was showing another cathedral now. This one was in Germany. The Englishman's voice droned on. "Cathedrals," the blind man said. He sat up and rolled his head back and forth. "If you want the truth, bub, that's about all I know. What I just said. What I heard him say. But maybe you could describe one to me? I wish you'd do it. I'd like that. If you want to know, I really don't have a good idea."

I stared hard at the shot of the cathedral on the TV. How could I even begin to describe it? But say my life depended on it. Say my life was being threatened by an insane guy who said I had to do it or else.

I stared some more at the cathedral before the picture flipped off into the countryside. There was no use. I turned to the blind man and said, "To begin with, they're very tall." I was looking around the room for clues. "They reach way up. Up and up. Toward the sky. They're so big, some of them, they have to have these supports. To help hold them up, so to speak. These supports are called buttresses. They remind me of viaducts, for some reason. But maybe you don't know viaducts, either? Sometimes the cathedrals have devils and such carved into the front. Sometimes lords and ladies. Don't ask me why this is," I said.

He was nodding. The whole upper part of his body seemed to be moving back and forth.

"I'm not doing so good, am I?" I said.

He stopped nodding and leaned forward on the edge of the sofa. As he listened to me, he was running his fingers through his beard. I wasn't getting through to him, I could see that. But he waited for me to go on just the same. He nodded, like he was trying to encourage me. I tried to think what else to say. "They're really big," I said. "They're massive. They're built of stone. Marble, too, sometimes. In those olden days, when they built cathedrals, men wanted to be close to God. In those olden days, God was an important part of everyone's life. You could tell this from their cathedral-building. I'm sorry," I said, "but it looks like that's the best I can do for you. I'm just no good at it."

"That's all right, bub," the blind man said. "Hey, listen. I hope you don't mind my asking you. Can I ask you something? Let me ask you a simple question, yes or no. I'm just curious and there's no offense. You're my host. But let me ask if you are in any way religious? You don't mind my asking?"

I shook my head. He couldn't see that, though. A wink is the same as a nod to a blind man. "I guess I don't believe in it. In anything. Sometimes it's hard. You know what I'm saying?"

"Sure, I do," he said.

"Right," I said.

The Englishman was still holding forth. My wife sighed in her sleep. She drew a long breath and went on with her sleeping.

"You'll have to forgive me," I said. "But I can't tell you what a cathedral looks like. It just isn't in me to do it. I can't do any more than I've done."

The blind man sat very still, his head down, as he listened to me.

I said, "The truth is, cathedrals don't mean anything special to me. Nothing. Cathedrals. They're something to look at on late-night TV. That's all they are."

It was then that the blind man cleared his throat. He brought something up. He took a handkerchief from his back pocket. Then he said, "I get it, bub. It's okay. It happens. Don't worry about it," he said. "Hey, listen to me. Will you do me a favor? I got an idea. Why don't you find us some heavy paper? And a pen. We'll do something. We'll draw one together. Get us a pen and some heavy paper. Go on, bub, get the stuff," he said.

So I went upstairs. My legs felt like they didn't have any strength in them. They felt like they did after I'd done some running. In my wife's room, I looked around. I found some ballpoints in a little basket on her table. And then I tried to think where to look for the kind of paper he was talking about.

Downstairs, in the kitchen, I found a shopping bag with onion skins in the bottom of the bag. I emptied the bag and shook it. I brought it into the living room and sat down with it near his legs. I moved some things, smoothed the wrinkles from the bag, spread it out on the coffee table.

The blind man got down from the sofa and sat next to me on the carpet.

He ran his fingers over the paper. He went up and down the sides of the paper. The edges, even the edges. He fingered the corners.

"All right," he said. "All right, let's do her."

He found my hand, the hand with the pen. He closed his hand over my hand. "Go ahead, bub, draw," he said. "Draw. You'll see. I'll follow along with you. It'll be okay. Just begin now like I'm telling you. You'll see. Draw," the blind man said.

So I began. First I drew a box that looked like a house. It could have been the house I lived in. Then I put a roof on it. At either end of the roof, I drew spires. Crazy.

"Swell," he said. "Terrific. You're doing fine," he said. "Never thought anything like this could happen in your lifetime, did you, bub? Well, it's a strange life, we all know that. Go on now. Keep it up."

I put in windows with arches. I drew flying buttresses. I hung great doors. I couldn't stop. The TV station went off the air. I put down the pen and closed and opened my fingers. The blind man felt around over the paper. He moved the tips of his fingers over the paper, all over what I had drawn, and he nodded.

"Doing fine," the blind man said.

I took up the pen again, and he found my hand. I kept at it. I'm no artist. But I kept drawing just the same.

My wife opened up her eyes and gazed at us. She sat up on the sofa, her robe hanging open. She said, "What are you doing? Tell me, I want to know."

I didn't answer her.

The blind man said, "We're drawing a cathedral. Me and him are working on it. Press hard," he said to me. "That's right. That's good," he said. "Sure. You got it, bub. I can tell. You didn't think you could. But you can, can't you? You're cooking with gas now. You know what I'm saying? We're going to really have us something here in a minute. How's the old arm?" he said. "Put some people in there now. What's a cathedral without people?"

My wife said, "What's going on? Robert, what are you doing? What's going on?"

"It's all right," he said to her. "Close your eyes now," the blind man said to me.

I did it. I closed them just like he said.

"Are they closed?" he said. "Don't fudge."

"They're closed," I said.

"Keep them that way," he said. He said, "Don't stop now. Draw."

So we kept on with it. His fingers rode my fingers as my hand went over the paper. It was like nothing else in my life up to now.

Then he said, "I think that's it. I think you got it," he said. "Take a look. What do you think?"

But I had my eyes closed. I thought I'd keep them that way for a little longer. I thought it was something I ought to do.

"Well?" he said. "Are you looking?"

My eyes were still closed. I was in my house. I knew that. But I didn't feel like I was inside anything.

"It's really something," I said.

STRATEGIES

Don't wait for inspiration. Inspiration is for amateurs; the rest of us just show up and get to work. . . . All the best ideas come out of the process; they come out of the work itself.

CHUCK CLOSE

Writing has laws of perspective, of light and shade just as painting does, or music. If you are born knowing them, fine. If not, learn them. Then rearrange the rules to suit yourself.

TRUMAN CAPOTE

I begin with the voices of those I care for, family or otherwise, and follow them until they drop off, until I have to create them in order to hear them. My writing is an echo.

OCEAN VUONG

CHAPTER FOUR

IMAGES

In this chapter you will:

- Distinguish showing from telling
- Generate vivid images in summary and in scenes
- Choose when to use scene and summary

Creative writing relies on images: three-dimensional mental pictures that inspire thoughts and feelings, movies in the reader's mind. As writers, that's what we are always trying to make happen in our reader's brain — a sustained *moving picture* that's real, visual, sensory, and alive, just like a dream is. The **image** is that movie in your mind; **imagery** is the term used to point to descriptive passages that activate the larger image your reader sees.

THE PRINCIPLES OF IMAGES

We all access these images — the alive, moving picture in our mind's eye — when we read, play, write creatively, or dream. When we listen to our friend tell a story, we may be able to see, in our mind's eye, the people and situation she's talking about. When children play, they are hooked into a live image. They are not pretending, they are riding a horse. They *are* riding a horse; they can feel its reins, sense its warmth, hear it whinny. The story as it plays out on our mental movie screen is physical; it's entirely real. Using images — creating live minimovies for your reader — is your essential go-to strategy as a writer.

> *The book is a thing in itself, and it is not me. There is no ego in it. I am glad that you sense that while I am in it and of it, I am not the book. It is much more than I am. The pictures have come to me out of some hugeness and sometimes they have startled me. But I am glad of them.*
> —JOHN STEINBECK

Your most powerful images will be those that *activate* the five senses. If asked, you could tell me what the desk chair you are sitting in right now feels like, and what sound it makes when you drag it across a tile floor. You could actually feel what it's like to touch the horse if you wanted to. Your images will have sound, dialogue, visuals, textures, tastes, and smells. And your reader will experience your work as though it's alive.

Images Are Active

Creative writing, at its core, uses people in action to create a powerful moving picture made inside another person's head when that person simply *reads words on a page*. Images are bundles of memory, emotion, action, physical details, and dialogue, put together smoothly for the reader to experience being transported fully into your world. In an image, everything happens at once, providing a rich, seamless experience. The reader is *there*. This is the essential difference—moving images—between what we call "creative" writing and other kinds of writing.

PRACTICE 1

NOTICING IMAGES IN ACTION

Listen to Jenifer Hixson read aloud her memoir, "Where There's Smoke," found online at *The Moth*. As you listen, notice what you see in your mind's eye. Now go through the piece, which begins on page 274, and see what you can determine about how she creates the moving image. What does she do or not do to enable her audience to *see*, to "be there"?

> *My task is to make you hear, feel, and see. That and no more, and that is everything.*
> —JOSEPH CONRAD

Reading Is Image Viewing

Read the following excerpts, or, if you can, have someone read them aloud to you while you close your eyes. As you read or listen to the selections, concentrate on the picture in your head. What do you see? When there isn't a picture in your head, what do you think *is* happening? Can you break down the different ways in which parts of your mind are activated? Can you isolate the "thinking" mind versus the "seeing" mind versus the "experiencing" mind?

Go slowly. Reading this way takes a lot of focus and a little practice. You are trying to watch what happens in your mind as you read.

1

I've never met, or personally known, anyone who was blind. This blind man was late forties, a heavy-set, balding man with stooped shoulders, as if he carried a great weight there. He wore brown slacks, brown shoes, a light-brown shirt, a tie, a sports coat. Spiffy. He also had this full beard. But he didn't use a cane and he didn't wear dark glasses. I'd always thought dark glasses were a must for the blind. Fact was, I wished he had a pair. At first glance, his eyes looked like anyone else's eyes. But if you looked close, there was something different about them. Too much white in the iris, for one thing, and the pupils seemed to move around in the sockets without his knowing it or being able to stop it. Creepy.

— RAYMOND CARVER, "Cathedral"

2

Will was on the station platform, leaning against a baggage truck. He had a duffle bag between his shoes and a plastic cup of coffee in his mittened hand. He seemed to have put on weight, girlishly, through the hips, and his face looked thicker to me, from temple to temple. His gold-rimmed spectacles looked too small.

My mother stopped in an empty cab lane, and I got out and called to Will.

— MARY ROBISON, "Pretty Ice"

3

He sat cross-legged, weeping on the steps
when Mom unlocked and opened the front door.
    O God, he said. *O God.*
    He wants to kill me, Mom.

— NATALIE DIAZ, "My Brother at 3 a.m."

Which of the passages above created the most vivid moving picture in your mind? What or whom do you remember "seeing"? One of the best ways to read as a writer is to actively notice: What *did* you see as you read?

Note that **active images** — scenes — are used by fiction and nonfiction writers, playwrights, and also poets. Although not all poems are scenes, many make use of the technique in order to provide dramatic interest and clarity for the reader. In Natalie Diaz's poem "My Brother at 3 a.m." on page 165, notice how she uses real time (3 a.m.) and a specific location to write a deft portrait of a brother troubled by hallucinations.

> *You can observe a lot by*
> *just watching.*
> —YOGI BERRA

Practice **close reading** in order to distinguish the difference between *knowing* and *seeing*. They are two different ways for the mind to apprehend information. Report writing explains: "My mother confronted me about the drinking," or, "My kid's coach was an amazing lecturer." Most writing tells or reports information. Nothing wrong with that at all, but it's very different from what we do. We create images, showing instead of telling. A mother walks her daughter down to the pond. It's a beautiful day. The daughter has a hangover; she is practically tiptoeing. The mother brings up the forbidden topic; this is the day she says out loud what no one has said out loud: "You have a drinking problem." It's image, and it's alive, moving.

An image is a container with action inside it. Notice that all of the image examples have three key ingredients:

- **Two people.** A man meets a blind man, a girlfriend picks up her boyfriend, a mother confronts/comforts a son in trouble.
- **Action.** People (entities) engaged in action, and speaking. If they are thinking, the thoughts are active, rich, specific, detailed, and action-oriented. (The girlfriend notices her boyfriend has changed *a lot* since she last saw him.)
- **Grounded in space and time.** A specific moment in time and a specific location bounds, or frames, each image—a living room in the evening, a train station platform at dawn, a doorstep after midnight.

These three elements create the three-dimensionality and the movement necessary for a reader to see an image.

Each person's set of experiences is different, so the picture you see when you are reading will vary from your teacher's, your friend's, the author's pictures. If you grew up in the southern United States, you'll read a story about driving on ice (Mary Robison's "Pretty Ice" appears at the end of this chapter on page 169) differently from a student who grew up in Montreal. The Montreal reader knows from experience that driving in winter on retread tires is incredibly dangerous. While some readers might miss some of the nuances, hopefully they still get a sense of the main action. Our job as writers is to create a living, moving image and to trust that the action that comes to life in the reader's mind is fairly close to what we had in mind.

When you read, try to notice when your brain is working in image mode. The more you read, though, the more wide-ranging your transporting experiences will be. If you don't see a lot right away, keep practicing. The more images you expose your brain to, the more perceptive you will become. A side benefit of this practice: You will see more nuances in real-life situations, too. Dating, job interviews, interactions with teachers and parents—you'll be reading them all as a writer does, alert and attentive to the little gestures and actions and specifics that reveal the inner lives and fascinating aspects of your subjects.

> *The culture is telling you to hurry, while the art tells you to take your time. Always listen to the art.*
> —JUNOT DÍAZ

Images Are the Opposite of Thought and Feeling

Let's define *thinking* as any nonvisual mental activity. Images are the *opposite* of thought. Feelings—the emotional states your characters experience—often come through the image itself; rarely do you need to tell your reader what someone is thinking or feeling.

The following chart shows, in the left-hand column, which kinds of writing work best in creative writing where we want the reader to have a sensory and emotional experience versus an intellectual one. On the right side of the chart are modes that work best in analytical writing.

Experiential (showing)	Analytical (telling)
Action	Commentary
Dialogue	Analysis
Description (imagery)	Explanations of feelings and thoughts
Insight	Researched reporting
Five senses	Exploration of ideas and opinions

Most beginning writers work from an analytical mind-set and they *overwrite* the thoughts in their first drafts and *underwrite* the images. Not surprising. Writing instruction in school, up until now, often has been limited to a focus on composing essays. Many of us haven't had encouragement or support or training in trusting our eyes and writing what is seen, *not* what is thought or felt. Many new writers don't trust their eyes to get the job done; they forget how potent reading is and how creative the human brain is—your reader *is* going to see it, and get it, and understand many layers of feeling and thought, without your interrupting the flow to explain.

You might try to exaggerate in the opposite direction. Try to overwrite the images. Try to be *too* visual, *too* sensory.

Here, you are practicing transporting yourself to another place and seeing. Thoughts suck the drama and the richness out of your writing and rob the reader of the pleasure of figuring things out.

Analytical writing isn't wrong, of course. We love well-written history, philosophy, psychology, and more, but it's just not what we're doing in this course. For example, in an essay for an anthropology course, you might write, "The Pueblo method of divorce can be as simple as this: A woman leaves her husband's moccasins on the doorstep. And it's over." In creative writing, using images, you want your reader to have the weight of those shoes, to be able to imagine the house, the marriage, the sky, the pain of the divorce for both parties—all that. And more. Images let you trigger whole worlds of consciousness in your reader.

> *Nothing exists in the intellect that has not first gone through the senses.*
> —PLUTARCH

When you write, put yourself there physically. Don't think, "Okay, my character is feeling really angry with her husband." Instead, see what you can see in order to show the feeling state:

> She brushed her skirt and sat on the bed with his shoes next to her. His toes seemed to be always in these shoes, in all his shoes—there were five dimples at the tops of each shoe, shiny, where the suede was worn away. She picked one of the moccasins up. They were always heavier than they appeared to be. She threw the shoe at the door.

Your images shouldn't be merely describing. They should *be the thing*. Experience the musty leather as you write; if you experience, your reader will, too. When you fully imagine that house, that marriage, the bedspread, the smells of the field, as a writer you have to paint some deft strokes, outline a few items, an emotion, the palm of a hand—and your reader will fill in the entire town. Eventually, as you gain practice using images, you can make your images so powerful that by describing a front porch, your reader will see the whole county and feel as though he or she has been there before.

In sum, don't write what you think. Write what you see.

Notice how in the works you have read so far for this class, the writer doesn't tell, explain, or preach. The writer shows. You, the reader, conclude for yourself.

Imagine, if instead of the comic, poem, and micro-memoir from Chapter One, we just heard about what the authors thought. We might have a list like this one:

Technology is dangerous and making robots could have dire consequences.

I feel terrible about all the poems I have not written; it's really weird for me as poet to reflect on all the time I've wasted and think about what could have been; I could have been an impressive poet.

After my dog died and I had to move from a house I loved, my life was really hard and I was super depressed all the time. I hated my new apartment and the neighbors kind of made me crazy in a way.

PRACTICE 2

READING FOR IMAGES

Read the micro-memoir "Counting Bats" by Thao Thai on page 168. With a highlighter (or by taking notes and making a list), mark every passage that is an image (where you see, or could see, a scene play out in your mind). Focus on where you see people or bats in action. Remember, dialogue such as "My grandfather promised. . ." is an action of speech. What percentage of the story is active images?

Generating Images

To create a live image to work from as a writer, it can be really helpful to set up the place and time you're going to be working with in your piece in advance. You can ground yourself in the images you'll be writing by first doing a **sketch** of what you will be writing and/or answering a set of questions. This preparation works well for stories, poems, comics, and plays. Instead of doing a rough draft, you might want to practice anchoring your creative writing in time and space before you write. You could save *hours* of revision time.

If you are writing a poem or memoir from personal experience, you'll answer the questions below for yourself. If you are writing a play or a fictional story using characters, pretend you are that person as you are answering the questions. These questions come from Lynda Barry; if this technique is appealing to you, her book *Syllabus* has more prompts to help you get into and stay inside of your images.

QUESTIONS TO ASK: Orienting Yourself in Images before Writing

Answer these orienting questions before beginning to write, either by making notes or by doing a drawing; use them to get grounded again when you are stuck.

1. Where are we? What room, neighborhood, town, county, place are we located?
2. What time is it? What minute, hour, day, month, year?
3. What is the weather outside like?
4. Who is "onstage"? Who just left? Who is nearby?
5. What just happened before this moment?
6. How old is each person "onstage"?
7. What are people wearing? What do they have in their hands? Are they standing or sitting? What is their posture like?
8. What is in the room/location? What "stuff" is around?
9. What's the atmosphere inside like (lighting, hot/cold, smoky, comfortable, etc.)? What is the dominant smell?
10. What is the dominant background sound?
11. As you gaze around the image, what else do you notice?

PRACTICE 3

VISUAL ANCHORING

Read Dylan Landis's list essay, "In My Father's Study upon His Death" on page 166. Draw the father's study, as best you can, from her list. Comment on which images in this list had the most powerful effect on you. Which ones allow you to see the most, visually? Does Landis address all five senses in her list? Compare your drawing and your reading notes with others in the class.

The drawing technique presented in the practice above is also extremely useful as you work to get grounded in your scene before you begin to write. And when you get stuck, it's useful to revisit your question list and drawing in order to get back into the scene.

PRACTICE 4

SKETCH TO MAKE A SCENE

Use an experience you had this week when you were with another person in a specific place at a specific time. Draw a sketch or make a list answering the orienting questions on page 148. Write a scene based on your answers to the questions.

CREATING WITH IMAGES

Creative writing is rooted in individuals, struggling and interacting with the physical world and others in that world. The first step is to ground your work from the outset in a specific space and time, focusing on sensory details that give us a full visual experience.

Focus on People in Action

It's easier to create interesting material that your reader can see when you have two or more entities to work with. Many writers begin with a character or themselves sitting alone with their thoughts — driving, waking up, staring out a window, or in nonspace.

> *Seeing is polysensory, combining the visual, tactile, and kinesthetic senses.*
> —ROBERT MCKIM

But people sitting by themselves alone thinking are difficult to bring to life for your reader. Thoughts aren't usually interesting enough on their own to sustain creative writing. While the person alone may feel intense emotions and drama, there's often not much drama for the reader to participate in. Marco Ramirez's "I am not Batman." (page 82) is a notable exception; notice how the playwright puts another character, the Drummer, on stage to create drama, conflict, action, and visual and sonic interest.

You are wise to consider beginning with two or more people — or entities — in **conflict** and to avoid people alone "onstage" in your pieces. In poetry, notice how active and alive the images are. Instead of static descriptions or emotions, the poems you've read so far burst with action. In John Brehm's "The Poems I Have Not Written" (page 43), trees bow their heads, the Tower of Babel sways, husbands repent, the wind changes course, the continent is papered with Brehm's poems — in nearly every line some very large and **significant dramatic action** takes place. "Buying Wine" (page 71) by Sebastian Matthews shows, in every stanza, people in action. Gwendolyn Brooks's "We Real Cool" (page 105) compresses powerful dramatic action — people are in motion through the entire poem.

Whether you are writing a play, a comic, a poem, fiction, or nonfiction, these ingredients—two people or entities in conflict, and something happening that we can see—give you the spark you need to activate and ignite your images.

PRACTICE 5

READING PEOPLE IN ACTION

Read Mary Robison's short story "Pretty Ice" on page 169. How much of the story features two or more people "onstage" in action? When the character Belle is alone, what makes those images active and interesting? Read the story a second time. Do some of the actions symbolize a character's inner state?

"Pretty Ice" is composed wholly of active images. When the story opens, Belle balances her accounts, reckoning her bank balance and the amount of love she has to give. Notice how the image of a person in action can also point to what's going on inside the character's psyche. While Belle is checking her funds, the reader wonders if she has money problems. Later, we wonder if she is perhaps settling for a man she doesn't really love because of her financial situation.

When Belle makes her way across the frozen pond that is her yard (life?), water seeps in her shoes. Does someone have "cold feet"? Yes. By focusing on people in action, the author creates, with images, a complex, fascinating portrait of two women, frozen, stunted by grief. The author of this story has knit these powerful **symbols** into the active images.

In every scene, the images reveal the conflicts between the characters. There's conflict between the mother and daughter, and then when the triangle is introduced, there's conflict between all three characters: Belle, her mother, and Will. The story conforms perfectly to the structural principles you learned in Chapter Three: rising action, complications, a crisis where there's a big turn of events, and a resolution (no train with a man on it is coming to this town again, in all likelihood; Belle will remain alone, encased in grief, frozen in her pretty ice.)

When Robison describes setting, it's never as mere background detail. The image that holds the setting matters to the story. Belle's mother's cigarette smoke blends with the acrid, yellow smoke of the dying midwestern town and Robison wants us to connect those descriptions. The mother is like the town. Belle's heading in the same direction.

Think from within Images

You can write using all images, and all active scenes, so the whole piece takes place before our eyes, like a movie. But sometimes you may want to include thoughts, reflections, and insights. How do writers use thoughts, then, in their work? Sparingly. And only when firmly, deeply anchored in the image. Make sure you have an image up and running, with action and moving pictures, *before* you offer the reader a thought, an insight, a conclusion, or a comment.

> *Merely to see is not enough. It is necessary to have a fresh, vivid, physical contact with the object you draw through as many of the senses as possible—and especially through the sense of touch.*
>
> —KIMON NICOLAÏDES

Notice how Robison places the backstory in "Pretty Ice" deep inside the story, after we have had plenty of time to sink into the sensory visual world of the story and to get to know its characters. And when we do come upon the backstory, Robison takes care to render that material in an active image in every case. We see the two characters of the parents as "mannequins, a pair of dolls." The paragraph of backstory, where Belle thinks back on her parents' lives, is all active image filled with movement and vivid description. When later we learn the father committed suicide, even that scene is delivered as active image: "He was found in his warm-up clothes—a pullover sweater and pleated pants." No feelings are given; no emotions, just images, miniscenes that allow us as readers to enter the moment that sheds light on the present, even though it's in the distant past.

PRACTICE 6

COMPARE: Image Versus Thought

Write a scene all in active images, completely free of any telling or explaining, feeling, emotion, or thinking. Then do the reverse, and write the same material all in summary, explanation, telling—no visuals. No dialogue. Try to keep the reader from seeing anything. Comment on what you notice in each version.

Use Specifics

Specific words—**concrete nouns**, **place names**, **proper nouns**, **active verbs**—are the fuel that feeds the image, keeping it alive and sparkly.

It's not enough for writers to "be descriptive." In fact, you have probably heard readers say, "The description goes on too long; you can skip it." It's very likely you have done some skipping or skimming yourself; most of us have.

Sentences that billow with very formal language and flowery word choices might seem specific. These kinds of sentences may draw praise from some teachers, friends, or parents not trained as creative writers. Actually, lots of *words* may block your reader's engagement with the piece:

The pulsating rivers plunged toward their ultimate and terrible death!

This is the story of heartache and heartbreak, of tumultuousness and terror and I want you to always remember, this is true, and real!

The joy of holding hands,
You are in my mind always
My heart beating and yours
Beating beating as one heart.

It's unlikely you really see any specific images in the passages above. What's blocking the images? Not thoughts this time, but language — **overwriting**. General or overblown language is as ineffective as passive thoughts when you are trying to get your reader fully absorbed in your writing.

In fact, more simple writing activates the brain's image-making machine most often. Instead of worrying about adjectives and beautiful word-picture-painting — "writerly things" — concentrate on where *you* are, in your mind's eye, when you write. Creative writing isn't about the writer. It's about the reader, having an experience, being somewhere, seeing through someone else. You don't report your emotions and thoughts; you activate those of your reader. Creative writing serves readers. It's not a stage for show-offs.

When writing in images, name the simple, actual things. Strive for **specificity**. Instead of writing *missing you*, you place your lover and yourself in your car, your last Friday night together, ever. Instead of *car*, you write *Angel's old Cadillac* or *the sedan with the human teeth marks*. Instead of writing *fruit*, write *five strawberries*. See the difference for the reader? See how *fruit* makes you think? You may or may not picture a fruit — you think *fruit* as a concept. That's absolutely contrary to the goals and pleasures of creative writing. Write *five strawberries*, and you've got them. Your mouth might even water. When you are in the image, writing what you see, write really, truly what you see. Be specific by looking carefully, naming the small parts, and keeping it simple.

Move Around in Images

Images are alive which means that things move in that picture inside the reader's head. Action takes place. Whether it's a poem, play, nonfiction piece, or story, the image has movement in it.

When you create an image (using your checklist from page 148), you create a solid starting point. Once you have launched the image, you need to make sure your camera *moves*.

If you started your image in the living room, where your mom is sitting in her favorite chair sleeping, after you have shown that scene, you need to move your camera. You need to get really, really close up so that we can see the pores of her skin, *or* you need to go somewhere else to capture something that is *more interesting*. Leave the room. No need to write boring. Film your way into the kitchen. Your dad fighting with your obnoxious older brother who refuses to lift a finger around the house? That could be good. Move in close and keep moving.

Note how in the poems we have read, **active verbs** power the poems forward — there's a lot of movement. In the plays we have looked at, even if a character is talking to the audience, there is dramatic action at each step of the way. In "Pretty Ice," every single scene contains action. Robison is skilled at watching her characters closely and capturing the tiny gestures and movements that reveal their true natures: the mom's honking, the way a man holds his coffee cup, the late night scribbling. In "Swerve," Brenda Miller's micro-memoir on page 124, every sentence contains an action that shows us the relationship physically and psychologically.

Read the story "Boys" by Rick Moody on page 219. Notice how there is always action, always lots of movement — the boys run around, in and out of the house, year after year, shooting a dog, itching and scratching, breaking out into pimples, calling names, torturing their sister. Notice where the camera is in each of these image flashes: positioned over the neighborhood, then, *whoosh*, down into a backyard, then in a church pew, right over the shoulder of one of the boys, then at the bathroom mirror, close up on a boy's face, then the camera, *whoosh*, tracking down the upstairs hallway as the boys chase their sister. The camera is *always moving. The distance between the camera and the subject is constantly changing.*

At first, it might feel awkward to walk around and film simultaneously. As you practice writing this way, focused on the moving image, you will feel more comfortable.

Amateurs tend to stay back. It may feel weird and intrusive and uncomfortable to get in people's faces. But that is what artists do. The amateur stands stock-still, and everything is filmed from the same distance. Excellent filmmakers vary the distance and so do writers. They open with a long shot, and we see the whole world. Then, for high impact, they close in. Then they pull out a little. Then they zoom in, and all we can see is part of a face. Part of a life. A secret inside view. Keep moving. Keep changing your angles. That's how you get the good stuff, the alive parts of your image.

One Sentence, One Action

Action feeds the image. Action keeps it alive. But often, while **tracking** actions and gestures, we get all tangled up.

> Nancy was rushing to get to class on time and she stumbled and fell while picking up her books from the sofa to get out the door on time.

What's confusing here is that the author thinks she is writing in the image, using action, nouns, and verbs. But she isn't. Because the human brain reads English sentences in a linear fashion, from left to right, we take in the order of events sequentially. If your image sequence is off, if your sentences try to handle too many actions, the reader won't be transported. He or she may be able to muscle through and *think* out what is happening, but that isn't what you want as a writer. You want the reader *to not work too hard*. The reader wants to just see what's happening. The reader doesn't want to have to sort out all the stage directions. That involves thinking, heavy lifting. Creative writing is all about *seeing*.

An important aspect of manipulating images is remembering the muscular possibilities and the linear limitations of the sentence. Do only one thing at a time:

> Harry grabbed the gin and tonic. He rushed down the driveway, spilling.

As opposed to:

> Harry, coming in the door, grabbed his drink and got undressed and changed into his soccer shorts.

It's physically impossible to come in a door and grab a drink *and* get undressed. This is summary. It's not a real image. It's a list of events. Good writers break down what they see and render what's important for the reader to notice.

Notice how in the readings in this chapter most of the sentences are devoted to one action, one thing. Readers are reading lines, in a linear fashion, from left to right. Sentences that try to do two things — "She walked in and put down her coat, and he read the comic book to his brother" — are not as effective as sentences that devote themselves to a single action, a single concept. Simplify your sentences and make them into straight lines, simple, sharp, clearly aimed at their target. You can still write complex sentences with complex actions. It's just a matter of tightly focusing your logic and lining it up with your tightly focused camera work. Isolate the action one thing at a time, and the sentence breaks the action down into bite-size pieces.

Kim Addonizio's "First Poem for You" on page 121 illustrates this point perfectly.

> I like to touch your tattoos in complete
> darkness, when I can't see them. I'm sure of
> where they are, know by heart the neat
> lines of lightning pulsing just above

A complex argument, a lot going on in this moment. But Addonizio lets her sentences do one thing at a time. I was going to do X. Instead I did Y, which caused Z.

Compare Addonizio's lines to typical nonimage sentences:

> I'm crazy about him. He is my soul mate.
> I know everything about him.

The poem goes one sentence at a time. One image, one step, and one line at a time. What happens first here? The speaker likes to touch her lover's tattoos when the room is dark, "when I can't see them." What happens next? She feels certain of where the tattoos are — she really knows her lover, and the lover's skin — it's a map she can read in the dark. What do we see next? A tattoo: lightning bolts. One thing at a time so that we, the readers, actually participate, co-creating the scene.

Instead of writing "I know everything about him" or "he is my soul mate," Addonizio, a skillful poet, shows in real time how she loves him and how he matters to her. When we write general sentences like "he makes my heart pound faster," we aren't really looking at our subject. When we write feelings and thoughts such as these, we often aren't transporting the reader into our image — we may even be shutting the reader out. Note how Addonizio's "First Poem for You" stems from those grounding questions on page 121. Where we are, what people look like, what they're doing and saying — and what they are yearning for — is visual and clear. See it before you say it, and let each sentence or line do one thing at a time, in sequence.

How do you move from one active image to another smoothly? We will cover a technique called **sliding**, where the writing smoothly moves the camera from one subject to another, at the end of this chapter. In general, try to minimize or remove "busy" transitions — people getting into and out of cars, leaving rooms, saying good-bye — unless something significant happens during the moment. Consider using **white space** instead, skipping two double lines. Or, simplify:

His father said, "One minute," and they climbed out of the car.

They went up wooden steps into the bar. Inside, it was dark and smelled of cigarette smoke and something stale and sweet.

Summary Images

In a short piece—a poem or a short-short story, for example—you can sustain one active image, and that can be your entire piece. In addition to scenic presentation, you have another choice: **summary images**.

In creative writing, summary is just as important as image-based scenes. **Summary** provides the connective tissue so that the images work together. Summary can increase the drama in a piece: Your reader learns new information that makes everything in this situation suddenly more complicated. Raymond Carver makes excellent use of summary in presenting the background story of the blind man and his wife. We didn't experience that material in real time, in scenes. The most important parts—she read to him, she liked it; she let him touch her face—are summarized for us as visual bullet points. Summary images increase conflict as they help the reader understand the relationships of the characters to each other and to the larger themes of the piece.

Summary also lets you cover big chunks of time deftly and vividly. We begin "Cathedral" at a very dramatic moment in time—the arrival of the blind man. We don't start the story any earlier, before the couple was married, or when they were in high school, or even the week before. We start when the blind man is arriving: "he was on his way to spend the night." We're plunged into the middle of the conflict. This technique is called **in medias res**, into the middle of things.

Carver next offers summary so we understand the context—just as exposition is used at the top of a play:

His wife had died. So he was visiting the dead wife's relatives in Connecticut. He called my wife from his in-laws'. Arrangements were made.

Summary differs from scene in three ways:

1. The events don't play out in real time in the movie in our mind.
2. Large chunks of time are presented (wife died, visit to Connecticut).
3. We don't see the specifics of action and dialogue. ("Arrangements were made.")

In creative writing, summary is:

1. Always interesting, well observed, specific, and detailed.
2. Inherently dramatic or increasing the tension in the rest of the story.
3. Increasing the depth of our understanding of the characters and their yearnings.

Summary can't be used as filler. It's not an opportunity for the writer to pile on general background information. Skillful summary presents snapshots of key moments, skidding over time in an interesting and targeted way in order to get to the next dramatic turn in the piece, which of course will be presented in a full-blown image.

Thao Thai uses summary exposition to open her micro-memoir "Counting Bats" on page 168:

I tell you, we've got bats. Not just one, which might be extraordinary. . .

And then moves quickly to an active image:

Four of them perch on the mosquito netting above me, claws gripping the fine, flossy strands that wind protectively around my head.

She creates a poetic rhythm, moving back to summary **exposition** in the next passage where we learn the author is from Vietnam and her grandparents have tried to westernize their home just for her visit. Then she offers an insight into her yearning: "I find this place terribly inconvenient." Using incredibly vivid summary, we see in our mind's eye how the bats emerged from a hidden place in the house during the remodel, "their wings stuck together from lack of use." Summary can be as beautiful and interesting as poetry.

Many stories are driven by scenes, with active images taking up most of the real estate on the page, as in "Cathedral" and most of the other pieces we've looked at. But some stories rely heartily on well-crafted summary.

Akhil Sharma's "Surrounded by Sleep" on page 174 is a short story about two brothers, Ajay and Aman. A terrible accident occurs and in medias res, we learn about the tragedy in the first sentence. Because the story is about family and culture, prayer and ritual, the past plays a significant role. Sharma relies on summary to deepen and enrich his tale:

Ajay's family had moved from India to Queens, New York, two years earlier. The accident occurred during the boys' summer vacation, on a visit with their aunt and uncle in Arlington, Virginia. After the accident,

Ajay's mother came to Arlington, where she waited to see if Aman would recover. At the hospital, she told the doctors and nurses that her son had been accepted into the Bronx High School of Science, in the hope that by highlighting his intelligence she would move them to make a greater effort on his behalf. Within a few weeks....

The same rules for effective scene-writing apply to summary: sharp word choice ("Ajay," "India," "Queens"), specific details ("Arlington," "Bronx High School of Science") character-revealing dialogue ("she told the doctors and nurses that her son had been accepted . . .") and powerful, urgent character yearning ("in the hope that by highlighting his intelligence . . ."). It's not a full-blown scene because it doesn't take place in one location during a specific period of time. Instead, summary is bullet points over a period time involving perhaps more than one location—summer vacation, home of relatives, hospital, a period of weeks.

Signal phrases that announce a summary image often have to do with time or character. *That summer* or *For five weeks it went on* are the kinds of cues that let the reader know how things generally went over the next chunk of time. *She always wanted to . . .* or *He never met a blind man . . .* deepen character yearning via summary.

PRACTICE 7

SCENE VERSUS SUMMARY: Akhil Sharma's "Surrounded By Sleep"

Read "Surrounded by Sleep" on page 174 and identify the sections that are in scene (specific moment in time that plays out in your mind's eye) versus summary. What do you notice about what Sharma elects to place in summary and what he places in scene?

Notice that in paragraph two of "Surrounded by Sleep," Sharma gives a summary, the backstory, an overview of how Ajay's family arrived at the pool that August afternoon. During this summary, what happens in your mind's eye? Does the screen go blank? Do you reason your way through this passage, as in a chemistry textbook? Or, do you *see* as you learn more information about the family?

Sliding

To move from summary to real-time image and back again, or to move from place to place, from image to image, in your poem or story or play, you learn to slide. **Sliding** is like smooth camera work, when moving your reader's attention from one scene or moment to another, panning slowly from the park swing set where two kids are playing, gently over to the mall parking lot across the street.

Writers who don't learn sliding may inadvertently confuse the reader. Sliding is the art of using transitions that are sensory and cinematic.

However, if the theme of your piece is dislocation, as in "Counting Bats," leaps and jumps from summary to scene to a question—"What drives a woman out of hiding?" give the reader a strong feeling of unease—and here the lack of slides or transitions serves the piece really well.

But if you have too many locations, not enough depth, no transitions, and no reason for those moves, your writing might be all over the place, and not in a good way. So, usually you'll want to slide from one type of moment to another in order to keep the reader's interest high. If you present each moment with the same level of detail, the same distance, the same steady scene or same steady summary, the piece could fall flat.

Marisa Silver, author of "What I Saw from Where I Stood" on page 279, is a master of the slide. Examine this short excerpt from her story, which you will read in full later, and simply notice the sliding action:

> I drove Dulcie's car to work the next day. When I got home that night, Dulcie had moved our mattress from our bed into the living room, where it lay in the middle of the floor, the sheets spilling over onto the carpet.

Silver slides from the narrator's workday into the apartment, which is where the next scene takes place, an important one. The reader doesn't need the workday, the car ride, or the character's entrance into the apartment, so Silver places that material in summary.

The next dramatic moment is a dialogue beat:

> "It's the rat," she said. "He's back."

The slide is the bridge that moves us from summary into scene: "When I got home that night, Dulcie had moved. . . ." We don't need to see the character get out of the car and enter the apartment—we need to see something important, something he sees: sheets spilling onto the floor. The reader needs these slides in order to seamlessly move through the piece.

Examine the following passage from Sharma's story, and notice where the slide from summary to scene occurs:

> Sometimes when Ajay arrived his mother was on the phone, telling his father that she missed him and was expecting to see him. . . . Ajay had thought of his parents as the same person: MummyDaddy. Now . . . Ajay sensed that his mother and father were quite different people. After his mother got off the phone, she always went to the cafeteria to get coffee for herself and Jell-O or cookies for him. He knew that if she took her coat with her, it meant that she was especially sad. . . .

That day, while she was gone, Ajay stood beside the hospital bed and balanced a comic book on Aman's chest. He read to him very slowly. Before turning each page, he said, "Okay, Aman?"

Hospital days often blur together. Sharma, in summary-image mode, uses the time cue "Sometimes . . ." so we are very clear this kind of behavior happens over a period of time. The summary gives us the texture of the characters' lives in a way that is both a) efficient and b) sensory. Here, Sharma summarizes Ajay's new insights into his parents, how he is seeing them as people, as more than just entities designed to meet his needs. Sharma doesn't stop and lecture to us, though. He stays deep in the moment by calling out the four main physical images from those days: coffee, Jell-O, cookies, and his mother and her coat. That's the key: Anchor summary in specific images—moving ones. When you have your specific images in place, you can hang insights and conclusions on them. Without the images, the summary becomes too heavy, it ceases to be art, and it becomes an essay. There's nothing wrong with essays. It's just not what we are doing here as creative writers. When we read creative writing, *imaginative* writing, we expect to have pictures play out in our minds. That's part of the deal.

Notice how Sharma slides from the generalized summary image to the full-blown "this is happening right now" image. The change happens so smoothly as Sharma freezes the frame on one day. In summary time, the mother walks outside. "That day, while she was gone . . ." is the line where Sharma bridges to scene. We've been seeing her come and go, do her coffee-and-coat routine, and one day, while she is out, Sharma anchors us firmly in real time, in an image we are going to be in for a while. We're going in for a closer look, back to Ajay in real time.

We're plunged into a live scene, a three-dimensional image with a floor, a ceiling, walls, all five senses. Sharma writes this scene by imagining for himself what it's like to see through Ajay's eyes. He doesn't write *about* the boy; he writes *from* the boy.

PRACTICE 8

WRITING A SLIDE

Try writing—fiction or nonfiction—a full-blown scene and moving into summary. Then try writing a passage of summary and flowing into a scene. What do you notice?

A WORD ON IDEAS

Sometimes writers have "ideas" for writing. When the idea is accompanied with a sensory spark—a bit of overheard conversation or an image of three

pink birds flying across a bold blue Florida sky
late afternoon — when the idea isn't in words
yet, it holds much promise. When you orient
in space and time and pursue the image — a
sheaf of poems stretched across the country,
a parrot explaining crucial questions for our
planet — most often you'll discover the writing
takes you to an interesting place.

> *I write hungry sentences
> because they want more
> and more lyricism and
> imagery to satisfy them.*
> —NATALIE DIAZ

But if the idea is a more abstract concept — "I want to write about
rejection" or "I have an idea for a trilogy of elf novels" — with no people or
action in it, it can be harder to launch.

For example, you have an idea for a poem about your grandmother.
Often, starting from the thought — Grandma was beautiful, even in old
age — is a difficult place to begin. It might be easier to start with a description of you and her, in a room, on a particular day, and create a sketch or
make a list of the sensory images: what her hands looked like, what she said
aloud, what she was reading or eating or watching on TV, working hard to
get every detail and every syllable accurate and clear on the page.

Get in the habit of working from images. The ideas will take care of themselves, and your writing will be fresher, richer, more original. And smarter.

Don't save up ideas: Collect the live images your mind dreams up and
note the details of what you see and hear every day. Practice noticing specifics and jotting down overheard bits of real-world dialogue.

Ideas come naturally; writing in images doesn't usually come naturally.
Practice taking notes and starting pieces from images, not ideas. Instead of
putting down all your thoughts, hoping to translate them into images later,
try taking notes that are images, honing your powers of observation. Try
to have the experience while writing — even when you are at the very, very
earliest note-taking stage — that you want your reader to have while reading.

Instead of asking "idea" questions to generate writing topics and creative
projects, ask "sense" questions: What did it feel like to the touch? What was
the taste in your mouth? What were the visual images from that day? Get
grounded in your body, and in the scene, and write from the five senses
rather than thinking, remembering, or drawing from other writers' images,
such as those you encounter on television or in film. Your key to success as a
creative writer rests inside your **sense memory**.

As a creative writer, one of the most powerful prompts for you to launch
yourself into the image is to rely on your sense of smell. Scent triggers
memory and the emotions attached to those memories; the neuroscience
on this effect is well documented. Doubtless, you've also been transported
by smells — scent memories lodge deep in our brains. Practice keeping track
of your body's reactions to things. A woman's perfume launches you back to

kindergarten and your love for Mrs. Vander K. When you notice the way a friend organizes the stuff under her kitchen sink, your mom's drinking problem comes flooding back to you — those bottles of alcohol hidden among the bottles of cleaning supplies. The way the sky looks right before it snows, and whoosh, there's childhood, the night your sister left, pregnant, the last night you ever saw her. It was that sky. Use these visual prompts for creative writing, rather than ideas.

WRITING PROJECTS

Poetry

1. Write an ode, imitating Ross Gay's "Ode to Sleeping in My Clothes" on page 164. Use his title and make your poem roughly the same length and shape. Pack the poem with active images and sensory details from your wardrobe. Attend to sound work every 3–8 syllables, as Gay does: "**cott**on sar**co**phagus"; "**rank** from the **day**."

Nonfiction

2. Using Dylan Landis's piece on page 166 as your inspiration, choose a time when you were experiencing strong emotion — grief or joy or passion or anger. In your mind's eye, enter a significant room you would have been in during this time — your friend's kitchen, your grandmother's bedroom. Feel your feelings, *but don't put any of them on the page*. Write a list piece that is a simply detailed inventory of the things you find in that room — all the images.

Fiction

3. Write a short story, 3–7 pages long, where you demonstrate the following techniques:
   - Active images (most of the story): scenes with two people
   - Conflict
   - One summary image
   - One slide

Drama

4. Write a scene for a play. Choose action images that serve as metaphor for the characters' inner experience.

IMAGES WORKSHOP

The following prompts will guide your discussion of your classmates' work.

1. In the student piece you are reading, highlight the places you truly see as "moving images," the alive parts of the piece, where you aren't reading words on a page as much as experiencing something, seeing.
2. Identify three to five places in the student piece where an image could be made more powerful, alive, and focused. Look for passages that rely on thoughts, feelings, explanations, or description.
3. Identify where the writer left out emotions, explanation, irrelevant description, or analysis. Did you understand the piece, even without these elements?
4. Identify your favorite image in this student's piece.

READINGS

Ross Gay
Ode to Sleeping in My Clothes

And though I don't mention it
to my mother
or the doctors
with their white coats
it is, in fact,
a great source of happiness,
for me, as I don't
even remove my socks,
and will sometimes
even pull up my hood
and slide my hands deep
in my pockets
and probably moreso
than usual look as if something
bad has happened
my heart blasting a last somersault
or some artery parting
like curtains in a theatre
while the cavalry of blood
comes charging through
except unlike
so many of the dead
I must be smiling
there in my denim
and cotton sarcophagus
slightly rank from the day
it is said that Shostakovich slept
with a packed suitcase beneath
his bed and it is said
that black people were snatched
from dark streets and made experiments
of and you and I
both have family whose life

savings are tucked 12 feet beneath
the Norway maple whose roots
splay like the bones
in the foot of man
who was walked to Youngstown, Ohio
from Mississippi without sleeping
or keeping his name
and it's a miracle
maybe I almost never think of
to rise like this
and simply by sliding my feet into my boots
while the water for coffee
gathers its song
be in the garden
or on the stoop
running, almost,
from nothing.

Natalie Diaz

My Brother at 3 a.m.

He sat cross-legged, weeping on the steps
when Mom unlocked and opened the front door.
  O God, he said. *O God.*
   He wants to kill me, Mom.

When Mom unlocked and opened the front door
at 3 a.m., she was in her nightgown, Dad was asleep.
  He wants to kill me, he told her,
   looking over his shoulder.

3 a.m. and in her nightgown, Dad asleep,
What's going on? she asked. *Who wants to kill you?*
  He looked over his shoulder.
   The devil does. Look at him, over there.

She asked, *What are you on? Who wants to kill you?*
The sky wasn't black or blue but the green of a dying night.
  The devil, look at him, over there.
   He pointed to the corner house.

The sky wasn't black or blue but the dying green of night.
Stars had closed their eyes or sheathed their knives.

My brother pointed to the corner house.
His lips flickered with sores.

Stars had closed their eyes or sheathed their knives.
O God, I can see the tail, he said. *O God, look.*
Mom winced at the sores on his lips.
It's sticking out from behind the house.

O God, see the tail, he said. *Look at the goddamned tail.*
He sat cross-legged, weeping on the front steps.
Mom finally saw it, a hellish vision, my brother.
O God, O God, she said.

Dylan Landis

In My Father's Study upon His Death

An article on Vincent Van Gogh, explaining that one year to the day before Van Gogh was born, his mother gave birth to another son, also named Vincent. The infant died and was upheld as a kind of angel, the most perfect and most adored son. The article suggests that Vincent, in second place, despaired of ever earning his mother's love and approval, and fell into lifelong depression.

A painting by my father of himself sitting with his own father — two thin men with somber, distracted faces, staring into separate distances, leaning away from each other in art as they did in life.

A file marked "Courage" containing clippings and book reviews in which my father has underlined *imperturbability, intention* and *fixed resolve*.

A file marked "Breathing and Emotions" containing my father's writings and a slip of paper on which he has tightly handwritten:

> *She takes your breath away*
> *You can breathe freely around him*
> *He suffocates me*
> *I gasped when I saw how she changed*
> *It knocked the wind out of me*
> *I'd like some breathing room*

An unlabeled file containing patient notes from my father's days as a psychoanalyst. The patient, now deceased, was a famous man, and the notes are faded and nearly illegible, but two phrases stand out as the shredder sucks in the pages: "The idiocy of fear." "I feel I ought to be better."

A photograph of my mother in her thirties, wearing a two-piece leopard-print bathing suit, vamping for the camera. (One room away, my mother now sleeps on the sofa, a tracheostomy tube jutting from her throat, a feeding tube snaking from her stomach.)

A fake book stamped *Main Street* and *Sinclair Lewis* in gold on the spine. It is hollow and contains an envelope on which my father has written "Emergency $300." The envelope holds a twenty-dollar bill. At one point it held $300. At another point it held $80, but an aide needed money for parking in New York City. My father was convinced that aides were stealing from him over the months of his long neurological illness. It is possible. Items not found in my father's study, or anywhere else: an ivory carving; a zippered money belt in which he kept a thousand dollars tucked away for decades.

78 artist's paint brushes, most stained blue and green, one fan-shaped and never used, arranged in several dense bouquets.

His final painting, made on a square of corrugated cardboard, a field of darkest blues and greens penetrated by a meandering white line.

Two files marked "Dylan," containing every letter I ever wrote my father.

WRITERS ON WRITING

DYLAN LANDIS

HEATHER SELLERS: How did you get the idea for writing this piece?

DYLAN LANDIS: My father had just died. So I did what writers do, even, or especially, at the worst of times. I got my notebook out. I walked alone into my father's study and wrote down every object that I saw. I just made a list, leaving all emotion out of it. I went through his files and described the things he had saved and the stories they told. I counted his paintbrushes. I wanted the list to be a portrait of the room, because the room was a portrait of my father.

HS: After the first draft, how much did you reshape the piece? What was your process?

DL: The original list was a sprawling mess. I *needed* that mess, though — I needed a huge mass so I could compress it. But how? A writer-friend helped me strip out 80 percent of my sentences. What remained was purely concrete and sensory detail, and some *unexpected* detail. The reader now had plenty of space to step in and use her imagination. My writer-friend also showed me that items in a list essay each have different meaning and weight. We treated them like tiles in a mosaic, moving them around, and by ordering them carefully we were able to build up slowly and powerfully to what this man cared about most.

Thao Thai
Counting Bats

I tell you we've got bats.

Not just one, which might be extraordinary — or two, which could be cute — not even three, a vaguely threatening almost-gang. But four. Four of them perch on the mosquito netting above me, claws gripping the fine, flossy strands that wind protectively around my head.

Four are points on a pirate-compass, ready to plunder.

You should know that these bats are not even a little ordinary. They came from the deep recesses of my childhood home in Vietnam, a thin, rectangular house on stilts, with rushing sewage below. My grandparents hired a man from the village to remove the squat toilet so that they could install a new, Western-style one for my benefit. For my convenience.

I find this place terribly inconvenient.

With the last clank of sledgehammer on porcelain, the bats emerged from beneath, angry and whitened by cement particles, their wings stuck together from lack of use. They took to the walls, they took to the ceilings. They fled into the dark.

My family gaped at one other. We thought we knew everything about this place.

The four bats are so close now I could reach out to touch their furry bodies, to poke them each in a beady eye. Bats can't bully *me*. Instead, I shake the mosquito netting. I create myself a little tempest. They rollick back and forth and still they stay fastened. Their eyes bore.

Is this blame? Is this retribution? I told them my comfort was more important than their home and now they are here to get me. Sweat gathers in the crease of my elbow. I'm feverish.

Beyond my makeshift bed, my grandparents sleep in their tightly enclosed bedroom. Beyond that, my village sleeps, and beyond that — the entire country of Vietnam. There's no sound except for the bats' slow progress across the netting. They switch positions. They're trying to find a break.

There is none, I say, shaking the netting a little more. Don't you know this house has no windows. They lose grip. Or I lose grip.

Count with me now.

Three days ago, I was in Saigon, city of honking mopeds and steaming street food. City of distended stomachs and rats and the damp heat of tropical summer. Seven days ago, I was in the States, typing frantically at a coffee shop in the cooling Midwest. Twenty years ago, I was here, in this house—wasn't I?—with bats scrambling beneath the bed where I slept. Now the bats are on top.

My grandfather promised that he would kill them in the morning, when they'd least suspect it. He said I could help. I imagine us with torches and nets, the flap of a wing close to my ear. What drives a bat out of hiding?

What drives a woman out of hiding?

The bats cross one another overhead, dignified, almost prancing in their delicacy. They think they are on their way to the opera. Hello, how are you. Hello, excuse me.

I'm the ground upon which bats tread. They aren't trying to get *at* me. They're trying to get *past* me. That difference is riveting. I am suspended between terror and its accompanying shadow, wonder.

Let's start again.

Four bats. Three days in the village. Two hours of sleeplessness. One woman in one small country one whole ocean away from one home that sits calm and safe and quiet at the bottom of one green, blessedly familiar hill.

What comes before one?

Without warning, the bats loosen their claws and take flight.

I could unhinge myself too and fly with them, already hollow and high, in another place, another plane of unfettered existence. Somewhere along the way, I might ask, Where is the sky, that dark, dimpled ceiling of my world?

Nowhere, I tell you. Nowhere comes before one.

Mary Robison
Pretty Ice

I was up the whole night before my fiancé was due to arrive from the East—drinking coffee, restless and pacing, my ears ringing. When the television signed off, I sat down with a packet of the month's bills and figured amounts on a lined tally sheet in my checkbook. Under the spray of a high-intensity lamp, my left hand moved rapidly over the touch tablets of my calculator.

Will, my fiancé, was coming from Boston on the six-fifty train—the dawn train, the only train that still stopped in the small Ohio city where I lived. At six-fifteen I was still at my accounts; I was getting some pleasure from transcribing the squarish green figures that appeared in the window of my calculator. 'Schwab Dental Clinic,' I printed in a raveled backhand. 'Thirty-eight and 50/100.'

A car horn interrupted me. I looked over my desktop and out the living-room window of my rented house. The saplings in my little yard were encased in ice. There had been snow all week, and then an ice storm. In the glimmering driveway in front of my garage, my mother was peering out of her car. I got up and turned off my lamp and capped my ivory Mont Blanc pen. I found a coat in the semidark in the hall, and wound a knitted muffler at my throat. Crossing the living room, I looked away from the big pine mirror; I didn't want to see how my face and hair looked after a night of accounting.

My yard was a frozen pond, and I was careful on the walkway. My mother hit her horn again. Frozen slush came through the toe of one of my chukka boots, and I stopped on the path and frowned at her. I could see her breath rolling away in clouds from the cranked-down window of her Mazda. I have never owned a car nor learned to drive, but I had a low opinion of my mother's compact. My father and I used to enjoy big cars, with tops that came down. We were both tall and we wanted what he called 'stretch room.' My father had been dead for fourteen years, but I resented my mother's buying a car in which he would not have fitted.

'Now what's wrong? Are you coming?' my mother said.

'Nothing's wrong except that my shoes are opening around the soles,' I said. 'I just paid a lot of money for them.'

I got in on the passenger side. The car smelled of wet wool and Mother's hair spray. Someone had done her hair with a minty-white rinse, and the hair was held in place by a zebra-striped headband.

'I think you're getting a flat,' I said. 'That retread you bought for the left front is going.'

She backed the car out of the drive, using the rear-view mirror. 'I finally got a boy I can trust, at the Exxon station,' she said. 'He says that tire will last until hot weather.'

Out on the street, she accelerated too quickly and the rear of the car swung left. The tires whined for an instant on the old snow and then caught. We were knocked back in our seats a little, and an empty Kleenex box slipped off the dash and onto the floor carpet.

'This is going to be something,' my mother said. 'Will sure picked an awful day to come.'

My mother had never met him. My courtship with Will had all happened in Boston. I was getting my doctorate there, in musicology. Will was involved with his research at Boston U., and with teaching botany to undergraduates. 'You're sure he'll be at the station?' my mother said. 'Can the trains go in this weather? I don't see how they do.'

'I talked to him on the phone yesterday. He's coming.'

'How did he sound?' my mother said.

To my annoyance, she began to hum to herself.

I said, 'He's had rotten news about his work. Terrible, in fact.'

'Explain his work to me again,' she said.

'He's a plant taxonomist.'

'Yes?' my mother said. 'What does that mean?'

'It means he doesn't have a lot of money,' I said. 'He studies grasses. He said on the phone he's been turned down for a research grant that would have meant a great deal to us. Apparently the work he's been doing for the past seven or so years is irrelevant or outmoded. I guess "superficial" is what he told me.'

'I won't mention it to him, then,' my mother said.

We came to the expressway. Mother steered the car through some small windblown snow dunes and down the entrance ramp. She followed two yellow salt trucks with winking blue beacons that were moving side by side down the center and right-hand lanes.

'I think losing the grant means we should postpone the wedding,' I said. 'I want Will to have his bearings before I step into his life for good.'

'Don't wait too much longer, though,' my mother said.

After a couple of miles, she swung off the expressway. We went past some tall high-tension towers with connecting cables that looked like staff lines on a sheet of music. We were in the decaying neighborhood near the tracks. 'Now I know this is right,' Mother said. 'There's our old sign.'

The sign was a tall billboard, black and white, that advertised my father's dance studio. The studio had been closed for years and the building it had been in was gone. The sign showed a man in a tuxedo waltzing with a woman in an evening gown. I was always sure it was a waltz. The dancers were nearly two stories high, and the weather had bleached them into phantoms. The lettering — the name of the studio, my father's name — had disappeared.

'They've changed everything,' my mother said, peering about. 'Can this be the station?'

We went up a little drive that wound past a cindery lot full of flatbed trucks and that ended up at the smudgy brownstone depot.

'Is that your Will?' Mother said.

Will was on the station platform, leaning against a baggage truck. He had a duffle bag between his shoes and a plastic cup of coffee in his mittened hand. He seemed to have put on weight, girlishly, through the hips, and his face looked thicker to me, from temple to temple. His gold-rimmed spectacles looked too small.

My mother stopped in an empty cab lane, and I got out and called to Will. It wasn't far from the platform to the car, and Will's pack wasn't a large one, but he seemed to be winded when he got to me. I let him kiss me, and then he stepped back and blew a cold breath and drank from the coffee cup, with his eyes on my face.

Mother was pretending to be busy with something in her handbag, not paying attention to me and Will.

'I look awful,' I said.

'No, no, but I probably do,' Will said. 'No sleep, and I'm fat. So this is your town?'

He tossed the coffee cup at an oil drum and glanced around at the cold train yards and low buildings. A brass foundry was throwing a yellowish column of smoke over a line of Canadian Pacific boxcars.

I said, 'The problem is you're looking at the wrong side of the tracks.'

A wind whipped Will's lank hair across his face. 'Does your mom smoke?' he said. 'I ran out in the middle of the night on the train, and the club car was closed. Eight hours across Pennsylvania without a cigarette.'

The car horn sounded as my mother climbed from behind the wheel. 'That was an accident,' she said, because I was frowning at her. 'Hello. Are you Will?' She came around the car and stood on tiptoes and kissed him. 'You picked a miserable day to come and visit us.'

She was using her young-girl voice, and I was embarrassed for her. 'He needs a cigarette,' I said.

Will got into the back of the car and I sat beside my mother again. After we started up, Mother said, 'Why doesn't Will stay at my place, in your old room, Belle? I'm all alone there, with plenty of space to kick around in.'

'We'll be able to get him a good motel,' I said quickly, before Will could answer. 'Let's try that Ramada, over near the new elementary school.' It was odd, after he had come all the way from Cambridge, but I didn't want him in my old room, in the house where I had been a child. 'I'd put you at my place,' I said, 'but there's mountains of tax stuff all over.'

'You've been busy,' he said.

'Yes,' I said. I sat sidewise, looking at each of them in turn. Will had some blackish spots around his mouth—ballpoint ink, maybe. I wished he had freshened up and put on a better shirt before leaving the train.

'It's up to you two, then,' my mother said.

I could tell she was disappointed in Will. I don't know what she expected. I was thirty-one when I met him. I had probably dated fewer men in my life than she had gone out with in a single year at her sorority. She had always been successful with men.

'William was my late husband's name,' my mother said. 'Did Belle ever tell you?'

'No,' Will said. He was smoking one of Mother's cigarettes.

'I always like the name,' she said. 'Did you know we ran a dance studio?'

I groaned.

'Oh, let me brag if I want to,' my mother said. 'He was such a handsome man.'

It was true. They were both handsome — mannequins, a pair of dolls who had spent half their lives in evening clothes. But my father had looked old in the end, in a business in which you had to stay young. He had trouble with his eyes, which were bruised-looking and watery, and he had to wear glasses with thick lenses.

I said, 'It was in the dance studio that my father ended his life, you know. In the ballroom.'

'You told me,' Will said, at the same instant my mother said, 'Don't talk about it.'

My father killed himself with a service revolver. We never found out where he had bought it, or when. He was found in his warm-up clothes — a pullover sweater and pleated pants. He was wearing his tap shoes, and he had a short towel folded around his neck. He had aimed the gun barrel down his mouth, so the bullet would not shatter the wall of mirrors behind him. I was twenty then — old enough to find out how he did it.

My mother had made a wrong turn and we were on Buttles Avenue. 'Go there,' I said, pointing down a street beside Garfield Park. We passed a group of paper boys who were riding bikes with saddlebags. They were going slow, because of the ice.

'Are you very discouraged, Will?' my mother said. 'Belle tells me you are having a run of bad luck.'

'You could say so,' Will said. 'A little rough water.'

'I'm sorry,' Mother said. 'What seems to be the trouble?'

Will said, 'Well, this will be oversimplifying, but essentially what I do is take a weed and evaluate its structure and growth and habitat, and so forth.'

'What's wrong with that?' my mother said.

'Nothing. But it isn't enough.'

'I get it,' my mother said uncertainly.

I had taken a mirror and a comb from my handbag and I was trying for a clean center-part in my hair. I was thinking about finishing my bill paying.

Will said, 'What do you want to do after I check in, Belle? What about breakfast?'

'I've got to go home for a while and clean up that tax jazz, or I'll never rest,' I said. 'I'll just show up at your motel later. If we ever find it.'

'That'll be fine,' Will said.

Mother said, 'I'd offer to serve you two dinner tonight, but I think you'll want to leave me out of it. I know how your father and I felt after he went away sometimes. Which way do I turn here?'

We had stopped at an intersection near the iron gates of the park. Behind the gates there was a frozen pond, where a single early-morning skater was skating backward, expertly crossing his blades.

I couldn't drive a car but, like my father, I have always enjoyed maps and atlases. During automobile trips, I liked comparing distances on maps. I liked the words *latitude, cartography, meridian*. It was extremely annoying to me that Mother had gotten us turned around and lost in our own city, and I was angry with Will all of a sudden, for wasting seven years on something superficial.

'What about up that way?' Will said to my mother, pointing to the left. 'There's some traffic up by that light, at least.'

I leaned forward in my seat and started combing my hair all over again.

'There's no hurry,' my mother said.

'How do you mean?' I asked her.

'To get William to the motel,' she said. 'I know everybody complains, but I think an ice storm is a beautiful thing. Let's enjoy it.'

She waved her cigarette at the windshield. The sun had burned through and was gleaming in the branches of all the maples and buckeye trees in the park. 'It's twinkling like a stage set,' Mother said.

'It is pretty,' I said.

Will said, 'It'll make a bad-looking spring. A lot of shrubs get damaged and turn brown, and the trees don't blossom right.'

For once I agreed with my mother. Everything was quiet and holding still. Everything was in place, the way it was supposed to be. I put my comb away and smiled back at Will—because I knew it was for the last time.

Akhil Sharma
Surrounded by Sleep

One August afternoon, when Ajay was ten years old, his elder brother, Aman, dove into a pool and struck his head on the cement bottom. For three minutes, he lay there unconscious. Two boys continued to swim, kicking and splashing, until finally Aman was spotted below them. Water had entered through his nose and mouth. It had filled his stomach. His lungs collapsed. By the time he was pulled out, he could no longer think, talk, chew, or roll over in his sleep.

Ajay's family had moved from India to Queens, New York, two years earlier. The accident occurred during the boys' summer vacation, on a visit with their aunt and uncle in Arlington, Virginia. After the accident, Ajay's mother came to Arlington, where she waited to see if Aman would recover. At the hospital, she told the doctors and nurses that her son had been accepted into the Bronx High School of Science, in the hope that by highlighting his intelligence she would move them to make a greater effort on his behalf. Within a few weeks of the accident, the insurance company said that Aman should be transferred to a less expensive care facility, a long-term one. But only a few of these were any good, and those were full, and Ajay's mother refused to move Aman until a space opened in one of them. So she remained in Arlington, and Ajay stayed too, and his father visited from Queens on the weekends when he wasn't working. Ajay was enrolled at the local public school and in September he started fifth grade.

Before the accident, Ajay had never prayed much. In India, he and his brother used to go with their mother to the temple every Tuesday night, but that was mostly because there was a good *dosa* restaurant nearby. In America, his family went to a temple only on important holy days and birthdays. But shortly after Ajay's mother came to Arlington, she moved into the room that he and his brother had shared during the summer and made an altar in a corner. She threw an old flowered sheet over a cardboard box that had once held a television. On top she put a clay lamp, an incense-stick holder, and postcards depicting various gods. There was also a postcard of Mahatma Gandhi. She explained to Ajay that God could take any form; the picture of Mahatma Gandhi was there because he had appeared to her in a dream after the accident and told her that Aman would recover and become a surgeon. Now she and Ajay prayed for at least half an hour before the altar every morning and night.

At first she prayed with absolute humility. "Whatever you do will be good because you are doing it," she murmured to the postcards of Ram and Shivaji, daubing their lips with water and rice. Mahatma Gandhi got only water, because he did not like to eat. As weeks passed and Aman did not recover in time to return to the Bronx High School of Science for the first day of classes, his mother began doing things that called attention to her piety. She sometimes held the prayer lamp until it blistered her palms. Instead of kneeling before the altar, she lay face down. She fasted twice a week. Her attempts to sway God were not so different from Ajay's performing somersaults to amuse his aunt, and they made God seem human to Ajay.

One morning as Ajay knelt before the altar, he traced an Om, a crucifix, and a Star of David into the pile of the carpet. Beneath these he traced an *S*, for Superman, inside an upside-down triangle. His mother came up beside him.

"What are you praying for?" she asked. She had her hat on, a thick gray knitted one that a man might wear. The tracings went against the weave of the carpet and were darker than the surrounding nap. Pretending to examine them, Ajay leaned forward and put his hand over the *S*. His mother did not mind the Christian and Jewish symbols—they were for commonly recognized gods, after all—but she could not tolerate his praying to Superman. She'd caught him doing so once several weeks earlier and had become very angry, as if Ajay's faith in Superman made her faith in Ram ridiculous. "Right in front of God," she had said several times.

Ajay, in his nervousness, spoke the truth. "I'm asking God to give me a hundred percent on the math test."

His mother was silent for a moment. "What if God says you can have the math grade but then Aman will have to be sick a little while longer?" she asked.

Ajay kept quiet. He could hear cars on the road outside. He knew that his mother wanted to bewail her misfortune before God so that God would feel guilty. He looked at the postcard of Mahatma Gandhi. It was a black-and-white photo of him walking down a city street with an enormous crowd trailing behind him. Ajay thought of how, before the accident, Aman had been so modest that he would not leave the bathroom until he was fully dressed. Now he had rashes on his penis from the catheter that drew his urine into a translucent bag hanging from the guardrail of his bed.

His mother asked again, "Would you say, 'Let him be sick a little while longer'?"

"Are you going to tell me the story about Uncle Naveen again?" he asked.

"Why shouldn't I? When I was sick, as a girl, your uncle walked seven times around the temple and asked God to let him fail his exams just as long as I got better."

"If I failed the math test and told you that story, you'd slap me and ask what one has to do with the other."

His mother turned to the altar. "What sort of sons did you give me, God?" she asked. "One you drown, the other is this selfish fool."

"I will fast today so that God puts some sense in me," Ajay said, glancing away from the altar and up at his mother. He liked the drama of fasting.

"No, you are a growing boy." His mother knelt down beside him and said to the altar, "He is stupid, but he has a good heart."

Prayer, Ajay thought, should appeal with humility and an open heart to some greater force. But the praying that he and his mother did felt sly and confused. By treating God as someone to bargain with, it seemed to him, they prayed as if they were casting a spell.

This meant that it was possible to do away with the presence of God entirely. For example, Ajay's mother had recently asked a relative in India to drive a nail into a holy tree and tie a saffron thread to the nail on Aman's behalf. Ajay invented his own ritual. On his way to school each morning, he passed a thick tree rooted half on the sidewalk and half on the road. One day Ajay got the idea that if he circled the tree seven times, touching the north side every other time, he would have a lucky day. From then on he did it every morning, although he felt embarrassed and always looked around beforehand to make sure no one was watching.

One night Ajay asked God whether he minded being prayed to only in need.

"You think of your toe only when you stub it," God replied. God looked like Clark Kent. He wore a gray cardigan, slacks, and thick glasses, and had a forelock that curled just as Ajay's did.

God and Ajay had begun talking occasionally after Aman drowned. Now they talked most nights while Ajay lay in bed and waited for sleep. God sat at the foot of Ajay's mattress. His mother's mattress lay parallel to his, a few feet away. Originally God had appeared to Ajay as Krishna, but Ajay had felt foolish discussing brain damage with a blue god who held a flute and wore a dhoti.

"You're not angry with me for touching the tree and all that?"

"No. I'm flexible."

"I respect you. The tree is just a way of praying to you," Ajay assured God.

God laughed. "I am not too caught up in formalities."

Ajay was quiet. He was convinced that he had been marked as special by Aman's accident. The beginnings of all heroes are distinguished by misfortune. Superman and Batman were both orphans. Krishna was separated from his parents at birth. The god Ram had to spend fourteen years in a forest. Ajay waited to speak until it would not appear improper to begin talking about himself.

"How famous will I be?" he asked finally.

"I can't tell you the future," God answered.

Ajay asked, "Why not?"

"Even if I told you something, later I might change my mind."

"But it might be harder to change your mind after you have said something will happen."

God laughed again. "You'll be so famous that fame will be a problem."

Ajay sighed. His mother snorted and rolled over.

"I want Aman's drowning to lead to something," he said to God.

"He won't be forgotten."

"I can't just be famous, though. I need to be rich too, to take care of Mummy and Daddy and pay Aman's hospital bills."

"You are always practical." God had a soulful and pitying voice, and God's sympathy made Ajay imagine himself as a truly tragic figure, like Amitabh Bachchan in the movie *Trishul*.

"I have responsibilities," Ajay said. He was so excited at the thought of his possible greatness that he knew he would have difficulty sleeping. Perhaps he would have to go read in the bathroom.

"You can hardly imagine the life ahead," God said.

Even though God's tone promised greatness, the idea of the future frightened Ajay. He opened his eyes. There was light coming from the street. The room was cold and had a smell of must and incense. His aunt and uncle's house was a narrow two-story home next to a four-lane road. The apartment building with the pool where Aman had drowned was a few blocks up the road, one in a cluster of tall brick buildings with stucco fronts. Ajay pulled the blanket tighter around him. In India, he could not have imagined the reality of his life in America: the thick smell of meat in the school cafeteria, the many television channels. And, of course, he could not have imagined Aman's accident, or the hospital where he spent so much time.

The hospital was boring. Vinod, Ajay's cousin, picked him up after school and dropped him off there almost every day. Vinod was twenty-two. In addition to attending county college and studying computer programming, he worked at a 7-Eleven near Ajay's school. He often brought Ajay hot chocolate and a comic from the store, which had to be returned, so Ajay was not allowed to open it until he had wiped his hands.

Vinod usually asked him a riddle on the way to the hospital. "Why are manhole covers round?" It took Ajay half the ride to admit that he did not know. He was having difficulty talking. He didn't know why. The only time he could talk easily was when he was with God. The explanation he gave himself for this was that just as he couldn't chew when there was too much in his mouth, he couldn't talk when there were too many thoughts in his head.

When Ajay got to Aman's room, he greeted him as if he were all right. "Hello, lazy. How much longer are you going to sleep?" His mother was always there. She got up and hugged Ajay. She asked how school had been, and he didn't know what to say. In music class, the teacher sang a song about a sailor who had bared his breast before jumping into the sea. This had caused the other students to giggle. But Ajay could not say the word *breast* to his mother without blushing. He had also cried. He'd been thinking of how Aman's accident had made his own life mysterious and confused. What would happen next? Would Aman die or would he go on as he was? Where would they live? Usually when Ajay cried in school, he was told to go outside. But it had been raining, and the teacher had sent him into the hallway. He sat on the floor and wept. Any mention of this would upset his mother. And so he said nothing had happened that day.

Sometimes when Ajay arrived his mother was on the phone, telling his father that she missed him and was expecting to see him on Friday. His father took a Greyhound bus most Fridays from Queens to Arlington, returning on Sunday night in time to work the next day. He was a bookkeeper for a department store. Before the accident, Ajay had thought of his parents as the same person: MummyDaddy. Now, when he saw his father praying stiffly or when his father failed to say hello to Aman in his hospital bed, Ajay sensed that his mother and father were quite different people. After his mother got off the phone, she always went to the cafeteria to get coffee for herself and Jell-O or cookies for him. He knew that if she took her coat with her, it meant that she was especially sad. Instead of going directly to the cafeteria, she was going to go outside and walk around the hospital parking lot.

That day, while she was gone, Ajay stood beside the hospital bed and balanced a comic book on Aman's chest. He read to him very slowly. Before turning each page, he said, "Okay, Aman?"

Aman was fourteen. He was thin and had curly hair. Immediately after the accident, there had been so many machines around his bed that only one person could stand beside him at a time. Now there was just a single waxy yellow tube. One end of this went into his abdomen; the other, blocked by a green bullet-shaped plug, was what his Isocal milk was poured through. When not being used, the tube was rolled up and bound by a rubber band and tucked beneath Aman's hospital gown. But even with the tube hidden, it was obvious that there was something wrong with Aman. It was in his stillness and his open eyes. Once, in their house in Queens, Ajay had left a plastic bowl on a radiator overnight and the sides had drooped and sagged so that the bowl looked a little like an eye. Aman reminded Ajay of that bowl.

Ajay had not gone with his brother to the swimming pool on the day of the accident, because he had been reading a book and wanted to finish it. But he heard the ambulance siren from his aunt and uncle's house. The pool was only a few minutes away, and when he got there a crowd had gathered around the ambulance. Ajay saw his uncle first, in shorts and an undershirt, talking to a man inside the ambulance. His aunt was standing beside him. Then Ajay saw Aman on a stretcher, in blue shorts with a plastic mask over his nose and mouth. His aunt hurried over to take Ajay home. He cried as they walked, although he had been certain that Aman would be fine in a few days: in a Spider-Man comic he had just read, Aunt May had fallen into a coma and she had woken up perfectly fine. Ajay had cried simply because he felt crying was called for by the seriousness of the occasion. Perhaps this moment would mark the beginning of his future greatness. From that day on, Ajay found it hard to cry in front of his family. Whenever tears started coming, he felt like a liar. If he loved his brother, he knew, he would not have thought about himself as the ambulance had pulled away, nor would he talk with God at night about becoming famous.

When Ajay's mother returned to Aman's room with coffee and cookies, she sometimes talked to Ajay about Aman. She told him that when Aman was six he had seen a children's television show that had a character named Chunu, which was Aman's nickname, and he had thought the show was based on his own life. But most days Ajay went into the lounge to read. There was a TV in the corner and a lamp near a window that looked out over a parking lot. It was the perfect place to read. Ajay liked fantasy novels where the hero, who was preferably under the age of twenty-five, had an undiscovered talent that made him famous when it was revealed. He could read for hours without interruption, and sometimes when Vinod came to drive Ajay and his mother home from the hospital it was hard for him to remember the details of the real day that had passed.

One evening when he was in the lounge, he saw a rock star being interviewed on *Entertainment Tonight*. The musician, dressed in a sleeveless undershirt that revealed a swarm of tattoos on his arms and shoulders, had begun to shout at the audience, over his interviewer, "Don't watch me! Live your life! I'm not you!" Filled with a sudden desire to do something, Ajay hurried out of the television lounge and stood on the sidewalk in front of the hospital entrance. But he did not know what to do. It was cold and dark and there was an enormous moon. Cars leaving the parking lot stopped one by one at the edge of the road. Ajay watched as they waited for an opening in the traffic, their brake lights glowing.

"Are things getting worse?" Ajay asked God. The weekend before had been Thanksgiving. Christmas soon would come, and a new year would start, a year during which Aman would not have talked or walked. Suddenly Ajay understood hopelessness. Hopelessness felt very much like fear. It involved a clutching in the stomach and a numbness in the arms and legs.

"What do you think?" God answered.

"They seem to be."

"At least Aman's hospital hasn't forced him out."

"At least Aman isn't dead. At least Daddy's Greyhound bus has never skidded off a bridge." Lately Ajay had begun talking much more quickly to God than he used to. Before, when he had talked to God, Ajay would think of what God would say in response before he said anything. Now Ajay spoke without knowing how God might respond.

"You shouldn't be angry at me." God sighed. God was wearing his usual cardigan. "You can't understand why I do what I do."

"You should explain better, then."

"Christ was my son. I loved Job. How long did Ram have to live in a forest?"

"What does that have to do with me?" This was usually the cue for discussing Ajay's prospects. But hopelessness made the future feel even more frightening than the present.

"I can't tell you what the connection is, but you'll be proud of yourself."

They were silent for a while.

"Do you love me truly?" Ajay asked.

"Yes."

"Will you make Aman normal?" As soon as Ajay asked the question, God ceased to be real. Ajay knew then that he was alone, lying under his blankets, his face exposed to the cold dark.

"I can't tell you the future," God said softly. These were words that Ajay already knew.

"Just get rid of the minutes when Aman lay on the bottom of the pool. What are three minutes to you?"

"Presidents die in less time than that. Planes crash in less time than that."

Ajay opened his eyes. His mother was on her side and she had a blanket pulled up to her neck. She looked like an ordinary woman. It surprised him that you couldn't tell, looking at her, that she had a son who was brain-dead.

In fact, things were getting worse. Putting away his mother's mattress and his own in a closet in the morning, getting up very early so he could use the bathroom before his aunt or uncle did, spending so many hours in the hospital — all this had given Ajay the reassuring sense that real life was in abeyance, and that what was happening was unreal. He and his mother and brother were just waiting to make a long-delayed bus trip. The bus would come eventually to carry them to Queens, where he would return to school at P.S. 20 and to Sunday afternoons spent at the Hindi movie theater under the trestle for the 7 train. But now Ajay was starting to understand that the world was always real, whether you were reading a book or sleeping, and that it eroded you every day.

He saw the evidence of this erosion in his mother, who had grown severe and unforgiving. Usually when Vinod brought her and Ajay home from the hospital, she had dinner with the rest of the family. After his mother helped his aunt wash the dishes, the two women watched theological action movies. One night, in spite of a headache that had made her sit with her eyes closed all afternoon, she ate dinner, washed dishes, sat down in front of the TV. As soon as the movie was over, she went upstairs, vomited, and lay on her mattress with a wet towel over her forehead. She asked Ajay to massage her neck and shoulders. As he did so, Ajay noticed that she was crying. The tears frightened Ajay and made him angry. "You shouldn't have watched TV," he said accusingly.

"I have to," she said. "People will cry with you once, and they will cry with you a second time. But if you cry a third time, people will say you are boring and always crying."

Ajay did not want to believe what she had said, but her cynicism made him think that she must have had conversations with his aunt and uncle that he did not know about. "That's not true," he told her, massaging her scalp. "Uncle is kind. Auntie Aruna is always kind."

"What do you know?" She shook her head, freeing herself from Ajay's fingers. She stared at him. Upside down, her face looked unfamiliar and terrifying. "If God lets Aman live long enough, you will become a stranger too. You will say, 'I have been unhappy for so long because of Aman, now I don't want to talk about him or look at him.' Don't think I don't know you," she said.

Suddenly Ajay hated himself. To hate himself was to see himself as the opposite of everything he wanted to be: short instead of tall, fat instead of thin. When he brushed his teeth that night, he looked at his face: his chin was round and fat as a heel. His nose was so broad that he had once been able to fit a small rock in one nostril.

His father was also being eroded. Before the accident, Ajay's father loved jokes—he could do perfect imitations—and Ajay had felt lucky to have him as a father. (Once, Ajay's father had convinced his own mother that he was possessed by the ghost of a British man.) And even after the accident, his father had impressed Ajay with the patient loyalty of his weekly bus journeys. But now his father was different.

One Saturday afternoon, as Ajay and his father were returning from the hospital, his father slowed the car without warning and turned into the dirt parking lot of a bar that looked as though it had originally been a small house. It had a pitched roof with a black tarp. At the edge of the lot stood a tall neon sign of an orange hand lifting a mug of sudsy golden beer. Ajay had never seen anybody drink except in the movies. He wondered whether his father was going to ask for directions to somewhere, and if so, to where.

His father said, "One minute," and they climbed out of the car.

They went up wooden steps into the bar. Inside, it was dark and smelled of cigarette smoke and something stale and sweet. The floor was linoleum like the kitchen at his aunt and uncle's. There was a bar with stools around it, and a basketball game played on a television bolted against the ceiling, like the one in Aman's hospital room.

His father stood by the bar waiting for the bartender to notice him. His father had a round face and was wearing a white shirt and dark dress pants, as he often did on the weekend, since it was more economical to have the same clothes for the office and home.

The bartender came over. "How much for a Budweiser?" his father asked.

It was a dollar fifty. "Can I buy a single cigarette?" He did not have to buy; the bartender would just give him one. His father helped Ajay up onto a stool and sat down himself. Ajay looked around and wondered what would happen if somebody started a knife fight. When his father had drunk half his beer, he carefully lit the cigarette. The bartender was standing at the end of the bar. There were only two other men in the place. Ajay was disappointed that there were no women wearing dresses slit all the way up their thighs. Perhaps they came in the evenings.

His father asked him if he had ever watched a basketball game all the way through.

"I've seen the Harlem Globetrotters."

His father smiled and took a sip. "I've heard they don't play other teams, because they can defeat everyone else so easily."

"They only play against each other, unless there is an emergency — like in the cartoon, when they play against the aliens to save the Earth," Ajay said.

"Aliens?"

Ajay blushed as he realized his father was teasing him.

When they left, the light outside felt too bright. As his father opened the car door for Ajay, he said, "I'm sorry." That's when Ajay first felt that his father might have done something wrong. The thought made him worry. Once they were on the road, his father said gently, "Don't tell your mother."

Fear made Ajay feel cruel. He asked his father, "What do you think about when you think of Aman?"

Instead of becoming sad, Ajay's father smiled. "I am surprised by how strong he is. It's not easy for him to keep living. But even before, he was strong. When he was interviewing for high school scholarships, one interviewer asked him, 'Are you a thinker or a doer?' He laughed and said, 'That's like asking, "Are you an idiot or a moron?" ' "

From then on they often stopped at the bar on the way back from the hospital. Ajay's father always asked the bartender for a cigarette before he sat down, and during the ride home he always reminded Ajay not to tell his mother.

Ajay found that he himself was changing. His superstitions were becoming extreme. Now when he walked around the good-luck tree he punched it, every other time, hard, so that his knuckles hurt. Afterward, he would hold his breath for a moment longer than he thought he could bear, and ask God to give the unused breaths to Aman.

In December, a place opened in one of the good long-term care facilities. It was in New Jersey. This meant that Ajay and his mother could move back to New York and live with his father again. This was the news Ajay's father brought when he arrived for a two-week holiday at Christmas.

Ajay felt the clarity of panic. Life would be the same as before the accident but also unimaginably different. He would return to P.S. 20, while Aman continued to be fed through a tube in his abdomen. Life would be Aman's getting older and growing taller than their parents but having less consciousness than even a dog, which can become excited or afraid.

Ajay decided to use his devotion to shame God into fixing Aman. The fact that two religions regarded the coming December days as holy ones suggested to Ajay that prayers during this time would be especially potent. So he prayed whenever he thought of it—at his locker, even in the middle of a quiz. His mother wouldn't let him fast, but he started throwing away the lunch he took to school. And when his mother prayed in the morning, Ajay watched to make sure that she bowed at least once toward each of the postcards of deities. If she did not, he bowed three times to the possibly offended god on the postcard. He had noticed that his father finished his prayers in less time than it took to brush his teeth. And so now, when his father began praying in the morning, Ajay immediately crouched down beside him, because he knew his father would be embarrassed to get up first. But Ajay found it harder and harder to drift in the rhythm of sung prayers or into his nightly conversations with God. How could chanting and burning incense undo three minutes of a sunny August afternoon? It was like trying to move a sheet of blank paper from one end of a table to the other by blinking so fast that you started a breeze.

On Christmas Eve his mother asked the hospital chaplain to come to Aman's room and pray with them. The family knelt together beside Aman's bed.

Afterward the chaplain asked her whether she would be attending Christmas services. "Of course, Father," she said.

"I'm also coming," Ajay said.

The chaplain turned toward Ajay's father, who was sitting in a wheelchair because there was nowhere else to sit.

"I'll wait for God at home," he said.

That night, Ajay watched *It's a Wonderful Life* on television. To him, the movie meant that happiness arrived late, if ever. Later, when he got in bed and closed his eyes, God appeared. There was little to say.

"Will Aman be better in the morning?"

"No."

"Why not?"

"When you prayed for the math exam, you could have asked for Aman to get better, and instead of your getting an A, Aman would have woken."

This was so ridiculous that Ajay opened his eyes. His father was sleeping nearby on folded-up blankets. Ajay felt disappointed at not feeling guilt. Guilt might have contained some hope that God existed.

When Ajay arrived at the hospital with his father and mother the next morning, Aman was asleep, breathing through his mouth while a nurse poured a can of Isocal into his stomach through the yellow tube. Ajay had not expected that Aman would have recovered; nevertheless, seeing him that way put a weight in Ajay's chest.

The Christmas prayers were held in a large, mostly empty room: people in chairs sat next to people in wheelchairs. His father walked out in the middle of the service.

Later, Ajay sat in a corner of Aman's room and watched his parents. His mother was reading a Hindi women's magazine to Aman while she shelled peanuts into her lap. His father was reading a thick red book in preparation for a civil service exam. The day wore on. The sky outside grew dark. At some point Ajay began to cry. He tried to be quiet. He did not want his parents to notice his tears and think that he was crying for Aman, because in reality he was crying for how difficult his own life was.

His father noticed first. "What's the matter, hero?"

His mother shouted, "What happened?" and she sounded so alarmed it was as if Ajay were bleeding.

"I didn't get any Christmas presents. I need a Christmas present," Ajay shouted. "You didn't buy me a Christmas present." And then, because he had revealed his own selfishness, Ajay let himself sob. "You have to give me something. I should get something for all this." Ajay clenched his hands and wiped his face with his fists. "Each time I come here I should get something."

His mother pulled him up and pressed him into her stomach. His father came and stood beside them. "What do you want?" his father asked.

Ajay had no prepared answer for this.

"What do you want?" his mother repeated.

The only thing he could think was, "I want to eat pizza and I want candy."

His mother stroked his hair and called him her little baby. She kept wiping his face with a fold of her sari. When at last he stopped crying, they decided that Ajay's father should take him back to his aunt and uncle's. On the way, they stopped at a mini-mall. It was a little after five, and the streetlights were on. Ajay and his father did not take off their winter coats as they ate, in a pizzeria staffed by Chinese people. While he chewed, Ajay closed his eyes and tried to imagine God looking like Clark Kent, wearing a cardigan and eyeglasses, but he could not. Afterward, Ajay and his father went next door to a magazine shop and Ajay got a bag of Three Musketeers bars and a bag of Reese's peanut butter cups, and then he was tired and ready for home.

He held the candy in his lap while his father drove in silence. Even through the plastic, he could smell the sugar and chocolate. Some of the houses outside were dark, and others were outlined in Christmas lights.

After a while Ajay rolled down the window slightly. The car filled with wind. They passed the building where Aman's accident had occurred. Ajay had not walked past it since the accident. When they drove by, he usually looked away. Now he tried to spot the fenced swimming pool at the building's side. He wondered whether the pool that had pressed itself into Aman's mouth and lungs and stomach had been drained, so that nobody would be touched by its unlucky waters. Probably it had not been emptied until fall. All summer long, people must have swum in the pool and sat on its sides, splashing their feet in the water, and not known that his brother had lain for three minutes on its concrete bottom one August afternoon.

CHAPTER FIVE

ENERGY

> ## In this chapter you will:
>
> - Develop specific strategies to maximize reader interest in your work
> - Manipulate point of view and pace
> - Minimize pitfalls that deplete energy in writing: predictability, cliché, abstraction, and passivity

Are you creating work readers are truly excited to read? Or are you writing stuff people read only because they feel they have to: It's for class, or they're polite, or they're your friend?

Most of us get bored fairly easily. Competing for our time and attention are pages and pages of great writing, social media, and work, a need for down time, many responsibilities and multiple distractions. As writers, we have to be exceptionally creative—perhaps more than ever before—in order to capture and keep our reader's attention. You can make *everything* you write more attractive to readers by paying attention to a core strategy: **energy**. Energy gives your writing power, drama, originality, and life. Energy is what makes your creative writing stand out from everyone else's. Building on skills from previous chapters—writing what you know and writing in images—this chapter presents specific methods for using energy to create work that is interesting and original.

THE PRINCIPLES OF ENERGY

Specific techniques allow you to increase the energy and interest level in all types of creative writing, whether you are creating a poem, a story, a micro-memoir, or a play. When we look at the kind of writing that appeals most to readers, we find four central principles of energy—subject choice, leaps, sparky words, and super-specifics. Writers create and modulate energy through:

1. **Subject choice.** A good writer can make any topic interesting. You already know that subjects that will lead to energetic writing are those (a) that you experience firsthand, (b) that you wonder about passionately, and (c) about which you are the sole expert. Here, you'll discover ways to use **heat** and **movement** to showcase the energy in a topic and rivet your reader.

2. **Leaps.** Good writers leave gaps on purpose so that readers have the pleasure of filling in pieces of the picture on their own. Leaping is one of the most effective energizing techniques available and one of the simplest to master.

3. **Sparky word choices.** Some words spark and sizzle and pop (like the words *spark*, *sizzle*, and *pop*). Other words (think of a legal brief, a handbook, or anything dull you have read lately) make the reader's eyes glaze over: "Student research abstract platform decisions will be considered until the mandatory deadline occurs." Did you even take that sentence in? Could anyone? No spark, no energy. When writers fail to attend carefully to the energy in each word, they risk losing the reader.

4. **Super-specifics.** We've talked already about the power of close observation and the necessity of using details and images—write what you see, not what you think. But there's more to that story. Choosing ultra-super-specific details and using them artfully, such as in **lists** and **litanies**, creates vital energy.

Nine Moves That Increase Energy	Nine Moves That Decrease Energy
• Movement	• Nothing happening
• Heat	• Predictability, sameness, steadiness
• Leaps and gaps that create reader engagement	• Thinking aloud on the page, musing—**filtering**
• Action that has consequences (something could go wrong)	• Extended discussions of feelings, emotions, mental states
• Dialogue that surprises us	• Explaining to the reader
• Sudden and unexpected word choices	• Lack of sparky words, action, or dialogue
• Up-close details that make a scene pop to life	• Vague or generalized writing—we can't see images
• Lists	• **Abstraction**—we can't see images
• Artful repetition	• Length

Refer to the chart to refresh yourself on the creative choices that typically increase energy and the choices that *may* run the risk of boring your reader.

Subject: Focus on What's Fascinating

What to choose for a subject? What only you know about, and no one else. Everyone knows what it is like to grow up, turn seven years old, struggle with a mother's rules. But no one knows

> *I merely took the energy it takes to pout and wrote some blues.*
> —DUKE ELLINGTON

what it was like to turn seven inside Apartment 8R on Prospect Avenue, where a kid sat on a cake, and the mother drank three martinis, and all this happened before noon. Close in on the subject matter you know best.

Most people know high school graduation, loneliness, flat tires. But no one knows *your* specific experience. It doesn't matter if you are writing poetry, fantasy fiction, love letters, short stories, or screenplays. And you do not need to write your autobiography. It's your specific repertoire of observations, access to human emotions, and the details that makes for an energized subject choice.

If you can *put* yourself there, using only the power of your mind — whether it's part of your autobiography or not — you can write it. You might be able to create energy and grip your readers by engaging with powerful subject matter quite far from your own everyday experience — you simply have to immerse yourself in your subject and be able to write what you see before you, *as though* it's coming from firsthand knowledge.

You can tell you have chosen a good, alive subject if it gives you energy to work on it. A good creative writing topic unnerves you a little. When a subject is alive, it's going to shift as you work, too. You'll start out writing about your relationship with a sibling and realize you are also writing about your parents' relationship. Some students feel uncomfortable with this fact — subjects shift and drift. But good subjects are alive, not static. If you already know everything you are going to say about your subject, you might struggle to keep the writing energized.

> *There is a vitality, a life force, an energy, a quickening, that is translated through you into action, and because there is only one of you in all time, this expression is unique.*
> —MARTHA GRAHAM

Tricky Topics. Some topics are hard to make interesting, though clever writers always find a way. Neighbors you know nothing about, historical figures you're only mildly familiar with, general settings, stereotypical characters — these are all energy black holes. Subjects that force you to write about passive conditions — dreaming, powerful but vague feeling states, falling asleep, waking up, sitting at a desk, driving — are extremely difficult to infuse with energy. Conversely, you can write energetically when your focus is on the material you have at hand: last night's brawl at the Dirty Parrot. Your rich aunt's summer visit to your trailer park. A pack of high school punks wreaking havoc after school, Robin Hood–style, in the Sunset Heights subdivision at the edge of Detroit — that's the kind of subject that is already infused with energy.

You don't need to reveal your deepest, darkest secrets, but you do need to make readers feel you are giving them your best stuff. What do you know about that is strange, interesting, unusual? What kinds of things have you seen that are outside of most people's normal day-to-day experience? Use a microscope to view your life, the lives of people you know, your past, and your family's history. If you haven't been to a war zone, it may be very difficult for you to create energy in your piece of writing. If all your images come from what you have learned from television, video games, and movies, your writing is likely to be flat and not energized with interesting, closely observed specifics and deeply personal passion.

This is especially true when you are writing speculative pieces. Be careful not to use the same worlds, the same subjects, and the same details everyone else uses. When you read Brenda Peynado's short story "What We Lost" on page 223 note how she creates energy by choosing a town and a family that are very realistic in many ways; she knows her subject and when events spin out of control, the energy comes from her ability to make her subject believable. We go along for the ride because we trust her; the piece has energy because the subject — a place where people are losing parts of themselves — is fresh and well observed and inherently fascinating.

Tricky topics also include those which your teacher and classmates may define as triggering or inappropriate. While no one wants to censor writers or block creative expression, a classroom and writing workshop is a specific community; instructors and students often set guidelines for subject matter based on their experience with how to best create a healthy, positive workshop that respects everyone in the class. Some schools also have specific policies around subject matter that you'll need to take into account.

Movement and Heat. **Movement** is energy. People and things in action are going to attract reader attention; passivity is going to cause your reader's attention to fade quickly. Look carefully in the subjects you choose for the places where there is movement — action: noses falling off, arms dropping off. Poems not written, but nevertheless leading happy lives in far-flung places. In Rick Moody's "Boys" on page 219, the writing focuses completely on the energy displayed in various physical actions and movement; the entire piece is a list of images of boys in motion. In "Genealogy," the poem by Betsy Sholl, the parents and the child careen through life, doing significant damage. Characters in "Pretty Ice" by Mary Robison on page 169 and "Surrounded by Sleep" by Akhil Sharma on page 174 are almost always on the move, even if it's simply across the room to get closer to the person who is in the most pain. Steer your focus as a writer, in every subject you choose, toward what is active, moving, and most alive within that subject.

But movement for the sake of movement, action without meaning, isn't enough. To keep your reader riveted to your pages, you must steer toward the **heat** in the action. Heat is the part of your subject that has the most power to affect other people. Heat involves telling the truth, even when that is painful. And to move toward the heat is to move toward the part of the subject that is most difficult, most intense, most pleasurable, most alive. Ira Sukrungruang brilliantly steers his piece, "Chop Suey," on page 74 toward the heat — that terrible moment when his mother is cruelly mocked. Vincent Scarpa's "I Go Back to Berryman's" on page 76 similarly focuses on what's most hot — difficult, unpleasant, even shocking — in the trailer park.

Every subject has dull facets and every subject has interesting active parts to it. You could write about writer's block — you sit there, you worry, you think about how lonely you are — and bore us quite easily. Or, you could write about writer's block as John Brehm does in his poem on page 43 and move directly into the part of the subject that has the most energy: There are *so many* poems not written, you could line them up and they'd stretch across the entire United States. And, not only are there so many, the unwritten poems are magnificent poems! They're better than the poems that he has written. The subject of writer's block can be energized by looking for movement and heat.

Jamila Osman uses the technique of heat in her micro-memoir "Fluency" on page 214. She writes deftly about two sexual assaults, both events pressed tightly into one sentence. In choosing a subject with so much heat, Osman creates a necessary connection to her reader: I'm worried about silence, she's saying. I'm worried about whispers and about silence. Brian Turner uses the technique of heat in his poem, "What Every Soldier Should Know," on page 213. He doesn't write *about* waking up in a war zone. He doesn't write about generally feeling scared. Every day, every hour, he shows us exactly what it's like to know you are in danger of being shot, of being blown up. He tightly packages all that heat in finely wrought couplets, loaded with details of his daily life; we feel the heat.

No matter how small or seemingly simple and everyday your subject, don't circle around, wasting time in the shower or having a character wake up: drive directly toward the most essential heat. Beth Ann Fennelly is expert at finding heat in her everyday subjects. In writing about her mother in "Two Phone Conversations," on page 216, she chooses two moments, drinking and trying to cover up drinking, to illustrate the heat in the mother's secrecy and also in their relationship. In "Why I'm Switching Salons," Fennelly focuses tightly on the heat that comes from shame and pride. She's been called out as vain. And she's not having it.

If you are writing flash and/or micro, you have to train yourself to focus on the heat in your subject—there's not room for *anything but the heat*. To be an excellent **miniaturist**, a writer of **flash** and **micro**—and it's harder than it looks—you have to couple interesting movement with true heat.

Leaps: The Energetic Power of Gaps

Creative writing isn't an explanation for things. It's a show. To keep your reader with you, you have to withhold the urge to explain. It can be hard to remember this because as writers we often get caught up in our words and ideas, perhaps falling a bit in love with the sound of our own voice. But the reader *wants* to figure things out. Spelling everything out, providing detailed transitions, explaining and reviewing and going over it again—that may be effective for your chemistry textbook or your term paper, but it's detrimental to creative writing. Explanation kills energy and it's annoying; it's like having someone telling you what you can know for yourself.

Instead of explaining things, focus on the power created by leaping from one thing to another: A **leap** is a quick move from one thing to something unexpected:

> One of my parents I drank, the other I dreamed.

Leaps are the places where the writer purposely leaves something out, skips ahead, or changes topic. Betsy Sholl, in "Genealogy" on page 213, does all three in her single-line poetry. Compare a sentence with no leaps, no movement, no surprise, and no juxtaposition:

> My mother is a very difficult person who creates many challenges for me in my life and my father similarly can be extremely difficult because he is complicated but I have hopes and dreams for our relationship at times but not always.

Leaps create **gaps.** A gap is when there's something on the page but you, the reader, know more than just what's on the page. You're able to fill in the blank space. In "Genealogy" the metaphors create gaps. We know the parents are complex and challenging; we have to fill in for ourselves exactly how.

In "Fluency," on page 214, Jamila Osman literally leaves gaps, using blanks instead of words; note how powerful it is as a reader when you are asked to fill in. Och Gonzalez leaves gaps in her micro-memoir "What I Do on My Terrace Is None of Your Business"—she leaps into the story and creates energy by allowing us to spy on her neighbor with her. The background situation is never explained. These gaps allow the reader to actively participate in creating the image, thought, or meaning. We "leap" to conclusions, and that's a large part of what makes reading so rewarding: We co-create the experience with the author.

Once you start using the leaping technique and attempt to create meaningful gaps for your reader to fill in, you will be amazed at how much explanation you can leave out. Readers are pretty savvy—they figure out a lot from just a few hints.

There are many places in your writing where you will want to deploy leaps. Here are a few suggestions.

Format Leaps. Even the way you lay your piece out on the page offers an opportunity to play with leaps and gaps. Notice in "What Every Soldier Should Know," on page 213 that the couplets (two-line stanzas) force the reader to make leaps from section to section—fourteen leaps! The poet, Brian Turner, didn't want the lulling calm of a prose poem or the warmth of long stanzas. Rapid-fire couplets keep the reader hopping, on the move, an effect that suits Turner's subject extremely well.

Compare the way "Boys" on page 219 looks on the page—giant blocks of text, no paragraph, no gaps—not one chance to pause, to catch your breath, to fill in your own reactions or assumptions. The author, Rick Moody, chooses to pack his single-paragraph short story about adolescent males with masses of action, and the relentlessness of the prose mirrors the relentlessness of this stage of life. He creates energy by *not* allowing your eye to leap or escape—there's no way out of growing up in "Boys."

Symbol Leaps. When you employ leaps in your work, you are comprehensible and interesting on the first reading, but the aware reader knows there's more there. The reader gets a full, confusion-free experience the first read. On a second and third reading, the piece reveals more information, more connections. For example, the first time you read Raymond Carver's "Cathedral" you may be more caught up in the dynamics between the characters. On a second and third read, you discover there are many layers in the piece—every single detail, every line of dialogue, and every bit of action has been chosen to create echoes to other parts of the story. The cathedral allows a sighted man to realize ways in which he has been blind; he makes a leap and so do we.

In "Pretty Ice," another short story that uses symbols — rich metaphors — throughout, multiple readings allow for more productive and memorable leaps to new meaning. Noticing a young tree encased in ice — that tree will never be right again — allows us to pair the young tree with a young woman encased in grief; she'll never develop properly either, likely never to experience love. The leaps set up by symbols make literature powerful and resonant.

> *When in doubt, make a fool of yourself. There is a microscopically thin line between being brilliantly creative and acting like the most gigantic idiot on earth. So what the hell, leap.*
> —CYNTHIA HEIMEL

Object Leaps. Read the following excerpt, from Jessica Shattuck's story "Bodies" which is presented in full at the end of this chapter on page 291.

> In the fluorescent light of the refrigerator, the halved parsnips look naked — pale and fleshy as limbs. Annie pauses before pulling them out. A refrigerator is like a hospital, a bright place that is not cheerful. A protective but uncertain place to wait.

Notice the leap: a woman opens a fridge and thinks of a hospital. She makes a leap from one object to another, and we understand something of the nature of her struggle. Compare the writing above to this prose excerpt from another writer, a beginning student.

> When the alarm clock went off, I woke up and I reached over and turned it off and got out of bed. I walked across the room and I went to the bathroom which was close by and when I went in, I turned on the light so I could see. I was wondering what I was going to do today. I was just waking up. I had a bad case of bedhead.

Which of these two excerpts has more energy? Why?

In the first example, we have leaps and surprises. In the second excerpt, we find a blow-by-blow description of a fairly typical morning — the opposite of leaping. Here, things are filled in completely, with no surprises. Everything is predictable and explained step-by-step, and the energy is low. Would you read this story in full by choice? Does the paragraph have any energy at all?

In the professional pieces included at the end of this chapter, you can find dozens of examples of object leaps — this technique is the fundamental to energized writing. Here are four examples of leaps:

If you hear gunfire on a Thursday afternoon,
it could be for a wedding, or it could be for you.

—WHAT EVERY SOLDIER SHOULD KNOW, page 213

A rider? A light turned on in his eyes, suddenly as blue as his scrubs. He put his fists up and bounced them, a cowboy bounding over the plains.
No, I said. *A writer.* Which now seemed to require a gesture, so I help up my imaginary pen and wiggled it.

—HEATING AND COOLING, "Small Talk at Evanston
General," page 215

. . . one boy wears a hat, the other boy thinks hats are ridiculous.

—BOYS, page 219

All a Vision Quest requires is a dash of mystical shaman, a spirit animal (wolf usually, but birds of prey are on the upswing this year), and the approximation of a peyote experience.

—WELCOME TO YOUR AUTHENTIC INDIAN EXPERIENCE™, page 226

When you keep your writer's eye tightly focused on things that don't go together, things that require the reader to build the bridge in her own mind, sparks fly.

Dialogue Leaps. One of the most important places you'll want to leap is in dialogue. Nothing is deadlier to creative writing than dialogue that explains and tells. It takes most writers some practice to leap in dialogue; most real-life conversations are filled with explanation and boring patches. You'll want to pay close attention to how real-life speech sounds while crafting your dialogue to keep the energy high.

Here, the dialogue lacks energy because it has no leaps or gaps. Everything spoken is exactly what the character means to say. This is seen as less effective and less interesting than dialogue that involves crafted leaps.

> JOEY: What's wrong, Emily? You look really sad. Are you blue because
>   you got a D—on your history test this morning in first period? It
>   seemed like you were really struggling with that test.
> EMILY: Thanks for noticing, Joey. That test was so hard. I'm really
>   feeling bad about this.
> JOEY: That is sad.
> EMILY: I may fail.
> JOEY: Wow. You might fail history?

Both characters are on the same topic, plodding along. Explaining. Carefully, slowly, boringly, filling in all the gaps. In good creative writing, dialogue does just the opposite: It bristles with energy because each character has his or her own agenda, and the agendas conflict, causing gaps, leaps. Good dialogue is like a tennis match. The energy moves back and forth, with equal force on both sides.

Consider this example of crisp, energetic dialogue from *The Sopranos* by James Manos Jr. and David Chase. Tony, the mob moss with a therapist, and his daughter Meadow, a high school student, are visiting colleges. Meadow comes out of the admissions office, and her father asks her how it went.

> MEADOW: They've got a 48 to 52 male-female ratio which is
>   great—strong liberal arts program, and this cool Olin Arts Center
>   for music. Usual programs abroad—China, India —
> TONY: You're just applying here and you're already leaving?

Notice the energy. Meadow is specific. She broadcasts her agenda. She leaps from social benefits to infrastructure to study abroad. Tony's agenda probably isn't for his daughter to enjoy the benefits of an equal male-female ratio. When he asks her for more information, the reader *leaps*: We know he doesn't care how she answers the question. He is not asking her *for more information*. There's a gap in what he says—on the surface—and in what he intends. Meadow lists what she likes about the college. She doesn't really care what her father thinks at this point. Tony doesn't want her to go away, to be too far out of his control. No filler. No explanation. The leaps and gaps leave plenty of room for the reader to figure things out—that's the pleasure of energy. We readers are set up by the author to know *more* than the characters themselves. The dialogue leaps, and we zip along to keep up.

By leaping, a writer generates **reader involvement**. Information about conflict, values, and character comes out between the lines. We readers (or viewers) know, without it being said—this information comes through in the gaps, called the **subtext**—that Tony wants his daughter to have a good education and a life that he understands. We can tell he is embarrassed by his lack of formal education. We sense he is afraid of her leaving home. It is clear that Meadow isn't afraid of her father. She's mostly concerned with her ability to enjoy the social benefits of her educational experience.

Line Leaps. In poetry, it can be helpful to think of *every single line* as leaping to some new place. If you think of lines as leaps, rather than opportunities for explanation (a prose move), your poetry will have more energy and more excitement.

In Lee Herrick's "My California" on page 72 notice what he leaves out: commentary on his complaints about issues in his home state and explanation about why farmer's markets are a symbol of healthy communities. He leaps from image to image, and you the reader fill in your own understanding of how he feels and what his opinions are.

In Kim Addonizio's "First Poem for You" (page 121), she leaps from line to line through the couple's love-making to imagining death as the only thing that could separate the two; she leaves out everything else. Natalie Diaz also uses the power of leaps to highlight the energetic signature of mental illness in a family in "My Brother at 3 a.m." (page 165). All she gives you is the brother and his dialogue, and the reader fills in the emotions of despair and grief and fear. She leaves all that off the page, trusting her reader to "get it."

PRACTICE 1

LEAPS IN DRAMA

Read Kristina Halvorson's play, "Now We're Really Getting Somewhere" on page 240. What do you know about the characters that's not actually on the page? Describe at least four different leaps or gaps you find in the play.

Sparky Word Choices

To create and sustain energy on the page, keep in mind that every word matters. With each word choice, you must deliver information-rich writing, using specific insider details and a vocabulary rich with specificity. We'll look at another way to achieve this goal — making sure everything is specific, detailed, vibrant, and visual — in the next section of this chapter.

As often as possible, you want to stud your writing with energy by choosing words that create a spark for your reader. A **sparky word choice** is a word choice that your reader didn't expect. Word choice is covered in more detail in Chapter Three; revisit page 88 for a refresher on this core component of creative writing.

Word packages are overly familiar phrases in which perfectly fine words lose energy because they are constantly yoked together: *beautiful blue eyes, red rose, gaping hole, awkward moment.* Word packages are the opposite of sparky word choices. Good writers enjoy busting up word packages and recombining their elements to create original effects: *gaping moment, awkward rose.* See the difference? When thinking about how to increase the energy of your writing, it's worth checking every single word you use to evaluate how much energy the word brings to your piece in relationship to the other words you've chosen.

You might have a great subject and terrific leaps on every level, but if the words you are using are dead, flat, or abstract, energy will leak out of your piece with a slow, steady *whoosh*.

It can be helpful to shine a spotlight on individual words in the professional pieces you read, looking for sparky word choices—words that have a pop. For example, in the short story "Welcome to Your Authentic Indian Experience™" by Rebecca Roanhorse on page 226, we can scan through the story and note each word that jumps off the page and create a list of sparking words—simple words, but not words you necessarily run into every day. These are words that create a tiny flash in the reader's mind, such as:

Vision Quest	*Crazy Horse Experience*
dash	*Sioux*
birds of prey	*artiste*
spirit animal	*Pima*
peyote	*bushy*
Trueblood	*loincloth*
Indian-sounding	*ass*
Depp	

Every single sentence in this short story has at least one sparky word, and often more:

"**DarAnne** and her **crew** will put you on the **guys-who-are-assholes** list…"

Roanhorse packs her prose with specific, interesting, lively words that have terrific energy, and her sentences sing.

PRACTICE 2

IDENTIFYING ENERGY IN WORDS

Rank each of the following words, using a scale of 0 to 10. A 10 is high octane, high energy; a 0 is a low-energy word, a word with very low pulse rate. Do you notice anything about what the 5+ words have in common?

Frizzed	Blue	Wondering	Spatula
Surge	Beautiful	Understanding	Apartment
Very	Flapjack	Important	It

Consider the differences between the two words in each of the following pairs:

road	avenue
jerk	unpleasant person
party	reception
fun	enjoyable
tunes	aural interlude

Many writers, when they are starting out, feel obligated to sound "writerly." They choose words that sound bookish and important, the right-hand column, above, rather than the left.

Some overly **writerly words** include many adverbs (*suddenly, finally, interestingly, absolutely*) and clichéd shortcuts to rendering emotions: *she furrowed her brow, he raised an eyebrow, tears streamed from her face, his jaw dropped.* Use what you learned in Part One, and write what you see: What does your character *really* do when he is frustrated, skeptical, or shocked? Use the words that describe your actual scene, not the general population's explanatory shorthand.

Consider the following paragraph by Rick Moody, from his energy-rich short story "Boys" on page 219.

> Boys enter the house, boys enter the house. Boys, and with them the ideas of boys (ideas leaden, reductive, inflexible), enter the house. Boys, two of them, wound into hospital packaging, boys with infant pattern baldness, slung in the arms of parents, boys dreaming of breasts, enter the house. Twin boys, kettles on the boil, boys in hideous vinyl knapsacks that young couples from Edison, NJ, wear on their shirt fronts, knapsacks coated with baby saliva and staphylococcus and milk vomit, enter the house.

Compare this to the following paragraph. What do you notice about the differences in word choices?

> They were just typical kids. You know kids. The normal American kind. The boy was thinking about how he just wanted the day to end so he could get out of school and get to the project. He had been dreaming about this project for years. It was so great to finally be so close. So close. And yet so far, too. It seemed as though he and his buddy would never be able to really get there. Those afternoons were slow.

PRACTICE 3

IDENITFYING SPARKY WORD CHOICES

Read through the pieces at the end of this chapter, and make a list of sparky words — words that pop out as you scan the work of professional writers. From Osman on page 214, you might choose something you've never seen before: *tskedtskedtsked*. From Halvorson on page 240 you might be sparked by "Sales Jack." Find at least twenty-five words that grab your attention because they emit energy, a true spark.

PRACTICE 4

IDENTIFYING SPARKY WORD COMBINATIONS

Read through the pieces included in this chapter, beginning on page 213 and ending on page 246. From the set of pieces, locate at least six phrases in all that do not usually occur in that combination. *Wild horses* and *thin man* are word packages. You are looking for fresh, unusual combinations such as *elephant pants*, *Sleeping Tubby and Snow Weight*, *shirtsleeves aglow with torchlight*.

Super-Specifics

One of the most common questions students and writers hear back from teachers and editors is this: *Can you be more specific?* To sustain energy in your creative writing, in every genre, you'll want to hone your ability to notice specific details and choose precise words to describe those details.

Read the poem "What Every Soldier Should Know" by Brian Turner on page 213. Notice how Turner provides *images* from the war, and it's the details — the **super-specific** examples — that give this poem its energy. The Arabic words are super-specific — we hear the language he hears every day. How much it costs to hire an attacker versus a killer, RPGs, parachute bombs, "a sticky gel of homemade napalm," chai — his poem is powerful and effective because it is loaded with *super-specifics* — there are carefully observed specific details in every single line of the poem.

In Brian Arundel's "The Things I've Lost," the author uses the technique of super-specifics to create his entire micro-memoir. The piece is a list of highly detailed, carefully observed super-specifics: "black beret" not hat, "round, purple sunglasses" not shades, "a quarter inch off the tip of my left thumb, in 1987, while slicing Muenster cheese on an electric Hobart slicer" not "hurt."

Notice the words Arundel doesn't use: *stuff, things, items, contents, belongings.* He is a master of the super-specific.

Good writers get the real name, the actual address, the specific phrase, and the right translation, because the energy in writing comes from that exactness. Vague details and sparse details suck energy from your writing.

PRACTICE 5

READING FOR SUPER-SPECIFICS

Working from the various pieces in this chapter, make a list of ten super-specifics that, in your opinion, bring the most energy to the writing in these pages.

Filters

Vague and **under-detailed** writing usually lacks energy, as does writing that is filtered through a thinking process. When a writer describes *thinking* (*wondered, reflected, worried, thought, etc.*), the energy often decreases, sharply. These **filters**—writing filtered through a mental activity—are passive; filters can be detrimental to strong, energetic writing.

Envision a short story about a college freshman's visit to his physics professor's office. The purpose of the visit is to go over a flunked test. As he waits for his prof to call him into the office, the student thinks to himself, "I don't like this guy. I dread seeing this man. I wish I were anywhere else. I feel anxious." Perhaps the writer of the story describes the moment like this: "He was worried."

No action, just a guy, in a chair, *thinking*. He's not thinking particularly interesting thoughts—they're pretty much what we might predict if we passed by and saw this kid and knew the situation. The reader isn't getting to look at anything interesting, just a student sitting in a chair. A potentially dramatic, perhaps even meaningful experience—a painful conversation about a failed test—is about to take place; why can't we see that instead? Instead of reporting on generalized thoughts—a filtered experience—it might be more interesting for us as readers if we got to see the most exciting part of this experience, the part where the scene **turns**, as the student cleverly convinces the prof to change the grade. Showing us filtered thoughts—this generalized report of generic mental activity—profoundly lacks energy.

Instead of people's static thoughts, a better choice is to use images. Brian Turner doesn't tell the reader his thoughts about getting killed as a soldier: "I was afraid of basically everyone; it was awful. I was really scared." He shows us his fear with a singularly powerful image:

and any one of them
may dance over your body tomorrow.

However, if the speaker or character in your piece is thinking thoughts that are energized, fresh, and interesting—unfiltered—by all means, take us inside their head. Brian Arundel shows the reader his own thought process by revealing precisely how he changes his mind about politics as he gets older: "The thought that officials were somehow more evolved than those who elect them: in 1972, listening to my father explain the Watergate burglary." He doesn't write: "I lost hope in government." He shows the energy of his mind at work.

For quick reference, here is a list of common filter words. Try to show action or lively energetic mental activity instead.

seems	*wonders*
acknowledges	*claims*
advises	*concludes*
agrees	*declares*
allows	*disputes*
answers	*feels*
asserts	*remarks*
believes	*thinks*

These words, while useful for writing essays for academic classes, are the *opposite* of the words creative writers use. Expository essays appeal to the intellect, the head. Creative writing relies on activating the five senses—the body.

The best way to avoid filters is to avoid writing about trite situations where the character will be left alone with their thoughts, prone to brooding: solo car trips, waking up, airplane travel, staring out windows. You can avoid filtering by simply always having two or three characters onstage at once, never one character doing nothing but thinking.

Because writers tend to be observant, thoughtful, introspective people, it's natural for them to record thinking, observing, watching, musing. This is a mistake. Readers don't want a filter, a block, an *entity* processing information for them. We want it to feel like *we are actually seeing and experiencing* this, that it's happening before our eyes and to figure the thinking out for ourselves.

MANIPULATING ENERGY

Choose energetic subjects. Set up your writing so that you can leave things out and invite readers to make their own connections—to leap. Pay close attention to every single word. Don't leave characters alone with nothing to do but think; avoid describing bland mental activity; show the precise energy of a thought process. Whether you are a minimalist poet or a lush, expansive novelist, these are the basic principles that allow you to infuse your writing with energy.

As you practice the techniques presented in this chapter, consider two additional methods for modulating energy in your work: pace and point of view.

Pace

By increasing the **pace** of action, you increase the energy. However, once your reader adjusts to the speed, the energy flattens out again. Varying pace is a key to sustaining energy. After about three beats, or three "points," the reader is adjusted. It's time to change things up again. In "Genealogy", on page 213, Sholl sets the pace with "One of . . . , the other . . ." and "One of . . . , the other. . . ." She varies the pace by inserting "I."

Pacing requires variety and also being attentive to how much time passes through your paragraphs or stanzas. In Rick Moody's story "Boys," the author presents the intense, fast coming-of-age arc of boys' lives. Moody speeds time up and then slows it down, varying the pace. Use pace to create the effect you want on your reader. What you don't want to do is *just write*, laying down sentences or lines of poetry block by block like so much cord wood, oblivious to pace.

> *Vary the pace — one of the foundations of all good acting.*
> —ELLEN TERRY

Good writers, the ones we read again and again, use the full continuum of pace, the full range, just like good musicians do. Practice moving from slow to fast, and to medium. Change how far, how close you are when you are looking at the scene before you. Take a step back. What do you see now? Move in closer than is polite. What senses are engaged now? Practice getting fluid with your mental "camera" as a writer, and watch what happens to the pace of your writing on the page.

As the writer, you must consciously calibrate pace based on the effect you want to achieve. You may intuitively know that when you want to increase the energy of your writing, you use short sentences to indicate fast-paced action:

Scott grabbed her wallet. He grabbed his keys. He ran out the door. He jumped in the car. She never saw him again.

And when you want to slow down the pace, in order to show a process that is taking place over a long period of time, use a long sentence as Arundel does in "The Things I've Lost," when describing a slow shift in his growing-up process:

> Self-pity and -importance, at least most days, while striving to look beyond the borders of my own desires in a steady ascent that some might refer to as maturation.

Notice how Arundel creates energy, following that long, slow sentence with a crisp, tight one:

> The desire to remain in this country: since 2004.

Writing everything at a slow pace will bore your reader. Writing everything at a breakneck speed will tire your reader. It's *variety* of pace — slowing down, speeding up, slowing way down — that keeps the human mind intrigued, on point. Think about how a roller coaster works. It's not all whooshing downhill at 150 miles an hour. There's the slow climb. A short fast dip. A quicker climb. A pause at the top — then the giant fall. Think about driving at exactly seventy-five miles an hour on the highway, your car set on cruise control. After a while, have you noticed how that speed feels almost slow? Compare the experience of barely even poking along at six miles an hour, and then suddenly peeling out, getting to sixty in six seconds. You're going slower than seventy-five, but which feels faster? Which is more exciting? The energy is in the change of acceleration, not in top speed.

Rick Moody is a master of pace. Watch how he speeds up time in this passage from the story "Boys." (Moody is also a musician.)

> Boys enter the house carrying their father, slumped. Happens so fast. Boys rush into the house leading EMTs to the couch in the living room where the body lies, boys enter the house, boys enter the house, boys enter the house.

Moody puts single-word phrases at the ends of his sentences ("slumped") and uses sentences with missing pieces ("Happens so fast"). Those techniques add speed to the story, which is one long paragraph, isn't it? He repeats the word *boys* — a lot — and lists make his sentences jolt, surge, and compress. In his paragraph, he covers a whole childhood, which ends with the death of a father. That's a large scope for a short-short story! Moody packs in the detail. He uses pace to force the reader through the story, headlong.

And also notice how much detail he includes: Edison, NJ; balsamic vinegar; the Elys' yard. Pump action bb gun, Stilton cheese, mismatched tube socks. He binds the reader to his words by making every single one bristle with super-specificity.

PRACTICE 6

PACED SENTENCES

Write a paragraph about something that is very slow-paced by its nature (traffic jam, weeding an entire garden). Use very short sentences—two, three, and four words long—to describe the action. Then write a paragraph about something that is nearly instantaneous (hitting a baseball, a quick good-bye kiss, spilling your coffee). Do this in at least three sentences, and each sentence should be extremely long.

PRACTICE 7

EXPERIMENTING WITH PACE

Increase the energy of your writing by telescoping time. Using Jamila Osman's memoir on page 214 as a model, write the story of your life, in images, from early childhood to now. Your story must be no longer than 200 words.

Camera Work

As a writer, you are always looking at something interesting—your subject—through a kind of lens: your mind's eye. But as creative writers we often take on viewing the subject through *someone else's eyes*: a character or a speaker. It's a specific person, not the writer, whose eyes we are seeing through. The location of the writer's camera—in the brain/mind/eye of the "seeing" character is called the **point of view**. Point of view simply refers to where you set your camera in order to transmit the scene being viewed by your reader. Paying attention to point of view is an important way to increase and control the energy in your work.

Writers will often choose a single consciousness to be inside of, and the author looks out at the world strictly through that person's eyes. The daughter/girlfriend in Robison's "Pretty Ice" is the point-of-view character in that story—we see her life and the other characters' lives through her eyes. In "The Great Silence," by Ted Chiang on page 79, the point-of-view character is a parrot; the first-person narration creates terrific energy as we get to see the world from this radically different point of view.

But you don't have to always limit yourself in that way. Brenda Peynado in "What We Lost" and Jarod Roselló in "Robot Camp" open out the lens; both use a "we" in places in their story to show that the "I" feels part of a group that is very much a collective character in the narrative. "Boys" on page 219 plants the camera in the collective mind of a group of boys—a kind of wide-angle lens, third person.

Pay attention to the camera work when you read. Where is the camera? What is being recorded? Where is the author? What is the reader directed to focus on? Does the camera move? Does the viewer of the scene change?

As always with creative writing, your job as writer is to pay attention to the experience your reader will have when they read your work. If you jerk the camera around a lot, it's probably going to be kind of interesting at first, and then maybe mostly annoying. The principle most writers follow when it comes to point of view is **consistency**. If you choose first person, and you choose a parrot, stick with that choice throughout your piece. If you choose third person, "Ajay never prayed much," stay with that point of view, not using *I* or *you*. It would be difficult for the reader to have the rules of the story change. That said, some writers experiment with point of view, and when done artfully and with purpose, point-of-view shifts can be interesting and effective.

For now, it might be helpful to consider two aspects of point of view — two settings on your camera — as you play with various energy effects that you can create — **proximity** and **intimacy**.

QUESTIONS TO ASK: Controlling Point of View

Proximity	Who is looking out at whom? How close is the viewing character to others?
Intimacy	Whose head are we in? How deep inside that head are we? Do we have access to all their thoughts and feelings, or just some?

Usually the greater the proximity and the more intimacy, the more energy you create.

In "The Great Silence" we are in a parrot's mind looking at the world. We don't know too much about the parrot's inner life or history, but we are very deep inside their current point of view. In "Genealogy," the poem by Betsy Sholl, the speaker is the daughter, looking at her parents — she's very close to them, and we know a great deal of intimate detail about her life. Compare these two pieces to "Surrounded by Sleep," the short story by Akhil Sharma. Here, a third-person point of view allows us to see the family as it struggles with the tragedy — we have some access to each family member. We know how the mother prays. We know the father loves jokes. But the character we are closest to, and know most deeply and intimately because we are given access to his thinking and his heart, is Ajay. This point of view is called third person limited — the camera can see a lot of external things but is limited to Ajay's internal experience.

Here's a chart you can use to help you clarify point of view.

Identifying Point of View

"Robot Camp"	"At first, I thought Robot Camp was a good idea . . ."	First Person
"Pretty Ice"	"I was up the whole night . . ."	First Person
"Surrounded by Sleep"	"One August afternoon when Ajay was ten years old . . ."	Third Person
"Welcome to Your Authentic Indian Experience™"	"You maintain a menu of a half dozen Experiences on your digital blackboard . . ."	Second Person

---

PRACTICE 8

EXAMINING POINT OF VIEW

Read the story "Rebecca Roanhorse's short story, Welcome to Your Authentic Indian Experience™" on page 226 and notice how the "you" creates energy. What are three ways the point of view increases the tension in the story? Are there any drawbacks, in your opinion, to second person?

Poetry tends to use the term *speaker* to identify who speaks in a poem (the speaker may or may not be the poet). In screenplays and drama, as the characters talk and behave, we observe them and make conclusions about their points of view on our own. They may tell us what they are thinking deep inside — and we may or may not be led to believe them. In graphic novels and comics, examine point of view by looking at where the "camera" is positioned. The close-up, the long shot, the dream sequence, the cityscape are all different points of view. Changing point of view in graphic forms adds energy.

Two other terms may be useful as you explore point of view:

Omniscience means that the point of view knows all and can go inside any head, any time, as superficially or deeply as they choose.

Objective describes an approach in which the point of view reports everything that happens as though we readers are perched on the shoulders of the characters—not inside their heads, but very close. So close that we can smell them and guess at their interior lives.

PRACTICE 9

EXPERIMENTING WITH POINT OF VIEW

Write the first paragraph of a story—fiction or nonfiction—from a first-person point of view, beginning with the word *I*. Then, try another version where you include a *we* in that first-person paragraph. Lastly, try one more version where you convert the paragraph to second person or third person. Write a brief explanation: Which point of view will allow for the most energy to come forward with this particular subject matter?

Too Much Energy?

Energy is about focus, and it's about control. What will happen in your reader's brain when you slow or increase the pace, choose words that spark, withhold information to create a gap, or leap ahead?

Think about some of the ways you use energy already. In a conversation, when things flag, get boring, or there's a long silence, you keep the energy going by asking more questions or introducing a more exciting topic. But if you keep all your conversations going all the time by just talking non-stop, if you suck up all the air in the room, your interlocutors grow tired, disinterested.

Conversation, like good writing, is a kind of game. It's passing a ball back and forth. Too much revelation at the wrong time is misplaced energy. Yelling when whispering would be appropriate is expending too much energy.

It's the same in writing. Modulation is what calibrates the amount of electricity in your work. You want the sparks to fly, but only when you have your readers exactly where you want them. Good writers work to control the energy flow.

As you may have already noticed, there is such a thing as too much energy: too many words, too many images, too much irrelevant information, too many full-throttle, high-pitched events, too much nonstop action, too many disturbing revelations. When readers get overwhelmed, they tune out. Manic, wild, out-of-control passages can be really fun to write, and a little fun to read—but probably not for too many pages.

Some beginning writers mistakenly believe that good writing is dense, incomprehensible, and obscure. Other writers rely on adjectives and adverbs, the stimulants of writing, in order to pep up their paragraphs. It may be counterintuitive at first, but flowery language and extra words actually work to destroy energy. Strong verbs and clearly visualized scenes will always do more to transport your reader than flash and verbiage.

Some writers resort to excessive embellishment—too many words per square inch. Writing in this hyperactive mode is like turning on all the lights in your house: It misses the point. Focus, highlight, and *modulate* the energy. Slowly dim the lights in the most special room in your house, and boom, you have our focus and attention.

Sometimes, using all your energy tools at once at full volume is a way of avoiding the truth of what you have to say, a way of putting off real writing. It's sometimes more fun to show off than to show up, unadorned, saying what's true, small, tender, and difficult.

Experiment with energy conservation.

Notice how few words Beth Ann Fennelly's micro-memoirs on page 215 use to pack a delicious and memorable punch. Notice how much dialogue alone can accomplish in creating high energy; Kristina Halvorson's play on page 240 is a powerful example. Notice how heavy reliance on a single tool—the repetition of *boys enter the house*—creates intense energy in "Boys" by Rick Moody on page 219. Similarly, the single-pointed focus on metaphor as a tool creates a poem filled with mysterious, dramatic, and meaningful gaps in "Genealogy" by Betsy Sholl. Consider choosing one tool to increase energy and focus tightly on creating effects with that single tool.

TROUBLESHOOTING ENERGY

The troubleshooting chart that follows will help you evaluate and control the level of energy in your creative writing. If you choose all the tools from the "Decreases Energy" column, you might still write a great piece but it might be harder to make that piece compelling for your reader.

	Increases Energy	Decreases Energy	Depletes Energy
Subjects	Subjects known intimately from real life.	Subjects known secondhand from friends, family members.	Subjects informed by television, movies, general assumptions and impressions. Feelings and emotions as subject.
Leaps	Leaps from one juicy piece of information to another.	Answers that fit the questions.	Explanation.
Word Choice	Specific, sharp, concrete nouns and action verbs.	General words, filler words. Adjectives, adverbs.	Abstract words, filtering verbs.
Conflict	Conflicting agendas.	Long answers. Agreement.	One person alone with thoughts.
Pace	Varied pace.	Even pace.	Lack of attention to pace.
Distance	Close-up camera work.	Long shots, pulling back, writing from far away.	Camera in one spot, never changes.
Point of View	Super specifics and action + dialogue from a single point of view.	Shifts between multiple points of view for reasons that aren't always clear.	Author talking, author reporting (point of view not a character or speaker). Filters.
Sentence Variation	Variety in sentence length, word choice.	Lack of variety in constructions.	Lack of attention to length and shape of sentences, sections.

WRITING PROJECTS

Micro-memoir

1. Write two micro-memoirs. First, imitate Beth Ann Fennelly's "Two Phone Conversations," with two conversations (cell, text, or in person) from your own life. Make sure you have gaps *in* the conversation as well as a leap *between* the two phone conversations. Next, try an imitation of "Why I'm Changing Salons" where your extremely short micro-memoir relies mostly on the gap between the title and the two lines of story. Ensure that the dialogue in your two-line story also includes a gap.

2. Imitate Jamila Osman's "Fluency": Write a memoir or a poem, no longer than one page, where you leave meaningful blanks, actual physical blanks, for the reader to fill in.

Poetry

3. Write a poem (or micro-memoir) entitled "What Every _____ Should Know." Fill in the blank with a subject you probably know more about than anyone else in the class — perhaps from one of the jobs you've held, "What Every Lifeguard Should Know" or "What Every Babysitter Should Know" or "What Every Mower of Lawns Should Know." Use fresh images and super-specifics to create energy.

Nonfiction

4. Write a list piece on one of the following subjects: what you lost, what you found, what you used to have but don't anymore, what you've purchased with your own money and regret, specific things/people you've loved. Make sure each item has some kind of movement and your piece uses ultra-super-specifics.

Fiction

5. Write a third-person, collective point-of-view short story in one paragraph, using repetition as Rick Moody does, in order to capture the energy of your subject choice in the a) sentence structures and b) format of the piece. Check your piece before submitting to make sure you haven't used any filters.

6. Write a speculative short story that uses leaps, super-specifics, and no filters.

Drama

7. Write a five-minute, five-page play based on three characters and an exaggerated situation (or not, if you work in a high-energy place) from your workplace. Read the work aloud before submitting. Do any of the lines explain? Does each line of dialogue create some kind of a gap—room for the audience to fill in?

ENERGY WORKSHOP

The prompts below will help you constructively discuss your classmates' work.

1. Try to find an example in your classmates' writing of each of the principles of energy, and explain why it works in the piece:
   a. Effective subject choice
   b. Leaps and gaps
   c. Sparky word choices
   d. Super-specific word choices
2. Identify any parts of the piece where the energy is affected by word packages, lack of movement, lack of heat, or use of explanation.
3. Identify a place in the student piece where the energy could be increased by moving the camera closer in on the people/place in the piece. Explain why this might work well.
4. Identify a passage in the student piece where the pace stays at about the same level for longer than it probably should.
5. Identify any filters.

READINGS

Betsy Sholl
Genealogy

One of my parents was a flame, the other a rope.
One was a tire, the other a dial tone.

In the night I'd wake to a hum and the faint
smell of burnt rubber.

One of my parents was a flag, the other a shoe.

The ideogram tattooed on my lower back
is the one for dog trying to run on ice.

One of my parents was a star already gone out,
the other a cup I carried into the night,
convinced it was fragile.

One of my parents I drank, the other I dreamed.

In the revolving door of my becoming,

one pushed from inside, one from without.
Thus, my troubled birth, my endless stammer.

One was an eyebrow, the other a wink.
How they amused each other.

One was a candle, the other a bird. I was ashamed
of not burning, embarrassed I couldn't fly.

I was a girl calling across the ice to a dog
she didn't have.

Brian Turner
What Every Soldier Should Know

> *To yield to force is an act of necessity, not of will;*
> *it is at best an act of prudence.*
> — JEAN-JACQUES ROUSSEAU

If you hear gunfire on a Thursday afternoon,
it could be for a wedding, or it could be for you.

Always enter a home with your right foot;
the left is for cemeteries and unclean places.

O-guf! Tera armeek is rarely useful.
It means *Stop! Or I'll shoot.*

Sabah el khair is effective.
It means *Good morning.*

Inshallah means *Allah be willing.*
Listen well when it is spoken.

You will hear the RPG coming for you.
Not so the roadside bomb.

There are bombs under the overpasses,
in trashpiles, in bricks, in cars.

There are shopping carts with clothes soaked
in foogas, a sticky gel of homemade napalm.

Parachute bombs and artillery shells
sewn into the carcasses of dead farm animals.

Graffiti sprayed onto the overpasses:
I will kell you, American.

Men wearing vests rigged with explosives
walk up, raise their arms and say *Inshallah.*

There are men who earn eighty dollars
to attack you, five thousand to kill.

Small children who will play with you,
old men with their talk, women who offer chai —

and any one of them
may dance over your body tomorrow.

Jamila Osman
Fluency

> *What would happen if one woman told the truth about her life? The world would split open.*
>
> — MURIEL RUKEYSER

We learned English faster than our parents, their tongues too old to take a new shape. Our tongues still coated in milk, this meant we didn't pray like they did, and God didn't answer when we called. English teachers *tskedtskedtsked* when our words lost letters: when ending became endin became the end. English was a world we rebuilt with our small hands. I was a girl, small and dark skinned. Nothing belonged to me except what came out of this mouth of mine.

When my cousin put his_____in my_____or when my uncle_____ed me in the living room of my own home and the strange man grabbed my_____last summer on the train I wanted to say stop but didn't know what language to say it in.

In Somalia we speak Somali, in America we speak English, or sometimes we speak nothing at all. All the women I know speak in whispers. When I try and tell some stories language turns to iron, heavy and rusting in the back of my throat. I bite my tongue and taste blood.

Silence was my first language. I am fluent in its cadences. I know the way quiet can pour out of a mouth like a rush of water in a season of drought.

Beth Ann Fennelly
HEATING & COOLING: 52 MICRO-MEMOIRS

One Doesn't Always Wish to Converse on Airplanes

but this tanned, fit couple—white-sweatered, like tennis pros—seemed eager to talk, so we talked. No, their final destination wasn't Denver. They'd continue to Hawaii after the layover. How awesome, I said, Hawaii. Is it a special occasion, an anniversary? They grinned at each other, like *You tell her. No, you.*

Their thing, it turned out, was scuba diving with metal detectors. They dove at popular honeymoon spots on Oahu, because, they said, the first time those rich Japanese brides hit the water, their new diamonds slid right off. The couple said they didn't always find a ring, but overall they'd found enough to fund their vacations.

"That's . . . wow," I said.

They grinned at each other again, and took a sip from their Bloody Marys, then she gave his biceps a squeeze. Her diamond ring broadcast sequins of light on the tray table. I envisioned how, after netting a big rock, they'd perform exceedingly athletic hotel sex. Their avarice was so unabashed that it was difficult to keep despising them, but I, large of righteousness and small of diamond, persevered all the way to Denver.

Small Talk at Evanston General

And what is it you do? he asked, after a moment of silence. My mother was in the bathroom exchanging her dress for the cotton gown.

I had the sense that he was asking to fulfill some kind of med school training: *Engage the patient's loved ones in conversation.*

Five outlandish occupations pinged through my head, all lies. But I knew I shouldn't mess with him. I needed to get him on our side and keep him there. *I'm a writer,* I said.

A rider? A light turned on in his eyes, suddenly as blue as his scrubs. He put his fists up and bounced them: a cowboy bounding over the plains.

No, I said. *A writer.* Which now seemed to require a gesture, so I held up my imaginary pen and wiggled it.

Oh, he said, all business again as my mother came out of the bathroom. *Well,* he said, *me too.* He untied her gown with one hand and slipped the black Sharpie from his pocket with the other, clamped it between his teeth to remove the cap, then drew dashes on my mother's naked chest, indicating where his scalpel would go.

Why I'm Switching Salons

"We can put on a topcoat with glitter," said the manicurist. "We've noticed you like attention."

Two Phone Conversations

—*I can't find my wine glass. My favorite wine glass.*
—The one with the glass beads glued on?
—*That's the one. I think the maid took it.*
—The maid didn't take it.
—*Yes, she did. The Polish maid. She took it.*
—The maid didn't take the wine glass, Mom. If she was going to steal, she'd steal something valuable. Jewelry or money. But she's not stealing. And she certainly didn't take your wine glass. You've misplaced it. It'll turn up.

* * *

—*I found my wine glass.*
—Yeah? Where?
—*In the cabinet. She put it back.*

WRITERS ON WRITING

BETH ANN FENNELLY

HEATHER SELLERS: What's your writing process when it comes to micro-memoir? Is it different from your poetry writing process?

BETH ANN FENNELLY: I like to write in the mornings, because that's that time that's easiest to cordon off from the rest of my noisy, busy, lucky life (three kids, a demanding teaching job, and lots of travel). My deal with myself is that, every morning possible, I have to be at my desk, calm and present and ready. That means I've kept my mental space unsullied—I haven't checked social media, listened to politics, opened the Visa bill. I've come to my desk closer to my dream state. I open my notebook, and read for inspiration, and I daydream and stare out the window. If nothing comes to me worth writing about, fine—I don't beat myself up, as long as I was there. This is basically the same for me no matter what genre I'm writing, though I read different books depending on the kind of inspiration I'm seeking.

HS: How much revision do you do? What's your revision process for micro-memoir?
BAF: I'm a huge reviser. When I was a younger writer, I didn't enjoy it as much, especially cutting—I guess my words seemed so unbearably precious that I couldn't imagine hitting DELETE. But now I like nothing better than cutting. If a piece is good at 500 words, could it be better at 400? Could it be great at 300? It's not always the case that a shorter piece is improved. But it usually is.

HS: What makes for a good subject choice for a micro-memoir?
BAF: I think one of the keys to writing successful short pieces is finding the right sized ideas. This doesn't mean the subject has to be light or thin—but even with heavy topics, one is taking on a smaller bit of it. I think the micro-memoir is great for focusing in on the moment, which is to say—a tiny text can dignify the small encounters that normally get overlooked in favor of the big, dramatic moments. Cushioning such a moment with white space—like a frame around a painting—asks the reader to study something she might not normally notice.

HS: Anything else you want to tell introductory creative writing students? Tips?
BAF: Titles are often important in tiny texts; they do heavy lifting because they take up a bigger percentage of the word count.

Also, because micro-memoirs are stripped of most exposition, rather like a joke, they can be a great place for humor. Humor, like rhythm, is created through syntax—paying attention to the ordering of information. The big difference is that micro-memoirs need to deepen, not cheapen, upon rereading.

The last thing I'd say is that micro-memoirs are fun because they're low stakes! If you're writing something that's only one paragraph, and it fails, so what? Throw it away and write another! And this freedom, paradoxically, can invite risk-taking. Instead of worrying and trying to sound like a genius, let's lower the stakes and be playful—it can lead us into writing something accidentally genius.

Brian Arundel
The Things I've Lost

Fleece hat and gloves: in the backseat of a Boston cab in 2002, before driving back to Maine. Round, purple sunglasses: in an Atlanta pool hall over drinks with Ashy, whose wife was determined to save their marriage by having a baby. A measurable dose of self-skepticism: at about 14, when I realized I was very good at both playing violin and baseball, while not necessarily everyone else was. A school-wide presidential election in sixth grade, after I was drafted to run by Mrs. Sticoiu, the most frightening teacher in the school, while I was out of town. A copy of *The Little Prince*, in Mrs. Sticoiu's class the previous year. A floppy disk that contained my paper on ideological subversion in Wendell Berry, the first essay I'd written after returning to graduate school following a four-year respite. A black scarf from Pigalle: somewhere in Maine before moving west.

The chance to kiss Leslie Wertmann, and, later, that redhead in seventh grade with a smile that could buckle steel — Kim, Christine, or Kathleen maybe — and the blonde at the freshman dance because I couldn't recognize flirtations, even when told that I looked like Bruce Springsteen. My virginity: in 1980, a couple weeks short of 16, in a ritual so brief, awkward and forgettable that I have, in fact, forgotten it. My heart, or so I thought, in 1985, when Susie dumped me; my naivete, three months later, when I learned that she'd slept with at least three other guys I knew while we'd been dating.

Belief that my mother was somehow more than human: in 1972, the first time I saw her fall down after getting drunk. Belief that my father was more than human: a few months beforehand, after learning that he'd had an affair and was being thrown out of the house. The belief that my sister was stable: 1976, when she began pointing at random objects and saying their names, a few months before getting arrested, the first of many times, for disturbing the peace by refusing to leave a Western Union office until they gave her a job. A ten-dollar bill on a DC subway in 1985, on my way home to my friend Tommy's, where I was staying after leaving my father's house — after he'd moved back in, once my mother remarried and moved south.

The chance, in 1986, to meet Raymond Carver: the only person invited to sit in on an interview, I instead drank all night with friends and overslept. A quarter-inch off the tip of my left thumb, in 1987, while slicing Muenster cheese on an electric Hobart slicer. My shit, figuratively, that same summer when Bob Weir sang "Looks Like Rain" just as my acid trip was peaking at a two-night Dead stand in Roanoke, Va. The Buick a friend had given me as a tax write-off in 1996, which I let someone take for a test drive without holding collateral.

The thought that officials were somehow more evolved than those who elect them: in 1972, listening to my father explain the Watergate burglary. Faith in politics — particularly a two-party system relegated to fundraising contests perpetuated by shallow sound bites, mudslinging and outright lies for the Mindless American Voter so that each party can pursue a majority with which to repress the other, with complete disregard for actually trying to improve the lives of citizens: gradually over time, culminating in 2000. Fundamental hope that Americans really would overcome their vacuity, fear and greed to evolve beyond sheep determined to re-elect George W. Bush: 2004.

The ability to drink until late at night and go to work the next day without feeling like I need to be zipped inside a body bag: sometime in my early thirties. General insecurity and inadequacy: during the past seven years, as I've tried to allow myself to be loved without guilt or judgment. Self-pity and -importance, at least most days, while striving to look beyond the borders of my own desires in a steady ascent that some might refer to as maturation. The desire to remain in this country: since 2004. A black beret: in a Minneapolis bar, just a few days before relocating to Georgia in 1993. A taste for soy sausage patties: inexplicably, sometime in the past six months, leading up to a Saturday brunch three weeks ago.

Rick Moody
Boys

Boys enter the house, boys enter the house. Boys, and with them the ideas of boys (ideas leaden, reductive, inflexible), enter the house. Boys, two of them, wound into hospital packaging, boys with infant pattern baldness, slung in the arms of parents, boys dreaming of breasts, enter the house. Twin boys, kettles on the boil, boys in hideous vinyl knapsacks that young couples from Edison, NJ, wear on their shirt fronts, knapsacks coated with baby saliva and staphylococcus and milk vomit, enter the house. Two boys, one striking the other with a rubberized hot dog, enter the house. Two boys, one of them striking the other with a willow switch about the head and shoulders, the other crying, enter the house. Boys enter the house, speaking nonsense. Boys enter the house, calling for Mother. On a Sunday, in May, a day one might nearly describe as *perfect*, an ice cream truck comes slowly down the lane, chimes inducing salivation, and children run after it, not long after which boys dig a hole in the backyard and bury their younger sister's dolls *two feet down*, so that she will never find these dolls and these dolls will *rot in hell*, after which boys enter the house. Boys, trailing after their father like he is the Second Goddamned Coming of Christ Goddamned Almighty, enter the house, repair to the basement to watch baseball. Boys enter the house, site of devastation, and repair immediately to the kitchen, where they mix lighter fluid, vanilla pudding, drain-opening lye, balsamic vinegar, blue food coloring, calamine lotion, cottage cheese, ants, a plastic lizard that one of them received in his Xmas stocking, tacks, leftover mashed potatoes, Spam, frozen lima beans, and chocolate syrup in a medium-sized saucepan and heat over a low flame until thick, afterwards transferring the contents of this saucepan into a Pyrex lasagna dish, baking the Pyrex lasagna dish in the oven for nineteen minutes before attempting to persuade their sister that she should *eat the mixture*; later they smash three family heirlooms (the last, a glass egg, *intentionally*) in a two-and-a-half hour stretch, whereupon they are sent to their bedroom, until freed, in each case thirteen minutes after. Boys enter the house, starchy in pressed shirts and flannel pants that *itch so bad*, fresh from Sunday School instruction, blond and brown locks (respectively) plastered down, but even so with a number of cowlicks protruding at odd angles, disconsolate and humbled, uncertain if boyish things—such as shooting at the neighbor's dog with a pump action bb gun and gagging the fat boy up the street with a bandanna and showing their shriveled boy-penises to their younger sister—are exempted from the commandment to *Love the Lord thy God with all thy heart and with all thy soul, and with all thy might, and thy neighbor as thyself.* Boys enter the house in baseball gear (only one of the boys can hit): in their spikes, in mismatched tube socks that smell like Stilton cheese. Boys enter the house in soccer gear. Boys enter the house carrying skates. Boys enter the house with lacrosse sticks, and, soon after, tossing a lacrosse ball lightly in the living room they destroy a lamp. One boy enters the house sporting basketball clothes, the other wearing jeans and a sweatshirt. One boy enters the house bleeding profusely and is taken out to get stitches, the other watches. Boys enter the house at the end of term carrying report cards, sneak around the house like spies of foreign nationality, looking for a place to hide the report cards for the time being (under the toaster? in a medicine cabinet?). One boy with a black eye enters the house, one boy without. Boys with acne enter the house and squeeze and prod large skin blemishes in front of their sister. Boys with acne treatment products hidden about their persons enter the house. Boys, standing just up the street, sneak cigarettes behind a willow in the Elys' yard, wave smoke away from their natural fibers, hack terribly, experience nausea, then enter the house. Boys call each other *retard, homo, geek*, and, later, *Neckless Thug, Theater Fag*, and enter the house exchanging further epithets. Boys enter the house with nose hair clippers, chase sister around the house threatening to depilate her eyebrows. She cries. Boys attempt to induce girls to whom they would not have spoken only six or eight months prior to enter the house with them. Boys enter the house with girls efflorescent and homely, and attempt to induce girls to sneak into their bedroom, as they still share a single bedroom; girls refuse. Boys enter the house, go to separate bedrooms. Boys, with their father (an arm around each of them), enter the house, but of the monologue preceding and succeeding this entrance, not a syllable is preserved. Boys enter the house having masturbated in a variety of locales. Boys enter the house having masturbated in train station bathrooms, in forests, in beach houses, in football bleachers at night under the stars, in cars (under a blanket), in the shower, backstage, on a plane, the boys masturbate constantly, identically, three times a day in some cases, desire like a madness upon them, at the mere sound of certain words, words that sound like other words, *interrogative* reminding them of *intercourse*, *beast* reminding them of *breast*, *sects* reminding them of *sex,* and so forth, the boys are not very smart yet, and, as they enter the house, they feel, as always, immense shame at the scale of this *self-abusive cogitation,* seeing a classmate, seeing a billboard, seeing a fire hydrant, seeing things that should not induce thoughts of masturbation (their sister, e.g.) and then thinking of masturbation anyway. Boys enter the house, go to their rooms, remove sexually explicit magazines from hidden stashes, put on loud music, feel despair. Boys enter the house worried; they argue. The boys are ugly, they are failures, they will never be loved, they enter the house. Boys enter the house and kiss their mother, who feels differently, now they have outgrown her. Boys enter the house, kiss their mother, she explains the seriousness of their sister's difficulty, *her diagnosis.* Boys enter the house, having attempted to locate the spot in their yard where the dolls were buried, eight or nine years prior, without success; they go to their sister's room, sit by her bed. Boys enter the house and tell their completely bald sister jokes about baldness. Boys hold either hand of their sister, laying aside differences, having trudged grimly into the house. Boys skip school, enter house, hold vigil. Boys enter the house after their parents have both gone off to work, sit with their sister and with their sister's nurse. Boys enter the house carrying cases of beer. Boys enter the house, very worried now, didn't know more worry was possible. Boys enter the house carrying controlled substances, neither having told the other that he is carrying a controlled substance, though an intoxicated posture seems appropriate under the circumstances. Boys enter the house *weeping* and hear weeping around them. Boys enter the house, embarrassed, silent, anguished, keening, afflicted, angry, woeful, *griefstricken.* Boys enter the house on vacation, each clasps the hand of the other with genuine warmth, the one wearing dark colors and having shaved a portion of his head, the other having grown his hair out longish and wearing, uncharacteristically, a tie-dyed shirt. Boys enter the house on vacation and argue bitterly about politics (other subjects are no longer discussed), one boy supporting the Maoist insurgency in a certain Southeast Asian country, one believing that *to change the system you need to work inside it;* one boy threatens to *beat the living shit out of the other,* refuses crème brûlée, though it is created by his mother in order to keep the peace. One boy writes home and thereby enters the house only through a mail slot: he argues that the other boy is *crypto-fascist,* believing that *the market can seek its own level on questions of ethics and morals;* boys enter the house on vacation and announce future professions; boys enter the house on vacation and change their minds about professions; boys enter the house on vacation and one boy brings home a *sweetheart,* but throws a tantrum when it is suggested that the *sweetheart* will have to retire on the folding bed in the basement; the other boy, having no *sweetheart,* is distant and withdrawn, preferring to talk late into the night about family members gone from this world. Boys enter the house several weeks apart. Boys enter the house on days of heavy rain. Boys enter the house, in different calendar years, and upon entering, the boys seem to do nothing but compose manifestos, for the benefit of parents; they follow their mother around the place, having fashioned their manifestos in celebration of brand-new independence: *Mom, I like to lie in bed late into the morning watching game shows*, or, *I'm never going to date anyone but artists from now on, mad girls, dreamers, practicers of black magic*, or *A man should eat bologna, sliced meats are important*, or, *An American should bowl at least once a year*, but these manifestos apply only for brief spells, after which they are reversed or discarded. Boys don't enter the house, at all, except as ghostly afterimages of younger selves, fleeting images of sneakers dashing up a staircase; soggy towels on the floor of the bathroom; blue jeans coiled like asps in the basin of the washing machine; boys as an absence of boys, blissful at first, you put a thing down on a spot, put this book down, come back later, *it's still there*; you buy a box of cookies, eat three, later three are missing. Nevertheless, when boys next enter the house, which they ultimately must do, it's a relief, even if it's only in preparation for weddings of acquaintances from boyhood, one boy has a beard, neatly trimmed, the other has rakish sideburns, one boy wears a hat, the other boy thinks hats are ridiculous, one boy wears khakis pleated at the waist, the other wears denim, but each changes into his suit (one suit fits well, one is a little tight), as though suits are *the* liminary marker of adulthood. Boys enter the house after the wedding and they are slapping each other on the back and yelling at anyone who will listen, *It's a party!* One boy enters the house, carried by friends, having been arrested (after the wedding) for driving while intoxicated, complexion ashen; the other boy tries to keep his mouth shut: the car is on its side in a ditch, the car has the top half of a tree broken over its bonnet, the car has struck another car which has in turn struck a third, *Everyone will have seen*. One boy misses his brother horribly, misses the past, misses a time worth being nostalgic over, *a time that never existed*, back when they set their sister's playhouse on fire; the other boy avoids all mention of that time; each of them is once the boy who enters the house alone, missing the other, each is devoted and each callous, and each plays his part on the telephone, over the course of months. Boys enter the house with fishing gear, according to prearranged date and time, arguing about whether to use *lures* or *live bait*, in order to meet their father for the *fishing adventure*, after which boys enter the house again, almost immediately, with live bait, having settled the question; boys boast of having caught fish in the past, though no fish has ever been caught: *Remember when the blues were biting?* Boys enter the house carrying their father, slumped. Happens so fast. Boys rush into the house leading EMTs to the couch in the living room where the body lies, boys enter the house, boys enter the house, boys enter the house. Boys hold open the threshold, awesome threshold that has welcomed them when they haven't even been able to welcome themselves, that threshold which welcomed them when they *had* to be taken in, here is its tarnished knocker, here is its euphonious bell, here's where the boys had to sand the door down because it never would hang right in the frame, here are the scuffmarks from when boys were on the wrong side of the door *demanding*, here's where there were once milk bottles for the milkman, here's where the newspaper always landed, here's the mail slot, here's the light on the front step, illuminated, here's where the boys are standing, as that beloved man is carried out. Boys, no longer boys, exit.

Brenda Peynado
What We Lost

We were losing parts of ourselves. A reporter discovered a trove of ears in a burlap sack. The leader said the papers were lying, and we weren't sure what was rumor and what was fact. What happened to me, what happened to my neighbors—that wasn't enough proof of all we had lost.

At first we knew only that we were missing pieces of ourselves. It was easy enough in the early days to say, Your hand? How strange. Are you sure you didn't misplace it somewhere?

We know now about the field of hands, planted in the ground and waving like a crop of corn. The farmers who lost their collarbones and couldn't shoulder any weight. The fishermen who lost their rotator cuffs and could no longer pull their catch to shore.

I myself lost my nose, and I can't smell or taste the poison in the water. My father is missing his thumbs and can't hold his tools. He spends his evenings telling stories of the old days, when things were better. My friend Salma lost her eyes. She lives in the district next to the leader's palace, where everyone has gone blind. She comes to my house led by Milito, who cannot hear: his ears were at the bottom of the bag the reporter discovered. Another friend, Darciel, lost his feet, and when he visits me, he claws himself up the hill, his body scraping on the sidewalk. After he says goodbye, he lets himself roll back down the hill. Many women lost their kidneys, and their eyes and skin became as yellow as gold. In the dialysis clinics they gossip as if they are in beauty parlors. And aren't they still beautiful, despite what they've lost?

Milito leads Salma up to my door. Darciel is not far behind, having just finished his scraping ascent up the hill. Salma smiles when I belt out my greeting.

In the afternoons the four of us, plus my parents, still drink lemonade in the shade of my porch. It's not really lemonade, not with fresh water as rare as it is. I crushed grapes with lemons to make it. A bird trills in the trees. We haven't heard such a thing in months—most birds have lost their wings and their voices—and we pause in reverence, except for Milito, who cannot hear it. Salma tilts her head in the direction of the song.

How did all this happen? It started with the natural world. First we lost most of the crops, and then the aquifers ran out of water. Then the empty aquifers collapsed into sinkholes, which made several neighborhoods disappear. But we weren't concerned back then. We closed our blinds. We were tired. Our leader had promised to fix what was broken, no matter what the cost.

My mother, who lost her teeth, creeps up behind me as I am filling a glass. She mumbles a litany of praise for the leader, how he has given us such delicious lemons. How great it is that he has taken the seeds so we don't have to pick them out.

I am tired of reminding her that without seeds we can't grow lemon trees and have to beg for our fruit.

My father, sensing an argument about to ruin our afternoon, changes the subject and talks about how strong he used to be, when he could still wield an ax. He talks only about the past now, so we humor him. Like my mother, he supports the leader because of all the problems that need fixing. He waves his hands as he talks: they look like paws without their thumbs.

I found the valley of noses myself, a few miles north of the city. They trembled in the wind, inhaling the smog. Was that my own nose calling to me from down in the valley? To reclaim it, I would have to fight the police. If I wanted to take back what was mine, I would have to start a revolution. But I was alone.

The decrees read every week at the shopping mall said that there was never any excuse for violence. Never mind how our fights over rainwater give the police an opportunity to beat us. Never mind our missing organs, which disappeared so slowly and silently we didn't even realize what was happening. Never mind our sick and injured dying in the gutters.

You knew that what went missing could be found: in a burlap sack or a palace. But if you tried to take back what was yours—the ear, the bone, the nose—the police would set upon you instantly, taking another part of you as punishment.

You knew when someone had tried, because suddenly their street would be a sea of white police helmets. You had to wonder about the police. They were people, too, people we knew well. One officer's wife said that there were chunks missing from her husband's back. So why were they so quick with the guns and the machetes?

When Darciel first lost his left foot, he went hopping through the streets looking for it. He thought he saw it in the gutter, but it floated away. Finally he found it in the water-treatment plant. It was there along with thousands of other feet bobbing on the surface of the water, yellow and green with fungus. Maybe it was the feet that poisoned our drinking water. When he reached in with a net to try to get his foot out, the police dragged him back and cut off his other foot.

Darciel regales us with accounts of what he's seen as he's crawled through the streets: A suburb of boys with no fingers playing soccer. Publishing houses filled with historians who have no memories and write their books in the present tense. A neighborhood—the one closest to the water-treatment plant—filled with people who have no brains. Farmers with drooping arms, picking wild raspberries with their toes, the juice dripping from their feet. A district of girls with no voices, who are coveted by marriageable men. When they raise the blinds in the morning, their mouths are open like O's. My mother says they're singing, but we remember how some songs can be screams.

I hand Darciel a cup of lemonade.

My mother asks him if he's ever thought of walking on his hands. It seems easy enough, she says.

No, Darciel says. I never want to forget what was done to me.

Traitor, my mother says, slamming the door on her way back into the house.

Milito fingers the guitar, playing a song that he still remembers from when he could hear. Sometimes the song is so off-key that we wince. Sometimes it's flawless, and we want to dance. Today the song sounds as clear as sparkling water.

You know what I love about us? Salma asks. We're still mostly the same. Look at us, enjoying a drink on the porch.

I cover my face with my hand. I don't want to be looked at. I was beautiful once.

My father scoffs. Milito helps Salma to the bathroom. Now we have to ask each other for help to do everything. (Except for Darciel, who refuses to let me push him in a wheelbarrow.)

Evening is falling. It's getting dark.

Darciel says he passed by the palace, and the windows from the ballroom gleamed with light. We wonder what the leader has lost. Some say he has lost nothing. My mother says he uses all of our missing parts for the good of the people. He is not to blame for everything that came before him. You didn't need that nose, she says. Nor Salma her eyes. She repeats the state-sponsored news about our soldier who was captured behind enemy lines: How he was being traded back one piece at a time. His kidney, an eye, and a hand were exchanged for the kidney, eye, and hand of one of our own citizens. Maybe that eye was yours, Salma, my mother says. You should be proud to help our soldiers come home.

Sometimes I wish my mother had lost her tongue instead of her teeth.

When my father goes inside, we make plans in hushed voices, and Milito reads our lips. A crawling man, a blind woman, a deaf man, and a woman without a nose—it will take all of us. We have rage enough for twenty.

We will sneak into the palace and release the arms to fight the police. The hearts to sound the alarm we should have heard long ago. The legs to carry our messages. And the eyes to bear witness.

Rebecca Roanhorse
Welcome to Your Authentic Indian Experience™

> *In the Great American Indian novel, when it is finally written, all of the white people will be Indians and all of the Indians will be ghosts.*
> —SHERMAN ALEXIE, *How to Write the Great American Indian Novel*

You maintain a menu of a half dozen Experiences on your digital blackboard, but Vision Quest is the one the Tourists choose the most. That certainly makes your workday easy. All a Vision Quest requires is a dash of mystical shaman, a spirit animal (wolf usually, but birds of prey are on the upswing this year), and the approximation of a peyote experience. Tourists always come out of the Experience feeling spiritually transformed. (You've never actually tried peyote, but you did smoke your share of weed during that one year at Arizona State, and who's going to call you on the difference?) It's all 101 stuff, really, these Quests. But no other Indian working at Sedona Sweats can do it better. Your sales numbers are tops.

Your wife Theresa doesn't approve of the gig. Oh, she likes you working, especially after that dismal stretch of unemployment the year before last when she almost left you, but she thinks the job itself is demeaning.

Our last name's not Trueblood," she complains when you tell her about your *nom de rêve.*

"Nobody wants to buy a Vision Quest from a Jesse Turnblatt," you explain. "I need to sound more Indian."

"You are Indian," she says. "Turnblatt's Indian-sounding enough because you're already Indian."

"We're not the right kind of Indian," you counter. "I mean, we're Catholic, for Christ's sake."

What Theresa doesn't understand is that Tourists don't want a real Indian experience. They want what they see in the movies, and who can blame them? Movie Indians are terrific! So you watch the same movies the Tourists do, until John Dunbar becomes your spirit animal and Stands with Fists your best girl. You memorize Johnny Depp's lines from *The Lone Ranger* and hang a picture of Iron Eyes Cody in your work locker. For a while you are really into Dustin Hoffman's *Little Big Man*.

It's *Little Big Man* that does you in.

For a week in June, you convince your boss to offer a Custer's Last Stand special, thinking there might be a Tourist or two who want to live out a Crazy Horse Experience. You even memorize some quotes attributed to the venerable Sioux chief that you find on the internet. You plan to make it real authentic.

But you don't get a single taker. Your numbers nosedive.

Management in Phoenix notices, and Boss drops it from the blackboard by Fourth of July weekend. He yells at you to stop screwing around, accuses you of trying to be an artiste or whatnot.

"Tourists don't come to Sedona Sweats to live out a goddamn battle," Boss says in the break room over lunch one day, "especially if the white guy loses. They come here to find themselves." Boss waves his hand in the air in an approximation of something vaguely prayer-like. "It's a spiritual experience we're offering. Top quality. The fucking best."

DarAnne, your Navajo co-worker with the pretty smile and the perfect teeth, snorts loudly. She takes a bite of her sandwich, mutton by the looks of it. Her jaw works, her sharp teeth flash white. She waits until she's finished chewing to say, "Nothing spiritual about Squaw Fantasy."

Squaw Fantasy is Boss's latest idea, his way to get the numbers up and impress Management. DarAnne and a few others have complained about the use of the ugly slur, the inclusion of a sexual fantasy as an Experience at all. But Boss is unmoved, especially when the first week's numbers roll in. Biggest seller yet.

Boss looks over at you. "What do you think?"

Boss is Pima, with a bushy mustache and a thick head of still-dark hair. You admire that about him. Virility. Boss makes being a man look easy. Makes everything look easy. Real authentic-like.

DarAnne tilts her head, long beaded earrings swinging, and waits. Her painted nails click impatiently against the Formica lunch table. You can smell the onion in her sandwich.

Your mouth is dry like the red rock desert you can see outside your window. If you say Squaw Fantasy is demeaning, Boss will mock you, call you a pussy, or worse. If you say you think it's okay, DarAnne and her crew will put you on the guys-who-are-assholes list and you'll deserve it.

You sip your bottled water, stalling. Decide that in the wake of the Crazy Horse debacle that Boss's approval means more than DarAnne's, and venture, "I mean, if the Tourists like it …"

Boss slaps the table, triumphant. DarAnne's face twists in disgust. "What does Theresa think of that, eh, Jesse?" she spits at you. "You tell her Boss is thinking of adding Savage Braves to the menu next? He's gonna have you in a loincloth and hair down to your ass, see how you like it."

Your face heats up, embarrassed. You push away from the table, too quickly, and the flimsy top teeters. You can hear Boss's shouts of protest as his vending machine lemonade tilts dangerously, and DarAnne's mocking laugh, but it all comes to your ears through a shroud of thick cotton. You mumble something about getting back to work. The sound of arguing trails you down the hall.

You change in the locker room and shuffle down to the pod marked with your name. You unlock the hatch and crawl in. Some people find the pods claustrophobic, but you like the cool metal container, the tight fit. It's comforting. The VR helmet fits snugly on your head, the breathing mask over your nose and mouth.

With a shiver of anticipation, you give the pod your Experience setting. Add the other necessary details to flesh things out. The screen prompts you to pick a Tourist connection from a waiting list, but you ignore it, blinking through the option screens until you get to the final confirmation. You brace for the mild nausea that always comes when you Relocate in and out of an Experience.

The first sensation is always smell. Sweetgrass and wood smoke and the rich loam of the northern plains. Even though it's fake, receptors firing under the coaxing of a machine, you relax into the scents. You grew up in the desert, among people who appreciate cedar and pinon and red earth, but there's still something home-like about this prairie place.

Or maybe you watch too much TV. You really aren't sure anymore.

You find yourself on a wide grassy plain, somewhere in the upper Midwest of a bygone era. Bison roam in the distance. A hawk soars overhead.

You are alone, you know this, but it doesn't stop you from looking around to make sure. This thing you are about to do. Well, you would be humiliated if anyone found out. Because you keep thinking about what DarAnne said. Squaw Fantasy and Savage Braves. Because the thing is, being sexy doesn't disgust you the way it does DarAnne. You've never been one of those guys. The star athlete or the cool kid. It's tempting to think of all those Tourist women wanting you like that, even if it is just in an Experience.

You are now wearing a knee-length loincloth. A wave of black hair flows down your back. Your middle-aged paunch melts into rock-hard abs worthy of a romance novel cover model. You raise your chin and try out your best stoic look on a passing prairie dog. The little rodent chirps something back at you. You've heard prairie dogs can remember human faces, and you wonder what this one would say about you. Then you remember this is an Experience, so the prairie dog is no more real than the caricature of an Indian you have conjured up.

You wonder what Theresa would think if she saw you like this.

The world shivers. The pod screen blinks on. Someone wants your Experience.

A Tourist, asking for you. Completely normal. Expected. No need for that panicky hot breath rattling through your mask.

You scroll through the Tourist's requirements.

Experience Type: Vision Quest.

Tribe: Plains Indian (nation nonspecific).

Favorite animal: Wolf.

These things are all familiar. Things you are good at faking. Things you get paid to pretend.

You drop the Savage Brave fantasy garb for buckskin pants and beaded leather moccasins. You keep your chest bare and muscled but you drape a rough wool blanket across your shoulders for dignity. Your impressive abs are still visible.

The sun is setting and you turn to put the artificial dusk at your back, prepared to meet your Tourist. You run through your list of Indian names to bestow upon your Tourist once the Vision Quest is over. You like to keep the names fresh, never using the same one in case the Tourists ever compare notes. For a while you cheated and used one of those naming things on the internet where you enter your favorite flower and the street you grew up on and it gives you your Indian name, but there were too many Tourists that grew up on Elm or Park and you found yourself getting repetitive. You try to base the names on appearances now. Hair color, eye, some distinguishing feature. Tourists really seem to like it.

This Tourist is younger than you expected. Sedona Sweats caters to New Agers, the kind from Los Angeles or Scottsdale with impressive bank accounts. But the man coming up the hill, squinting into the setting sun, is in his late twenties. Medium height and build with pale spotty skin and brown hair. The guy looks normal enough, but there's something sad about him.

Maybe he's lost.

You imagine a lot of Tourists are lost.

Maybe he's someone who works a day job just like you, saving up money for this once-in-a-lifetime Indian Experience™. Maybe he's desperate, looking for purpose in his own shitty world and thinking Indians have all the answers. Maybe he just wants something that's authentic.

You like that. The idea that Tourists come to you to experience something real. DarAnne has it wrong. The Tourists aren't all bad. They're just needy.

You plant your feet in a wide welcoming stance and raise one hand. "How," you intone, as the man stops a few feet in front of you.

The man flushes, a bright pinkish tone. You can't tell if he's nervous or embarrassed. Maybe both? But he raises his hand, palm forward, and says, "How," right back.

"Have you come seeking wisdom, my son?" you ask in your best broken English accent. "Come. I will show you great wisdom." You sweep your arm across the prairie. "We look to brother wolf—"

The man rolls his eyes.

What?

You stutter to a pause. Are you doing something wrong? Is the accent no good? Too little? Too much?

You visualize the requirements checklist. You are positive he chose wolf. Positive. So you press on. "My brother wolf," you say again, this time sounding much more Indian, you are sure.

"I'm sorry," the man says, interrupting. "This wasn't what I wanted. I've made a mistake."

"But you picked it on the menu!" In the confusion of the moment, you drop your accent. Is it too late to go back and say it right?

The man's lips curl up in a grimace, like you have confirmed his worst suspicions. He shakes his head. "I was looking for something more authentic."

Something in your chest seizes up.

"I can fix it," you say.

"No, it's alright. I'll find someone else." He turns to go.

You can't afford another bad mark on your record. No more screw-ups or you're out. Boss made that clear enough. "At least give me a chance," you plead.

"It's okay," he says over his shoulder.

This is bad. Does this man not know what a good Indian you are? "Please!"

The man turns back to you, his face thoughtful.

You feel a surge of hope. This can be fixed, and you know exactly how. "I can give you a name. Something you can call yourself when you need to feel strong. It's authentic," you add enthusiastically. "From a real Indian." That much is true.

The man looks a little more open, and he doesn't say no. That's good enough.

You study the man's dusky hair, his pinkish skin. His long skinny legs. He reminds you a bit of the flamingos at the Albuquerque zoo, but you are pretty sure no one wants to be named after those strange creatures. It must be something good. Something ... spiritual.

"Your name is Pale Crow," you offer. Birds are still on your mind.

At the look on the man's face, you reconsider. "No, no, it is White" — yes, that's better than pale— "Wolf. White Wolf."

"White Wolf?" There's a note of interest in his voice.

You nod sagely. You knew the man had picked wolf. Your eyes meet. Uncomfortably. White Wolf coughs into his hand. "I really should be getting back."

"But you paid for the whole experience. Are you sure?"

White Wolf is already walking away.

"But ..."

You feel the exact moment he Relocates out of the Experience. A sensation like part of your soul is being stretched too thin. Then, a sort of whiplash, as you let go.

The Hey U.S.A. bar is the only Indian bar in Sedona. The basement level of a driftwood-paneled strip mall across the street from work. It's packed with the after-shift crowd, most of them pod jockeys like you, but also a few roadside jewelry hawkers and restaurant stiffs still smelling like frybread grease. You're lucky to find a spot at the far end next to the server's station. You slip onto the plastic-covered barstool and raise a hand to get the bartender's attention.

"So what do you really think?" asks a voice to your right. DarAnne is staring at you, her eyes accusing and her posture tense.

This is it. A second chance. Your opportunity to stay off the assholes list. You need to get this right. You try to think of something clever to say, something that would impress her but let you save face, too. But you're never been all that clever, so you stick to the truth.

"I think I really need this job," you admit.

DarAnne's shoulders relax.

"Scooch over," she says to the man on the other side of her, and he obligingly shifts off his stool to let her sit. "I knew it," she says. "Why didn't you stick up for me? Why are you so afraid of Boss?"

"I'm not afraid of Boss. I'm afraid of Theresa leaving me. And unemployment."

"You gotta get a backbone, Jesse, is all."

You realize the bartender is waiting, impatient. You drink the same thing every time you come here, a single Coors Light in a cold bottle. But the bartender never remembers you, or your order. You turn to offer to buy one for DarAnne, but she's already gone, back with her crew.

You drink your beer alone, wait a reasonable amount of time, and leave.

White Wolf is waiting for you under the streetlight at the corner.

The bright neon Indian Chief that squats atop Sedona Sweats hovers behind him in pinks and blues and yellows, his huge hand blinking up and down in greeting. White puffs of smoke signals flicker up, up and away beyond his far shoulder.

You don't recognize White Wolf at first. Most people change themselves a little within the construct of the Experience. Nothing wrong with being thinner, taller, a little better looking. But White Wolf looks exactly the same. Nondescript brown hair, pale skin, long legs.

"How." White Wolf raises his hand, unconsciously mimicking the big neon Chief. At least he has the decency to look embarrassed when he does it.

"You." You are so surprised that the accusation is the first thing out of your mouth. "How did you find me?"

"Trueblood, right? I asked around."

"And people told you?" This is very against the rules.

"I asked who the best Spirit Guide was. If I was going to buy a Vision Quest, who should I go to. Everyone said you."

You flush, feeling vindicated, but also annoyed that your co-workers had given your name out to a Tourist. "I tried to tell you," you say ungraciously.

"I should have listened." White Wolf smiles, a faint shifting of his mouth into something like contrition. An awkward pause ensues.

"We're really not supposed to fraternize," you finally say.

"I know, I just … I just wanted to apologize. For ruining the Experience like that."

"It's no big deal," you say, gracious this time. "You paid, right?"

"Yeah."

"It's just …" You know this is your ego talking, but you need to know. "Did I do something wrong?"

"No, it was me. You were great. It's just, I had a great grandmother who was Cherokee, and I think being there, seeing everything. Well, it really stirred something in me. Like, ancestral memory or something."

You've heard of ancestral memories, but you've also heard of people claiming Cherokee blood where there is none. Theresa calls them "pretendians," but you think that's unkind. Maybe White Wolf really is Cherokee. You don't know any Cherokees, so maybe they really do look like this guy. There's a half-Tlingit in payroll and he's pale.

"Well, I've got to get home," you say. "My wife, and all."

White Wolf nods. "Sure, sure. I just. Thank you."

"For what?"

But White Wolf's already walking away. "See you around."

A little déjà vu shudders your bones but you chalk it up to Tourists. Who understands them, anyway?

You go home to Theresa.

As soon as you slide into your pod the next day, your monitor lights up. There's already a Tourist on deck and waiting.

"Shit," you mutter, pulling up the menu and scrolling quickly through the requirements. Everything looks good, good, except … a sliver of panic when you see that a specific tribe has been requested. Cherokee. You don't know anything about Cherokees. What they wore back then, their ceremonies. The only Cherokee you know is …

White Wolf shimmers into your Experience.

In your haste, you have forgotten to put on your buckskin. Your Experience-self still wears Wranglers and Nikes. Boss would be pissed to see you this sloppy.

"Why are you back?" you ask.

"I thought maybe we could just talk."

"About what?"

White Wolf shrugs. "Doesn't matter. Whatever."

"I can't."

"Why not? This is my time. I'm paying."

You feel a little panicked. A Tourist has never broken protocol like this before. Part of why the Experience works is that everyone knows their role. But White Wolf don't seem to care about the rules.

"I can just keep coming back," he says. "I have money, you know."

"You'll get me in trouble."

"I won't. I just …" White Wolf hesitates. Something in him slumps. What you read as arrogance now looks like desperation. "I need a friend."

You know that feeling. The truth is, you could use a friend, too. Someone to talk to. What could the harm be? You'll just be two men, talking.

Not here, though. You still need to work. "How about the bar?"

"The place from last night?"

"I get off at 11 p.m."

When you get there around 11:30 p.m., the bar is busy but you recognize White Wolf immediately. A skinny white guy stands out at the Hey U.S.A. It's funny. Under this light, in this crowd, White Wolf could pass for Native of some kind. One of those 1/64th guys, at least. Maybe he really is a little Cherokee from way back when.

White Wolf waves you over to an empty booth. A Coors Light waits for you. You slide into the booth and wrap a hand around the cool damp skin of the bottle, pleasantly surprised.

"A lucky guess, did I get it right?"

You nod and take a sip. That first sip is always magic. Like how you imagine Golden, Colorado must feel like on a winter morning.

"So," White Wolf says, "tell me about yourself."

You look around the bar for familiar faces. Are you really going to do this? Tell a Tourist about your life? Your real life? A little voice in your head whispers that maybe this isn't so smart. Boss could find out and get mad. DarAnne could make fun of you. Besides, White Wolf will want a cool story, something real authentic, and all you have is an aging three-bedroom ranch and a student loan.

But he's looking at you, friendly interest, and nobody looks at you like that much anymore, not even Theresa. So you talk.

Not everything.

But some. Enough.

Enough that when the bartender calls last call you realize you've been talking for two hours.

When you stand up to go, White Wolf stands up, too. You shake hands, Indian-style, which makes you smile. You didn't expect it, but you've got a good, good feeling.

"So, same time tomorrow?" White Wolf asks.

You're tempted, but, "No, Theresa will kill me if I stay out this late two nights in a row." And then, "But how about Friday?"

"Friday it is." White Wolf touches your shoulder. "See you then, Jesse."

You feel a warm flutter of anticipation for Friday. "See you."

Friday you are there by 11:05 p.m. White Wolf laughs when he sees your face, and you grin back, only a little embarrassed. This time you pay for the drinks, and the two of you pick up right where you left off. It's so easy.

White Wolf never seems to tire of your stories and it's been so long since you had a new friend to tell them to, that you can't seem to quit. It turns out White Wolf loves Kevin Costner, too, and you take turns quoting lines at each other until White Wolf stumps you with a Wind in His Hair quote.

"Are you sure that's in the movie?"

"It's Lakota!"

You won't admit it, but you're impressed with how good White Wolf's Lakota sounds.

White Wolf smiles. "Looks like I know something you don't."

"You wave it away good-naturedly, but vow to watch the movie again.

Time flies and once again, after last call, you both stand outside under the Big Chief. You happily agree to meet again next Tuesday. And the following Friday. Until it becomes your new routine.

The month passes quickly. The next month, too.

"You seem too happy," Theresa says one night, sounding suspicious.

You grin and wrap your arms around your wife, pulling her close until her rose-scented shampoo fills your nose. "Just made a friend, is all. A guy from work." You decide to keep it vague. Hanging with White Wolf, who you've long stopped thinking of as just a Tourist, would be hard to explain.

"You're not stepping out on me, Jesse Turnblatt? Because I will—"

You cut her off with a kiss. "Are you jealous?"

"Should I be?"

"Never."

She sniffs, but lets you kiss her again, her soft body tight against yours.

"I love you," you murmur as your hands dip under her shirt.

"You better."

Tuesday morning and you can't breathe. Your nose is a deluge of snot and your joints ache. Theresa calls in sick for you and bundles you in bed with a bowl of stew. You're supposed to meet White Wolf for your usual drink, but you're much too sick. You consider sending Theresa with a note, but decided against it. It's only one night. White Wolf will understand.

But by Friday the coughing has become a deep rough bellow that shakes your whole chest. When Theresa calls in sick for you again, you make sure your cough is loud enough for Boss to hear it. Pray he doesn't dock you for the days you're missing. But what you're most worried about is standing up White Wolf again.

"Do you think you could go for me?" you ask Theresa.

"What, down to the bar? I don't drink."

"I'm not asking you to drink. Just to meet him, let him know I'm sick. He's probably thinking I forgot about him."

"Can't you call him?"

"I don't have his number."

"Fine, then. What's his name?"

You hesitate. Realize you don't know. The only name you know is the one you gave him. "White Wolf."

"Okay, then. Get some rest."

Theresa doesn't get back until almost 1 a.m. "Where were you?" you ask, alarmed. Is that a rosy flush in her cheeks, the scent of Cherry Coke on her breath?

"At the bar like you asked me to."

"What took so long?"

She huffs. "Did you want me to go or not?"

"Yes, but ... well, did you see him?"

She nods, smiles a little smile that you've never seen on her before.

"What is it?" Something inside you shrinks.

"A nice man. Real nice. You didn't tell me he was Cherokee."

By Monday you're able to drag yourself back to work. There's a note taped to your locker to go see Boss. You find him in his office, looking through the reports that he sends to Management every week.

"I hired a new guy."

You swallow the excuses you've prepared to explain how sick you were, your promises to get your numbers up. They become a hard ball in your throat.

"Sorry, Jesse." Boss actually does look a little sorry. "This guy is good, a real rez guy. Last name's 'Wolf'. I mean, shit, you can't get more Indian than that. The Tourists are going to eat it up."

"The Tourists love me, too." You sound whiny, but you can't help it. There's a sinking feeling in your gut that tells you this is bad, bad, bad.

"You're good, Jesse. But nobody knows anything about Pueblo Indians, so all you've got is that TV shit. This guy, he's ..." Boss snaps his fingers, trying to conjure the word.

"Authentic?" A whisper.

Boss points his finger like a gun. "Bingo. Look, if another pod opens up, I'll call you."

"You gave him my pod?"

Boss's head snaps up, wary. You must have yelled that. He reaches over to tap a button on his phone and call security.

"Wait!" you protest.

But the men in uniforms are already there to escort you out.

You can't go home to Theresa. You just can't. So you head to the Hey U.S.A. It's a different crowd than you're used to. An afternoon crowd. Heavy boozers and people without jobs. You laugh because you fit right in.

The guys next to you are doing shots. Tiny glasses of rheumy dark liquor lined up in a row. You haven't done shots since college but when one of the men offers you one, you take it. Choke on the cheap whiskey that burns down your throat. Two more and the edges of your panic start to blur soft and tolerable. You can't remember what time it is when you get up to leave, but the Big Chief is bright in the night sky.

You stumble through the door and run smack into DarAnne. She growls at you, and you try to stutter out an apology but a heavy hand comes down on your shoulder before you get the words out.

"This asshole bothering you?"

You recognize that voice. "White Wolf?" It's him. But he looks different to you. Something you can't quite place. Maybe it's the ribbon shirt he's wearing, or the bone choker around his neck. Is his skin a little tanner than it was last week?

"Do you know this guy?" DarAnne asks, and you think she's talking to you, but her head is turned towards White Wolf.

"Never seen him," White Wolf says as he stares you down, and under that confident glare you almost believe him. Almost forget that you've told this man things about you even Theresa doesn't know.

"It's me," you protest, but your voice comes out in a whiskey-slurred squeak that doesn't even sound like you.

"Fucking glonnies," DarAnne mutters as she pushes past you. "Always making a scene."

"I think you better go, buddy," White Wolf says. Not unkindly, if you were in fact strangers, if you weren't actually buddies. But you are, and you clutch at his shirtsleeve, shouting something about friendship and Theresa and then the world melts into a blur until you feel the hard slap of concrete against your shoulder and the taste of blood on your lip where you bit it and a solid kick to your gut until the whiskey comes up the way it went down and then the Big Chief is blinking at you, How, How, How, until the darkness comes to claim you and the lights all flicker out.

You wake up in the gutter. The fucking gutter. With your head aching and your mouth as dry and rotted as month-old roadkill. The sun is up, Arizona fire beating across your skin. Your clothes are filthy and your shoes are missing and there's a smear of blood down your chin and drying flakes in the creases of your neck. Your hands are chapped raw. And you can't remember why.

But then you do.

And the humiliation sits heavy on your bruised up shoulder, a dark shame that defies the desert sun. Your job. DarAnne ignoring you like that. White Wolf kicking your ass. And you out all night, drunk in a downtown gutter. It all feels like a terrible dream, like the worst kind. The ones you can't wake up from because it's real life.

Your car isn't where you left it, likely towed with the street sweepers, so you trudge your way home on sock feet. Three miles on asphalt streets until you see your highly-mortgaged three-bedroom ranch. And for once the place looks beautiful, like the day you bought it. Tears gather in your eyes as you push open the door.

"Theresa," you call. She's going to be pissed, and you're going to have to talk fast, explain the whole drinking thing (it was one time!) and getting fired (I'll find a new job, I promise), but right now all you want is to wrap her in your arms and let her rose-scent fill your nose like good medicine.

"Theresa," you call again, as you limp through the living room. Veer off to look in the bedroom, check behind the closed bathroom door. But what you see in the bathroom makes you pause. Things are missing. Her toothbrush, the pack of birth control, contact lens solution.

"Theresa!?" and this time you are close to panic as you hobble down the hall to the kitchen.

The smell hits you first. The scent of fresh coffee, bright and familiar.

When you see the person sitting calmly at the kitchen table, their back to you, you relax. But that's not Theresa.

He turns slightly, enough so you can catch his profile, and says, "Come on in, Jesse."

"What the fuck are you doing here?"

White Wolf winces, as if your words hurt him. "You better have a seat."

"What did you do to my wife?!"

"I didn't do anything to your wife." He picks up a small folded piece of paper, holds it out. You snatch it from his fingers and move so you can see his face. The note in your hand feels like wildfire, something with the potential to sear you to the bone. You want to rip it wide open, you want to flee before its revelations scar you. You ache to read it now, now, but you won't give him the satisfaction of your desperation.

"So now you remember me," you huff.

"I apologize for that. But you were making a scene and I couldn't have you upsetting DarAnne."

You want to ask how he knows DarAnne, how he was there with her in the first place. But you already know. Boss said the new guy's name was Wolf.

"You're a real son of a bitch, you know that?"

White Wolf looks away from you, that same pained look on his face. Like you're embarrassing yourself again. "Why don't you help yourself to some coffee," he says, gesturing to the coffee pot. Your coffee pot.

"I don't need your permission to get coffee in my own house," you shout.

"Okay," he says, leaning back. You can't help but notice how handsome he looks, his dark hair a little longer, the choker on his neck setting off the arch of his high cheekbones.

You take your time getting coffee—sugar, creamer which you would never usually take—before you drop into the seat across from him. Only then do you open the note, hands trembling, dread twisting hard in your gut.

"She's gone to her mother's," White Wolf explains as you read the same words on the page. "For her own safety. She wants you out by the time she gets back."

"What did you tell her?"

"Only the truth. That you got yourself fired, that you were on a bender, drunk in some alleyway downtown like a bad stereotype." He leans in. "You've been gone for two days."

You blink. It's true, but it's not true, too.

"Theresa wouldn't …" But she would, wouldn't she? She'd said it a million times, given you a million chances.

"She needs a real man, Jesse. Someone who can take care of her."

"And that's you?" You muster all the scorn you can when you say that, but it comes out more a question than a judgment. You remember how you gave him the benefit of the doubt on that whole Cherokee thing, how you thought "pretendian" was cruel.

He clears his throat. Stands.

"It's time for you to go," he says. "I promised Theresa you'd be gone, and I've got to get to work soon." Something about him seems to expand, to take up the space you once occupied. Until you feel small, superfluous.

"Did you ever think," he says, his voice thoughtful, his head tilted to study you like a strange foreign body, "that maybe this is my experience, and you're the tourist here?"

"This is my house," you protest, but you're not sure you believe it now. Your head hurts. The coffee in your hand is already cold. How long have you been sitting here? Your thoughts blur to histories, your words become nothing more than forgotten facts and half-truths. Your heart, a dusty repository for lost loves and desires, never realized.

"Not anymore," he says.

Nausea rolls over you. That same stretching sensation you get when you Relocate out of an Experience.

Whiplash, and then …

You let go.

Kristina Halvorson
Now We're Really Getting Somewhere

CHARACTERS

JEN, mid 20s. Cynical, unhappy.
BETHANY, mid 20s. Unhappy, trying hard not to be.
ELAINE, late 20s. Jen and Bethany's supervisor, trying hard in general.
JACK, late 20s. Sales guy. Nice enough.

SETTING

At work.

TIME

Today.

> *Lights up on a conference table. Jen is waiting for someone. Bethany walks in and proceeds to pile tons of office crap on the table — files, legal pads, water bottle, Diet Coke, coffee — is she here for a three-day summit? They barely look at each other, having already gone through their morning greetings earlier. They are waiting. Waiting.*

JEN: This sucks.

BETHANY: You always say that.

JEN: This always sucks.

BETHANY: You just need to adjust your expectations.

JEN: I don't think it's unreasonable to expect that the person who schedules these meetings would actually show up on time.

BETHANY: But she never does.

JEN: And, it sucks.

BETHANY: It could be worse.

JEN: That's how I should adjust my expectations? By thinking it could be worse?

BETHANY: Why not? Look. Elaine is late. And while she's late, I'm sitting here, happily chatting with my friend Jen and getting paid to do it. You, on the other hand, are all worked up over something that happens every single time we have our weekly meeting. Who's better off? Me. Why? Very low expectations.

JEN: Amazing.

BETHANY: You just need an attitude adjustment.

JEN: I need to have my attitude surgically removed.

> *(Elaine enters the room with her pile of meeting files.)*

ELAINE: Good morning! Sorry I'm late.

BETHANY: No problem!

JEN: No problem.

ELAINE: So, how were your weekends?

BETHANY: SO great.

ELAINE: Great! Jen, how was yours?

JEN: Exhausting, short, awful.

ELAINE: (*Wasn't listening.*) Great.

BETHANY: Did you do anything fun?

ELAINE: Nope! So! Let's go ahead and get started.

BETHANY: (*Peeling an orange.*) Anybody want an orange? I have like twelve of them in my bag.

ELAINE: You know, before we begin, I should let you both know that I've asked Jack to join us for a few quick moments this morning.

JEN: (*Pause.*) Jack?

BETHANY: Sales Jack?

ELAINE: Well, of course sales Jack.

JEN: Sales Jack is coming here? Now?

BETHANY: But, this is our Monday morning meeting. OUR Monday morning meeting. I mean, this is supposed to be our safe place.

ELAINE: Well, you two brought up what I consider to be some very important issues last week, and I thought it would be beneficial for the four of us to begin a mutual dialogue.

BETHANY: But, Elaine, we hate him.

ELAINE: Oh, you do not.

BETHANY: Oh, yes. We do.

JEN: You just need to adjust your expectations.

BETHANY: I did. I can't adjust any lower with him.

ELAINE: So, while we're waiting for Jack, let's look at what's on everybody's plate this week.

JEN: Wait, what are we supposed to say to Jack?

ELAINE: Whatever you think will help.

JEN: Help what?

ELAINE: The situation.

JEN: Elaine, I'm sorry, but the situation is that he's totally incompetent, he makes our jobs impossible, and he should be fired.

ELAINE: I don't think that will help the situation.

BETHANY: I don't care if he's incompetent. I just hate him.

ELAINE: But what's behind that?

BETHANY: Yesterday, I had this really important question? So I e-mailed him, and I left him about twelve voice mails, and he never called me back. Just totally ignored me. He always does that.

JEN: He does.

BETHANY: I mean, he's sales, and we're customer support, right, but he never tells us anything that's going on until suddenly somebody calls with this out-of-control problem, and they're like, "Oh, Jack said I should just call you." Hello, I don't know what's going on, I've never even heard of them before, and obviously, I look like a total idiot. Oh, and the way he always calls us his "girls"—I mean, I'm not a feminist or anything, but that totally bugs. "Just call my girls, they'll take care of you." God! He makes me want to, I don't know, throw things, or, or shoot somebody.

JEN: Awesome. (*Pause.*) Sorry.

ELAINE: Well. It seems that perhaps the core issue here is actually a simple personality conflict.

JEN: Um. I like him OK.

ELAINE: Great!

JEN: He doesn't mean to be insensitive. I think he has a good heart.

ELAINE: Yes, I think he does.

JEN: I just think he's utterly incompetent and should be fired.

BETHANY: Or shot. (*Oops—puts her hands over her mouth.*)

ELAINE: OK. Let's talk facts. Jack is the sales specialist for our region, agreed. We are his assigned customer support specialists, agreed. Clearly we need to be able to work as a team, together. Agreed? I'm not asking you to *like* Jack . . . I'm just asking you to treat him with the respect he deserves, as a person who is doing his best. Right? You said it yourself, he has a good heart. He's doing the best that he can.

(*Bethany and Jen consider this. She's probably right.*)

ELAINE: We are all doing the best that we can.

BETHANY: I will do my best to be nice to Jack.

JEN: But we still need to talk about the stuff you were saying. Elaine, you're the team leader . . . just, please be sure to bring that stuff up, OK?

ELAINE: Absolutely.

(*Jack enters.*)

JACK: Good morning, ladies!

ELAINE: Jack! Good morning. Thanks for stopping by.

BETHANY AND JEN: Hey.

JACK: No problem. So, what I miss?

ELAINE: Oh, nothing, really, we've just been chatting about our weekends.

JACK: And how were they?

BETHANY: SO great.

ELAINE: Thanks for asking.

JACK: Jen, how was yours?

JEN: Fabulous. Thanks.

JACK: Great.

ELAINE: (*Pause.*) So. Jack. We thought it would be helpful for the four of us to talk this morning about a few different issues that have come up.

JACK: You have some issues.

ELAINE: Well, not ISSUES, issues.

JACK: Great.

ELAINE: Great. So, Jack. I've asked you here today because the three of us would like to chat about what it is we can do to help make your job easier. That is to say, what could we do to help make you as effective as possible at what you do?

JACK: That's awfully nice.

ELAINE: We're all on the same team. Your team.

JACK: Right.

BETHANY: (*Pause.*) I think what we kind of want to know is, is there anything we could be doing to *partner* with you, with the customers. It just seems like maybe, I don't know, maybe we should be working more closely together.

JACK: I'm not sure I'm following.

(*Bethany looks to Elaine for help. Elaine smiles blankly.*)

BETHANY: Um, well. Like when a customer has a problem, do you think that, I don't know, maybe you could tell us what's going on, you know, before they call us?

JACK: Sure!

BETHANY: Oh. Great.

JACK: Anything else?

JEN: (*Giving it a try.*) Jack. I guess maybe we're feeling like we should be more closely involved with the sales process from the start. And that way we can be more familiar with the customers and the specific issues they're facing . . .

JACK: (*Interrupts Jen after "customers."*) You know, no offense meant here, but after nearly ten years in professional sales, I think I can handle my customers. I just don't think your department really understands what all is involved in pre-sales, which is fine. That's why I'm in sales and you're in support, right? Sales is a multi-layered process that can't always be predicted or precisely measured. I really don't see where it is you feel you need to be "brought in."

BETHANY: But when you're working with the customers and they have a problem and you give them our number . . .

JACK: Exactly. It's great to know I can count on your team no matter what. Really, if I need anything, I'll let you know.

ELAINE: Perfect. Great.

JEN: I don't, um, I don't really feel like this exactly resolves what Bethany is getting at.

ELAINE: What else do you need to hear, Jen?

JEN: Well, Jack (*She's going to go for it.*) . . . do you like your job?

JACK: Sure. Sure, I like my job.

JEN: Because, well, we try really hard to help your customers, and well, I guess I don't see you trying very hard. At anything. Ever.

ELAINE: Now, Jen, let's not . . .

JEN: What I want to say here, Jack, is that what we don't, I don't really see in you is passion. For what you do.

JACK: I don't think passion was in my job description.

JEN: Well, obviously, but . . .

JACK: I sell telecommunications equipment to companies with two hundred and fifty employees or less. There's only so much to get excited about there.

ELAINE: Jack, Jen is certainly not questioning your commitment . . .

JEN: Let's take Bethany, here. Bethany is a customer support specialist for a telecommunications company. When people ask her what she does, and she tells them, they say, "That's great!" But they might be thinking, it would be within their rights to think, "Well, this person isn't exactly changing the world with that, now is she?" But the thing is, I think in Bethany's mind, she *is* changing something, doing some good for somebody. Let's say there's this one guy who's in, I don't know, Kenosha or something . . . this one guy is out there, trying his best daily to accomplish some stupid set of menial tasks, and every day he is absolutely counting on being able to pick up the phone that you sold him and knowing he can make a call. And one day, his phone, our phone, fails him. And that day, maybe Bethany talks to him, answers his questions, and fixes the problem. Now the phone works, and she's made one of the 10 million problems this guy has just because he's a human being go away. And knowing Bethany? She'll be grateful that she was given the opportunity to help.

That kind of thinking. That's passion. That's what makes Bethany a great person — no, a great woman — to work with. Commitment. Cooperation. Common courtesy. That's what we want from our team members.

(*No one knows what to say. In the silence, Bethany chugs her entire Diet Coke and crushes the can with one hand.*)

ELAINE: Jack, we're on your team.

JACK: Right.

ELAINE: Aren't we, girls?

JEN: That's it? "Girls"?

ELAINE: Thanks so much for coming by this morning, Jack.

JEN: We're not going to talk about this?

ELAINE: We just did, and it's late, and Jack needs to get going.

JACK: Thanks, Elaine.

JEN: Amazing. Absolutely amazing.

ELAINE: Jen, we can continue this conversation . . .

JEN: You know, we always talk, and shit always comes up, and everyone is nice, and no one ever says anything because we don't want anything to disrupt this illusion we have of forward movement. Which, what does that mean anyway? What exactly are we measuring to determine movement? Do you even know?

ELAINE: We're all done here.

JEN: We are not done.

ELAINE: We're done, I say we're done.

JEN: You know, Bethany is convinced that Jack is the problem because he's so clued out 98 percent of the time, but it's really you. It's the way you just smile and nod and say we're all doing our best, we're all on the same team, we all need to respect each other —

ELAINE: Jen, let's try to keep our emotions under control . . .

JEN: You say, "We need to be patient, we need to stick together," and then nothing ever changes because you're so worried about pissing somebody off, like somehow that would move us backward if there were tension or conflict or God *forbid* someone got angry . . .

ELAINE: You know, don't blame me because you're an unhappy person. I like my job here. I like coming in to a place every day where I know everyone is nice, and professional, and respectful, and we all like each other.

JEN: And nothing ever changes, does it, Elaine?

ELAINE: What is so wrong with things the way they are? Why does anything need to change?

JEN: Oh, you're right. Shitty sales, fucked-up nonexistent communication, general mediocrity everywhere you turn, what's wrong with that?

ELAINE: Oh, and you are so much better than that.

JEN: No, Elaine, I'm not. I'm shitty and I'm mediocre. But I don't want to be. I want to be passionate. I want to be inspired. I want to know that what I do means something, that there is an effect, a shift, even a goddamn ripple . . .

ELAINE: But listen to me, Jen. As your team leader, I'm telling you, there is. You contribute. You make a difference. I'm telling you, you matter.

JEN: But I don't respect you.

(*Stunned silence. Elaine musters what little remaining dignity she can, picks up her pile of files and legal pads, and walks out.*)

JACK: Hey, 9:30 already? Whoa, time flies when you're having fun. So. I guess I'll just see you around. Jen? For what it's worth . . . I think you're doing a great job. (*Jack exits. Bethany and Jen sit together. Finally, Bethany gathers up her crap and simply exits. Jen sits at the table and begins to recite to herself, perhaps adding movement or volume as it builds.*)

JEN: I'm doing the best that I can. I'm doing the best that I can. I'm doing the best that I can. I'm doing the best that I can.

CHAPTER SIX

TENSION

In this chapter you will:

- Develop effective strategies for modulating conflict in all genres
- Heighten reader interest by attending to internal and external tension points
- Create more complex writing by utilizing layers and façades

THE PRINCIPLES OF TENSION

Tension is the state of being stretched tight; it occurs when two forces oppose each other.

Visually, tension looks like this, where one element is pulled in two opposing directions:

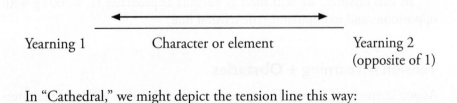

| Yearning 1 | Character or element | Yearning 2 (opposite of 1) |

In "Cathedral," we might depict the tension line this way:

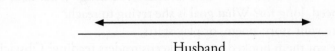

| | Husband | |

| Husband loves wife, loves status quo | | And husband dislikes wife's friend, resists change |

247

In "Genealogy," the tension line might be charted as:

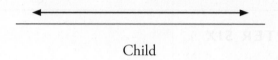

Child

My parents shape me —   I long to shape
it's inevitable   my own identity

It can be helpful to keep this visual image—a single entity pulled in two different directions, two intentions, or two opposing energies—in mind as you apply the concepts in this chapter to your own writing.

Our focus as writers is on intentionally creating oppositions in every aspect of the piece of work. But for those of us trained to "yes, and . . ." our way through life, this "no, but . . ." approach to creating runs counter to how we normally speak and act, and so it can take some effort to actively craft tension. Unlike the strategies you've learned so far—using the movie in your mind as a focus point, writing with images as an anchor, using language to generate energy—building tension doesn't always come naturally or quickly. However, intentionally designed tension is crucial to successful creative writing.

In fact, one of the most common reasons editors cite for rejecting pieces of creative writing—even pieces that are otherwise beautifully written—is lack of tension. Tension keeps readers off balance, making them guess, forcing them to wait, allowing them to worry, or to wonder, or to hope. Good writers infuse their writing with tension at *every* opportunity: In the title, the first line of the poem and every line after, the first sentence of narrative and every sentence after, the opening words of dialogue in the play and every single beat.

In this chapter, we will look at various approaches to working with oppositions and manipulating the tension line.

Tension = Yearning + Obstacles

As you learned in Chapter Three, to create a conflict that will hold the interest of readers, a writer hones in on the character's **yearning**: What does this person desire, need, long for? What goal is she trying to reach?

That's where your story, poem, or play starts.

After you've got them hooked in, what keeps readers reading? Obstacles. As the character or speaker moves closer to what they want, obstacles pull or push the main character *directly* away from their goal, making it more and more difficult for the yearning to be met. Once the person (or entity, say, a

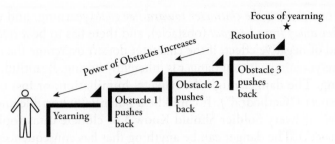

Figure 6.1 Character Yearning Met with Obstacles

parrot) gets what they want—overcoming the final obstacles—the piece is over.

To build the **tension** through a piece of creative writing, it can be helpful to use the above diagram in Figure 6.1 to map your poem, story, or play.

Robert McKee, the renowned screenwriting teacher, describes **obstacles** as the world pushing back on a person's desire, want, yearning, or need. The narrator of "Cathedral" yearns to keep the status quo; he resists growth and change. The world pushes back: His wife had a life before they were married, and one of her friends, a blind man, is coming to visit, staying in their house. The speaker in "What Every Soldier Should Know" yearns to speak the language and respect the customs of the foreign place he is in—"Always enter a home with your right foot; / the left is for cemeteries and unclean places." But the world pushes back and pushes back hard: RPG, bombs under overpasses, parachute bombs. Notice how in both the short story and the poem, the obstacles progress—increase—in terms of their level of difficulty for the speaker or character. Readers expect tension to build.

> *My writing is always [prompted by] this whole series of questions that I'm asking myself: Why does this happen? Why does that person behave that way? What is the impact of that behavior? How is that person going to change? What's going to be the catalyst to their change?*
> —JACQUELINE WOODSON

If there is no danger, if nothing of consequence will happen, if the main character doesn't get what she wants, there is no tension. *This is a common error.* It's only when you combine yearning or desire (the thing a character or speaker most wants—growth and maturity, more meaningful interpersonal connection with others, money, to score points, to get out of a relationship, to stay in a relationship until death do us part) and obstacles that have some amount of risk or danger that you create tension. You have to have both forces—one *pulling the character toward her goal* (yearning) and the other *pushing her away from her goal* (obstacle), and there has to be *a consequence*, some kind of negative effect, if the character doesn't overcome the obstacle.

Desire/yearning without danger is inherently boring. Beautiful, perhaps. But boring. The danger might be naivete, humiliation, or loss of respect or self-respect ("Cathedral"). It could be a potentially horrible and violent death ("What Every Soldier Should Know") or climate catastrophe ("The Great Silence"). The danger can be anything that has consequences that are significant for the parties involved. Love—a good thing, but one that has massive risks and consequences—can be overwhelming; it may be dangerous to even contemplate loving someone permanently, for the rest of your life ("First Poem for You").

You must have all three components: strong desire/yearning, interesting obstacles pushing back against that yearning, and some consequences, a "So what?" For example, you might have a young character with a strong desire—to impress his mom. But unless the world is pushing back—a hurtful, racist comment ("Chop Suey" on page 74)—there's not much tension, and therefore not much of a story: You've got a mother and a son standing around in a bowling alley. Conversely, you might infuse a lot of danger into your writing—apocalypse on the horizon, people losing limbs and parts of themselves—but unless there is a strong, clear, single-pointed yearning, the tale will likely fall flat.

Your obstacles—the risk factors—needn't be murders, car chases, or battlefields. Often it is subtle, small obstacles that actually create the most tension: a mother honking the car horn at 6:00 a.m., someone who hangs up on you unexpectedly, a hard no from a good friend.

PRACTICE 1

IDENTIFYING TENSION

Choose one of the pieces in this chapter (or read as assigned by your instructor). What are the two central forces pulling in opposite directions in the piece?

Tension, Stakes, and Cause/Effect

Read the following example, and rate the tension contained in this passage on a scale of 0 to 5, with 0 being very little tension, and 5 being quite tense and interesting:

> I wake up when my alarm goes off and I get out of bed. It's 7:47 a.m. I can't believe I have to go to work. I will be late. I get dressed, and drive—the traffic is terrible. I stop by my aunt's. I get out of my car.

I see my aunt waiting for me in the yard. She is wearing tan clamdiggers and her black shirt complements her dark olive skin and her black hair. Her Teva-saddled feet are next to a white ball. Sneaky sees me, wagging his tail. When he reaches me I pick him up.

The piece seems fine, in many ways. It's doing all of the things you've learned in this textbook so far: showing action, movie-in-mind, describing people, using specific detail. There is energy from staying in one point of view. However, there is some filtering: "I can't believe I have to go to work." And the verbs are weak and unsparky: *is* and *are*. The characters are doing things, in action—to some extent. And there are specific details—"clamdiggers" and Tevas. But somehow, the piece falls flat. So flat that many readers rate this writing as a 0 in tension. Others rate it a 1 or a 2—they're mildly interested in what will happen with the aunt and this dog. While there will probably some pieces from this textbook that you remember long after the course ends, it's fairly certain this will not be one of them.

The main reason perfectly nice writing falls flat is because of lack of true tension. The yearning, obstacles, and consequences must be set into a matrix of cause and effect. In our example above, there is no meaningful cause and effect. The character yearns to get to work on time, but nothing happens when they don't. The character stops to see an aunt—but there's no yearning on the page. So, the reader cares *not at all.*

There are four components to building effective tension in a matrix of cause and effect:

1. A person or entity, with a strong need for something (a yearning both internal and external)
2. Obstacles block that yearning
3. **Consequences** that matter: When they don't get what they yearn for, there's a clear, discernable effect
4. A meaningful rhythm of **cause and effect**. Because of x, y happens; because of y, the character must now actively change course in order to reach the object of her desire.

In the example above, with the late-to-work employee, their aunt, and the dog, we do not have a clear yearning on the part of the "I." All we are given is events. Drive to aunt; aunt is there; dog walks over. We don't have true obstacles—traffic can make one late, but there don't appear to be any consequences for this person, for lateness or really for anything else. In fact, we're not shown any consequences for any of these actions, and therefore they feel unimportant. Why are you at your aunt's home? What's the point? Why are you telling us that the dog comes over to you? If you go to your aunt's home, there has to be a reason that matters, regarding your yearning. If the dog comes over, it has to matter, somehow. And, these events—aunt, dog, lateness—have to create new problems—**cause**. Those new problems have to matter and relate to the yearning: **effect**. The passage falls flat because the action lacks all four of the key ingredients of tension.

Action isn't yearning. Events aren't obstacles. Random events (heavy traffic, lousy job) aren't consequences. An arrival at a house with a dog walking over to greet you is not cause and effect. It's meaningless: the reader will ask—so what?

How do you move from "So what?" to "What's next?" You may find it helpful to plan your poem, story, or play on paper, making notes or sketching the four elements of tension before you begin. It's okay if the elements change as you work; that's common. Many writers find studying professional examples to see how the four elements work together to be the most effective way to improve the quality of tension in their writing.

Examine this passage from Marisa Silver's story "What I Saw from Where I Stood":

> Dulcie is afraid of freeways. She doesn't like not being able to get off whenever she wants, and sometimes I catch her holding her breath between exits, as if she's driving past a graveyard. So, even though the party we went to last week was miles from our apartment in Silver Lake, we drove home on the surface streets.

How would you rate the level of tension in this paragraph compared to the one above? This paragraph has more tension than the earlier example about a person driving across town to see their aunt. What contributes to the tension in Silver's passage?

1. *Yearning.* Dulcie is afraid. There is immediately a yearning—to be safe—and a real, present, and clear threat that is specific to this person. If she has to go on a freeway, she's going to freak out. She feels trapped on freeways; she holds her breath between exits. The yearning is internal (desire) and external (an action).
2. *Obstacles.* The "I" (the narrator of the story) catches Dulcie "holding her breath." That makes him tense. It makes us tense. They have to take inefficient routes to avoid freeways.
3. *Consequences.* Dulcie's fears may take a toll on the narrator. How long can they continue to take the long way, adjust their lives because of her anxiety?

4. *Cause and effect.* We're worried about the effect of all of Dulcie's fears and yearning on the narrator. We're worried about Dulcie, this woman who is afraid of freeways—*something* caused that to happen to her.

Three simple sentences. Quite a bit of tension. How? The focus is on the character's desire—Dulcie wants safety; the world doesn't provide that. The stakes are clear: She holds her breath (which makes us hold our breath)—you can't live without breathing. She wants to breathe—she just needs to be able to exit when she feels panicky. The narrator might want to be helpful to her—we do not yet know and that in itself creates some tension. How much can he really offer? How does he feel about her?

When you open your piece with clear, interesting, and original problems and questions, as this piece opens, and you imply cause and effect, you offer your reader a tension line as a through line. We want to keep reading.

The Elements of Tension

Component	Considerations
1. PERSON: A person with a problem.	Be specific. Provide name, age, situation, setting, cultural/social information.
2. YEARNING: The person wants something specific—a strong desire for something they must have.	What the person wants drives the tension. Ideally, the character/speaker has an external, physical desire that parallels or contrasts with an interior, psychological yearning.
3. OBSTACLES: The person has to be thwarted by obstacles that keep her from getting what she wants. Obstacles can be opponents (another person or people interfering with the goal) or internal/external forces (grief, fear, weather, etc.).	When the person gets what she wants, the piece is over, the tension is resolved. During the piece, don't let the character get what she wants and/or keep creating new needs, new wants. Your job as a writer is to move her closer to her need, and to keep increasing the difficulty posed by the obstacles.
4. STAKES: What the person wants is important—it has to matter to her, greatly.	What are the consequences of the unmet need? What if she doesn't get what she wants? How bad will it be? If your character doesn't care about what happens to them, the reader won't either.

Notice that in "What I Saw From Where I Stood," as in most, things start bad—fear of freeways—and the writer keeps giving more information that *increases* the tension. Moving in closely again on that excerpted passage, notice that in addition to the freeway fear, Dulcie holds her breath. The party is far away (higher stakes). Notice how Silver, the writer, is dialing up the tension one notch at a time, one sentence at a time.

Cause and effect drives the tension line in Jenifer Hixson's memoir, "Where There's Smoke," on page 274. A fight with her partner causes Jenifer to flee; because she's fleeing domestic violence, she's motivated to help another woman who appears to be in the same situation; because she helps the woman, they bond and the woman is motivated to take her to her apartment; because she sees the woman's apartment, and her child, she's motivated to reconsider her life in complex ways.

PRACTICE 2

EXAMINING TENSION IN FICTION

Identify the central character in "What I Saw from Where I Stood" by Marisa Silver on page 279. Identify his yearnings (interior and exterior), the obstacles that block his yearnings, and what's at stake (what could go wrong). Make a statement about the chain of cause and effect (how one event causes another) in the story. Find words or phrases that support each component. If you feel you need more practice with these techniques, examine the short stories, perhaps in a small group or with a partner, "Surrounded by Sleep" and "Bodies."

PRACTICE 3

EXAMINING TENSION IN POETRY

Read "Abecedarian Requiring Further Examination of Anglikan Seraphym Subjugation of a Wild Indian Rezervation" by Natalie Diaz on page 273. Identify the central yearning of the speaker in the poem, the obstacles that block the yearning, and what's at stake (what could go wrong). Quote the line of poetry that best exemplifies each aspect of tension.

MAINTAINING TENSION

Work with at Least Two Characters/Elements

Most writers don't automatically create tension; it's a skill that has to be developed. We've examined a tension template—yearning + obstacles + consequences + cause and effect—that you can use as you work to set up your creative writing to ensure there is interest for your reader. As you design and structure your piece, you're looking at tension throughout the whole.

Now we will look at ways to keep your piece taut, to ensure there is tension on the micro level, in every line, on every page.

First, consider always writing with two or three elements or characters so that you can have "sides." When you write about one person who is alone, you tend to rely on thoughts. It's harder to create tension with a character alone onstage, lost in thought—difficult but not impossible; in "I am not Batman," Marco Ramirez creates dramatic interplay between his solo speaker and the drums and the special effects on stage. The monologue details a powerful, fraught story with menacing characters and hope. The boy isn't thinking—he's talking (action). His yearning is incredibly strong, and the tension gets higher as we learn about obstacles in his past and the terrible obstacles in his current situation. He's on a high floor: consequences. The drums and smoke onstage create a terrific pulse of cause and effect.

As a rule, however, a character alone with their thoughts is boring. Twos are more interesting—a game is afoot. "Boys" by Rick Moody relies on a double, an us-versus-them: There's "the boys" and then there is everyone else. Kim Addonizio's "First Poem for You" is like most love poems, focused on the dynamics between two people with a lot at stake: their hearts. Tracing the tattoos *causes* the speaker to think about permanence. Dylan Landis's "In My Father's Study upon His Death" is a story of a father and a daughter, and though the father has just died, he lives on in his belongings *causing* the daughter to see who he really was. Twos work well and threes are almost always inherently interesting—because there is so much more opportunity for *problems* to arise. Notice how tension is created in Mary Robison's "Pretty Ice" because there are three characters, each with a yearning that creates obstacles for the other characters. Natalie Diaz's "My Brother at 3 a.m." relies on a triad: the brother, the sister, and the mother, each with a competing agenda. Akhil Sharma's "Surrounded by Sleep" has three pulse points—parents, grieving healthy brother with a damaged brother, and high tension.

PRACTICE 4

EXAMINING TENSION IN NONFICTION

Jenifer Hixson's memoir, "Where There's Smoke" on page 274 is an instructive example of how to create tension. Read it (and/or listen to her spoken-word version on YouTube). How does Hixson create tension by using two characters, herself and the other young woman? Make a statement about her use of yearning for each character and obstacles for each character. If it's easier for you, instead of writing a paragraph, try mapping both of the women's yearning for an object of desire and the mounting obstacles each faces, by using the diagram on page 249 as your model; you'll do a map for each woman separately.

PRACTICE 5

EXAMINING TENSION IN DRAMA

Read "Now We're Really Getting Somewhere" by Kristine Halvorson on page 240. What is Jen's yearning? What are the obstacles to her yearning? What is Bethany's yearning? What are her obstacles? Do the obstacles increase in intensity for each character as the play progresses? What other factors in the play create tension?

Match Your Opponents

Perhaps you have left a football game at half time because the score is so uneven. Unless you are related to one of the players (yearning!), virtually nothing is at stake when the score is 108–15 at the half. As a writer, the same rule applies. Unless the strong yearning of your main character is opposed by equally strong obstacles — people or events — throughout the piece, the stakes will drop. When you have a blow-out, you risk losing your reader. The "sides" in the power struggle that your piece explores should probably be equally matched.

In a great game, the kind you stay into triple overtime in pouring rain to see finalized because it's so exciting, the sides are evenly matched. One team pulls ahead by a point. Then the other team scores three. Super close. We are on the edges of our seats, then standing, nervous the whole time. We constantly wonder and worry. *Who is going to win?* And, more important, *How are they going to get from where they are now to that win?* Each play is riveting. Because the stakes are so high, and the teams are so evenly matched, every step, every pass, every glance matters.

In "Pancakes" by Peter Morris on page 303, Buddy is an unemployed philosophy major who is good with words, good at argument, but less effective with job-hunting. Sam is a businessman with a mean streak; he seems to lord his accomplishments over his roommate. Each one has strengths. Each one has weaknesses. They drive each other crazy. They're opposites, to be sure — and, weirdly, equally matched. In the end, Buddy turns out to have more of a mean streak than Sam ever could have imagined: he's actually a psychopath.

Tension in Poetry

Good poems burst with tension — in their word choice, lines, themes, and imagery. Poets knit tension into every aspect of their poems, even the title.

Take a close look at "Abecedarian Requiring Further Examination of Anglikan Seraphym Subjugation of a Wild Indian Rezervation" by Natalie Diaz on page 273. Notice all of the places in this poem where there is tension—a force moving in one direction with a counterforce pulling in an opposing direction:

1. **Form:** This poem is written in the form of an **abecedarian**—a form that requires each line to begin with the next letter of the alphabet. In a poem about literacy, probing both inequity in terms of access and stereotypes about Native Americans, to use a form that is based on the English alphabet creates irony and therefore tension.
2. The **title** creates tension for the reader because it's hard to read. A poem's title is supposed to help you understand the poem. We have to study the title, much as one does when learning a new language. Words are awkwardly misspelled and there are words we have to look up, such as *seraphim* and *Anglican*. Tension occurs here because we're not accustomed to high-level vocabulary pulling us in one direction (to the dictionary) while misspelled words pull us in the opposite direction (questioning the intelligence and editing skill of the speaker). Did you notice that in this alphabet poem, the poet cleverly used all the letters of the alphabet in the title? There's another level of tension: taking the abecedarian form and pushing it further by creating the alphabet yet again, hidden in the title. The title itself serves as a flashlight into the poem, introducing the key tensions, in all their complexity, in this piece.
3. **Situation:** The opponents in the poem about poverty on a reservation, where whites who run the church as well as the dominant political structure are engaged in a high-stakes battle.
4. **Questions** posed to the speaker pack tension into the poem, forcing the reader to consider possible answers.
5. The **tone** of the speaker's voice is filled with tense dictums ("Quit bothering with angels") and ominous cautions ("Remember what happened last time?" and "You better hope . . ."). The speaker is sarcastic in places revealing deep tensions between what the white families experience and what the Native American families experience, on this particular reservation.

In sum, tension in prose and drama is maintained by working with two or three characters or elements and matching the characters equally so there's a power struggle. In poetry, tension is downloaded into every word, every line, every image, and the tone and syntax of the poem. Even the title introduces elements of tension: "First Poem for You" (New lover—will it last? How many poems will the relationship produce?) and "My Brother at 3 a.m." (Not a time of night you probably want to be experiencing conflict.) Notice how the titles of these poems point to situations where there's more than one person involved and the situation itself is unstable, potentially fraught with tension.

MANIPULATING TENSION

Much of what you are doing when you work to increase the tension in a piece of creative writing is *creating oppositions.*

Creating Oppositions

The simplest way to create an **opposition** is to take two qualities in the work and set them against each other. You can create oppositions by carefully choosing the **setting** for each piece you write:

- An Anglican church's Christmas pageant on a Native American reservation
- A beautiful beach in Hawaii where a woman tells her husband she wants a divorce
- A beloved father's office, filled with his art and private personal files — his life — immediately after his death (rather than a dead body in a funeral parlor or a morgue)

In each of these cases, the setting, the action, and the situation clash together, presenting an opportunity for more obstacles.

In addition to creating oppositions between setting and situation, tension is created by showing the reader oppositions within characters. No one is probably all good or all bad. Sam, in "Pancakes," is a jerk — really awful — but he has loaned Buddy money in the past and helped him along.

The good guy has to have some weaknesses and flaws. The steadfast boyfriend in "Pretty Ice" is devoted but passive, and unsuccessful professionally. The blind man in "Cathedral" is thoughtful and a good friend to the wife; he tugs at his beard oddly and falls asleep in front of the television set. Brian Arundel's speaker, the soldier in "What Every Soldier Should Know," wants to speak the local language and bond with the local kids; he also very much wants to stay alive. You're well served to find tension — forces that oppose each other — in each character in your creative writing.

This is crucial in memoir, too, when you are writing about yourself. You'll need to see yourself objectively and interrogate

> *I want to write the story that will zero in and give you intense, but not connected, moments of experience*
> —ALICE MUNRO

your weaknesses as well as your strengths. If you describe yourself as well-meaning, hard-working, and kind, and your mother is portrayed as unpleasant, withholding, and downright mean, the reader may feel like you are just complaining. Try to see your part in the problems; try to see the yearning in the other people in your life. Och Gonzalez, in "What I Do on My Terrace Is None of Your Business," is shut down, lonely, grieving, and isolated. She's also open to a moment of hope and grace. Without both of those yearnings pulling in opposite directions, the piece would lack tension.

PRACTICE 6

READING FOR COMPLEX CHARACTERIZATION

Read "Chop Suey" on page 74, "The Things I've Lost" on page 217, and "I Go Back to Berryman's" on page 76. In each of these three pieces, the speaker—the "I"—is the author himself. What is the main strength or positive aspect of the person in this story? What is the main weakness or blind spot the author is showing about this version of himself at this point in time? What's the tension between those two aspects of the person?

Consider the power of **visual juxtapositions** as a third way to manipulate tension. If the kittens are terribly cute, and you smile when you play with them, and their ribbons are pink, and it's your birthday and you love kittens, you are putting cuteness next to delight next to adorableness. There is simply no tension. If you are severely allergic to cats and hate the color pink, we suddenly have an element of tension. The drum set in "I am not Batman." is a powerful visual juxtaposition that adds tension to Ramirez's play. In "Pancakes," a benign meal of milk and pancakes belies violent interpersonal tension. In "The Great Silence" a parrot discusses astrophysics. **Juxtaposition**—putting things that don't go together next to each other—creates tension.

In addition to creating oppositions, there are three additional strategies you can use to imbue your work with necessary tension:

1. **Modulate tension:** Adjust the temperature.
2. **Create layers:** Echo patterns of imagery to create meaning.
3. **Install façades:** Indicate things aren't what they seem.

In this next section, we'll take a close look at each of these techniques.

Thermostat Control: Adjusting the Temperature

The secret to creating tension, in life and on the page, is to *vary the heat in the situation.* Ups and downs are going to keep your readers on their toes, turning the page to see what happens next. Things start out problematic, then they get a little better, then a lot worse, then really good, then the bottom falls out. In real life it's called "being jerked around."

But for your reader, productive tension is created by these ups and downs, the carefully structured back and forth of increasing tension and then releasing the tension. This up-and-down is the rhythm of creative writing. Don't let your reader adapt. Once the reader adjusts to the emotional tenor of one line, you have to change it up again. Be thoughtfully unpredictable. Don't let your piece remain at the same tension level for long.

Reread the poem "Buying Wine" by Sebastian Matthews on page 71 and refer to Figure 6.2 on the next page. Notice the tension level in the first stanza. A choice is always imbued with some tension; here the choice is backseat or Wine Mart. Each one has pluses and minuses. Somewhat arbitrarily, we could assign a number to that level of tension, on a scale of 0 to 5. Let's say it's a 2. Because the speaker in the poem is a child, either choice is at least a little scary.

In the second stanza, the tension goes down—the boy is in the store, trailing Dad, and things look good, orderly, even familiar, "like bat racks." The tension is perhaps a 1. But not for long. In stanza 3, the cart is "ever-filling"—and this is not good and it's getting worse because the father is "unkempt" and pretty much flinging liquor into the cart in the aisle. Tension in stanzas 3 through 5 could be said to dial up quickly; 2, 3, and then 4. In stanza 5, Matthews ratchets the tension meter back down—the speaker, a child, sees his father shopping here as he shops at the meat store. Things are okay, aren't they? We're just shopping for food. It's good to match wines and food, put a pinot grigio with scallops . . . right? The tension dances down to near 1.

Notice the leap that occurs between stanzas 7 and 8. While the boy is adjusting to his father's wine-shopping ritual, he slips into a reverie, remembering other wine store trips where he made the other choice and stayed in the car. Whenever a writer switches locations, pops into a flashback, moving back in time and space, the reader experiences a tension shift. "Often, we'd stay in the car" moves the tension from 1 back up to 2 or 3, and then in the second line of stanza 8—notice the tension shift in that "dwindling capacity to believe our father" comment. Boom. This isn't a kid who still worships his dad. This is a kid who has been disappointed by this dad many, many times. That statement charges the poem with energy, intensity.

That intensity is increased—to a 5, perhaps, on the tension meter—in the next stanza, where the kids in the backseat are imagined as free from the car, roaming. Unsupervised offspring of an alcoholic father, "like horses" for a moment, and anything could happen. Lots of tension here. Which drops back down when the boys are, sadly, drawn to the liquor store window, to peek in, glimpse "snippets of [the] father's profile." They want to be like him.

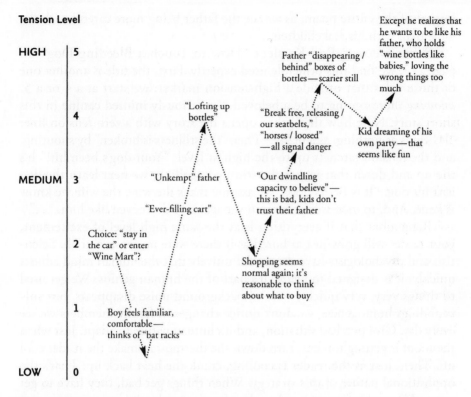

Tension Level

HIGH | 5

Except he realizes that he wants to be like his father, who holds "wine bottles like babies," loving the wrong things too much

Father "disappearing / behind" boxes of bottles — scarier still

4

"Lofting up bottles"

"Break free, releasing / our seatbelts," "horses / loosed" —all signal danger

Kid dreaming of his own party—that seems like fun

MEDIUM | 3

"Unkempt" father

"Our dwindling capacity to believe"— this is bad, kids don't trust their father

"Ever-filling cart"

Choice: "stay in the car" or enter "Wine Mart"?

2

Shopping seems normal again; it's reasonable to think about what to buy

1

Boy feels familiar, comfortable— thinks of "bat racks"

LOW | 0

Figure 6.2 Map of tension in Sebastian Matthews's poem "Buying Wine" on page 71

They want to be with him. They want to be free. The tensions in the poem are further dialed up a notch in the line when he disappears "behind the tall cardboard stacks" as if he's being swallowed up by liquor, which, in fact, he is.

Tension level ranges from 1 to 5. The arrows represent the direction of the tension; the length of the arrows indicates how much the tension increases or decreases.

When the kid loads up his own cart in stanza 12, do you see that as more or less drastic than the preceding stanza? Some readers will say it's just as tense: a 4 or a 5. Because the boy is hurt so deeply in the preceding stanza, seeing his dad disappear, other readers will see this stanza as less tense — a kid acting like a kid. Readers will react differently; what's important for you as the writer is to keep *changing* the intensity.

When the speaker is dreaming of parties, some readers may feel this is the most tense part of the poem because it's so easy to imagine the speaker going down a bad path. Others will believe that the final image, of the father holding "wine bottles like babies in his hands," creates the deepest emotional impact of the entire poem, as we see the father being more careful with the wine than with his real children.

When we read Rod Kessler's "How to Touch a Bleeding Dog" on page 277, we find this principle used expertly. First, the title is another one of those titles that provide a high-tension marker: we start at a 4 or a 5, *knowing* there's going to be a beloved and seriously injured canine in this short story. Note how the author opens the story with a zero tension line: "It begins as nothing, as a blank." Then "the stillness is broken" by shouting, and the tension ratchets up to the highest level: "Your dog's been hit!" It's the up and down that makes the story compelling; we next learn the dog isn't his dog. "It is Beth's dog." We assume that's the wife, the wife we know is gone. And, to increase the tension yet again: "I don't even like him. . . ."

Remember that if everything is at the same high level of excitement, your reader will grow just as bored as if there were no tension at all. Scientists and psychologists have shown definitively that the human mind adjusts quickly; it is designed to *adapt*. It's part of the human genius. We get used to things very, very quickly—loud background noise disappears, our surroundings homogenize, we don't notice changes in family members we see every day. Give us a bad situation, and it's human nature to adapt. Just when the room is getting too hot, turn down the thermostat; make the reader cool off. Then, just as the reader is cooling, crank the heat back up. That's the oppositional nature of this strategy. When things get bad, they have to get worse. When they get worse, they then have to get better.

The following chart lists various elements of a piece of writing, presenting ways for adjusting the thermostat and modulating tension.

Adjusting the Temperature: Ways to Decrease and Increase Tension

Decreases Tension	Increases Tension
Agreement	Disagreement
Safety	Danger
Things are okay	Things are not okay
Generalization	Specific information; intimate details
One thing is going on	Two or three things happening at once
Linear, chronological exposition	Leaps
Moving ahead as expected	Reversals

Having all needs met, ease, simplicity	Wanting something badly, needing, yearning
Overcoming obstacles easily	Thwarted again and again
Solution = resolution	Solution to problem creates new problem
Explanation, telling	Mystery, withholding
Static character, doing nothing	Character in action
Character alone with thoughts	Character in a triangle with two other characters
Speeches, interior dialogues	Crisp dialogue based on an argument
One technique used at length (all description, all dialogue, all interior thoughts . . .)	Variety of techniques (dialogue first, then description, then interior thoughts, then more dialogue . . .)
All long or all short sentences or lines	Short sentences or lines mixed up with longer ones
Seeing the big picture; long shots	Seeing things from *very* close up

---

PRACTICE 7

NO TENSION VERSUS HIGH TENSION

Write a short poem, a paragraph of fiction or nonfiction, or a brief dialogue scene from a play. Make sure it has absolutely no tension. Now, do the opposite: Write in the same genre, but this time include as many tension techniques as possible.

Layers: Adding Dimension

Layers provide important fuel for tension. Layers are two or more facets and they echo each other, reinforcing the meaning and power of your piece of writing. They give it depth and also tension, as the reader works to make surprising connections. You can layer images and you can also create layers by using character triangles.

Layering with Images. **Image layers** are images that repeat throughout the piece in surprising and unexpected places: in the past and the present, for example, or in various settings and situations in the piece. Layers of images infuse your writing with meaning, interest, and excitement. Imagine coming

> *I believe more in the scissors than I do in the pencil.*
> —TRUMAN CAPOTE

upon a stack of halved parsnips (they look like white carrots) in the fridge — not really very interesting on its own.

Add another layer: a young woman with cancer, who has to cook these parsnips for a wealthy family, where there may be adultery, deceit, neglect — a family with emotional cancers — and you've got something rife with tension. The previously plain image is now layered, and three-dimensional. To the young woman with cancer, these innocuous parsnips look like naked human limbs, maybe dead, in the fluorescent light of the refrigerator. That's layering.

In "Bodies" on page 291, when Jessica Shattuck describes Annie's view of little Anthony, her charge, Annie sees the old man in the tiny five-year-old. "He is five years old, blond, and freckled, with close-set blue eyes. Something about his mouth and his stubby but prominent little nose hints already at the old man he will be — stubborn, soft-spoken, a little unforgiving." Annie is aware of death when she opens the fridge, she's aware of age and dying even when she sees a little kid. The themes of the story — who talks, who forgives, what gets passed on — are layered onto the description of a five-year-old.

In "Counting Bats" on page 168, Thao Thai layers four images: first, of the four bats perched on the mosquito netting above her head with images from her trip to Saigon (rats, damp heat) and then, thirdly, her time in the States (coffee shop) and lastly, her childhood, twenty years earlier, with bats "scrambling beneath the bed." It's beautiful writing, richly layered with related images, creating a powerful, memorable three-dimensional portrait bursting with tension.

Shattuck uses image layers in her story to show how all-encompassing living with cancer can be. Thai uses image layers to make a powerful statement about how the past is always part of the present — you can't escape it.

Bottom line: If you provide only one layer in your writing, readers will not find the tension in your piece, and will grow bored at best, and stop reading at worst. Girl goes to party wearing favorite outfit, has fun, meets great guy, parties all night, has to dash to work late the next day — that's just one layer. Person wakes up, goes to work at Starbucks, hates job — that's just one layer. You must have more than one layer of images, connecting and complicating your tension line, in order to transform these series of events into something that has true, meaningful drama.

Poets are experts at using layers. For example, we can identify repeating images in "Abecedarian Requiring Further Examination of Anglikan Seraphym Subjugation of a Wild Indian Rezervation" by Natalie Diaz on page 273 and see just how layers create tension. "Angels don't come to the reservation" the poet announces. But other animals with wings do come by, such as bats and owls, winging in with their own complex and layered mythologies. She continues to layer the angel/flight image pattern, describing who gets the best part in the Christmas pageant. She layers "jailbird"—another thing that flies—into her poem, and we see just how tension abounds as whites both stay out of and profoundly create trouble while the life is very different for those on the reservation.

Brian Arundel uses the image-layering technique to create depth and tension in "The Things I've Lost" by listing experiences, feelings, and personal items he's left behind, creating a portrait of who he is now out of the images of who he used to be and is no longer.

PRACTICE 8

READING FOR IMAGE LAYERS

Jenifer Hixson expertly uses image layers in "Where There's Smoke" on page 274. Find and list examples of images in the story that are used in more than one place, creating tension.

Layering with Triangles. As a writer, you can use the technique of triangles to keep tension high. A **triangle** is three people—characters or entities—all involved in the same situation, each of whom represents a different agenda. Their individual yearnings conflict with one another.

Creative writers typically avoid having one character alone with their thoughts because it's difficult to keep the tension going. It's easier to create tension when we can see two people in conflict with each other, presenting desires that are at odds. Better yet is creative writing that involves three points of conflict, or three forces. In a sophisticated or longer piece, writers layer one triangle over another triangle to create dimensions. This is the premise of most ensemble dramas. Consider *Friends*, the television sit-com that's been on the air since 1994, lasting ten seasons and still widely watched in reruns. Two sets of three—three males, three females—allows for endless combinations of triangle tensions.

Note how triangles form the basic tensions in "Pretty Ice"—mother, daughter, fiancé. In "Bodies," there's a Cleo-Annie-Jay triangle as highlighted in Figure 6.3 on the next page. Annie is drawn to Jay. Cleo is married to Jay. Jay is attracted to and repelled by Annie—she scares him, her illness scares him, she lives in his house, cares for his children (more attentively than Cleo, the mother of his children). Cleo loves Jay, relies on Annie. This is a love triangle, but it's also a triangle created by *complex* human relationships. Good creative writing relies on relationship triangles. Pieces with just one character, or two characters in a simple relationship, may not hold reader's interest as readily as triangle pieces.

> *Don't write about the things that you remember, but the things that you wish you could forget.*
> —SANDRA CISNEROS

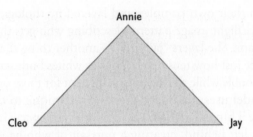

Figure 6.3 Tension triangle in Jessica Shattuck's story "Bodies." Annie, Jay, and Cleo form a triangle. There will always be tension whenever these three are together at the same time.

Shattuck is a very skilled writer. She uses triangles to create friction in her main characters and amplifies those tensions with yet another triangle, the Michele–Cleo–Jay triangle. The Michele–Cleo–Jay triangle provides the subplot, the undercurrent, and this triangle operates as the catalyst for the story. Michele, Cleo's niece, is in love with Jay, who maintains a secret relationship with the girl. Annie is stunned, as we are, by this secret triangle. Anthony is quite literally stuck in the middle of these adult relationships, which make a complex web around him.

Groups of three add dimension, excitement, possibility, and interest. Threes always work.

In Rod Kessler's "How to Touch a Bleeding Dog," the triangle that opens the story with high tension is the husband, our narrator, his dog, and his deceased wife. There's another triangle with the neighbor, his dog, and the husband. And another at the veterinarian's office: the vet, the husband, and the dog. Kessler uses the principle of triangles throughout the story, riveting the reader to the page.

Jenifer Hixson works triangles to her advantage in "Where There's Smoke." The first triangle is her partner (from whom she is fleeing), herself, and the woman who needs a light. The next triangle is herself, the woman, and the man (and child) behind door number four. It's the triangles — vastly different and conflicting yearnings, three different ways — that create the powerful, memorable tension in this piece.

PRACTICE 9

READING FOR TRIANGLES

Read back through pieces you've studied in earlier chapters. Choose two pieces.
List each of the triangles you find in both. Remember, the triangle is created from identifying the conflicting yearnings in three different characters/speakers/entities.

Layering Dialogue and Action.   Some beginning writers fill whole pages with direct dialogue, including long conversations that often don't create images in the reader's mind. No images; no tension. People yakking away mindlessly, or people stating the obvious in direct dialogue, is not going to be rich enough for creative writing. Long speeches, monologues, and he said/she said predictable dialogues weaken good creative writing. Writer and teacher Robert Boswell explains that while we probably say three thousand lines of dialogue out loud every day in our regular lives, perhaps twenty of those lines are worthy of including in a piece of literature. Like everything else in your poem, story, or play, dialogue has to have layers.

Not only do you have to choose the most interesting lines of dialogue for your work, you have to accompany the speech with interesting action. Tension is created when dialogue and action are layered, not predictable. You are cautioned to *not* use the action as a way to explain the dialogue. Equally deadening to tension: when the dialogue explains the action.

Here's an example of unlayered dialogue and action:

"I love you," he said. He handed her the flowers and the card.
"Thank you," she said. She opened the card. "So beautiful!"
"Thanks," he said, and leaned over to give her a kiss. "You know I love you."
"Yes, I love you," she said, and she kissed him back, with pleasure.

There's no reason to use dialogue to render the happy moment. There are no layers here between the dialogue and the action and there's very little, if any, tension in the scene. Save dialogue for the places in your story or poem, memoir or play where the emotions are mixed, and tease out the tension by layering the dialogue and action. For example, here is dialogue and action layered to create tension:

He handed her the anniversary card. "I'm leaving the marriage."

Or:

"Yes, I love you," she said, and she kissed her husband, holding her phone over his shoulder, and eyeing the screen to see if her boyfriend had texted the photo.

In poetry, we see the layering technique between what's said — "Gabriel? Never heard of him" — and what's happening — a car thief named Gabe passes through town while a privileged pageant rehearses. In drama, layering action and dialogue is the foundation of a great play. Sam clearly isn't sharing a single bite—his words could not be clearer. Buddy sits at the table anyway, drawing closer and asking "Why won't you give me some of those pancakes?" Terrific tension.

Note the basic tension line that governs this strategy is always in play, and what's said is pulling in a different direction from what the speaker is actually doing:

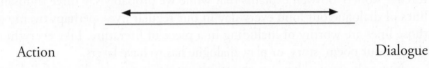

Action   Dialogue

Tension

Dialogue never occurs outside human action. When we speak we use our full body, our face moves around, and our arms and gestures and habits punctuate our phrases. We interrupt, we slam the book on the table, we cross our arms, we roll our eyes, scoot our chair back, stroke the arm of our partner—all that is part of the conversation. Dialogue can't be separated from action, and so action is automatically a crucial part of *what is said*. To increase tension, you create layers and oppositions between these two energies.

PRACTICE 10

READING FOR DIALOGUE–ACTION LAYERS

Read aloud just the dialogue—nothing else—from the short story "Bodies" by Jessica Shattuck on page 291. What do you notice about the dialogue? Now go back through and highlight some of the actions that attend each spoken bit. How do the actions create oppositions with the dialogue and therefore the tension?

A final note on keeping the tension high in action and dialogue layers: Avoid using clichés—overly familiar dialogue expressions, things people never *really* say. And avoid not just spoken clichés but also **action clichés**, called emotional shorthand: raised eyebrows, grimaces, smiles, winks, pounding fists. Those are all **shortcuts**, cartoon gestures for real emotions, and a sign of potentially lazy writing.

Action–dialogue units need to have freshness and truth in them.

The takeaway? You'll create the most tension when you also invoke some kind of opposition between what is said and what's done.

> *I like sentences. While some writers are driven by images or scenes or characters, it's when I get a sentence in my head that I feel that there's a story I need to write.*
>
> —TED CHIANG

Façade

A **façade** is a false front. People in real life and characters in books don't always do and say exactly what they mean. Readers take pleasure in reading action and dialogue that is a façade and knowing more than a character or speaker knows about themselves. In writing, the technique of having characters say and do things other than what they actually mean is called *façade*.

Sometimes a person knows full well that they're creating a false front.

"Hey, how's it going," your friend says, but we can tell by her tone, how she is hanging her shoulders and dragging her toe around, making a bored circle, that she doesn't care how you are doing at all. She just wants you to ask her how *she's* doing. The "false front" she is putting up by asking you how it's going covers up what she really means. In Rod Kessler's "How to Touch a Bleeding Dog," the character lies to the vet when he says, "Beats me." He knows he's lying; he owns it.

But in other cases, a person doesn't know themselves well enough to be able to discern their true emotions; they unknowingly create façades. In "Pretty Ice" on page 169, Mary Robison uses the façade technique throughout the story. The young woman tells us she is taking pleasure balancing her accounts; we suspect she's actually worried about money and conflicted about this engagement as we see that she's not getting herself or her apartment ready for her fiancé's arrival. When she leaves to go and pick him up at the train station, she refuses to look in the mirror. The author is giving us a hefty clue: Here's a person who won't look at herself. When the mother begins to hum, annoying her daughter, we have another façade — casting doubt on Will's arrival and then her humming is annoying; she's doing it accidentally on purpose, it seems. Then the mother asks for more explanation on what Will does for work and the daughter answers coldly, "It means he doesn't make a lot of money."

Lots of façade creates delicious tension throughout this story. The daughter says she is looking forward to seeing her fiancé but she's been up all night; she doesn't have a car — her mother is taking her to the train station. The daughter's yard is frozen; her heart is frozen. The mother promises not to ask Will about the money situation — façade: Those words are practically the first ones out of her mouth.

Dialogue and action work in concert to create façade. The reader feels the tension between what is declared on the page and what's really felt and yearned for by the people in the piece.

Examine this scene from Marisa Silver's "What I Saw from Where I Stood":

"We saw them," she said. "We know what they look like."

"They weren't killers. They were thieves. There's a difference, I guess," I said.

"No," she said, twisting her straight brown hair around her finger so tightly the tip turned white. "It doesn't make sense."

Dulcie needs things to be exact.

In the passage above, Dulcie's dialogue lines are interesting because we have to pay attention to understand what they are about. She hides as much as she reveals when she talks. The reader is *drawn in*. These are not talking heads, making a point to serve the writer's goal. These are stressed-out people, in pain, trying to communicate. They say the wrong thing, or try to impress the cops, or come off as serious and devoted, when really they are terrified inside.

Dulcie is real to the reader. She is saying things that do make sense and that don't make sense, all at the same time. She is experiencing a great deal of tension inside herself. We feel for her.

Read the dialogue further on:

"I should have noticed them tailing me," Dulcie said now. "How could I not notice a car that close?"

"Don't do that," I told her. "Don't think about what could have happened."

"I have to think about it," she said. "How can you not think about it? We were this close," she said, holding her fingers out like a gun and aiming at my chest.

Dulcie's companion tells her not to worry about "what could have happened." But that isn't what she is worried about. When people are tense, they misunderstand. They hear what they need to hear. Their own motives and concerns come out in the dialogue. He's trying to help. With her actions, she "shoots" her partner, and we see that behind her words there is so much more going on.

"We were this close," Dulcie says. In that line there is façade—she's not just talking about the people in the van. She's talking about the baby, lost, too.

Usually, we reveal a lot more than we think we do when we talk to other people. When we are stressed and tense (those are the moments worthy of dramatizing through creative writing), our internal censors are less able to protect us. We say too much, or not enough. We don't mean to, but we reveal our deepest feelings and desires. "Now it doesn't matter why I clean up. Or whether," Ron Kessler's narrator states in "How to Touch a Bleeding Dog." We know it actually does matter, quite a lot; this is grief. This is depression talking. Façade.

> *Writing a book is like driving a car at night. You can only see as far as your headlights go, but you can make the whole trip that way.*
>
> —E. L. DOCTOROW

"'It's not what you think, Jay begins.'" In "Bodies" Annie knows more about what's going on in this home than the family realizes, and she creates a façade when she says, "It's not my business." She says it's not her home, but she does live there. Tension seeps and surges through the technique of façade.

In Beth Ann Fennelly's micro-memoir "Two Phone Conversations," she relies heavily on the façade technique to create tension. When the mother claims the maid put the wine glass back, we know full well that's not what happened and we know what is happening: The mother has a memory or a drinking problem. Or both. All that in four words: *She put it back.*

PRACTICE 11

READING FOR FAÇADE

Reading through the pieces included in this chapter, find two examples of façade, one where a character is saying something other than what they mean — façade dialogue — and another where a character is doing something that contradicts their stated yearning — façade in action.

WRITING PROJECTS

Poetry

1. Think of a dramatic situation that involves, for you personally, something to do with writing, reading, the alphabet, or literacy — something personal that you care about a lot. Perhaps you have dyslexia, or you come from a bi- or trilingual home. Write about your passion and struggles with spoken word, or teaching someone to read, for example. List the most dramatic, tension-filled images related to your topic and create an abecedarian. Use image layers.

Nonfiction

2. Consider a time in your life when you met someone whose life turned out to be very different from what you assumed; through the writing, explore, in scenes, how you were changed after meeting this person. Focus on your yearning. And try to find an image layer to pull through the piece, as Hixson does in "Where There's Smoke."

Fiction

3. Write a story that uses the tensions of a close game. The only subject you can't use is that of an actual sporting event. Write about a bad

friend-date, awkward shopping with your father, babysitting a nightmare child; let the ups and downs—the tension—be inspired by the forward/backward rhythm of a fantastically close game, one that goes into triple overtime. Consider surprising your reader by letting the apparently weaker person win.

Drama

4. Try writing a short play with only two characters at a meal; rely heavily on façade. Before you begin, consider plotting out both characters' yearnings and the obstacles the other character will place in their path during this meal where neither character says what they mean.

TENSION WORKSHOP

The prompts below will help you constructively discuss your classmates' work.

1. Does the piece contain yearning and obstacles? Does the piece contain consequences (unwanted effects if the desire isn't met)?
2. Does the piece have elements of tension in the title and in every line? Explain.
3. Create a tension map for the piece, assigning a number to represent the amount of tension in each paragraph (for prose) or line (for poetry and drama). Does the piece "flatline" (the same number repeats) in certain places? How could the numbers vary more? In which one place do you suggest the author work hardest to increase the tension?
4. What's the central tension?
5. What parts of the piece display the most tension? What techniques is the writer using that create the most tension?
6. Identify three places in the piece where there could be more tension.
7. List at least two uses of triangles or potential triangles that could be developed.
8. Read just the dialogue aloud. Does it sound natural? Do you find layers in what is said and what is really meant? Do you find oppositions? Is the dialogue tension-filled or predictable? Note the best use of dialogue and say why. Note the weakest passage of dialogue and say why.
9. Has the writer used the façade technique? Where might the writer try to use façade more fully or boldly?

READINGS

Natalie Diaz

Abecedarian Requiring Further Examination of Anglikan Seraphym Subjugation of a Wild Indian Rezervation

Angels don't come to the reservation.
Bats, maybe, or owls, boxy mottled things.

Coyotes, too. They all mean the same thing—
death. And death

eats angels, I guess, because I haven't seen an angel
fly through this valley ever.

Gabriel? Never heard of him. Know a guy named Gabe though—
he came through here one powwow and stayed, typical

Indian. Sure he had wings,
jailbird that he was. He flies around in stolen cars. Wherever he stops,

kids grow like gourds from women's bellies.
Like I said, no Indian I've ever heard of has ever been or seen an angel.

Maybe in a Christmas pageant or something—
Nazarene church holds one every December,

organized by Pastor John's wife. It's no wonder
Pastor John's son is the angel—everyone knows angels are white.

Quit bothering with angels, I say. They're no good for Indians.
Remember what happened last time

some white god came floating across the ocean?
Truth is, there may be angels, but if there are angels

up there, living on clouds or sitting on thrones across the sea wearing
velvet robes and golden rings, drinking whiskey from silver cups,

we're better off if they stay rich and fat and ugly and
'xactly where they are—in their own distant heavens.

You better hope you never see angels on the rez. If you do, they'll be
  marching you off to
Zion or Oklahoma, or some other hell they've mapped out for us.

Jenifer Hixson
Where There's Smoke

I reached over and secretly undid my seat belt. And when his foot hit the brake at the red light, I flung open the door, and I ran. I had no shoes on. I was crying. I had no wallet. But I was okay because I had my cigarettes. And I didn't want any part of freedom if I didn't have my cigarettes.

When you live with someone who has a temper — a very bad temper — a very, very bad temper — you learn to play around that. You learn, *This time, I'll play possum, and next time I'll just be real nice, or I'll say yes to everything.*

Or you make yourself scarce, or you run. And this was one of the times when you just run.

And as I was running, I thought, *This was a great place to jump out,* because there were big lawns and cul-de-sacs.

Sometimes he would come after me and drive and yell at me to "get back in, get back in!"

And I was like, *No, I'm outta here. This is great.* And I went and hid behind a cabana, and he left.

And I had my cigarettes.

I started to walk around this beautiful neighborhood. It was ten-thirty at night, and it was silent and lovely. There was no sound, except for sprinklers. And I was enjoying myself. Enjoying the absence of anger, and enjoying these few hours I knew I'd have of freedom.

Just to perfect it, I thought, *I'll have a smoke.* And then it occurred to me, with horrifying speed, *I don't have a light!*

Just then, as if in answer, I see a figure up ahead. *Who is that? It's not him. Okay. They don't have a dog. What are they doing out on this suburban street?*

And the person comes closer, and I can see it's a woman. Then I can see she has her face in her hands. Oh, she's crying. And then she sees me, and she composes herself. And she gets closer, and I see she has no shoes on. She has no shoes on, and she's crying, and she's out on the street.

I recognize her, though I've never met her.

And just as she passes me, she says, "You got a cigarette?"

And I say, "You got a light?"

And she says, "Damn, I hope so."

And then she digs into her cutoffs in the front. Nothing. Then digs in the back. And then she has this vest on that has fifty million little pockets on it, and she's checking and checking, and it's looking bad. It's looking very bad. She digs back in the front again, deep, deep, and she pulls out a pack of matches that have been laundered at least once.

We open it up, and there is *one match* inside.

Oh my God, it's like NASA now. *How we gonna do it?* And we hunker down. We crouch on the ground. *Where's the wind coming from?* We're stopping. I take out my cigarettes. *Let's get the cigarettes ready.*

"Oh, my brand," she says. Not surprising.

We both have our cigarettes at the ready. She strikes once. Nothing. She strikes again. *Yes!* Fire. Puff. Inhale. Mmmm. The sweet kiss of that cigarette.

And we sit there, and we're loving the nicotine, and we both need this right now, I can tell. The night's been tough.

Immediately we start to reminisce about our thirty-second relationship:

"I didn't think that was gonna happen."

"Me neither."

"Oh, man, that was close."

"I'm so lucky I saw you."

"Yeah."

Then she surprises me by saying, "What was the fight about?"

And I say, "What are they all about?"

And she says, "I know what you mean. Was it a bad one?"

And I say, "You know like, medium."

"Oh."

And we start to trade stories about our lives. We're both from up north. We're both kind of newish to the neighborhood (this is in Florida). We both went to college — not great colleges, but, man, we graduated.

And I'm actually finding myself a little jealous of her because she has this really cool job washing dogs. She had horses back home, and she really loves animals, and she wants to be a vet.

And I'm like, "Man, you're halfway there!"

I'm a waitress at an ice cream parlor. I don't know where I want to be, but I know it's not that.

And then it gets a little deeper, and we share some other stuff about what our lives are like. Things that I can't ever tell people at home. This girl, I can tell her the really ugly stuff, and she understands how it can still be pretty. She understands how nice he's gonna be when I get home, and how sweet that'll be.

We are chain-smoking off each other. "Oh, that's almost out. Come on . . ."

We go through the entire pack until it's gone.

Then I say, "You know what? This is a little funny, but you're gonna have to show me the way to get home." Because although I'm twenty-three years old, I don't have my driver's license, and I just jumped out right when I needed to.

And she says, "Well, why don't you come back to my house, and I'll give you a ride?"

"Okay, great."

We start walking. And we get to this corner with lots of lights, and the roads are getting wider and wider, and there are more cars. I see lots of stores — you know, Laundromats and dollar stores and EmergiCenters.

And then we cross over US-1, and she leads me to some place, and I think, *No.*

But, yes.

Carl's Efficiency Apartments. This girl lives here.

And it's horrible, and it's lit up so bright, just to illuminate the horribleness of it. It's the kind of place where you drive your car right up, and the door's right there, and there are fifty million cigarette butts outside. There are doors one through seven, and you just know behind every single door there's some horrible misery going on. There's someone crying or drunk or lonely or cruel.

And I think, *Oh, God, she lives here. How awful.*

We go to the door — door number four — and she very, very quietly keys in. As soon as the door opens, I hear the blare of a television, and on the blue light of the television, the smoke of a hundred cigarettes in that little crack of light.

I hear a man, and he says, "Where were you?"

She says, "Never mind. I'm back."

And he says, "You all right?"

And she says, "Yeah, I'm all right."

And then she turns to me and says, "You want a beer?"

And he says, "Who the *fuck* is that?"

And she pulls me over, and he sees me, and he says, "'Oh. Hey."

I'm not a threat.

Just then he takes a drag off of his cigarette, a very hard drag — the kind that makes the end of it really heat up hot, hot, hot. And long. And it's a little scary. And I follow the cigarette down, 'cause I'm afraid of that head falling off. And I'm surprised when I see, in the crook of his arm, a little boy, sleeping. A toddler. And I think, [*gasps*].

And just then the girl reaches under the bed and takes out a carton, and she taps out the last pack of cigarettes in there. On the way up, she kisses the little boy, and then she kisses the man.

And the man says again, "You all right?"

And she says, "Yeah. I'm just gonna go out and smoke with her."

And so we go outside and sit amongst the cigarette butts and smoke.

I say, "Wow. That's your little boy?"

"Yeah, isn't he beautiful?"

"Yeah, he *is*. He is beautiful."

"He's my light. He keeps me going," she says.

We finish our cigarettes. She finishes her beer. I don't have a beer, 'cause I can't go home with beer on my breath. She goes inside to get the keys. She takes too long in there getting the keys, and I think something must be wrong.

She comes out, and she says, "Look, I'm really sorry but, um, like, we don't have any gas in the car. It's already on 'E,' and he needs to get to work in the morning. I'm gonna walk to work as it is. So what I did was, here, look, I drew out this map for you. You're like a mile and a half from home. If you walk three streets over, you'll be back on that pretty street, and you just take that and you'll be fine."

She also has wrapped up, in toilet paper, seven cigarettes for me — a third of her pack, I note. And a new pack of matches.

And she tells me, "Good-bye," and "that was great to meet you," and "how lucky," and "that was fun," and, you know, "let's be friends."

And I say, "Yeah, okay." And I walk away.

But I kinda know we're not gonna be friends. I might not ever see her again. And I kinda know I don't think she's ever gonna be a vet. And I cross, and I walk away.

And maybe this would have seemed like a visit from my possible future, and scary, but it kinda does the opposite. On the walk home I'm like, *Man, that was really grim over there. And I'm going home now to my nice boyfriend, and he's gonna be so extra-happy to see me. And we have a one-bedroom apartment. And we have two trees, and there's a yard. And we have this jar in the kitchen where there's loose money that we can use for anything. We would never, ever run out of gas. And I don't have a baby, you know? So I can leave whenever I want.*

I smoked all seven cigarettes on the way home. And people who have never smoked cigarettes just think, *Ick, disgusting and poison.* But unless you've had them and held them dear, you don't know how great they can be, and what friends and comfort and kinship they can bring.

It took me a long time to quit . . . that boyfriend. And then to quit smoking. But sometimes I still miss the smoking.

Rod Kessler

How to Touch a Bleeding Dog

It begins as nothing, as a blank. A rose light is filtering through the curtains. Rosy and cozy. My blanket is green. My blanket is warm. I am inside. Inside is warm. Outside is the dawn. Outside is cold. Cold day. My arm reaches for a wife who is no longer there.

The stillness is broken by the voice of a neighbor, yelling from the road outside. "The dog! Your dog's been hit!" It's the farmer down the road, keeping farmer's hours. "The dog!"

It's not my dog, but it's my responsibility. It is Beth's dog. I don't even like him, with his nervous habit of soiling the kitchen floor at night. I used to clean up after the dog before Beth came yawning out of our bed, and that was an act of love, but not of the dog. Now it doesn't matter why I clean up. Or whether.

Beth's dog is old and worn. He smells like a man given to thin cigars. Beth found him at the animal shelter, the oldest dog there.

I find the dog quivering on his side where he limped from the road. He has come to the garden gate, where the rose bushes bloom. A wound on his leg goes cleanly to the bone, and red stains appear here and there on the dull rug of his coat. He will not stand or budge when I coax him. A thick brown soup flows out of his mouth onto the dirt.

On the telephone, the veterinarian asks me what he looks like, and I say, stupidly, like an old Airedale. He means his wounds. After I describe them, he instructs me to wrap the dog in something warm and rush him over.

I make a mitten of the green blanket and scoop weeds and clods as well as the dog. The dew on the grass looks cool, but the blood that blossoms on the blanket is warm and sick. He is heavy in my arms and settles without resistance in my car. He is now gravity's dog.

Driving past the unplowed fields toward town, I wonder if my clumsiness hurt the dog. Would Beth have touched him? The oldest dog in the shelter! It's a wonder that she thought having a dog would help.

The veterinarian helps me bring the dog from the car to the office. We make a sling of the blanket, I at the head. We lay him out on a steel-topped table. I pick weeds and grass from the blanket and don't know what to say.

The veterinarian clears his throat but then says nothing.

"He's my wife's dog," I say. "Actually, he came from the shelter over on High Street. He wasn't working out, really. I was thinking of returning him."

The veterinarian touches a spot below the dog's ear.

"Maybe," I continue, "maybe if it's going to cost a lot . . ."

"I don't think you have to make that decision," says the veterinarian, who points out that some papillary response is missing. "He's dying," he says. "It's good you weren't attached to him."

Beth, I remembered, enjoyed taking the dog for rides in the car.

"These breaths," the veterinarian is saying, "are probably his last."

He seems relieved that he needn't bother to act appropriately for the sake of any grief on my part. He asks, "Did he run in the road a lot?"

"Never," I say. "He never ran at all."

"What do you make of that?"

"Beats me," I say, lying. I watch the dog's chest rise and fall. He's already far away and alone. I picture myself running out into the road.

I watch my hand volunteer itself and run its finger through the nap of his head, which is surprisingly soft. And, with my touch on him, he is suddenly dead.

I walk back to the car and am surprised by how early in the day it still is. Blood is drying on the green blanket in my hand, but it will come off in the wash. The blood on the carpet of the car is out of sight, and I will pretend it isn't there. And then there's the touch. But soon the touch, too, will be gone.

Marisa Silver
What I Saw from Where I Stood

Dulcie is afraid of freeways. She doesn't like not being able to get off whenever she wants, and sometimes I catch her holding her breath between exits, as if she's driving past a graveyard. So, even though the party we went to last week was miles from our apartment in Silver Lake, we drove home on the surface streets.

I was drunk, and Dulcie was driving my car. She'd taken one look at me as we left the party, then dug her fingers into my pants pocket and pulled out my keys. I liked the feel of her hand rubbing against me through my jeans; she hadn't been touching me much lately.

I cranked open the window to clear my head as we drove through Santa Monica. Nice houses. Pretty flowers. Volvos. Dulcie and I always say we'd never want to live out here in suburbia, but the truth is, we can't afford to, not on our salaries. Dulcie's a second-grade teacher in Glendale, and I'm a repairman for the telephone company.

When we reached Hollywood, things got livelier. There were skinny guitar punks patrolling the clubs on the strip with their pudgy girlfriends in midriff tops and thigh-high black skirts. A lot of big hair, big breasts, boredom. Farther east, there were boys strutting the boulevard, waiting to slip into someone's silver Mercedes and make a buck. One leaned against a fire hydrant and picked at his sallow face, looking cold in a muscle T-shirt.

We hit a red light at Vermont, right next to the hospital where Dulcie lost the baby, a year ago. She'd started cramping badly one night. She was only six months pregnant. I called the emergency room, and the attendant said to come right over. By the time we got there, the doctors couldn't pick up a heartbeat. They gave Dulcie drugs to induce labor and the baby was born. He was blue. He was no bigger than a football.

Dulcie looked up at the hospital and then back at the road. She's a small girl and she sank behind the wheel, getting even smaller. I didn't say anything. The light turned green. She drove across Vermont and I nodded off.

I woke up when a car plowed into us from behind. My body flew towards the windshield, then ricocheted back against my seat. Dulcie gripped the wheel, staring straight ahead out the windshield.

"Something happened," she said.

"Yeah," I heard myself answer, although my voice sounded hollow. "We had an accident."

We got out to check the damage and met at the back of the car. "It's nothing," Dulcie said, as we studied the medium-sized dent on the fender. It was nothing to us, anyway; the car was too old and beat-up for us to feel protective of it.

Behind me, I heard the door of a van slide open. I hadn't thought about the people who'd hit us, hadn't even noticed if they bothered to stop. I started to wave them off. They didn't need to get out, apologize, dig around for the insurance information they probably didn't have. But when I turned around, there were four or five men in front of me. They were standing very close. They were young. I was beginning to think that Dulcie and I should just get back into our car and drive away, when the van's engine cut out and a tall guy wearing a hooded sweatshirt called back towards it. "Yo, Darren! Turn it on, you motherfucker!"

His cursing seemed to make his friends nervous. Two of them looked at their feet. One hopped up and down like a fighter getting ready for a bout. Someone was saying "Shit, shit, shit" over and over again. Then I heard "Do it, do it!" and a short, wide kid with a shaved head and glow-in-the-dark stripes on his sneakers pulled out a gun and pointed it at my face. It didn't look like the guns in movies. Dulcie screamed.

"Don't shoot. Please don't shoot us!" Her voice was so high it sounded painful, as if it were scraping her throat.

"Your keys!" the tall one shouted. "Give us your motherfucking keys!"

Dulcie threw the keys on the ground at their feet. "Please! I don't have any money!"

"I'll get it," I heard myself say, as if I were picking up the tab at a bar. I was calm. I felt like I was underwater. Everything seemed slow and all I could hear was my own breathing. I reached into my back pocket and pulled out my wallet. I took out the bills and handed them over. The tall guy grabbed the money and ran back to the van, which made me feel better until I noticed that the kid with the shaved head was still pointing the gun at me.

That's when I got scared. As though someone had thrown a switch, all the sound returned, loud and close. I heard the cars roaring past on Sunset. I heard Dulcie screaming "No! No! No!" I heard an argument erupt between two of the guys. "Get in their car! Get in their fucking car or I'll do you too!" I grabbed Dulcie's hand, and I pulled her around the front of our car, crouching low. I could feel the heat of the engine under the hood. The van revved up. I stood, bringing Dulcie up with me, and there, on the driver's side, no more than three feet away, was the kid with the shaved head. He had the gun in one hand and Dulcie's keys in the other. I could see sweat glistening over the pimples on his face.

"Hey!" he said, looking confused. "What the fuck?"

Then it was as if I skipped a few minutes of my life, because the next thing I knew, Dulcie and I were racing down a side street toward the porch lights of some bungalows. We didn't look back to see if we were being followed. Sometimes Dulcie held my hand, sometimes we were separated by the row of parked cars. We had no idea where we were going.

After the police and their questions, and their heartfelt assurance that there was nothing at all they could do for us, we took a cab back to our apartment in Silver Lake. Dulcie was worried because the crack heads — that's what the police called them — had our keys, and our address was on the car registration. But the police had told us that the carjackers wouldn't come after us — that kind of thing almost never happened.

Still, Dulcie couldn't sleep, so we sat up all night while she went over what had happened. She'd seen the van on the street earlier, but hadn't it been in front of us, not behind? Why had they chosen our car, our sorry, broken-down mutt of a car? How close had we come to being shot?

"We saw them," she said. "We know what they look like."

"They weren't killers. They were thieves. There's a difference, I guess," I said.

"No," she said, twisting her straight brown hair around her finger so tightly the tip turned white. "It doesn't make sense."

Dulcie needs things to be exact. You have to explain yourself clearly when you're around her, so she's probably a good teacher. For a minute I wondered whether she wished we had been shot, just for the sake of logic.

She'd done this after losing the baby, too, going over and over what she might have done to kill it. Had she exercised too much? Not enough? Had she eaten something bad? She wanted an answer, and she needed to blame someone; if that person turned out to be her, that would still be better than having no one to blame at all. A few days after the delivery, a hospital social worker called to check on her. She reassured Dulcie that what had happened hadn't been her fault. It was a fluke thing, the woman said. She used the word *flukish*.

"I should have noticed them tailing me," Dulcie said now. "How could I not notice a car that close?"

"Don't do that," I told her. "Don't think about what could have happened."

"I have to think about it," she said. "How can you not think about it? We were this close," she said, holding her fingers out like a gun and aiming at my chest.

I drove Dulcie's car to work the next day. When I got home that night, Dulcie had moved our mattress from our bed into the living room, where it lay in the middle of the floor, the sheets spilling over onto the carpet. She'd taken a personal day to recover from the holdup. Her eyes were red, and she looked as though she'd been crying all afternoon.

"It's the rat," she said. "He's back."

A month earlier, a rat had burrowed and nested in the wall behind our bed. Every night, it scratched a weird, personal jazz into our ears. We told the landlord and he said he would get on it right away, which meant: You'll be living with that rat forever, and if you don't like it there're ten other people in line for your apartment. I checked around the house to make sure the rat couldn't find a way inside. I patched up a hole underneath the sink with plywood and barricaded the space between the dishwasher and the wall with old towels. After Dulcie was sure that there would be no midnight visitor eating our bananas, she was okay with the rat. We even named him — Mingus.

She wasn't okay with it anymore.

"He's getting louder. Closer. Like he's going to get in this time," she said.

"He can't get in. There's no way."

"Well, I can't sleep in that room."

"It's a small apartment, Dulcie." The living room was smaller than the bedroom, and the mattress nearly filled it.

"I can't do it, Charles. I can't."

"All right. We can sleep anywhere you want," I said.

"I want to sleep in the living room. And I want you to change the message on the answering machine," she said. "It has my voice on it. It should have a man's voice."

"You're worried about the rat hearing your voice on the machine?"

"Don't make fun of me, okay? Those guys know where we live."

Later that night, I discovered that she wanted to sleep with all the lights on.

"I want people to know we're home," she said. "People don't break in if they think you're there."

We were lying on the floor on our mattress. She felt tiny, so delicate that I would crush her if I squeezed too hard or rolled the wrong way.

"You don't mind, do you?" she said. "About the light. Is it too bright?"

She'd let me throw one of my shirts, an orange one, over the fixture hanging from the ceiling. It gave the room a muffled, glowy feel.

"No," I said. I kissed her forehead. She didn't turn to me. Since the baby, we've had a hard time getting together.

Dulcie sat up again. "Maybe it's a bad idea," she said. "Maybe a thief will see the light on at four a.m. and think that we're actually out of town. I mean, who leaves their light on all night when they're home?"

"No one."

"You know," she said, "I saw in a catalogue once that you could buy an inflatable man to put in a chair by your window. Or in your car. You could put him in the passenger seat if you were driving alone."

She looked at me, but I didn't know what to say. To me, driving with a plastic blow-up doll in the seat next to you seemed very peculiar.

"Lie down," I said, stroking her back beneath her T-shirt. Her skin was smooth and warm.

She lay down next to me. I turned over on my stomach and laid my hand across her chest. I liked the feel of the small rises of her breasts, the give of them.

Dulcie's milk had come in two days after the delivery. The doctor had warned her that this would happen and had prescribed Valium in advance. I came home from work and found Dulcie, stoned, staring at her engorged breasts in the bathroom mirror. I'd never seen anything like it. Her breasts were like boulders, and her veins spread out across them like waterways on a map. Dulcie squeezed one nipple, and a little pearl of yellowish milk appeared. She tasted it.

"It's sweet," she said. "What a waste."

For the next two days, she lay on the couch holding packs of frozen vegetables against each breast. Sometimes we laughed about it, and she posed for a few sexpot pictures, with the packs of peas pressed against her chest like pasties. Other times, she just stared at the living room wall, adjusting a pack when it slipped. I asked her if her breasts hurt, and she said yes, but not in the way you'd think.

I slid my hand off Dulcie's chest, turned back over, and stared at the T-shirt on the light fixture.

"Did you know," she said, "that when you're at a red light the person next to you probably has a gun in his glove compartment?"

"Defensive driving," I said, trying for a joke.

"Statistically speaking, it's true. Until yesterday, I never thought about how many people have guns," Dulcie said. "Guns in their cars, guns in their pocketbooks when they're going to the market, guns . . ."

A fly was caught between the light and my T-shirt. I could see its shadow darting frantically back and forth until, suddenly, it was gone.

The next evening as I was driving home from work, someone threw an egg at my car. I thought it was another holdup. I sucked in so much air that I started to choke and almost lost control. Two kids then ran by my window. One was wearing a Dracula mask and a cape. The other one had on a rubber monster head and green tights. I'd forgotten it was Halloween.

Dulcie takes holidays pretty seriously, and when I got home I expected to see a cardboard skeleton on the door, and maybe a carved pumpkin or two. Usually she greets the trick-or-treaters wearing a tall black witch hat that she keeps stashed in a closet the rest of the year. When she opens the door, she makes this funny cackling laugh, which is kind of embarrassing but also sweet. She's so waifish, there's not much about her that could scare anybody. But when I got home and climbed the outside stairs to our second-floor apartment, there was nothing on our door and the apartment was dark.

"What are you doing with all the lights off?" I asked when I got inside. She was sitting at the kitchen table, her hands folded in front of her as if she were praying.

"Shut the door," she said. "A whole pack of them just came. They must have rung the bell five times."

"They want their candy."

"We don't have any."

"Really? You didn't buy any?"

"Charles, we don't know who any of these people are," she said slowly, as if I were six years old. "I'm not going to open my door to perfect strangers."

"They're kids."

"What about the ones who come really late?" she asked. "All those teenagers. They're looking for trouble."

I sat down and reached across the table for her hands. "It's Halloween, Dulcie. It's just kids having fun."

"Plenty of people aren't home on Halloween. This is just going to be one of those places where nobody's home."

The doorbell rang.

"Dulcie—"

"Sh-h-h!" She hissed at me like a cat.

"This is ridiculous." I got up.

"Please, Charles!"

The bell rang again. I grabbed a box of cookies from the shelf and went to the door. A little kid was walking away, but he turned back when he heard the door open. He was six, eight years old. An old man I recognized from the neighborhood, maybe his grandfather, stood a few steps behind him.

The boy wore a cowboy outfit—a fringed orange vest over a T-shirt with a picture of Darth Vader on it, jeans mashed down into plastic cowboy boots, and a holster sliding down over his narrow hips. He took a gun out of the holster and waved it around in the air.

"Bang," he said, without enthusiasm.

"You got me," I answered, putting my hands to my chest and pretending to die.

"It's a fake gun," the boy said. "No real bullets."

"You mean I'm not dead?" I tried to sound amazed, and I got a smile out of the kid.

The grandfather said something impatiently in another language, Russian or maybe Armenian.

"Trick or treat," the boy said quietly. He held out a plastic grocery sack with his free hand.

I looked into the bag. There were only a few pieces of candy inside. Suddenly the whole thing made me sad. I offered my box of mint cookies.

The boy looked back at his grandfather, who shook his head. "I'm only allowed to have it if it's wrapped," the boy said to me.

I felt like a criminal. "We didn't have a chance to get to the store," I said, as the boy holstered his gun and moved off with his grandfather.

When I went back inside, Dulcie was standing in the middle of the dark living room, staring at me. Three months after the baby died, I came home from work and found her standing in that same place. Her belly underneath her T-shirt was huge, much bigger than when she'd actually been pregnant. For one crazy second, I thought that the whole thing had been a mistake, and that she was still pregnant. I felt a kind of relief I had never felt before. Then she lifted her shirt and took out a watermelon from underneath it.

A group of kids yelled "Trick or treat!" below us. They giggled. Someone said "Boo!" then there was a chorus of dutiful thank-you's. I heard small feet pound up the rickety wooden stairway to the second-floor apartments. I walked over to Dulcie and put my arms around her.

"We can't live like this," I said.

"I can," she said.

Dulcie went back to work three days after the carjacking. I dropped her off at school in my car, and she arranged for one of her teacher friends to give her a lift home. I took it as a good sign, her returning to work. She complains about the public school system, all the idiotic bureaucracy she has to deal with, but she loves the kids. She's always coming home with stories about cute things they did, or about how quickly they picked up something she didn't think they'd understand the first time. She was named Teacher of the Year last spring, and a couple of parents got together and gave her this little gold necklace. Her school's in a rough part of Glendale. The necklace was a big deal.

She was home when I got off work, sitting on the couch. She waved a piece of pink paper in the air.

"What's that?" I said.

"We're not allowed to touch the children anymore," she said.

"What are you talking about?"

She told me that a parent had accused a teacher of touching his daughter in the wrong way. Social Services came in, the works. When they finally got around to questioning the girl, she told them the teacher had just patted her on the back because she answered a question right.

"Now the district's in a panic — they don't want a lawsuit every time some kid exaggerates. So, no touching the students."

"That's nuts," I said. "Those kids need to be hugged every once in a while. They probably don't get enough affection at home."

"That's a racist generalization, Charles," she said. "Most of the parents try hard. They love their kids just as much as you and I would."

Neither of us said anything. Dulcie hadn't brought up the idea of our having kids since we'd lost the baby. She had just stepped on a grenade, and I was waiting through those awful seconds before it explodes.

"This is a fucked-up town," she said finally.

I wasn't sure what had made her say this. The school thing? The carjacking?

"Maybe if we turn on the TV we'll catch a freeway chase," I said.

"Or a riot."

"Or a celebrity bio."

She started laughing. "That's the real tragedy," she said. "The celebrity bio."

We laughed some more. When we stopped, neither of us knew what to say.

"I'm not racist," I said at last.

"I know. I didn't mean that."

"I may be prejudiced against celebrities, though."

She squeezed out a smile. It was worth the stupid joke.

The next Saturday, Dulcie called an exterminator. She'd decided that we should pay for one out of our own pocket, because she'd read that some rats carry airborne viruses.

"People died in New Mexico," she said. "Children too."

It turns out that the exterminator you call to get rid of bugs is not the kind you call to get rid of a rat. There's a subspecialty — Rodent Removal. Our rodent remover was named Rod. Rod the Rodent Remover. I was scared of him already.

When he came to the door, he was wearing a clean, pressed uniform with his name on it. "Rod," I said, "thanks for coming."

"It's really Ricardo, but I get more jobs as Rod. Ricardo is too hard for most people to remember. You have a problem with rats?" he said helpfully.

"Yeah. In here." I opened the door wider and led him into the apartment. "It's not really *in* the apartment, but we hear it from in here."

If Ricardo thought it was strange that the mattress was on the living room floor, he didn't say anything. Dulcie was waiting for us in the bedroom.

"It's there," Dulcie said, pointing to a gray smudge where the head of our bed frame met the wall. "He's in there."

Ricardo went over and tapped the wall with his knuckle. Dulcie held her breath. There was no sound from the rat.

"They usually leave the house during the day," Ricardo said.

"How does he get in?" Dulcie said.

Ricardo raised his finger toward the ceiling. "Spanish tile roof. Very pretty, but bad for the rat problem," he said. "They come in through the holes between the tiles."

"So there's nothing we can do?" Dulcie asked, alarmed.

"We can set a trap in the wall through the heating vent there," Ricardo said, pointing to the one vent in our entire apartment, which was, unhelpfully, in the hallway outside our bedroom.

"Then he'll die in the wall?"

"It's a bad smell for a few days, but then it goes away," Ricardo said.

I could see that none of this was making Dulcie feel any better.

"Or I can put a trap on the roof," Ricardo said.

"Do that," Dulcie said quickly.

"Okay," he said. "Now we have a plan."

He reached into his pockets and took out two yellow surgical gloves. Dulcie was horrified, the gloves confirming her suspicions about disease. But Ricardo smiled pleasantly. This was a guy who dealt with rats every day of his life, and it didn't seem to faze him.

"Why do they come inside?" Dulcie said, as we followed Ricardo towards the door. "The rats. Why do they live in the walls? There's no food there."

"To keep warm," Ricardo said. "Sometimes to have their babies."

He smiled and gave us a courtly nod as I let him out. When I turned back, Dulcie was still staring at the closed door, her hand over her mouth.

"It's just a rat," I said. I touched her shoulder. She was shaking.

A month after the baby died, the mailman delivered a package that I had to sign for. We don't get a lot of packages, so it was an event. The box was from a company called La Tierra. The name sounded familiar, but I couldn't place it; I was about to call back into the apartment for Dulcie when I remembered. La Tierra was the name of the company that cremated the baby.

"What is it?" Dulcie said from behind me. "Who was at the door?"

I turned around. This will kill her, I thought.

"What is it?" she said again, holding out her hand.

I had no choice but to hand it to her. She looked at it. Her face crumpled. "It's so light," she said finally.

I went to put my arms around her, but she stepped back. Then she started laughing. Her laughter became the kind of giggling you can't turn off. She bit her lips and clenched her teeth, but the giggles kept coming, as if they were tickling her insides in order to get out.

"You probably thought it was something from your mom," she said through her laughter. "Or some freebie from a computer company. Oh, my God," she said. "Can you believe this is our life?" I smiled, but it was that weird, embarrassed smile you offer when you feel left out of a joke.

We decided to take the ashes to the beach and scatter them on the water. We drove out to the Ventura County line, to a beach called El Pescador. You have to climb down a steep hillside to get to it, and there's usually no one there, especially in the off season. We parked and scrambled unsteadily down the trail. We were so busy concentrating on not falling that we didn't see the ocean until we were at its level. We both got quiet for a moment. The water was slate gray, pocked by the few white gulls that every so often swooped down to the surface and then rose up again. There were no boats in the ocean, only a couple of prehistoric oil derricks in the distance. "I think we should do it now," Dulcie said.

We opened the box. Inside was some Styrofoam with a hole gouged out. Nestled inside that hole, like a tiny bird, was a plastic bag filled with brown dust. There could not have been more than a tablespoonful. I took the bag and handed the box to Dulcie. Then I kicked off my shoes, rolled up my jeans, and walked out into the water. When I was calf deep, I opened up the bag. I waited for something to happen, for some gust of wind to kick up and take the ashes out to sea. But the day was calm, so I finally dumped the ashes into the water at my feet. A tiny wave moved them towards the shore. I worried that the ashes would end up in the sand, where somebody could step all over them, but then I felt the undertow dragging the water back towards the sea.

"I think that's the bravest thing I've ever seen a person do," Dulcie said as I came out of the water.

As we headed back to the trail, she picked up a smooth stone and slipped it into her pocket. Halfway up the path, she took the stone out and let it drop to the ground.

A week after the holdup, the police called. They had found our stolen car. Once the kids run out of gas, the officer explained, they usually abandon the car rather than pay for more. He gave us the address of the car lot, somewhere in South Central.

"Go early in the morning," the officer warned. "Before they get up."

"'They'?" I asked.

"You a white guy?" the policeman asked.

"Yeah."

"You want to be down there before wake-up time. Trust me."

Dulcie said it was a self-fulfilling prophecy. Everybody expected things to be bad, so people made them bad. She saw it at her school. The kids who were expected to fail, well, they blew it every time out, even if they knew the work cold.

Still, we took the officer's advice and went down to the lot at seven in the morning. I admit I was nervous, driving through those streets. You like to think you're more open-minded than that, but I guess I'm not. I kept thinking about drive-by shootings and gangs and riots and all the things you read about, thinking, Those things don't happen near where I live, so I'm okay.

We found our car. It was a mess. It had been stripped; even the steering wheel was gone. There was every kind of fast-food wrapper scattered on the back seat, and French fries and old hamburger buns on the floor. You get hungry when you're high. It wasn't worth the price of towing, so we signed it over to the pound and left it there.

As I drove Dulcie to work, I told her the police had asked us to come identify the suspects in a lineup.

"But they'll know it was us who identified them," she said. "They know where we live."

"They were busy getting high. I don't think they were memorizing our address."

"I don't even remember what they looked like. It was dark."

"Once you see some faces, it might come back."

"Charles, don't make me do this. Don't make me!" she cried.

"I'm not going to make you do anything. Jesus. What do you think I am?"

She didn't answer me. I dropped her off at the school. She got out and walked towards the front door, then turned to wave at me, as if it were any regular day, as if we weren't living like some rat trapped in our own wall.

I took the day off. I'd already used up my sick days, and I knew we couldn't throw away the money, but I thought I'd go crazy if I had to be nice to a customer or listen to some technician talk about his bodacious girlfriend or his kid's troubles in school.

I didn't have a plan. I picked up a paper and got breakfast at a hipster coffee shop on Silver Lake Boulevard. There were a lot of tattooed and pierced people eating eggs and bacon; they looked as though they were ending a night, not beginning a day. I tried to concentrate on my paper, but nothing sank in. Then I got back into my car. I ended up driving along Vermont into Griffith Park, past the roads where guys stop to cruise, all the way up to the Observatory. I parked in the empty lot and got out.

The Observatory was closed; it was still early. I was trying to think of something to do with myself when I saw a trail heading up into the hills. The path was well worn; on the weekends, it was usually packed with tourists and families making a cheap day of it. But that morning I had it to myself. I wanted to walk. I walked for hours. I felt the sun rise up, and I saw the darkness that covered the canyons lift, as if someone were sliding a blanket off the ground.

By the time I stopped, others were on the trail—runners, or people walking their dogs, some kids who were probably playing hooky. I looked out over the canyon and thought about how I could go either way: I could stay with Dulcie and be as far away from life as a person could be, or I could leave.

I had been looking forward to the baby. I didn't mind talking to Dulcie about whether or not the kid should sleep in bed with us, or use a pacifier, or how long she would nurse him, or any of the things she could think about happily for days. I got excited about it, too. But I had no idea what it meant. What was real to me was watching Dulcie's body grow bigger and bigger, watching that stripe appear on her belly, watching as her breasts got fuller and that part around her nipples got as wide and dark as pancakes. When the doctors took the baby out of her, they handed him to me without bothering to clean him up; I guess there was no point to it. Every inch of him was perfectly formed. For a second, I thought he would open his eyes and be a baby. It didn't look like anything was wrong with him, like there was any reason for him not to be breathing and crying and getting on with the business of being in the world. I kept saying to myself, This is my baby, this is my baby. But I had no idea what I was saying. The only thing I truly felt was that I would die if something happened to Dulcie.

A runner came towards me on the trail. His face was red, and sweat had made his T-shirt transparent. He gave me a pained smile as he ran past. He kicked a small rock with his shoe, and it flew over the side of the canyon. For some reason, I looked over the edge for the rock. What I saw from where I stood was amazing to me. I saw all kinds of strange cactus plants—tall ones like baseball bats, others like spiky fans. There were dry green eucalyptus trees and a hundred different kinds of bushes I couldn't name. I heard the rustle of animals, skunks or coyotes, maybe even deer. There was garbage on the ground and in the bushes—soda cans, fast-food drink cups, napkins with restaurant logos on them. I saw a condom hanging off a branch, like a burst balloon. For some reason, the garbage didn't bother me. For all I knew, this was one of those mountains that was made of trash, and it was nature that didn't belong. Maybe the trash, the dirt, the plants, bugs, condoms—maybe they were all just fighting for a little space.

I got home before Dulcie. I dragged the mattress back into the bedroom. I took my shirt off the light fixture in the living room and put it in the dresser. When Dulcie came back, she saw what I had done, but she didn't say anything. We ate dinner early. I watched a soccer game while she corrected papers. Then I turned off the lights in the living room, and we went into the bedroom. She knew my mind was made up, and she climbed into bed like a soldier following orders. When I snapped off the bedside lamp, she gave a little gasp.

We lay quietly for a while, getting used to the dark. We listened for the rat, but he wasn't there.

"You think the traps worked?" she said.

"Maybe."

I reached for her. At first it was awkward, as though we were two people who had never had sex with each other. Truthfully, I was half ready for her to push me away. But she didn't, and, after a while, things became familiar again. When I rolled on top of her, though, I felt her tense up underneath me. She started to speak. "I should go and get—"

I put my fingers on her mouth to stop her. "It's okay," I said.

She looked up at me with her big watery eyes. She was terrified. She started again to say something about her diaphragm. I stopped her once more.

"It's okay," I repeated.

I could feel her heart beating on my skin. I could feel my own heart beating even harder. We were scared, but we kept going.

Jessica Shattuck
Bodies

In the fluorescent light of the refrigerator, the halved parsnips look naked—pale and fleshy as limbs. Annie pauses before pulling them out. A refrigerator is like a hospital, a bright place that is not cheerful. A protective but uncertain place to wait.

"What are you doing?" Anthony says. He's standing in the doorway.

"Starting dinner," Annie says, flicking on the lights. They both blink in the sudden brilliance.

Anthony climbs up onto one of the tall stools on the other side of the kitchen island. He is five years old, blond, and freckled, with close-set blue eyes.

Something about his mouth and his stubby but prominent little nose hints already at the old man he will be—stubborn, soft-spoken, a little unforgiving.

The music of *The Lion King* drifts toward them from the playroom.

"Not in the mood for the movie?" Annie asks.

Anthony shrugs and lays his head down on his outstretched arm.

Annie dabs small pieces of butter on the parsnips, draining water from the dish. Outside the window, twenty stories below, there is a bright stream of traffic on Fifth Avenue. Beyond that, Central Park is black—lit paths twist through it like constellations. She rinses beans, wraps bread in aluminum foil, rubs garlic and pepper on steaks, washes the pretty purple-and-white salad leaves whose name she can never remember. She and Anthony are comfortable with silence. When she first moved in with his family, he made her nervous. He is an intense child, with a sharp, scrutinizing gaze, and his frankness can be almost cruel. Annie tried to protect herself with chatter, elaborately inventive games, even bribes. But they are friends now. She feels more at home around Anthony than around anyone else she knows.

"Will you read to me?" Anthony asks after the steaks are in the broiler and the beans are steaming on the stove.

Annie looks at the clock. "For five minutes," she says.

"Yes, yes, yes," he chants, sitting up straight now.

Annie is in what her doctor refers to as the "hunker down and wait" period of treatment for Stage III Hodgkin's lymphoma. For the most part, she has been lucky. She has gone through ten remarkably smooth cycles of chemotherapy; the success has yet to be determined, but the side effects have been mild. Her straight, pale-brown hair is thinner, but she still has it. Though she needs at least twelve hours of sleep a day, she is not constantly exhausted. She takes her pills every morning—vitamins, herbs a Chinese doctor prescribed, green algae. She eats kale and radishes and drinks a full gallon and a half of water a day. She lives like someone who has built a home on the San Andreas Fault: She takes what small, possibly ridiculous precautions she can, and then chooses not to think about it.

Until November, Annie worked as a secretary for Anthony's mother, Cleo. Cleo is the creative director of a large international advertising agency—the first woman in the company's history to have this role. She is tall and levelheaded and big-boned, but glamorous. She works fifteen hours a day, and most weekends as well. She is an adept psychoanalyst of the public mind. "That'll make people think of getting old. People don't want to think of getting old," she'll say about a mockup of an ad for a real-estate Web site. Suddenly everyone will realize that the little boy bouncing his ball down the walk into his grandmother's garden reminds them of their lost childhoods — of time passing, of old dreams, and of dying. Cleo will substitute a girl for the boy, an older brother for the grandmother, and it will become an entirely different story. Annie would like to crawl into Cleo's confidence and curl up in her powerful vision of the world as an infinitely malleable, manageable place.

Annie's own days at the agency have been put on indefinite hold, and she misses them — the feeling of purpose and efficiency. Now she lives with Cleo and her family in their penthouse on Fifth Avenue, which has lots of extra room. It is a perfect arrangement, really; Annie did not have many people she could move in with when she got sick. There was her high-school sweetheart, who is now her ex-husband, in San Diego, and her brother, Todd, in Long Beach. But the last time she saw Todd he locked her in the closet and broke a bottle against the door. And her ex-husband has found God.

Besides, Cleo and her husband, Jay, need someone in addition to their babysitter to look after their two children. Mrs. Tibbs, they worry, will teach the children bad grammar and imperfect diction. Now Annie reads them stories and plays interesting, educational games, and is careful to choose her words exactly, hold on to silent "g" 's, never say "gonna" or use "real" as an adjective. She is used to this from the office — the only difference is that it is no longer a work-related necessity but something she has to do at home, because that is what Cleo and Jay's apartment has become.

Annie has made it to page 5 of *Goodnight Moon*, Anthony's favorite book, when the doorbell rings. "No," Anthony says, putting his hand on her hip as she starts to get up. "No." He is clingy and uncertain in the evenings.

"I have to get the door," Annie says gently. "It might be important."

But it is Cleo's niece Michele, who lives with her mother, Cleo's sister, two buildings down.

"Hi," Michele says with a bright, insincere smile. "Is Cleo home yet?" She peers over Annie's shoulder into the apartment as if Annie might not be trusted to tell the truth. Michele's mother drifts in and out of rehab programs, and Cleo worries about her niece. She is a beautiful girl: blond, long-legged, with perfectly straight, well-proportioned features. Tonight she is wearing a short, hot-pink skirt and impossibly high platform heels. Around Michele, Annie feels dumpy, prudish, and overwhelmingly average — average height (five feet five), average prettiness (small nose, brown eyes, and pale skin), average age (thirty-two), and average-sized breasts (34B). She remembers that she has not showered in two days, that her sweater is pilly, that her jeans are baggy at the knees.

"Not yet," she says. "Would you like to come in and wait for her?"

"Story!" Anthony demands from the couch.

Annie hopes Michele will say no.

"I can't," Michele says. "I'm on my way downtown, but I wanted to give her this." She holds out a thick silver-paper envelope with writing in metallic gold. "My sweet-sixteen party. At Au Bar," she adds, unable to restrain herself.

"Ooh," Annie says, "that'll be nice," hoping this is an appropriate response. But it sounds fraudulent, schoolteacherish. "I'll give it to her."

"Thanks," Michele breathes, and flashes another studied smile. "Say hi to Jay."

Annie closes the door behind her and walks back over to Anthony.

"O.K.," she says, settling onto the sofa. "Where were we?"

"Here," Anthony says, squirming closer, collapsing against her as soon as she leans back. She is thankful for his helplessness.

Since it is Thursday night, they are all eating together. This is Cleo's rule. Sundays and Thursdays, they dine at seven so that Anthony and his baby sister, Eden, can join them and afterward Cleo can put them to bed. On other nights, Cleo and Jay eat late, or have dinner engagements, or, often, Cleo is out of town. Tonight, Cleo has brought pink and orange dahlias home from the florist on Madison, which Annie has arranged in the center of the table. In the candlelight, they project pointed orange shadows onto the walls.

"What did you do, invite Alain Ducasse over to cook?" Jay says, surveying the food. "This looks fantastic." Jay is tall and in his early forties. He is technically good-looking, but there is something about him that seems still unformed, as if he had never, for even a moment, experienced pain.

"Abble, abble, abble, abble," Eden chants from her high chair. Saliva runs down her lower lip.

"Did you work out with Mel today?" Cleo asks Jay, wiping Eden's chin with her napkin. Mel is Jay's trainer. "I thought that was Monday, Wednesday, Friday."

"Bumped it up—Thursdays, too," Jay says, helping himself to a steak. Jay sold his Internet company for "a bundle," as he likes to say, before the market went bust, and since then he has devoted himself to "independent projects," which originally consisted of learning to play the guitar, writing a how-to (in his case, how to sell your startup company for millions) book, and getting in shape. Now his projects consist entirely of getting in shape—kick-boxing class, weight lifting, training for the New York marathon. In the four months since Annie moved in with them, he has gone way past "in shape." His muscles, which are by nature invisible, have become hard and round and move like an animal's beneath his skin. He can bench-press two hundred and thirty pounds and run to the tip of Manhattan and back in an hour and twenty minutes.

"Four times a week?" Cleo asks, her eyebrows raised.

"What's that supposed to mean?" Jay demands.

"Nothing," Cleo says. "Did you have a chance to call the Hornbys?"

Cleo is so smooth. Jay will have to run after this question now. He is volatile, but easily distracted. Annie has seen him agitated, cranky, even nasty a few times, but she has never seen Cleo so much as ruffled.

"They're coming on Saturday." Jay turns to Anthony and tousles his hair. "With Davey-boy, so you'll have a friend, too."

"I don't like him," Anthony says, slumping back in his chair.

"But he's your buddy," Jay says with a mixture of surprise and disappointment. "He's a good guy."

"Why not?" Cleo asks at the same time.

Anthony grunts and kicks the table leg. Annie has begun to notice that he is different with Cleo. Less communicative. More petulant. Gently, Annie stills his leg under the table.

"Na, na, na, na," Eden begins chanting. She has been released from her high chair and is crawling around under the table. Then she sits down and begins sucking on the remote control of Jay's new stereo.

"She loves to put things in her mouth," Annie says, removing the remote control gently from Eden's grasp.

"Well!" Jay says, standing up. "Just like your mother, aren't you?" He laughs and wiggles one of Eden's fat toes.

"Could you get the salt while you're up?" Cleo asks, with no hint that she has heard.

Annie suspects that Cleo and Jay have a wild and theatrical sex life. There is all of Jay's working out. There are his crass jokes. There is the way he smells when he comes into the kitchen for breakfast before showering. But these are merely complements of something Annie sees in Cleo. She is too confident, too invulnerable to be seductive. But when she is relaxed, when she and Jay come in from an evening out at a benefit, or a day of sailing on the Sound, there is something raw about her—a loose, substantial physicality that reminds Annie of a high-school athlete. It is slightly masculine. Unabashedly sexual.

The first time Annie thought about this, an image of Cleo, bent over, her brown hair trailing on the floor, popped into her mind. She was being fucked from behind. She was wearing a bustier and garters, and her wide pale feet with their unpainted toenails looked inanimate. The image was so vivid that Annie almost can't remember whether she has actually seen it. She imagines that Cleo likes frilly nighties in little-girl colors. That Jay, with his newly built body, comes out of the bathroom shirtless, in black briefs. That Cleo is coy, that Jay will do anything to get a blow job—David

Hasselhoff impersonations, handsprings, a wrestling move in which he pins Cleo roughly against the headboard. It is both comical and dangerous. And Annie is shocked at how readily it springs into her imagination.

"Stop doing dishes," Cleo says, coming into the kitchen from the children's room. "Mrs. Tibbs will do those in the morning. You have better things to do."

"I like doing dishes," Annie says.

"Anthony would like you to go in and give him a kiss goodnight."

Annie tries to interpret Cleo's voice. Lately, when Cleo wants to read Anthony a story, he says no, he'd rather have Annie. Cleo turns it into a joke—you're a more fun mommy than I am, she says. But here, alone in the kitchen, Annie feels tension spring up between them like a wire. It makes Annie nervous; beneath Cleo's unflappable exterior, Annie has noticed lately, she has a capacity for cruelty.

"O.K." Annie wipes her hand on the dish towel and adds, "I feel a little woozy," which she does not, as if somehow this could make things equal.

Anthony's bedroom is at the far end of the apartment, across the darkened living room with its glass doors that lead out to a roof garden and the hollow rush of the city. Anthony is lying on his back, staring at the glow-in-the-dark stars Jay arranged on the ceiling in the shape of a baseball. "I knew you'd come," he says, turning onto his side as soon as she opens the door.

"Well, you asked for me, right?" Annie says gently. She sits down on the edge of his bed and can feel his legs, warm under the covers, pushing against her back.

"It's too dark," he says. "I want to sleep with the light on."

"Why?" Annie says. "Darkness is good. It's nothing to be afraid of."

"I'm not afraid," he says rolling onto his back. His voice has an anxious hitch to it, though.

"That's good."

"What is 'afraid'?" Anthony asks.

All around her the room is full of indistinguishable objects and flickering shadows from the roof garden—living things blowing, husk-like, in the March wind. A siren howls from below, muffled by the distance it has to travel.

"Annie?" Anthony is looking at her, his eyes demanding.

"It's a feeling," she says. "It's a way you feel." The words come out sounding thick and automatic. She concentrates on the pressure of his knee, bony and hard against the small of her back. "I think you know," she adds softly, when her voice seems more like her own again.

When she leans over to kiss him, he clasps her cheeks in his small damp hands. "Sleep tight," she whispers. Anthony doesn't let go. "Sleep tight," she repeats, gently peeling off his fingers.

In the front hall, Cleo has on the long tailored coat, gray slacks, and platform sneakers she refers to as her plane PJs. "Asleep?" she asks cheerfully. She already has more important things to think about.

"Almost," Annie says.

"I'm catching the red-eye. Be back Saturday at noon." She puts on a gray felt hat.

"You leaving, babe?" Jay comes in from the living room holding the *Wall Street Journal* in one hand.

"Mm-hmm," Cleo smiles, adjusting the hat just in time for Jay to knock it askew by enveloping her in his arms for a newspaper-crumpling bear hug and a kiss.

Cleo laughs and kisses him back. A firm but restrictive press of the lips.

"Call when you get there?" Jay says over his shoulder, already walking away across the hall.

"I will." Cleo makes a what-can-you-do face at Annie as she tucks her hair behind her ears and pulls the hat back into place. "Oh, will you make sure Mrs. Tibbs gets the envelope I put on the counter?"

Annie nods.

"You O.K.?" Cleo fixes Annie with her gaze, but there is something prohibitive about it, just as there was in her kiss.

"Yes," Annie says. "Have a safe trip."

"Be strong, kiddo." Cleo gives Annie a cool, dry kiss on the cheek.

Annie forces a smile and then closes the door after her.

In the kitchen she has the desire—the first in a long time—for a drink. She has not touched alcohol since she was diagnosed. In high school, there were two or three times she got really drunk—an exhilarating, freeing drunk where she became loud, sexy, and silly, the kind of girl who took drama instead of typing. This was a long time ago, when she was a Californian. When she was still living in Long Beach, answering phones at the tattoo parlor her brother worked at, and imagining she would go to design school, marry someone famous, live in a mansion. It was before junior college, before Todd really lost it, certainly before New York.

Annie opens Cleo and Jay's liquor cabinet, pulls out the Johnnie Walker, pours herself a glass. It tastes sharp and pure as medicine. Then she turns on the tap to finish the dishes. With her hands immersed in the warm water, the whiskey hot inside her, she tries to listen to her body—tries to feel the movement of her blood, the labored breathing of her cells. But she feels nothing—not even the beating of her heart.

"Hey, why don't you turn a light on?" Jay is standing in the doorway, where Anthony stood before.

"Oh," Annie says. "I forgot." But this isn't true. She has chosen the darkness. Seeing clearly seems like a distraction; she is surrounded by other people's clutter.

Jay flips the switch from the doorway but he hesitates before entering. Annie has the feeling he is afraid she is crying.

"Vitamins," he says. "Forgot my vitamins."

Annie wipes her face with her sleeve. She takes another sip of whiskey.

"Should you be drinking that—with—you know, your treatment and all?" Jays says the word "treatment" as if it were a euphemism for something sordid. He pours four pills as fat as roaches into his palm. In the refrigerator, bottles of zinc, vitamins C, A, and B, iron, protein powder, and Strong Body Multitabs occupy an entire shelf of the door.

She and Jay have never addressed her illness, a reticence that is not exactly strange but tiring. Cleo, with her strong sense of calm, her reliance on order and the ability to manipulate, has always been the arbiter of conversations about Annie's health. Jay usually pretends not to be listening, as if it were some other intimate, distinctly feminine problem they were discussing. "He doesn't get it," Cleo told Annie once. The comment was slightly unnerving—what was it, exactly, according to Cleo, that Jay didn't get?

Now, instead of looking at her, he occupies himself with a carton of skim milk.

"Here," Annie says, handing him a glass. When he pours the milk, the muscles under his taut, sallow skin rise and subside. Annie feels a corresponding rise of something unidentifiable in her gut.

"Your heart rate must be low," she says unsteadily.

"Forty-nine at rest." Jay brightens. "Last year it was seventy-two. Count it," he says, extending his arm.

Annie wraps her fingers around his warm wrist. His pulse crawls as sluggishly as ink through water. Annie counts forty-nine but doesn't let go. "Fifty, fifty-one, fifty-two, fifty-three," she recites out loud and tightens her grip. She concentrates on the flawless rhythm of his blood working its way through his body, nourishing his bones and muscles—she would like to absorb it, gobble it up, make it her own. Jay looks at her quizzically but doesn't pull away. She raises his wrist to his chest, bending his arm at the elbow, and watches his biceps swell. Suddenly, she can imagine it, pressed against her collarbone—his arm wrapped heavily around her neck and her teeth grazing the pale, damp, almost womanly skin at the crook of his elbow. Her own low breathing, she realizes when the hum of the refrigerator switches off, is the loudest sound in the room.

"Annie," Jay says, peeling her fingers from his wrist. "I think you need to get some sleep."

Annie removes her hand. "Maybe." She is surprisingly unembarrassed, even when she sways slightly against the door frame. She can feel Jay's eyes following her across the floor.

In the morning, Annie fixes herself breakfast. Early buds have appeared overnight on the trees in the Park, and the ground looks black and wet with spring. Friday mornings are when she usually goes in to see Dr. Tatel, but this week she is going in on Monday because Dr. Tatel is going out of town. This small irregularity feels exciting—evidence that she is well enough to be rescheduled.

In the last few months, she has learned how to turn her body over to medical science as if it were a sick pet. She can be poked and prodded now without feeling judged by the hands examining for error, can watch her blood coil up out of her arm without getting nauseated, can take the cold metallic sting of the stethoscope without feeling light-headed at the idea of her own beating heart. She has had practice, after all. She went to the emergency room at least four times with her brother before he took off. "Annie," he would joke afterward, "you watch those doctors like you're in training."

From the kitchen, Annie can hear Jay grunting on his chin-up bar. In about an hour, he will come out of the study and walk around the apartment, stretching his elbows behind his head, picking up newspapers and magazines, tossing them back down. At about eleven, he will try to sit at the computer and "organize his notes" before he goes to the gym at two o'clock, but will end up online playing a pro-sports betting game based on the stock market instead.

Annie puts on her sneakers and jacket to go for a walk. She has not left the apartment for four days. On Fifth Avenue, she is quickly swept up in the rush of taxis, buses, tourists, shoppers, and can collectors rattling their metal carts over the uneven sidewalk. At the corner of Park and Sixty-fifth Street, there is a Japanese man with thick glasses trying to feed a chocolate popsicle to a pigeon with a stump instead of a foot. Almost half the pigeons collecting tentatively around him have mutant feet—grotesque, fleshy bulbs or string-tangled toes. Annie can barely look at them, but at the same time cannot look away. She watches them hop around the cracked concrete eating invisible morsels, pecking at each other, and clumsily, violently, trying to mate. Why have they chosen this meagre, earthbound existence when they could be airborne, soaring up above the garbage and pollution—beyond the need to fight over an old man's crumbs?

It is almost noon by the time Annie realizes she is too cold to stay out any longer. The sun is flat and white and the budding trees cast a blurry shade on the path. Annie heads uptown, suddenly worried that she has exhausted herself, although she feels quite all right. Nannies and baby carriages and strollers have taken over the sidewalk. Nursery schools and half-day programs are getting out — it is the hour of the under-five-year-old. In the apartment, Jay will be fixing lunch — a protein shake, a bowl of cottage cheese, a chicken breast, and iceberg lettuce. The image of his biceps gathering into a round knot and then releasing under her hand appears in her mind. The thick skin, the light hairs, the full, invincible blue-green veins. Mrs. Tibbs will not bring Anthony home for another half hour.

Annie greets Philipe, the doorman. She suspects he sees her as some sort of charity case of Jay and Cleo's, or, worse yet, as a freeloader. But today her self-consciousness has vanished. Crossing the black and white marble tiles she feels transparent, like one of those tiny clear fish whose slippery bodies filter and refract light, break it into dancing pieces. A clammy layer of perspiration has built up on her lower lip and under her shirt, where the raggedy, nylon-covered underwire of her bra sits against her rib cage. Anticipation — Annie recognizes the same fluttering feeling that rose in her last night.

The elevator opens directly into the apartment, which takes up half the building's twentieth floor. It is bright inside, full of sunlight, dust particles hovering, visible in the air. She has started to shrug her coat off before she realizes there is a hysterical voice coming from the living room. Annie freezes with the coat around her elbows.

"Michele, you can't — " Jay's voice interrupts the higher sound of the girl's voice.

"I can't? Oh, really, I can't? You don't know anything about what I can do, Jay. You don't know shit about me." There is the sucking sound of the sliding door to the roof deck being opened.

The hazy bubble of expectation that has carried Annie upstairs bursts in an instant. Of course Jay has been sleeping with Michele. Hasn't she known this all along? It is her first thought, followed immediately by the urge to back up and away — to get into the elevator, go down to the lobby, out onto the cold street.

"Jesus Christ," Jay says. "What are you? Don't — "

But Annie is no longer listening to the words, just to the tense, terrified sound of his voice, which propels her forward, silently, across the sun-bright floorboards. When she gets to the entrance of the living room, she can see Jay standing in the open expanse of the sliding door and beyond him Michele, looking as though she's about to climb up onto the chest-high brick wall that marks the edge of the terrace. Her hair is pulled back in a severe ponytail that the wind is blowing up in all directions. She looks frightened, a little haggard. And she is high. Annie recognizes the signs from when she lived with Todd.

Both Jay and Michele turn at the same time to look at Annie, although she is not aware of having said anything. "Annie—" Jay says. It is possible that he is crying; his face has an ashen, uncomposed look to it. Annie averts her eyes. He is cowering in the doorway of his own living room, sucked dry by his own fear. The wall Michele is standing at is not even at the edge of the roof—beyond it there are several yards of tar and loose gravel.

Michele says nothing to Annie, but turns to Jay, wide-eyed with a new burst of rage. "You're probably sleeping with her, too. Aren't you? You're probably fucking her right under Cleo's nose. That's convenient. You don't even have to worry about the future, you sick asshole."

"No, no, no," Jay protests, and Annie stands absolutely still, bracing herself against the blow implicit in Michele's words. But they seem to float above her.

The girl looks almost shocked herself, still breathing too fast, but quiet now.

"I'm not dying," Annie says calmly. "I'm waiting."

She is aware of a new edge in her voice. A light, powerful feeling begins to course through her. She can feel her own blood finally—she is aware of its quick rhythm in the channels of her veins. She is aware of its feeding her bones and tissues, rushing from one region of her body to another, fuelled by something bright and strong and weightless, impervious to treatment or disease. It is as if some door had opened inside her and she could hear everything—not just her own heartbeat but the hollow, coddled ticking of Jay's body, the more chaotic, unformed racing of Michele's, and the troubled cacophony all three of them are making. The sound is real and essential and utterly irrelevant. It makes her think of the time her brother gave her a tattoo—a spindly leaf and its shadow curving along the jutting bone of her ankle. It had hurt like nothing she'd known before, and she'd squirmed and bit her lip until it was bloody, feeling nothing but the prick of the needle against delicate nerve endings, the burn of the ink under her skin. That's not you, Todd had said, pointing at her ankle. That's your body —leave it for a minute and come back.

"In fifteen minutes, Anthony will be coming home," Annie says to Michele. "And then Eden. You'd better go home before that."

From his place at the glass door, Jay is watching her.

"What makes you such an expert at what I should do?" Michele says. "You just live here. This isn't even really your home." But her voice is losing its conviction.

"No, it's not," Annie replies. "But I know you should leave now. You should go home and get some rest."

Michele heaves a deep sigh and runs her hand over her hair in a habitual gesture. "If I leave, it's for her sake, not yours, Jay," she says, in a voice that trembles, straining to be haughty. "And for poor Anthony. I'm sorry he has a twisted fuck of a father like you." Then she takes a few steps across the terrace and past Jay into the living room — stiff, careful steps shaped by some combination of pride and restraint. She plucks her leather jacket up off the sofa and walks across the beige-and-white Chinese carpet, leaving faint gray footprints on the plush surface which Carolita, the cleaning lady, will have to spend hours on her hands and knees scrubbing to remove. The thought flits through Annie's mind involuntarily.

When Michele gets to Annie, she pauses, close enough for Annie to smell the acrid, strung-out scent of her sweat. "Don't let him touch you," she says fiercely. There are little bubbles of saliva in the corners of her mouth. In a moment, she is gone, and the heavy oak door to the elevator vestibule clicks shut.

When Annie turns back toward Jay, he has sunk down onto the sofa with his knees wedged in against the coffee table and his head in his hands. He looks too big and ungainly for the spot he has climbed into. The curve of his back has the slump of defeat. What could she ever have thought his body had to offer?

"It's not what you think," Jay begins. "Michele is on something. She's upset—" He breaks off under Annie's gaze.

"It's not my business," she says. "It isn't my home."

"Of course it is. You live here. You take care of Anthony."

Jay shifts his gaze out toward the terrace in a self-conscious, nearsighted way. Looking at him, Annie is filled with the knowledge of things outside this room, of hospital waiting rooms and of the bowels of complicated machines that can see through flesh to what lies beneath it, of wet sidewalks and empty hallways, of the smell of new leaves and spring earth and grease coming out of coffee-shop air vents, of babies in the Park and the serious yellow of taxis and how simple it all looks from above. She is filled with the knowledge of loneliness and suspense and courage. Unlike this man protected by the mantle of good health and good fortune, she knows what is required not to be afraid.

Jay ventures a nervous glance up at her. His face is still pale and covered with a thin sheen of sweat. "I'm sorry—" he begins. "I'm sorry about what Michele—"

"It's all right," Annie interrupts. "It doesn't matter." And she means it.

From the hall, there is the whirr of the elevator door opening and the sound of Anthony's high, excited voice, then Mrs. Tibbs's lower, wearier murmur of response. In a moment, Anthony is rushing toward Annie, flushed with fresh air and emotion. He is waving a sheet of paint-stiffened paper so that colored chips fall from it to the floor. "For you — " He is panting. "I made this. I didn't know if you'd be here."

Peter Morris
Pancakes

CHARACTERS

SAM, a businessman, late 20s–early 30s.
BUDDY, an unemployed man, late 20s–early 30s.

SETTING

An apartment.

TIME

The present.

Lights up on the table and two chairs. On the table are a butter dish, a knife and fork, a bottle of syrup, a glass of milk and a plate with an enormous stack of pancakes—four dozen at least. Sam sits at the table eating. He wears a blue business suit with a white shirt and red tie. Buddy enters, running in and sliding to a stop. He wears boxer shorts and a tee shirt and has a severe case of "bed head." He takes a deep breath, inhaling the pancake aroma, then crosses to the table and sits. He stares at Sam. There are several moments of silence with nothing being heard but the sound of Sam eating.

BUDDY: Good?
SAM: Uh huh.
BUDDY: They look good.
SAM: (*His mouth full.*) They are good.

    (*Silence.*)
BUDDY: Make 'em from scratch?
SAM: (*Mouth still full.*) Bisquick.
BUDDY: Bisquick is good.
SAM: I like Bisquick.

BUDDY: Makes a lotta pancakes.

SAM: I guess.

BUDDY: That's a lotta pancakes.

SAM: I like pancakes.

(*Silence. Buddy watches Sam pour more syrup on his pancakes. Buddy stands and exits. Sam continues to eat.*)

BUDDY: (*Offstage.*) There's no more Bisquick.

(*No response. Sam just smiles.*)

BUDDY: I said, there's no more Bisquick.

SAM: (*His mouth full.*) So?

(*Buddy re-enters with empty Bisquick box.*)

BUDDY: You used it all up.

SAM: I know.

BUDDY: You could've left me some.

SAM: Well, I didn't.

BUDDY: That sucks. I live here too, you know.

SAM: Just barely.

BUDDY: You gonna bring that up again?

SAM: Just reminding you.

BUDDY: I don't need to be reminded. (*Silence. Buddy sits at the table opposite Sam.*)

BUDDY: Why won't you give me some of those pancakes?

SAM: Because they're mine.

BUDDY: You can't possibly eat them all.

SAM: Just watch me. (*He shoves an entire pancake in his mouth.*)

BUDDY: It's not fair.

SAM: Says you.

BUDDY: You have to give me some.

SAM: I do not. Who said I do? It's not a law. It's not in the Declaration of Independence or the Constitution. Nowhere do they say I have to give you some of my pancakes. What they *do* say is that everyone—*everyone*—is entitled to his own pancakes. This is a land of opportunity. Anyone is free to go out and get all the pancakes he can get his hands on.

BUDDY: What about the Bible?

SAM: What about it?

BUDDY: "Love thy neighbor"?

SAM: That only means you have to love him, not feed him.

BUDDY: You're taking it too literal. You're missing the spirit of the thing.

SAM: Spirit, schmirit, it doesn't say a fucking thing about pancakes.

BUDDY: I can't believe you're not going to give me any.

SAM: Make your own.

BUDDY: There's no more Bisquick.

SAM: Then eat something else.

BUDDY: There *is* nothing. Nothing but some pickle relish and a box of baking soda. I can't make anything out of that.

SAM: Not my problem.

BUDDY: Is that your attitude? "Not my problem"? You're satisfied so to hell with everybody else?

SAM: Not everybody else—just you. (*He resumes eating.*)

BUDDY: Look at you, stuffing your face. You should be ashamed.

SAM: Leave me alone. I'm trying to eat.

BUDDY: So am I! Only I have no food!

SAM: (*Stands and confronts Buddy.*) Then do something about it. Don't stand around begging. That's all you ever do and I'm sick of it. You want some food? Go get it.

BUDDY: Fine! I will! (*Buddy storms out. Beat. Sam sits back down and resumes eating. Buddy storms back in.*) Do you have ten bucks?

SAM: What?

BUDDY: Can you loan me ten bucks?

SAM: On top of the back rent you already owe me?

BUDDY: I said I'd pay you.

SAM: How? You have no job.

BUDDY: I'm looking.

SAM: Look harder.

BUDDY: I just need a little loan.

SAM: What about the big one I've already given you? I've been carrying you for months now but I'm through with it. Do you hear me? I work hard for my money, Buddy.

BUDDY: I'd be happy to work for mine too if someone would just let me. But I can't find a job, OK? I've looked and I've looked and I can't find a job. There's just not a big market these days for philosophers.

SAM: Then do something else.

BUDDY: But I was a philosophy major in college.

SAM: People don't need philosophers.

BUDDY: Yes, they do. They just don't know it. But they will. One day they'll wake up with a spiritual malaise, then they'll need me.

SAM: What the hell is a spiritual mayonnaise?

BUDDY: Malaise! Not mayonnaise! Spiritual malaise! And people like you are gonna get it bad! Trust me! Then I'll be in big demand! You wait and see!

(*Pause. Buddy, realizing he is becoming unhinged, pulls himself together. He sits on the floor and begins meditating in the lotus position. Sam just looks at him.*)

SAM: You don't wanna work, do you?

BUDDY: (*In the same rhythm as his chanting.*) Yes, I do.

SAM: You don't. If you did, you wouldn't be sitting around unwashed, unshaved and undressed on a weekday.

BUDDY: It's eight o'clock in the morning.

SAM: Early bird catches the worm.

BUDDY: I don't want worms. I want pancakes.

SAM: Then earn them.

BUDDY: How?

SAM: You can do a little job for me.

BUDDY: What kind of little job?

SAM: You can shine my shoes.

BUDDY: You want me to shine your shoes?

SAM: I'll give you a pancake for each shoe.

BUDDY: One pancake for each shoe.

SAM: That's the offer.

BUDDY: Is that what you want, to humiliate me? Demean me? Well, forget it! I won't do it! I won't! I want at least two pancakes per shoe!

SAM: Deal.

BUDDY: Deal.

(*They shake hands.*)

BUDDY: Take off your shoes.

SAM: No.

BUDDY: Then how am I supposed to shine them?

SAM: Get down on your knees.

BUDDY: What?

SAM: Get down on your knees and shine my shoes.

BUDDY: Are you serious?

SAM: You want some pancakes, don't you?

BUDDY: You know I do.

SAM: Then get down on your knees.

BUDDY: Sam, please.

SAM: Down!

(*Silence. Buddy gets down on his knees.*)

BUDDY: What do I use to shine them with?

SAM: (*Deliberately, biting each word.*) Your tongue.

BUDDY: No.

SAM: (*Dangling a pancake in Buddy's face.*) Mmmmm, these are so good.

BUDDY: I won't do it.

SAM: They're so light and fluffy, sweet and delicious. Mmmm-mmmm-mmmm.

BUDDY: You're a pig.

(*Sam pushes Buddy over with his foot.*)

SAM: (*Seething.*) Watch your mouth, Buddy. You're only here thanks to my good graces. I could've thrown you out months ago. I could throw you out right now. But I won't. Because I pity you. Do you hear me? You're pathetic. Look at you, about to kiss my feet for some lousy pancakes.

BUDDY: I'm hungry. All I've eaten in the last week were some stale Saltines.

SAM: Those were *my* stale Saltines. Bought and paid for with my money. And you didn't even say thank you, did you?

BUDDY: (*Weakly.*) Thank you.

SAM: What was that?

BUDDY: Thank you. I said thank you.

SAM: That's better. (*Sam sits. Buddy slowly gets up off the floor.*) What is it with guys like you? You've always got your hand out. Soft, fleshy hands that haven't seen a day of work.

BUDDY: I need help.

SAM: "The Lord helps those who help themselves." Now *there's* a Bible quote for you.

BUDDY: That's not from the Bible.

SAM: Well, it should be. Now stop bothering me.

BUDDY: How can you be so heartless when you have so much? Look at you, you have all the pancakes.

SAM: That's right. They're all mine. And what, I should just give them to you?

BUDDY: You could share them.

SAM: Why in hell would I want to do that?

BUDDY: It might make you feel good.

(*Sam bursts out laughing. Buddy watches in silence.*)

SAM: That's the stupidest thing I ever heard.

BUDDY: Some people find great solace in charity.

SAM: What they find, Buddy boy, is a tax deduction. No one does anything without getting something in return. Now, can all the philosophical mumbo jumbo. I have to finish eating. I have a morning conference. They're putting me in charge of the national ad campaign for Good Will. (*He resumes eating.*)

BUDDY: Good Will. They're putting you in charge of "good will." Well, that's just perfect. It's like putting a fox in charge of the hen house.

SAM: (*His mouth full.*) Very funny.

BUDDY: It is. It's hilarious. But I just can't bring myself to laugh. It's a very amusing paradox but I just can't laugh. I'm too weak. I'm hungry and light-headed and I just don't have the strength to laugh. But it is funny. Not slap-your-thigh funny but wry and ironic. Only God could make a joke like that. The same God that gets a kick out of holocausts and plagues and famines. What a sense of humor that guy's got. He gave you all the pancakes and he gave me none.

SAM: That's life. Some of us have pancakes and some of us have not.

BUDDY: Yup, and you have them. You're the pancake king.

SAM: That's me.

BUDDY: Here, your majesty, why don't I give you some more syrup?

SAM: I don't want any more syrup.

BUDDY: Sure you do. Everybody wants more syrup. (*He picks up the bottle of syrup and begins pouring it on Sam's head.*)

SAM: What the fuck!

BUDDY: And butter? What about some more butter? (*Buddy picks up the butter knife and plunges it in Sam's gut—one, two, three times. Sam falls to the floor.*) You want pancakes? Here, eat some pancakes! (*Buddy begins shoving pancakes into Sam's mouth. He coughs and hacks and begins choking.*) Have another! And another! And another!
(*Suddenly, Sam's body goes limp. Buddy sits in his chair and begins ravenously eating pancakes.*)

BUDDY: Hungry. So hungry. (*After a moment he looks down at Sam's body.*) You were right, the Lord does help those who help themselves. (*He kicks the lifeless body then resumes eating the pancakes.*)
(*Fade to black.*)

CHAPTER SEVEN

PATTERN

In this chapter you will:

- Build sound patterns to create emphasis and meaning
- Develop meaningful visual repetitions on the page
- Design and add layers to your writing with two powerful pattern tools: anaphora and lists

Pattern—artful, intentional repetition of significant components—has a number of important functions in creative writing. First, pattern is a system of road signs or signals for your readers, designed to move them through your piece smoothly while guiding their attention to the most important parts of the work. Patterns can be aural, appealing to the reader's ear to create meaning, flow, and smoothness. Patterns can also be visual: Writers shape the way their pieces appear on the page or screen to create additional layers of meaning and interesting effects that appeal to the eye.

Pattern is part of what makes art different from real life. Real life rambles and is often random. Pattern contains a piece, helps give it a **shape**. A thoughtfully designed and patterned piece is more likely to be read, reread, and remembered.

When you were in secondary school, it's likely you were taught to write in three stages: generate, write, rewrite. You were supposed to brainstorm ideas, then write them all out, and

> *I consider myself a farmer of patterns.*
> —ALEXANDER GORLIZKI

then revise. Few creative writers work this way, however. The writing process is a lot messier than teachers told us in school, and the writing process can be a lot more fun than slogging through those three stages in lock-step. One of the ways you may enjoy the writing process more is to keep an eye on patterns as you work. Attending to patterns—intentionally creating repetitions of sound, image, and rhythm—provides an alternate way of working, one that's much more organic and alive than the old write-and-revise model. In fact, you can use pattern to design and create your work as well as to layer and shape work-in-progress.

Working with pattern may not come easily to you, especially at first. Try to be patient with yourself as you learn this new strategy. Many of us have been taught that repetition, like imitation, is a fault and a flaw. You may have an unconscious bias against or some preconceptions about repetition. "It's a pattern of behavior." "You're stuck in a pattern." But pattern in creative writing is repetition with a purpose. When we accuse someone of repetition, we imply that he or she is using a pattern without purpose, repeating design elements that either are not worthy of repetition (recall the classic all-pattern song "99 Bottles of Beer on the Wall") or are repeated mindlessly, without a larger goal.

> *Art is the imposing of a pattern on experience, and our aesthetic enjoyment is recognition of the pattern.*
> —ALFRED NORTH WHITEHEAD

Intentionally repeating yourself is brave. Repeating yourself calls attention to what you are saying. It takes some confidence to believe that your sounds, images, gestures, and ideas are worth echoing and deserving of emphasis. The artful use of pattern is how you make a great poem out of a good poem; it's how you make fiction out of a stack of anecdotes, how you shape a play from snatches of dialogue. When you make patterns—with words, phrases, gestures, dialogue, and images—you make art.

In Part Three, Genres, you will find a series of writing projects that offer excellent practice in pattern, including **anaphora** and **list**. No matter what genre you are most interested in working on—novels, screenplays, comics, nonfiction—you'll be well served if you train in the principles of pattern. If you've been poetry-averse, this is a good time in your training to grab hold of some foundational poetic skills in order to strengthen your writing across the board. Just as football players sometimes study ballet in order to strengthen precision and control, as a writer you want to try writing in tight, pattern-rich poetic forms such as the **ghazal**, **pantoum**, **sestina**, **sonnet**, and **villanelle**. These recipes, included in Chapter Ten, beginning on page 446, are essentially short courses in all the techniques presented in this chapter. Some students find the recipes for these pattern-intensive pieces daunting at first, but with just a little patience and a sense of play, you will discover a useful set of literary tools that will pay off as you work in any genre.

PATTERN BY EAR

Rhymes and Other Echoes

The most common pattern we find in creative writing is sound work: the linking of words by echoing **consonants** and **vowels**. If both the consonants and the vowels in two words echo, you have a **rhyme**; if one or the other echoes, you have **consonance**, **assonance**, or **alliteration**. As discussed previously, writers in all genres—comics, screenplays, memoir, essay, novels, as well as poetry—pay attention to **sound patterns**.

Perhaps the first pattern we encounter as young readers is rhyme. As small children, we were especially drawn to pattern, and we found things that repeated and rhymed especially pleasing: "Red fish, blue fish, old fish, new fish" is vastly more memorable, delightful, and intriguing to the ear than "miscellaneous finned creatures varying in color." As we grow older, we draw much pleasure from song lyrics, where rhyme abounds. Rhyme gives us pleasure. Rhyme provides a pattern so that we can memorize a piece of writing, carrying it with us always. The keys to using rhyme effectively are:

1. Rhyme words that are significant in the piece (and no other words).
2. Rhyme unexpected words.
3. Unless writing in a specific form, with rules, don't always rhyme the end word in the line or the sentence.
4. Use rhyme strategically in all genres.

Rhyming is a powerful flashlight; the purpose is to call attention to significant words. Rhyming for the sake of rhyming, however, can be annoying:

> You are the one I love.
> More than the stars above.

The verse seems clunky, forced, amateurish, because the sole reason the word *above* is being used is to rhyme with *love*. It sounds goofy to describe stars and love this way when there are so many more interesting ways to talk about one's lover. But this novice writer is not concerned with the image or even the reader. Nothing really pops into our reading mind when we read or hear these two lines. We can't see *above*—the word is the opposite of a specific image, forcing us as readers to think rather than see. The ear may be satisfied, but that is never enough in creative writing. Eyes, ears, mind's eye, touch—the whole sensory system has to be activated. Rhyming is the most overt sound pattern, but if it is to be truly effective, the rhyming words need to be fresh, natural, surprising, clear, and interesting, so that you are carrying through all the principles you've learned in the previous chapters.

In contrast to the *love–above* rhyme, consider the rhymes from the first six lines of Gregory Orr's poem "The River," which appears in full on page 332.

> *For constructing any work of art you need some principle of repetition or recurrence; that's what gives you rhythm in music and pattern in painting.*
>
> —NORTHROP FRYE

I felt both pleasure and a shiver
as we undressed on the slippery bank
and then plunged into the wild river.

I waded in; she entered as a diver.
Watching her pale flanks slice the dark
I felt both pleasure and a shiver.

Shiver and *river* rhyme, but not in a predictable way. Both words belong in the poem and add to the story in the poem. Both words create a visual and tactile image for the reader. And, importantly, Orr doesn't limit himself just to words that rhyme. In the poem, he creates a matrix of repeating sounds so that the rhyming words don't stick out weirdly. The words *pleasure* and *shiver* echo, as do the "s" sounds in *undressed* and *slippery*. The rhyming words are knit into the sound pattern of the overall poem. *Pleasure, plunged,* and *pale* create a sound pattern (alliteration), echoing through the poem, and *pleasure, shiver,* and *diver* connect, nearly rhyming, adding richness to the subtle, sensual texture of soundscape in the poem. Orr orchestrates **exact rhymes** (*shiver* and *river*) along with **near rhymes** and echoes (*bank, dark/diver, shiver*) to create sophisticated, surprising sounds that aren't singsong, predictable, pointless, or clichéd. Orr is sneaky: He gives the reader a visual pattern — *diver, shiver* — called a **sight rhyme** in order to add another layer to the poem.

Note that the poet repeats only significant words: *river* and *shiver*. The poem is about skinny-dipping, and it's also about taking another kind of dive: the leap into a new relationship. The words *river* and *shiver* amplify Orr's meaning and serve to create, through pattern, subtext for the poem. If he had repeated words like *lump* and *clump*, we would experience a completely different set of meanings, a different poem. If he had rhymed random words — *and, the, he* — we wouldn't have a significant pattern. The words a writer repeats shine light where he wants the reader to focus their attention.

Look back at Natalie Diaz's poem "Abecedarian Requiring Further Examination of Anglikan Seraphym Subjugation of a Wild Indian Rezervation" on page 273. Diaz brings style and creativity to her use of rhyme and other sound echoes. She avoids predictable rhymes at the ends of lines. Instead, she repeats words *within* the line: "death. And death" (line 4) and "eats angels, I guess, because I haven't seen an angel" (line 5). She deploys a sophisticated soundscape of consonants and vowels throughout the poem — *boxy, coyotes, grow like gourds, Nazarene, organized* — creating a tapestry with echoing sounds of language.

Attention to the sound patterns of language is one of the most important features that distinguish creative writing from writing that informs,
instructs, records, or explains. It's important to note that rhyme and sound
echoes are *not* just for poets—a common misconception.

Consider this line of fiction from short-story writer Aimee Bender:

> The walk home from school was a straight line and the boy was not the
> wandering kind.

Notice the near-rhyme. Bender's use of pattern—rhyming *line* and *kind*—
makes the sentence interesting, fresh, and intriguing—good moves for a
first sentence. The author is signaling to the reader: This will be fun, beautiful, and interesting. An experienced writer is at the helm.

At the end of this chapter, you'll read a short story by Ken Liu on
page 337, "Paper Menagerie." Notice how he uses sound echoes in the opening sentences: "sobbing" and "soothed"; "bedroom" and "breakfast table."
And in the nonfiction piece by Julie Hakim Azzam on page 333, notice how
a published writer uses sound patterns to create a matrix of meaning and a
flow throughout the piece of writing. In the first section, this author uses
consonance: "seventh" and "social"; "family" and "father's family"; "classroom
commenting" alongside assonance: "trace" and "flags." But it's her bold use of
direct, overt repetition—"Palestine," "Palestinian," and "Palestine"—three
times in three lines—that underscore the piece's meaning. By naming a state
whose identity is questioned three times, the
author creates energy and tension. The official
state exists? Doesn't exist? She insists her reader
say the name three times, bringing the word,
and therefore the place, into existence.

> *Happiness is the longing for repetition.*
> —MILAN KUNDERA

Recall Marco Ramirez's use of pattern in "I am not Batman" on page 82.
This playwright is expert at having his BOY character repeat and echo,
creating a pattern with dialogue lines: "And my navy blue polo shirt?—"
he says, before a long description of the shirt, followed by "—*that* blue
polo shirt?—" The repetition adds intensity and drama; we lean forward:
Repeated things are important things.

Rhyming, using sound echoes, and repeating significant words: Pattern is how writers make meaning. Again, while poetry brings sound to the
foreground, plays, screenplays, comics, and fiction and nonfiction also rely
heavily on sound echoes. Attention to sound is what distinguishes creative
writing from basic writing.

You might be thinking to yourself, "Do I really have to look at every single
vowel, every single letter?" Yes, actually. You do. Sound is going to come out
of your piece, whether you want it to or not. You have a chance to shape
the way your reader feels. All the sounds in your piece need to flow together

artfully. Pattern matters, and not just for poets and playwrights. Few writers are willing to leave the sound of their piece to chance.

| PRACTICE 1 |

SOUND ECHOES IN PROSE

Choose any piece of prose in this textbook and make a list of sound echoes, word repetitions, and direct rhymes that you find in the first three or four paragraphs or sections. Write a short statement on how these sound patterns contribute to the meaning of the piece.

| PRACTICE 2 |

SOUND ECHOES IN POETRY

Read Randall Mann's "Pantoum" on page 332. How many repeating sounds do you find in the poem? How do the sound echoes — repetitions, rhymes, assonance, consonance, alliteration — create patterns that convey meaning?

| PRACTICE 3 |

SOUND ECHOES IN DRAMA

Reread any play in this book. Find ten examples of sound echoes — places where important words are emphasized by the use of a repeating sound in nearby words.

> *Refrain is one of the most valuable of all form methods. Refrain is a return to the known before one flies again upwards. It is a consolation to the reader, a reassurance that the book has not left his understanding.*
> —JOHN STEINBECK

Word Order

Creating meaning in sentence patterns and then varying those sentence patterns creates energy and power and increases tension. Notice the difference between "Good is what I am" and "I am good." Reread each sentence aloud. Do they sound the same? Do they even mean the same thing? Does the first version have implications that the second one doesn't?

Compare:

He came. He saw. He conquered.

To:

He woke up when his alarm clock went off. Boy oh boy it pretty much looked to be a great day. He wondered what to wear and got up and brushed his teeth and washed his face. He then got into his clothes. Go for it, little dude!

Syntax is the order of the words in the sentence. In the first example, notice how the syntax echoes—it makes a pattern. Each sentence is two words, the parts of speech echoing. The second example doesn't pay attention to syntax. The writer hasn't thought about how to make a pattern with the sentences themselves. The syntax—the order of the words in the sentences—feels spontaneously invented, off the top of the author's head, and not well thought out at all. The second writer is perhaps missing an opportunity to make his writing reader-friendly, powerful, and effective.

Installing a pattern of syntax can make even the most simple, basic writing come (at least a bit) to life:

Woke up. Got dressed. Washed body. Am dude: Lo. Now faced world.

Syntax matters to writers in the same way reading music matters to composers and strategy matters to military generals. The word *syntax* comes from the Greek word *tassein*, meaning "to arrange" (the word *tactics* is closely related). To write "with syntax" means to write "with tactics." The order of the words creates a pattern and that pattern matters. Writers must *choose* the order of words, and shape patterns in word order, instead of leaving this all to chance. The syntax—the kinds of sentences you choose and the order of words in your sentences—must create a pattern that *goes with* or somehow comments on what you are describing in your piece of writing.

Let's look at Aimee Bender's sentence again:

The walk home from school was a straight line and the boy was not the wandering kind.

Notice how she repeats the same verb, *was*, and sets up the syntax of the sentence so that its two parts mirror each other. How differently we would feel about this sentence if she wrote, "The boy walked home. He really didn't get lost much cuz he was super shy and risk-averse."

Many new writers rely on one basic sentence structure, learned early on. Their basic dance step uses the subject–verb–object or subject–verb–modifier syntax. Like this:

She left the building.

He woke up and got in the shower.

Janet sang loudly.

There is nothing inherently wrong with this syntax pattern. But when a writer uses only that one pattern, the writing falls flat.

In the following example from Tobias Wolff's best-selling memoir *This Boy's Life*, notice how the author uses the basic pattern, inserts a variation, and returns to the basic pattern.

So I passed the hours after school. Sometimes, not very often, I felt lonely. Then I would go home to Roy.

In this memoir, the speaker is struggling with an abusive stepfather. He tries to create a normal life on his own after school, messing around outside, hanging out alone, avoiding his own house. When he feels lonely (not what he desires, not what he expects his life to be like), Wolff uses an atypical sentence pattern to emphasize the unusual, the not-okay-ness—"sometimes, not very often"—the sentence begins with a stutter-step, pauses—we breathe differently when we read it. It's a little jolt, a little break. The return to subject–verb–object/modifier matches the sense of inevitability—Tobias has nowhere else to go. He has to go home. Messing around with the basic sentence pattern creates energy and power.

Note how each sentence has a syntax that supports the meaning the writer wants to get across. Tobias has to go home eventually. But it's not just home—it's home *to Roy*. Ending the sentence with those two words—*to Roy*—avoids the predictable pattern ("I went home") and makes a strong and chilling point. Roy is at the end of the day; Roy is at the end of the sentence.

PRACTICE 4

SYNTAX PATTERNS IN PROSE

Write a short analysis of the syntax—word order—and sound and word pattern (repetition) Brenda Miller uses in her memoir, "Swerve," on page 124.

While prose writers attend carefully to the patterns of sentences and word order, these principles come to the fore in poetry.

The poet E. E. Cummings inverts word order so frequently that it becomes his signature move. Here is Cummings's poem about a mouse, poisoned by someone who doesn't want mice in the house.

E. E. Cummings
(Me up at does)

Me up at does

out of the floor
quietly Stare

a poisoned mouse

still who alive

is asking What
have i done that

You wouldn't have

What's important to remember is that our point of view is inverted in this poem — we are the mouse, looking up at the human. The words are reversed, and so is our usual perspective — we don't typically identify with rodents. The syntax is jerky; words seem to be missing. Do you almost hold your breath — choke? — as you read the poem? Another pattern to notice: Why are some words capitalized? Do the capitalized words form a pattern you can make sense of?

Readers appreciate "figuring out" the puzzle that is pattern, but the harder the puzzle is, the more payoff there needs to be. The mouse poem above is, like the mouse's life, quite brief. Poetry is compressed, and the reader is expected to reread, and stay with trick, complex syntax, knowing there will be a purpose and a payoff.

Read the poem "What lips my lips have kissed, and where, and why" by Edna St. Vincent Millay on page 333. You'll want to read the poem aloud and to read it several times. First you'll notice the poet uses an intricate pattern of sound echoes to create an aural matrix for her sonnet. She achieves flow and beauty by linking and repeating consonants and vowels in a pattern. Note also the end rhymes create a specific pattern (called a Petrarchan or Italian sonnet). She uses all one-syllable words for her rhymes and that creates a rhythmic pattern, too, with each line coming to a firm pause on that heavy beat. Within the lines, too, we find repetitions of words ("lips" and "lips" in line 1; "one by one" in line 10) and also the pattern of sounds: "ghosts," "sigh," and "boughs," "before." It's a masterful example of the power of pattern in creative writing: Every single line has sound echoes connecting the words in the line to each other and to other words in the poem. Not only does the thoughtfully designed pattern cause this poem to flow, each repetition underscores meaning in the poem. Those single-syllable end words emphasize the loneliness that is the subject of this powerful, memorable poem. And the syntax — that weird inversion at the opening of the poem, "What lips my lips have kissed, and where, and why" forces the reader to feel a little disoriented — *what's happening now? what has happened? whose lips did what?* And those are the *exact* same questions the poet/speaker is asking of her own experience. The syntax of that first sentence in the poem delays the subject of the sentence. So, the subject itself is "forgotten" for a moment, mirroring the forgetting that is a hallmark of aging and loss itself.

PRACTICE 5

SYNTAX PATTERNS IN POETRY

With a partner or as a class, read Randall Mann's "Pantoum" on page 332. Make a list of the kinds of sentences he uses (subject–verb–object, interrogative, etc.). How does he use and break syntax patterns to underscore the meaning of his poem?

Rhythm

Rhythm-less writing = boring writing.

Law briefs lack rhythm. Memos from your boss lack rhythm. Bureaucratic writing lacks rhythm. Those kinds of writing are trying to be neutral as they deliver information. Creative writing is the opposite, trying to be interesting, lively, memorable, and enjoyable to read. Rhythm is the pattern tool that lets you do that. Creative writers use **rhythm** to punctuate, highlight, and emphasize content and to keep the reader engaged in the piece.

Notice the differences in rhythm in the following two samples, one from a textbook, the other from the novel *Risk Pool* by Richard Russo:

> The preceding section illustrates important relationships between numerous cohesive devices worthy of further study.

> My father, unlike so many of the men he served with, knew just what he wanted to do when the war was over. He wanted to drink and whore and play the horses.

The rhythm in these two sentences is *very* different. The first is very monochromatic in tone, droning on in part because the rhythm is flat. The second sentence bounces, moves, pulses. It has an interesting beat to it; it startles us as much as the subject matter startles us.

A beginning writer may write:

> My father was a party animal.

Russo, again, an experienced novelist, writes:

> He was celebrating life. His.

In the second example, Russo uses the familiar, typical subject–verb–object construction, but he slams on the brakes in the sentence that follows; instead of writing two S-V-O/M sentences in a row, he slaps down a one-word sentence. Both sentences begin with the sound of the letter *h*, creating a sound pattern that is counterpointed by the rhythms in the opposing sentences. Four words juxtaposed with one word: *his*. Russo creates humor and energy with sound and syntax, and he creates rhythm.

Notice the rhythmic patterns Julie Hakim Azzam establishes in her micro-memoir, "How to Erase an Arab," on page 333. Each section opens with the same pattern: "Seventh grade, social studies — ," "Seventh grade, the kitchen," "Eighth grade, the kitchen." In the small sections that make up each "headline," Azzam varies her sentence patterns. When she wants to emphasize a particular moment, she uses much shorter sentences and direct dialogue. "'Palestine isn't a country,'" and "My parents exchange a glance," and "Nobody ever does." The last sentence in the memoir is an incomplete sentence: "Over and over." If all the sentences were short or incomplete, the dramatic spotlight effect would be lost.

> *Meter is like the abstract idea of a dance as a choreographer might plan it with no particular performers in mind; rhythm is like a dancer interpreting the dance in a personal way.*
> —JOHN FREDERICK NIMS

Meter. In poetry, the pattern of rhythms is called **meter**. Just like a speedometer, meter measures how fast you are going, and it gives you information on which syllables or beats are stressed (emphasized) and which ones aren't. That's good information to have. Many new writers resist learning meter — it is complex, and the vocabulary is off-putting — *spondee* and *trochee* and *pentameter*. But if your class decides to spend some time on meter, try to remember this: Meter isn't a strict set of rules. Meter is feedback. It's information you get about how your poem is going to play out for the reader. Meter is a tool. It's not a prison. Your class may go in-depth with meter; many students find the website For Better for Verse to be extremely helpful when learning meter.

If you choose to learn one meter, focus on **iambic pentameter**: ten syllables per line, with accented, or stressed, syllables in a specific pattern, described below.

Many poems are written in iambic pentameter. The term sounds fancy, but it isn't highbrow or obscure. It's our daily rhythm. It's a very natural way for many (not all) speakers of English to put words together. Like the two-step in dance, or 4/4 time in music, it's a common pattern of beats that English easily falls into: Chaucer, Shakespeare, Milton, Frost, and Stephen Crane wrote in iambic pentameter.

> *I would sooner write free verse as play tennis with the net down.*
> —ROBERT FROST

An iamb is a *da-DUM* sound; two syllables together, with the stress (the stress is the weight or the emphasis) on the second one, as in the word *adore*. The names Heather and Jacob are *not* iambs. "Heh-THERE" sounds wrong. "Ja-COBE" sounds funny.

In English we usually begin sentences with an article—*the, an, a*—so the natural rhythm follows: the house, an egg, a boy. *Da-DUM, da-DUM, da-DUM.*

Set next to each other in a row, in a sentence, iambs always make a pattern:

i-AM-bic ME-ter GOES like THIS.

Some people say that iambic pentameter echoes the pattern of a heartbeat (*da-DUM da-DUM*) or footfalls when people walk.

Pentameter means, simply, five units, so iambic pentameter means five *da-DUM*s per line, which is ten syllables per line, as in:

My mistress' eyes are nothing like the sun;

Why five? Like *da-DUM*s, units of five are natural, too. We count in fives for a good reason (five fingers). There might be another reason: Take a deep breath. A very deep breath. Now take a deep breath again, and this time, count how many times your heart beats. The poet John Frederick Nims calls iambic pentameter "a breathful of heartbeats." Have you taken CPR? What is the ratio of breaths to chest compressions, the substitute heartbeats?

If one purpose of poetry is to resuscitate the human soul, to give us back ourselves, it's no surprise that iambic pentameter has become our most common rhythm.

PRACTICE 6

MAKING FRIENDS WITH IAMBIC PENTAMETER

Read Millay's sonnet, "What lips my lips have kissed, and where, and why" on page 333. Mark the stressed syllables in each line. A stressed syllable is one that has emphasis—you read it a little louder, a little longer, a little heavier than the nearby syllables; it's all relative. It's easier to do this aloud and with a partner. Next, try writing four lines of your own in iambic pentameter.

There are many meters you can learn if you wish to pursue poetry at a more advanced level. For now, know that readers like iambic pentameter. It's reassuring, predictable, steady, controlled, and clear. Iambic pentameter is like jeans and a tee shirt—it's a great practical go-to pattern. Meter makes poems easier to understand and memorize. Just as with rhyme, it's crucial that you make sure the words and syllables that are stressed or accented are the most important words in the poem. Avoid emphasizing *the* and *and* and *have*. Simply paying attention to this one small trick will increase vastly the power of your writing.

Free Verse. When you write poetry with no rules about the number of syllables in a line or stresses or line length, when you are not following a preexisting pattern, you are writing **free verse**. (**Blank verse** is quite different from free verse. Blank verse is *unrhymed* lines of iambic pentameter.)

You probably do not want to write in iambic pentameter all the time. I recommend though that you *try* writing in meter, just as an experiment, before abandoning this powerful pattern tool. After writing a few poems using a metrical rhythm recipe, such as iambic pentameter, then reject it as a pattern for your work if you like. That's fine. Free verse is just as popular as iambic pentameter; however, it can be more difficult to write a powerful, memorable free verse poem because there is more pressure on you as the writer to build meaningful patterns via the subtle work of image, sound echoes, and rhythm.

Because poetry demands structure, the free verse poet has to invent ways to create structures to avoid writing "prose with line breaks." Here's where your training in pattern comes into play. If you choose to abandon meter, you can create meaningful patterns in your poetry in order to emphasize meaning, underscore key words, and create pleasing rhythms and sound echoes for the reader by attending to:

1. The natural rhythm in each line—does it fit with the meaning of the line?
2. Patterns of sound echoes and rhyme in unexpected, meaningful places throughout the poem
3. Repetitions of key images
4. The shape of the poem on the page—does it support the overall meaning of the poem?

PATTERN BY EYE

Object Patterns

In addition to using sound and rhythm, creating patterns that appeal to the reader's ear, writers also create patterns out of objects or images to make the work more meaningful and cohesive. This is called a **unified pattern of imagery**.

> *The ear tends to be lazy, craves the familiar and is shocked by the unexpected; the eye, on the other hand, tends to be impatient, craves the novel and is bored by repetition.*
> —W. H. AUDEN

Take an inventory of the specific details, the objects, the "stuff" in your piece. Is there too much stuff that doesn't fit, isn't really necessary? Do you need to have a garage sale? Or does your piece need a personal shopper to add more carefully chosen objects to layer meaning into your piece?

> *Usually I begin with an image or a phrase; if you follow trustfully, it's surprising how far an image can lead.*
>
> —JAMES MERRILL

Many beginning writers need *more* stuff in their stories, poems, and plays. They refer to general worlds, but they don't populate these worlds with the details of real life, thereby missing an opportunity not just to be energetic but to create a complex, interesting, layered pattern of imagery.

Common mistake: The writer describes *everything*. But the reader doesn't want to read details that are there for no real reason. Don't just stick random stuff into your writing. Choose objects and images that go with or work against the "stuff" in your piece, making interesting visual patterns. A cigarette, a broken baby stroller with a baby in it, a half-empty warm beer can—those objects are telling a story that's already interesting. Those carefully chosen objects make a pattern that affects the reader: a pattern of danger, neglect. The takeaway? Objects and images make a pattern all on their own, and that pattern creates meaning for your reader.

The easiest way to learn more about creating a pattern of objects or images is to read as a writer. First, divide a sheet of paper into two columns, one labeled "Animate Objects" and the other "Inanimate Objects." Review the story "Bodies" by Jessica Shattuck on page 291. As you come to each object in the story, record it in the appropriate column. Listing all these objects, fill up your columns like this:

Object Patterns in Jessica Shattuck's "Bodies"

Animate Objects	Inanimate Objects
Long-legged, blond, shiny Michele	Halved parsnips like limbs
Glamorous, big-boned, cool Cleo, creative director for a giant ad agency	Refrigerator like a hospital
Intense, frank Anthony, the kid	Gallon and a half of water a day
Drooling Eden, the baby	Pilly sweater, baggy jeans, pills, vitamins
Animal-like Jay	Black Central Park
Annie, her body like a sick pet, sneakers, jacket	Pink and orange dahlias projecting pointy orange shadows on the walls

The pattern of objects tells us a lot about the deeper layers of the story. The objects are signals, creating a kind of lighted pathway for the reader. The objects, when strung together, make meaning. That's the power of pattern.

Review your object patterns worksheet and notice the pairs that emerge. Michele, looking at the vegetables and seeing limbs. Cleo, hospital. Anthony, too much water. The people in this story — animate objects who have health, sexuality, and beauty — are accompanied by objects that evoke artifice, insensitivity, greed. The weaker characters — young Anthony, sick Annie — are trying, but drowning, turning limp. We know this partly because they are associated with objects that are losing strength or suffocating.

The pattern makes meaning.

Look at the inanimate objects. Do they create a visual pattern? Do you hear echoes? Yes.

When pulled out and strung together, these objects spell out decay, loss, and fear, among other things.

By naming creepy inanimate things at regular intervals throughout her story, Shattuck creates a background sound track that is thrumming, unnerving, slightly menacing, unpleasant. The reader has an uneasy feeling. That feeling is underscored by the pattern, and the breaks in the pattern. Shattuck includes *Goodnight Moon* and the sound track to *The Lion King*: moving, heartfelt pieces. The wholesome sweetness of these objects breaks the image pattern, breaks the sirens and the low-level fighting, underscoring the betrayal, sadness, and decay. To use heavy, dark, sad music in this story could have tipped the whole thing into melodrama.

If Shattuck had chosen to call our attention to the nice, brilliant nephew, the cute white doves in Central Park, the cheerful children in strollers, the helpful doorman in his pressed red suit, the fresh bread from the bakery on 107th Street, the crisp white paper it comes in — and all those things exist in this world, too — the tone of the piece, our feelings when we read, would be *quite* different.

A meaningful pattern of objects is key to a successful piece of creative writing.

When writing a piece set in a house, you don't describe every single room or list everything in the fridge. You choose the items that go with the other items, items that underline or highlight the feeling you want to evoke in the reader. You are a set designer. You can bring in only *a few specific objects*. What do you select to best amplify the drama, your themes? The objects are going to create a pattern — you want to control that pattern. When you

> *Never use three words when one will do. Be concise. Don't fall in love with the gentle trilling of your mellifluous sentences.*
> —COLSON WHITEHEAD

bring in flowers, you bring in clashing colors, to echo Michele and Cleo. Instead of providing beauty, these flowers make scary Halloween shadows, like weapons, on the walls. Everything you bring onto your set, you use. The gift of the flowers contrasts with and bounces off Anthony's gift in the final sentence of the story, the painting, so thick with color that pieces of it are falling off as he gives it to Annie. Notice the patterns: Saliva on Eden's face at the beginning of the story pairs with Michele's "little bubbles of saliva in the corners of her mouth" at the end of the story; Michele is a baby, a dangerous baby. Anthony is curved in a sofa at the beginning of the story; Jay is "sunk down into the sofa with his knees wedged against the coffee table and his head in his hands." This pattern of imagery sharply underlines the differences in our desire to be comforted and our ability to give and receive love.

So you do what good set designers (and home stagers) do. You have a storehouse of stuff, and you pull out different items until you find a pattern. Because creative writing appeals in large part to a reader's visual experience, taking care to layer objects that create patterns of meaning is crucial.

PRACTICE 7

OBJECT PATTERNS IN PROSE

Read "Paper Menagerie" by Ken Liu on page 337. Make a list of the animate and inanimate objects. Then, write a short analysis of the patterns the objects create. For example, the paper animals the mother makes (animate *and* inanimate) are part of the *paper* pattern in the story: The father found the mother in a *paper* catalogue.

PRACTICE 8

OBJECT PATTERNS IN POETRY AND DRAMA

Choose a poem or a play and create a list of the animate objects (people, animals) and the inanimate objects (images, things). Write a short description of the patterns and what they suggest about the meaning of the piece.

Gesture Patterns

One of the most intriguing patterns to work with is that of movement—human physical movement or gestures—throughout your piece. Consider the story of Cinderella, as told in Disney's movie version for children. The first gestures are Cinderella's, dancing around the house getting her chores done. Imagine the footwork of the tale—that's the pattern we are tracking now. The next movement pattern is the festive dance of birds and the fairy godmother, getting her ready for the ball. Another dance, with a different shape or pattern to it. It relates to the grand ball where Cinderella *dances* again, for real this time, with the Prince. The final dance: It's the community's turn, as everyone is thrown into a tizzy while the Prince fits the slipper, whirling through the town with his entourage until he finds his match. Tracking and working to align and intensify the patterns of movement in your creative writing allows you to cleverly connect the parts of your piece. Movement attracts the reader. Movement patterns in your writing reinforce theme and meaning.

When the pattern changes, we have the same reaction as when a poet using iambic pentameter inserts a rhythm break such as "Hark! Hark!" into an otherwise metrically perfect line. We pay attention.

Consider the patterns of gestures in Rick Moody's story "Boys" on page 219. Throughout the entire story, the boys are running and swooping and diving and dashing, tossing and digging, scratching and hollering. So when they stop, stand still, and whisper, that break in the pattern heightens tension and gathers our attention as readers; the writer creates meaning and makes a major point through the gesture pattern.

Notice the opening pattern of gestures in "Bodies" (look back at the opening paragraph on page 291). Annie makes dinner, turns on lights, a child lays his head down on his arm. Annie moves quietly through the kitchen, promises him attention; the boy sits up straight. Summary flashback: Annie moves carefully through her days at Cleo's, dancing with her illness. Notice the pattern: In the first section (before the space break), we see up close Annie's moves through her life — they are tender, evenly paced, smooth. In the second section, the patterns her feet make on the floor of her life are the same. They have been static for a long time — since she got sick — and we see the dance from above, from farther back. Pattern. Pattern. Then, in the third section, the pattern changes, yes? The doorbell rings. Anthony puts his hand on his hip — two staccato gestures, boom, boom. It's like a time change in music, a couple of quick leaps in dance. Enter Michele. She *peers, breathes, flashes,* and Anthony is *demanding, shouting, squirming, collapsing*. This is a new sequence, a new pattern. Notice the contrast, and how energy is created by establishing a pattern firmly and then changing it dramatically.

PRACTICE 9

GESTURE PATTERNS IN PROSE

In Rick Moody's story "Boys" on page 219, the movements and gestures are easy to track. Make a list of the gestures you find in the story. These will be different from the verbs you collected earlier; *gestures* refers to actions made by human bodies. What patterns do the gestures create? Another story that uses gesture patterns to create rich layers of meaning is "Pretty Ice" by Mary Robison on page 169. For extra practice, track gesture patterns in that story or Ken Liu's "Paper Menagerie."

PRACTICE 10

GESTURE PATTERNS IN POETRY

In poetry, a form that relies so heavily on compression, gestures almost always create patterns that aid the reader's understanding of the meaning. List each gesture (person in action) in "The River" by Gregory Orr on page 332. Make a brief statement about layers of meaning in the poem simply based on the gestures and what each implies.

PRACTICE 11

GESTURE PATTERNS IN DRAMA

In a play, the actions performed by the actors — their gestures — usually play out a pattern of meaning. Choose any play in this textbook, and focus on the actions the characters display. Some actions will be written in the stage directions: "(*He aims the gun up at the sky.*)" Others you will infer from what the character is doing while he speaks (wolfing breakfast). After you have created your list of gestures, make a short statement about the pattern created by the gestures alone.

Creative writing creates, through movement, a kinetic, dramatic experience for the reader to focus on. Attending to gesture patterns increases the depth, meaning, energy, and drama in your writing.

Pattern on the Page

Another important aspect of pattern is the way the elements of your writing play out visually on the page and screen. What's the pattern on the page created by your paragraphs, your stanzas? How will your work appear if it's read on a small or large screen?

When you design the way your writing looks on the page, you take into account a number of considerations. Your instructor (or your editor or publisher) may have specific requirements in terms of word count, feasibility of text and image, font size, and so on. And you as the artist and creator must consider how the format you are working with, taking into account whatever external constraints are placed on you (budget, assignment requirements), supports the meaning of your piece.

Consider the visual patterns your work creates: How does your piece look on the page to the reader's eye?

Giant blocks of text aren't friendly to readers. If your paragraphs are taking up whole pages, is there a reason, as we saw with "Boys" and "I Go Back to Berryman's"? Or, if there isn't a thematic reason, instead of using giant blocks of text, is there a meaningful way you can initiate a more pleasing pattern of white space, indents, and breaks?

Pattern determines the way the piece looks on the page, and it's worth paying attention to designing a form — a shape — for your work that augments the meaning of the work itself.

Betsy Sholl chose couplets and one- and three-line stanzas to shape her poem about a girl and her two parents — form follows function. When writing poetry, notice the way your stanzas create a pattern on the page. Does the poem *look* shaped? Does the poem have the same number of lines per stanza and lines about the same length? Or are you deliberately changing the pattern of your lines in order to make a point? Is that purpose well thought out or random? If your line breaks are unconscious and your creative writing sprawls across the page for no good reason, you might be underutilizing the power of the page or screen. Check again: Are your lines ragged on purpose? Or just because you haven't attended to that pattern yet?

Form is like asbestos gloves that allow you to pick up material too hot to handle otherwise.

—ADRIENNE RICH

White space matters. White space acts as a rest does in music; the reader gets to pause, to breathe. White space alternating with short blocks of text speeds the pace (a staccato effect). Repeated visual elements — big blocks of text (paragraphs, stanzas, speech) with white space — create a polished, professional look and invite the reader in. The piece feels crafted, not dashed off. Long sections of text with no white space breaks are more difficult, and the reader may become lost. Most writers employ white space and additional patterns, such as sound, syntax, and rhythm, to help the reader stay engaged and on track through a long section.

The visual outline, or pattern, involves blocks of text and blocks of white space. Because as writers we are so limited by these two tools, it's absolutely essential that we attend to the nuances of shape — the way the piece looks on the page.

Take a look at the essay "How to Erase an Arab" by Julie Hakim Azzam on page 333. The pattern created on the page is quite noticeable. Short sections with newspaper headlines "title" blocks of prose. Azzam draws short sections, almost like stanzas, from poetry. She takes headlines from the newspaper, a collagist's move. She shares scenes from her life, her family's life: memoir moves. The newspaper headlines work as a kind of voice-over — a dramatist's move. Mixing and matching various patterns from across the genres, Azzam invents a fresh new form to hold her singular personal story.

Consider the giant, consuming block of text on page 76 that Vincent Scarpa uses to tell the story of growing up in a trailer park; he felt trapped and the block of text physically entraps the reader, too. A. Van Jordan's "af•ter•glow" on page 71 is formatted to physically look like a dictionary definition; inside the block of text, he implants/marks to denote lines of poetry banging around inside the definition, creating a new visual pattern on the page.

Sebastian Matthews's poem "Buying Wine" on page 71 has long lines and is long, as are liquor store aisles, as is childhood. In Gwendolyn Brooks's "We Real Cool" on page 105 and E. E. Cummings's "(Me up at does)" on page 316 are made of quick bright lines, just a few words each, that skitter down the page, and the reader tumbles down through the poem, too. In each case the physical layout of the piece of writing visually **mirrors** the subject matter itself.

PRACTICE 12

PATTERN ON THE PAGE

Thumb through this textbook. Which pieces are most inviting to read, in terms of pattern on the page? Least inviting? How does noticing what invites you as a reader inform how you think about pattern in your own works? Write a one-page piece where the pattern on the page underscores the meaning of the piece.

Though my poems are about evenly split between traditionally formal work that uses rhyme and meter and classical structure, and work that is freer, I feel that the music of language remains at the core of it all. Sound, rhythm, repetition, compression—these elements of my poetry are also elements of my prose.

—FLOYD SKLOOT

In sum, when designing the pattern your piece will create on the page, don't settle for your first instinct. Play a little. We writers have two elements: text and white space. (Your instructor may also encourage drawing.) How much pattern can you eke out of your options without distracting or alarming your reader? As always, pattern supports, complements, and underscores the theme and purpose of the piece.

Two additional pattern techniques are well worth learning and practicing. These two techniques, lists and anaphora, allow you to make meaning, hold reader interest, and play with the shape of your writing on the page to create drama and depth.

Lists. A list is an inventory of items. Lists are one of the oldest forms of creative writing; they're simple, reader-friendly, and a terrific way to practice the image-based techniques you've learned so far in this course. You can use a list within a piece, to add texture and specificity, to round out a character description or establish setting, or your list can provide the structure for a whole piece that stands on its own. Jordan's "af•ter•glow" on page 71 is a list of possible and poetic definitions for the word at hand. Brian Arundel's

"The Things I've Lost" on page 217 is a list piece using objects to tell a personal story of growth and maturation; Azzam's "How to Erase an Arab" on page 333 is a piece patterned from a list of five headlines the author chose from the *New York Times* over a period of thirteen years. Each headline prompts the author to reveal a little more of her personal story. As Azzam and her family struggle to understand the complexities of war, history, identity, politics, violence, and memory, it makes perfect sense for her to tell her story in headlines and snippets, as she grasps for clarity and understanding in brief glimpses between bombings.

If you are stuck as a writer, try conceiving your piece as a list; lists are our go-to, jump start, no-fail writing prompt. Lists work because they're pattern-based.

Working from patterns — whether sound, rhythm, images and objects, gestures, or structurally, as with a list — is often much more generative and effective than working from "ideas" or other abstract concepts.

> *I'm supposed to be writing another novel in English about Indian Americans. I haven't done that. I may never do that again. I think that what I have been truly searching for as a person, as a writer, as a thinker, as a daughter, is freedom.*
>
> —JHUMPA LAHIRI

Anaphora. "Boys" by Rick Moody on page 219 is a list short story (all the stuff these particular boys do) that uses **anaphora** to create a pattern that gives shape to the whole piece. Anaphora is the repetition of a word or key words that appear at the beginning of a sequence of lines or sentences. Anaphora is discussed in full in Chapter Ten beginning on page 429.

Anaphora creates a sonic pattern, because we repeat the words or phrases over in our mind, and it also creates visual pattern on the page, whether you use it in poetry, at the beginning of a sequence of lines, or in prose, as Moody does.

The reader's eye is attracted to visual pattern; you will want to experiment with anaphora in every genre, including comics, playwriting, and screenwriting.

Note the powerful use of anaphora in Marco Ramirez' "I am not Batman" on page 82. After his first sentence, Ramirez has the boy start every line of dialogue with the word *and*:

"And if you squint …
"And if you look up high enough …
"And up there, a place …
"And I'm freakin' *Batman.*
"And I gots Batmobiles and Bat-a-rangs …
"And my navy blue polo shirt?

He breaks the pattern for three beats, and then returns to it:

"And nobody pulls out a belt ..."

Anaphora adds elegance and pressure to the words of the boy. He turns the boy's pain and lament into art by imposing this pattern on the dialogue. The play turns into a kind of prayer, or litany, or lament because of the repetition.

Joy Harjo's poem "She Had Some Horses" uses anaphora. Take a look at the poem (the first part is reprinted here in this textbook; you can read the whole poem online) on page 372. Note the visual look on the page. Anaphora is a pattern that invites the reader in. The poem looks like a song; it has a refrain. Read the poem aloud and notice the effect of the anaphora, raising up the words, framing them, and underscoring the meaning of the poem in complex and interesting and original ways.

WRITING PROJECTS

Experiments

1. Make a long and detailed list of stuff in from your childhood bedroom, or your current sleeping quarters, or another place — a coffee shop, gym, library — where you spend a lot of time. Choose the most surprising, peculiar, and unexpected items, and use the list of objects as a pattern to organize a piece that tells the story of your life. Aim for ten list items and ten short sections. See page 452 for additional information on list pieces.
2. Imitate Julie Hakim Azzam's piece, "How to Erase an Arab," on page 333. For a week, collect headlines from social media and news outlets. Create a piece with sections headed by these quotes, telling the story of your life as prompted by these sound bites. Aim for five to ten sections.
3. Write a short piece (a poem, story, memoir, or prose poem) in which you use a lot of inverted syntax. Make your piece about a situation that is upside down, or tell it from a perspective that is the opposite of what we expect.
4. Write a piece that uses anaphora in every line. Use the guidelines on page 432.

Poetry

5. Write a pantoum, creating sound patterns within the lines as well as at the end. Use the guidelines on page 460.

6. Write a sonnet, creating sound patterns within the lines as well as at the line ends. Use the guidelines on page 472 in Chapter Ten: fourteen lines of iambic pentameter. It's challenging, but very likely worthwhile. Because of its compression (140 syllables!), many student writers report that writing a sonnet changes the way they approach creative writing across the board.

Fiction

7. Write a short story using anaphora, as Moody does: Many of the sentences in your piece will start with the same noun or phrase.
8. Write a short story that begins with images from one of your own personal earliest memories—a sound, smell, or gesture; use those images as a pattern to trace a coming-of-age story for an invented character; Liu's "Paper Menagerie" can serve as your model, if that's helpful to you.

Drama

9. Write a scene for a play that uses anaphora and an object pattern as well a gesture pattern.

PATTERN WORKSHOP

The prompts below will help you constructively discuss your classmates' work.

1. Read your peer's work and highlight or underline patterns of rhyme and sound echo in this piece.
2. Locate at least three repeated consonant patterns and three repeated vowel patterns that serve to unify the piece or emphasize words in a special way.
3. Comment on the rhythm in the piece.
4. When you look at the work on the page, do you notice any interesting visual patterns? Any awkward widows or orphans, lines left stranded at the bottom or top of a page, or space breaks? Can you find places or ways the writer could rework the piece in order to make it more visually interesting?
5. List the objects referred to in the writing. Can you think of a way—either by substituting objects or by naming more specific, more specialized versions of the objects already named—to create a pattern? Do the same for the gesture patterns (human/animal movements).

READINGS

Gregory Orr
The River

I felt both pleasure and a shiver
as we undressed on the slippery bank
and then plunged into the wild river.

I waded in; she entered as a diver.
Watching her pale flanks slice the dark
I felt both pleasure and a shiver.

Was this a source of the lake we sought, giver
of itself to that vast, blue expanse?
We'd learn by plunging into the wild river

and letting the current take us wherever
it willed. I had that yielding to thank
for how I felt both pleasure and a shiver.

But what she felt and saw I'll never
know: separate bodies taking the same risk
by plunging together into the wild river.

Later, past the rapids, we paused to consider
if chance or destiny had brought us here;
whether it was more than pleasure and a shiver
we'd found by plunging into the wild river.

Randall Mann
Pantoum

If there is a word in the lexicon of love,
it will not declare itself.
The nature of words is to fail
men who fall in love with men.

It will not declare itself,
the perfect word. *Boyfriend* seems ridiculous:
men who fall in love with men
deserve something a bit more formal.

The perfect word? Boyfriend? Ridiculous.
But *partner* is . . . businesslike—

we deserve something a bit less formal,
much more in love with love.

But if partner is businesslike,
then *lover* suggests only sex,
is too much in love with love.
There is life outside of the bedroom,

and lover suggests only sex.
We are left with *roommate*, or *friend*.
There is life, but outside the bedroom.
My *friend* and I rarely speak of one another.

To my left is my roommate, my friend.
If there is a word in the lexicon of love,
my friend and I rarely speak it of one another.
The nature of words is to fail.

Edna St. Vincent Millay
What lips my lips have kissed, and where, and why

What lips my lips have kissed, and where, and why,
I have forgotten, and what arms have lain
Under my head till morning; but the rain
Is full of ghosts tonight, that tap and sigh
Upon the glass and listen for reply,
And in my heart there stirs a quiet pain
For unremembered lads that not again
Will turn to me at midnight with a cry.

Thus in the winter stands the lonely tree,
Nor knows what birds have vanished one by one,
Yet knows its boughs more silent than before:
I cannot say what loves have come and gone,
I only know that summer sang in me
A little while, that in me sings no more.

Julie Hakim Azzam
How to Erase an Arab

"Israeli General Says Mission is to Smash P.L.O. in Beirut"
Seventh grade, social studies — On the family tree, next to the names of my
father's family, I write locations of birth: Lebanon, Palestine, Syria. I trace

flags from my atlas. There is no Palestinian flag in the book, but I know how to draw it. When the teacher walks around the classroom commenting, all she says about mine is: "Palestine isn't a country."

Palestine is a place where memories and stories are born. *Do I remember Gaza or my grandmother's stories about Gaza?* Palestine is a phantom limb that continues to send pain signals through the nerves.

"District Starving in Beirut Battle Gets Food Aid; Early Effort Thwarted"

Seventh grade, the kitchen — Jodie's brown eyes are open wide; her mouth opens, then abruptly shuts. My grandmother pauses from dicing onions and hands her a glass of water. When grandmother hands me a glass, I turn it and drink from the side her fingers haven't touched. I hold the water in my mouth. Despite drinking from the other side, I can still taste the onion.

After I close the door to my room, Jodie lets escape the thing she's been holding inside.

"Who was that brown woman in your kitchen?"

My grandparents, refugees, recently arrived at the airport after a bomb destroyed their Beirut apartment. My grandfather is so thin his skin hangs from his body. I wonder if it will slide to the floor. After establishing herself in the kitchen, grandmother begins prolific production, a *compensatory cooking,* my mother says. Out of the kitchen comes freshly baked pita bread, huge trays of kafta, overflowing bowls of salad.

My mouth waters, but I tell her I want McDonald's. *Give me Hamburger Helper, macaroni and cheese, hot dogs.* I push her food aside.

"Palestinians Exit Lebanon in Droves"

Eighth grade, the television — My family moves the following year, and when the teacher assigns the same family ancestry project, I ask my father if I can change our ancestry. The idea comes to me while watching Brian Boitano and Brian Orser battle for the gold in the winter Olympics in Calgary.

The only way I can discern one Brian from the other is by their differently colored outfits, yet I want to be part of the Brians. I want to be so confident I kick down the door of every room, to cry proud tears of victory under a flag whose validity is neither questioned nor a metonym for violence. I am willing to offend, to jettison Palestine.

My parents exchange a glance. "All right."

Instead of drawing the green cedar tree that adorns the Lebanese flag, or the flag of a stateless people, I get out my red marker and begin to draw a maple leaf.

"Car Bomb on West Beirut Street Leaves 25 Dead and 180 Injured"

Tenth grade, the foyer—Nicole steps into the foyer to pick me up and is met by my father, who asks her if she knows what is going on in Lebanon. She squints, trying not to appear stoned.

My father points a finger and yells about *typical Americans* and *ignorance* and *privilege* and *nobody here notices*.

The day before, my uncle and his friends stood walking on a West Beirut street. A car bomb detonated and killed them all. According to the *Times*, "most of the dead were unidentified."

When we get into her large, rust-colored Impala, Nicole snorts, "The fuck was that?" No clue, I mumble, but I know that history is a house I must live in. As the ignition cranks, I imagine it. Maybe the men were talking about Amal or infighting among the Palestinians. Perhaps over cigarettes, they commiserated over the mundane: wives, kids gone stir-crazy, food shortages. They didn't notice the unassuming Peugeot or Fiat.

Nobody ever does.

"Wrecked by Years of Civil War, Beirut is Rising from the Ashes"

University, near Lake Placid—From bare ground, my father erects a house near the site of the 1980 Winter Olympics. He selects wood, casement, granite, and marble. My Muslim father attends Catholic mass, and makes friendly introductions with neighbors. If they ask, he tells them he is Greek. Or Italian.

It's bad to lie your way through life. *But this is easier, better.* What's worse is how it keeps happening. We build it—our lives, a city, a home—we break it down. Over and over.

*(Note: All headlines are from the *New York Times* between 1982 and 1995)

WRITERS ON WRITING

JULIE HAKIM AZZAM

HEATHER SELLERS: What inspired you to write this piece?

JULIE HAKIM AZZAM: Honestly, I have a hard time finishing pieces that I start and need a firm goal and external deadline to hold myself accountable. I saw a call for short pieces of nonfiction in *Brevity* magazine, and decided that I'd try to answer that call by writing something that would draw on my experiences growing up Arab American in the Midwest. I had no idea what I would write, but I knew that I had to write something.

HS: Can you describe to us your process in creating the piece? How did you shape it, how much revision did you do, etc.?

JHA: Once I figured out that I was going to structure my piece along the lines of newspaper headlines, I found actual headlines and then wrote a paragraph that could correspond to each one. I then printed them out and cut them up with scissors and started rearranging their order on my desk. I wasn't sure how to arrange these headlines and paragraphs. Should I do so in chronological order? I also had too many headlines and paragraphs to meet the publisher's requirements of 750 words so I had to figure out which ones to keep and which ones to let go. Physically manipulating the structure with my hands gave me a break from staring at the computer screen but it also got me thinking about organization in a different way.

HS: How do you decide what genre to work in?

JHA: As this was a memoir piece, I wanted to write something that didn't try to be anything other than me, and capture how I think about and process things, and not mimic what I see others doing, as I am so tempted to do. I have always loved newspapers, clip stories to remember for later (either paper stories or virtual bookmarks and reading lists) and have long considered myself a "news junkie." One day I thought, if you're so into reading the news, then why not structure a piece that pays homage to how you process your rather emotional heritage and family history with the context of a dry, facts-only newspaper headline?

The editors classified this piece as "experimental," but in truth, it's how I think about my family's history. What was most earth-shattering for me as a writer in this process was becoming aware of my own ways of seeing and contextualizing things and then accepting that this way was not only acceptable, but a good way in which to structure my writing. It was a form of self-acceptance, really, which is what I think the piece is about.

HS: Most difficult thing about writing this piece?

JHA: The most difficult thing was writing about something private for such a public forum. (I'm a very private person and even something as small as a social media post can get me regretting sharing personal information — it's completely neurotic, I know!) As soon as I submitted the work to *Brevity*, I wanted to take it back for that same reason. I figured I'd get rejected so I wouldn't have to worry about the feeling that I'd "overshared" personal information on my family. In truth, I have not shared this piece with my family and I am 100 percent okay with that. While I don't think I've misrepresented my family in my piece, I do struggle with how something I write that includes my family will affect them. I can't say that I've resolved that issue, or that my way of resolving the issue was a good one.

HS: What advice do you wish you'd gotten early on as a writer?

JHA: Trust yourself and believe that your quirky, unique way of seeing and experiencing the world is something worth capturing, replicating, thinking about, and sharing with others through your writing. For my whole life, people have told me that I "see things sideways," and I fought to correct that and see things their way. It was a revelation when I could come to terms with the fact that readers like it when things are presented in new and different ways.

Ken Liu

Paper Menagerie

One of my earliest memories starts with me sobbing. I refused to be soothed no matter what Mom and Dad tried.

Dad gave up and left the bedroom, but Mom took me into the kitchen and sat me down at the breakfast table.

"*Kan, kan,*" she said, as she pulled a sheet of wrapping paper from on top of the fridge. For years, Mom carefully sliced open the wrappings around Christmas gifts and saved them on top of the fridge in a thick stack.

She set the paper down, plain side facing up, and began to fold it. I stopped crying and watched her, curious.

She turned the paper over and folded it again. She pleated, packed, tucked, rolled, and twisted until the paper disappeared between her cupped hands. Then she lifted the folded-up paper packet to her mouth and blew into it, like a balloon.

"*Kan,*" she said. "*Laohu.*" She put her hands down on the table and let go.

A little paper tiger stood on the table, the size of two fists placed together. The skin of the tiger was the pattern on the wrapping paper, white background with red candy canes and green Christmas trees.

I reached out to Mom's creation. Its tail twitched, and it pounced playfully at my finger. "*Rawrr-sa,*" it growled, the sound somewhere between a cat and rustling newspapers.

I laughed, startled, and stroked its back with an index finger. The paper tiger vibrated under my finger, purring.

"*Zhe jiao zhezhi,*" Mom said. *This is called origami.*

I didn't know this at the time, but Mom's kind was special. She breathed into them so that they shared her breath, and thus moved with her life. This was her magic.

Dad had picked Mom out of a catalog.

One time, when I was in high school, I asked Dad about the details. He was trying to get me to speak to Mom again.

He had signed up for the introduction service back in the spring of 1973. Flipping through the pages steadily, he had spent no more than a few seconds on each page until he saw the picture of Mom.

I've never seen this picture. Dad described it: Mom was sitting in a chair, her side to the camera, wearing a tight green silk cheongsam. Her head was turned to the camera so that her long black hair was draped artfully over her chest and shoulder. She looked out at him with the eyes of a calm child.

"That was the last page of the catalog I saw," he said.

The catalog said she was eighteen, loved to dance, and spoke good English because she was from Hong Kong. None of these facts turned out to be true.

He wrote to her, and the company passed their messages back and forth. Finally, he flew to Hong Kong to meet her.

"The people at the company had been writing her responses. She didn't know any English other than 'hello' and 'goodbye.'"

What kind of woman puts herself into a catalog so that she can be bought? The high school me thought I knew so much about everything. Contempt felt good, like wine.

Instead of storming into the office to demand his money back, he paid a waitress at the hotel restaurant to translate for them.

"She would look at me, her eyes halfway between scared and hopeful, while I spoke. And when the girl began translating what I said, she'd start to smile slowly."

He flew back to Connecticut and began to apply for the papers for her to come to him. I was born a year later, in the Year of the Tiger.

At my request, Mom also made a goat, a deer, and a water buffalo out of wrapping paper. They would run around the living room while Laohu chased after them, growling. When he caught them he would press down until the air went out of them and they became just flat, folded-up pieces of paper. I would then have to blow into them to re-inflate them so they could run around some more.

Sometimes, the animals got into trouble. Once, the water buffalo jumped into a dish of soy sauce on the table at dinner. (He wanted to wallow, like a real water buffalo.) I picked him out quickly but the capillary action had already pulled the dark liquid high up into his legs. The sauce-softened legs would not hold him up, and he collapsed onto the table. I dried him out in the sun, but his legs became crooked after that, and he ran around with a limp. Mom eventually wrapped his legs in saran wrap so that he could wallow to his heart's content (just not in soy sauce).

Also, Laohu liked to pounce at sparrows when he and I played in the backyard. But one time, a cornered bird struck back in desperation and tore his ear. He whimpered and winced as I held him and Mom patched his ear together with tape. He avoided birds after that.

And then one day, I saw a TV documentary about sharks and asked Mom for one of my own. She made the shark, but he flapped about on the table unhappily. I filled the sink with water, and put him in. He swam around and around happily. However, after a while he became soggy and translucent, and slowly sank to the bottom, the folds coming undone. I reached in to rescue him, and all I ended up with was a wet piece of paper.

Laohu put his front paws together at the edge of the sink and rested his head on them. Ears drooping, he made a low growl in his throat that made me feel guilty.

Mom made a new shark for me, this time out of tin foil. The shark lived happily in a large goldfish bowl. Laohu and I liked to sit next to the bowl to watch the tin foil shark chasing the goldfish, Laohu sticking his face up against the bowl on the other side so that I saw his eyes, magnified to the size of coffee cups, staring at me from across the bowl.

When I was ten, we moved to a new house across town. Two of the women neighbors came by to welcome us. Dad served them drinks and then apologized for having to run off to the utility company to straighten out the prior owner's bills. "Make yourselves at home. My wife doesn't speak much English, so don't think she's being rude for not talking to you."

While I read in the dining room, Mom unpacked in the kitchen. The neighbors conversed in the living room, not trying to be particularly quiet.

"He seems like a normal enough man. Why did he do that?"

"Something about the mixing never seems right. The child looks unfinished. Slanty eyes, white face. A little monster."

"Do you think *he* can speak English?"

The women hushed. After a while they came into the dining room.

"Hello there! What's your name?"

"Jack," I said.

"That doesn't sound very Chinesey."

Mom came into the dining room then. She smiled at the women. The three of them stood in a triangle around me, smiling and nodding at each other, with nothing to say, until Dad came back.

Mark, one of the neighborhood boys, came over with his Star Wars action figures. Obi-Wan Kenobi's lightsaber lit up and he could swing his arms and say, in a tinny voice, "Use the Force!" I didn't think the figure looked much like the real Obi-Wan at all.

Together, we watched him repeat this performance five times on the coffee table. "Can he do anything else?" I asked.

Mark was annoyed by my question. "Look at all the details," he said.

I looked at the details. I wasn't sure what I was supposed to say.

Mark was disappointed by my response. "Show me your toys."

I didn't have any toys except my paper menagerie. I brought Laohu out from my bedroom. By then he was very worn, patched all over with tape and glue, evidence of the years of repairs Mom and I had done on him. He was no longer as nimble and sure-footed as before. I sat him down on the coffee table. I could hear the skittering steps of the other animals behind in the hallway, timidly peeking into the living room.

"*Xiao laohu*," I said, and stopped. I switched to English. "This is Tiger." Cautiously, Laohu strode up and purred at Mark, sniffing his hands.

Mark examined the Christmas-wrap pattern of Laohu's skin. "That doesn't look like a tiger at all. Your Mom makes toys for you from trash?"

I had never thought of Laohu as *trash*. But looking at him now, he was really just a piece of wrapping paper.

Mark pushed Obi-Wan's head again. The lightsaber flashed; he moved his arms up and down. "Use the Force!"

Laohu turned and pounced, knocking the plastic figure off the table. It hit the floor and broke, and Obi-Wan's head rolled under the couch. "*Rawwww*," Laohu laughed. I joined him.

Mark punched me, hard. "This was very expensive! You can't even find it in the stores now. It probably cost more than what your dad paid for your mom!"

I stumbled and fell to the floor. Laohu growled and leapt at Mark's face.

Mark screamed, more out of fear and surprise than pain. Laohu was only made of paper, after all.

Mark grabbed Laohu and his snarl was choked off as Mark crumpled him in his hand and tore him in half. He balled up the two pieces of paper and threw them at me. "Here's your stupid cheap Chinese garbage."

After Mark left, I spent a long time trying, without success, to tape together the pieces, smooth out the paper, and follow the creases to refold Laohu. Slowly, the other animals came into the living room and gathered around us, me and the torn wrapping paper that used to be Laohu.

My fight with Mark didn't end there. Mark was popular at school. I never want to think again about the two weeks that followed.

I came home that Friday at the end of the two weeks. "*Xuexiao hao ma?*" Mom asked. I said nothing and went to the bathroom. I looked into the mirror. *I look nothing like her, nothing.*

At dinner I asked Dad, "Do I have a chink face?"

Dad put down his chopsticks. Even though I had never told him what happened in school, he seemed to understand. He closed his eyes and rubbed the bridge of his nose. "No, you don't."

Mom looked at Dad, not understanding. She looked back at me. "*Sha jiao* chink?"

"English," I said. "Speak English."

She tried. "What happen?"

I pushed the chopsticks and the bowl before me away: stir-fried green peppers with five-spice beef. "We should eat American food."

Dad tried to reason. "A lot of families cook Chinese sometimes."

"We are not other families." I looked at him. *Other families don't have moms who don't belong.*

He looked away. And then he put a hand on Mom's shoulder. "I'll get you a cookbook."

Mom turned to me. "*Bu haochi?*"

"English," I said, raising my voice. "Speak English."

Mom reached out to touch my forehead, feeling for my temperature. "*Fashao la?*"

I brushed her hand away. "I'm fine. Speak English!" I was shouting.

"Speak English to him," Dad said to Mom. "You knew this was going to happen some day. What did you expect?"

Mom dropped her hands to her side. She sat, looking from Dad to me, and back to Dad again. She tried to speak, stopped, and tried again, and stopped again.

"You have to," Dad said. "I've been too easy on you. Jack needs to fit in."

Mom looked at him. "If I say 'love,' I feel here." She pointed to her lips. "If I say '*ai*,' I feel here." She put her hand over her heart.

Dad shook his head. "You are in America."

Mom hunched down in her seat, looking like the water buffalo when Laohu used to pounce on him and squeeze the air of life out of him.

"And I want some real toys."

Dad bought me a full set of Star Wars action figures. I gave the Obi-Wan Kenobi to Mark.

I packed the paper menagerie in a large shoebox and put it under the bed.

The next morning, the animals had escaped and took over their old favorite spots in my room. I caught them all and put them back into the shoebox, taping the lid shut. But the animals made so much noise in the box that I finally shoved it into the corner of the attic as far away from my room as possible.

If Mom spoke to me in Chinese, I refused to answer her. After a while, she tried to use more English. But her accent and broken sentences embarrassed me. I tried to correct her. Eventually, she stopped speaking altogether if I were around.

Mom began to mime things if she needed to let me know something. She tried to hug me the way she saw American mothers did on TV. I thought her movements exaggerated, uncertain, ridiculous, graceless. She saw that I was annoyed, and stopped.

"You shouldn't treat your mother that way," Dad said. But he couldn't look me in the eyes as he said it. Deep in his heart, he must have realized that it was a mistake to have tried to take a Chinese peasant girl and expect her to fit in the suburbs of Connecticut.

Mom learned to cook American style. I played video games and studied French.

Every once in a while, I would see her at the kitchen table studying the plain side of a sheet of wrapping paper. Later a new paper animal would appear on my nightstand and try to cuddle up to me. I caught them, squeezed them until the air went out of them, and then stuffed them away in the box in the attic.

Mom finally stopped making the animals when I was in high school. By then her English was much better, but I was already at that age when I wasn't interested in what she had to say whatever language she used.

Sometimes, when I came home and saw her tiny body busily moving about in the kitchen, singing a song in Chinese to herself, it was hard for me to believe that she gave birth to me. We had nothing in common. She might as well be from the moon. I would hurry on to my room, where I could continue my all-American pursuit of happiness.

Dad and I stood, one on each side of Mom, lying on the hospital bed. She was not yet even forty, but she looked much older.

For years she had refused to go to the doctor for the pain inside her that she said was no big deal. By the time an ambulance finally carried her in, the cancer had spread far beyond the limits of surgery.

My mind was not in the room. It was the middle of the on-campus recruiting season, and I was focused on resumes, transcripts, and strategically constructed interview schedules. I schemed about how to lie to the corporate recruiters most effectively so that they'll offer to buy me. I understood intellectually that it was terrible to think about this while your mother lay dying. But that understanding didn't mean I could change how I felt.

She was conscious. Dad held her left hand with both of his own. He leaned down to kiss her forehead. He seemed weak and old in a way that startled me. I realized that I knew almost as little about Dad as I did about Mom.

Mom smiled at him. "I'm fine."

She turned to me, still smiling. "I know you have to go back to school." Her voice was very weak and it was difficult to hear her over the hum of the machines hooked up to her. "Go. Don't worry about me. This is not a big deal. Just do well in school."

I reached out to touch her hand, because I thought that was what I was supposed to do. I was relieved. I was already thinking about the flight back, and the bright California sunshine.

She whispered something to Dad. He nodded and left the room.

"Jack, if—" she was caught up in a fit of coughing, and could not speak for some time. "If I don't make it, don't be too sad and hurt your health. Focus on your life. Just keep that box you have in the attic with you, and every year, at *Qingming*, just take it out and think about me. I'll be with you always."

Qingming was the Chinese Festival for the Dead. When I was very young, Mom used to write a letter on *Qingming* to her dead parents back in China, telling them the good news about the past year of her life in America. She would read the letter out loud to me, and if I made a comment about something, she would write it down in the letter too. Then she would fold the letter into a paper crane, and release it, facing west. We would then watch, as the crane flapped its crisp wings on its long journey west, towards the Pacific, towards China, towards the graves of Mom's family.

It had been many years since I last did that with her.

"I don't know anything about the Chinese calendar," I said. "Just rest, Mom."

"Just keep the box with you and open it once in a while. Just open—" she began to cough again.

"It's okay, Mom." I stroked her arm awkwardly.

"*Haizi, mama ai ni—*" Her cough took over again. An image from years ago flashed into my memory: Mom saying *ai* and then putting her hand over her heart.

"Alright, Mom. Stop talking."

Dad came back, and I said that I needed to get to the airport early because I didn't want to miss my flight.

She died when my plane was somewhere over Nevada.

Dad aged rapidly after Mom died. The house was too big for him and had to be sold. My girlfriend Susan and I went to help him pack and clean the place.

Susan found the shoebox in the attic. The paper menagerie, hidden in the uninsulated darkness of the attic for so long, had become brittle and the bright wrapping paper patterns had faded.

"I've never seen origami like this," Susan said. "Your Mom was an amazing artist."

.The paper animals did not move. Perhaps whatever magic had animated them stopped when Mom died. Or perhaps I had only imagined that these paper constructions were once alive. The memory of children could not be trusted.

It was the first weekend in April, two years after Mom's death. Susan was out of town on one of her endless trips as a management consultant and I was home, lazily flipping through the TV channels.

I paused at a documentary about sharks. Suddenly I saw, in my mind, Mom's hands, as they folded and refolded tin foil to make a shark for me, while Laohu and I watched.

A rustle. I looked up and saw that a ball of wrapping paper and torn tape was on the floor next to the bookshelf. I walked over to pick it up for the trash.

The ball of paper shifted, unfurled itself, and I saw that it was Laohu, who I hadn't thought about in a very long time. "*Rawrr-sa.*" Mom must have put him back together after I had given up.

He was smaller than I remembered. Or maybe it was just that back then my fists were smaller.

Susan had put the paper animals around our apartment as decoration. She probably left Laohu in a pretty hidden corner because he looked so shabby.

I sat down on the floor, and reached out a finger. Laohu's tail twitched, and he pounced playfully. I laughed, stroking his back. Laohu purred under my hand.

"How've you been, old buddy?"

Laohu stopped playing. He got up, jumped with feline grace into my lap, and proceeded to unfold himself.

In my lap was a square of creased wrapping paper, the plain side up. It was filled with dense Chinese characters. I had never learned to read Chinese, but I knew the characters for *son*, and they were at the top, where you'd expect them in a letter addressed to you, written in Mom's awkward, childish handwriting.

I went to the computer to check the Internet. Today was *Qingming*.

I took the letter with me downtown, where I knew the Chinese tour buses stopped. I stopped every tourist, asking, "*Nin hui du zhongwen ma?*" *Can you read Chinese?* I hadn't spoken Chinese in so long that I wasn't sure if they understood.

A young woman agreed to help. We sat down on a bench together, and she read the letter to me aloud. The language that I had tried to forget for years came back, and I felt the words sinking into me, through my skin, through my bones, until they squeezed tight around my heart.

Son,

We haven't talked in a long time. You are so angry when I try to touch you that I'm afraid. And I think maybe this pain I feel all the time now is something serious. So I decided to write to you. I'm going to write in the paper animals I made for you that you used to like so much.

The animals will stop moving when I stop breathing. But if I write to you with all my heart, I'll leave a little of myself behind on this paper, in these words. Then, if you think of me on Qingming, *when the spirits of the departed are allowed to visit their families, you'll make the parts of myself I leave behind come alive too. The creatures I made for you will again leap and run and pounce, and maybe you'll get to see these words then.*

Because I have to write with all my heart, I need to write to you in Chinese.

All this time I still haven't told you the story of my life. When you were little, I always thought I'd tell you the story when you were older, so you could understand. But somehow that chance never came up.

I was born in 1957, in Sigulu Village, Hebei Province. Your grandparents were both from very poor peasant families with few relatives. Only a few years after I was born, the Great Famines struck China, during which thirty million people died. The first memory I have was waking up to see my mother eating dirt so that she could fill her belly and leave the last bit of flour for me.

Things got better after that. Sigulu is famous for its zhezhi *papercraft, and my mother taught me how to make paper animals and give them life. This was practical magic in the life of the village. We made paper birds to chase grasshoppers away from the fields, and paper tigers to keep away the mice. For Chinese New Year my friends and I made red paper dragons. I'll never forget the sight of all those little dragons zooming across the sky overhead, holding up strings of exploding firecrackers to scare away all the bad memories of the past year. You would have loved it.*

Then came the Cultural Revolution in 1966. Neighbor turned on neighbor, and brother against brother. Someone remembered that my mother's brother, my uncle, had left for Hong Kong back in 1946, and became a merchant there. Having a relative in Hong Kong meant we were spies and enemies of the people, and we had to be struggled against in every way. Your poor grandmother—she couldn't take the abuse and threw herself down a well. Then some boys with hunting muskets dragged your grandfather away one day into the woods, and he never came back.

There I was, a ten-year-old orphan. The only relative I had in the world was my uncle in Hong Kong. I snuck away one night and climbed onto a freight train going south.

Down in Guangdong Province a few days later, some men caught me stealing food from a field. When they heard that I was trying to get to Hong Kong, they laughed. "It's your lucky day. Our trade is to bring girls to Hong Kong."

They hid me in the bottom of a truck along with other girls, and smuggled us across the border.

We were taken to a basement and told to stand up and look healthy and intelligent for the buyers. Families paid the warehouse a fee and came by to look us over and select one of us to "adopt."

The Chin family picked me to take care of their two boys. I got up every morning at four to prepare breakfast. I fed and bathed the boys. I shopped for food. I did the laundry and swept the floors. I followed the boys around and did their bidding. At night I was locked into a cupboard in the kitchen to sleep. If I was slow or did anything wrong I was beaten. If the boys did anything wrong I was beaten. If I was caught trying to learn English I was beaten.

"Why do you want to learn English?" Mr. Chin asked. "You want to go to the police? We'll tell the police that you are a mainlander illegally in Hong Kong. They'd love to have you in their prison."

Six years I lived like this. One day, an old woman who sold fish to me in the morning market pulled me aside.

"I know girls like you. How old are you now, sixteen? One day, the man who owns you will get drunk, and he'll look at you and pull you to him and you can't stop him. The wife will find out, and then you will think you really have gone to hell. You have to get out of this life. I know someone who can help."

She told me about American men who wanted Asian wives. If I can cook, clean, and take care of my American husband, he'll give me a good life. It was the only hope I had. And that was how I got into the catalog with all those lies and met your father. It is not a very romantic story, but it is my story.

In the suburbs of Connecticut, I was lonely. Your father was kind and gentle with me, and I was very grateful to him. But no one understood me, and I understood nothing.

But then you were born! I was so happy when I looked into your face and saw shades of my mother, my father, and myself. I had lost my entire family, all of Sigulu, everything I ever knew and loved. But there you were, and your face was proof that they were real. I hadn't made them up.

Now I had someone to talk to. I would teach you my language, and we could together remake a small piece of everything that I loved and lost. When you said your first words to me, in Chinese that had the same accent as my mother and me, I cried for hours. When I made the first zhezhi *animals for you, and you laughed, I felt there were no worries in the world.*

You grew up a little, and now you could even help your father and I talk to each other. I was really at home now. I finally found a good life. I wished my parents could be here, so that I could cook for them, and give them a good life too. But my parents were no longer around. You know what the Chinese think is the saddest feeling in the world? It's for a child to finally grow the desire to take care of his parents, only to realize that they were long gone.

Son, I know that you do not like your Chinese eyes, which are my eyes. I know that you do not like your Chinese hair, which is my hair. But can you understand how much joy your very existence brought to me? And can you understand how it felt when you stopped talking to me and won't let me talk to you in Chinese? I felt I was losing everything all over again.

Why won't you talk to me, son? The pain makes it hard to write.

The young woman handed the paper back to me. I could not bear to look into her face.

Without looking up, I asked for her help in tracing out the character for *ai* on the paper below Mom's letter. I wrote the character again and again on the paper, intertwining my pen strokes with her words.

The young woman reached out and put a hand on my shoulder. Then she got up and left, leaving me alone with my mother.

Following the creases, I refolded the paper back into Laohu. I cradled him in the crook of my arm, and as he purred, we began the walk home.

CHAPTER EIGHT

INSIGHT

In this chapter you will:

- Develop a practice of reading for insight and reflection
- Experiment with methods for deepening your work
- Examine your writing for three pitfalls: overexplaining, judging, and preaching

So far, you've practiced creating vivid, image-based work filled with energy and tension, made more memorable and meaningful through the use of various patterns. You've tried new genres and played with form. You've traded work with fellow writers and likely improved your talent for giving as well as receiving feedback on pieces in progress. There's one more strategy to consider applying as you continue your study of the craft of writing, one often overlooked in manuals and craft books: insight.

How do you generate writing that is insightful — truly fresh, thoughtful, and necessary? When many thousands — millions — of websites publish writers and self-publishing options beckon and countless libraries are stuffed with volume after volume, page after page, it can be daunting to think that you personally have anything of value to add. How do you contribute something that's worth reading? When you're concerned about the overall power of your work, or whenever you are doubting your ability to say something new, consider using the strategy of insight to generate new writing and shape work in progress.

Insight results not from "deep thoughts" or isolated genius but rather from writers simply paying close attention to themselves and to their experience of the world of nature and people. Insight essentially boils down to a writer observing carefully, up close and in depth and then questioning what it is one sees. Things other people might pass right by are the source for writers' insights. Insight requires slowing down and staying with what you *don't* know. It sounds counterintuitive, right? But most people hurtle so quickly through life that they risk missing some of the more interesting aspects and conclusions one can draw. Writing slows us down, asks us to pay attention. And insight simply means capturing what is missed when we're rushing through, distracted, not really paying attention.

Of course you can't take a piece in progress and just decide to make it more insightful. Wisdom doesn't work that way. In fact, if you try to "put in" insight, you might end up writing clichés or oversimplifying what's potentially complex and interesting in your work. This chapter presents some principles and techniques that will help you generate and layer work that is complex, thoughtful, and meaningful.

> *Your assumptions are your windows on the world. Scrub them off every once in a while, or the light won't come in.*
> —ISAAC ASIMOV

Creative writers are explorer-discoverers, finding insights as they work rather than working from conclusions and then using the work to illustrate canned or packaged ideas. Good writers don't sit down and just quickly come up with brilliant insights, sticking in bits of wisdom here and there throughout a piece of writing as though mixing gelled fruit into a fruitcake batter.

Insight is a process. The writing itself makes us wiser, and insight is a kind of dance between knowing what you want to say and letting the writing take you to a new place of discovery. As William Stafford describes in *Writing the Australian Crawl*:

> *There is only one trait that marks the writer. He is always watching. It's a kind of trick of mind and he is born with it.*
> —MORLEY CALLAGHAN

> A writer is not so much someone who has something to say as he is someone who has found a process that will bring about new things he would not have thought of if he had not started to say them. That is, he does not draw on a reservoir; instead he engages in an activity that brings to him a whole succession of unforeseen stories, poems, essays, plays.

READING FOR INSIGHT

Most writers agree that the best way to increase your ability to be more observant and more original on the page is through reading.

Read the short memoir "Control" by Dana Spiotta on page 374. Notice how she uses a framework of insights to structure the piece. Like any good storyteller, she begins with her strong yearning and high stakes: This is the last week of her family restaurant's high season, and they have to make enough money to get through winter when the restaurant is closed. Using action images and her mind's eye, Spiotta shows how her day—this really important day—begins: "I contemplate the floor chart as I would a puzzle—." That's an insight: She sheds *light* into her thinking process. There's tension—she's got a young child to take care of and she's got to plan for the seatings that night exactly right, to maximize profits. "I have the run times; I can be precise," is the next insight she offers. She knows herself, she knows what she is good at, and she knows she *has* to be good at this. There are mouths to feed.

The next insights come from her careful observation of the restaurant business—the food Clem, her husband, makes doesn't really matter if the service isn't flawless. Here's the insight line: "Although a great restaurant experience must include great food, a bad restaurant experience can be achieved through bad service alone." That's wisdom on the page. Notice her confident tone. Notice how she ends with the most important part of the sentence: "bad service." This wisdom is so important to the essay that she follows this insight line with another: "Ideally, service is invisible. You notice it only when something goes wrong." Spiotta, the author, uses her careful observations to show us *inside* herself and her world.

In every paragraph, she gives us images so we can see the restaurant life for ourselves. She uses action—"stamp the flames out" and "whisk it away"—and she uses enabling details and all five senses—"green-peppercorn-bourbon sauce," a kiss, and all the tastes and smells and sounds of a busy restaurant. There's conflict in every paragraph and building tension. And, in every paragraph, the author gives us another insight:

> Restaurants require concentration and timing. A badly handled problem during a rush can cascade and send the whole dining room careening toward disaster.
>
> Because there is so much I can't control, I am a maniac about the details I can control.
>
> . . . the staff eats pasta concocted out of whatever didn't sell at dinner.

Even simple observations—the second seating is calmer, the opera talent come in late and stay late and bring it loud—show that the writer is paying close attention; she is continually producing insight.

The most significant insight of all comes at the very end of the piece. Spiotta surprises us with an unexpected **turn**—a jump in time: "Years later. . . ." Here's the big reveal: She's been guilty about neglecting her daughter, stressed about balancing everything, all these years. But her daughter remembers those days fondly. She treasures them. There's so much richness and wisdom here. Parents often can't know what affects their children, or how. A young girl appreciates joy, perhaps feels secretly proud that joy belongs to her in a way—her parents created this night, this space, this community. None of that is stated. It doesn't need to be. The images do the work, building on insight and generating wisdom.

Now read Julia Koets's poem "Boys" on page 369. It's a list poem—a list of the boys she's dated. There's a rich layer of insight in the poem, informed by the fact that the speaker in the poem is not attracted to boys; she's in love with another girl. Note the **pattern** of gestures in the poem. Koets *shows* her journey into the boy-world by describing the boys through their movements—how they paint their rooms, mess around with motorcycles, cook, and spill. She uses **images** to show her relationship to boys: She keeps some too long, collecting them as one collects found treasures, "like sand dollars, starfish." She chooses couplets because the poem is about couples, creating **energy** and **tension**. Notice how those hyphenated phrases in the final couplet denote and attempt to put disparate things into one thing. The poet uses **syntax** to generate insight. And, that final image of the two kids not being able to find the path back creates a powerful layer of wisdom in this poem: When we're young, we're searching for the path to our identity, our sexuality, our self-knowledge.

We read to gain insight into others. And we read to gain insight into ourselves; our own experiences can click into focus when we read powerful literature.

When you are reading *specifically* to increase your own insight, you might consider taking notes on the following as you read. How is the text helping you

1. see something in a new or fresh way (for example, a woman's grief, a boy's experience of racism)?
2. learn new subject matter (for example, what it's like in 1960s Cleveland, what it's like to have a child born with a heart defect, how to make a robot)?
3. understand, through a character, some aspect of your own nature you have not really noticed before?
4. come to doubt something you previously held as fact (such as, after reading "Cathedral," your belief that people don't really change)?
5. appreciate that something is more complex than you originally thought?
6. tolerate something you didn't think you'd be able to (a difficult poem, a very long story, or subject matter, such as domestic violence, war, or cruelty)?

Consider keeping a reading journal where you record your insights along these lines.

For example, Raymond Carver's short story "Cathedral" on page 125 contains numerous insights, small and large, into how sighted people behave around people with impaired vision and how married people behave in general, resulting in wisdom about human growth and the potential for people to change their vision of the world. This wisdom is always embedded in the characters, their action and dialogue, and the setting itself. In your insight journal, you can note what you learn through reading and how the insight was delivered by the writer.

In presenting her portrait of truants in "We Real Cool" on page 105, the poet Gwendolyn Brooks presents insight into the romanticized attitudes toward death held by members of a gang. She doesn't talk about her subject; she has the subject itself speak. And Marisa Silver's short story "What I Saw from Where I Stood" on page 279 plays out hard-won insights into just how complex it is to be young, in love, living in a large city, and up against some of life's toughest questions — the action of the story illustrates her ideas. Gregory Orr focuses his poem "The River" on page 332 around insights into the exact nature of desire, and the risk we take when we fall — or in this case leap — into love. Many people might not think there's much to learn from listening to truants or anxiety-ridden young people, quirky, struggling robot campers or skinny-dipping couples carried along by a river.

Creative writers, however, know that examining everyday human situations — no matter how superficial or weird or sensual or sad or hilarious or fantastical they might appear to someone else — is of great value. In sum, insight is *looking within*, literally, and reading — and taking notes while reading — helps us with that process.

PRACTICE 1

READING FOR INSIGHT

Examine the short story "White Angel" by Michael Cunningham on page 376. Insight is looking within: moments where a character sees inside of others or himself or moments when the story causes the reader to see something inside themselves. What are three examples of insight indirectly or directly stated in the piece?

PRACTICE 2

ACTIVELY OBSERVING PERSONAL INSIGHTS

Choose one of your favorite selections from this book. Write a brief statement about what you like about the piece and why. Then, describe two insights you gleaned from the reading.

PRINCIPLES OF INSIGHT

When it comes to reading and writing for insight, writers rely on two core principles: accuracy and generosity.

Accuracy

To employ the strategy of insight in your writing, you'll practice a kind of laser-like, dead-on accuracy in your observations and details. Comedian Jerry Seinfeld's television show *Seinfeld* was popular partly because Seinfeld and his friends on the show spent an enormous amount of time simply observing and then naming, with great precision, everyday things we experience all the time but never notice: the low talker, the close talker. That's in large part what "smart" is: accurate. Noticing tiny true things that everyone else glides by. Seeing closely. You don't have to be "deep." You just have to get it *exactly* right.

> *A writer's mind seems to be situated partly in the solar plexus and partly in the head.*
>
> —ETHEL WILSON

How? By paying close attention to your subject.

In your writing, strive for a kind of scientific accuracy (describing things exactly as they are) and psychological accuracy (presenting human behavior exactly as you see it, not slanting actions one way or the other to make a particular point). What you discover *by writing* will always be more revealing, more likely to produce insight than what you *think of ahead of time*. The image work you did in Chapter Four is the best way to practice insight. To allow the deeper insights to come to the surface, practice looking closely at scenes and settings, and pay particular attention to what you see. Simply noticing and carefully naming what you actually see—as many of the writers in this book have done—is a fantastic way to work your observational muscles and present fresh insights to your reader. Observation *is* wisdom.

When you focus on accurately rendering just what you see, pay special attention to each of these areas: gestures and dialogue. Often, these are the places wisdom comes shining through.

Gestures. Actions speak louder than words. When you write about people, write from close up, and focus tightly on their gestures—how they move their bodies and what those gestures imply about what they want and how they are feeling. You want to focus on action—it's our behavior that reveals our character. What kind of things, large and small, do the people you are writing about do? How exactly do they do it, and what tiny distinctions do you notice between one person's little actions and another's way of doing the exact same thing? Focus less on facial expressions—wrinkled brows, crinkly smiles, and raised eyebrows—which almost everyone does roughly the same way to demonstrate feelings of worry, happiness, and disapproval. Those gestures are not well observed enough for the creative writer; they don't offer much if any opportunity for insight. Instead, focus on the specific way a father walks wildly down the aisle in the liquor store; the way a poet talks in his mind to his alter ego, his suit; the exact way a younger brother defers to his older brother. What do you see? If you look closely and record, you'll likely create a layer of revelatory insight.

PRACTICE 3

INSIGHT THROUGH GESTURES

Examine Mary Robison's "Pretty Ice" on page 169. For the mother, the daughter, and her fiancé, make a list of two or three gestures—the physical behaviors of the characters—and how each reveals an insight into that person's psychology. For example, the mother honks the horn repeatedly. What insight into that kind of person does this gesture show? Will smokes the mother's cigarettes. What does that gesture perhaps reveal about his nature? Do the same for Michael Cunningham's "White Angel" on page 376 and list the gestures that show us insights into the deeper nature of the characters. Explain.

Dialogue. In addition to the insights that come from watching human behavior as closely and carefully as a scientist, you also find insight by listening to exactly how people talk. Avoid writing down what you *think* people sound like; instead, be like a reporter and capture the exact things people say. Rather than giving your characters lines, let *them* surprise you.

Your characters may or may not speak wisdom. But your reader will find your insights into human behavior compelling if you record the ways in which people say and misstate what they mean, often hiding what they really think. In Raymond Carver's "Cathedral" on page 125, the wife says to the blind man, "I want you to feel comfortable." He replies that he is comfortable. That dialogue has wisdom in it. The author is using the dialogue to say something deeper about the blind man's character, our definitions of comfort, and surface social interactions. The blind man doesn't need anyone's help to feel at ease. He is deeply at ease in who he is. He is, truly, comfortable. It's the others who aren't, but they don't know it.

The reader gleans insight about people through their words.

PRACTICE 4

INSIGHT THROUGH DIALOGUE

Read "Two Hearts" by Brian Doyle on page 375. Make a list of a) the insights in the dialogue and b) the insights that come through piece as a whole. Comment on your findings.

Generosity

Perhaps you used to write for yourself, and maybe you still do. But now you are doing something different: You write for readers. Good writers are generous to their readers, creating work that flows and is clear and enjoyable to read, and filled with surprises, careful observation, and precise word choices. But writers are generous to their characters and subjects as well. Good writers make sure they include compassion and complexity in each piece of writing. If a character is all good or all bad, the reader will probably rebel and perhaps even start to side with your villain, or turn against your shining angel girlfriend character because, frankly, no one is that perfect and she makes us sick. Give your villains some good qualities. Give your heroes a few small flaws, and at least one large one: We are *all* flawed.

If you write from "on high," hypercritical of everyone and everything you write about, showing humans only at their most petty, most violent, most unaware, you will likely not be writing lasting, insightful work. Recall Raymond Carver's story "Cathedral" on page 125. Carver is generous in his insights. He shows Robert's annoying qualities as well as his good ones. He does the same for the wife and, most importantly, for the narrator. The narrator has a lot of limitations. But he has some good points, too. Carver explores all the dimensions in his characters. We don't always act in ways that get us what we want. Sometimes, we can't see what's right in front of us. We put on acts, try to impress others, when really we are insecure, afraid. Carver, like any highly evolved human, is generous to the narrator. He sees the man's limitations as well as the context for those limitations. He shows the reader what the narrator is trying to do. When the narrator fails, Carver shows us his pain. He shows his humanity.

Smart writers seek to understand human flaws, see weakness and strength, and balance their description by looking at a moment from many sides. Even artists famous for a dark or despairing view of the world, such as Franz Kafka or Quentin Tarantino or Sylvia Plath, thread humor or compassion or earnest attempts at human connection into their work. They are generous with compassion and empathy. "If it could happen to you, it could happen to me." That's the basic premise of *generosity* in art, and that's why art connects us.

Instead of judging people as good or bad, work to understand the how and why of the people on your pages.

PRACTICE 5

EXPLAIN GENEROSITY

Write a short statement explaining three ways in which Cunningham, the author of "White Angel" on page 376, is generous to his characters. Where, specifically in the story, does he overtly offer *insight* into a character instead of judgment?

PRACTICING INSIGHT

Here are seven straightforward, practical avenues to creating insight on the page. You can use these insight techniques to improve pieces in progress, to start new pieces in any genre, to get unstuck, or to practice and build your observational skills. Aim to try each one on its own, at least once. In a polished, finished piece of writing, you'll likely layer in more than one of the following wisdom moves.

Reflect on Your Personal Experience

Most writers, when they are starting out, feel they don't *know* enough to be considered Wise and Writerly. Even experienced writers may doubt they have enough to say or important things to say. For most writers, the feeling of having something to say varies daily, even hourly. Often, on any day we feel empowered to write, when we sit down to create a scene, we feel dumb, blocked, empty. Pointless.

The most important thing a writer can do to develop wisdom and insight is to trust that if she pays attention to her own experience in the world, if she looks long enough at the very things in front of her and closely enough at her own life and the lives of those she knows, then she will have a fairly good chance of writing some interesting stuff — whether it's fantasy fiction or a realistic short story or an experimental digital poem. This method for cultivating insight doesn't mean you are stuck writing only from personal experience. It means you work from life, starting close to home, writing what you know intuitively and emotionally, and working out from there. Remember: You have been in relationships with all kinds of people — brilliant, limited, powerful, mean, beautiful, spiritual, petty, stupid. As a writer — especially if you work in speculative and fantasy-based genres — you combine and recombine details and experiences from observations you gather as you reflect on your own life.

You don't need to know more than you know right now in order to get started on insight. The great writers of the world have simply focused very tightly on the insights they can glean from what is right before them: Zora Neale Hurston's African American Floridians north of Orlando, living their lives. Ernest Hemingway's kid up north in Michigan, fishing, hunting, falling in love. Jay McInerney's superficial, greedy New York City partyers. Amy Tan's mother–daughter struggles in a tightly knit Chinese American family. Great writers look long and hard at what's in front of them, instead of thinking that wisdom is out of reach, or lofty, or pulled from thin air.

> *A writer's duty is to register what it is like for him or her to be in the world.*
> —ZADIE SMITH

Ask Questions

Instead of *answering* big questions on the page, insightful creative writing often *poses* questions. Artists, like children, ask many questions — huge, ridiculous, sacred, amazing, inappropriate, tiny, potent, unanswerable questions. Creative writing often points to conclusions even as it resists coming up with pat answers. Creative writing isn't afraid of a little mystery. Why your ex behaved that way isn't ever going to be revealed. It's just not. But looking closely at the how and why of the tension between the two of you may well generate something more useful and interesting for both you and your readers. Questions usually lead us closer to the truth, toward deeper insights, and into the realm of wisdom. Asking the right question — specific, targeted, precise — *is* wisdom. When writing pretends to have all the answers, readers often keep the work at arm's length. Certainty can close things down, end things too quickly, cut off the very curiosity that keeps us learning, moving us toward insight. In fact, asking the right questions is often wiser — and more difficult, truth be told — than coming up with answers.

> *You never know what you will learn 'til you start writing. Then you discover truths you never knew existed.*
> —ANITA BROOKNER

Getting in the habit of questioning — staying open to not knowing longer and longer — gives you a direct line to your innate wisdom. Practice letting your work pose small pointed questions, as well as giant life-mystery questions, so the reader remains engaged, active, surprised, and wondering right along with you. The secret here is to make sure your questions take place from within images — in scenes, in real places at real points of time.

Instead of having "great ideas" or answers for writing projects, get in the habit of asking questions about human behavior and motivation. Notice how Brenda Miller in "Swerve" and Jenifer Hixon in "Where There's Smoke" don't preach or judge; they pose questions about the most mysterious and confusing aspects of their experience.

Good questions are usually not the first ones you think of. Use listing as your technique — before, during, and after writing — in order to generate insight-bearing questions. Wise questions often come in clusters — not freewriting, not thinking out loud, but a calculated, forceful deepening of the narrator's hopes and considerations.

Instead of recording your feelings in your journal, get in the habit of keeping a writer's notebook in which you ask questions. You can use this notebook to explore the questions that keep you up at night. Asking questions that don't have easy answers — or possibly any answers at all — is a great reason to start a piece of writing.

Writers spend time asking questions. We're the ones who pause on the street and say, "Wait. Stop. Did you notice that? Do you wonder why?"

PRACTICE 6

READING FOR QUESTIONS

Read Brian Doyle's memoir "Two Hearts" on page 375. The author asks a question in the piece, but many other questions are implied. Make two lists—one of overt questions and one of implied questions. In what ways do the questions the piece raises generate insight? Do the same for Michael Cunningham's "White Angel" on page 376 and Joy Harjo's "She Had Some Horses" on page 372: What questions are these writers asking through their works?

PRACTICE 7

PERSONAL QUESTION LIST

Set your timer for ten minutes. By hand, quickly write a list of every single question that has crossed your mind in the past twenty-four hours. Leap from big questions (*Is there a God?*) to mundane ones (*Will I eat pizza for dinner?*). Be as specific as you can: not "Will coats go on sale?" but "Will the North Face jacket still be $299 in November or will it be marked down 20 percent and can I even afford it then?" Type up your list, and share your list with a classmate. Discuss: Are any insights or wisdom implied in this list?

Reverse Expectations

Writing that lacks insight is usually flat and predictable writing. A simple strategy for adding a shot of insight to your writing is to be purposefully and boldly counterintuitive: Reverse yourself. Take what you wrote and say the opposite.

Let's say your poem opened this way:

> I struggle to say
> How I feel each morning
> When you awaken next to me

Using the reversal technique, you'd write something like this:

> I don't struggle to say
> What I didn't feel last night
> When I slept away from myself
> Un-next to dreamed awake you

Which version is fresher and more surprising? Which version is more engaging? Often, the reverse version is more fun, livelier, more unexpected, and perhaps wiser. There is something intriguing about that notion of "sleeping away from oneself." The writer can ask herself, "What does that mean?" Perhaps it means that the relationship she is writing about takes her too far away from her core self, who she really is. Maybe she likes who she is when she spends the night with this person, but maybe she doesn't. Or maybe she's talking about the profound loneliness she feels when she is alone or, even worse, with someone but still feeling really alone. The reverse opens up possibilities. And in possibility, there is almost always an arrow pointing toward insight.

John Brehm uses the reverse course technique in his poem on page 43 by listing all the poems he has *not* written. Joy Harjo uses reversals in part one of her masterful poem "She Had Some Horses" by upending, inverting, and reversing our regular sense of what a horse stands for. "She had horses who had no names/She had horses who had books of names." When two things cancel each other out like this, we call it a **paradox.** Harjo uses paradox to create insight into a woman's life. We all have experiences—with relationships, or substances, or emotions—that contain both a joyful, healing side and a dark, terrible side. Pablo Neruda, in "Ode to My Suit" on page 370, takes the intriguing visual notion of how our clothes take on something of our own bodies, our own shapes, when we wear them every day, and he reverses it: The clothes are affecting him, too.

Self-help books would like us to believe human experience is simple; problems can be solved with logical thought and commonsense behavior changes. But most of life doesn't fit into orderly boxes like that. It's more challenging and more complex. Reversals allow you to name those complexities with depth and accuracy.

| PRACTICE 8 |

INSIDE OUT INSIGHT

Take a piece you wrote earlier in the semester. Copy over each line, but this time, say the opposite. Bring both versions to a writing partner or small group. Is one more successful? Ultimately, you may choose to meld the two versions, using the strongest lines from each piece to make a new version.

Create Deep Context

Above, you experimented with reversing your field. Another way to layer in depth in your writing is to set your work in a **context** that's significant and powerful. Even though you are just a simple lad from Coldwater, Michigan, and your childhood wasn't bad, when you set your writing in the larger cultural and political landscape around you, meaning is automatically created. Creating context means that you pull the camera lens back, way back, in space and in time, and you consider the decades and centuries of history that are behind your piece of writing. You consider the location of your piece, and you see the big picture that frames the events you're looking at. Your town may rest on Native American lands, and some research on the history of the place where your work is set could add insight and importance. Your characters may be affected by a water crisis, wrought by lead pipes and corrupt city officials. Climate change affects everyone, as does racial violence and #MeToo.

Joy Harjo uses powerful, surreal, and archetypal images — "maps drawn of blood," "fur and teeth" and horses waltzing on the moon — to set her poem "She Had Some Horses" on page 372 in a historical and psychological context. The "she" whose experiences are described in the poem is a personal *she* — one woman's experience in a specific culture and landscape, but also a larger, universal *she*. The horses in the poem stand for many things — men, ideas, longings, parts of self, times of life. Each line in the poem offers a deep, fresh, rich insight into the speaker's experience and our larger fraught and mysterious human experience.

Similarly, Pablo Neruda uses the dramatic events in Chilean and international politics as the backdrop for his poem, "Ode to My Suit" on page 370. He keeps the images and details very personal and very specific, but all the while he is talking about the threats to his life in ongoing political upheaval and war. He's writing about his suit, his life as a poet, and much, much more.

Your creative writing is situated in a context. No matter how small, how sleepy, how "regular" your place may seem, events there take place against a backdrop that has historical, political, and cultural implications. Setting your memoir or story or poetry in the context where you live and investigating all the forces that shape and have shaped that place is a powerful and perhaps necessary task for every writer. Don't be fooled into thinking your place doesn't have historical significance. Every place has a past, and that past, when rendered with detail and insight and passion, is potentially fascinating. Don't be intimidated by what you don't know: Few people take the time to look into their own history or the history of the place where they now live. To bring insight into your work, go epic. Consider how the current story you're focused on interacts with (contradicts or mirrors) the history of the people in this place where you are situated.

"White Angel" by Michael Cunningham on page 376 provides a great example of how authors use cultural context to deepen and enrich the insight readers can find in their works. Here the author uses the cultural backdrop of the 1960s to provide a metaphor for the chaos and breakdown and loss and heartbreak in the family in his story, as well as in the individual character of the younger brother.

PRACTICE 9

READING FOR DEEP CONTEXT

Reread "White Angel" on page 376. Describe the references to history and culture. Make a statement about how these specific uses of cultural context create metaphors for the individual experiences in the story.

Surprise Yourself

Your wisdom is in you, deep inside, often lurking just under the busy thoughts you walk around with all day. Since insight is in you, actively "looking inside" to let that quieter wisdom emerge often works. You need time for reflection. You need time off-screen, uninterrupted. Some writers use Freedom or SelfControl or other apps to make sure they have focused time to work deep.

Sometimes writers find that when they try to be "wise," they get lucky; more often, however, they end up sounding hollow, shallow, or pat. You need to have some strategies for sneaking up on the vault inside you where your wisdom rests, protected. Often, it's when you don't know what you are about to say that the deeper, more arresting truth comes out on the page. Here are several techniques for sneaking up on your own insight, to spring a trap to release the gold that is in you.

1. **Write by hand.** This is a great way to surprise yourself with what you know, deeply. Writing by hand slows your mind down to the pace of wisdom. Also try working with your nondominant hand. Take an image you'd like to pursue or revise a piece that isn't working by writing it, slowly, with your nondominant hand. Some students have had great luck by having one character (or part of self) ask a question in writing, using the dominant hand; then another character answers the questions, using the nondominant hand. It's important to keep your hand moving, to not stop and think.

2. **Fill in the blank.** Fill-in-the-blank activities (like the one you did in on page 67 with "Genealogy") let you move fast so you have less control over what you want to say. This exercise often works best if your teacher reads the prompts and you have only about one minute to write — no time to think, just let your pencil do what it wants to do. If you are

forced to write quickly by hand, you'll surprise yourself; many students find working quickly, by hand, with guided prompts allows surprising wisdom to come forward.

3. **List questions.** Creating a list of questions on the page—in a poem, in a play, or in prose—can jumpstart a stalled piece. A question list can even serve as the form for a complete piece of writing. Questions are dramatic: They can plunge the reader into depth. Notice how powerful the phrase "I wonder . . ." is in Neruda's "Ode to My Suit" on page 370. Note the use of questions to God in Doyle's "Two Hearts" on page 375: "Why did you break my boy?" And in Cunningham's deeply moving short story, "White Angel," the climax of the story turns into a poignant question: "Why don't you stay a minute?"

While these practices might seem like games or gimmicks, they've worked surprisingly well for many writers. The goal is to tap into your unconscious, to resist knowing and planning, and to create situations where you're surprised by what comes forward. As Robert Frost famously said, no surprise for the writer, no surprise for the reader.

Create Subtext

The text is what's on the surface in a piece of writing. The **subtext** is what is beneath the surface. In good writing, the writer works hard to choose words that can be interpreted more than one way, words that come with weight and depth, with a lot of substance beneath the top layer. Imagine an iceberg, part of it poking above the surface of the sea but most of it submerged. An insightful piece of writing almost always has subtext. All genres of creative writing use subtext, as do songs, dinner conversations, and political negotiations. You're well-served, as a writer but also as a human, to hone your ability to pay attention to what's being said and also to what's *really* being said.

The opening of Mary Robison's short story "Pretty Ice" on page 169 provides a compelling example of subtext.

> *If a writer knows enough about what he is writing about, he may omit things that he knows. The dignity of movement of an iceberg is due to only one-ninth of it being above water.*
> —ERNEST HEMINGWAY

I was up the whole night before my fiancé was due to arrive from the East—drinking coffee, restless and pacing, my ears ringing. When the television signed off, I sat down with a packet of the month's bills and figured amounts on a lined tally sheet in my checkbook. Under the spray of a high-intensity lamp, my left hand moved rapidly over the touch tablets of my calculator.

Belle, the narrator, is waiting for her fiancé's visit. She doesn't seem romantic, relaxed, or happy. She's anxious. She's doing her bills. She's *taking account*. Subtext means that whatever your characters are doing, there's an implied metaphor. What they're doing is interesting on the surface. But it's also interesting beneath the surface. What isn't Belle doing? Sleeping. Shaving her legs. Getting the apartment ready so it's nice for her fiancé. Because there is a gap between her behavior and what we expect her behavior to be, we wonder about the subtext. *Why is she restless and pacing? Does she have money worries? Does she love this guy for the right reasons? Maybe she's just anxious. But why?*

Providing subtext is one powerful way authors illuminate their writing with insight. In the next paragraph, Belle's mother arrives. There's been an ice storm. Her mother honks. (Subtext: The mother is impatient, thoughtless, and oblivious — it's 6:15 in the morning. What does that say about her daughter? About their relationship? Why isn't the daughter — a grown woman — driving herself to pick up her fiancé?) We see that Belle has a very expensive ivory Mont Blanc pen. Money worries. Expensive pen. We learn that she hasn't gotten ready for her fiancé's arrival — she hasn't slept, she doesn't shower. Strange. Kind of awful. The story unfolds, and nine-tenths of the story is subtext. We are able to gather a lot of information and insight by paying careful attention to what's beneath the surface, all of which the author has carefully placed there, palpable though just out of view.

PRACTICE 10

READING FOR SUBTEXT

Neruda's "Ode to My Suit" on page 370 is a terrific poem for practicing reading for subtext. Read the poem several times and at least once aloud. Make a list: Which images and gestures in the poem stand for something deeper, or point to another layer?

Rely on Form

Form — templates for pieces of creative writing, such as the ode, the sonnet, or the three-act play — provides you as a writer with an insight-generating machine. Form forces you into corners you wouldn't normally go into as a writer, and thereby allows deeper wisdom in you to spring forth. Many writers resist form only to find that of all their poetry, their sonnets are actually the strongest poems. Not having any shape and not having any rules to follow sounds creative and, well, wonderful. But sometimes, when we don't have a recipe or a shape to fill, our writing sprawls, our ideas fall flat, and we churn out cliché characters, cliché details, well-worn ideas. Form is a terrific on-ramp to wisdom.

Notice how effectively Joy Harjo uses form for "She Had Some Horses" on page 372. She uses **anaphora**—repeating the first words of each line: *She had horses*. . . . She uses **refrain**—repeating a line ("She had some horses.") after each stanza. Those two formal devices, both relying on the power of repetition, turn the poem into a **litany**, a list that is actually a prayer, a song, or a chant. The repetitions create a platform for the striking, disturbing, stunningly original images in each line. They give the reader a break and at the same time frame and showcase the action images. The form is wise in itself: We must honor the beautiful and the terrible.

Pablo Neruda uses form, too, to make a powerful political statement in a very stealthy way. He lives in a regime where poets and artists can be (and are) assassinated. He encodes messages about the power of art, the necessity of writing, and his own fears about his life in a classic form, the **ode**. The ode is an ancient form, and it has many variations and definitions; the basic form of an ode is to praise something simple using powerful language. Through the ode form, the suit comes to represent something of the poet's inspiration: his soul.

In Part Three of this book, you'll find an introduction to fourteen forms for creative writers to practice. Keep in mind that form, while sometimes tricky to learn at first, often pays off magnificently when it comes to providing a vehicle for insight.

THREE PITFALLS

When you are working with insight as a strategy for your creative writing, try to avoid a few common pitfalls. Literature isn't a code; it isn't designed to hold hidden meanings that torture readers. And poems aren't soapboxes; essays aren't sermons; short stories aren't propaganda pieces. Close observation generates meaning. If you follow your images, hew closely to accuracy, and steer toward empathy, your work will be insightful and rich. Sometimes, however, without even realizing it, we preach, overwrite, or neglect to respect our readers' intelligence. Here are the three most common ways writers fail to serve their readers, and what to do instead.

1. **Avoid preaching.** If you center your story, poem, or play on a single idea, from a single vantage point (abortion should be legal, homelessness is bad), you are likely writing a sermon or a position paper. Didactic writing—writing that instructs the reader—is not creative writing. Pontificating is the opposite of what art intends to do. Harjo doesn't say "Native American women are very oppressed and struggling." She

creates a much more complex statement about human experience. Neruda doesn't say "Politicians are threatened by poets because we tell the truth." He shows us, carefully and thoughtfully, the complexity of his situation as a writer. Creative writing teaches by showing people involved in actions, from very close up, so that the reader sees things about her or his own life simply by watching these moments and overhearing the dialogue. The less the writer states directly, the more powerful the creative writing. It's not effective to have a character in a play or a speaker in a poem expound an idea you love or dislike—there's not enough tension to hold the reader's interest for long, unless perhaps she agrees with you, and then what's the point?

UNWISE   Your personal diatribe on the conflict in Syria (You've never been there, but you read a lot online.)

WISE   A poem from the point of view of a soldier-friend of yours, who is struggling with how to act back here at home. The scene takes place while the two of you are shooting pool at the local pub, and you capture her actual dialogue and the reactions of others who were there that night in the pub.

2. **Avoid overwriting.** Do not use overly poetic or writerly diction. If you are writing in order to sound smart or be "poetic" by using lots of words you don't normally use in conversation, trying to sound lofty, trying too hard to be difficult and complex, you will sound amateurish, not wise.

If you are writing in a flowery or fancy way, readers may conclude that you are trying to be ironic or funny. If they read you at all. Pretentious is the opposite of wise.

UNWISE   "It's been a long and winding road, this life I've lived, with ups and downs and ins and outs, terrible troubles, and truly amazing, wildly stupendous, drug-induced, God-seeing mind benders. I'm a seeker, a lover, a poet, and a cluster of consciousness the likes of which no one has ever seen!"

WISE   "We lived then in Cleveland, in the middle of everything. It was the sixties—our radios sang out love all day long." (Michael Cunningham, "White Angel.")

3. **Avoid stating the obvious.** *Show a lot, tell a little, never explain,* the writer Dinty Moore teaches. Treat your reader as a smart, informed, savvy person. Readers want to figure things out. They want to come up with multiple interpretations of events—just as we do in real life.

There's nothing for the reader here, in this sample poem:

Life is a mystery
We do not know why
We struggle so much
And then we die.

Compare to Brian Doyle's powerful memoir, "Two Hearts," on page 375:

The heart is a railroad station where the trains are switched to different tracks. A normal heart switches trains flawlessly two billion times in a life; in an abnormal heart, like Liam's, the trains crash and the station crumbles to dust.

By using images to explain a complex medical mystery, and a metaphor to help us understand, Doyle allows the reader *insight* into the human heart literally and figuratively. We understand the depth of the crisis this family is in. But it's not *explained* to us. It's shown, brilliantly.

The writers we love rarely explain what is perfectly clear to readers: it was hard, it was great, it was upsetting, people were shocked. Trust. Your. Reader.

PRACTICE 11

CUTTING EXPLANATION

Look back at a piece you wrote earlier this semester, in any genre. Can you find sentences that are purely explanation? You know it's explanation if the sentence can be cut, and the reader doesn't miss it at all; they already get the point. If it's more useful to do this with a peer, trade work and cut explanation; sometimes it's clearer when others are explaining than when you are yourself.

WRITING PROJECTS

Experiment

1. Write a piece that is a list of questions. Make sure each of your questions is surprising, fresh, unexpected, and *super-specific to your life*—not one that you could imagine anyone else asking. Try to include images—specifics, concrete words—in as many of the questions as you can. However old you are—that's how many questions you should write.

Poem

2. Write an ode to a piece of clothing—you're actually talking *to* the item in this poem. Have the ode be *indirectly* about a social or political issue, or an environmental or societal concern that's very important to you. Don't talk about the issue overtly. Use your relationship to the clothing item to play out your concerns.

Memoir

3. Reflect on one of your jobs. Make a list of all the insights and observations about customers, your coworkers, and yourself that come from taking some time to look carefully at yourself and at how things run in this place of business. Write a short memoir about an important, specific moment in time when you were working: your last day, the last night of high season. Layer in your insights; be open to discovering new ones as you write. Make sure to include enabling details, the five senses, and a hard turn at the end.

Fiction

4. Take a truism or piece of generally held wisdom ("Look before you leap" or "Power tends to corrupt, and absolute power corrupts absolutely") and write a short story, no longer than 750 words, using concrete details, dialogue, and images/scenes that prove the truism false.

Drama

5. Write a five- or ten-minute play based on "White Angel." But set the play in contemporary times, choosing a cultural context that is well known to you, and current and relevant to the story you want to tell about families and teenagers today.

INSIGHT WORKSHOP

The prompts below will help you read and discuss your classmates' work.

1. In the student piece you are reading, try to highlight two examples of accuracy, places where the writer names something small that we take for granted or just don't notice because we don't pay close enough attention.

2. Try to find two examples of generosity, where the writer shows both the good and the bad, or at least two different sides, in a character, speaker, or situation.

3. Note passages where the writer asks questions that are then left unanswered. Or suggest places where questions could be used to provoke insight.

4. Note a place where you are surprised—in a good way.

5. Identify a place where the author uses subtext or could try using more subtext.

6. Identify any passages in the student's work that preach, overexplain, state the obvious, or sound grandiose or forced, as though the writer is trying too hard and not trusting his or her own voice and inner wisdom.

7. Identify your favorite piece of insight in this piece.

READINGS

Julia Koets
Boys

There were boys whose time I wasted. I didn't know it
at the time. Boy who drove a black car fast, boy who

wore a rubber band around one wrist, across-a-river
boy, boy I kissed underwater. I kept some boys too long,

like sand dollars, starfish. Boy who painted his bedroom floor,
boy who fixed up motorcycles, boy who loved the girl I loved,

chrysanthemum-tattoo-on-his-back boy, boy like a shell
I took home to put to my ear to hear home, put to my mouth

to call myself there. Boy who wore a watch to bed,
boy who cooked spaghetti, sauce spilled down his shirt,

cheese-toast-in-the-oven boy, yard-strewn-with-yellow-leaves
boy, beach-so-dark-we-couldn't-find-the-path-back boy.

WRITERS ON WRITING
JULIA KOETS

HEATHER SELLERS: How did you get the idea for this poem "Boys"?

JULIA KOETS: At the time that I wrote "Boys," I was writing several series of villanelles, and I'd often start a new villanelle with a phrase or an image that I couldn't get out of my head. While "Boys" obviously isn't a villanelle, I did write a very early partial draft of the poem in that form. I got the idea for "Boys" because I was thinking about the first two lines of the poem: "There were boys whose time I wasted. I didn't know it at the time." Writing villanelles changed the way I think about repetition. It was the repetition of the word "time" in these lines that kept me writing. In writing so much about queer desire and temporality in my second poetry collection, I often felt guilt about how long it took me to understand my sexuality and to talk openly about it. I worried I had led certain men on in relationships I'd had in high school and into my mid-twenties, and yet I also realized that "I didn't know it at the time."

HS: Did you come to the poem with a particular insight or gain any specific insights while working on the poem?

JK: I came to the poem with a question, with multiple questions, with something I couldn't stop thinking about. I came to the poem seeking a kind of insight. I heard someone once say that you shouldn't go into a piece of writing knowing what you're going to say because then there won't be any surprise in the piece. The reader won't see the moment of insight happen in the work because there wasn't a moment of insight in the writing process.

HS: How much shaping or revision did this poem require? Can you describe your process drafting and shaping the piece?

JK: I just went back and found an early draft of this poem because I couldn't remember how much I'd revised it over time. It's a strange thing to see lines that I cut several years ago. I'd completely forgotten that they were ever there. Along with cutting several lines and phrases and playing with some of the line breaks, in revision I added the dashes between certain words (chrysanthemum-tattoo-on-his-back boy). In adding the dashes, the place, the image, or the action became more intrinsically linked to each particular boy. The dashes also changed the pacing of the poem. Reading the revised poem aloud, I can't help but speed up in those particular moments. The dashes help create a certain momentum in the poem, a momentum that echoes the anxiety I felt looking back on these particular relationships.

HS: What do you like best about this piece?

JK: I like that the tension in the poem translates when I read the poem out loud.

HS: Any advice to student writers for writing with depth and insight?

JK: Write into the questions you have. Some of my favorite pieces I've written are pieces I was afraid to write, pieces I felt conflicted about.

Pablo Neruda

Ode to My Suit

Every morning, suit,
you are waiting on a chair
to be filled
by my vanity, my love,
my hope, my body.
Still
only half awake
I leave the shower
to shrug into your sleeves,

my legs seek
the hollow of your legs,
and thus embraced
by your unfailing loyalty
I take my morning walk,
work my way into my poetry;
from my windows I see
the things,
men, women,
events and struggles
constantly shaping me,
constantly confronting me,
setting my hands to the task,
opening my eyes, creasing my lips,
and in the same way,
suit,
I am shaping you,
poking out your elbows,
wearing you threadbare,
and so your life grows
in the image of my own.
In the wind
you flap and hum
as if you were my soul,
in bad moments
you cling
to my bones,
abandoned, at nighttime
darkness and dream
people with their phantoms
your wings and mine.
I wonder
whether some day
an enemy
bullet
will stain you with my blood,
for then
you would die with me,
but perhaps
it will be

less dramatic,
simple,
and you will grow ill,
suit,
with me, with my body,
and together
we will be lowered
into the earth.
That's why
every day
I greet you
with respect and then
you embrace me and I forget you,
because we are one being
and shall be always
in the wind, through the night,
the streets and the struggle,
one body,
maybe, maybe, one day, still.

Joy Harjo
She Had Some Horses (excerpt)

I. She Had Some Horses

She had some horses.
She had horses who were bodies of sand.
She had horses who were maps drawn of blood.
She had horses who were skins of ocean water.
She had horses who were the blue air of sky.
She had horses who were fur and teeth.
She had horses who were clay and would break.
She had horses who were splintered red cliff.

She had some horses.

She had horses with eyes of trains.
She had horses with full, brown thighs.
She had horses who laughed too much.
She had horses who threw rocks at glass houses.
She had horses who licked razor blades.

She had some horses.

She had horses who danced in their mothers' arms.
She had horses who thought they were the sun and their
bodies shone and burned like stars.
She had horses who waltzed nightly on the moon.
She had horses who were much too shy, and kept quiet
in stalls of their own making.

She had some horses.

She had horses who liked Creek Stomp Dance songs.
She had horses who cried in their beer.
She had horses who spit at male queens who made
them afraid of themselves.
She had horses who said they weren't afraid.
She had horses who lied.
She had horses who told the truth, who were stripped
bare of their tongues.

She had some horses.

She had horses who called themselves, "horse."
She had horses who called themselves, "spirit," and kept
their voices secret and to themselves.
She had horses who had no names.
She had horses who had books of names.

She had some horses.

She had horses who whispered in the dark, who were afraid to speak.
She had horses who screamed out of fear of the silence, who
carried knives to protect themselves from ghosts.
She had horses who waited for destruction.
She had horses who waited for resurrection.

She had some horses.

She had horses who got down on their knees for any saviour.
She had horses who thought their high price had saved them.
She had horses who tried to save her, who climbed in her
bed at night and prayed as they raped her.

She had some horses.

She had some horses she loved.
She had some horses she hated.

These were the same horses.

Dana Spiotta
Control

It's August, 2007, the final week of our restaurant's high season. My three-year-old daughter, Agnes, pulls me out of bed at seven o'clock. I follow her down the steps that lead from our living space to the restaurant space, on the ground floor of our house. The pine tables and floors gleam in the morning sun. As she eats her oatmeal and I drink my coffee, I study the reservation book. I know it will be the busiest night of the summer. I contemplate the floor chart as I would a puzzle — could we somehow squeeze in one more party? Our business flows from the Glimmerglass Opera, in nearby Cooperstown, so I make calculations about when people will arrive after the matinée and when others will leave for the evening curtain. I have the run times; I can be precise.

After breakfast, Agnes plays pick-up sticks with red cocktail straws while I polish a mountain of flatware. We have owned the place for four years, and I have learned that the food my husband, Clem, makes from the robust local ingredients of upstate New York — the roasted summer beets, the pork side ribs he prepares with skin on so the fat crackles when you bite into it, the buttercup-squash bread pudding with espresso ice cream — doesn't matter if the front of the house isn't right. Although a great restaurant experience must include great food, a bad restaurant experience can be achieved through bad service alone. Ideally, service is invisible. You notice it only when something goes wrong.

And things have gone wrong: a waiter lost his balance and smashed a full tray of glasses into the bar ice bin just as a huge round of drink orders came in; a woman got locked in the bathroom and had to be rescued by a waiter unscrewing the doorknob mid-rush; a choking man needed the Heimlich maneuver to dislodge a piece of food (which looked, as it flew out of his mouth, just like the safety posters); a bread basket placed too close to a votive ignited a small bonfire. My role is to remain calm, to throw the basket to the floor, stamp the flames out with my clog, and then whisk it away as if noting had happened. Restaurants require concentration and timing. A badly handled problem during a rush can cascade and send the whole dining room careering toward disaster.

At noon, Agnes loves to watch as Clem portions the meat and fish, slicing through the smooth slabs of flesh. Later, the babysitter takes her to the playground. I restock the bar cooler and use a hand-lever press to squeeze lemon and lime juice. I sit by one of the floor-to-ceiling windows in the dining room and fold napkins. It is a simple, flat fold that hides the edges. Clem roasts garlic cloves, boils cardamom pods, and simmers the green-peppercorn-bourbon sauce for his steak dish. A sweet caramel tang waves through the dining room. I set the tables, placing each napkin an inch from the edge. Because there is so much I can't control, I am a maniac about the details I can control.

At three, my waiters finish the setup. Just before five, I carry a tray upstairs with dinner for Agnes and the babysitter: goat-cheese-and-caramelized-onion tarts, creamed spinach, Pellegrino, and apple slices. I kiss Agnes good night and go downstairs.

We open the doors and in they come. After the pre-opera crush, the calmer second seating arrives. The light fades and people linger. The babysitter leaves at ten. Agnes's bedroom is above the dining room. A low rumble of voices reaches her room, but she always sleeps through it. In the lull before the after-opera bar rush, the staff eats pasta concocted out of whatever didn't sell at dinner. At eleven-thirty, our late crowd arrives—mostly the opera talent coming in to unwind after the performance. The line cook prepares the simple late-night menu and Clem helps me with the bar. Whenever I look up, six new faces are eager to order. Clem lines up glasses and mixes drinks. Under the noise, I hear Agnes crying on the baby monitor that sits on a shelf behind us. I make my way though the thick crowd. There is no time to comfort her, so I scoop her up and carry her downstairs. She stops crying, and I take orders with her on my hip. Clem makes the drinks and shakes his head, laughing. She is warm against me and falls asleep.

Later, I put Agnes back to bed, close the door, and pause at the top of the stairs. The candlelight flickers across the wood, and I hear the murmur of voices. At two-thirty, the last people leave. I finger the big stack of receipts. We are hoping the busy summer will pay for the slow winter of writing, of free time, of playing with Agnes.

Years later, after we have given up the restaurant, whenever I ask Agnes what she remembers about it, she always mentions that one night. I cringe, but she recalls it like this: you carried me through the dining room, and the crowd of people parted to let us through. The people smiled at me; they were all happy.

Brian Doyle

Two Hearts

Some months ago my wife delivered twin sons one minute apart. The older is Joseph and the younger is Liam. Joseph is dark and Liam is light. Joseph is healthy and Liam is not. Joseph has a whole heart and Liam has half. This means that Liam will have two major surgeries before he is three years old.

I have read many pamphlets about Liam's problem. I have watched many doctors' hands drawing red and blue lines on pieces of white paper. They are trying to show me why Liam's heart doesn't work properly. I watch the markers in the doctors' hands. Here comes red, there goes blue. The heart is a railroad station where the trains are switched to different tracks. A normal heart switches trains flawlessly two billion times in a life; in an abnormal heart, like Liam's, the trains crash and the station crumbles to dust.

So there are many nights now when I tuck Liam and his wheezing train station under my beard in the blue hours of night and think about his Maker. I would kill the god who sentences him to such awful pain, I would stab him in the heart like he stabbed my son, I would shove my fury in his face like a fist, but I know in my own broken heart that this same god made my magic boys, shaped their apple faces and coyote eyes, put joy in the eager suck of their mouths. So it is that my hands are not clenched in anger but clasped in confused and merry and bitter prayer.

I talk to God more than I admit. "Why did you break my boy?" I ask.

I gave you that boy, he says, and his lean brown brother, and the elfin daughter you love so.

"But you wrote death on his heart," I say.

I write death on all hearts, he says, just as I write life.

This is where the conversation always ends and I am left holding the extraordinary awful perfect prayer of my second son, who snores like a seal, who might die tomorrow, who did not die today.

Michael Cunningham
White Angel

We lived then in Cleveland, in the middle of everything. It was the sixties — our radios sang out love all day long. This of course is history. It happened before the city of Cleveland went broke, before its river caught fire. We were four. My mother and father, Carlton, and me. Carlton turned sixteen the year I turned nine. Between us were several brothers and sisters, weak flames quenched in our mother's womb. We are not a fruitful or many-branched line. Our family name is Morrow.

Our father was a high school music teacher. Our mother taught children called "exceptional," which meant that some could name the day Christmas would fall in the year 2000 but couldn't remember to drop their pants when they peed. We lived in a tract called Woodlawn — neat one- and two-story houses painted optimistic colors. Our tract bordered a cemetery. Behind our back yard was a gully choked with brush, and beyond that, the field of smooth, polished stones. I grew up with the cemetery, and didn't mind it. It could be beautiful. A single stone angel, small-breasted and determined, rose amid the more conservative markers close to our house. Farther away, in a richer section, miniature mosques and Parthenons spoke silently to Cleveland of man's enduring accomplishments. Carlton and I played in the cemetery as children and, with a little more age, smoked joints and drank Southern Comfort there. I was, thanks to Carlton, the most criminally advanced nine-year-old in my fourth-grade class. I was going places. I made no move without his counsel.

Here is Carlton several months before his death, in an hour so alive with snow that earth and sky are identically white. He labors among the markers and I run after, stung by snow, following the light of his red knitted cap. Carlton's hair is pulled back into a ponytail, neat and economical, a perfect pinecone of hair. He is thrifty, in his way.

We have taken hits of acid with our breakfast juice. Or rather, Carlton has taken a hit and I, considering my youth, have been allowed half. This acid is called windowpane. It is for clarity of vision, as Vicks is for decongestion of the nose. Our parents are at work, earning the daily bread. We have come out into the cold so that the house, when we reenter it, will shock us with its warmth and righteousness. Carlton believes in shocks.

"I think I'm coming on to it," I call out. Carlton has on his buckskin jacket, which is worn down to the shine. On the back, across his shoulder blades, his girlfriend has stitched an electric-blue eye. As we walk I speak into the eye. "I think I feel something," I say.

"Too soon," Carlton calls back. "Stay loose, Frisco. You'll know when the time comes."

I am excited and terrified. We are into serious stuff. Carlton has done acid half a dozen times before, but I am new at it. We slipped the tabs into our mouths at breakfast, while our mother paused over the bacon. Carlton likes taking risks.

Snow collects in the engraved letters on the headstones. I lean into the wind, trying to decide whether everything around me seems strange because of the drug, or just because everything truly is strange. Three weeks earlier, a family across town had been sitting at home, watching television, when a single-engine plane fell on them. Snow swirls around us, seeming to fall up as well as down.

Carlton leads the way to our spot, the pillared entrance to a society tomb. This tomb is a palace. Stone cupids cluster on the peaked roof, with stunted, frozen wings and matrons' faces. Under the roof is a veranda, backed by cast-iron doors that lead to the house of the dead proper. In summer this veranda is cool. In winter it blocks the wind. We keep a bottle of Southern Comfort there.

Carlton finds the bottle, unscrews the cap, and takes a good, long draw. He is studded with snowflakes. He hands me the bottle and I take a more conservative drink. Even in winter, the tomb smells mossy as a well. Dead leaves and a yellow M & M's wrapper, worried by the wind, scrape on the marble floor.

"Are you scared?" Carlton asks me.

I nod. I never think of lying to him.

"Don't be, man," he says. "Fear will screw you right up. Drugs can't hurt you if you feel no fear."

I nod. We stand sheltered, passing the bottle. I lean into Carlton's certainty as if it gave off heat.

"We can do acid all the time at Woodstock," I say.

"Right on. Woodstock Nation. Yow."

"Do people really *live* there?" I ask.

"Man, you've got to stop asking that. The concert's over, but people are still there. It's the new nation. Have faith."

I nod again, satisfied. There is a different country for us to live in. I am already a new person, renamed Frisco. My old name was Robert.

"We'll do acid all the time," I say.

"You better believe we will." Carlton's face, surrounded by snow and marble, is lit. His eyes are bright as neon. Something in them tells me he can see the future, a ghost that hovers over everybody's head. In Carlton's future we all get released from our jobs and schooling. Awaiting us all, and soon, is a bright, perfect simplicity. A life among the trees by the river.

"How are you feeling, man?" he asks me.

"Great," I tell him, and it is purely the truth. Doves clatter up out of a bare tree and turn at the same instant, transforming themselves from steel to silver in the snow-blown light. I know at that moment that the drug is working. Everything before me has become suddenly, radiantly itself. How could Carlton have known this was about to happen? "Oh," I whisper. His hand settles on my shoulder.

"Stay loose, Frisco," he says. "There's not a thing in this pretty world to be afraid of. I'm here."

I am not afraid. I am astonished. I had not realized until this moment how real everything is. A twig lies on the marble at my feet, bearing a cluster of hard brown berries. The broken-off end is raw, white, fleshly. Trees are alive.

"I'm here," Carlton says again, and he is.

Hours later, we are sprawled on the sofa in front of the television, ordinary as Wally and the Beav. Our mother makes dinner in the kitchen. A pot lid clangs. We are undercover agents. I am trying to conceal my amazement.

Our father is building a grandfather clock from a kit. He wants to have something to leave us, something for us to pass along. We can hear him in the basement, sawing and pounding. I know what is laid out on his sawhorses—a long raw wooden box, onto which he glues fancy moldings. A single pearl of sweat meanders down his forehead as he works. Tonight I have discovered my ability to see every room of the house at once, to know every single thing that goes on. A mouse nibbles inside the wall. Electrical wires curl behind the plaster, hidden and patient as snakes.

"Shhh," I say to Carlton, who has not said anything. He is watching television through his splayed fingers. Gunshots ping. Bullets raise chalk dust on a concrete wall. I have no idea what we are watching.

"Boys?" our mother calls from the kitchen. I can, with my new ears, hear her slap hamburger into patties. "Set the table like good citizens," she calls.

"Okay, Ma," Carlton replies, in a gorgeous imitation of normality. Our father hammers in the basement. I can feel Carlton's heart ticking. He pats my hand, to assure me that everything's perfect.

We set the table, spoon fork knife, paper napkins triangled to one side. We know the moves cold. After we are done I pause to notice the dining-room wallpaper: a golden farm, backed by mountains. Cows graze, autumn trees cast golden shade. This scene repeats itself three times, on three walls.

"Zap," Carlton whispers. "Zzzzzoom."

"Did we do it right?" I ask him.

"We did everything perfect, little son. How are you doing in there, anyway?" He raps lightly on my head.

"Perfect, I guess." I am staring at the wallpaper as if I were thinking of stepping into it.

"You guess. You guess? You and I are going to other planets, man. Come over here."

"Where?"

"Here. Come here." He leads me to the window. Outside the snow skitters, nervous and silver, under streetlamps. Ranch-style houses hoard their warmth, bleed light into the gathering snow. It is a street in Cleveland. It is our street.

"You and I are going to fly, man," Carlton whispers, close to my ear. He opens the window. Snow blows in, sparking on the carpet. "Fly," he says, and we do. For a moment we strain up and out, the black night wind blowing in our faces—we raise ourselves up off the cocoa-colored deep-pile wool-and-polyester carpet by a sliver of an inch. Sweet glory. The secret of flight is this—you have to do it immediately, before your body realizes it is defying the laws. I swear it to this day.

We both know we have taken momentary leave of the earth. It does not strike either of us as remarkable, any more than does the fact that airplanes sometimes fall from the sky, or that we have always lived in these rooms and will soon leave them. We settle back down. Carlton touches my shoulder.

"You wait, Frisco," he says. "Miracles are happening. Fucking miracles."

I nod. He pulls down the window, which reseals itself with a sucking sound. Our own faces look back at us from the cold, dark glass. Behind us, our mother drops the hamburgers sizzling into the skillet. Our father bends to his work under a hooded lightbulb, preparing the long box into which he will lay clockworks, pendulum, a face. A plane drones by overhead, invisible in the clouds. I glance nervously at Carlton. He smiles his assurance and squeezes the back of my neck.

March. After the thaw. I am walking through the cemetery, thinking about my endless life. One of the beauties of living in Cleveland is that any direction feels like progress. I've memorized the map. We are by my calculations three hundred and fifty miles shy of Woodstock, New York. On this raw new day I am walking east, to the place where Carlton and I keep our bottle. I am going to have an early nip, to celebrate my bright future.

When I get to our spot I hear low moans coming from behind the tomb. I freeze, considering my choices. The sound is a long-drawn-out agony with a whip at the end, a final high C, something like "ooooooOw." A wolf's cry run backward. What decides me on investigation rather than flight is the need to make a story. In the stories my brother likes best, people always do the foolish, risky thing. I find I can reach decisions this way, by thinking of myself as a character in a story told by Carlton.

I creep around the side of the monument, cautious as a badger, pressed up close to the marble. I peer over a cherub's girlish shoulder. What I find is Carlton on the ground with his girlfriend, in an uncertain jumble of clothes and bare flesh. Carlton's jacket, the one with the embroidered eye, is draped over the stone, keeping watch.

I hunch behind the statue. I can see the girl's naked arms, and the familiar bones of Carlton's spine. The two of them moan together in the dry winter grass. Though I can't make out the girl's expression, Carlton's face is twisted and grimacing, the cords of his neck pulled tight. I had never thought the experience might be painful. I watch, trying to learn. I hold on to the cherub's cold wings.

It isn't long before Carlton catches sight of me. His eyes rove briefly, ecstatically skyward, and what do they light on but his brother's small head, sticking up next to a cherub's. We lock eyes and spend a moment in mutual decision. The girl keeps on clutching at Carlton's skinny back. He decides to smile at me. He decides to wink.

I am out of there so fast I tear up divots. I dodge among the stones, jump the gully, clear the fence into the swing-set-and-picnic-table sanctity of the back yard. Something about that wink. My heart beats fast as a sparrow's.

I go into the kitchen and find our mother washing fruit. She asks what's going on. I tell her nothing is. Nothing at all.

She sighs over an apple's imperfection. The curtains sport blue teapots. Our mother works the apple with a scrub brush. She believes they come coated with poison.

"Where's Carlton?" she asks.

"Don't know," I tell her.

"Bobby?"

"Huh?"

"What exactly is going on?"

"Nothing," I say. My heart works itself up to a hummingbird's rate, more buzz than beat.

"I think something is. Will you answer a question?"

"Okay."

"Is your brother taking drugs?"

I relax a bit. It is only drugs. I know why she's asking. Lately police cars have been browsing our house like sharks. They pause, take note, glide on. Some neighborhood crackdown. Carlton is famous in these parts.

"No," I tell her.

She faces me with the brush in one hand, an apple in the other. "You wouldn't lie to me, would you?" She knows something is up. Her nerves run through this house. She can feel dust settling on the tabletops, milk starting to turn in the refrigerator.

"No," I say.

"Something's going on," she sighs. She is a small, efficient woman who looks at things as if they give off a painful light. She grew up on a farm in Wisconsin and spent her girlhood tying up bean rows, worrying over the sun and rain. She is still trying to overcome her habit of modest expectations.

I leave the kitchen, pretending sudden interest in the cat. Our mother follows, holding her brush. She means to scrub the truth out of me. I follow the cat, his erect black tail and pink anus.

"Don't walk away when I'm talking to you," our mother says.

I keep walking, to see how far I'll get, calling, "Kittykittykitty." In the front hall, our father's homemade clock chimes the half hour. I make for the clock. I get as far as the rubber plant before she collars me.

"I told you not to walk away," she says, and cuffs me a good one with the brush. She catches me on the ear and sets it ringing. The cat is out of there quick as a quarter note.

I stand for a minute, to let her know I've received the message. Then I resume walking. She hits me again, this time on the back of the head, hard enough to make me see colors. "Will you *stop*?" she screams. Still, I keep walking. Our house runs west to east. With every step I get closer to Yasgur's farm.

Carlton comes home whistling. Our mother treats him like a guest who's overstayed. He doesn't care. He is lost in optimism. He pats her cheek and calls her "Professor." He treats her as if she were harmless, and so she is.

She never hits Carlton. She suffers him the way farm girls suffer a thieving crow, with a grudge so old and endless it borders on reverence. She gives him a scrubbed apple, and tells him what she'll do if he tracks mud on the carpet.

I am waiting in our room. He brings the smell of the cemetery with him, its old snow and wet pine needles. He rolls his eyes at me, takes a crunch of his apple. "What's happening, Frisco?" he says.

I have arranged myself loosely on my bed, trying to pull a Dylan riff out of my harmonica. I have always figured I can bluff my way into wisdom. I offer Carlton a dignified nod.

He drops onto his own bed. I can see a crushed crocus, the first of the year, stuck to the black rubber sole of his boot.

"Well, Frisco," he says. "Today you are a man."

I nod again. Is that all there is to it?

"*Yow*," Carlton says. He laughs, pleased with himself and the world. "That was so perfect."

I pick out what I can of "Blowin' in the Wind."

Carlton says, "Man, when I saw you out there spying on us I thought to myself, *yes*. Now *I'm* really here. You know what I'm saying?" He waves his apple core.

"Uh-huh," I say.

"Frisco, that was the first time her and I ever did it. I mean, we'd talked. But when we finally got down to it, there you were. My brother. Like you *knew*."

I nod, and this time for real. What happened was an adventure we had together. All right. The story is beginning to make sense.

"Aw, Frisco," Carlton says. "I'm gonna find you a girl, too. You're nine. You been a virgin too long."

"Really?" I say.

"*Man*. We'll find you a woman from the sixth grade, somebody with a little experience. We'll get stoned and all make out under the trees in the boneyard. I want to be present at your deflowering, man. You're gonna need a brother there."

I am about to ask, as casually as I can manage, about the relationship between love and bodily pain, when our mother's voice cuts into the room. "You did it," she screams. "You tracked mud all over the rug."

A family entanglement follows. Our mother brings our father, who comes and stands in the doorway with her, taking in evidence. He is a formerly handsome man. His face has been worn down by too much patience. He has lately taken up some sporty touches—a goatee, a pair of calfskin boots.

Our mother points out the trail of muddy half-moons that lead from the door to Carlton's bed. Dangling over the foot of the bed are the culprits themselves, voluptuously muddy, with Carlton's criminal feet still in them.

"You see?" she says. "You see what he thinks of me?"

Our father, a reasonable man, suggests that Carlton clean it up. Our mother finds that too small a gesture. She wants Carlton not to have done it in the first place. "I don't ask for much," she says. "I don't ask where he goes. I don't ask why the police are suddenly so interested in our house. I ask that he not track mud all over the floor. That's all." She squints in the glare of her own outrage.

"Better clean it right up," our father says to Carlton.

"And that's it?" our mother says. "He cleans up the mess, and all's forgiven?"

"Well, what do you want him to do? Lick it up?"

"I want some consideration," she says, turning helplessly to me. "That's what I want."

I shrug, at a loss. I sympathize with our mother, but am not on her team.

"All right," she says. "I just won't bother cleaning the house anymore. I'll let you men handle it. I'll sit and watch television and throw my candy wrappers on the floor."

She starts out, cutting the air like a blade. On her way she picks up a jar of pencils, looks at it and tosses the pencils on the floor. They fall like fortune-telling sticks, in pairs and crisscrosses.

Our father goes after her, calling her name. Her name is Isabel. We can hear them making their way across the house, our father calling, "Isabel, Isabel, Isabel," while our mother, pleased with the way the pencils had looked, dumps more things onto the floor.

"I hope she doesn't break the TV," I say.

"She'll do what she needs to do," Carlton tells me.

"I hate her," I say. I am not certain about that. I want to test the sound of it, to see if it's true.

"She's got more balls than any of us, Frisco," he says. "Better watch what you say about her."

I keep quiet. Soon I get up and start gathering pencils, because I prefer that to lying around trying to follow the shifting lines of allegiance. Carlton goes for a sponge and starts in on the mud.

"You get shit on the carpet, you clean it up," he says. "Simple."

The time for all my questions about love has passed, and I am not so unhip as to force a subject. I know it will come up again. I make a neat bouquet of pencils. Our mother rages through the house.

Later, after she has thrown enough and we three have picked it all up, I lie on my bed thinking things over. Carlton is on the phone to his girlfriend, talking low. Our mother, becalmed but still dangerous, cooks dinner. She sings as she cooks, some slow forties number that must have been all over the jukes when her first husband's plane went down in the Pacific. Our father plays his clarinet in the basement. That is where he goes to practice, down among his woodworking tools, the neatly hung hammers and awls that throw oversized shadows in the light of the single bulb. If I put my ear to the floor I can hear him, pulling a long low tomcat moan out of that horn. There is some strange comfort in pressing my ear to the carpet and hearing our father's music leaking up through the floorboards. Lying down, with my ear to the floor, I join in on my harmonica.

That spring our parents have a party to celebrate the sun's return. It has been a long, bitter winter and now the first wild daisies are poking up on the lawns and among the graves.

Our parents' parties are mannerly affairs. Their friends, schoolteachers all, bring wine jugs and guitars. They are Ohio hip. Though they hold jobs and meet mortgages, they think of themselves as independent spirits on a spying mission. They have agreed to impersonate teachers until they write their novels, finish their dissertations, or just save up enough money to set themselves free.

Carlton and I are the lackeys. We take coats, fetch drinks. We have done this at every party since we were small, trading on our precocity, doing a brother act. We know the moves. A big, lipsticked woman who has devoted her maidenhood to ninth-grade math calls me Mr. Right. An assistant vice principal in a Russian fur hat asks us both whether we expect to vote Democratic or Socialist. By sneaking sips I manage to get myself semi-crocked.

The reliability of the evening is derailed halfway through, however, by a half dozen of Carlton's friends. They rap on the door and I go for it, anxious as a carnival sharp to see who will step up next and swallow the illusion that I'm a kindly, sober nine-year-old child. I'm expecting callow adults and who do I find but a pack of young outlaws, big-booted and wild-haired. Carlton's girlfriend stands in front, in an outfit made up almost entirely of fringe.

"Hi, Bobby," she says confidently. She comes from New York, and is more than just locally smart.

"Hi," I say. I let them all in despite a retrograde urge to lock the door and phone the police. Three are girls, four boys. They pass me in a cloud of dope smoke and sly-eyed greeting.

What they do is invade the party. Carlton is standing on the far side of the rumpus room, picking the next album, and his girl cuts straight through the crowd to his side. She has the bones and the loose, liquid moves some people consider beautiful. She walks through that room as if she'd been sent to teach the whole party a lesson.

Carlton's face tips me off that this was planned. Our mother demands to know what's going on here. She is wearing a long dark-red dress that doesn't interfere with her shoulders. When she dresses up you can see what it is about her, or what it was. She is responsible for Carlton's beauty. I have our father's face.

Carlton does some quick talking. Though it's against our mother's better judgment, the invaders are suffered to stay. One of them, an Eddie Haskell for all his leather and hair, tells her she is looking good. She is willing to hear it.

So the outlaws, house-sanctioned, start to mingle. I work my way over to Carlton's side, the side unoccupied by his girlfriend. I would like to say something ironic and wised-up, something that will band Carlton and me against every other person in the room. I can feel the shape of the comment I have in mind but, being a tipsy nine-year-old, can't get my mouth around it. What I say is, "Shit, man."

Carlton's girl laughs at me. She considers it amusing that a little boy says "shit." I would like to tell her what I have figured out about her, but I am nine, and three-quarters gone on Tom Collinses. Even sober, I can only imagine a sharp-tongued wit.

"Hang on, Frisco," Carlton tells me. "This could turn into a real party."

I can see by the light in his eyes what is going down. He has arranged a blind date between our parents' friends and his own. It's a Woodstock move — he is plotting a future in which young and old have business together. I agree to hang on, and go to the kitchen, hoping to sneak a few knocks of gin.

There I find our father leaning up against the refrigerator. A line of butterfly-shaped magnets hovers around his head. "Are you enjoying this party?" he asks, touching his goatee. He is still getting used to being a man with a beard.

"Uh-huh."

"I am, too," he says sadly. He never meant to be a high school music teacher. The money question caught up with him.

"What do you think of this music?" he asks. Carlton has put the Stones on the turntable. Mick Jagger sings "19th Nervous Breakdown." Our father gestures in an openhanded way that takes in the room, the party, the whole house — everything the music touches.

"I like it," I say.

"So do I." He stirs his drink with his finger, and sucks on the finger.

"I *love* it," I say, too loud. Something about our father leads me to raise my voice. I want to grab handfuls of music out of the air and stuff them into my mouth.

"I'm not sure I could say I love it," he says. "I'm not sure if I could say that, no. I would say I'm friendly to its intentions. I would say that if this is the direction music is going in, I won't stand in its way."

"Uh-huh," I say. I am already anxious to get back to the party, but don't want to hurt his feelings. If he senses he's being avoided he can fall into fits of apology more terrifying than our mother's rages.

"I think I may have been too rigid with my students," our father says. "Maybe over the summer you boys could teach me a few things about the music people are listening to these days."

"Sure," I say, loudly. We spend a minute waiting for the next thing to say.

"You boys are happy, aren't you?" he asks. "Are you enjoying this party?"

"We're having a great time," I say.

"I thought you were. I am, too."

I have by this time gotten myself to within jumping distance of the door. I call out, "Well, goodbye," and dive back into the party.

Something has happened in my small absence. The party has started to roll. Call it an accident of history and the weather. Carlton's friends are on decent behavior, and our parents' friends have decided to give up some of their wine-and-folk-song propriety to see what they can learn. Carlton is dancing with a vice principal's wife. Carlton's friend Frank, with his ancient-child face and IQ in the low sixties, dances with our mother. I see that our father has followed me out of the kitchen. He positions himself at the party's edge; I jump into its center. I invite the fuchsia-lipped math teacher to dance. She is only too happy. She is big and graceful as a parade float, and I steer her effortlessly out into the middle of everything. My mother, who is known around school for Sicilian discipline, dances freely, which is news to everybody. There is no getting around her beauty.

The night rises higher and higher. A wildness sets in. Carlton throws new music on the turntable — Janis Joplin, the Doors, the Dead. The future shines for everyone, rich with the possibility of more nights exactly like this. Even our father is pressed into dancing, which he does like a flightless bird, all flapping arms and potbelly. Still, he dances. Our mother has a kiss for him.

Finally I nod out on the sofa, blissful under the drinks. I am dreaming of flight when our mother comes and touches my shoulder. I smile up into her flushed, smiling face.

"It's hours past your bedtime," she says, all velvet motherliness. I nod. I can't dispute the fact.

She keeps on nudging my shoulder. I am a moment or two apprehending the fact that she actually wants me to leave the party and go to bed. "No," I tell her.

"Yes," she smiles.

"No," I say cordially, experimentally. This new mother can dance, and flirt. Who knows what else she might allow?

"Yes." The velvet motherliness leaves her voice. She means business, business of the usual kind. I get myself out of there and no excuses this time. I am exactly nine and running from my bedtime as I'd run from death.

I run to Carlton for protection. He is laughing with his girl, a sweaty question mark of hair plastered to his forehead. I plow into him so hard he nearly goes over.

"Whoa, Frisco," he says. He takes me up under the arms and swings me a half-turn. Our mother plucks me out of his hands and sets me down, with a good farm-style hold on the back of my neck.

"Say good night, Bobby," she says. She adds, for the benefit of Carlton's girl, "He should have been in bed before this party started."

"*No*," I holler. I try to twist loose, but our mother has a grip that could crack walnuts.

Carlton's girl tosses her hair and says, "Good night, baby." She smiles a victor's smile. She smooths the stray hair off Carlton's forehead.

"*No*," I scream again. Something about the way she touches his hair. Our mother calls our father, who comes and scoops me up and starts out of the room with me, holding me like the live bomb I am. Before I go I lock eyes with Carlton. He shrugs and says, "Night, man." Our father hustles me out. I do not take it bravely. I leave flailing, too furious to cry, dribbling a slimy thread of horrible-child's spittle.

Later I lie alone on my narrow bed, feeling the music hum in the coiled springs. Life is cracking open right there in our house. People are changing. By tomorrow, no one will be quite the same. How can they let me miss it? I dream up revenge against our parents, and worse for Carlton. He is the one who could have saved me. He could have banded with me against them. What I can't forgive is his shrug, his mild-eyed "Night, man." He has joined the adults. He has made himself bigger, and taken size from me. As the Doors thump "Strange Days," I hope something awful happens to him. I say so to myself.

Around midnight, dim-witted Frank announces he has seen a flying saucer hovering over the back yard. I can hear his deep, excited voice all the way in my room. He says it's like a blinking, luminous cloud. I hear half the party struggling out through the sliding glass door in a disorganized, whooping knot. By that time everyone is so delirious a flying saucer would be just what was expected. That much celebration would logically attract an answering happiness from across the stars.

I get out of bed and sneak down the hall. I will not miss alien visitors for anyone, not even at the cost of our mother's wrath or our father's disappointment. I stop at the end of the hallway, though, embarrassed to be in pajamas. If there really are aliens, they will think I'm the lowest member of the house. While I hesitate over whether to go back to my room to change, people start coming back inside, talking about a trick of the mist and an airplane. People resume their dancing.

Carlton must have jumped the back fence. He must have wanted to be there alone, singular, in case they decided to take somebody with them. A few nights later I will go out and stand where he would have been standing. On the far side of the gully, now a river swollen with melted snow, the cemetery will gleam like a lost city. The moon will be full. I will hang around just as Carlton must have, hypnotized by the silver light on the stones, the white angel raising her arms up across the river.

According to our parents the mystery is why he ran back to the house full tilt. Something in the graveyard may have scared him, he may have needed to break its spell, but I think it's more likely that when he came back to himself he just couldn't wait to get back to the music and the people, the noisy disorder of continuing life.

Somebody has shut the sliding glass door. Carlton's girlfriend looks lazily out, touching base with her own reflection. I look, too. Carlton is running toward the house. I hesitate. Then I figure he can bump his nose. It will be a good joke on him. I let him keep coming. His girlfriend sees him through her own reflection, starts to scream a warning just as Carlton hits the glass.

It is an explosion. Triangles of glass fly brightly through the room. I think for him it must be more surprising than painful, like hitting water from a great height. He stands blinking for a moment. The whole party stops, stares, getting its bearings. Bob Dylan sings "Just Like a Woman." Carlton reaches up curiously to take out the shard of glass that is stuck in his neck, and that is when the blood starts. It shoots out of him. Our mother screams. Carlton steps forward into his girlfriend's arms and the two of them fall together. Our mother throws herself down on top of him and the girl. People shout their accident wisdom. Don't lift him. Call an ambulance. I watch from the hallway. Carlton's blood spurts, soaking into the carpet, spattering people's clothes. Our mother and father both try to plug the wound with their hands, but the blood just shoots between their fingers. Carlton looks more puzzled than anything, as if he can't quite follow this turn of events. "It's all right," our father tells him, trying to stop the blood. "It's all right, just don't move, it's all right." Carlton nods, and holds our father's hand. His eyes take on an astonished light. Our mother screams, "Is anybody *doing* anything?" What comes out of Carlton grows darker, almost black. I watch. Our father tries to get a hold on Carlton's neck while Carlton keeps trying to take his hand. Our mother's hair is matted with blood. It runs down her face. Carlton's girl holds him to her breasts, touches his hair, whispers in his ear.

He is gone by the time the ambulance gets there. You can see the life drain out of him. When his face goes slack our mother wails. A part of her flies wailing through the house, where it will wail and rage forever. I feel our mother pass through me on her way out. She covers Carlton's body with her own.

He is buried in the cemetery out back. Years have passed — we are living in the future, and it's turned out differently from what we'd planned. Our mother has established her life of separateness behind the guest-room door. Our father mutters his greetings to the door as he passes.

One April night, almost a year to the day after Carlton's accident, I hear cautious footsteps shuffling across the living-room floor after midnight. I run out eagerly, thinking of ghosts, but find only our father in moth-colored pajamas. He looks unsteadily at the dark air in front of him.

"Hi, Dad," I say from the doorway.

He looks in my direction. "Yes?"

"It's me. Bobby."

"Oh, Bobby," he says. "What are you doing up, young man?"

"Nothing," I tell him. "Dad?"

"Yes, son."

"Maybe you better come back to bed. Okay?"

"Maybe I had," he says. "I just came out here for a drink of water, but I seem to have gotten turned around in the darkness. Yes, maybe I better had."

I take his hand and lead him down the hall to his room. The grandfather clock chimes the quarter hour.

"Sorry," our father says.

I get him into bed. "There," I say. "Okay?"

"Perfect. Could not be better."

"Okay. Good night."

"Good night. Bobby?"

"Uh-huh?"

"Why don't you stay a minute?" he says. "We could have ourselves a talk, you and me. How would that be?"

"Okay," I say. I sit on the edge of his mattress. His bedside clock ticks off the minutes.

I can hear the low rasp of his breathing. Around our house, the Ohio night chirps and buzzes. The small gray finger of Carlton's stone pokes up among the others, within sight of the angel's blank white eyes. Above us, airplanes and satellites sparkle. People are flying even now toward New York or California, to take up lives of risk and invention.

I stay until our father has worked his way into a muttering sleep.

Carlton's girlfriend moved to Denver with her family a month before. I never learned what it was she'd whispered to him. Though she'd kept her head admirably during the accident, she lost her head afterward. She cried so hard at the funeral that she had to be taken away by her mother — an older, redder-haired version of her. She started seeing a psychiatrist three times a week. Everyone, including my parents, talked about how hard it was for her, to have held a dying boy in her arms at that age. I'm grateful to her for holding my brother while he died, but I never once heard her mention the fact that though she had been through something terrible, at least she was still alive and going places. At least she had protected herself by trying to warn him. I can appreciate the intricacies of her pain. But as long as she was in Cleveland, I could never look her straight in the face. I couldn't talk about the wounds she suffered. I can't even write her name.

CHAPTER NINE

SHAPE

In this chapter you will:

- Distinguish revision and shaping from editing and proofreading
- Practice a variety of hands-on shaping and revision strategies for improving your writing-in-progress
- Address common pitfalls in order to more easily shape your work into a successful final draft

Rarely do our words tumble out in polished and perfect order, with a meaningful structure all of their own. Thus, shaping a piece of writing is a crucial part of the creative process. But when and how do we make changes? Should we work on the sentence level, smoothing each sentence before going on to the next? Do we just hammer out a rough draft, and then assess what works and what doesn't? How does one even know when a piece is finished?

> *The main reason for rewriting is not to achieve a smooth surface, but to discover the inner truth of your characters.*
> —SAUL BELLOW

PRINCIPLES OF SHAPE

In this chapter, you'll learn **shape** as a strategy that can help you create a flexible and generative writing process that works across genres and suits your particular personality. Shape is defined as the work a writer does on the word level, the sentence and line level, and all throughout the whole of a piece, from initial conception to finished product, to create a smooth, professional, polished piece of original writing.

As you proceed to shape and complete the writing projects you've begun, it may be helpful to keep in mind that a useful shaping process is one that allows the writer:

1. To learn and build confidence for the *next* writing project
2. To make the work better not worse
3. Flexibility to try various shaping strategies to see if they work or not
4. A built-in way to find out what's working, and what's not
5. To have fun creating and experimenting

Sometimes revision feels like a kind of punishment after a lot of hard work has already been done. You put all this effort into a piece of writing, and then you're told to take it apart, start over, or make radical changes. That can be really hard to do and, especially early on, quite disheartening. Good writers know how to apply a range of creative approaches to their work in order to make it better, and they have learned how to tolerate frustration and failed attempts.

In the material that follows, you'll discover how and when to shape your writing, you'll examine some of the pitfalls that can bog down the process, making it hard to finish a piece, and you'll shadow one student's writing process as she works on her short story-in-progress using the revision tools that work best for her. In the end, you'll develop strategies that work best for you.

Shaping, Editing, and Proofreading

We shape our writing as we work, adding scenes, striking dialogue, manipulating the tension. And, before we send a piece off to our writing group, post it for workshop, turn it in to our instructor, or send it off to a literary magazine in hopes of publication, we carefully go over the piece again and again, trying out:

- Different combinations of words
- Various kinds of sentences (syntax)
- Options for titles
- The best scenes in the best order
- Cuts
- New material

As we work on a piece, we're constantly honing the dialogue, improving the power and consistency of the rhythm and meter, striving to make each beat interesting and evocative. Polishing, starting anew, and searching carefully for the perfect word—this messy, ongoing process is a process of shaping writing into a form that feels right.

Revision—literally *seeing again*—is part of the shaping process, but seeing the piece afresh is not the only thing a writer does before calling the work complete. It's important, as you set out to build a productive shaping process for yourself, that you understand revision involves many kinds of critical assessment, small and large, and that writers shape their work both as they write and after the first draft is complete.

And, it's important to distinguish various types of revision from editing and proofreading. Editing, which is covered later in this chapter, is an entirely separate process from revision. **Editing** is the act of making micro changes on the word and sentence level, correcting grammar, and correcting for consistency in tense and subject-verb agreement. Editing involves tightening sentences, deleting unintentional repetitions, sharpening details, smoothing out sentences, and perfecting word choice. Editing is comparable to cleaning up your room. Revision is deciding afresh which room you actually want to live in, spending time hunting for the perfect furnishings for that space, and arranging them in a pleasing configuration. **Proofreading** is the very final step in your shaping process. Proofreading is checking a text for typos, grammar, spelling, and accidental errors. Proofreading is like dusting and polishing that beautiful room, so nothing distracts the eye.

> *Moments of pure inspiration are glorious, but most of a writer's life is, to adapt the old cliché, about perspiration rather than inspiration. Sometimes you have to write even when the muse isn't cooperating.*
>
> —J.K. ROWLING

To grow as a writer, it's crucial that you make these distinctions between revision, editing, and proofreading. You'll want to work on these three separate tasks at the appropriate times in your writing process. You probably want to spend more time shaping than you may be spending right now (and this chapter shows you how). You certainly don't need to spend time proofreading an early draft. Editing at the sentence level too soon—before you really know what your piece means on a deeper level, before you have your basic images clear and stable, and a good solid sense of the structure—is probably a waste of time. The three different processes use different parts of your brain and have very different purposes: Revision solidifies, editing strengthens, and proofreading perfects.

This pyramid shows you roughly how much time you can expect to spend on each stage.

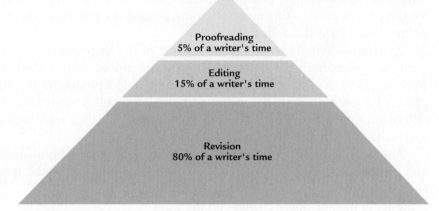

Figure 9.1 Amount of Time Typically Spent Revising, Editing, and Proofreading

Revision = Seeing Again

Revision means "re-seeing." In Latin, the word *revisere* means "to look again, to visit again." It comes from the word *videre*—"to see," as in *vision*. So revision actually means taking a new look at your whole piece, seeing it as the reader might see it. Picking over each word isn't re-seeing (that's editing). To truly revise a piece of writing, you have to find ways to read your work so that you can actually experience what the reader would experience in their mind's eye when they read your work.

Because it can be really difficult to take your own hopes for the piece out of the equation, many writers take their pieces to a small group or a workshop and get feedback to help them see from different angles, to help them understand how the reader sees their work.

The goal of revision is to intensify the work so that it makes a moving picture inside the reader's mind. You are trying to make the reader forget she is reading at all—you want her to have an *experience*. Reviewing the material in Chapter One and Chapter Four can be helpful as you delete the parts of your work that are not transporting the reader (but rather explaining things to him) and to make more visual and interesting the parts that aren't active and alive.

Most published works go through dozens and dozens of drafts to get the words on the page working in such a way that the reader doesn't see the words, they see the experience you want them to have in their mind. To do this work requires time and patience. Author James Dickey says that it takes him 50 drafts to get the poem well crafted and structured and then another 150 to make it sound spontaneous!

Shaping by Strategy

Instead of thinking of revision as an impossible task or a wall of frustration, it can be helpful to think of revision as a shaping process, made up of many smaller activities, and to approach the work systematically, first working through the strategies step-by-step. This book is set up so that you can apply each of the core features of creative writing you've studied to every piece you write in a logical and productive way. First, you create with **images**, so you can produce a play or poem or story that is visually compelling, in motion. Then, you work to infuse those images with more **energy**. Next, you overtly increase the **tension** — every word, every line, every panel. As you move the piece of writing toward completion, you go through your words once again, increasing the **patterns** and echoes in every aspect of the piece: sound echoes, word repetitions, visual patterns, and so on. Lastly, you go through the piece yet again, working out ways to improve the depth and meaning in your piece, developing its **insights** as you shape the work into a final form.

Figure 9.2 shows precisely how to use the five strategies of creative writing as a scaffold for shaping your work to completion. While not every

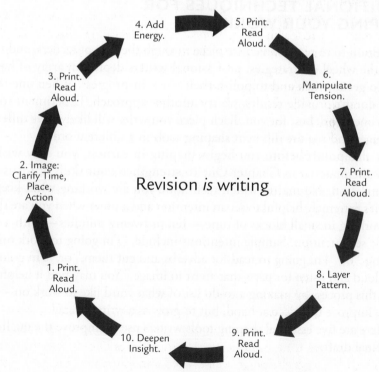

Figure 9.2 Revision Process Using the Strategies for Creative Writing

writer works with a hard copy, students who take the time to print and read aloud often get stuck less often, and many have better results more quickly. Ten steps is a lot of steps, but the more you practice, the smoother your writing process will be. The wheel of strategies *really* works!

Start with a hard copy of your poem, story, or play. Read it aloud, and then use what you learned in your study of **images**. Make changes by hand on your hard copy, if you can, and then continue through the steps.

PRACTICE 1

Reflecting on Your Revision Process

Write a short paragraph describing your revision process. What do you do when you revise a piece of writing, exactly? Write a few sentences on your revision challenges. When it comes to revision, what is hardest for you? Have you had successful revision experiences? Make a list of the three-to-five steps that are most useful to you — steps that really work for you when revising goes well.

ADDITIONAL TECHNIQUES FOR SHAPING YOUR WORK

In addition to re-seeing an entire piece through the eyes of readers, and then using the wheel of strategies, professional writers deploy an array of handy tools to get unstuck and to polish their work-in-progress. When one technique doesn't provide results, we try another approach. Experiment to see which ones work best for you. Each piece you write will likely have different challenges and require different shaping tools in a different order.

At this point, before you begin shaping in earnest, you may wish to review the material in Chapter One to strengthen your skills of focus and concentration. No matter which technique you are working with, keep in mind it's extremely helpful to set an intention and a timer when you are shaping, working in small blocks of time — ten or twenty minutes — with a very specific set intention. Sample intentions include, "I'm going to work on the opening," or, "I'm going to read for adverbs and cut them," or, "I'm going to read aloud and listen for parts that aren't in image." You may find it helpful to begin this process by making a to-do list of what you'd like to work on — not just to improve the piece at hand, but to grow as a writer overall.

Here are five essential shaping tools writers use to improve the quality of their final draft.

Look Closer

Your go-to strategy when revising is to take each molecule of the writing — each line, each bit of dialogue, each panel, every sentence and paragraph, and see if you can make it more specific, more vivid, more relevant, and more exciting by improving your powers of observation. Look more closely and more carefully at what you are actually writing about, and choose straightforward words and vivid details that are more accurate, more careful, and more precise.

For example, when shaping a piece of flash fiction she titled "Pogo Sticks," a student writer named Courtney Clute decided to use the look-closer technique to revise her opening paragraph, which read, in the original:

> My mom said we could use our new pogo sticks and so we went to the park. I couldn't wait.

When her writing group read this first draft, they told her they needed to see the pogo sticks (not everyone in the group knew what a pogo stick even is), and they needed to see the characters.

When Courtney took the time to look closer, she saw the pogo sticks clearly. She remembered details from her own pogo stick childhood. She revised her opening this way:

> Our mother brought home two pogo sticks from a garage sale. We were young, my sister 10 and me 7, and our mom hadn't bought us anything new in a long time. The padding on the handlebars was peeling, and the exposed metal was spotted with rust. They both still had the hand-written price stickers on them: $5.

Because she looked more carefully at the "stuff" in her story, Courtney's new version contains images, energy, tension, and subtext—we see how the family is struggling; we access the yearning of the girls to have a normal-ish childhood, and to play.

"Look closer" is such a powerful technique that it may become your mantra as a writer. Looking closer will almost always improve your writing.

Work by Hand

Many writers dictate or tap out work on their phones; other writers compose and revise in a word-processing program. These devices are wonderful—until they aren't. Sometimes, writing on a device simply lets you go too fast and write too much. And, worse, it's almost too easy to delete on a device.

You'll absolutely use these tools, but don't neglect the old-fashioned way: The power of a pencil and a sheet of paper can be grounding and peaceful. When you are stuck, consider writing some of your piece by hand. Some writers find writing by hand to be the only way they can create work that is thoughtful, original, and interesting. Others use writing by hand as a way to address trouble spots or get unstuck. You don't need fancy paper or a Mont

Blanc pen; printer paper or a composition notebook and a pencil will do quite nicely.

Instead of revising on keyboard and screen large or small, try printing out what you have written and reread it kindly, as though it was written by a beloved, respected friend. Make your revisions with pen or pencil. Working by hand will slow you down, which immediately puts you in closer touch with the pace and focus the reader will be bringing to your page. Many students are surprised by how much better the handwritten work is than typed text. It's quick and easy to enter the edits into your phone or word processor. It sounds slow but it's often actually much quicker than the "type–delete–type–delete–stare at blank screen" method because you'll make visible forward progress.

Be Bold: Let Go

Weak writing is not a crisis. Author Greg Neri says he is successful because he is able to "tolerate my own suckedness for longer periods of time than most people." Learning to tolerate your own early drafts — often "bad" writing — is all part of the process of producing good writing. Many successful writers explain their success this way: "My bad writing doesn't bother me that much, and it's a good thing because there is tons of it." Try to welcome your weaker efforts with love — they are part of your process and not a problem. *Even for professional writers, most first drafts have numerous flaws.* Let go of the idea that it needs to come out perfect or nearly so the first time. That's simply not how writing works.

And, when you produce something that just isn't working, instead of trying to revise it, you may decide to simply let it go. That's an important part of growing as a writer. Not everything needs to be revised and shaped to perfection because not every piece you create is going to be worthy of all the time and effort required to shape it to completion.

Sometimes what's required is *letting go of your original ideas so new images can come forward.*

One student, Deion Matthews, wrote a long poem about a character's ongoing nightmare-ish visions. It was an attempt to bring to life fear, violence, and jealousy. The poem was over six pages — and still not complete, in the author's opinion — and filled with lines such as these from page one:

> Pulsing, vibrating, terror-stricken, in corners
> the desire entwines with VIOLENCE and black hatred HATRED
> the undone ending never comes   phantoms
> the yearning for dawn's light and the grace an angel NEVER COMES!

The writers in his writing group admired the author's attempt to put strong feelings on the page. But when it came time to re-see and look closer, Deion realized he was just done with this poem. It was what it was. Making things more clear would actually ruin the poem. He wanted the murky, strange feeling, and this wasn't a reality-based poem; he was done. So, he just let go of the untitled opus and moved on to his next writing project.

Invest in your growth as a writer by choosing to shape your strongest work. For the weaker or more mysterious, super-complex pieces, consider moving on (at least for now) and letting go. It's almost always easier to start a new piece fresh rather than labor over a revision when the first draft is ultra-abstract.

Sketch

As you learned in the beginning of this book, instead of drafting, you're wise to begin your writing process with a quick sketch of your scene (no drawing talent is required—in your mind's eye, you just want to clearly visualize a "movie" of what you are writing), listing the five senses that are present in this scene, and *then* beginning the writing. The key is to be very clear when and where your image is taking place before you start writing. You might want to sketch out various options until you find a scene that has tension and energy.

When you are shaping your work-in-progress, usually the sentences aren't the primary problem: Weak writing is often simply not well-visualized. Later in this chapter, you'll look closely at one student's shaping process. This particular student writer, Meghan Wilson loved her first draft (the opening appears on page 407)—at first. But after her first peer workshop, she realized that while she was in love with the words, the writing was abstract and a bit extra. Her readers didn't really understand what was important in the situation. Meghan resisted revision. For a week, she moved sentences and words around (see page 403, Perfectionism, for an example). When she came to me for help, as her teacher I suggested she try the sketching tool: I encouraged her to make a diagram of the scene she wanted to write before she began writing.

Meghan was polite but she didn't really think drawing first and writing second would work; ultimately, she decided to give sketching a try. She drew her scene. You can see how she did this by turning to page 400; later in the chapter, we examine her shaping process step by step.

Sketching forces you to look closely, and to see again. For this writer, sketching made revision and final shaping more fun and much more doable.

Sketching gets you out of sentence-level revision. Many pieces of writing need to be more fully grounded in space and time; shaping sentences doesn't help the piece because sentences aren't the problem. A lack of image is the problem.

When Meghan drew what she wanted to write, she was surprised what the sketch showed her. When she looked at her original quick sketch—a girl walking down a staircase—she could see how static and unfocused the scene actually was. When Meghan looked at the scene again, she realized that starting her short story with the stair descent was boring and pointless, visually and thematically. Revising the sentences in that piece might have never shown her what she needed to see.

She began a second sketch. When she drew the scene again, she left out the staircase and instead drew the scene her character was headed to. Total time invested so far? About five minutes.

Figure 9.3 shows what Meghan drew during her second attempt at sketching before writing.

Figure 9.3 Meghan's Sketch of Family Fighting in the Living Room

She drew what she could and noted other sensory details—the clock ticking at 8:00 p.m. on prom night; the stairs, couch, and front door forming a triangle—and her new opening is vibrant, funny, and visually rich. Just as filmmakers storyboard their scenes and graphic novelists picture the story frame by frame, you should get in the habit of seeing by sketching each part of your stories, poems, plays, and essays. It's a quick way to jump-start truly effective writing—you don't have to rework lots and lots of stuff. See the scene before you write and as you rewrite.

After looking and seeing again, Meghan stopped trying to fix the stair sentence, and she started her story with the living room scene. The rest of the story? It pretty much wrote itself once she was on the right track.

For dramatic works—plays, monologues, screenplays, and comics/graphic novels—you can storyboard each scene, doing a quick sketch to locate the triangle of tension, and zoom in on the sensory images (sights, smells, sounds, textures, and tastes) for each scene, as in the example above.

Cut

Originally I titled this section "Cut, Cut, Cut." But you don't need to read the word "cut" three times. Cutting is not a difficult concept. So, I cut two words. One "cut" is enough to get the point across.

> *Life is a field of corn. Literature is the shot of whiskey it distills down into.*
>
> —LORRIE MOORE

The most effective way to shape your work is to improve the images—to make everything visual, clear, active, and alive. The second most powerful tool you have as a shaper is your cutting tool. Strike everything you can. Here's a checklist, as you read over your piece again and again, of places you can cut extra words, sentences, and even full passages so your work is lean, taut, powerful, and concise. As you work to shape your final pieces, try to delete as many of these as you can:

- Adverbs
- Adjectives
- Explanations
- Meaningless repetitions
- Extra description
- Set-ups and conclusions
- Commentary
- Long passages of musing (no action)

Write to the bone.

When Jennifer Schelter was working on her micro-memoir, titled "Pretty Dumb," she felt she was finished until she read the work aloud into her phone, recording her voice, and then playing it back. She was stunned at what she heard.

> In fourth grade I was always trying to get the answers from other kids by sitting next to them and copying their work. I always sat close to the smart kids. I was terrified of not-knowing. I was worried about getting caught but more worried about not getting into a college or something like that and my mother being mad. When Mrs. Purdy announced 'test' I Velcroed myself to Kate Felsen.

The piece went on. And on. Jennifer heard herself "talking," not really creating images for the reader.

She printed out the page and cut everything she could by drawing a line through everything that wasn't a visual image. This is what she ended up with:

> In fourth grade, Mrs. Purdy said, 'Test.' I Velcroed myself to Kate Felson. I squinted to see her handwriting. I wrote as fast as I could. Then I looked back to her page again. I heard pencils spelling things I could not spell. I heard the buzz of fluorescent lights.

> *The best writing comes not when you want to say something but when you want to find something.*
> —ANDRE DUBUS III

Jennifer decided that in the future, she'd try more writing by hand, in an effort to keep from going too fast and perhaps overwriting. And, she now prints out her pages and uses a pencil to circle the visual parts, and to cross out the extra parts. It's just how she works best — writing more than she needs, knowing she'll be fine with deleting stuff later.

PRACTICE 2

PERSONALIZED REVISION

From the list of techniques, above — Look Closer, Work by Hand, Be Bold: Let Go, Sketch, and Cut — which ones suit you and your work habits the best? Which ones do you find less effective? Write a paragraph of explanation. Then, share one example of a passage of writing, first the original draft and then a shaped version, using one of the techniques. Write a brief paragraph explaining why you chose that technique and how you feel about the results.

PITFALLS

Shaping a piece from initial concept through to its final form is difficult even for seasoned writers. In addition to adding specific techniques to your tool box, it can be helpful to learn about the common obstacles many writers face, and how to work around them.

Perfectionism

Writers often struggle to revise, spending hours getting nowhere fast. For many, revision goes something like this. The writer writes a sentence:

> She went down the stairs.

And then the writer checks Instagram, texts a friend, goes for a run, comes back, and rereads the sentence. Something is off. So the writer deletes that sentence:

> ~~She went down the stairs.~~

She writes a new sentence, quite similar to the original, hoping it's better. Now the sentence has action and emotion. Right?

> She went down the stairs, quickly, sighing heavily.

Then she reads it. It's worse. And she deletes:

> ~~She went down the stairs, quickly, sighing heavily.~~

And she writes another new sentence, and another, and each one is *worse*—not better—than the previous ones:

> Downstairs. She decided: She had to get downstairs!
> ~~Downstairs. She decided: She had to get downstairs!~~
> "I'm coming down!" she announced. And so she descended the stairs.
> ~~"I'm coming down!" she announced. And so she descended the stairs.~~

Only to end up, an hour later, with her original sentence:

> She went down the stairs.

This tortured writer might conclude two things: Writing is hard, and revision is a waste of time.

But all this crossing out and fiddling with words—is this revision? No, moving words around and trying out versions of the same sentence over and over is not really revision at all.

Anxiety and Fear

Many beginning writers start their revision process by reading the first sentence of their piece and then immediately feel two powerfully contradictory emotions: "It's fine" and "It sucks." What to do next? There's often a deer-in-headlights effect, where the writer is frozen, uncertain what move to make next. Any move he makes could make the piece worse. What move would be best?

Is it any wonder that a quick round of Candy Crush or doing laundry suddenly seems like a great idea? We have less fear when the task before us has clear steps. For example, laundry is usually not scary; it's clear and it's fairly easy. You fill the washer with water, toss in a pod, put in clothes.

The truth is that your piece is fine, and yes, it could be better, too. That's kind of weird—that two opposite things are true at once. The brain experiences some friction, some tension when two things seem to be cancelling each other out. Often, we feel anxious in these situations. We may even shut down completely and quit trying to shape our piece of writing.

Instead of starting with the first sentence, and then freezing up or freaking out and redoing that opening sentence over and over and over, it may be helpful for you to come up with a set of directions, personalized just for you, for shaping your work.

Practice shaping numerous different pieces using the strategies and techniques in this chapter. Which ones do you like the most? Which ones produce the best effects for you? Use shaping as a way to get to know yourself and your writing better.

> I'm very aware that an asteroid could kill us all tomorrow. But I create works of art that take years and years to finish. So it's an enormous act of faith to start a project.
> —LIN-MANUEL MIRANDA

Overwhelm

If you are overwhelmed, simply choose one shaping strategy to focus on at a time, set your timer, and set your intention. To locate the part of the piece that most needs attention, read your piece aloud, or have someone read it to you. Did you hear a slightly lengthy, flat, boring description? Apply the strategy of Energy to that passage. Did you hear a confusing passage, where you aren't even sure what you meant? Apply the strategy of Image to that section. Did you hear a spot where nothing is really happening? Apply the strategy of Tension to that passage. Go slowly. Go one step at a time.

If that approach still feels too overwhelming, do what many published writers do: Start fresh. Instead of trying to salvage a mediocre piece, experienced writers start anew. It's sometimes faster, easier, and more fun to start an assignment over, from scratch. Set that first version to the side. Re-see what you want to write, sketch it, focus on the sensory experiences you want your readers to create in their minds as they read, and begin in a new way. In fact, when you write this new version, your brain will still remember much of the first version. It's not wasted time—you aren't starting over with nothing. The first version still exists. Sometimes it's easier not to be married to it. Starting a new version, based on the previous version, frees you up from your mistakes and allows room for new creativity to emerge.

Instead of liking or hating your work, and spending time in a terrible endless sea of confusion, aim to shift your focus of building a revision practice that you can stick with, one that is a good fit for you personally. Small steps, clear goals, and the use of a timer are your best weapons against becoming overwhelmed.

> *Always dream and shoot higher than you know how to. Don't bother just to be better than your contemporaries or predecessors. Try to be better than yourself.*
> —WILLIAM FAULKNER

Darlings

There's a famous quote passed down by many writers and teachers, originating from a 1914 lecture on the craft of writing by Arthur Quiller-Couch, titled "On Style." He cautions writers, before sending off their manuscripts to publishers, to "Murder your darlings." This means writers have to work hard to strike out elaborate turns of phrase, to avoid overwriting or relying on inside jokes and flowery phrasings that are fun to write and pleasing to the writer. This "extraneous Ornament" bogs down the reader, according to Quiller-Couch. For many writers, this is absolutely the most challenging part of shaping: the clipping off of perfectly lovely bits of writing—deleting your favorite passages. But these pet phrases and decorative or overly emotional or inappropriately comic elements often must go.

Here's one student's experience with murdering a darling. He originally wrote:

> My coat pulled me down to the ground as though I were wearing boots of concrete cement.

This writer loved—*loved*—his simile, the concrete boots. He did not want to take the image out of his memoir. Members of his writing group gently pointed out the concrete boot thing is one of his go-to phrases. It's hard to understand how a coat on one's body can feel like wearing heavy shoes. Almost. But not really. Ultimately, he murdered his darling and replaced the sentence with:

My coat was heavy and smelled of old rain.

Dramatic, quirky metaphors and outrageous similes can be fun to write and maybe, for some readers, fun to read—once.

They had the voice of a dog trying not to vomit violently while barking.

She entered the room like a hailstorm over Kansas in the summer but not really.

As long as you have text on the page, you have something you can revise.
—JERICHO BROWN

But if your phrasings take the reader out of the situation at hand, these elaborate phrases may be actually weakening your work, calling attention to your cleverness at the expense of the writing. Examples of this error abound on the internet; search "worst metaphors." Perhaps your class will have a contest: Who can create the most strained, overtly hilarious, trying-too-hard sentence?

PRACTICE 3

MURDER YOUR DARLINGS

Read through your recent writing projects, and collect any phrases that seem precious to you; specifically, turns of phrase or word combinations that you love but may be seen as "darling," unnecessary, decorative, elaborate, or calling too much attention to themselves by the reader. Share your collection of darlings with others. Can you imagine deleting these phrases from your work?

SHAPING A STORY: A WRITER AT WORK

Writers learn what shape is by practicing, by reading, and by getting feedback from instructors and other writers. But when it comes down to actually revising a piece of writing, all writers do it their own way. Examining how other writers shape works-in-progress may help you build your skills and confidence, as you come up with the methods that work best for your work ethic, your personality, and your writing style.

Letting Go

Meghan Wilson, the student writer who fell in love with the sketching technique, first began her untitled short story this way:

> I closed my eyes to time. I succumbed to it. I let it creep along, and then be picked up by an accelerating wind. When I finally had the courage to open my eyes, time was gone. I let the years fly by, and I eternally scarred my parents in that process of growing up. There were countless arguments, and although I can't remember them, they always ended the same way: badly.
>
> Those treacherous adolescent years have long since passed, and I've actually become proud of who I developed into because of them. It was my parents who, as I found out, would simply not let it go.

Meghan chose this short story to work on for her final portfolio because she really liked the subject—a teenage girl's super-hard high school experience, complete with sex, and mean girls. First, Meghan used the sketching method for revision (see her sketch on page 400). Then, she used the strategy wheel (see page 395), and she went through her story one strategy at a time, in short, timed sessions, usually printing a hard copy for each step, but not each time.

> *The key for me . . . was to get back into my body. If I could figure out what my foot was doing, if I could feel how it was to sit in the blue chair, I could get back into the scene. . . . And that was how I got unstuck.*
> —CHARLIE WALTER

Once Meghan had Images in mind from her sketch, she began her work with Energy. She reviewed the concepts of energy (see Chapter Five), and she reread her short story, still untitled, out loud with these three Energy questions in mind.

- Was the subject interesting? Superbly personal and important to her? *Absolutely yes.*
- Did she know the subject extremely well? *Yes, the characters in the story were based on events she'd witnessed in her own high school*
- Were the words specific and the verbs grounded and muscular? *She thought so, yes. At least in part.*

"*Succumbed, accelerating, scarred, developed*—I thought this all sounded really momentous and dramatic and exciting," Meghan told me. But when she reread her opening again, aloud, she cringed. Reading aloud was the key part of the process for her. It was hard to do — painful — but incredibly helpful. She realized, "You can't even see who this is! It just sounds so overblown, and like, what are we even talking about? The winds of time? What even is that? It sounds like a bad college application essay! I don't know what I was thinking when I wrote this. I liked it a lot at the time. But what is the wind? This isn't really how I want to sound. Windy."

Applying the Wheel of Strategies

As Meghan looked at her short-story opening with Energy in mind, she realized that yes, the sentences had a lot of energy and power, but there was a lot of metaphor — stuff the readers couldn't really see, though they could probably relate. But what was treacherous? What was scarring? What was argued over? Meghan felt it would be more effective to show one of the battles, in real time. For the story to be truly effective, she thought that she needed to *show* the conflict, and not say, in the second paragraph, "I've actually become proud of who I developed into." First of all, it seemed kind of bogus, and second, Meghan thought if this was the story she was going to tell, that information should be on the last page should be on the last page and in a scene.

So, with those goals in mind, she decided to use the wheel of strategies in order this time. She'd realized she had a scene, but it wasn't the right one for the story she was actually trying to tell. So she went back to Images, setting her timer. She decided to start with a sketch of an image of the most painful high school moment she could easily imagine — and, surprisingly, it had nothing to do with parents. It was waking up late. Figure 9.4 shows what she drew.

As she wrote, starting completely fresh, she tried to shift from abstract, vague writing in the original draft to something that was in action, in scene, making sure her piece took place in an actual space and at a specific time of day. After she did her drawing, she wrote:

> The midday sunlight seeps through open spaces where the bedroom blinds aren't closed. A stream of light hits the center of my right eye, and I bury my face in the depths of my down pillow. I reach up with one hand, drawing the blinds completely closed. I'm not getting out of bed today. I'm not going to school. I turn over on my belly and pull my dirty hair into a tousled ponytail. I rest my thick dully throbbing head in my palm trying to talk myself out of getting sick. My eyelashes feel like I'm wearing lead mascara. How can I be this tired? I scan my bedroom. My thoughts are a muddled mess.

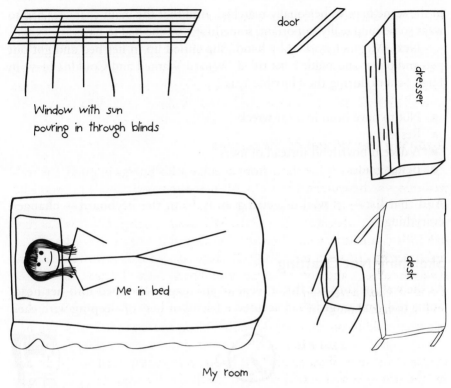

Window with sun pouring in through blinds

door

dresser

Me in bed

desk

My room

Figure 9.4 Meghan's Sketch of Character Waking Up

Getting Feedback

When she reread this piece the next day, she felt it was a lot better than the first draft. She took her revision to her writing group in class (the piece she took in was quite a bit longer than the excerpt above). The three members of the group felt the piece was in image, and that was good, but one group member said a character waking up was pretty much a cliché. Plus, it violated one of the principles of images: to avoid having characters onstage, in scene, alone with their thoughts. "Nothing happens," Meghan said to her group. "It takes place in real time, which is what I wanted, but there's not really any tension." Meghan realized she had no triangles (for more on triangles, see page 265 in Chapter Six). She was in scene, but it was a boring scene. But she was in scene! She was making progress.

Next, Meghan felt she needed to actually sit down and review Chapter Six, Tension. What struck her as she reread the chapter was that the opponents in the scene have to be equally matched. And that the main character had to want something really important, something that she had to have.

Next, Meghan worked by hand. She curled up in her bed and got out pen and paper and made a list titled "What I Wanted and Couldn't Have in High School during the Horrible Year":

- Not to have been in a car wreck
- Respect
- A decent boyfriend instead of users
- Better grades

And that list—as well as getting away from the keyboard—changed everything.

Sketching Not Drafting

As she was making her list, a scene—an image—popped into her head. Some really mean girls had accused a friend of hers of sleeping with their

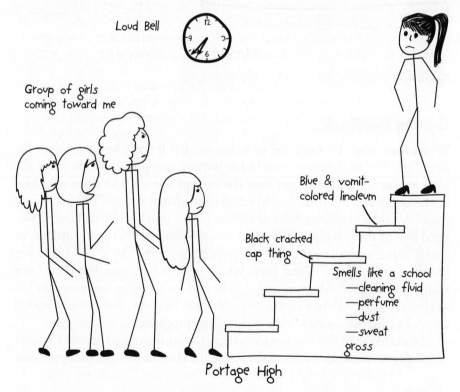

Figure 9.5 Meghan's Sketch of Mean Girls at Portage High School

boyfriends—it was like a bad teen movie. It made her face burn just to think of it now—and she hadn't thought of that day in a long time.

Meghan went back to her image-making shape tool and sketched a quick floor plan with notes.

A truant high schooler, lurking by the stairwell, ditching class, freaking out when an army of powerful popular junior girls, dressed alike, barrel down the hall like they are the princesses of Portage High.

Meghan made a list of the sounds, sights, textures, and smells from that day at school, that single moment. And she started her new draft this way:

At Portage Central

Start by any given stairwell because after the tardy bell dings over the PA there usually aren't any educators around and the Hall Walkers are smoking the last cigarette down to the filter or crushing a Styrofoam cup into the trash receptacle, and they'll be out soon but not soon enough. So it's you, the walls and stairs, and a couple of girls a year or two older round the corridor now like bloodhounds. One gnarls her lip at you, kick-starts the whole thing.

The girl next to her, let's say it's football season this time around, is wearing an old basketball jersey the athletic department sold to students that year, and a short torn jean skirt, tube socks, all yellow and blue, yes, she'll be the one to speak up first.

You know the caricature and now you've got to make a decision depending on whether or not they keep walking. Are you going to walk to class? Are they stopping? Sometimes they'll keep walking and brush into you as they walk by and in a voice so low you could've misheard she'll say, Meghan Wilson, yeah right.

They stop, in unison, and the dark haired girl (what sets her apart from the rest is that she claims she is half Russian/half Japanese), slants her body backward and places a hand on her jutted out hip, the other stands next to her, five or six inches shorter, mouth open, nose flared, the one who would be the bat boy on the baseball team, if this were a spectator sport. She forces some laughs it seems like, when the Japanese/Russian says, "Ohmygod Sara. She's wearing the same sweatshirt I wore yesterday."

The shorter one will echo, "The same one," before she bobbles her head in your direction and says, well, spits, "Burn that shit. We do not dress like sluts."

So you say something you've never said before but you've rehearsed it and you're nervous and don't quite get the catch-phrase spot-on but you say: Please shut the fuck up.

This is when you're late. This is how you're late. This is exactly the beginning of the whole thing.

PRACTICE 4

COMPARING MEGHAN WILSON'S DRAFTS

Compare Meghan Wilson's voice in her first, second, and third drafts. How would you describe the speaker in the first piece? In the second? In the third? How would you describe this kind of shaping process, starting over, and sketching, rather than reworking sentences one by one? Does Meghan's revision style seem harder than the one you typically employ? Easier? Do you think the second piece is better than the first? How? How not? Share your thoughts in a few paragraphs, and quote from Wilson's writing to back up your points.

Building a Personal Process

Instead of writing in general about something that happened long ago and far away, Meghan plunged herself into the heart of the conflict—a young high school girl, trapped by a gang of "mean girls." She eschewed all filters and generalities and wrote a single fast-paced scene, with specific word choices and close-up camera work. It took her multiple tries and four different shaping sessions, but when Meghan began the final version, excerpted above, she didn't stop writing for three hours! She completed ten pages, by hand, and made very few changes when she entered her work into the computer. The piece ended up in her portfolio. She wrote in her artist's statement:

> I was, I realize now, all these months after making this portfolio, just really scared to tell the truth. I mean, I was calling it fiction, but all of this was so close to home from the beginning. Even in the story version, originally, her name is Meghan! Oh my god. I was scared to go for the heart of the scene, so I screwed around with the waking up crap. It was really, really, really hard to relive those moments with those girls. And face who I was then. I cried. But, I also knew, when I was writing—I know this sounds . . . whatever. I knew this—with the fuck you—this is what I wanted to write. The truth. But it was hard. It was. Worth it though. Yeah, it took me like seven tries. I'm not even showing you the really bad ones!

The hardest thing about revision is seeing where it needs to go next. To me, the poem often feels done. But my peers push me to keep working.

—ANNALISE MABE

Shaping invites you to move in between the strategies, trying one, then trying another, then going back, trying again. You'll have to pick up different tools at different times in order to break through frustration, false starts, and into your deepest truths. Shaping asks you to be patient, flexible, honest, bold, and brave, or, in a word, creative.

In sum, instead of revising sentences, try reshaping the images themselves, choosing exciting visuals, changing camera lenses so you are using the telephoto, getting closer to your liveliest, most interesting subjects. Approaching revisions this way — with your senses, reconsidering what's really going on in the piece and why you are telling it — is hard work. But it's more efficient work, more rewarding, and ultimately more fun than crossing out a sentence and writing it over again, which often just feels like punishment.

| PRACTICE 5 |

ASSESSING YOUR REVISION PROCESS

After you shape one of your pieces, perhaps for your final portfolio, write two paragraphs on which strategies you used to revise and describe your experience with revision. What did you learn as a writer, in shaping this piece that you will be able to use in your next writing project?

EDITING AND PROOFREADING

Editing and proofreading are almost the opposite of shaping. Editing and proofreading are late-stage activities — the very last things a writer does before showing the work. Shaping and re-seeing are messy and wild, exactly like writing itself. Editing and proofreading require a hard copy, a pencil, and a kind of sitting-up-straight focus. You use a different head for these two tasks.

> *Writing is about hypnotizing yourself into believing in yourself, getting some work done, then un-hypnotizing yourself and going over the material coldly.*
>
> —ANNE LAMOTT

But all three of these activities have one thing in common. In each case, the writer must have strategies for dealing with unhelpful judgmental thoughts. She has to concentrate when she is working, and to cultivate a *helpful* focused concentration, she must postpone judgmental thoughts.

Revision is re-seeing and deep dreaming. Editing is making sure that the grammar and syntax are correct; that your verbs are in the appropriate tense; that your facts are accurate, sentences aren't clunky, line breaks are most effective, lines scan metrically, and titles are fresh and fitting. Editing is like giving your piece its annual physical examination. Are all the systems working properly? After you have re-seen your work and chosen the best scenes and images, worked hard to tell your story or perfect your poem, honed the opening and closing, polished the dialogue, and deepened the significance — only then are you ready to edit. Shaping works on the deep interior of the piece — the bones and the guts and the brain of the work. Editing checks to make sure that all the systems are hooked up to each other properly so we have a cohesive, smoothly running, healthy whole.

Proofreading is checking the skin. Proofreading is picking over the *surface* of your piece (as opposed to further illuminating the interior, as you do in writing and revising). Proofreading is the *opposite* of getting inside the piece and re-seeing all those alive moving images—it's the final check in the mirror before you go out the door. No awkward milk mustache. No bedhead. No bizarrely wrinkled pants, hanging threads, distracting mismatched socks. It's all surface stuff, but it's incredibly important. If you have a stain on your shirt during a job interview, it's going to distract the interviewer and define you as a sloppy person. Your words and experience won't be taken seriously. If you have typos, misspelled words, missing page numbers, or strange indents, your reader will be distracted. They want to be transported by your play, engaged by your story, blown away by your poetry. Your writing must be proofread so that the reader can have a relaxing experience. You owe it to your reader. Proofread. Smooth. Polished. Professional. Tip: Proofread backward, starting at the end of the piece and looking for errors so that you are not caught up in the story or progression, but are more able to focus on the surface. Also, it's easier to find errors in other people's work than in your own. (Did you find any mistakes in this textbook? Please let me know: sellersh@usf.edu.)

To proofread properly, go over every single syllable carefully with your eyes. Read the piece forward and backward. Literally, go from bottom to top at least twice so that you are more likely to find errors and less likely to be so caught in the "dream" you have worked so hard to create that you are blind to errors. And ask your writing group, or a partner, to look at your work, too. *Writers work with other writers.* It's well known that it's much harder to find mistakes in your own writing than that of others.

QUESTIONS TO ASK: Editing for Flow

Is your writing edited and ready to turn in, post, or send out? Consider the following questions before you submit your work.

1 Is your writing clear? Is it easy to understand who is talking, who is in the piece, where we are, and what is happening? (See Chapter One.)

2 Do you rely on weak verbs such as *to be* verbs, *should, could, would, might,* and *may*?

3 Do you overuse filters, words that describe mental activity, such as *seemed, felt, realized,* and *thought*? (See "Filters" on page 201.)

4 Do you explain too much?

5 Do you include too much description?

6 Do you use unnecessary adverbs?

Your instructor probably will have specific guidelines for turning in work. Various assignments and magazines and editors also have specific guidelines and format requirements. Always follow them to the letter.

Ask your instructor and your readers what errors they see most often in your work, and concentrate on correcting those. Consult your grammar handbook and learn why you make those mistakes and how to fix them. To progress as a writer, now is the time to learn the rules of grammar and style. Neither editors nor employers nor publishers will take your work seriously if it is plagued with serious grammar problems.

QUESTIONS TO ASK: Proofreading for Common Grammar Errors

Use your grammar handbook to check for the following common mistakes.

1. Have you chosen the word you meant to use? Frequently confused word pairs include *lie* and *lay*, *less* and *fewer*, *it's* and *its*, *that* and *which*, and *they're* and *their*, *your* and *you're*.
2. Do your subjects and verbs agree?
3. Do you have any misplaced modifiers?
4. Are there unintentional sentence fragments?

QUESTIONS TO ASK: Proofreading for Submitting Your Work

Sometimes you'll receive specific guidelines for preparing your work. Even if you don't, you should always address the following conventions.

1. Do you need a title page? If so, have you created one?
2. Are your pages numbered?
3. Are your margins at least one inch wide at the left, right, top, and bottom of every page?
4. Is the spacing between sentences, sections, and stanzas consistent?
5. Have you included any necessary headers and footers?
6. Have you followed punctuation conventions, especially for dialogue?
7. Have you checked your spelling?
8. Have you checked separately for typographical errors? For instance, you may have typed *from* instead of *form* or *then* instead of *than*. Spell checkers won't catch these errors since the words are spelled correctly. They just aren't the ones you intended to use.

WRITING PROJECTS

Experiment

1. Take a "failed" piece, one that you like, perhaps, but simply can't figure out how to improve. Decide to let it go. Don't delete it. Instead, devise a ritual for letting this piece go — for now. Some writers store these pieces in a special folder called "Attempts" or "The Trunk." (Every successful writer has a stack of "failures.") Write a paragraph on your process of letting go.

Fiction/Nonfiction/Poem/Drama

2. Choose one of your pieces. Use the diagram on page 395, and work through the wheel of strategies, one at a time, in order to shape the piece anew. Write a process statement — several paragraphs — where you explain what changes you made, tell why you made them, and reveal what your experience has been, shaping by strategy.

Fiction/Nonfiction/Poem/Drama

3. Choose a piece to re-see and shape, using the sketching technique, detailed on page 399. If the piece has more than one location, use the sketching technique, noting the five senses your main character or speaker experiences, for each new part of the piece.

Nonfiction/Drama

4. Take a poem, and recast it into a micro-essay or micro-memoir of 500–750 words, using three techniques in this chapter: sketching, working by hand, and looking closer.

Poem/Drama

5. Choose one of your plays from the semester, or write a one-page play. Then, turn your play into a fifteen- to thirty-line poem.

Fiction/Nonfiction

6. Take a piece of prose from the semester, fiction or nonfiction, and note the word count. Print the piece out, and work from a hard copy. You must now cut the piece exactly in half. Strike out extra sections, then sentences of explanation. Then work on the word level, cutting adjectives, adverbs — anything nonessential. Level up: Cut the piece in

half *again*. Compare your versions—which one is stronger and why? Write a paragraph of observation.

Drama

7. Take one of your plays, and recast it using only action, no dialogue. Then, try the play again as though for radio: Use only dialogue, no other sounds or action. Compare your versions: What did you notice? Write a paragraph of observation.

Poem

8. Take any of your free-verse poems and try the poem in a form. Choose from villanelle, pantoum, or sonnet. Write a paragraph of observation comparing the two poems. Which is more successful and why?

Fiction/Nonfiction/Poem/Drama

9. Edit and then proofread one of your pieces in final draft. How many changes did you make in editing? In proofreading? Write a brief paragraph on what kinds of changes you made and why. Explain what you did in the editing process and how that differed from your proofreading process. Now, trade pieces with another writer in your class. Edit and then proofread their piece. Write a brief paragraph: How many changes did you suggest in your peer's work? Did you do more editing or more proofreading? Is it easier to edit and proofread your own work or someone else's? Why?

SHAPE WORKSHOP

The prompts below will help you constructively discuss your classmates' work.

1. Read the piece aloud. Indicate all the parts that are "in image": that is, where you can *see* what's on the page as an image in your mind's eye.

2. Note any places where there are too many words or where the writer has trailed off into excess commentary or description. Often, revision involves simply cutting out extraneous material.

3. Reread the piece. Pretend it's a tiny movie. Make a list of the scenes—the visual, sensory moments—that the piece takes you through. Which are the most dramatic items on your list? Is the writer willing to cut the less dramatic sections, or replace them with new sections, or find a way to increase the depth and tension in these passages?

4. Review the Troubleshooting Energy checklist on page 210. In which places does the piece have good energy? In which places does the energy flag?

5. What patterns do you notice in this piece? Can you find visual patterns? Sound patterns? Where could the writer use pattern more actively?

6. Look back at Questions to Ask: Editing for Flow (see page 414). How does this piece of writing address the first three questions? How could it do so more overtly?

7. What is the single most memorable visual image from this piece of writing? What will you still be able to "see" in your mind's eye, perhaps long after this course has ended?

FORMS

I'm yet to find the correct name for this "condition"—hybrid writer, form merger, genre fluid—but I've stopped feeling like an imposter when someone tells me they're a novelist or an essayist. My writing life parallels my medical career—I'm a generalist.

LEAH KAMINSKY

I go around and take elements from different genres that can serve my needs. Not feeling as a writer that you're serving the genre, but that the genre is serving you.

CARMEN MARIA MACHADO

You write what you want to write in the way that it has to be.

ANNE CARSON

CHAPTER TEN

FINDING FORM

> ## In this chapter you will:
>
> - Build confidence and develop your creative abilities by studying a wide range of forms
> - Use form templates to compose new work
> - Modify, combine, and invent new forms to create innovative original pieces of writing

FORMS: RECIPES FOR WRITERS

This chapter presents a detailed guide to working in fourteen different forms, many of which can be developed in more than one genre.

By now, you're familiar with the four traditional genres used by writers in contemporary Western literature: poetry, creative nonfiction/memoir, fiction, and drama. You've looked at subgenres in each category: flash fiction, micro-memoir, free verse, and formal poetry, such as the sonnet and the villanelle. You've also considered comics and perhaps spoken word. This chapter helps you extend and deepen your practice in each of these genres and also invites you to experiment, combine, invent, and hybridize as you define yourself as a writer on the page and online, now and in the future.

> *Twitter is the perfect form for poetry.*
>
> —AI WEIWEI

Think of a form as a blueprint or a recipe for a specific kind of writing project. For example, a writer working in the genre of poetry may choose to create poems in the sonnet form or free-verse form. A playwright practices in various forms, including two-parters, ten-minute plays, or one-act plays, a common short form of play. Other writers push the boundaries of genre and create their work in between the traditional categories, writing in forms such as prose poems, spoken word, monologues in verse (rap is one example), or stories so short (the six-word story is a popular form, easily found online) that on the page they're indistinguishable from poetry. Other forms of creative writing refuse to fit neatly into the four main genres: comics, Twitter Moments, digital stories, digital poems, video essays, graphic novels, vouvelles, and text-and-image experiments, to name a few. But practicing the various forms presented here, across the genres—traditional and nontraditional—expands your skill and your vision as a writer. It's often been said that there's nothing new to say, only new ways to say it.

Because some writers come into creative writing with very fixed ideas about the genres they love most—*I am a poet,* or *I was born to craft plays*—some students dread certain forms, perhaps the sonnet or the essay because of a negative experience earlier in their education, or just a lack of familiarity with the breadth and range possible. But writers are people who, simply put, write. A strong writer can produce good work, on deadline, in *any* form.

So challenge yourself to write a piece in each of the forms presented in this chapter. Once again, this kind of cross-training in form strengthens your writing in surprising ways. A fiction writer improves her ear when creating a scene for a screenplay. Poets learn necessary aspects of narrative structure by writing short stories. Creative nonfiction writers *must* practice the basics of scene and characterization in order to create vivid, compelling, character-rich essays; for them, immersion in the craft of fiction is essential. Nonfiction tells the truth, but in a way that's story-forward and drama-rich. Poets and dramatists share a love for how words *sound* aloud; fantasy writers practice the ultra-challenging forms of sonnet and villanelle in order to hone their ability to create intricate, thrilling plots and structures.

You may likely discover you are capable of much more than what lies within the bounds of an early genre choice. Expanding your skillset and your range of tastes is not only the mark of a mature writer, it's also rewarding and fun.

You may try working with forms as writing projects throughout the course, choosing, say, one form per week, in order to apply the techniques you are learning in Part Two, Strategies. Or, at the end of the course, once you have practiced a wide range of creative writing activities and you have your craft techniques more or less mastered, you might create a portfolio of pieces, choosing from the genre-specific projects in this chapter. If you are working on your own, it's recommended you work through the forms in order. First, read the recipes included in this book. Then, read a few samples in this textbook and online and in other books. Then, practice the form *at least once* before you judge whether or not you like it.

> *I don't have much interest in writing if there are not opportunities to crack open the inherited forms. The writing I love to read most does this as well. I'm a form junkie.*
> —LIDIA YUKNAVITCH

Writing in the Genres

Form means shape and refers to the final structure of your piece of writing. What parts make it up? How are the parts put together? That's form. **Genre** means kind or type and refers to the specific category your writing fits into (or doesn't). Fiction, nonfiction, prose, poetry, and drama are examples of popular genres. There are subgenres, categories within the larger genres. For example, fantasy, horror, and detective fiction are all subgenres in fiction. The subgenres have categories within them, too. Epic fantasy, super hero, and magical realism are fantasy subgenres.

In this chapter, you essentially have a recipe book you can use to create pieces in various genres. Some forms are genre-specific, such as **pantoum**, **sestina**, **sonnet**, **and villanelle** — all forms of poems. But many forms can be used across genres, such as **abecedarius**, **anaphora**, **braid**, and **list**. Some forms, such as **journey**, list, and **monologue**, can be used to construct whole pieces, or they can be used as elements in a larger piece.

With these fourteen forms, you can build an entire writing life.

Table of Forms by Genre

	Poetry	Fiction	Drama	Nonfiction
Abecedarius	X	X		X
Anaphora	X	X	X	X
Braid	X	X	X	X
Graphic		X		X
Flash		X		X
Ghazal	X			
Journey	X	X	X	X
List	X	X		X
Monologue	X	X	X	X
Pantoum	X			
Play/Screenplay	X		X	
Sestina	X			
Sonnet	X			
Villanelle	X			

Figure 10.1 This table shows how various forms can be used across genres.

> *Passion, beauty,*
> *intensity—everything*
> *I care about in art—is*
> *made possible through the*
> *discipline of distance. Or, to*
> *say it another way: Powerful*
> *feeling in art takes place*
> *only through the particular*
> *kind of distance known*
> *as form.*
> —STEVEN MILLHAUSER

How to Create with Form

Forms are not confining, they are road maps. Form can often help you take your writing to unexpected places. Here are three strategies for getting the most out of your work with form.

Read, Read Again, Then Write. Read the form recipe straight through, carefully. Then, read at least two examples of the form you are going to be writing in. If you can, try to find diverse examples of each form, one example that breaks the rules, one that is a perfect example. Look for examples across the genres, too. And, when you notice a writer breaking the rules of a form, take a moment to reflect on why they might be doing so.

Try Each Form at Least Twice. The first time you try a form, focus on mastering the form itself, and attempt to conform to the guidelines carefully. You aren't trying to write great literature. You're just trying to pick up some new moves and understand how the form works. The second time you try a new form, it's healthy to intentionally break the rules (once you know exactly how they work). Your reader will consider it poor "form" if you make a hash of the guidelines, breaking the rules willy-nilly. But, after you've mastered a form, artfully experimenting with the template in order to create a fresh new form keeps creative writing *creative*. Many writers try a sequence in each form—a series of list pieces, a series of sonnets or monologues, in order to develop a cohesive body of work.

Begin Boldly. A recent study on perfectionism tested two groups of college students in their ability to read and then summarize a paragraph in a timed trial. The first group was made up of self-proclaimed perfectionists—hard-driving overachievers. The second group self-identified as "take it easy, like to have a good time" students. Professors who didn't know the groups' identities read the results of both groups. The self-proclaimed perfectionists *performed significantly worse than their counterparts!* They had trouble getting started. They kept starting over. They freaked out and often couldn't grasp the main point of the paragraph. The more easygoing students actually understood the deeper meaning of the reading and quickly wrote clear summaries.

Don't stress out trying to intellectually understand all aspects of the form. Read the recipe for the form you are working with straight through and then don't worry about what you don't understand. Plunge in! Begin writing your piece, consulting the recipe and the textbook and your models as you go, just as you would when cooking a meal using a recipe. You don't need to understand everything at once and it's okay if you are confused. Just start writing. The form rules will fall into place.

When it comes to forms, *not* trying too hard actually turns out to be a good thing.

A Note on Poetry

Many students, at first, find poetry to be the most challenging genre. Then, after learning and practicing a few times, they often produce such compelling work in the more demanding forms of verse that they change their minds, opening up to poems in a new way or even converting from another genre over to poetry. One student writer, Lakin Smith, said this about poetic form: "I'm not going to lie. At first I hated the sonnet. I hated the pantoum. I really hated villanelles. And then, at the end of the class, when I looked back over my work, those are my best pieces. I don't write that way—I'm not that confined all the time now—but what I learned about being compressed and using imagery changed the way I write forever." Other students have observed that poems, while often a struggle to write at first, usually come out more successfully because the forms require more time and effort. Yes, these poetic forms are sometimes harder, but because they require concentration and effort, many students find that once they "crack the code," poetry is a rewarding genre, one that feeds their writing in all other genres for years to come.

CREATING A PORTFOLIO OF FORMS

The forms that follow are sequenced alphabetically. You might want to try a piece of writing in each form, or perhaps you will focus on three or four genres: fiction, poetry, nonfiction, drama, working through various forms.

Each of the forms presented here requires you to use all the strategies from the course—Images, Energy, Tension, Pattern, Insight, and Shape. Because they are complex shapes, with varying design and skill challenges, the forms will each require several writing sessions. Remember the wheel of strategies you can use for shaping your work on page 395, and work through each strategy intentionally as you create your final piece. You'll also want to consider using the drawing techniques presented in Chapter Nine, Shape, as you plan your pieces and as a method for getting unstuck while you work in more demanding forms.

Lastly, students often keep this textbook on their shelf along with other writing guides because this chapter works well as a set of prompts for now and in the future. When you are blocked as a writer or simply seeking some new inspiration, returning to this chapter and picking a form at random can be a terrific jump-start to a stalled writing practice. There are endless combinations available to you as you play with form.

If you are in a multi-genre course that is featuring four genres, your final portfolio of forms might look like this:

Two Poems:	Pantoum, Sestina, Sonnet, and/or Villanelle
One Flash Fiction:	Incorporating Anaphora and/or Braid
One Memoir/Nonfiction:	Incorporating Abecedarius and/or List
One Drama:	Monologue or Five-minute play/Screenplay

Figure 10.2 A Traditional Portfolio of Forms

If you are in a multi-genre course of study that privileges experiment, hybridization, and innovation, your final portfolio might look more like this:

Any Genre:	Abecedarius
Any Genre:	Comic/graphic or text and image
Any Genre:	Journey
New Form:	A poem that is an invented new form of the student's design using elements of Pantoum, Sestina, Sonnet, and/or Villanelle in a completely new way
New Genre:	A piece in a form the student creates and names, in any genre or in a genre of their own invention. May be digital or have digital elements.

Figure 10.3 An Experimental Portfolio of Forms

FOURTEEN FORMS

ABECEDARIUS

An abecedarius is a piece of writing that is organized using the letters of the alphabet. For example, in a short story, the first sentence starts with the word *A* or a word beginning with *a*, the first word of the second sentence begins with the letter *b*, the first word of the third sentence begins with *c*, and so on for twenty-six sentences; the first word of the final sentence begins with *z*. In a poem, the first letter of each line is *a, b, c, d, e,* and so on, and the poem is twenty-six lines long. The lines may be of any length, but poets often keep the lines about the same length. In a memoir, the writer could label short sections with title words in alphabetical order, writing a paragraph of their personal story to go with each word.

Throughout history, people have used the alphabet to send coded messages and to communicate profound secrets, as well as to write trivial, superficial, goofy poems. The 119th Psalm is an abecedarius in Hebrew; Geoffrey Chaucer, Ezra Pound, and many other writers throughout the ages have used the form to great effect. The abecedarius can be silly or simplistic, but it can also be quite complex, beautiful, and intricate, with long lines or even paragraphs or chapters using the letters of the alphabet in sequence.

Tip #1: Avoid using words that correspond to the letters from your very first abecedarian book: "A is for Apple, B is for Boy, C is for Cat, D is for Dog." Your piece may slip into a sing-song or predictable rhythm if you choose those ultra-familiar words to shape your piece.

Tip #2: The hardest words to find good matches for are those starting with the letters *q, x,* and *z*. What are the most predictable choices? *Queen, xylophone,* and *zebra*. Avoid those words. If your reader can predict your word, your choice probably isn't fresh enough; predictable choices can bore readers.

Tip #3: A successful abecedarius doesn't strain: If you don't use the word *zuegmas* in your daily life, then you probably won't be able to create a smooth, thoughtful abecedarius. The alphabetical words should blend in with the rest of the poem so the reader doesn't even notice the abecedarian form.

You're well served to make lists from a search online, using a word-finding tool, so you have a stockpile of words, especially for the tricky letters, to choose from as your build your piece.

But it's probably just as helpful to keep working, from your own life, to get words that you actually use. *Xanthum gum*. On my desk right now is a snack wrapper with that word on it: *xanthum*. I see that word every day. So I look it up, and now I'm thinking that my abecedarius might be about food allergies. But before I start writing, I make lists of words that start with the remaining tricky letters. And I want lists of five to ten words so that I have some freedom to make different choices, depending on how my piece is unfurling.

What counts as a word? You get to decide. For example: *Ex-boyfriend.* Does *ex* count as the letter "x"? It *sounds* as though it starts with an "x." Because the sound of words is as important as how they look on the page, I'm going to use *ex-boyfriend* in my abecedarian.

Reading the Abecedarius

Read Natalie Diaz's "Abecedarian Requiring Further Examination of Anglikan Seraphym Subjugation of a Wild Indian Rezervation" on page 273. Now read the poem aloud, and again. It's a complex and richly textured poem. Did you notice the abecedarius form when you first read the poem? In a good abecedarius, the reader will be so caught up in the images and insights and pattern and sound work that they will not notice the form. Observe how the use of **enjambment**—ending lines in a poem mid-sentence, rather than ending lines with periods, at the end of a sentence—adds to the form: When we listen to the poem being read aloud and when we read the poem on the page, we don't notice the letter scheme as much because of the enjambment.

The abecedarius is a form that allows you to play with language and letters in all their glory. It embraces puns, double meanings, hidden messages, acrostics, codes, and wordplay. Notice Diaz's use of language.

Lastly, the abecedarius is related to the acrostic, in which the first letters of the lines spell a word. In a double acrostic, the final letters of each line or sentence also render the alphabet (forward or backward) or spell a word that has special meaning once you've read the piece.

You might also enjoy Edward Lear's "Alphabet" and Edgar Allan Poe's fascinating "A Valentine to _____," an acrostic that uses the first letter of his beloved's name as the first letter of the first line, the second letter of her name as the second letter of the second line, and so on, so that her name is spelled out on the diagonal from the top left to the bottom right of the poem. Another type of alphabet poem makes every word in the line begin with the same letter ("Andrea ate aardvark and") and progresses through the alphabet line by line.

But the abecedarius form is not limited to poetry. In addition to the alphabetical sentence technique mentioned at the outset of this form, fiction and nonfiction writers use section headings placed in alphabetical order to create pieces with twenty-six short sections. Clever writers come up with all kinds of ways to use the alphabet to build a form.

Further Reading

In This Book	Highly Recommended
• "Abecedarian Requiring Further Examination of Anglikan Seraphym Subjugation of a Wild Indian Rezervation" by Natalie Diaz (page 273)	• "Son of Mr. Green Jeans: An Essay on Fatherhood, Alphabetically Arranged" by Dinty W. Moore • "Abecedarius" by Pia Aliperti • "Another Poem for S." by Jessica Greenbaum

Writing an Abecedarius

1. You can come up with your own topic for this form; often, writers use something that has to do with words or literature: reading, writing, learning the alphabet, video gaming as an education, etc. If you are stuck with no subject, choose a friend or family member and write your piece to this person, someone you love or perhaps someone who is in need of comfort. Focus on the tensions and difficulties in the relationship (for example, a grieving friend who sometimes finds solace in faith, but not lately; a father-son relationship that is marked by neglect and misunderstanding, not fitting into the popular culture's definitions of fathering).
2. You might title your piece: "An Abecedarius for _____," and fill in the name of the person you are writing your piece to in the blank.
3. Begin your first line or section with a word that begins with the letter "B."
4. If you are writing a poem, remember to use enjambment. Don't end each line in the poem with a period—let your sentences wrap around to the next line. If you are writing a short story or poem, you might be using the next letter of the alphabet to start each sentence or you might be working in alphabetically titled sections—each section is an image, a little micro-story.
5. Avoid strained word choices (words you wouldn't normally use in your daily conversations), and avoid **inverted syntax** (mixing up the natural order of the words to fit the pattern). For example, you can't say "Zipper, my own, was broken." And try to stay away from simplistic word choices: "A wonderful man was my father./Boy, was that guy great."

ANAPHORA

Anaphora is the repetition of the first words in each line or sentence. As a form based on repetition, it's one of the most powerful ways to structure a piece of writing. Writers in all genres use anaphora to increase the energy, tension, insight, and overall power of their work. You can use anaphora when you want to make a strong point and have your readers remember your words. One of the most famous examples of anaphora is from Martin Luther King Jr.'s "I Have a Dream" speech:

> **I have a dream** that one day this nation will rise up and live out the true meaning of its creed: "We hold these truths to be self-evident: that all men are created equal." **I have a dream** that one day on the red hills of Georgia the sons of former slaves and the sons of former slaveowners will be able to sit down together at a table of brotherhood. **I have a dream** that one day even the state of Mississippi, a state sweltering with the heat of injustice, sweltering with the heat of oppression, will be transformed into an oasis of freedom and justice. **I have a dream** that my four little children will one day live in a nation where they will not be judged by the color of their skin but by the content of their character. **I have a dream** today.

Essayists and speechwriters, poets and politicians, even parents all use the device when they want to make a point, a big point: "*You are not* leaving this house. *You are not* playing Zelda. *You are not* leaving your room! *You are not!*"

Novelists use anaphora to establish authority, indicate profundity, and create energy. Perhaps the opening of Charles Dickens's *A Tale of Two Cities* is familiar to you:

> **It was** the best of times, **it was** the worst of times, **it was** the age of wisdom, **it was** the age of foolishness, **it was** the epoch of belief, **it was** the epoch of incredulity, **it was** the season of Light, **it was** the season of Darkness, **it was** the spring of hope, **it was** the winter of despair, **we had** everything before us, **we had** nothing before us, **we were all going direct** to Heaven, **we were all going direct** the other way. . . .

Reading Anaphora

Perhaps you have been told in a writing class, "Don't repeat yourself!" In grade school, you might have been mocked: "Stop repeating yourself. Stop repeating yourself. Stop repeating yourself." Anaphora is a form that *requires* you to repeat yourself. Notice the intentional use of repetition in the works you read and how the repetition affects you as a reader.

PRACTICE 1

ANAPHORA IN POETRY

A. Van Jordan invented a form, the dictionary poem. In his invented form, he uses anaphora. Read A. Van Jordan's dictionary poem, "af•ter•glow" (page 71). Where do you find anaphora? Underline each example. How many times does the poet use this form? What's the effect of all those repetitions? Write a paragraph response.

PRACTICE 2

ANAPHORA IN NONFICTION AND FICTION

Read "I Go Back to Berryman's" by Vincent Scarpa (page 76). This piece is written in the form of anaphora. Where do you see the form? Underline each example. What is the effect on the reader of the words that are repeated? Compare this author's use of anaphora to Michael Cunningham's in the opening of his short story "White Angel" (page 376). Notice how Cunningham captures the tightness of the brothers by repeating the word *we*. Do you see anaphora elsewhere in "White Angel"? Write a paragraph on each piece, describing the effect the anaphora has on you as a reader.

In "White Angel," anaphora underlines how bound the younger brother is to his older brother. He thrives on the *we*. But by repeating *we*, Cunningham also indicates that the brothers' experiences are the experiences of a generation and a subculture: At this age, in these times, on these drugs, you aren't an *I*—you're a *we* and part of something larger, and nothing, nothing could be sweeter. Pulling out the sentences that use the first-person plural pronouns, the poetry of Cunningham's prose becomes clear:

> We lived in Cleveland
> Our radios sang out love all day long
> We were four
> Between us were several brothers and sisters
> We are not a fruitful or many-branched line
> Our father . . . , our mother . . .
> We lived in a tract
> We have taken hits of acid with our breakfast juice

Anaphora can be as radically repetitive or as subtle as you wish. Author Michael Martone created a whole book of anaphora in his parody of contributor notes, titled *Michael Martone*, in which his own name, Michael Martone, appears over and over and over. Joe Brainard's book *I Remember* is an entire memoir in which each sentence begins with the words *I remember*. You may wish to explore the Poetry Foundation's section on anaphora at poetryfoundation.org.

With its focus on pattern, anaphora magically allows you to increase the depth and insight of your work, to stay with images longer to maximize their power, and to sustain energy and tension. It's a powerful technique for opening and closing a piece. It's loud, it's certain, and it's compelling. Anaphora is terrific form to use in every genre.

Further Reading

In This Book	Highly Recommended
• "Boys" by Rick Moody (page 219) • "af•ter•glow" by A. Van Jordan (page 71) • "I Go Back to Berryman's" by Vincent Scarpa (page 76) • "White Angel" by Michael Cunningham (page 376) • "The Things I've Lost" by Brian Arundel (page 217) • "Genealogy" by Betsy Sholl (page 213) • "We Real Cool" by Gwendolyn Brooks (page 105)	• "America" and "Howl" by Allen Ginsberg • *The Delight Song of Tsoai-talee* by N. Scott Momaday • *Song of Myself* by Walt Whitman • "The Tyger" by William Blake • *I Remember* by Joe Brainard • "Sonnet 66" by William Shakespeare

Writing an Anaphora

Anaphora is a form that amplifies whatever you are writing about. So for your anaphora, choose a topic you feel strongly about, something that is very personal to you. Here are some options.

1. Memoir anaphora: Think of a *we* you identified with strongly, a group you were very much a part of—a lifeguard crew in the summer of 2019; the high school "vaping behind the gym" girls; your rugby team; your basic training class. Write a memoir, letting the reader in on the very particular images that detail your exploits and passions, beginning each line with "We" and showing the group in action.

2. Write an anaphora piece that uses one of the following as the beginning for each line. In each case, write specific details, actions, and images. Name names. However old you are, that's how many lines your piece will have:

   - I used to _____, but now _____.[1]
   - I am so sorry _____ (*List the things you are sorry for that no one even knows you did.*)
   - I am not sorry I _____ (*List all the things you've done that have caused fallout for others, but it was worth it.*)
   - Every night we _____
   - I wish I never _____
   - I remember _____

---

[1]This prompt is adapted from *Rose, Where Did You Get That Red?* by Kenneth Koch.

3. Use anaphora to revise a work-in-progress. Take one of your works-in-progress and apply anaphora to the opening and the closing by choosing a key sentence and repeating the first words in that sentence throughout. Read the new version of your piece aloud. Do you prefer the new version or the old one? What's lost? What's gained?

BRAID

A braided piece uses different strands—usually three separate story lines or topics—and alternates sections sequentially among the three subjects. Think of how hair is braided, or bread, such as challah, or, if you grew up in the southern United States, maybe you braided the three strands of pine needles. The reader learns one beat from story A, then one beat from story B, and then one beat from story C. Then, usually, the story lines progress in order, and we get the next part of story A, then story B, then story C.

In a braided piece of writing, the three strands each have equal weight, and often the writer will form the piece of writing out of sections that are roughly the same length. A braided piece differs from a piece with a plot and a subplot. In the braided piece, each section matters as much as the other sections, and each of the narratives is fragmented—spliced among the two other strands in a neat pattern. Each topic is revealed to the reader slowly. As their third strand, writers often use someone else's voice—research, words from brochures or travel journals, and so on. This external voice is part of what gives the braid its depth and texture. You can use the braid form to create a whole book, such as Amy Fusselman's *The Pharmacist's Mate*, or as Beth Ann Fennelly does in *Heating and Cooling: 52 Micro Memoirs*, or a single standalone story or essay, such as JoAnn Beard's "The Fourth State of Matter", or a poem. This is a most flexible form: You can braid a poem or a play or a comic or a graphic novel.

The simplest stories—the ones little kids love, and the ones they tell—are usually *not* braided. The baby duck is lost, the duck needs its mother, the duck is lonely, the mother duck appears with snacks. No braid—it's a one-shot deal. When kids relate their dreams, it's usually a single, unlayered sequence, with no braiding: The monster was big, he was purple, he ate the family, then we went to the moon, we found a lot of candy there, and it was good. No braids here. Not a lot of dimension. Very little is expected of the reader.

Braids—story lines interwoven to create the whole piece—add depth, energy, layers, tension, and insight to your writing. Braids allow you to establish and play with pattern. For most readers, a good piece of writing usually needs to have more than one thing going on. Braiding is an easy, effective way to keep your reader reading—he's always waiting for the next part of the story to unfold. The juxtapositions between the story lines create depth, surprise, subtext, and meaning.

Reading Braids

When you read braided pieces, you first want to identify the two or three story lines. The author Amy Fusselman used three strands to create a braid for her book *The Pharmacist's Mate*. The three story lines include a) her trying to get pregnant, b) her coping with grief after her father dies, and c) verbatim excerpts from her father's journals (he was a pharmacist's mate when he served in the military). The three braids — pregnancy, grief, and her father's diary entries — weave together in interesting and meaningful ways. While Fusselman wants to create new life — to get pregnant — there's been a terrible end of life: the loss of her father. We get to meet her father — she brings him to life for us — through his journal entries, kept while he was serving on a ship, ministering to others' health needs. Each moment in one story line is juxtaposed with moments in the others, both visually and emotionally. The reading experience is tension-filled and very powerful. Once your readers "get" your structure, a braid keeps them engrossed, as they figure out how the disparate parts relate.

Here is the exact structure of Fusselman's piece:

STRAND A   Yearning for a family of her own

STRAND B   Grieving for her father

STRAND C   Journal entries from her father in the military

When Fusselman sat down to form her book, she used a single paragraph from each story line, and she alternated them, one after the other, until she was done.

Some writers write out each story separately and then cut each story line into sections, laying them out in the ABC alternating sequence. Others work one section at a time. In a delicious form mash-up, some writers, like Dinty Moore, combine braiding with abecedarius. Moore's "Son of Mr. Green Jeans: An Essay on Fatherhood, Alphabetically Arranged" braids four threads: 1) his own coming of age as a boy and as a parent himself, 2) his father's lessons and rules, 3) bizarre and fun facts from extreme nature, and 4) pop culture references relating to fathering. He includes descriptions of questionable fathering wisdom from 1950s sitcoms, ones that were likely playing in the background of the author's childhood. He doesn't rotate his four strands in a predictable pattern. Instead, Moore uses the alphabet to create headings for sections such as "Bees," "Carp," "Divorce," "Emperor Penguins," and so forth, and he tells his four stories in very short paragraphs — just a sentence or two — from A to Z. He sometimes has several animal sections in a row, then he jumps to an image from his own life, and then to his father's Irish history.

When student writer Charlie Walter began his braided memoir, he made three lists of subjects from his personal life:

STRAND A   Dramatic scenes from his hearing loss/medical doctor saga

STRAND B   Dramatic scenes from trying out for a rock band

STRAND C   Dramatic scenes from his attempts to learn to play guitar

He had about ten images for each strand. When Charlie was composing his braided essay, he carefully spliced them together in an ABC ABC ABC pattern; the final memoir had nine short sections. As he worked, at first he felt that his braids didn't really relate enough. But in the final piece, the sections interrelate in surprising and interesting ways. In a climactic scene about his ear surgery, the lights go out when he is in the hospital. That scene dovetails with Charlie's musical debut in front of five hundred people—the lights go on and suddenly Charlie *can't* see his audience. He also can't hear well. The auditorium suddenly seems like another kind of operating theater. The juxtapositions between sections in a braid can spark exciting new ideas and insights. The writer has to trust the form.

Because braids keep your story moving crisply forward, braids are good for topics that are heavy: your mom's cancer, your profound anxiety disorder, the death of your high school girlfriend. Often those subjects, treated alone, can grow ungainly and sentimental and feel overwhelming or too heavy for your reader. Braids force leaps, and leaps keep your writing fresh and fascinating. Essentially, a braid is a mosaic of discrete, independent images that work together to form a cohesive whole. Try combining three subject matters that don't quite go together, and see what happens when you braid.

Playwrights use braiding: Three characters each take turns offering monologues, rotating in turn. Poets braid, using stanzas to separate out the sections of the various threads. Three sections (just as with hair-braiding) work extremely well. Two sections can work well, too. More than four is asking a lot of your reader—they have to hold a great deal of material in their head. Keep your sections crisp, visual, energetic, tension-filled, and short.

Further Reading

Highly Recommended

- "Braided Essays" by Nicole Walker
- "Swimming" by Joel Peckham
- "A Braided Heart" by Brenda Miller
- "When We Played" by Matthew Komatsu
- "Time and Matter Overcome" by Eula Biss
- "Braiding" by Li Young-Lee

Writing a Braid

1. Make a list of moments in your life that have been most difficult for you. They should be action-oriented, not thought-oriented—you need moments when you were doing something around other people. Dating, auditioning, getting engaged (a different kind of auditioning, right?), buying a new car, dealing with a judge during a court case, moving out from your apartment and into a new place, your first day on the curling team, being the daughter of a bipolar mother at your sister's wedding, the time when your anger management class went horribly wrong—you want a list of lively, dramatic, and specific difficulties. Trying to choose a major, deciding to go to law school, thinking about how weird your family is—those more abstract feeling states are hard to braid because they are made of thoughts taking place in your head, not scenes and images. You need passions that take you out into the world. Things you don't do well but care about immensely are good subjects for braiding because they inherently lend themselves to tension-filled scenes.

2. Discuss your list of images with a writing partner and/or your instructor. They can tell you what's most interesting to them. Choose two topics.

3. For each topic you choose, make a list of all the dramatic images that make up this story line. For example, in the "Failed to Ever Talk to Emily" story, the key images are the day you first saw her in Health Dynamics; the day you fell down the stairs and she was standing at the bottom and she didn't laugh; the week you spent preparing to talk to her out, but each day you walked right past her and pretended you didn't know her; the day when you sat next to her in class and said, "Dude, hey." Using your mind's eye, cast over this story from day one, when it all started, which may be a few years back. Do this for both of your story lines. If you don't like your images or you want to change your mind, review your list of ideas and choose a different strand to work with. Once you decide on the two best topics, make a list of about five to ten action scenes for each topic.

4. For your third braid, use text someone else has written (citing your sources, of course). You can use family letters or someone's journal (as long as you have permission). One student wrote about the tragic death of her roommate (braid A) and her own depression (braid B). For braid C, she interspersed quotes from brochures at the health center, which were inadvertently hilarious and added levity but also some political commentary: Not a single brochure was even remotely helpful. Another student writer, Christian Piers, used his great-great-uncle's journals, which told of the family's coming to America on a ship called *The Albatross*; while on this long sea journey, the uncle fell in love and got married. Christian braided short, lively excerpts from the journals

with two personal stories: his (consistently disastrous) social life and his participation in a historic college tug-of-war. When Christian showed the class his pieces, which he didn't think went together well, he was shocked at what his classmates noticed. First of all, he was a lot like his uncle. Second, the river over which the epic tug-of-war took place was the same river *The Albatross* had come up 150 years earlier! Christian had not made the connection. And that was just on page 1. Trust your separate braids to work together; let them create surprise, meaning, pattern, and depth on their own.

Brainstorm ideas for your braid C, drawing from science texts, found texts, old magazines from your grandmother's garage, vintage etiquette books for girls or boys, travel guides, or brochures from your campus health office. If you are writing about a video game obsession, the online cheat codes and attendant commentary might be braid C. If you are writing about your shopping compulsion, the guidelines from Consumer Credit Counseling might create an ironic counterpart. If you are writing about your autistic brother and your own struggles to bring creativity into your life, your braid C might draw from recent neuroscience exploring creativity and the autistic brain.

5. Working from your lists of images, write the images from your three topics and alternate them ABC ABC ABC ABC ABC so that you end up with fifteen short sections. Each of your five sequences will contain one scene (or line, stanza, or paragraph, depending on which genre you are working in) from each of the three strands, in order.

Try your braid in the genre of memoir, as suggested here. If you like, try your next braid as a play or a poem. Consider writing a braided micro-memoir and braided flash fiction.

COMICS AND GRAPHIC NARRATIVES

Comics and graphic narratives are stories or poems using a combination of text and image. Drawing skill can vary widely in this form. Creative writers—even those with weak drawing skills—can learn a lot from practicing storytelling in this form, which has surged in popularity. Writer Annalise Mabe explains: "Some writers collaborate with artists. Other writers learn how to draw or have always drawn. The styles range from very realistic to very cartoony and simplistic, so really, anyone can comic (yes, it's a verb too)."

> *Cartooning is not really drawing at all, but a complicated pictographic language intended to be read, not really seen.*
>
> —CHRIS WARE

Graphic and comic poems and narratives can be humorous, fictional, serious, historical, ridiculous, memoir, instructional, fantastic. In some examples, the artwork is quite impressive and inventive; in others, stick figures and rough sketches contribute to the visual charm of the form.

Reading Comics and Graphic Narratives

From the comics in daily newspapers, to the longer, richer Sunday comics, to Marvel comic books, manga, *Peanuts* and Fantagraphics anthologies, and on to the prize-winning books by Art Spiegelman (*Maus*) and Marjane Satrapi (*Persepolis*), the house of graphic works is a many-roomed mansion. Some people adore reading this form; however, others feel challenged trying to track both a visual and a verbal narrative.

Some graphic stories are designed specifically for electronic readers. And, of course, some video games are essentially interactive graphic novels, some of them wildly innovative and sophisticated in terms of not only the visual elements but also the story and philosophy behind the visuals.

This is an important form to study. Its power has saturated the publishing industry, with new textbooks in composition, physics, and speech-making using the conventions of the graphic novel. Challenge yourself to read widely in this genre and branch out from your stable of beloved favorite authors. Creators who have crossover appeal include Marguerite Abouet, author of *Aya*; Erika Alexander, author of *Concrete Park*; and Taneka Stotts, who edited *Beyond: The Queer Sci-Fi and Fantasy Comic Anthology*. You may be interested in GB Tran's *Vietnamerica: A Family's Journey*, the Hernandez Brothers' *Love and Rockets* series, Chester Brown's *I Never Liked You*, graphic short stories by Adrian Tomine, and Gabrielle Bell's "Book of" series (*Book of Sleep, Book of Insomnia, Book of Black*, and others). Bell is well known for creating a comic a day for a month and then making booklets of these works. Two highly respected print publishers of graphic works are Drawn and Quarterly and Fantagraphics; you can examine their catalogs for new and classic examples. Online, look for comics at *Hobart* and *The Rumpus*. Each time you search, you may find that a new zine pops up, featuring artists from around the world.

The classic resource on how to develop work in this form is Scott McCloud's *Understanding Comics: The Invisible Art*, an outstanding textbook in comic form. Lynda Barry's comic books on craft are also extremely helpful, especially *One! Hundred! Demons!, What It Is, Syllabus*, and *Making Comics*—a terrific introduction. Alan Moore's *Writing for Comics* and Jessica Abel and Matt Madden's *Mastering Comics* are two popular high-quality resources.

Further Reading

In This Book	Highly Recommended
• "Robot Camp" by Jarod Roselló (page 29)	• *Fun Home* by Alison Bechdel • *Sacred Heart* by Liz Suburbia • *Far Arden* by Kevin Cannon • *Nimona* by Noelle Stevenson • *Skim* by Mariko Tamaki

Writing a Comic or Graphic Narrative

This flexible form encompasses a wide range of possibility. You might create a single-panel comic, with your image and text in one frame. Common forms include the three-panel strip, the four-panel strip, and multiple strips stacked on top of each other or combined together to tell a story, as in Sunday newspaper comic sections. Then there are comic books (usually twenty-two-page booklets), anthologies of comics, web comics, and long-form graphic novels and graphic memoirs.

In creating the form, you'll notice that it has a lot more in common with plays and screenplays than with other traditional genres. Screenplays and graphic works are both visual forms, driven by strong storytelling interlaced with powerful images: the perfect training ground for a new writer.

PRACTICE 3

CREATING A SIMPLE COMIC

Divide a sheet of paper into four squares. Using no text — only images — in each square (and ignoring your limitations as a visual artist for now — just use stick figures if you like), answer these four questions with a quick drawing, one in each panel:

1. Who are you?
2. Where are you from?
3. Who is your family?
4. What do you do?

Remember — you can't use any words. Set a timer and limit yourself to five minutes for the comic. Members of your class may post or choose to hang their drawings on a wall of the classroom to share them and get to know one another better.

> ### PRACTICE 4
>
> #### NINE-PANEL COMIC
>
> Divide a sheet of paper into nine equal frames (a giant tic-tac-toe grid). Using text and image in the frames (some panels might be just text or just image), take us through your day today, starting with breakfast and projecting on into the evening. Set a timer: Limit yourself to ten minutes to make this comic.

Creative writers also use comics and graphic narratives as a tool for close reading, creating a visual outline of a story or poem in order to see its working parts cleanly and clearly. Writers also create graphic representations of narratives and novels using comic techniques—this is called storyboarding and it's a quick and effective way to see if you have enough action, and if the plot builds and makes sense, saving hours and hours of writing time.

> ### PRACTICE 5
>
> #### USING COMICS TO CLOSE READ NARRATIVE
>
> Working from an existing text, re-create the story in a nine panel comic. You don't need drawing talent—stick figures are fine. Choose "Where There's Smoke" on page 274 or "Cathedral" on page 125. Which nine scenes do you *have to have* in order to tell this story? Practice placing abbreviated core bits of the dialogue in panels and relying mostly on action. Your task is to isolate the key scenes in a story. Share your comics with classmates and discuss differences in approach.

"Reverse engineering" or storyboarding existing work helps you better understand how to structure your own creative writing. It works for poems too.

> ### PRACTICE 6
>
> #### USING COMICS TO CLOSE READ POETRY
>
> Reread "Buying Wine" on page 71. Create a four-panel comic of the poem, using text sparsely, if at all. Share your comic with classmates and discuss your choices.
>
> You can also use comics to plan your own work; many writers rely heavily on storyboarding.

> ### PRACTICE 7
>
> #### STORYBOARDING YOUR NARRATIVES
>
> Take one of your existing stories or essays and use it to create a four- or nine-panel comic of your piece of writing. Write a short statement on what you observe about the strengths and weaknesses in your existing story after you have looked at it through this lens. Now, plan your next story or essay using a four- or nine-panel comic to predict which scenes you will write.

Comics are not just a great tool for writers. To write a longer or a full-length graphic novel, graphic memoir, or graphic short story or comic, the first decision you have to make is a very straightforward one: Will you use a story you've already written and convert it into the format required for a graphic novel? Or will you create a brand-new story?

As you decide which route to take, you will most likely choose to write a fast-moving, hard-hitting, character-driven tale with an exciting linear plot. You'll probably follow the journey form (see page 449) or the traditional three-part conflict–crisis–resolution structure (see page 99). But you might choose a more meditative or poetic approach, using lists, anaphora, or a more impressionistic structure. The house of comics is huge and all styles are welcome.

In a graphic narrative, you don't have the time or space to include descriptions of setting, interior thoughts, reactions, or detailed histories of the characters, their conflicts, or their world. Everything has to move — fast — and you will be using dialogue and action scenes to make things move.

Read your story draft and imagine each interior or descriptive passage as one of these three options:

- Create dialogue scenes. (Can one character ask another a question to get this information across?)
- Cut the passage. (Can you delete most of the backstory and save only the sentences that are crucial for reader understanding?)
- Simplify. (Can you pare the story down to its essential bones?)

Cut dialogue scenes where conversation is filler. Conversations in which nothing is moving forward don't work in graphic novels any better than they do in prose. Shorten or eliminate as many conversations as you can — any talking that isn't significant should be deleted. Writing sparingly is excellent training for any writer. (Maybe all novelists should have to try their projects as graphic novel scripts.)

Translate dialogue into quick strokes. In a graphic novel, dialogue is a series of swift, short sentences. The dialogue bubbles are very small, and the art takes up most of the room in each frame, so there's not a lot of room for chit-chat. As a general rule, budget yourself to forty words maximum per panel. Try not to go over budget.

Storyboard your project. Once you have streamlined and pared down your story to basic speech and action, the fun begins. Think of your story's steps in terms of pages. Each page is its own micro-world. A graphic novel or memoir is often ninety-six physical pages, printed front and back, for a total of 192 content pages. Pages that face each other relate events in the reader's mind in a different way than do back-to-back pages. With physical books, when you turn the page, there's a beat, a pause.

You'll want to practice setting story steps out on pages so you get a feel for the flow of your book. Even if you are practicing with a shorter graphic work, storyboard each page so that you know the shape of your project.

You don't necessarily need art talent to do this kind of work, though of course it helps. And the more you draw, the better you will get, just as with your writing craft. Meanwhile, your training as a poet (having to get a lot of information into a small space in a meaningful and interesting way) will serve you well. Your training as a story writer is your foundation. You can do sketches or simply use words to practice building pages. In fact, many successful graphic novelists and memoirists collaborate with artists; very few people are highly skilled in both *story structure* and *drawing*. But you can create evocative, interesting images by hand—you'll be surprised at how much you already know. Lastly, consider using graphic elements in poems and texts. Bruce Eric Kaplan's *I Was a Child* is a perfect example of how drawings can enhance a story.

FLASH

Is it possible to write a novel in six words? Ernest Hemingway allegedly wrote what he called a novel in a sentence:

> For sale: baby shoes, never worn.

Is this a novel? A short story? Based on the sentence, what do you know about the situation? Whether or not authorship can be attributed to Hemingway, these six words serve to illustrate just how much a writer can accomplish in a tiny amount of space. In the digital age, brevity is ever more relevant—Tumblr, blogs, and Twitter all help flash and micro-forms flourish. Print and online literary magazines also feature high-quality, critically acclaimed flash and micro-forms, and these small tableaus create a growing canon in the field of creative writing.

Flash fiction is a short story that is 2,000 words or fewer. The stories are sharply focused, imagistic, and tightly wound pieces of prose, usually centered around intense moments of human experience. Some practitioners set the word limit at 750 words, others at 250 words. Nano-fiction is even shorter: 100 words or fewer. Flash fiction came into its own in the 1990s; some key anthologies of the genre include *Sudden Fiction*, *Flash Fiction*, and *Micro Fiction*.

Short nonfiction has long been a mainstay in periodicals and newspapers. As a form for creative writers, it began to flourish anew in the 1990s. *In Short*, *In Brief*, and *Short Takes* featured writers such as Naomi Shihab Nye, Michael Ondaatje, Terry Tempest Williams, Denis Johnson, and Russell Edson, many of whom published prose poems before the terms "brief essay," "flash nonfiction," and "micro-memoir" gained wide acceptance. Micro-memoir has this in common with prose poetry: It's short, with tightly packed language and concise imagery. Micro-memoir uses quick scenes; it turns on action. *The Rose Metal Press Field Guide to Writing Flash Nonfiction*, edited by Dinty Moore, lists journals that are well known and well respected for their focus on flash and micro: *DIAGRAM*, *Hippocampus*, and *Sweet: A Literary Confection*. *Creative Nonfiction* features an ongoing "#cnftweet" competition called "Tiny Truths," which requires that stories be no longer than 140 characters.

Flash pieces aren't excerpts from longer works. They stand on their own. They require urgency, intensity, and a high level of energy. Dinty Moore explains:

> Imagine there is a fire burning deep in the forest. In an essay of a conventional length, the reader begins at the forest's edge, and is taken on a hike, perhaps a meandering stroll, into those woods, in search of that fire. The further in the reader goes, with each page that turns, the more the reader begins to sense smoke in the air, or maybe heat, or just an awareness that something ahead is smoldering.
>
> In a very brief essay, however, the reader is not a hiker but a smoke jumper, one of those brave fire fighters who jump out of planes and land 30 yards from where the forest fire is burning. The writer starts the reader right at that spot, at the edge of the fire, or as close as one can get without touching the actual flame. There is no time to walk in.

Short pieces need to be highly compressed, filled with tension, and carefully observed. They're often filled with lyrical language. The author's intention is always to have the story linger in the reader's mind.

PRACTICE 8

CREATING A SIX-WORD FLASH

Take one of the short stories you've written and tell the story in six words. You can choose six words from the existing story, or translate the story into six words. Share the new short story with your peers. As you respond to their six-word stories, note what's gained and what's lost.

Reading Flash Fiction and Micro-Memoir

Flash fiction and micro-memoir, because they share some of the compression of poetry, will reward the reader who spends time going over the piece, reading more than once, reading aloud. In most of these pieces, as with poetry, you will find one or two hard "turns" — changes in direction. Because these are narratives, look for dialogue, conflict, and scene — just as in a full-length story or memoir.

PRACTICE 9

GETTING FAMILIAR WITH BREVITYMAG.COM

One of the most respected websites for flash nonfiction and micro-memoir is Brevitymag.com. The site features many examples of the form as well as craft essays, in which writers discuss strategies for succeeding with these jewel-like pieces. Scan through the website and locate two pieces you really enjoy. Write a brief, two-paragraph commentary on what you like about these two pieces and share with your classmates.

In creative writing, it's often said that the tighter the container, the more powerful the emotions the author can present to the reader. Because the flash form is compressed, writers are able to write about powerful, overwhelming subjects—betrayal, domestic abuse, lives imploding. In a longer work, the reader might be overwhelmed with unrelenting heaviness. In flash, hot bursts of intensity work extremely well.

Before you begin your flash piece, reread the flash/micro work in this textbook. Take some time to annotate each of these pieces, noting in the margins where you see 1) images, 2) energy, 3) the details that provide clues to the conflict, and 4) the patterns the author has used.

After you've read flash and micro, and closely studied some examples, it's time to write your own.

Further Reading

In This Book	Highly Recommended
• Selections from *Heating and Cooling* by Beth Ann Fennelly (pages 215 and 216)	• "The Rememberer" by Aimee Bender
• "How to Erase an Arab" by Julie Azzam (page 333)	• "Lost" by Pamela Painter
• "I Go Back to Berryman's" by Vincent Scarpa (page 76)	• "The Deck" by Yusef Komunyakaa
• "How to Touch a Bleeding Dog" by Rod Kessler (page 277)	• *Brevity* magazine (online) https://brevitymag.com
• "Swerve" by Brenda Miller (page 124)	• *In Brief: Short Takes on the Personal* edited by Judith Kitchen and Mary Paumier Jones
• "The Things I've Lost" by Brian Arundel (page 217)	• *Short: An International Anthology of Five Centuries of Short-Short Stories, Prose Poems, Brief Essays, and Other Short Prose Forms* edited by Alan Ziegler
• "Two Hearts" by Brian Doyle (page 375)	
• "Chop Suey" by Ira Sukrungruang (page 74)	
• "Counting Bats" by Thao Thai (page 168)	
• "What I Do on My Terrace Is None of Your Business" by Och Gonzalez (page 45)	• World's Best Short Short Story Contest at *The Southeast Review*

Writing Flash Fiction

1. Work with a designated word limit: one sentence, 250 words, 500 words, or 750 words.
2. For your subject, choose a moment of high intensity, and *do* think in scene: For inspiration, focus on the moment you quit your job, the moment you got busted for cheating, the last car ride you took with your wildest friend, the moment you realized he wasn't just wild, but actually dangerous. Choose something you know well.
3. Consider beginning in action and staying in action. Consider a strong turn in the last sentences, a change in direction that will surprise your reader and create that necessary moment of insight — the "flash."

Writing Micro-Memoir

When writing micro-memoir, you can follow the same approach you use for writing flash fiction, with a very important caveat: You can't make anything up. If you use direct dialogue, in quotation marks, it should be exactly what was spoken. If you can't remember exactly what was said, you might use italics for the dialogue or adopt Brenda Miller's technique in "Swerve": "I would apologize for the eggs being overcooked, and for the price of light bulbs, and for the way the sun blared through our trailer windows and made everything too bright. . . ." She clearly indicates what was said, but she doesn't put it in direct dialogue. She doesn't have the exact quotations. And what matters is the content, and the fact that she said these things many, many times.

Beth Ann Fennelly is expert at being extremely brief, and her micro-memoirs sparkle like diamonds because of it. Note how she chooses a single, pointed moment or she uses two moments, back to back, to tell a larger story. And, notice how Julie Azzam uses pattern, as a poet would, to create an interesting way of telling her deeply personal story.

Here are the keys to writing successful micro-memoir:

1. Use specific details set in a strong action line.
2. Use dialogue lines that reveal character and are surprising and interesting.
3. Use pattern and repetition to create a structure.
4. Strive for a strong turn at the end.
5. Be as brief as possible.

In both flash fiction and micro-memoir, there are some important ground rules:

1. Surprise endings do not work. Some endings have been used so often that they are no longer effective: "And then he woke up." "And then her alarm went off." "And then she was dead." Moreover, lines like

these don't work because the reader has just experienced a trick, not a meaningful exchange of emotion in image.

2. Don't go over the word count, adjust your font or margins, or bend the rules in any other way.

3. Don't write about thoughts and feelings (there are always exceptions). Flash fiction and micro-memoir are mini-movie forms. Use characters, scene, action, and dialogue, and stick with the presentational mode.

4. Don't label your story; think of the title as the first line of the piece — it should show your story already in motion. The title is going to do a lot of the heavy lifting in your flash and micro.

GHAZAL

The ghazal is a nonlinear poem written in long-line couplets (two-line stanzas) in which the end word or end words in the second line of each stanza repeat or echo. There are usually five to twelve couplets in a ghazal, though the poem can be of any length. The first stanza has a different rule than the rest of the stanzas: Both lines in the first stanza end with the same word. That end word is used to end the *second line* of all the following stanzas. Here's an example of how this works:

Stanza one:

> Here's an example of how the repeating words work in stanza **one**.
> The end words in both lines of this stanza repeat, but only for this **one**.

Stanza two, stanza three, stanza four, etc.:

> Here's an example of how the repeating words work in the other stanzas.
> The repeating word is at the end of every *second* line — neat! — every
>   single **one**.

There's no rhyming at the end of the line in a ghazal. Instead the rhyming words — two or three or four syllables of rhyming — appear in the second lines, all through the poem, *right before the repeating end word*.

With the rhyme scheme added, the first two stanzas of the ghazal look like this:

Blue Ghazal

My eyes are pale _____. Sometimes I am Lapis Lazuli, and I'm
    deep **blue**.
Guess the color of my rooms and clothes from the clue, **man, right? Blue**.
Rain in Florida pours down every day in summer, music and terror.
Everyone else is inside; I'm dancing in the drops; I **am bright blue**.

Note how the first stanza differs from the rest of the stanzas—the end words match. The rest of the stanzas will have two or more rhyming syllables *before* the repeating end word in the second line. But only the second line, from stanza two on, has the rhyme and the repeating end word.

PRACTICE 10

LEARNING THE FORM OF A GHAZAL

Locate "Hip-Hop Ghazal" by Patricia Smith online at www.poetryfoundation.org. Print a copy and carefully underline the repeating words at the ends of the lines and note the rhyme scheme in the second lines. This is a perfect model for a ghazal.

In addition to the interesting word patterns, the ghazal has another important feature. The couplets are not written in a straightforward story format. In the ghazal, each couplet is a mini-poem, meant to stand on its own, almost like a proverb or a saying, only very loosely related to what has come before. So the idea is to leap around, covering many topics, always coming back to the key repeating words in line 2 of every stanza. Ghazals are always written in couplets, usually five to twelve stanzas (ten to twenty-four lines) in length, but they can be much longer.

When you are choosing your subject for this poem, it's helpful to know a little bit about its history. The ghazal comes from Persian poetry; it flourished in the Middle East between 1100 and 1500. The form appears in Arabic, Urdu, and Turkish traditions. In Arabic, *ghazal* (pronounced "guzzle") means "the talk of boys and girls." In their earliest versions, ghazals focused on flirting, chatting up, expressing affection for a lover with this poetic song form. Later poets used the ghazal for spiritual, philosophical, and religious purposes. There is a long tradition of ecstatic spiritual ghazal, focusing on the mystical aspects of devotion to one's God. The form became popular in the Western world in the 1960s. So for your ghazal, you may want to work in that tradition and focus on the topics of love, having fun hanging out with friends, spirituality, or religion.

One last feature to pay attention to. Often the author of a ghazal will work their name into the last stanza of the poem, in effect "signing" the ghazal. Notice how Patricia Smith refers to herself in her last stanza of "Hip-Hop Ghazal." Other writers sew their name into the final couplet in subtle ways; for example, in a ghazal I wrote recently, in the final couplet I refer to the small flowering shrub, heather, which grows outside the booksellers' stand at my local market.

Reading Ghazals

The ghazal is associative (like a list). Instead of taking one idea and developing it as in a sonnet or a story, the poet takes disparate images and lays them next to each other, as you might on your coffee table—your personal arrangement of beautiful or intriguing objects. The two-line stanzas (couplets) sit in the reader's mind side by side, not to develop a linear argument, but to refract off each other. It's a list poem and it's a collage poem.

Read a few more ghazals online. Agha Shahid Ali is a renowned practitioner. You might enjoy "Derecho Ghazal" by Luisa Igloria, and "Red Ghazal" by Aimee Nezhukumatathil. These along with many more excellent examples of the ghazal can be found at the Poetry Foundation website. Print out and annotate your favorites, noting in the margins what each couplet boils down to, and underlining the sound repetitions. When you read ghazals, don't try to figure out a story. There really isn't one. Approach the ghazal as you would a mosaic, or a collage. Enjoy each stanza as its own little mini-poem.

As you read, notice how poets create variations on the repeating word, such as *red*, *read*, *dread*, *bred*, *reddened*, and *unread* as ghazal author Aimee Nezhukumatathil does. Notice how poets also use ear rhyme, as poet Ellen Doré Watson does in her ghazal "Ghazal," rhyming the words *core* and *corps*, which is an interesting and creative way of bending the rules and earning style points. Feel free to do the same when you write your ghazal, choosing words like *son* and *sun* or *be* and *bee*, words that sound alike but have different meanings.

Further Reading

Highly Recommended

- "Hip-Hop Ghazal" by Patricia Smith
- "Hustle" by Jericho Brown
- "Red Ghazal" by Aimee Nezhukumatathil
- "Where You Are Planted" by Evie Shockley
- "Many" by Agha Shahid Ali
- "Derecho Ghazal" by Luisa Igloria

Writing a Ghazal

1. Choose your subject. Usually the title of a ghazal names the subject: "Red Ghazal" or "Hip-Hop Ghazal."
2. Each stanza is made of one couplet (two lines). Plan on writing five to fifteen couplets on your subject; seven is typical. Considering enjambment: wrapping your lines within the couplet, and also consider

enjambment between stanzas. Just make sure you follow the rules for end words and the rhyme scheme.

3. Each couplet in the poem is close to the same length. The lines are long, at least fourteen syllables. Each couplet is a separate poem.
4. Repeat the same end word at the end of both lines in the first couplet.
5. Create rhyming syllables for the two to four syllables *before* the end word at the end of the second line in each succeeding couplet.
6. Put your name in the final couplet. Historically, the last couplet is the "signature" couplet, in which the poet "sews" in their own name.)

As you shape your ghazal, here are some tips:

- Make your lines long and all about the same length.
- Write about your current important obsessions, faith, politics, or love—and make sure to use images and specific visual details.
- Don't try to tell a story. Think of your couplets as spokes on a wheel, or beads on a string.

JOURNEY

The journey is a basic structure often used by short story writers, storytellers, epic poets, screenwriters, and novelists. It describes a character (hero or antihero) who embarks on a quest and returns changed in significant ways. Journeys are portrayed in many genres, including short poems, epic novels, graphic novels, and movies.

The journey is the basic story recipe for much of the world's folklore, myths, and literatures; journey is also the foundational structure for many sacred texts. Joseph Campbell has written extensively on the journey story shape, and his book *The Hero with a Thousand Faces* is required reading in many film schools. Video games rely heavily on the journey structure, as do many popular and critically acclaimed television series and movies, such as *Game of Thrones, Breaking Bad, The Matrix,* and *Aladdin. Harry Potter, Lord of the Rings,* and the video games *Legend of Zelda* and *Final Fantasy* are all examples of journey, brought to artistic perfection. *The Wizard of Oz* is a fantastic example of the journey, and beginning writers can learn a great deal by analyzing the film using the journey's elements. Many famous musicians and performers study journey in order to bring depth and meaning to their creations, to give their work universal reach and staying power, and to appeal to a wide audience. It's to your advantage as a creative writer to practice the journey form.

Reading Journeys

The basic journey story requires you to start with a character who is called the hero. Traditionally, the hero has a strong character and is very likable. In most contemporary works, the hero is just as often an antihero, someone who is outside the norms of society. In *Breaking Bad*, the high school teacher who runs a meth lab (in order to pay his medical bills and provide for his family) is a wonderful example of an antihero. The husband in Raymond Carver's "Cathedral" (page 125) is an antihero—he is an unlikable person with biases and flaws, but he nonetheless embarks on a journey toward *seeing*, and at the end of the story, we see that he is transformed. Poems, too, can use the journey effectively as an organizational strategy. The hero in "Buying Wine" by Sebastian Matthews (page 71) is a boy who loses his innocence but gains some insight as he journeys with his father through the liquor store. In "Swerve" (page 124), Brenda Miller is on both a literal and a metaphorical journey. As the hero, she realizes that her journey has taken her into an underworld, and she emerges, she hopes, with wisdom.

In general, the journey breaks down into three stages. Notice the bones of the traditional conflict–crisis–resolution structure here, which is addressed in full in Chapter Three. Here are the three stages:

I. SEPARATION	The hero leaves the world he or she knows, sometimes known as the "ordinary world."
II. INITIATION	The hero has adventures and victories and learns a secret knowledge.
III. RETURN	The hero comes back to the ordinary world with a gift.

PRACTICE 11

READING JOURNEY STORIES

Read "What I Saw from Where I Stood" by Marisa Silver (page 279) or "Cathedral" by Raymond Carver (page 125). Track the stages of separation, initiation, and return. Describe, in a paragraph, where you see each stage, and make a few comments about the use of the journey structure in this story.

You can also analyze your favorite movies, games, and shows, looking for these aspects of the classic journey story, as journey is the most commonly used form for narrative in our culture. As you view, take notes. Can you find the scene that denotes the beginning of separation? The scene that acts as the climax of the initiation? The scene that holds the most important moment in the return?

The **visitation** structure is a variation of journey—its opposite, or inverse. In this structure, the hero—the person who is going to experience the most significant change in the story—is *visited by someone or something that will allow him or her to experience a character transformation.* "Cathedral" can be read as a classic visitation because the husband's journey takes place in his own living room; the travel he does is interior and psychological. He ends up far different from the callous, shut-down man he was at the beginning of the story because of the catalyst: the blind man's *visit.* The classic movie *E. T.* is a visitation story, as are *Toy Story, Jurassic World, Avengers: Age of Ultron,* and *Avatar.* In this textbook, Jessica Shattuck's story "Bodies" (page 291) is a visitation story, too, as is Mary Robison's "Pretty Ice" (page 169). As you study these stories, locate the stages of the hero's journey.

> *I write because I want to have more than one life.*
>
> —ANNE TYLER

Further Reading

In This Book	Highly Recommended
• "What I Saw from Where I Stood" by Marisa Silver (page 279) • "Swerve" by Brenda Miller (page 124) • "Buying Wine" by Sebastian Matthews (page 71) • "Where There's Smoke" by Jenifer Hixson (page 274)	• "Marriage" by Gregory Corso • "What I Have Been Doing Lately" by Jamaica Kincaid • "The Swimmer" by John Cheever • *Interpreter of Maladies* by Jhumpa Lahiri

Writing a Journey

Before you write, you may want to practice outlining a couple of journey stories, using the stages above. Then choose a journey of your own to write. The form works extremely well for graphic novels, screenplays, plays, longer short stories, and novels. But you can also create a poem or myth or folktale or children's book that follows the journey structure. (Try analyzing *Where the Wild Things Are,* by Maurice Sendak, through the lens of journey.)

To write a journey, follow these steps:

1. First, choose a hero, someone who is likable but flawed. Imagine a world that will throw the hero into a series of complications for which they are completely unprepared.

2. Provide a quirky helper, and make a list of trickster figures who have motivation for blocking the hero's quest. What do they—the tricksters or villains—lose if the hero gains the gift?

3. Imagine the list of challenges carefully so that you can arrange them in a compelling order.

   a. Brainstorm various challenges that might confront your hero (use the sketching technique from page 399).

   b. Consider interesting settings that will be visually and metaphorically rich as your characters embark on their quest. For example, if your hero is a bride and her quest is the wedding dress, you could visit all the bridal shops in your area and collect details for great scenes for the journey.

   c. Think about how bad things could get: At the bottom of the diagram is a near death, a crucifixion, or some kind of transformation that is violent and traumatic. The hero emerges from this powerful experience *changed*. How? What physical manifestation of the hero's new "gift" could you create? Take some time to plan out various options.

   d. When the hero returns to the ordinary world with his or her gift, it may take some time to restore the ordinary world to order. The hero still faces challenges. What are they?

Remember: You don't have to use all of the steps, but the quest schema gives you a solid foundation of workable story steps.

LIST

Lists direct, even dominate, our daily lives: lists of contacts and to-dos, your grocery list, the college graduation requirements checklist, the bucket list. And, using a list is a simple, straightforward way to structure a piece of creative writing, equally useful for both prose and poetry. Lists of questions, lists of wants, lists of fears, lists of tiny details, lists of gestures, lists of overheard dialogue on the subway, lists of regrets, lists of apologies, lists of images—anything that forces you to stay focused on a single subject will potentially generate a powerful piece of writing.

The list form, like the journey form, is ancient. These two forms, list and journey, are the two most common ways of structuring a piece of literature, and they both work for every genre. Like the journey, listing is also an ancient form, used in the Bible, for example, in Song of Solomon, in which a lover lists everything he loves about his partner. Parts of the *Iliad* are a list.

Today, listing is relevant for a wide range of authors. Some of the forms you've already studied, such as abecedarius and anaphora, are forms of listing, too. Lists can be used to structure lectures, formal essays, educational materials, and text-and-image experiments based on the quirkiest of passions. For example, take a look at "Why the Mantis Shrimp Is My New Favorite Animal" at The Oatmeal. It's a list.

If you are stuck or blocked as a writer, here's my hearty recommendation: Make a list. Anyone can make a list. Lists can be of any length, and in poetry, they can be rhymed or unrhymed. In the famous list poem "Jubilate Agno" by Christopher Smart (1722–1771), the author lists everything his beloved cat does when he wakes up in the morning. Here is a very brief excerpt from the poem:

> For first he looks upon his fore-paws to see if they are clean.
> For secondly he kicks up behind to clear away there.
> For thirdly he works it upon a stretch with the fore-paws extended.
> For fourthly he sharpens his paws by wood.

The list of cat behaviors goes on for several pages, and the energy comes from the author's ability to notice, with such fine observational skills, just what his cat does and exactly how he does it.

The keys to success with the list are threefold: superbly close observation, generous detail, and a subject matter on which you are the primary expert.

Reading Lists

Lists are usually easy and enjoyable to read because the form is so simple, direct, and pure. The form can be used for prose or poetry. The title is extremely important; not only does the title give a clue to the topic of the list, but it often points to the subtext of the list. In creative writing, a good list is greater than the sum of its parts.

You might be interested in reading list poems by Walt Whitman and Allen Ginsberg. If you like surreal poetry, you might enjoy list poems by James Tate, such as "The List of Famous Hats."

Memoirist Marion Winik wrote an entire book titled *The Glen Rock Book of the Dead* using the list form. In the table of contents, she lists everyone she knows who has died: The Neighbor, The Eye Doctor, The Driving Instructor, The Realtor, The Virgin. Each chapter is a page or two long, and the entire memoir works as a wonderfully moving, even funny (not depressing) exploration of life. Fiction writer Lorrie Moore uses lists in her

454 CHAPTER TEN Finding Form

short stories "How to Talk to Your Mother (Notes)" and the "Kid's Guide to Divorce."

The list is one of the most flexible and welcoming forms. When you are stuck as a writer, try listing. The form comes with one simple caveat: In every sentence, use skillful observation (or the list quickly becomes boring).

PRACTICE 12

READING A LIST MEMOIR

Reread Brian Arundel's "The Things I've Lost" (page 217) a list memoir. What kinds of things does he include in his list? Which surprise you the most? Which specifics in the essay reveal the most about the author's persona, in your opinion? What keeps you reading the list? Write a paragraph and discuss your observations with your peers.

Further Reading

In This Book	Highly Recommended
• "Boys" by Rick Moody (page 219) • "The Things I've Lost" by Brian Arundel (page 217) • "In My Father's Study upon His Death" by Dylan Landis (page 166) • "I Go Back to Berryman's" by Vincent Scarpa (page 76) • "How to Erase an Arab" by Julie Azzam (page 333)	• *The Glen Rock Book of the Dead* by Marion Winik • "Going to the Movies" by Susan Toth • "Jubilate Agno" by Christopher Smart • *Lists of Note: An Eclectic Collection Deserving of a Wider Audience* compiled by Shaun Usher • "Things to Do in the Belly of the Whale" by Dan Albergotti

Writing a List

Here is a list of prompts for list pieces. You can try them in poetry or prose, or as comics or for writing a play.

1. Ten Things I Do Every Day. (Check out Ted Berrigan's original poem, "10 Things I Do Every Day," online.)
2. Things to Do at _____. (Fill in the blank with a place you know really well that most people do not know at all, like your dad's apartment, or Fireman's Field on Roosevelt Island, or the fire escape behind 4D.)
3. Thirteen Things to Do While Looking at the Moon.

---

[2] From Kenneth Koch.

4. A list that uses this prompt: "I used to _____, but now I _____." How many lines long = However old you are.[2]
5. A list of things associated with your favorite season. (Make sure each item is extremely specific to you and not one of the first five items that everyone thinks of—no beaches, no first snowfall, no autumn leaves, no daffodils.)
6. A list in which each line or sentence begins with the words "My mother said . . ." or "My father said . . ."
7. A list of images in which you show bedtime for seven nights in a row, or breakfast for seven days in a row, or driving to campus over the course of a week, or going food shopping, etc.

The key to writing a great list is to use images and super specific details.

MONOLOGUE

Monologues are stories meant to be presented by the author or a reader onstage, on video, radio, or television. Spoken word and rap are forms of monologue. In a play, when the performer talks to the audience, it's a monologue; when he talks to himself ("to be or not to be"), it's a soliloquy. Monologues can be memoir, drama, or fiction. Monologues are usually character-driven, with a literary structure in which we identify with one main character, and they interact with other people in the story (who are offstage, or implied) through conflict. Usually a monologue has a climactic moment and a denouement, or resolution.

Contemporary writers usually avoid overt "And then I came to realize . . ." moments, but they show change—change in the main character's outlook, or development, or situation. In contemporary monologue, the main character—usually the speaker, but not always—learns something surprising, something different than what we were expecting. "That's always what we're going for, something surprising, a surprising situation—where somebody comes to a conclusion that you wouldn't expect," writes Ira Glass in *Radio: An Illustrated Guide*, his guidebook to producing stories for radio (a comic book instructional manual illustrated by Jessica Abel).

Monologue is an inherently dramatic form—you must write in scene and image, with energy and high tension. Pattern will help your reader follow along. You don't have much room to preach, rant, think, emote, reflect, muse, or share feelings and memories. You're not a teller; you're a *shower*. You're up there to render a gripping, visual, fresh, evocative story. You can't go into characters' thoughts as you would in fiction or memoir. You have to show, through action, everything that is interesting—you're making a movie with your words so that the images and actions play out in your listener's mind.

Reading Monologues

Shakespeare wrote dozens of brilliant and memorable monologues; you may choose to study his work carefully, especially if you are thinking of writing for the stage. If you are new to this material, perhaps start with Egeus's monologue in Act One of *A Midsummer Night's Dream*, "Full of vexation I come, with complaint."

You'll "read" with your ears. You might have a chance to see a live spoken word or storytelling event, or stand-up or slam. That's a wonderful way to see how this form works. Remember comedians are using this form to create their art. Listening to your favorite comedians and paying close attention to how they render their material in spoken form will aid you greatly.

PRACTICE 13

LISTENING TO MONOLOGUES ON PODCASTS

Listen to some monologues. *The Moth* and Glynn Washington's *Snap Judgment* are excellent sources for monologues, as is *This American Life*. On *This American Life*, try listening to "Squirrel Cop" and "Just Keep Breathing." Notice how each story is told as a sequence of actions. Not thoughts, not ideas, not commentary: actions. And the actions are framed by brief interpretation: "I didn't think it was that bad." "I just wanted to impress her." "All I wanted was to be the hero." Choose your favorite monologue from a podcast and write a paragraph description of what you learned about this form from your listening experience.

PRACTICE 14

LISTENING TO JENIFER HIXSON'S MONOLOGUE

Listen to Jenifer Hixson's "Where There's Smoke" online on *The Moth* or view it on YouTube. Notice what you see in your mind's eye as you listen. Then read it in print form on page 274. Make a list of five techniques she uses in order to get you to see the scenes. Write a paragraph of commentary to accompany your list: What makes this monologue successful?

Because monologue is performed, it can be helpful to move between different kinds of scenes, to juxtapose humorous scenes, emotional scenes, beautiful scenes, with reflection or questions. And because the audience is listening, not reading, you have to be extremely clear about where things take place, when, and who is present, both in your opening and as you move through the piece.

Further Reading/Listening

In This Book	Highly Recommended
• "Where There's Smoke" by Jenifer Hixson (page 274)	• "Santaland Diaries" by David Sedaris on "This American Life" • "Snap Judgment, a podcast from Glynn Washington." • *Potluck Podcast Collective* • *The Moth*

Writing a Monologue

1. Start with a series of events that are highly visual and intensely dramatic: the details before, during, and after you or your character lost her job; a trip to the doctor that does not go well; a fight in which you come to realize you are actually in the wrong.

2. A monologue is not a rant, not a confession, not a sermon, and not thoughts and feelings. It's a series of action scenes, framed by questions and insights. Write out your scenes, paying special attention to clarity: Where are we? Who is "onstage"? Because your audience is listening, you need to be especially concerned with accuracy and ease of understanding.

3. Usually, a monologue contains two turning points so that the story we think we are hearing isn't the story we are actually hearing—things change direction, and then they change direction *again*. Here are some questions that might help you deepen your story and find those key turning points:

    a. What does your speaker (and the speaker may be you or an invented character) think she wants more than anything in this moment?

    b. What does she *really* want? Attend closely to the gap between the answers to the questions in a and b—you're bound to find story juice in that gap.

    c. What are the action steps that externally show those two different levels of want?

    d. What's the worst-case scenario for this character/speaker? Set that up. Then make that happen: Show the worst-case scenario scene playing out. *Then* show us why that worst-case scenario was actually the best thing that could have happened. There are your two turns.

Record yourself reading your monologue. Most people deliver their monologues too quickly. Ask your peers to listen to your polished monologue. Have them note where they laughed, where they really saw the events you are narrating "play out" in their mind's eye, and where they were confused or unclear. Revise, and read your monologue again to the class.

Monologues are usually measured by time, not by word count or page count. It takes about two minutes to read a typical double-spaced page aloud. Five minutes is a good length for your first monologue.

PANTOUM

The pantoum is a poem composed of four-line stanzas (quatrains); the form requires you to repeat whole lines, instead of simply rhyming words. Originally a Malayan form of poetry with Persian and Chinese influences, the pantoum has been around for more than five hundred years. Poet John Ashbery is credited with bringing the form to the United States in the 1950s.

Instead of telling a linear story, the pantoum repeats itself and zigzags, forcing the reader to circle back and revisit. It's the opposite of classic dramatic structure; pantoums move in spirals. A pantoum is also the opposite of the conflict–crisis–resolution structure. A pantoum is devoted to circling, interlocking, unfolding. In pantoum, the journey *is* the destination. It's a perfect form for those experiences in your life you wish to write about that just don't fit into classic dramatic structure.

Here are the features of this form:

- Written in **quatrains** (four lines per stanza)
- *abab* rhyme scheme (lines 1 and 3 rhyme; lines 2 and 4 rhyme)
- Poem can be any length
- Repeating lines: line 2 and 4 of each stanza = lines 1 and 3 of the next stanza, all through the poem
- The last line of the poem = the first line of the poem

As with most forms, it's easier to understand the rules after reading a few samples, and then just starting to write your poem, rather than stressing out over the intricacies.

Poetry is against gravity.
—AI WEIWEI

Reading Pantoums

Some pantoums follow the structure to the letter; others vary the pattern. You're encouraged to write a classic, rule-following pantoum first, and then write poems that bend the rules to create new effects.

The pantoum is often clearer and more interesting when it is read aloud.

PRACTICE 15

READING A PANTOUM: Natalie Diaz's poem "My Brother at 3 a.m."

Read Natalie Diaz's poem "My Brother at 3 a.m." (page 165). In what ways does she take moves from the pantoum's recipe, and how does she alter the form? Do the alterations make sense to you? How so? She uses quatrains and a series of interlocking repeated lines to create a powerful portrait of a family with a very troubled brother/son. Why might the options offered by the pantoum — overlapping, interlocking, repetition — be an excellent choice of form for this topic?

PRACTICE 16

LISTENING TO A PANTOUM: Laure-Anne Bosselaar's "Stillbirth"

Locate the poem "Stillbirth," by Laure-Anne Bosselaar online. Read the poem several times aloud. What do you notice about the patterns? Write a paragraph description of how you see the form working in this poem.

It's helpful to annotate the stanzas of each pantoum, paying attention to what's happening on the level of language and also carefully discerning what's happening on a practical level in the poem. In Laure-Anne Bosselaar's "Stillbirth," a woman hears someone call out a person's name on a crowded train station platform. That name happens to be the name she gave her unborn child, years earlier. Chilled, she leaps into the car, and though it makes no sense, and she knows it, she can't help but search for the face of her grown daughter — impossible. But there it is, the irrational mind in all its power. In stanza 2, reality sets in: Of course her daughter, born dead (notice how the title shines a light, like a flashlight, down the spine of the poem, helping us understand what is happening), can't be on the train.

In stanza 3, the power of the pantoum form kicks in. Pantoum is a good form to use when writing about the recursive nature of memory, PTSD, difficult relationships, the things that haunt us, as the images pop up unexpectedly and keep coming back up. "No one in that car could have been you." She has told us — and herself — this before. She's trying to convince herself — to get what she knows as true to coincide with what she *feels* could be true. The speaker of the poem apparently has calculated how old the baby would now be. She confides to us — and her unborn daughter — "I sometimes go months without remembering you." Each stanza adds more detailed information. In stanza 4, we learn what she was told by the nurses and doctors: *Don't get attached.* And those powerful, chilling, terrible words repeat in stanza 5.

Bosselaar makes subtle shifts in her repeating lines. As you reread the poem, study those shifts. Here, as always, the guiding principle applies: If you are going to break the rules, you have to have a great reason. Do you think that her changes to the form improve the poem? Do they seem like mistakes or failures or wholly intentional? How can you tell?

As you read and listened, you were probably aware of the repetitions, the urgency, and the circling. Words and lines are repeated. These are poems about obsession. They keep going over certain images again and again. Whatever haunts us, annoys us, excites us — that's the province of the pantoum.

What do you notice about the "recipe" when you listen, compared to when you read the pantoum on the page? As with all structures, if the structure is truly effective, it's not the most prominent feature of the piece. The tension, the energy, the images — those are what you pay attention to. The pleasure and impact of a pantoum are in how the lines recur and surprise us when they fit together in unusual ways. So don't worry if you don't notice the structure right away. That's always a sign the poet has been successful!

It's important always to both see and hear a pantoum — to see the structure and hear its effect.

Further Reading

In This Book	Highly Recommended
• "Pantoum" by Randall Mann (page 332) • "My Brother at 3 a.m." by Natalie Diaz (page 165)	• "Parent's Pantoum" by Carolyn Kizer • "Pantoum in Wartime" by Marilyn Hacker • "Another Lullaby for Insomniacs" by A. E. Stallings

Writing a Pantoum

The pantoum *repeats whole lines* rather than words. The lines in a pantoum can be of any length.

Line 1	*a*
Line 2	*b*
Line 3	*a*
Line 4	*b*
Line 5	*b* [exactly the same line as line 2]
Line 6	*c*
Line 7	*b* [exactly the same line as line 4)
Line 8	*c*

Line 9   *c* [exactly the same as line as line 6)
Line 10   *d*
Line 11   *c* [exactly the same as line as line 8)
Line 12   *d*

And so on.

You can end whenever you like — some pantoums are *pages* long. However, a four-stanza pantoum is common, and in the final stanza, you may simply repeat lines 1 and 3 from the first stanza, or you can write new lines. You have options. Rhyme is optional but usually follows *abab, bcbc, cdcd,* etc., rhyme scheme.

Again this all sounds very complicated, but it's not. It's easier to write a pantoum than to think about it. Choose a topic and just get started. It will all come together as you write.

For your subject, choose something that is inherently repetitive, something that bores you out of your mind: a bad lecture, a tedious summer painting houses, your car that constantly breaks down. Write about swimming laps. Teaching kids to write the letter *a*. Grief is a worthwhile topic for a pantoum because of the way humans grieve. We feel we are making progress, healing from a loss, and then something snaps us back again, and we're gob-smacked by memories. Addiction, as in Diaz's pantoum on page 165, is a meaningful subject choice because of the spiraling nature of that illness. Insomnia, obsession, and other recurring things in your life will find a home in the pantoum form.

Watch the pantoum turn your boredom or despair into something humorous, weirdly fascinating, or beautiful. The pantoum gives you a lens for looking at repetition; you might be surprised at what you discover about the same-old, same-old. What images, in your heart of hearts, deep inside your secret self, do you turn over and over and over day and night? That's a good topic for a pantoum.

1. To get started, make a list of twenty-five things that cause your mind or body to go over the same ground, again and again. Work quickly — take no more than ten minutes to work on this list. With three minutes left, if you don't have twenty-five items, press yourself to come up with *anything*. If the last items don't "fit," just write them down anyway.
2. Pick a subject from your list that has a lot of *energy* for you.
3. List the *images* you see when you look closely at this subject. Then write two lines. These first two lines, which will give birth to all the other lines in the pantoum, affect what the pantoum does to the reader: It makes the

reader feel edgy, nervous, a bit boxed in. Many poets begin with "cast-off" lines from other poems, so as to not start with a blank page. When you write a pantoum, you need only two lines you like to get going.

For your first pantoum, follow the recipe above, exactly. It's okay to get a little frustrated when you first start writing your pantoum. Learning a new dance step or a new guitar lick is hard at first, but then you have a feeling of "breaking the code." Know that once you get your two basic lines, the pantoum *will* bow to you.

> *I like using forms like pantoums because I feel a set form, far from being restrictive, is very liberating and forces your imagination to explore possibilities it might not otherwise consider.*
> —SOPHIE HANNAH

Once you have tried the traditionally structured pantoum, use the basic recipe to make your own kind of pantoum. Break the rules, invent your own structure to support what you want to say. Use the pantoum's interesting back-and-forth structure to inspire you in a new creative direction. Sometimes when you break the rules, that breach becomes the most interesting part of the pattern. Musicians do this frequently. Consider a live performance, where a singer will substitute another word, maybe a rhyme, or maybe something else altogether, into a part of the song everyone knows by heart. This is part of the fun—the surprise, the play. And it calls the listener's (or reader's) attention to something important.

Alternative pantoums are inspired by the pantoum form but deviate in interesting ways. So try at least one pantoum that loosely follows the recipe, breaking out of the form at several key points; for example, allow the pantoum to break out of the form when you yourself are breaking out of your obsession.

PLAY/SCREENPLAY

Most plays and films you'll find in your local theaters and cinemas are full length—usually three to five acts, or about two hours long. And, most playwrights and screenwriters begin with making five- or ten-minute plays, one-acts, or films called "shorts."

A film short or brief or one-act play often features only one, two, or three characters, because new artists are almost always on a tight budget and a tight schedule; managing large casts is unrealistic. Conflict is introduced, it builds to a crisis, and resolves itself in a limited space and time. Your first play or screenplay might have one scene that takes up the whole play, or any number of short scenes. The ten-minute play, a more recent subgenre of the one-act, is very popular, especially for new actors and new writers. And, for aspiring filmmakers, there are terrific collections of award-wining short films to watch for inspiration; search for "Oscar-winning shorts," "festival-winning shorts," and "short of the week."

Reading Plays and Screenplays

Almost always, a play shows a character experiencing some kind of internal change. Just as in the journey structure, which governs so much of fiction and memoir, dramatic structure shows a central character in a conflict, going through dramatic moments of struggle that lead up to some kind of dramatic insight, reversal, or explosion; "I am not Batman." on page 82, and "Pancakes" on page 303 in this book are prime examples. But onstage, this journey is compressed. Everything takes place more quickly than in a novel or memoir. Reading a play aloud takes much longer than reading it silently, and audiences usually don't like to sit still for very long—especially if not much is happening on stage. In a play, everything has to be crisp and exciting, visual, tense, and dramatic. Even the opening must be powerful. In a play, especially a one-act, it's essential that a major conflict has already occurred, offstage, just before the play actually opens, and we, the audience, are plunged right into the thick of things.

The playwright and screenwriter imagine the setting, the costumes, the accents, even specific types of actors or actual actors in the roles, and describe all of these before the play actually begins. Ultimately, though, when the play is performed, the playwright's vision is interpreted by many other people, all of whom have their own creative ideas. When you write your play or screenplay, definitely see, in your mind's eye, all of the images as they unfold onstage—hear the sounds, foresee the lighting—every detail. And be prepared to let much of that go when your play is produced!

> *I think a playwright realizes after he finishes working on the script that this is only the beginning. What will happen when it moves into three dimensions?*
>
> —DON DELILLO

PRACTICE 17

READING PLAYS FOR CONFLICT, TENSION, AND SETTING

Read Peter Morris's "Pancakes" (page 303). What has already happened to establish conflict and tension offstage before the play starts? How do you imagine the stage set? Read Kristina Halvorson's "Now We're Really Getting Somewhere" (page 240). What has already happened to establish conflict and tension offstage before the play starts? How do you imagine the stage set? Write two paragraphs, one for each play, explaining your observations.

Further Reading

In This Book	Highly Recommended
• "Now We're Really Getting Somewhere" by Kristina Halvorson (page 240) • "I am not Batman." by Marco Ramirez (page 82) • "Pancakes" by Peter Morris (page 303)	• *Take Ten: New 10-Minute Plays* edited by Eric Lane and Nina Shengold • *Story* by Robert McKee • *Making a Good Script Great* by Linda Seger • *The Screenwriter's Problem Solver* by Syd Field • *The Script Lab* (https://thescriptlab.com)

Writing a Play

1. Start with characters in a setting. You can take one of your pieces from the semester—a short story or memoir—and use that as your starting point. Or you can use one of the plays in this book to brainstorm characters and conflicts for your plays. To write a one-act or ten-minute play, you typically start with one to three characters in immediate and fairly intense conflict, and a setting. You want to imagine the play taking place before an audience.

2. Imagine the play on a real stage. Make a list of the props, costumes, lighting effects, sounds, and anything else you need for your play. You will probably want to keep your ideas for lighting and props and atmospherics fairly simple—at first. Think in terms of a few strong "statement" props for your setting—a lamp, a chair, a stuffed animal, and a bucket of water might be all you need. Think of symbol props for your characters, too—the woman is in a evening gown, though it's morning; the guy is in his pajamas, holding a cocktail. Make sure the props and setting are *possible*. These limits—budget, time, space—actually force you to be more creative, so most writers welcome them! If you have classmates perform your play in the classroom, take those limitations into account and make them work to your advantage dramatically.

3. Work hard on your story. You will probably use classic story structure to keep your audience engaged and alert, but you can consider other options. If the writing is brilliant and the images unforgettable, a ten-minute rant, with one person onstage, might work perfectly. Usually, two or three characters in conflict give you enough material for a one-act. Work out a series of escalating events, with the characters at odds with each other.

4. Write the dialogue. Keep it short and realistic. In real life, people don't listen to each other carefully, they rarely speak in complete sentences, and their character is revealed not only by what is said, but by what is *not* said.

5. Write the physical action. Show your characters moving around in space, in conflict with the setting. You need to "block" out your characters' movements and gestures. Silence, pauses, and simple sound effects create a kind of sound score for your play, a third level of potential drama and tension you will want to exploit.

6. Rehearse. Not so much for the actors, but for you. Just as the fiction writer and memoirist replay their scenes over and over in their mind's eye, honing their images, recasting the scene again and again by focusing, sketching, seeing, and re-seeing, the playwright runs through the play with live actors. You don't need trained actors; friends or classmates will do a fine job. As they read their lines, you can find out what works, what feels flat, and what sounds tinny or off. Also, have the actors follow the stage directions so that you can see where the lulls are in your script and can work to hone the physical drama so that it emphasizes and underscores the verbal drama. Actors are famous for giving authors and directors (that's you for now) lots of free advice—take what's useful. Know that many plays are changed even after they open to a Broadway audience. Shown as "previews" before paying customers, many plays are revised for weeks while they are running.

7. Lighting is an important tool, though again you'll want to keep things simple for your one-act, using darkness and light, and perhaps "fading" light, to call attention to key moments. Dialogue, physical action, light, and the aural effects of sound and silence give you four different strands to script. So you can see that ten minutes of theater takes an *enormous* amount of work!

8. Format your final script (see Tips for Formatting a Play below). To format a play you turn in as part of your classwork in creative writing, use the play on page 303 as an example (unless your instructor gives you other directions). At the top of the first page, list the characters by name and give a brief description of their station in life, age, and important characteristics. Then describe the setting, quickly and briefly. For each bit of dialogue, place the speaker's name on the left side of the page, in all caps. Do not use quotation marks for dialogue, and type it all the way across the page. Tip: One page of a script is equal to about one minute of running time. If your characters are having a fight using lots of one-word sentences and back-and-forths, that's going to speed things up (a good thing!). But to maintain the tension, be sure to vary the pace, and intersperse lengthier patches of dialogue with the rapid-fire bits.

TIPS: Formatting a Play

1. The name of the person talking appears in all capital letters on the left-hand side of the page. Capitalize the entire name of a character each time she or he appears. You may use the play Pancakes as a model for formatting.

2. Write a brief, tight, evocative description of each setting before that scene unfolds. You want to establish the mood, key visual cues (e.g., there has to be a window because this character flew in through a window), and any emotions that might be crucial for the actors to show onstage.

3. For scene changes, identify new settings with the details needed.

TIPS: Formatting a Screenplay

1. The name of the person talking is centered on the page. Capitalize the entire name of a character each time they appear.

2. Write a brief, tight, evocative description of each setting before the drama of that scene unfolds. You want to establish the mood, key visual cues (e.g., there has to be a window because this character flew in through a window), and any emotions that might be crucial for the actors to show on screen.

3. Identify new settings with the details that are crucial to include each time the scene changes or the camera moves in closer or farther out.

SESTINA

The sestina is a poem that uses six stanzas of six lines each, with the end words in each line repeating in a specific pattern throughout the poem. The Italian poets Petrarch and Dante made the form famous (and Dante gave it its name). As with the pantoum, poets often write sestinas when they want to tackle topics involving obsession. When you land on the right topic, you render a haunting experience, the kind of feeling and worry that are very hard to talk about in regular conversation.

Reading Sestinas

Read the sestina "Liner Notes for an Imaginary Playlist" by Terrance Hayes (page 121). Read silently, and then have someone read the sestina aloud while you just let your mind take in the images. Read this long poem once more, and notice the pattern, the way words are repeated. You will notice that the poem has six stanzas, each with six lines, plus a little ending stanza of three lines, like a *P.S.* on a letter. If you want to read additional sestinas, you will find an excellent collection at *McSweeney's Internet Tendency*, including "To My Friend, the Christian Pop Star in Nashville" by K. Judith Mowrer, "O Light, Red Light" by Cathy Park Hong, "How to Build a Sestina Template in Microsoft Excel" by Daniel Ari, and "I'm Obsessed with My Wife" by Nicole Steinberg, along with dozens of others.

The sestina adds a slightly more intricate pattern of words to the brooding, worrying, obsessive feeling that you get from a pantoum or a ghazal. Safe to say, if you like Sudoku or Mad Libs, you will love the sestina. Writing a sestina is like a filling-in-puzzle-pieces project.

A sestina uses six different words as the end words for the lines in each stanza. However, each stanza uses the end words in a different pattern. All the lines in the poem end with one of those six specified words. The order is dictated by the recipe:

STANZA 1	STANZA 2	STANZA 3	STANZA 4
a	f	c	e
b	a	f	c
c	e	d	b
d	b	a	f
e	d	b	a
f	c	e	d

STANZA 5	STANZA 6	FINAL STANZA	
d	b	ab	
e	d	cd	
a	f	ef	
c	e		
f	c		
b	a		

The final stanza is three lines long and uses all six words—but now two of the repeating words appear in each line, one halfway through the line and one at the end. You'll use the two words in the line.

You will be surprised at the things you are able to say; limiting your word choices actually increases your creativity. Your lines do not need to be long. Poet Ciara Shuttleworth wrote a sestina titled "Sestina" that consists of one-word lines, following the pattern.

In a good sestina, the pattern isn't completely obvious; it's supposed to be subtle, a little hidden. If the poet is doing her job, being super specific, using enjambment, and adding new information in each stanza, the reader notices the images and the feelings the poem creates, not the overt pattern. Only upon close rereading does the structure, or recipe, become clear.

PRACTICE 18

READING A SESTINA

Label the sestina in this book on page 121 (or use another sestina you've found that you enjoy) with the corresponding letters from the recipe above. Do you notice any variations? Do they add anything to the meaning of the poem? Write a paragraph describing the sestina form as it plays out in the poem you are analyzing.

Further Reading

In This Book	Highly Recommended
• *Liner Notes for an Imaginary Playlist* by Terrance Hayes (page 121)	• *To My Friend, the Christian Pop Star in Nashville* by K. Judith Mowrer • *The Buffy Sestina* by Jason Schneiderman • *Sestina* by Elizabeth Bishop • *Sestina* by Ciara Shuttleworth

Writing a Sestina

Poet John Ashbery once said that writing a sestina is like riding downhill on a bicycle and having the pedals push your feet. Keep your sense of play and your sense of humor as you explore this form.

1. Make a list of six solid end words, words that leave you some flexibility: *code, mean, shallow, mist, body, read.* Hayes chose solid, simple, clear, concrete words that punch out his theme. And, he plays with the language, punning and bending, adding surprise and music: *red* and *reed* work with *read. Man* and *Amen* resound. He goes for subtle rhymes and echoes: *code, cold, coat, coast.* Hayes uses the form as a scaffolding, but he plays within its strictures and keeps the form fresh and new.

Avoid words that will work in only a few situations, like *hasenpfeffer*. Choose words you won't mind hearing over and over. Words that do double duty, like *read* and *sail* (a noun and a verb) give you more flexibility. To come up with a collection of good, usable end words that will work in many different situations, you can draw from your own poetry. Or you can use the end words used by other sestina writers as you learn the form. Remember that plain, clear, concrete words are easier to work with as you knit your stanzas together.

2. Next, choose for your topic something that weighs on your mind, something that you go over again and again: failed love, running track, worrying about the future.

3. Study the pattern, and place your end words on the page. Remember: The letters stand for the word at the end of each line. Note the logic of the pattern: Stanza 2 takes the *a b c* end words and intersplices *d e f* end words in reverse order. If all this patterning gives you a headache, don't worry about it. Just follow the guide on page 467, and write your lines to fit those end words.

4. For the final stanza, you can follow the recipe above and write three lines. When a poem recipe shows two letters, as above, it means that you put the *a* word (the word that ended your first line in stanza 1, your second line in stanza 2, etc.) in the middle of the line, and your *b* word (the same word you used in *b*, above) at the end of line 1 of this final stanza. Line 2 of the final stanza, *c d*, puts the *c* word in the middle of the line and the *d* word at the end; line 3, the last line of the whole poem, places the *e* word in the middle of the line, and your poem ends with whatever word you have been using in the *f* slot. Or you can make your final stanza just one line long, as Wesli Court does in "The Obsession" (easily found online).

The challenge of the sestina is to draw attention *away from* (not toward) the end words (the repeating words). So poets often break their lines so that the phrases with the repeating word flow down into the next line.

> You can't eat language but it eases thirst.
> —BERNARD MALAMUD

After trying a classic sestina, play a little and fudge the rules. Sometimes, for example, poets omit the final three-line stanza. That is okay. Other poets use closely related words to make patterns—*light, night, enlightened,* or *sun, son, sunned.* Try a strict sestina first; then play with form, breaking the rules in interesting and fresh ways.

SONNET

The sonnet is a fourteen-line poem, usually composed of lines that are ten syllables in length. Enduring topics for the sonnet are politics, love, and religion, but poets have written sonnets on every imaginable subject. The sonnet is one of the most well-known and best-loved forms of poetry in the Western world. Shakespeare, Milton, and Wordsworth are well known for their sonnets, along with literary superstars such as Dylan Thomas, Gerard Manley Hopkins, and Elizabeth Barrett Browning. But many contemporary poets, including Kim Addonizio, Terrance Hayes, and Denis Johnson, also write exciting and innovative sonnets. The form isn't stuffy or dusty; it's powerful and compressed, yet allows great range.

> *Life has been your art. You have set yourself to music. Your days are your sonnets.*
>
> —OSCAR WILDE

The word *sonnet* comes from an Italian word, *sonetto* (a "little sound" or "song"), from the Latin root *sonus* ("sound"). That etymology is important because when you read sonnets, you will notice that the poet pays close attention to the sounds of the words, certain kinds of rhymes, and the patterns of vowels and consonants. The rhythm in a traditional sonnet is the meter of iambic pentameter—five feet, which is ten syllables in every line, and every other syllable is accented. Traditional rhyme schemes for the sonnet vary greatly, but the most popular is the one that William Shakespeare used: *abab, cdcd, efef, gg*. Contemporary sonnets may not follow the rhyme scheme or syllable count; however, they almost always have fourteen lines and two strong turns. Some poets create interlocking sonnets, where the last line of the first sonnet is used as the first line of the second sonnet, and so on. Interlocking sonnets often contain fourteen poems, and this is called a crown of sonnets.

The sonnet requires a poet to look at things in a specific way and to develop a concept with a particular focus. Sonnet writing is not simple—but it is very rewarding, once you practice a bit.

Reading Sonnets

In addition to its special focus on sound, the sonnet gives both the poet and the reader an interesting way to look at anything. The sonnet is basically a *way of thinking.* You introduce your thoughts and feelings about a topic in the first eight lines; then you look at it in a different way in the last six lines. Make a strong turn between the first section of the sonnet and the second section. The last two lines, usually called the *couplet*, provide a surprising resolution to the two competing ideas presented. Phillis Levin writes that the sonnet is "a meeting place of image and voice, passion and reason."

When you read sonnets, pay attention to the rhyme, the turn, and the final couplet. Those three aspects of the sonnet create the rich layers and meanings in the poem. Here are the basic rules of the form:

> *Every mood of mind can be indulged in a sonnet; every kind of reader appealed to. You can make love in a sonnet, you can laugh in a sonnet, you can lament in it, can narrate or describe, can rebuke, can admire, can pray.*
> —LEIGH HUNT

- The sonnet consists of fourteen lines.
- It is often written in iambic pentameter (ten syllables per line).
- The rhyme scheme varies but is often *abab, cdcd, efef, gg,* or *abba, abba, cdcdcd.*
- The poem contains a turn at line 9 (introduction of a new, related subject, a shift in meaning, or a change in the direction or tone).
- There's often another turn in lines 11 and 12, especially if the rhyme scheme denotes a final couplet.

If you want to read more contemporary sonnets for inspiration, you can easily find many online. Try works by Kim Addonizio, Molly Peacock, Denis Johnson, Gail White, Rhina Espaillat, A. E. Stallings, and Cornelius Eady.

PRACTICE 19

STUDYING THE SONNET FORM IN KIM ADDONIZIO'S "FIRST POEM FOR YOU"

Read Kim Addonizio's sonnet "First Poem for You" (page 121). The first time you read it, did you realize it was a sonnet? Count the lines and the syllables. Does this poet stick to the 140-syllable limit? Where does she go over and why? What rhyme scheme is she using? Lastly, see if you can find the two turns. Remember, usually the first turn is at line 9, and there's another turn at line 11. Write a paragraph identifying and discussing the features of Addonizio's sonnet.

Kim Addonizio, an experienced poet, bends a few of the rules. Here's another example of the sonnet, written by Debra Wierenga.

Let Sleeping Boys Lie

Saturday morning, my living room's
wall-to-wall sleeping bags and bodies —
beautiful boys flung down in the ruins
of Risk's plastic troops and cannons and countries.

Newly furred arms and legs at odd angles,
they lie where they fell among the black cords
of digital war machines in tangles
that trail like barbed wire across the floor.

Mothers at Troy, Antietam, Agincourt,
stepped just this way over still limbs
of silent young men, making sure
with wild glances each one was not him—
O God, let his wars be always in fun.
Let this soldier, my son, sleep fiercely on.

Notice the careful use of iambic pentameter—(nearly all) ten-syllable lines
with a specific rhythm. Note the rhyme scheme: *abab, cdcd, efef, gg.* Some
of the rhymes are near rhymes, adding texture and slight unpredictability,
while paying careful attention to sound. Most importantly, this sonnet is a
perfect example of how sonnets use turns. Note in line 9 the radical voice
change and new subject matter; the poet is comparing her relationship to
her sleeping sons, while a war rages overseas, to countless mothers through
history, who are indeed losing their own sons to battles. And, in line 11,
notice how the poet again makes a radical shift in her tone: here, in the second turn, she addresses God directly with a prayer—*please save my son.*

The two poets, Addonizio and Wierenga, are using classic sonnet subject
matter—big emotions and the huge timeless topics of love and fear of death. The
tight container of sonnet holds the powerful feelings elicited by the subject matter.

Further Reading

In This Book	Highly Recommended
• "First Poem for You" by Kim Addonizio (page 121) • "Let Sleeping Boys Lie" by Debra Wierenga (page 471)	• "Fatigues" by David Livewell • "Sonnet 18" by William Shakespeare • "The Silken Tent" by Robert Frost • "Fairy Tale Logic" by A. E. Stallings • "Those Winter Sundays" by Robert Hayden

Writing a Sonnet

Because the sonnet is especially useful for more difficult topics—unrequited
love, political statements, religious questions—it's often hard to write at first.
Stay with it. It's better to write four or five sonnets before you decide whether

you like this form. Be patient with yourself, and allow plenty of time. Most poets work on demanding form poems in a series of short sessions, writing by hand for twenty to thirty minutes, stepping away, and coming back.

1. Start by listing topics in three categories — love, politics, religion (or spirituality). Because sonnets are about ideas, you may be tempted to just start writing. But it will be easier if you work from images. Make lists of *objects or people*. Try for ten items in each of the three categories. Here's a sample of one student's sonnet topic list, in progress:

Love	Politics	Religion
First-grade crush — can't remember name; redhead	Age of Supreme Court justices	Sunday hikes in dunes — nature is my church
Current partner, K.	Why no one votes	Prayer in school debate
Ex-partner, A.	Campus election for homecoming king?	Next-door neighbor was a minister
Love for my dad	Racism on campus	Boyfriend took me to synagogue
Grandfather	My brother, who is a 25-year-old mayor of a large town	Family holiday traditions
Charlie — my dog	Free speech	
Love for nature — kayaking		
Coming out		
Sibling		

After you make your lists, ask a classmate which ones he or she would like to know more about. Circle those. Then circle the three that are most interesting to you.

2. Now, for one of your topics, create a list of images that you associate with that topic.

3. Using the drawing technique, begin with a specific place and a specific time, and start your sonnet in action.

4. Writing a sonnet is similar to doing a puzzle with words. You have ten syllables per line to spend, so you might want to make a little fill-in-the-blank. (Tip: It's easier to do this work by hand than on the computer.) Make a grid with fourteen lines, ten blanks on each line. Then turn your first image into a line. Remember: You can spread the words in your first image into the next line (enjambment). At this point, it's less important that you worry about the rhythms of your lines — but do adhere closely to the *ten-syllable maximum* rule. Your instructor may introduce you to iambic pentameter — the *da dum, da dum, da dum* emphases on syllables found in Shakespeare's sonnets.

However, you will notice that if you stick to exactly ten syllables, your lines will have a natural rhythm.

5. Play out your first image. You can use online rhyming dictionaries to help you work out the rhymes suggested by the end words you have established in your first lines. If those words are too hard to rhyme, then simply go back and fiddle around with your lines. It can be frustrating and time-consuming. But it's always a great way to practice creative focus and concentration. Writing sonnets is exercise, and while not always pleasant, exercise is good for you.

> *He is a fool which cannot make one sonnet, and he is mad which makes two.*
> —JOHN DONNE

The sonnet will force you to come up with images, word choices, patterns, and thoughts that would not have occurred to you otherwise.

As you go over your sonnet and work on the words, make sure you send your poem in one direction in the first eight lines, and then in another direction for the next six lines. Perhaps in the opening of your sonnet you have argued that Tinder is mind candy, harmless, fun—a good way to relax at the end of the day. Then in the second part of the poem, you must *turn*. Moving in the opposite direction, you say that Tinder isn't really fun, relaxing, helpful, or harmless at all. In fact, you may conclude something very surprising about your Tinder addiction, something you would have never thought of without the sonnet as your guide. A sonnet provides *a way to think*.

VILLANELLE

The villanelle is a nineteen-line poem with a pattern of repeated lines and two rhymes. Poet Annie Finch says, "The villanelle is one of the most fascinating and paradoxical of poetic forms, quirky and edgy yet second to no other European form but the sonnet in importance; prone to moods of obsession and delight; structured through the marriage of repetition and surprise."

> *Poetry is not an expression of the party line. It's that time of night, lying in bed, thinking what you really think, making the private world public; that's what the poet does.*
> —ALLEN GINSBERG

Developed in Italy, where it was the basic pattern for folk songs, the villanelle became quite popular in France in the seventeenth century.

The nineteen lines of this form are presented in five tercets (three-line stanzas), completed by a quatrain (a four-line stanza).

Reading Villanelles

Without studying the form or reading ahead, take a moment to read aloud the villanelle on page 332 by Gregory Orr, "The River." And search for Theodore Roethke's famous example of a villanelle, "The Waking," online.

PRACTICE 20

READING VILLANELLES

Read the two villanelles "The River" and "The Waking" again. Annotate the poems so that you see the repetition and rhyme scheme clearly by labeling the rhyme scheme and noting any other kinds of repetition or pattern. Then, write a paragraph in which you answer the following questions: What seems to be the formal structure? What do you think the rules of the villanelle are going to be? What appeals to you about the sounds and music in the poems? What are the most striking differences in these two poems?

After you have read the villanelles, familiarize yourself with the following recipe. The nineteen lines can be of any length. There is no set meter. But there is a rhyme scheme and there are repeating lines. Ultimately, when you follow the recipe, the villanelle will have five tercets (three-line stanzas), one final stanza that is a quatrain (four-line stanza). Throughout the poem there are two sets of rhyming words, plus two refrains.

STANZA 1	STANZA 2	STANZA 3
A^1 — refrain	A	a
b	b	b
A^2 — refrain	A^1 — refrain	A^2 — refrain

STANZA 4	STANZA 5	STANZA 6
A	a	A
b	b	b
A^1 — refrain	A^2 — refrain	A^1
		A^2

In the table, a capital letter indicates that the whole line is repeated; a lowercase letter indicates that a word is rhymed or repeated. In the villanelle recipe, the symbol A^1 indicates the first line of your poem, and each time it's repeated, you use *the exact same line* again — the poem truly writes itself. The symbol A^2 indicates a new line, but the end word *rhymes* with the end word in A^1.

Sandwiched in between those repeating lines is also a rhyme scheme: *aba* for the tercets and *abaa* for the quatrain. As you read, you probably won't overtly notice the structure if the villanelle is doing its job.

It sounds like a kind of overwhelming nightmare; it's not, really. As always, it's easiest to begin a form poem by reading an example and then labeling the lines so you can see the form. The notation is confusing and frustrating until you practice writing a few. Be patient.

The successful villanelle has refrain (repeated) lines that blend and flow into the poem. As you read, the lines change meaning in their varied contexts.

Further Reading

In This Book	Highly Recommended
• *The River* by Gregory Orr (page 332) • *Do Not Go Gentle into That Good Night* by Dylan Thomas (page 123)	• *One Art* by Elizabeth Bishop • *The House on the Hill* by Edwin Arlington Robinson • *The American on His First Honeymoon* by Rita Mae Reese • *Zombie Blues Villanelle* by Tim Seibles • *Women's Work* by Julia Alvarez

Writing a Villanelle

Like the pantoum, the villanelle almost writes itself, once you have settled on two lines that you think are interesting enough to repeat (and that rhyme). The two lines need to go together but also be wholly independent of each other so that at the end, when they show up side by side, the reader will be both surprised and satisfied. Be patient with yourself as you write your villanelle—you are building new writing muscles as you work in this form, and you will surely feel some resistance, annoyance, and frustration. Let that be part of your writing and learning process. Most students find that in each case—pantoum, ghazal, sestina, villanelle—learning *about* the poem is difficult, much more difficult than actually writing it. Try taking older, failed poems and reworking them into one or more of these forms. And allow yourself to break the rules and reinvent the forms—to claim these techniques for yourself.

> *Pay attention only to the form; emotion will come spontaneously to inhabit it. A perfect dwelling always finds an inhabitant.*
> —ANDRÉ GIDE

Keep your lines about the same length. For topics, try writing about sisters, brothers, a river, or a job one of your parents had when he or she was young, titled "My Mother the _____" or "My Father the _____."

THE WRITING LIFE

The most important thing for any aspiring writer, I think, is to read! And not just the sort of thing you're trying to write, be that fantasy, SF, comic books, whatever. You need to read everything.

GEORGE R. R. MARTIN

I just kept thinking, if I can just keep practicing these sentences, then they'll get better. And that's exactly what happened.

ELIZABETH STROUT

One of the things I've learned this far into a life in language is to be grateful about all of this. Just to be able to do this work, to meet people along the way, to celebrate other writers, to live in a life of words? I can't tell you how grateful I am for that gift.

ADA LIMÓN

CHAPTER ELEVEN

REACHING READERS

In this chapter you will:

- Discover strategies for building a writing community, including reading your work publicly and subscribing and submitting to literary magazines
- Reflect thoughtfully on your own writing process in order to clarify strengths and weaknesses and set realistic writing goals in an artist's statement
- Construct chapbooks and/or portfolios

Painters show their work to the public at gallery openings. Piano students play for audiences at recitals. Actors build their performance for opening night. As writers, we bring our work—off our screens, out of the writing workshop—into the world through live readings and via literary magazines and other forms of publication. How do you know when your work is ready for a wider audience?

PREPARING TO PUBLISH

You've written *a lot*. You've created, revised, edited, proofread, and polished—it's been fun, and it's been frustrating and hard, too—and now you most likely have a body of work to share with others. You're wise to ask a trusted teacher or experienced writers if your work is ready to publish. Also, it can be helpful to clarify your expectations and your reasons for sharing your work with the world.

Bringing work to an audience offers you opportunities to learn more as a writer. Submitting work to a magazine or preparing a piece for reading aloud gives you a chance to evaluate your writing carefully; seen in this light, sharing your work can be a really helpful part of your shaping process. Creative writing is about more than self-expression: You want your audience to be entertained, deeply moved, intrigued, or all three, and imagining your audience's reactions—for real—can help you make your work more vibrant and clear and compelling.

Try to pay attention to audience reactions in a way that lets you gain insight into your own work. It's hard, but work to set your ego aside and keep your curiosity out front. What aspects of your writing are connecting with others? What parts of your work aren't hitting the mark as you'd like? Public reaction can be really helpful to you as you return to the writing studio and continue shaping your work. Ultimately, sharing your work with others is a community-building conversation. It's meaningful to offer your work to others, and for you to receive their writing, cheering on your fellow writers. Creative writers thrive on supporting each other and connecting through live readings and literary magazines, social media, blogs, YouTube recordings, and so on.

You have a number of ways to take your work to readers. Here are the three main ways:

1. Give a live reading of your creative writing (in class, at your school's student center, in a local coffee shop, etc.).
2. Publish or share in a digital or print format.
3. Create a digital or print chapbook or portfolio of your work to share with your instructor, classmates, or more widely.

Performing, tweeting, blogging, and creating and distributing limited print editions of your work are all forms of publication. So, in the service of learning your craft, at some point (usually toward the end of a course), it's a good idea both to celebrate and to take stock of what you have done, hone one or more strong pieces, stand back, and put the work out there to see how it's received by the larger community, whether that's your teacher and full class or a public venue, a class magazine, or a professional literary publication/ website.

LIVE READINGS

Attending a Live Reading

Many writers say that nothing allows them to see their work more clearly than reading it aloud before an audience. When you read your work to a live audience, all the flaws in a piece of writing can suddenly show up—if only to you—and new ways back into the piece might become obvious to you.

Consider this situation: There's a sentence in your story you love, you adore it, it's your favorite. When your piece is discussed in class, everyone loves the line. It's not until you read the work aloud in front of a group of people that you realize the truth: The sentence has nothing to do with your story. Out it goes (maybe it's the first line of a new piece). During a live reading, you'll be able to see things about your writing that you can't see any other way. Sometimes you will read aloud a sentence slightly differently than how it appears on the page, and you'll realize that you've landed on a smoother syntax. You'll see readers sometimes making little marks as they read.

You'll also be able to get immediate feedback. Are people on their phones while you are reading? Or do you have them riveted to your words, fully attentive? The feedback is crucial to your growth as a writer.

> A word after a word after a word is power.
> —MARGARET ATWOOD

Some writers feel they should wait until they are really, really good before they attempt some form of public presentation. However, presenting your work after writing intensively for even just a few months is a great way to educate yourself about your writing process—again, nothing else gives you quite this experience.

Before you read your own work aloud, attend a few live readings by professional authors, as well as watching author readings online, so you can see what you like, learn to avoid pitfalls, and get a feel for how various authors talk about their work, read, and behave. Some people just don't read their work well. You can learn from them what *not* to do. But some readings are thrilling. Just as established comics try out new material in tiny clubs, writers sometimes read from a new piece or even a work-in-progress in order to try it out, to get information about what is working in the piece and what is not. Again, nothing reveals the sweet spots and the weaknesses in a piece of writing more than reading it aloud before a live audience.

> The secret to being a writer is that you have to write. It's not enough to think about writing or to study literature or plan a future life as an author. You really have to lock yourself away, alone, and get to work.
> —AUGUSTEN BURROUGHS

While live is always best, try online resources such as *This American Life*, *The Moth*, TED Talks, and YouTube, especially if the area where you live doesn't offer a lot of live literary readings. Search for your favorite authors or the ones in this textbook; Joy Harjo and Jenifer Hixson are famous for giving terrific performances of their work. And search for the specific types of work you want to be exposed to, such

See plays you don't expect to like. Let yourself be surprised. A great playwriting teacher once told me, "There's nothing really to learn from watching a masterpiece. There's plenty to learn from watching something imperfect." Take notes, think about what you'd do differently.

—MARCO RAMIREZ

as poetry slam and hip-hop at the Nuyorican Poets Café (www.nuyorican.org). Or try a search for "best spoken word performances."

Some writers have a "read aloud" version of their work that differs from the published or printed version; often the "read aloud" version is shorter, and the writer puts in cues and markers for clarity, for example, placing the character names ahead of the dialogue lines and repeating characters' names more frequently so listeners are never confused.

Going to a live reading and staying present for the duration requires fairly intense concentration. Know that it's okay to space out . . . to mentally drift. It's really hard to listen carefully at a high level for a sustained amount of time, especially if you are someone who does not regularly go to live readings. Gently bring yourself back to the performance when you notice that your mind has wandered. And don't beat yourself up. It's actually the writer's job to keep you riveted!

TIPS: Attending a Live Reading

1. If possible, do some background reading on the authors who are presenting—you'll get more out of the event.

2. Take notes on images you like, lines you respond to. Taking notes helps you listen actively.

3. Observe what this reader does onstage that is particularly compelling. Do they have any speech or body language behaviors that are distracting?

4. When the author is finishing up, try to think of a question or a comment for them. You might jot it down in your notebook. During the question-and-answer period or afterward at the book-signing table, you can ask the question or make the comment.

PRACTICE 1

ATTENDING A LIVE READING

Before you read your work aloud to an audience, attend a live reading. Take notes during the reading and after. Write a paragraph reaction, answering the questions in the four prompts under "Tips" above. Include at least one question (whether or not you asked it aloud) for the author.

Giving a Live Reading

When you prepare your own work to read live, whether it's just to your class or to a larger audience, here are some strategies to keep in mind.

1. **Plan.** Make sure you know exactly what you are going to read, and what you are going to say when you take the stage. Some authors jump right in. Others announce the genre and title, and then jump in. Some begin with a short poem or paragraph by another writer, honoring and giving credit to an author who has inspired them. Prefacing your own reading with someone else's words pays homage to that person and at the same time serves to calm your nerves: You start your reading with a proven winner. You might have people to thank, or some needed background information to offer the audience before you begin your reading. Plan out everything you are going to say carefully.

2. **Practice.** You will want to practice before a mirror. Record yourself and listen to your reading carefully. This will help you make changes in the writing as well as in your presentation style. A supportive friend or family member who is willing to listen while you read your piece and offer constructive suggestions as well as praise can be extremely useful. Before you go live, practice extensively to rehearse your "off-the-cuff" remarks, work out your timing, and figure out the best pieces to read.

3. **Time yourself.** Going over the allotted time is completely out of bounds. For new writers, quick readings — five-minute, three-minute, two-page, or poem-and-a-page-of-prose readings — work best. Make sure your planned introductory remarks fit into your allotted time.

4. **Get comfortable.** Arrive early. If it's permitted, practice speaking into the microphone; ask for guidance on where to hold or how to wear the mic. Make sure your voice reaches the back row and that you are clear on where you are supposed to sit, stand, and read when the time comes.

5. **Connect.** You'll want to speak clearly and slowly, vary the pitch of your voice, avoid sounding monotone, and make eye contact. Whether you are reading from a device or hard copy, make sure the text isn't a barrier between you and your audience; know your piece well enough so that you can look up and make a connection with your listeners.

6. **Exit with grace.** Have an exit strategy. Slow down, way down, as you read the last words or lines of your piece. When you are done, look directly at the audience, say "thank you," and leave the stage.

Am I prolific? I'm not sure. I am persistent. Or maybe it's that I have no standards! It's something different than being prolific because it's very difficult. Every book I've published has taken me such a long time and I'm so unsure about all of them.

—KAZIM ALI

After you give your live reading, you may want to take a few minutes to make some notes on your text, marking places that you may want to consider revising — places where you stumbled, or got an unexpected laugh, or places where you could sense you may have confused the audience. If anything read rough, you will want to make a note. Later, you can decide if you want to revise your piece or if you just need to practice reading those parts aloud so they are smoother.

A class reading is a friendly, effective way to practice sharing your work. Some classes hold live readings at the end of the semester, and members of the class invite friends, teachers, and family.

Lastly, know that most people are nervous when they read their work. It's normal and okay to be nervous; you can use that energy in your performance. If you have shaped your work, practiced your reading, made sincere attempts to connect with your audience, and entered into this process with an openness to learning everything you can as a writer, you can't fail. You will gain confidence as you continue to give live readings.

LITERARY MAGAZINES: PRINT AND DIGITAL

Editors are constantly looking for new, undiscovered writers. Every magazine wants to be able to say it published the first story by the next Ernest Hemingway or the new Jhumpa Lahiri. New writers should explore as many of the so-called little or literary magazines as time allows, both print and digital. To get a good sense of what editors and readers are interested in, read through the pieces published in magazines devoted to showcasing new writers.

How do you find these literary magazines? Numerous online guides can help you. It's my strong opinion that when you are beginning as a writer, you should not pay reading fees or send money to anyone, ever, when you submit your work. While some magazines charge reading fees so they can stay afloat, I advise you to publish some pieces in magazines that do not charge reading fees, so that you are certain your technique is at a professional level *before* you send money. Ideally, you will be paid, even a token sum, for some of your pieces; use those funds to pay reading fees down the road. Don't go in the hole. Some scam artists and disreputable outfits might promise to publish your work in an anthology — for a fee. Run, don't walk, away.

Rely on Guides and Directories

The following resources are reputable and comprehensive guides to help you locate reputable journals. First, locate journals that look interesting to you. Then, read their submission guidelines (easily found on the magazine's website) to see if they are open to receiving work by new writers or unpublished writers. Then — and this is the crucial step — read several issues of that magazine before submitting your work to its editors. Do you still love this magazine? Would you be proud to be in it? Is your work a good fit? Is your writing at the same level of quality as the work it is publishing? If in doubt, ask your instructor, experienced writers, or trusted peers.

WebdelSol.com. Web del Sol is a comprehensive directory for information pertaining to literary magazines. You'll find creative writing news, reviews of literary magazines, and magazine rankings such as "Top 50 Literary Magazines and Metazines."

Clmp.org. The Community of Literary Magazines and Presses is also a directory that catalogues independent literary publishers. Like independent bookstores or independent record labels, these publishers focus on publishing indie poetry, fiction, and creative nonfiction, and they are mission-driven, meaning that their main concern is long-term, quality relationships with authors and small but devoted audiences, not ads, dollars, or fame. Emerging voices and hybrid and experimental art forms that are overlooked by mainstream magazines can find a home through *The CLMP Directory*. The site is also a good guide to writing conferences.

> *I just try to warn people who hope to get published that publication is not all it is cracked up to be. But writing is. Writing has so much to give, so much to teach, so many surprises. That thing you had to force yourself to do — the actual act of writing — turns out to be the best part.*
>
> —ANNE LAMOTT

Writersmarket.com. *Writer's Market* offers detailed information on a wide range of markets that pay writers to write. At your reference library, track down *Writer's Market*, a large, multitiered reference work. Historically, one volume is devoted to the novel and short story markets, another to the children's literature market, and another to the poetry market. In addition, it offers helpful articles on how to write attention-getting queries.

Pw.org. *Poets and Writers* is a fantastic resource for new writers. Online you'll find an excellent search engine for literary magazines; each magazine

> *I didn't love being rejected,*
> *but my expectations were low*
> *and my patience was high.*
>
> —ELIZABETH GILBERT

describes what kind of work it is currently looking for. This is also an invaluable resource for those interested in researching grants for writers, summer workshops, writing conferences, and contests.

Newpages.com. NewPages is a respected site that provides information on literary journals, publishers, and creative writing programs. The site's call-for-submission page is updated regularly.

PRACTICE 2

RESEARCHING LITERARY MAGAZINES

Visit two of the resources listed here and spend some time exploring the sites. Write a brief review of each of your two sites—what was most useful here for you as a writer? What are two or three things that surprised you as you dug deeper into the sites? Then make a brief list: In what ways are the two sites you chose different from each other? Did you like one better than the other? Lastly, create a list of three to five literary magazines you discovered via these sites that you will explore further, in order to research them as possible places where you will submit your work.

Research a Wide Range of Publications

Magazines are like towns—each one has its own personality, its own look and feel. Travel widely as a reader; exploring as many literary magazines as you can is empowering for you as a writer. You'll find some authors who inspire you to keep writing. And you may also say, "Hey, I can write this well."

If you search for "best literary magazines," "top ten literary magazines," or "best new literary journals," you will find that some titles keep appearing; check those out and read the work they are publishing to get a good feel for what the editors are looking for. Many magazines have special issues on topics they announce in advance such as the body, race, or climate change. Other magazines offer features that can inspire your writing, such as six-word Twitter stories or video essays.

And I encourage you to consider print magazines. Independent bookstores often stock local zines alongside internationally known literary magazines that feature the work of writers and artists you may not find elsewhere. Consider subscribing to a high-quality print literary magazine such as *The Paris Review, Image, Lapham's Quarterly, Prairie Schooner,* or *The Gettysburg Review.* In addition to participating in the community of writers in a significant way, magazines usually waive reading fees for subscribers.

PRACTICE 3

EVALUATING LITERARY MAGAZINES

Explore a recent issue of a print or online literary magazine, one listed above or one that you find on your own. Write a mini-review of the magazine and share it with your class, perhaps on a discussion board, so that others can decide if they want to explore this magazine or possibly submit work to it in the future.

Submit Your Work

Before you submit your work for publication, take it through as many rounds of workshops, writing groups, shaping, and editing as best as you can. The manuscript must be without error — many editors simply won't read past the first page if they spot grammar mistakes, typos, missing page numbers, or any failure to follow the magazine's submission requirements.

Magazines receive hundreds of manuscripts a week. Many of these are quickly discarded, without being read from beginning to end; experienced editors often know instantly whether the answer is "maybe" or "no." Editors may glance at the first page of a story or the first lines of a poem and decide immediately that the work does not have enough energy, pattern, or tension to keep reading. If the work is static, cliché, or grammatically challenged, it's probably going to be a "no." Editors won't do your work for you. Editors edit *magazines*. You edit your work. Send your best, most polished pieces.

When your manuscript is ready — really ready — read the submission guidelines for the magazine carefully. Follow the guidelines to the letter. Pay special attention to the magazine's policy on **simultaneous submissions** and **multiple submissions**. These are two different things. A simultaneous submission is a piece of writing you submit to different journals for consideration *at the same time.* If a magazine says they do not take simultaneous submissions, you must honor that policy. Multiple submissions occur when a writer sends several pieces of writing to a single magazine at the same time. Some magazines allow this; many do not. Read the fine print closely.

You'll want to stay organized, keeping track of each piece you submit, to where, when, and what you hear back from the editors. Many magazines use a free online submissions manager called Submittable; you'll want to open an account there. But not all magazines use Submittable, so you should keep track of your publishing life in a file or note on your phone or tablet. Know that many magazines take six months or even up to a year — sometimes longer! — to get back to you. While you are waiting, you are writing new pieces, honing your craft.

You may wish to start your submitting process with your school's literary magazine. If your school doesn't yet have a literary magazine, maybe it's time for you and your friends to start one online. Next, research local and then regional markets for creative writing. Visit locally owned bookstores for zines and journals with a regional focus. Be realistic about which publications might be a good fit for your work, stay creative, and have fun choosing where to submit your work. Most writers start small and close to home, steadily building a résumé of more prestigious publications.

An important note to keep in mind: If you have published your work on your blog or elsewhere on social media, it's usually considered published. Many magazines won't consider work that's already published—read their submission guidelines carefully.

Get Rejected

You will. Lots. It's not a problem and it doesn't mean your work is bad. Embrace rejection as part of the process of getting published. *Most* work is rejected; most magazines accept less than 10 percent of what they receive, and usually it's closer to a 1 percent to 2 percent acceptance rate. Many magazines receive hundreds of manuscripts *per week*. Remember, *rejection isn't feedback*—it's the publishing process, playing out. Maybe the magazine just published a poem on your topic, or maybe you misread the guidelines and the magazine doesn't actually publish plays. You really have no way of knowing if the piece was rejected because of the quality of the writing or the taste of the editor. Those of us who have published books—multiple books—still have work rejected by literary magazines *all the time.* Submitting is a process of finding the right home for your best work, and working, all the while, to improve your craft.

When a piece comes back, look at it gently but carefully. Can you improve it? Often, a rejection note changes your relationship to the piece. You read with a colder eye and are more willing to cut weaker parts. You read like an editor, asking editor-type questions: *What's the experience of reading this like? Why would my subscribers be interested in this? Where's the energy, the tension, the insight in this piece? Is it smooth, fresh, creative, evocative, polished?*

You may wish to do as other writers have done and start a spreadsheet titled "My 100." Your goal? To amass one hundred rejections before you even begin to complain about how hard it is to get published. One hundred rejections is a good measure that you are taking your work seriously. Make sure, as you are meeting your goal, that you are reading magazines carefully, keeping a close eye on the quality of your work—are you improving?—and your ability to assess if a magazine is a good fit for your subject matter and your talents.

Many nonwriters think they would never be able to handle rejection. But as all artists and athletes know, a high level of rejection and failure is built into our profession; rejection is simply part of the deal. It means at least you are in the game. Yes, rejection might indicate that you are sending your work out too early — it needs more revision, more attention. Or the rejection of a piece might mean that a particular editor just doesn't like this kind of piece, even though your writing is fantastic. You don't like everything you read. Some published works — perhaps in this very textbook — might make you wonder, *What is so great about this? I don't get it.*

> *Close the door. Write with no one looking over your shoulder. Don't try to figure out what other people want to hear from you; figure out what you have to say. It's the one and only thing you have to offer.*
>
> —BARBARA KINGSOLVER

Not all editors need to adore your work; just one editor does. Don't give editors, and rejection, more power than they really have: Just because an editor likes or dislikes your work doesn't mean it's good or bad. Great works go unpublished. Flawed works find publishers and readers.

Work on what you can control: your commitment to always improving your craft and your persistence. You'll probably resubmit your work (revising and improving along the way) many times before it finds a good home. Enjoy the process.

PORTFOLIOS AND CHAPBOOKS

Portfolios

In art classes, the end of the semester provides an opportunity to show the body of work you have created, shaped, and polished, so that others can see what you do. In writing classes, we often use a portfolio at the end of the semester for the same purpose. Your instructor evaluates your growth by examining this portfolio of your strongest pieces. Most important, by thinking about what you've created during the course, you can gain valuable insights into your strengths and weaknesses as a writer and can take stock of where you want to go next.

A portfolio is a sampling of your best work — your best poems, short-shorts, a short play, an outstanding essay. Sometimes a portfolio contains an artist's statement or other reflective writing in which you discuss your process and your habits of mind as a writer. Portfolios can be copied for each class member or simply discussed with your instructor.

For this course, you may be asked to create a portfolio presenting five separate pieces — in any genre — that best demonstrate your skill, in turn, with:

1. Images
2. Energy
3. Tension
4. Pattern
5. Insight

Your instructor may ask you to include at least two or three genres (or not).

PRACTICE 4

EVALUATING YOUR SKILLS

In preparation for a portfolio, or as a self-reflective opportunity, choose a piece from the semester that best demonstrates each of the five key creative writing strategies, listed above. Explain why the piece you have chosen best exemplifies your skill with this particular strategy, and give at least two examples, for each strategy, from your piece, that show techniques at work. Use different pieces of writing for each of the five strategies and make sure to quote examples from your works.

Alternatively, your portfolio might require you to demonstrate facility with a number of different genres, such as:

1. Flash fiction
2. Memoir
3. Free verse poem
4. Formal poem
5. Hybrid, comic, or five-minute play

PRACTICE 5

OBSERVING GENRE SKILLS

Write a self-reflection that is based on what you learned from practicing different genres. Your instructor may have specific directions. Reread the pieces you wrote in various genres. Going one genre at a time, choose a single piece that represents your best work in that genre. Explain why. Then write a paragraph about what you learned specifically from working in this genre that carries over into your other writing. Support your self-observations with examples.

Some instructors ask students to submit ten pages of original work, revised from the work they've been doing in this course, that demonstrate the course concepts. Regardless, use the portfolio as rehearsal for your publication process, taking this opportunity to shape and revise, to hone and polish, so you take your work to the next level before departing the course.

As an alternative to the portfolio, some creative writing classes design their own literary magazine. The entire class can serve as an editorial board, selecting a piece from each class member, working from portfolios of submitted works in either print or digital formats. Or small writing groups can publish print or digital literary magazines, each with its own vision, personal flair, and mission.

Chapbooks

Another way to collect your best work is to create a chapbook. A chapbook is a small book, like a pamphlet, stapled and photocopied, and sold or given away. The name derives from "cheap books," popular in Great Britain in the eighteenth and nineteenth centuries, where "chapmen" (peddlers) made up inexpensive publications—often just a single sheet of paper folded to make eight, sixteen, or twenty-four pages—to sell.

Simplicity and economy are hallmarks of the chapbook, and for poets, flash writers, and hybrid writers, especially, professionally published chapbooks remain a popular and widely respected mode for distributing new work. Chapbooks can be sold or given away at live readings. Some creative writing classes ask each participant to create enough copies of their individual chapbooks so that all students have one. If you would like to look at some excellent examples, search for publishers who specialize in chapbooks. RopeWalk Press, Rose Metal Press, and Black Lawrence Press are well-known, well-respected examples; there are many more. A chapbook that is made into a high-quality, professionally printed book is called an artist's book. Examine the Center for Book Arts (centerforbookarts.org) for more information on how writers turn their work into art, taking the publishing process into their own hands.

The type of chapbook most often submitted in creative writing classes usually has a simple cover on regular paper or card stock and may include illustrations by the author, clip art, or other graphic design elements. The chapbook also has a table of contents and often, in the back, a short biographical note about the author. A chapbook can be printed on

8½ × 11 inch paper with a landscape orientation so that the pages can then be folded and saddle-stapled. Using the search term *bookletize*, search online or in your word processing program for directions on how to create multiple copies of chapbooks. The article "DIY: How to Make and Bind Chapbooks," on the *Poets and Writers* website (pw.org), is a good introduction to making chapbooks.

A class chapbook—essentially a joint portfolio to which each student contributes one of his or her best pieces of writing—is another way to publish your work. The class decides on the guidelines. For example, each person might submit up to three pages of creative writing. Students decide who will organize the selections, who will proofread, and who will prepare the table of contents. Depending on the budget, the class can print extra copies so that each class member, the instructor, and friends and family have a chance to read this work or the work can be published online.

If you continue with creative writing, you can hand out chapbooks of your work (or your writing group's work) at your live readings, just as musicians may offer copies of their music at live performances.

Publishing your own work in a portfolio or chapbook helps you maintain high standards for revision and editing. While the process is time-consuming, it provides invaluable information to you as a writer. When you prepare work for public consumption, you learn to let go of things that were hard to cut during earlier revisions. That long poem has to fit onto one page? You might realize that what everyone has been saying all along, that the last four stanzas simply aren't needed, is actually spot on. Or you choose to start your story in the middle because you see that the beginning is merely preface after all.

Creating portfolios and chapbooks forces you to look at your work with a cold eye, and that is often the most helpful feedback you can get as a writer—the lessons you discover for yourself.

Artist Statements

At the end of the semester, it's a good idea to take stock of what you have learned, how far you have come. Your instructor may ask you to write an **artist's statement**—a reflective essay on what you set out to learn, how you have grown as a writer and a reader, and what concerns and considerations you will continue to explore, after the class. This statement may be included in your portfolio, chapbook, or class publication, or posted in a discussion.

To write an artist's statement, gather all of your writing from the semester. And as you read it over, take notes.

Look at how your writing process has matured, and take stock of the techniques you have now that you didn't have before. Look also at your exercises and the feedback you received from other writers. What patterns do you notice? What did you *not* know when this course opened? As you read, notice what makes you cringe or wince. Were you trying to sound writerly? Confident? Intrepid? Teacher-pleasing? Try to articulate the small, specific ways you've grown and changed as a writer — and a reader.

The reflective work you do in an artist's statement isn't easy. It might be helpful to talk through your observations with someone who knows you well — an instructor, adviser, or trusted mentor or friend. But this self-assessment work is essential to your growth as a writer — and your development as a thoughtful, engaged person in the world. These types of questions and this kind of thinking and writing serve as terrific practice for the writing you will do in the future, whether it's on the job, evaluating yourself and others, or in applications for graduate school, grants, or other programs or employment.

If you are feeling stuck, you might read some conversations with writers; interviews with the writers you most admire are easily found online and in *The Paris Review Interviews*.

QUESTIONS TO ASK: Writing an Artist's Statement

Consider the following fourteen questions when writing about your own work, whether for self-reflection or to include as an artist's statement to submit at the end of the term. You'll want to write at least a paragraph for each answer.

1. What were your assumptions about "being a writer" before you took this class?
2. What are two ways your understanding of what "being a writer" has changed?
3. Have your goals as a writer changed?
4. What's the most important thing you have learned during this course?
5. As you reread your early work for this class, what do you notice?
6. What piece of writing are you most proud of? Why?
7. What are three specific ways this course has helped you read more closely?

(Continues on next page)

QUESTIONS TO ASK: Writing an Artist's Statement (*continued*)

8 What have you learned about your writing habits?

9 Do you see yourself as part of a writing community? Do you prefer to work in isolation, focusing on the work and reading?

10 What's the most important thing you learned about getting and giving feedback about work-in-progress?

11 What techniques, authors, or exercises have been most useful to you?

12 What insights have you gained into the practice and art of creative writing?

13 Has your voice changed? Is your writing truer, deeper, better?

14 What authors do you want to read now? Has that changed from when you started the course?

CHAPTER TWELVE

WRITING RESOURCES

Instagram for up-and-coming authors, books on how to write your novel in thirty days (and lose weight in the process), websites listing calls for manuscripts from high-power literary agents, magazines promising publication and lucrative possibilities in "Six Quick Steps" — information for writers is abundant. How do you sort through the screens and pages of material to find trustworthy, high-quality information on building a writing life? It's not easy. This chapter serves as a guide to digital and print resources you can use as a jumping-off place. The resources listed here are ones that other writers and teachers of creative writing have cited as helpful. You will also certainly find additional valuable resources on your own.

As a writer, your best resources are always your dedicated daily writing practice — the ten minutes or two hours you spend on your craft — and your writing group. To supplement your daily writing habit, you may want to collect writing books for further study, use Twitter or Instagram to create community after your writing class ends, create your own blog and share it on social media, and locate publishing markets open to new writers. Remember: Do not send money for any reason in order to publish your work, have it edited, or enter a contest that requires fees unless your instructor has assured you it is a reputable and worthy venue.

Rather than rushing to publish, you might want to purchase a few good-quality books on writing and select some discerning blogs or feeds to monitor regularly. Keep in mind that if you self-publish your work digitally, you may not be able to publish it elsewhere.

> *Don't be seduced into thinking that that which does not make a profit is without value.*
>
> —ARTHUR MILLER

SMART SEARCHING

A quick Google search will reveal thousands of writing websites on the internet. So how are you supposed to know what is good and what is garbage? By developing good searching skills. A few tips will help you refine your search and separate the good, the bad, and the ugly.

The "Advanced Search" feature on Google lets you narrow down your results. Try limiting the search to domains ending in .edu or .org—these sites are affiliated with reputable, noncommercial enterprises. Use quotation marks in your search to find exact phrases (e.g., *daily writing prompts, creative writing MFA programs, contemporary sonnets, flash fiction,* or *slam poetry in Arkansas*). In the example shown in Figure 12.1, a student wanted to find daily writing prompts for fiction or nonfiction writing. He wanted a .org domain but didn't want to be linked to a blogspot site.

To find good advice on writing, search for interviews with your favorite author. Literary magazines often publish excellent interviews with authors, and these interviews frequently appear online. For example, the websites

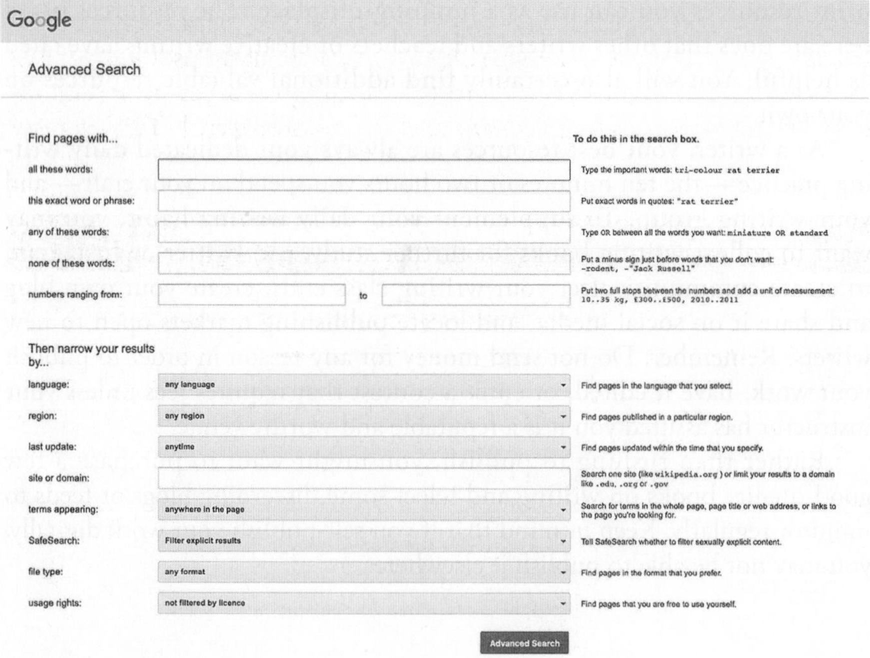

Figure 12.1 Google Advanced Search

for *The Paris Review* and *The Believer* have excellent archives of author interviews. *Brevity*, the online-only journal for flash nonfiction and micro-memoir, has a section devoted to craft essays. Also, check out podcasts such as *Fresh Air* and *Longform* to hear authors and artists in conversation.

To hear great storytelling and spoken word, download podcasts from *The Moth*, *Snap Judgment*, *Radiolab*, *This American Life*, *Serial*, and *The Story*. Search for "TED Talks to Inspire Creativity" and discover TED Talks by brilliant and motivating authors from around the world, such as Elizabeth Gilbert, Young-ha Kim, Amy Tan, Isabel Allende, and Chimamanda Ngozi Adichie.

High-quality websites are often connected to universities, writing programs, and nonprofit writing projects. Check out the websites for top writing programs such as the Vermont College of Fine Arts, the Iowa Writers' Workshop, Bennington College, the University of Michigan, the University of Arizona, and the UCLA Extension Writers' Program. Many of the official sites for these programs will link you to their own publications and other excellent writing sites.

In addition to a Google search, go to your school's library and use academic databases to find the most reputable writing resources. Reference librarians are your best resource for help with your search. Most colleges and universities have access to a selection of academic databases, which require a subscription. Academic databases tend to provide results from scholarly journals. You will discover fewer articles from popular magazines and more articles geared toward serious writers. Two particularly useful databases are Project MUSE and JSTOR. Project MUSE gives access to several literary magazines, including *Callaloo* and *Prairie Schooner*. JSTOR is more

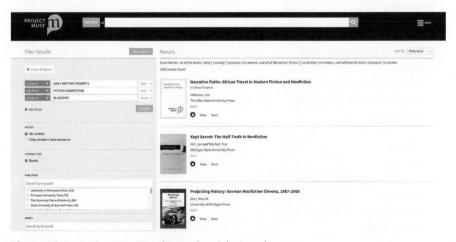

Figure 12.2 Project MUSE Advanced Article Search

academic than Project MUSE, but it is a good resource for finding articles on authors. As with Google, the advanced search features are extraordinarily helpful. You can browse by discipline, journal, author, title, keyword, or date of publication.

SOCIAL MEDIA

You will feel insecure and jealous. How much power you give those feelings is entirely up to you.
—CHERYL STRAYED

You've probably already considered the numerous resources on Twitter, Instagram, and other digital platforms. Most major journals, presses, and literary organizations are active on social media. Here are some suggestions for useful hashtags and handles to search to get you started:

Hashtags

#amwriting
#askagent
#author
#comics
#creativenonfiction
#editing
#inktober
#nanowrimo (National Novel Writing)
#napowrimo (National Poetry Writing)
#novels
#poetry
#poets
#pubtip (publication tips)
#scifi
#vss (very short story)
#wip (work-in-progress)
#writegoal
#writequote
#writer
#writers
#writerwednesday
#writing
#writingtips (writing advice)
#wrotetoday

The following hashtags are chats used as meeting places:

#bookstagram
#journchat
#kidlitchat
#litchat
#mybookfeatures
#scifichat
#storycraft

Twitter
@theoffingmag

> The Twitter account for *The Offing*, an online journal from the *Los Angeles Review of Books*, actively updates its followers on issues in writing and craft. This feed shares articles and creative essays from its own journal and other online sources that can be used in the creative writing classroom.

@NarrativeMag

> Follow this account to stay up-to-date on the latest publications by *Narrative Magazine*. Founded in 2003, *Narrative* aims to advance online literature.

@poetswritersinc

> A popular way to learn about hundreds of opportunities for new writers.

@Poetry_Daily

> You probably already follow your favorite poets; this account will expose you to terrific new voices.

@mcsweeneys

> *McSweeney's Quarterly Concern*, *Internet Tendency*, and *Books* are all discussed on this feed. The *Internet Tendency* articles are regularly posted to provide comic relief and writing inspiration.

@submittable
This account for Submittable, a submission manager tool, tweets open submission calls for writers.

RESOURCES

Creativity and Inspiration

If you are interested in increasing your creative powers, or you just want to read about artists, writers, and how they work, many resources are available. Each book and website on this list is accessible, lively, fascinating, and packed with useful information on what it is to "be creative." If you are stuck, these resources are extremely useful in helping you work through a block. Many of them have specific exercises that you can try in order to develop new creative muscles.

In Print

Ayan, Jordan E. *Aha! 10 Ways to Free Your Creative Spirit and Find Your Great Ideas.*
Baldwin, Christina. *Life's Companion: Journal Writing as a Spiritual Practice.*
Barry, Lynda. *Syllabus.*
Bayles, David, and Ted Orland. *Art and Fear: Observations on the Perils (and Rewards) of Artmaking.*
Brande, Dorothea. *Becoming a Writer.*
Gilbert, Elizabeth. *Big Magic: Creative Living beyond Fear.*
Gourevitch, Philip, ed. *The Paris Review Interviews.*
Lamott, Anne. *Bird by Bird: Some Instructions on Writing and Life.*
Maisel, Eric. *Fearless Creating: A Step-by-Step Guide to Starting and Completing Your Work of Art.*
Ueland, Barbara. *If You Want to Write.*

Online

Duotrope [www.duotrope.com]

> This resource aids writers in the submission process. It provides a searchable aggregate of information on literary journals. Users disclose statistics from their submitting experience. This information allows Duotrope to provide insider information, such as expected response time. The site charges a monthly membership fee.

Entropy [https://entropymag.org]

> A community space for writers at all levels, this site features reviews, interviews, calls for new work, and dozens of other helpful resources. Entropy is committed to creating safe spaces, valuing diverse beliefs, and supporting marginalized writers and readers.

Images: Seeing More Closely

The books listed here present different approaches to the "images" method presented in this textbook. In *How to Use Your Eyes*, James Elkins explains in great detail his philosophy of seeing—the art of looking more closely at the world and the people in it—with numerous visual examples to support his points. In *Zen Seeing, Zen Drawing*, visual artist Frederick Franck teaches how to enter that focused state in which you can see the aliveness in the image. Although Franck is talking to visual artists, his principles also apply to the work creative writers do.

In Print

Cassou, Mitchell. *Point Zero: Creativity without Limits.*
Elkins, James. *How to Use Your Eyes.*
Franck, Frederick. *Zen Seeing, Zen Drawing: Meditation in Action.*
Ganim, Barbara, and Susan Fox. *Visual Journaling.*

Self-Expression and Personal Writing

The assignments in this textbook are designed to help you write more effectively for others. Many creative writers also enjoy writing for themselves in a journal, in a blog, or as an informal daily practice. The following books and sites can help you go further with the writing you do just for yourself.

In Print

Adams, Kathleen. *Journal to the Self: Twenty-Two Paths to Personal Growth.*
Aronie, Nancy Slonim. *Writing from the Heart: Tapping the Power of Your Inner Voice.*
Cameron, Julia. *The Right to Write: An Invitation and Initiation into the Writing Life.*
Cerwinske, Laura. *Writing as a Healing Art.*
Goldberg, Natalie. *Writing Down the Bones: Freeing the Writer Within.*
Heard, Georgia. *Writing toward Home: Tales and Lessons to Find Your Way.*
Hughes, Elaine Farris. *Writing from the Inner Self.*
Joselow, Beth Baruch. *Writing without the Muse: 50 Beginning Exercises for the Creative Writer.*

Online

750 Words [750words.com]

> 750 Words is an online journaling site aimed to keep you writing 750 words every day. It has an interesting point system and many analysis tools that can tell you all about your writing.

Literary News

A key to writing is to immerse yourself in the literary world around you, not only by reading ferociously but also by keeping up-to-date on literary news. The following websites are great resources for headlines, reviews, interviews, and tips.

Literary Hub [lithub.com]

A website devoted to curating in one place the vast amount of literary news available online. Partnering with publishers, presses, and booksellers, Literary Hub provides original content, excerpts, and the latest news from the book world.

NewPages [newpages.com]

A guide to the world of the independent press. NewPages provides news and reviews on publications, bookstores, and periodicals, as well as resources for writers, such as a list of MFA programs and a list of blogs by published writers.

Poets and Writers [pw.org]

The website for *Poets and Writers Magazine*. The magazine itself is a must-read for creative writers interested in literary publishing. Both the magazine and the website are portals into the world of writing.

The Business of Writing: Agents, Freelancing, Book Proposals, and Publishing

You can find dozens of books on the business aspects of writing. Consider the 80/20 rule, and spend 80 percent of your writing time working on your craft and the remaining 20 percent on exploring markets, agents, and publishers. Here is a selection of the most useful resources devoted to helping you publish your work.

In Print

Begley, Adam. *Literary Agents: A Writer's Guide.*
Herman, Jeff, and Deborah Levine Herman. *Write the Perfect Book Proposal: 10 That Sold and Why.*
Higgins, George V. *On Writing: Advice for Those Who Write to Publish (or Would Like To).*
Lerner, Betsy. *The Forest for the Trees: An Editor's Advice to Writers.*
Lyon, Elizabeth. *Nonfiction Book Proposals Anybody Can Write: How to Get a Contract and Advance before Writing Your Book.*

Lyon, Elizabeth. *The Sell-Your-Novel Tool Kit: Everything You Need to Know about Queries, Synopses, Marketing, and Breaking In.*

Online

Agent Query [agentquery.com]

> Often recognized by *Writer's Digest* as one of the best websites for writers, Agent Query is an online database of hundreds of literary agents. In addition, Agent Query offers several helpful guides on the world of publishing, as well as a list of the best places to send your work, both in print and online.

The Association of Writers and Writing Programs [awpwriter.org]

> The Association of Writers and Writing Programs is a useful guide to schools, programs, and writing conferences—a must for those wanting to continue their education after undergraduate studies. The website for the AWP offers many useful databases for discovering writing programs and conferences. The organization also offers a useful print publication. Student discounts are available.

The Authors Guild [authorsguild.org]

> Members of the Authors Guild receive legal support, including contract reviews and health insurance discounts. Though membership is required for those benefits, nonmembers viewing the Authors Guild website will get the latest legal news in the publishing world.

Community of Literary Magazines and Presses [clmp.org]

> The Community of Literary Magazines and Presses website is an excellent resource for those interested in independent literary publication. The site lists websites for all of its member publications.

P&W Literary Agents Database [pw.org/literary_agents]

> Agents are listed with contact information and submission guidelines and are organized according to what sort of literature they are interested in representing.

Writers Guild of America [wga.org]

> This site is a very useful introduction to the business side of creative writing, with links where you can "ask the expert," learn to write for television, and connect with other writers. Especially helpful is the guide to internet developments of special interest to writers, which is updated monthly.

APPENDIX: TERMINOLOGY FOR CREATIVE WRITERS

Creative writers use a specialized vocabulary when talking about work-in-progress and when reading other writers' works, both student and professional. Here are some of the key words that you will hear frequently this semester and in your future writing and literature classes.

Alliteration: Repeated consonant sounds. Example: *Bring back baby.*

Assonance: Repeated vowel sounds. Example: *Oh no, don't let go, Jo-Jo.*

Backstory: Information about the characters' pasts that enriches the reader's understanding of the story's present.

Beat: A moment when something happens.

Block: A fear-based "freeze" reaction stemming from a lack of understanding of how the human brain engages with a writing process, as in "writer's block." See Lack of Focus (p. 22).

Cliché: Predictable choices—familiar words, stereotypical characters, and formulaic plots—that should be avoided in creative writing. To avoid clichés, try taking the fifth exit on the highway, not the first.

Complication: The practice of ordering beats so the situation gets more intense as the piece progresses. For example, imagine that you're late to class and you can't find a parking space. If you then hit a golf cart, that's a complication.

Conflict: The opposing elements in a piece of writing; without conflict, a piece usually lacks tension. (See Chapter Six.)

Couplet: A two-line stanza. See "We Real Cool" (p. 105).

Creative Nonfiction: True stories written with the dialogue, characterization, scene, and conflict common to fiction. Though these strategies are borrowed from fiction, they are used to present real situations instead of invented stories.

Direct Dialogue: The conversation of a character who is talking in real time. Direct dialogue is indicated by quotation marks. Example: *"I just published six poems," Emily Anne said.*

Enjambment: A poetry technique in which lines are wrapped so that they don't end with periods. See "First Poem for You" (p. 121).

First Person: The "I" point of view. See "How to Touch a Bleeding Dog" (p. 277).

Free Verse: A type of poem written without rhyme, with no rules for counting syllables, line length, or rhythm.

Genre: A category of artistic composition: a particular type of writing. There are many different literary genres, including poems, flash fiction, fan fiction, plays, detective novels, graphic novels, comic books, monologues, radio plays, and so on. (See Chapter Ten.)

Indirect Dialogue: Summarized dialogue. Indirect dialogue does not use quotation marks. Example: *The student said that she had writer's block and that it was cray-cray.*

Memoir: Personal writing about one's own life, often using scenes, dialogue, and insight, to tell a compelling story of interest to readers.

Metaphor: A comparison between two unlike things in order to make a point about a character, setting, or deeper insight. Example: *She's such a sunny person.* This person isn't actually being called the star at the center of our solar system but is being described as bright and warm.

Monologue: A story or speech spoken or delivered by one speaker. Comedians such as Jim Gaffigan and Wanda Sykes perform monologues, as do characters in plays and in other kinds of stories.

Narrator: The person telling the story.

Omniscience: A point of view in which the narrator is able to go into any character's perspective and make comments about the world of the story from an all-knowing perspective. In one of his novels, Tolstoy even went into a dog's point of view.

Point of View: The person or perspective from which a story is told. In addition to omniscience, types of points of view include first person ("I"), second person ("you"), and third person ("he," "she," or "they").

Prose: Works of fiction and nonfiction usually written in sentences and paragraphs, as distinct from poetry and drama.

Prose Poem: A poem where the lines extend over to the right margin. It is more like a paragraph than a traditional poem, where the lines may vary in length. Prose poems often make heavy use of images and sound work and are often less concerned with narrative drive, tension, conflict, and character. See "af•ter•glow" (p. 71).

Protagonist: The main character of a story, usually the one to whom the most happens in a story, the one who tells the story, or the one with whom we identify most closely.

Quatrain: A grouping for four lines in a poem, set off by space breaks from other groups of lines. Pantoums are written in quatrains.

Scene: A combination of visuals, action, dialogue, and setting. A scene creates a movie in the reader's mind: a box of space with time passing inside it. Something happens in the box, and the scene concludes.

Second Person: The point of view from the "you" perspective. Example: *You walk in. You sit down. You can tell she's upset. You don't know why.*

Setting: The place where the piece happens in space and time.

Stanza: A group of lines in a poem, set off by space breaks from the other groups of lines. *Stanza* means "room" in Italian.

Subtext: The meaning beneath the surface. Subtext is not overtly stated but is quite clear. For example, in a scene where a woman is chopping carrots harshly and speaking to her husband, the subtext may be that she is angry with her husband.

Summary: A technique used to move through time quickly or give background information efficiently instead of painting a detailed scene.

Third Person: A point of view that uses pronouns such as *he, she,* and *they.* Example: *He walked in. He could see she was upset. He didn't know why.*

Tone: the combined effect of the speaker's general feeling or attitude and the language being used in the piece.

Turn: In a piece of literature, there will often be a change in direction. In prose, the plot may *turn* in an unexpected direction, often at a climactic point. In poetry, the *turn* is called "the volta" — a place in the poem where the tone, or intention, or subject matter changes or even reverses.

Voice: A writer's style, including types of sentences, vocabulary, and tone — essentially, how a writer writes. A writer might have a very informal, edgy, conversational, in-your-face voice or might have a very mannered, detached, formal voice.

Acknowledgments

Kim Addonizio, "First Poem for You." Copyright © Kim Addonizio. Used with permission.

Brian Arundel, "Things I've Lost." Copyright © Brian Arundel. Used with permission.

Julie Hakim Azzam, "How to Erase an Arab," *Brevity*, Issue 53, Fall 2016. Copyright © 2016 by Julie Hakim Azzam. Used with permission.

"Writers on Writing" Feature, Julie Hakim Azzam interview. Used courtesy of Julie Hakim Azzam.

John Brehm, "The Poems I Have Not Written," from *Sea of Faith*. Copyright © 2004 by The Board of the University of Wisconsin System. Reprinted by permission of the University of Wisconsin Press.

"Writers on Writing" Feature, John Brehm interview. Used courtesy of John Brehm.

Gwendolyn Brooks, "We Real Cool." Copyright © Brooks Permission. Reprinted by consent of Brooks Permissions.

Raymond Carver, "Cathedral," from *Cathedral* by Raymond Carver. Copyright © 1981, 1982, 1983 by Tess Gallagher. Used by permission of Alfred A. Knopf, an imprint of the Knopf Doubleday Publishing Group, a division of Penguin Random House LLC. All rights reserved.

Ted Chiang, "The Great Silence," from *Exhalation: Stories,* compilation copyright © 2019 by Ted Chiang. Used by permission of Alfred A. Knopf, an imprint of the Knopf Doubleday Publishing Group, a division of Penguin Random House LLC. All rights reserved.

E. E. Cummings, "me up at does." Copyright © 1963, 1991 by the Trustees for the E. E. Cummings Trust, from *Complete Poems: 1904-1962* by E. E. Cummings, edited by George J. Firmage. Used by permission of Liveright Publishing Corporation.

Michael Cunningham, "Bobby," from *A Home at the End of the World* by Michael Cunningham. Copyright © 1990 by Michael Cunningham. Reprinted by permission of Farrar, Straus and Giroux.

Natalie Diaz, "Abecedarian Requiring Further Examination of Anglikan Seraphym Subjugation of a Wild Indian Rezervation," from *When My Brother Was an Aztec*. Copyright © 2012 by Natalie Diaz. Reprinted with the permission of The Permissions Company, LLC on behalf of Copper Canyon Press, www.coppercanyonpress.org.

Natalie Diaz, "My Brother at 3 a.m.," from *When My Brother Was an Aztec*. Copyright © 2012 by Natalie Diaz. Reprinted with the permission of The Permissions Company, LLC on behalf of Copper Canyon Press, www.coppercanyonpress.org.

Brian Doyle, "Two Hearts," excerpted from *Leaping: Revelation & Epiphanies*, 10th Anniversary Edition by Brian Doyle (Loyola Press, 2013) © Brian Doyle. Reprinted with permission of Loyola Press, www.loyolapress.com.

Beth Ann Fennelly, "One Doesn't Always Wish to Converse on Airplanes," "Small Talk at Evanston General," "Two Phone Conversations," and "Why I'm Switching Salons," from *Heating and Cooling: 52 Micro-Memoirs*. Copyright © 2017 by Beth Ann Fennelly. Used by permission of W. W. Norton & Company, Inc.

"Writers on Writing" Feature, Beth Ann Fennelly interview. Used courtesy of Beth Ann Fennelly.

Neil Gaiman, "Tips for Writing." Text Copyright © 2010 by Neil Gaiman. Reprinted by permission of Writers House LLC acting as agent for the author.

Ross Gay, "Ode to Sleeping in My Clothes," *The Massachusetts Review*, Volume 53, Issue 1, Spring 2012. Copyright © 2012 by The Massachusetts Review. Used with permission.

Och Gonzalez, "What I Do on My Terrace Is None of Your Business," *Brevity*, April 22, 2019. Copyright © 2019 by Och Gonzalez. Used with permission.

"Writers on Writing" Feature, Och Gonzalez interview. Used courtesy of Och Gonzalez.

INDEX